A Companion to Literature from Milton to Blake

Blackwell Companions to Literature and Culture

This series offers comprehensive, newly written surveys of key periods and movements and certain major authors, in English literary culture and history. Extensive volumes provide new perspectives and positions on contexts and on canonical and post-canonical texts, orientating the beginning student in new fields of study and providing the experienced undergraduate and new graduate with current and new directions, as pioneered and developed by leading scholars in the field.

A COMPANION TO LITERATURE FROM

MILTON
TO
BLAKE

EDITED BY **DAVID WOMERSLEY**

Fellow and Tutor in English Literature, Jesus College, Oxford

Copyright © Blackwell Publishers Ltd 2000
Editorial matter, selection and arrangement copyright © David Womersley 2000

First published 2000

2 4 6 8 10 9 7 5 3 1

Blackwell Publishers Ltd
108 Cowley Road
Oxford OX4 1JF
UK

Blackwell Publishers Inc.
350 Main Street
Malden, Massachusetts 02148
USA

British Library Cataloguing in Publication Data

A CIP catalogue record for this book is available from the British Library.

Library of Congress Cataloging-in-Publication Data

A companion to literature from Milton to Blake / edited by David Womersley.
p.   cm. – (Blackwell companions to literature and culture; 7)
Includes bibliographical references and index.
ISBN 0-631-21285-X (alk. paper)
1. English literature – 18th century – History and criticism.   2. English literature – Early
modern, 1500–1700 – History and criticism.   3. Literature and society – Great Britain – History.
I. Womersley, David.   II. Series.

PR441.C66 2001   820.9 – dc21   00-031018

Typeset in 11 on 13 pt Garamond 3
by Best-set Typesetter Ltd., Hong Kong
Printed in Great Britain by T.J. International Padstow, Cornwall
This book is printed on acid-free paper

Contents

PART TWO   Readings

Introduction

The period covered by this *Companion* is framed by profound crisis. It begins with the conflicts of the mid-seventeenth century, which Clarendon remembered as a convulsion that came close to overturning all the pillars of the state. Beginning his history of the rebellion, he warns his reader that:

> the hand and judgment of God will be very visible, in the infatuating a people (as ripe and prepared for destruction) into all the perverse actions of folly and madness, making the weak to contribute to the designs of the wicked, and suffering even those by degrees, out of the conscience of their guilt, to grow more wicked than they intended to be; letting the wise to be imposed upon by men of no understanding, and possessing the innocent with laziness and sleep in the most visible article of danger; uniting the ill, though of the most different opinions, divided interests, and distant affections, in a firm and constant league of mischief; and dividing those whose opinions and interests are the same into faction and emulation, more pernicious to the public than the treason of the others: whilst the poor people, under pretence of zeal to Religion, Law, Liberty, and Parliaments, (words of precious esteem in their just signification,) are furiously hurried into actions introducing Atheism, and dissolving all the elements of the Christian Religion, cancelling all obligations, and destroying all foundations of Law and Liberty, and rendering not only the privileges but very being of Parliaments desperate and impossible.

Clarendon, of course, was no dispassionate observer of these events, and his firm Stuart loyalties naturally disposed him to deplore them. But even those writers who embraced the cause of Parliament in the struggle, such as Milton, or those whose loyalties were, at least at the outset, more ambiguous and fluctuating, such as Marvell, recognized that this was a struggle which reached to, and transformed, the very foundations of the nation. This had been Cromwell's paradoxical achievement, at least as Marvell's musing intelligence had registered it:

And, if we would speak true,
   Much to the Man is due.
Who, from his private Gardens, where
He liv'd reserved and austere,
      As if his highest plot
      To plant the Bergamot,
Could by industrious Valour climbe
To ruine the great Work of Time,
      And cast the Kingdome old
      Into another Mold.

At the end of the period, the French Revolution struck many observers as an even more radical rupture. In one sense it cut the present off from the past; in another, it elevated the present until it rivalled the wonders of the ancient world, and thus emancipated modern Europe from any tutelage to ancient magnificence. Fanny Burney wrote to her father in October 1789 that 'there is nothing in old history that I shall any longer think fabulous; the destruction of the most wonderful empires on record has nothing more wonderful, nor of more sounding improbability, than the demolition of this great nation, which rises up against itself for its own ruin – perhaps annihilation'. Edmund Burke also registered the magnitude of the event, although in a less balanced, more distraught and distracted key:

> But the age of chivalry is gone. – That of sophisters, oeconomists, and calculators, has succeeded; and the glory of Europe is extinguished for ever. Never, never more, shall we behold that generous loyalty to rank and sex, that proud submission, that dignified obedience, that subordination of the heart, which kept alive, even in servitude itself, the spirit of an exalted freedom. The unbought grace of life, the cheap defence of nations, the nurse of manly sentiment and heroic enterprize is gone! . . . now all is to be changed. All the pleasing illusions, which made power gentle, and obedience liberal, which harmonized the different shades of life, and which, by a bland assimilation, incorporated into politics the sentiments which beautify and soften private society, are to be dissolved by this new conquering empire of light and reason. All the decent drapery of life is to be rudely torn off. All the super-added ideas, furnished from the wardrobe of a moral imagination, which the heart owns, and the understanding ratifies, as necessary to cover the defects of our naked shivering nature, and to raise it to dignity in our own estimation, are to be exploded as a ridiculous, absurd, and antiquated fashion.

As was the case with Clarendon and the Civil War, Burke was no objective spectator of the French Revolution. But in presenting developments in France as a break in the continuity of civilization in Western Europe, he shared common ground with his opponents on the other side of the question. Tom Paine also saw the significance of the Revolution in terms of its abolition of the past. In *Common Sense*, the pamphlet he had published in 1776 at the outset of the American War of Independence, Paine had evinced an understanding of the phenomenon of Revolution which adumbrated what he would later see happening, on a larger scale, in France. In 1776 he had noted that, in the wake of hostilities, 'our style and manner of thinking have undergone a revolution. We see with other eyes; we hear with other ears; and we think with other thoughts, than those we formerly used'; and he went on to express his sense of historical rupture in the most explicit manner when he suggested that 'by referring the matter from argument to arms, a new aera for politics is struck; a new method of thinking hath arisen. All plans, proposals, &c. prior to the nineteenth of April, i.e. to the commencement of hostilities, are like the almanacks of the last year; which, though proper then, are superceded and useless now'. Fourteen years later, Paine depicted the French Revolution as the child of the American conflict, which sustained and strengthened its inward and outward transformations of men and institutions:

> From a small spark, kindled in America, a flame has arisen, not to be extinguished. Without consuming, like the *Ultima Ratio Regum*, it winds its progress from nation to nation, and conquers by a silent operation. Man finds himself changed, he scarcely perceives how. He acquires a knowledge of his rights by attending justly to his interest, and discovers in the event that the strength and powers of despotism consist wholly in the fear of resisting it, and that, in order *'to be free, it is sufficient that he wills it'*.

The Revolution therefore marked an epoch in human affairs: 'The insulted German and the enslaved Spaniard, the Russ and the Pole, are beginning to think. The present age will hereafter merit to be called the Age of reason, and the present generation will appear to the future as the Adam of a new world.' The Revolutionary Calendar adopted in France on 7 October 1793 was, in this respect, simply an unusually direct translation of ideology into practice.

Between these two upheavals on first a national, and then a continental, scale, there intervened what for many years was presented as an historical and literary mill-pond. *The Peace of the Augustans* was the phrase chosen by George Saintsbury for the title of a book – a peace which over time came to seem more of a slumber. Historians, too, tended to see this period as one of consolidation, in which had occurred *The Growth of Political Stability in England* – the phrase J. H. Plumb used for the title of his Ford Lectures. However, for academics there is no incitement quite like an orthodoxy, and in due course both historians and literary scholars began to draw attention to aspects of the period which had been scanted, overlooked or suppressed. For instance, it was noted that, for a time of alleged calm, the occurrence of two armed rebellions (1715 and 1745), a successful revolution (1688), a change of ruling dynasty with the accession of the Hanoverians in 1714 and a series of international conflicts in and even with Britain's colonies looked curious. Was there really such consensus of political outlook amongst Britons in this period? And if there was, was it really as it had been described? Meanwhile, literary scholars were tunnelling on several fronts. Neglected groups of writers, such as women and labourers, began to receive their due, while at the same time tensions and contradictions were teased out of the works of the canonical figures. Gradually a period which had seemed monochrome to a fault began to emerge as increasingly parti-coloured. Was the literary culture of the eighteenth century overwhelmingly metropolitan? Look at the proliferation of provincial presses. Was it a time of growing enlightenment and secularization? Look at the popularity of religious books, and the way in which political attitudes at this time were so often suffused with or grounded on religious precepts. And this increasing plurality of study was accompanied by an increasing plurality of approach, as the volatile gases of theory eventually solidified into a range of stances from which the critic, faced by a literary work, might choose. Both kinds of resulting diversity – diversity of subject matter and diversity of approach – are reflected in the contributions to this *Companion*.

It is a familiar move in introductions to volumes such as this so to draw attention to the way recent scholarship has replaced unity with plurality. Often the matter is left there, as if fragmentation were good in and of itself, and the generation of an increasingly particularized and exceptionalist vision was a legitimate end of scholarship, rather than being just the natural (and, to that extent, insignificant) outcome of professional specialization. But, for a number of reasons, we might be unwilling to repose in the shards of earlier syntheses, and might wish instead to look forward to syntheses to come. In the first place, it is likely that much of this diversity is more apparent than real, and arises because current academic mistrust of grand narrative has inhibited the integrating impulse which must be an important part of scholarly endeavour. In due course, we may expect that the findings on particular authors or groups of authors which presently seem incommensurable with broader perspectives will in fact become assimilated. Second, the scepticism about generalization which is abroad seems at times to reject the urge to achieve a broader vision by assuming that nothing less than a totally comprehensive account of the field in question will suffice. But lower-order generalizations are surely possible, and may be useful in gathering together material that would otherwise lie dispersed. We may try to identify broad trends. For instance, the commercialization of literature, which Pope deplored in *The Dunciad*, can be viewed in a more benign light and welcomed as a means whereby literature broadened and renewed itself, generating new forms and digesting new experience. Here the novel is central, at one level because of its appetite to include aspects of life hitherto un- or under-represented in literature, but also because of its urge to regulate, order and place the material for which it hungered. At times the diversity which the novel could embrace might seem to imperil conspectus. But we should not forget that the aspect of *Tom Jones* which its early readers most admired was its plot; that is to say, the pattern which ultimately contained and bestowed significance upon its luxuriance of incident.

The opening lines of the first epistle on Pope's *An Essay on Man* eventually assumed this form:

> Awake, my ST. JOHN! leave all meaner things
> To low ambition, and the pride of Kings.
> Let us (since Life can little more supply

Than just to look about us and to die)
Expatiate free o'er all this scene of Man;
A mighty maze! but not without a plan;
A Wild, where weeds and flow'rs promiscuous shoot,
Or Garden, tempting with forbidden fruit.

But in the first edition of 1733, Pope had published something significantly different:

Awake, my LÆLIUS! leave all meaner things
To low ambition, and the pride of Kings.
Let us (since Life can little more supply
Than just to look about us and to die)
Expatiate free o'er all this scene of Man;
A mighty maze! of walks without a plan;
Or Wild, where weeds and flow'rs promiscuous shoot,
Or Garden, tempting with forbidden fruit.

The most important change comes in line 6. At first, Pope had suggested that there was no perspective from which the bewildering diversity of the world could be grasped as a unity. His first thoughts had assured him that life was 'A mighty maze! of walks without a plan'. But later that same year, in the second edition 'Corrected by the Author', the sentiment was reversed. Pope now affirmed that, despite appearances, coherence did exist and might be glimpsed. On reflection, life was in fact 'A mighty maze! but not without a plan'.

Whether we construe the final form of that line, dictated by Pope's second thoughts, as a pious hope or a well-grounded assertion is less interesting than the small drama created by taking the two forms of the line together. The promptness with which the bewitchment of diversity is followed, checked and corrected by the adherence to unity both says something about the period as a whole, and guides us in our study of it. The Augustan appetite for extending the range of experience which literature might address, and for generating new literary forms in response to expanding horizons, was intoxicating and at times even imperilling. It was accompanied, however, by a determination to resolve, digest and order: to hold the maze and the plan in a single thought. This *Companion* has been designed to encourage similar acts of discrimination and comprehension in those who study the diverse and compelling literature of the 'long' eighteenth century.

David Womersley
Jesus College, Oxford

Notes on Contributors

Ros Ballaster is Fellow in English Literature at Mansfield College, Oxford. She is author of *Seductive Forms: Women's Amatory Fiction from 1684 to 1740* (1992) and has edited Delarivier Manley's *New Atlantis* (1992) and Jane Austen's *Sense and Sensibility* (1995). She is preparing a book entitled *Fabulous Orients: Representations of Turkey, China and India in England, 1660–1760*. Her research interests include feminist criticism, popular media and Restoration and eighteenth-century writing.

Richard Braverman teaches in the Department of English and Comparative Literature at Columbia University. He is the author of *Plots and Counterplots: Sexual Politics and the Body Politic in English Literature, 1660–1730* (1993) and numerous articles on Restoration and eighteenth-century literature and culture.

Alun David was a British Academy Postdoctoral Fellow at Corpus Christi College, Oxford.

Peter Davidson is Chalmers Regius Professor of English at the University of Aberdeen. His research interests apart from seventeenth-century poetry are the three kingdoms in the seventeenth century and the early-modern visual arts. He is co-editor of the imminent publication, an *Anthology of Early Modern Women Poets*.

Martin Dzelzainis is Reader in Renaissance Literature and Thought at Royal Holloway, University of London. He has edited *John Milton's Political Writings* (1991), and, with Warren Chernaik, *Marvell and Liberty* (1999). He is currently working on *The Rehearsal Transpos'd* for a forthcoming edition of Marvell's prose works.

David Fairer is Professor of Eighteenth-century English Literature at the University of Leeds. In addition to his work on Pope he has published several essays on early romanticism. He has edited *The Correspondence of Thomas Warton* (1995) and co-edited

Eighteenth-century Poetry: An Annotated Anthology (1999). He is currently writing a book entitled *English Poetry of the Eighteenth Century*.

Christine Gerrard is a Fellow and Tutor in English at Lady Margaret Hall, Oxford. She is the author of *The Patriot Opposition to Walpole: Politics, Poetry, and National Myth* (1994) and co-editor of *Eighteenth-century Poetry: An Annotated Anthology* (1999). She is currently completing a critical biography of the author and entrepreneur Aaron Hill (1683–1750).

Nick Groom is Senior Lecturer in Post-medieval Literature at the University of Bristol. He is the author of *The Making of Percy's Reliques* (1999) and the editor of *Thomas Chatterton and the Romantic Culture* (1999). His new book, *The Forger's Shadow*, will be published in 2001.

Brean Hammond is Professor of English at the University of Nottingham. He is author of several books and articles on eighteenth-century topics, including *Professional Imaginative Writing in English, 1670–1740* (1997). He is a former editor of the *British Journal for Eighteenth-century Studies*.

Thomas Healy is Professor of Renaissance Studies at Birkbeck College, London. He is the author of *Richard Crashaw* (1986), *Christopher Marlowe* (1994) and *New Latitudes: Theory and English Renaissance Literature* (1992). He has edited the *Longman Critical Reader on Andrew Marvell* (1998), and co-edited *Literature and the English Civil War* (1990) and *The Arnold Anthology of British and Irish Literature in English* (1997). He is currently completing a book entitled *The English Boat*.

David Hopkins is currently Reader in English Poetry at the University of Bristol. His publications include *John Dryden* (1986), *The Routledge Anthology of Poets on Poets* (1994) and selections from Dryden, Ovid and Homer in the Everyman Poetry series. He has recently co-edited volumes 3 and 4 of the *Poems of John Dryden* in the Longman Annotated English Poets series.

Thomas Kaminski is Associate Professor of English at Loyola University in Chicago. He is the author of *The Early Career of Samuel Johnson* (1987) as well as a number of articles on eighteenth-century English literature.

Bridget Keegan is an Associate Professor of English at Creighton University in Omaha, Nebraska. She is the editor of *Literature and Nature: Four Centuries of British and American Nature Writing* (2000) and one of the editors of the forthcoming *English Labouring-class Poets, 1700–1900*. She has written several articles on labouring-class poets, and, in particular, on John Clare.

Malcolm Kelsall is Professor of English at Cardiff University. His publications include *Jefferson and the Iconography of Romanticism: Folk, Land, Culture and the Roman-*

tic Nation (1999), *Byron's Politics* (1987) and an edition of Congreve's *The Way of the World* (1981). He is currently writing a study of the Irish country house and Unionist literature in the nineteenth century.

Paulina Kewes is lecturer in English at the University of Wales, Aberystwyth. She has published widely on seventeenth- and eighteenth-century drama, publishing history, Rochester, Dryden and Rowe. She has written *Authorship and Appropriation: Writing for the Stage in England, 1660–1710* (1998) and her current book is provisionally entitled *The Performance of History: Theatrical Representations of the Past in Early-modern England*.

Tom Keymer is Elmore Fellow in English Language and Literature at St Anne's College, Oxford. His publications include the Oxford World Classics editions of Fielding's *Joseph Andrews* and *Shamela* (1999) and, with Alice Wakely, Richardson's *Pamela* (in press).

Paddy Lyons teaches in the English Literature Department, Glasgow University, and at Instytut Anglistyki, Warsaw University. His work on the Restoration includes *Congreve's Comedies* (1982) and (with Fidelis Morgan) *Female Playwrights of the Restoration* (1991). His edition of Rochester (1993) was the first to give a full text of the verse-play *Sodom: or the Quintessence of Debauchery*. His other interests include Irish studies, twentieth-century literature and theory.

Anne McDermott is Senior Lecturer in English at the University of Birmingham. Her main research studies are in eighteenth-century literature, history and philosophy, with a special interest in Samuel Johnson, women's writing, lexicology and the history of language. Recent publications include Johnson's *A Dictionary of the English Language* on CD-ROM (1996).

Jon Mee is Margaret Candfield Fellow in English at University College, Oxford, and also a Lecturer in English. He is the author of *Dangerous Enthusiasm: William Blake and the Culture of Radicalism in the 1790s* (1992) and co-editor of the *Oxford Companion to the Romantic Age* (1999). He is currently writing a book to be called *Romanticism, Enthusiasm and Regulation*.

Dafydd Moore is Lecturer in English in the School of Humanities and Cultural Interpretation, Faculty of Arts and Education, at the University of Plymouth. He has published a number of articles on the intellectual, political and literary contexts and impacts of the poems of Ossian.

David Nokes is Professor of English Literature at King's College, London. His recent books include *John Gay* (1995) and *Jane Austen* (1997) and his television adaptations include *Clarissa* (1991) and *The Tenant of Wildfell Hall* (1996).

David Norbrook is Professor of English at the University of Maryland. His publications include *Poetry and Politics in the English Renaissance* (1984) and *Writing the English Republic: Poetry, Rhetoric and Politics, 1627–1660* (1999). He is currently editing Lucy Hutchinson's *Order and Disorder* for Blackwell.

Karen O'Brien is Reader in English and American Literature at the University of Warwick. She is the author of *Narratives of Enlightenment: Cosmopolitan History from Voltaire to Gibbon* (1997) and of a forthcoming study of feminist debates in eighteenth-century British literature. She is currently writing a study of poetry and the British empire, 1650–1800.

Anita Pacheco is a Lecturer in the Department of Humanities at the University of Hertfordshire. She researches in early modern women's writing and seventeenth-century Protestantism. She has written articles on Aphra Behn, edited *Early Women Writers: 1600–1720* (1997) and co-edited *Grace Abounding with Other Spiritual Autobiographies* (1998). She is presently editing *The Blackwell Companion to Early Modern Women's Writing*.

Murray Pittock has held the Chair in Literature at the University of Strathclyde since 1996, and is currently head of the Glasgow–Strathclyde School of Scottish Studies. His main research is on Jacobitism and British identities and his most recent book is *Celtic Identity and the British Image* (1999).

Sarah Prescott is a Lecturer in English at the University of Wales, Aberystwyth, where she specializes in Restoration and eighteenth-century literature. She has published articles on eighteenth-century women writers and is currently completing a book on the subject. She is presently guest editor of a special issue on Augustan women writers for the journal, *Women's Writing*.

Claude Rawson is the Maynard Mack Professor of English at Yale University and an Honorary Professor at the University of Warwick. His recent books include *Satire and Sentiment, 1660–1830* (1994, 2000) and, edited with H. B. Nisbett, *The Cambridge History of Literary Criticism, Vol. 4: The Eighteenth Century* (1997). His *God, Gulliver, and Genocide* will appear in 2001.

Joad Raymond is a Lecturer in English Literature at the University of East Anglia. His research interests cover Renaissance and seventeenth-century poetry, journalism and political writing, and his publications include *The Invention of the Newspaper: English Newsbooks, 1641–1649* (1996). He is presently completing a study of pamphleteering, polemic and public opinion between 1588 and 1688.

Bruce Redford is University Professor at Boston University. His special interests include literature and the visual arts during the seventeenth and eighteenth centuries.

He is the author of *The Converse of the Pen* (1986) and *Venice and the Grand Tour* (1996) and the editor of *The Letters of Samuel Johnson* (five vols, 1992–4).

Valerie Rumbold is a Senior Lecturer in English at the University of Birmingham. She is author of *Women's Place in Pope's World* (1989) and editor of *Alexander Pope: 'The Dunciad' in Four Books* (1999). With Julian Ferraro and Nigel Wood she is currently working on an edition of Pope's poetry for the Longman Annotated English Poets series.

Stuart Sherman is Associate Professor of English at Fordham University. He is editor of the section on the Restoration and the eighteenth century in the *Longman Anthology of British Literature* (1998). His book, *Telling Time: Clocks, Diaries and English Diurnal Form* (1996), received the American Society for Eighteenth-century Studies' Louis Gottschalk Prize for book of the year. He is currently writing *News and Plays: Evanescences of Page and Stage, 1620–1779*.

Jane Spencer is a Senior Lecturer in English Literature at Exeter University. Her research interests are in feminist literary history from the seventeenth to the nineteenth century. Her publications include *The Rise of the Woman Novelist* (1986), *Elizabeth Gaskell* (1993), an edition of Aphra Behn's *The Rover and Other Plays* (1995) and *Aphra Behn's Afterlife*, a study of Behn's influence on the eighteenth century (2000).

Michael F. Suarez, SJ, is Associate Professor of English at Fordham University and Tutor in English at Campion Hall, Oxford. He is editor of Robert Dodsley's *A Collection of Poems by Several Hands* (1997) and co-editor of *Making Meaning: Selected Essays of D. F. McKenzie* (forthcoming 2002) and of *The Cambridge History of the Book in Britain, 1695–1830* (forthcoming 2004). He is associate editor of *The Oxford Companion to English Literature* (2000) and of *The Oxford Chronology of English Literature* (forthcoming 2001).

Katherine Turner is Lecturer in English at St Peter's College, Oxford. She has edited *Selected Poems: Thomas Gray, Charles Churchill & William Cowper* (1998) and has written articles on various aspects of eighteenth-century literature. She is currently completing a study of *British Travel Writers in Europe, 1750–1800: Authorship, Gender and National Identity* (forthcoming 2001).

Ann Jessie Van Sant, Associate Professor in the Department of English and Comparative Literature at the University of California, Irvine, is the author of *Eighteenth-century Sensibility and the Novel: The Senses in Social Context* (1993). Her current project is a book tentatively called *Women's Bodies, Women's Stories*.

Simon Varey works in fund raising at UCLA. He has written five books on eighteenth-century English literature and is preparing an edition of Smollett's translation of *Gil Blas* for the Georgia edition of the works of Smollett. He joined the *Scriblerian* as an editor in 1997.

Nicholas von Maltzahn is Professor of English at the University of Ottawa. He is the author of *Milton's History of Britain: Republican Historiography in the English Revolution* (1991) and numerous articles on English history and politics in the seventeenth and eighteenth centuries. He is now preparing a fuller study of *Milton and His Readers: The Making of a National Poet, 1650–1750.*

Peter Walmsley is an Associate Professor of English at McMaster University. He is the author of *The Rhetoric of Berkeley's Philosophy* (1990) and has recently completed a book on John Locke and Restoration science.

Abigail Williams is a Senior Scholar at St Hugh's College, Oxford. She is currently completing a D.Phil. thesis on early Whig poetry and patronage. Forthcoming publications include articles on the politics of literary enthusiasm in the early eighteenth century, and on Scriblerian satire. Her next research project is to be a study of the cultural politics of John Dennis's criticism.

Sue Wiseman teaches in the School of English and Humanities, Birkbeck College, University of London.

David Womersley is Fellow and Tutor in English Literature at Jesus College, Oxford. His research interests include Gibbon, Burke, Johnson, literary Whiggism, Elizabethan history plays and the history of literary criticism. His books on Gibbon include *The Transformation of the Decline and Fall of the Roman Empire* (1988) and the Penguin edition of *The Decline and Fall* (1994). Another recent publication is *Restoration Drama: An Anthology* (2000) published by Blackwell. He is currently completing a study of Gibbon's reputation for Oxford University Press.

David Wootton is Professor of Intellectual History at Queen Mary and Westfield College, University of London. He has edited *Republicanism, Liberty and Commercial Society* (1994) and *Locke's Political Writings* (1993) and edited and translated Machiavelli's *Selected Political Writings* (1994), More's *Utopia* (1998) and Voltaire's *Candide* (2000).

Brian Young is a Lecturer in Intellectual History at the University of Essex. He is the author of *Religion and Enlightenment in Eighteenth-century England* (1998) and a co-editor of *History, Religion and Culture and Economy, Polity, Society: Essays in British Intellectual History* (2000). He is currently at work on a study of history, religion and empire, 1740–1840.

PART ONE
Contexts, Issues and Debates

1

Literature, War and Politics, 1642–1668

Martin Dzelzainis

I

On 12 March 1642, the Prince of Wales (the future Charles II) attended a lavish reception at Trinity College, Cambridge. After dinner there was a performance of *The Guardian*, a comedy composed at just a week's notice by one of the fellows, Abraham Cowley (1618–87). Among those attending were George Villiers, second Duke of Buckingham (1628–1687), and his younger brother Francis (1629–1648). Taken into the royal family after their father, the king's favourite, was assassinated in 1628, the Villiers brothers had been educated by the prince's own governors, Brian Duppa, Bishop of Chichester, and William Cavendish, Earl of Newcastle, before furthering their studies at Trinity in 1641. Fellow-poets at Cambridge who would have been keen to see Cowley's latest work included his friend, Richard Crashaw (1612–1649), and Thomas Stanley (1625–1678). Like Cowley and Crashaw, Andrew Marvell (1621–1678), another Trinity poet, had contributed verses to Συνωδια, *sive Musarum Cantabrigiensium Concentus et Congratulatio* (1637), a volume congratulating the king and queen on the birth of their fifth child (see Marvell, 1972, 199–202). But by 1642 Marvell was living in London and so probably missed the event. Among those performing may well have been Martin Clifford (d. 1677), who had befriended Cowley at Westminster School before entering Trinity in 1640. According to the poet Joseph Beaumont, things went well with the prince showing 'all signs of a great acceptance which he could, and more than the University dared expect' (Nethercot, 1931, 74).

The occasion was nevertheless overshadowed by developments elsewhere, as Cowley acknowledged in the Prologue:

Who says the Times do Learning disallow?
'Tis false; 'twas never honour'd so as now.
When you appear, great Prince, our night is done:
You are our Morning-star, and shall b'our Sun.

But our Scene's *London*, now, and by the rout
We perish if the Roundheads be about:
For now no ornament the head must wear,
No Bays, no Mitre, not so much as Hair.
How can a Play pass safely, when we know,
Cheapside-Cross falls for making but a show?
Our onely hope is this, that it may be
A Play may pass too, made *ex tempore*.
Though other Arts poor and neglected grow,
They'll admit Poetry, which was always so.
Besides, the Muses of late time have bin
Sanctifi'd by the Verse of Master *Prin*.
   But we contemn the fury of these days,
And scorn as much their Censure as their Praise.
Our Muse, blest Prince, does onely on you relie.
                    (Cowley, 1650, sig. A2r–v)

By virtue of the royal presence, Cambridge is exempt from the malaise that afflicts learning generally, whereas London is terrorized by Roundheads with all the usual puritan prejudices against images, the arts, the theatre and the bishops. The satirical edge to Cowley's Prologue and Epilogue to *The Guardian* gave them a political value beyond the immediate occasion, and they went straight into print, the first of several works in which he attacked religious radicalism.

   What the two poems could not register (beyond a loaded remark in the Epilogue to the effect that if the play had offended the prince then 'we've now / Three hours done treason here' (Cowley, 1650, sig. F3)) was the full extent of the political crisis then unfolding. In January the king had made his ill-fated attempt to arrest five members of the House of Commons, a step which 'lost Charles London' (Kenyon, 1966, 195). Hence the staged withdrawal north to York, from which the prince broke off in order to visit Cambridge. Moreover, on 5 March – the day Cowley began work on *The Guardian* – the two Houses passed the Militia Ordinance, declaring that

> there hath been of late a most dangerous and desperate design upon the House of Commons, which we have just cause to believe to be an effect of the bloody counsels of Papists and other ill-affected persons, who have already raised a rebellion in the kingdom of Ireland; and by reason of many discoveries we cannot but fear that they will proceed not only to stir up the like rebellion and insurrections in this kingdom of England, but also to back them with forces from abroad. (Gardiner, 1979, 245)

The king's departure from London thus marked a turning point; after this, as Conrad Russell remarks, 'the major task is not to explain why there was a civil war: it is to explain why there was not a civil war for another eight months' (Russell, 1991, 454).

   War broke out in August 1642 and before long those who had gathered to see Cowley's play were scattered to the winds. The Villiers brothers enlisted in the Royalist army but after the defeat at Lichfield Close in April 1643 their appointed guardian, the Earl of Northumberland, sent them on a grand tour of Europe. Cowley left for Oxford by the spring of 1643, and by 1645 was in France, like Stanley, who had slipped away from England in 1642, and Crashaw, who abandoned his fellowship at Peterhouse in 1644. Other royalist intellectuals were not so fortunate; some were killed in action (Sidney Godolphin), died after being captured (William Chillingworth), succumbed to fever (George Aglionby, William Cartwright, Dudley Digges) or committed suicide (Sir John Suckling). The whole process of cultural decimation was epitomized by Viscount Falkland's suicidal gallantry at Newbury in 1643: rather than 'make *Lawrels* for the *Conquered*', a traumatized Cowley simply abandoned his epic poem, *The Civil War* (Cowley, 1915, 9).

It is of course true that many volumes of Cavalier poetry were published throughout the 1640s. More often than not, however, publishers were retrieving or recycling material from the 1630s or even earlier: for example, Thomas Carew, *Poems* (1640, 1642); Suckling, *Fragmenta Aurea* (1646); Richard Corbett, *Certain Elegant Poems* (1647) and *Poetica Stromata* (1648); and William Cartwright, *Comedies, Tragi-Comedies, with other poems* (1651). While such publications might have served to reiterate Cavalier values, it remains the case that far fewer new ones were being *written* (see Thomas, 1991). The closed world that generated this kind of coterie verse no longer functioned, at least in wartime. The publishing of previously private material also testifies in its own way to the enormous expansion of the public sphere in terms of access and generic diversity that took place in the 1640s (see Smith, 1994; Achinstein, 1994; Raymond, 1996). These Cavalier volumes now jostled for attention in a marketplace in which printed materials performed every conceivable kind of speech act: they informed, declared, petitioned, vindicated, remonstrated, censured, answered, reviewed, observed, animadverted, queried and questioned. It is fitting therefore that arguably the single most influential pamphlet of the Civil War was Henry Parker's unimposingly titled *Observations upon Some of His Majesties Late Answers and Expresses* (1642).

Yet it would be a mistake to conclude that the Cavaliers simply resigned themselves to the ascendancy of prosaic Roundhead values. As I hope to show, this was not true of the author and audience of *The Guardian*. However, this will not become apparent unless we first dispel some common assumptions about the period. The first of these concerns the stereotypes of Cavalier and Roundhead. Recent scholarship has shown that royalist literary culture, far from being rendered ineffectual by its own aesthetic, proved capable of generating a 'poetics of resistance' (Loxley, 1997, 223–34). Conversely, David Norbrook's recent *Writing the English Republic: Poetry, Rhetoric, and Politics, 1627–1660* (1999) has gone a long way towards excavating the poetics of republicanism, the burying of which was one of the major preoccupations of the restored monarchy, and of the literary establishment thereafter. The second assumption is that the topic of politics in this period is coterminous with, and exhausted by, the opposition between the royalists and the parliamentarians. However, it is clear that many of the most intense and significant political exchanges of the time took place *within* rather than between these groups. What we need to keep in the forefront of our minds is that, for the duration of the Civil War and Interregnum, each camp was ideologically divided within itself. Indeed, the aim of this essay is to try to bring out the implications of this fact for our understanding of the group of Cambridge writers that I have been discussing so far. But before doing so something needs to be said in general about these internal divisions.

In the case of the parliamentarians, the main fault-line was visible in a conflict of war aims. Having come close to defeat in 1643, the parliamentary leadership sought to recruit the Scots army (originally mobilized in 1638 to fend off attempts to impose an Anglican liturgy). But the Scots had their own agenda, for 'what Calvinists all over Europe in the late sixteenth and early seventeenth centuries wished to do was to *capture* their monarchs and use their power to establish a Presbyterian system of Church government' (Tuck, 1993, 203). These objectives were inscribed in the first three articles of the Solemn League and Covenant (September 1643); first, 'to bring the churches of God in the three kingdoms to the nearest conjunction and uniformity', or, in other words, to introduce Scottish Presbyterianism into England and Ireland; second, to 'endeavour the extirpation of Popery, prelacy . . . superstition, heresy, schism, profaneness'; and third, 'to preserve and defend the King's Majesty's person and authority, in the preservation and defence of the true religion and liberties of the kingdoms' (Gardiner, 1979, 268–9). The loose drafting of the third article allowed for endless debate over which clause was subordinate to which: did true religion take precedence over preserving the king, or vice versa? More importantly, there were those in the parliamentary coalition, especially in the New Model Army, who saw no need for a political settlement which included a monarchical element (at least not one as embodied in Charles I), or those (the Independents) who resented any attempt to impose religious uniformity. Much of what Milton wrote from 1643 onwards, for example, can only be comprehended in terms of his increasing hostility to the Presbyterian project as a whole (see Dzelzainis, 1999).

The royalists' failure to press home their early military advantage was the result of comparably deep divisions. The nucleus of the royalist party that Charles acquired in 1641–2, as Thomas Hobbes later observed, 'had declaimed against ship-money and other extra-parliamentary taxes, as much as any; but when they saw the Parliament grow higher in their demands than they thought they would have done, went over to the King's party' (Hobbes, 1990, 117). Advisers like Edward Hyde, Falkland, and Sir John Culpepper were anxious above all to preserve the constitutional reforms that the Long Parliament had extracted from the king. In Hobbes's view, however, their constitutionalism 'weakened their endeavour to procure him an absolute victory' because 'they thought that the government of England was not an absolute, but a mixed monarchy; and that if the king should clearly subdue this Parliament, that his power would be what he pleased, and theirs as little as he pleased: which they counted tyranny'. Sheer intransigence would have served the king far better than 'reasonable declarations' (Hobbes, 1990, 114–15, 116).

Further rifts opened up once the king surrendered in 1646. His negotiations with various elements of the parliamentary coalition were complicated by the conflicting advice he received from the exiles in Paris and elsewhere (see Tuck, 1993, 270). Henrietta Maria and her advisers urged a settlement either with the Independents (promising them religious toleration) or with the Scots and Presbyterians (promising them to implement the first article of the Covenant). But another faction opposed any deal which compromised the Church of England in the slightest: their leader, Hyde, urged that Charles be kept to 'a resolution of riding out this storm by those principles which will better defend him (whatever new politicks are read) than a union with either faction'. To begin with at least, the king agreed, assuring William Murray in October 1646 that he was 'confident that Religion will much sooner regaine the Militia, then the Militia will Religion' (Dzelzainis, 1990, 516–17). But the king's figure of speech, antimetabole, is all-too-easily inverted: how long would it be before he was confident that an army would do more to secure religion than religion would do to secure an army?

Hyde's quarrel with the queen's party was not simply about religion. He seems to have had almost as much trouble coming to terms with their philosophy. When he fulminated against those 'in France, who (comforting themselves with their old subtle resolutions, of breaking any agreement as soon as it shall be in their power) do heartily wish . . . that the king would sign every article' (Dzelzainis, 1990, 517), he was in part protesting about a generation of moral relativists who no longer lived by the values he recognized (for an insistence to the contrary on Hyde's 'modernity', see Trevor-Roper, 1989, 211–12). One paradox here is that the thinker to whom this younger set was most drawn actually belonged to the generation *before* Hyde (1609–74); namely, Thomas Hobbes, who was born in the year of the Armada, 1588, and died in 1679. Not surprisingly, Hyde's own relationship with Hobbes became increasingly strained before snapping in the 1650s (see Dzelzainis, 1989). What we need to look at next therefore is how the group of writers broken up in 1642 managed the increasingly complex demands of war and politics in the later years of the decade and beyond.

II

The Trinity cohort in fact began to reassemble itself quite quickly, albeit in different configurations. By the autumn of 1643 Marvell had embarked on what turned into a four-year tour of Holland, France, Italy and Spain. In the winter of 1645 to 1646, his path crossed that of the two Villiers at Rome, where Buckingham was presiding over a 'Poetical Academy', and it has been suggested that Marvell's satire on one of the members of the academy, the Catholic priest-poet Richard Flecknoe, was a bid for Buckingham's patronage (see Chaney, 1985, 348; Norbrook, 1999, 167–8). Paris not Rome, however, was unquestionably the nerve centre of émigré activity. The Marquis of Newcastle – Buckingham's old mentor and the patron of Hobbes – arrived there in the spring of 1645, and immediately joined the court of Henrietta Maria. When the Prince of Wales ended his journey into exile there the following summer (significantly, Hyde did not accompany him from Jersey but stayed behind), Newcastle arranged for him to be taught mathematics by Hobbes, who was also tutoring Buckingham as well as the son and nephew of the poet Edmund Waller (Tuck, 1993, 321–2; Sommerville, 1992, 21). By 1646, Cowley was not only handling Henrietta Maria's confidential correspondence but also 'managed a vast Intelligence in many other parts' ('An Account of the Life and Writings of Mr Abraham Cowley. Written to Mr M. Clifford', Cowley 1668a: unpaginated). Naturally, the circle was tolerant of Catholicism, and this was especially true of Hobbes and Cowley, whose friend Crashaw had converted to Rome. In his *Ode on the Death of Mr. Crashaw*, Cowley indulgently remarked that

> His faith perhaps in some nice tenets might
> Be wrong; his life, I'm sure, was in the right.
> And I myself a Catholic will be,
> So far at least, great saint, to pray to thee.
>   (Maclean, 1974, 335)

This kind of *rapprochement*, however, only deepened Hyde's suspicions about the 'new politicks' at Paris.

When hostilities ceased in June 1646 some émigrés took the opportunity to return to England. Thomas Stanley moved into the Middle Temple in 1646, while his cousin, Richard Lovelace, returned at around the same time after spending three years in Holland and France. Marvell came back the following year and seems to have associated with members of Stanley's literary circle (on Stanley and Marvell, see Kelliher, 1978, 33–4). Before long, Buckingham too was allowed to return to his estates with his brother. Like many others, they may simply have assumed that in the normal course of events the king's military defeat would be followed by a political settlement, only to be confounded in December 1647 when the king signed an Engagement with the Scots: in return for their military intervention on his behalf, he agreed to introduce 'Presbyterial government' for three years (see Gardiner, 1979, 347–52). By the following spring, civil war had broken out again.

An early notable casualty was Buckingham's brother, killed in a skirmish near Kingston in July 1648, and commemorated by Marvell in 'An Elegy upon the Death of My Lord Francis Villiers'. But many other high-ranking victims were to follow since the war was prosecuted with exceptional severity. After every set-piece battle or siege, as Morrill points out, 'the leading royalists were tried and executed' (21). By refusing to accept that his defeat in 1646 represented a divine judgement, and resorting to arms a second time, Charles had sealed his reputation as a 'man of blood', and those guided by the Bible had no doubt what this entailed: 'the land cannot be cleansed of the blood that is shed therein, but by the blood of him that shed it' (Numbers 35:33; see Crawford, 1977). The cleansing process began in December 1648 when the Army purged Parliament just as the Presbyterian majority seemed on the verge of restoring Charles to power. By 30 January 1649, Charles had been tried and executed, and by 19 May, after the office of king and the House of Lords had been abolished, England was declared a republic.

These were truly cataclysmic events. As was evident to most observers, however, the removal of Charles I from the scene did not mean that the war was over. It would end only when the English republic had subdued the Irish and the Scots or, conversely, they had helped the royalists to topple the republican regime in England. Cromwell's campaign in Ireland had largely removed one factor from the equation by mid-1650, so when the Scots began to make overtures to Charles II, the 'Louvrians' (so-called after the palace where Henrietta Maria now held court) responded positively (see Tuck, 1993, 322–3). Newcastle and Buckingham backed the initiative, as did Cowley: 'the mutual necessity of an accord is visible; the King is perswaded of it, and all Mankind but two or three mighty tender Consciences about him' (Cowley to Henry Bennet, 30 April 1650; Cowley, 1967, II, 345).

Cowley's narrative of events in 1650 can be extracted from the intelligence summaries he provided for Bennet. In prose of compelling poise and clarity, he kept Bennet abreast of developments in France (itself in the throes of civil war), and Holland (where the negotiations with the Scots were taking place) as well as significant events in Ireland, Scotland and England. His main anxiety was whether an agreement would be reached at Breda before the Commonwealth sent an army to Scotland. Late in April he reported that the 'Affairs of *Ireland* do every day grow worse and worse', and that Cromwell 'conceives himself very near the end of his work there' (Cowley to Bennet, 30 April 1650; Cowley, 1967, II, 345). In June, at the very moment that Marvell was composing 'An Horatian Ode upon Cromwell's Return from Ireland', Cowley despatched a crisp analysis of the intelligence reports:

> *Cromwell* was receiv'd with great Triumph and Magnificence at *London*; and it is believed, will have some new great Title conferr'd upon him (as Protector of the People's Liberty, or some such like) on purpose to put out *Fairfax*, and give the Command of all into his Hands. (Cowley to Bennet, 21 June 1650; Cowley, 1967, II, 348)

The effect of the passive constructions ('was receiv'd', 'is believed') is to cast Cromwell in the role of recipient, one who in due course 'will have' further honour 'conferr'd upon him'. But the phrase 'on purpose' reveals him as an active orchestrator of events. On re-reading, the auxiliary 'will' (giving future form to 'have') takes on instead the sense of Cromwell's *intending* to have happen something that serves the 'purpose' of ousting Fairfax as Lord General. So a sentence which began with a Roman military triumph ends in a Renaissance political conspiracy to gain 'Command of all' under cover of 'the People's Liberty'. Before long Cowley is reporting that, as predicted, '*Fairfax* has laid down his Commission, they say, because he would not enter with his army into Scotland . . . and *Cromwell*, you may be sure, is made General, and already gone from *London* towards the *North*' (Cowley to Bennet, 16 July 1650; Cowley, 1967, II, 349). Cowley's Cromwell is thus an open book (at least to those versed in the literature of reason of state) compared to the enigma of Marvell's 'Horatian Ode' – an out-and-out Machiavellian whereas this is only one aspect, though a significant one, of Marvell's portrait (see Vickers, 1989).

Crucially, however, there is a lacuna in the correspondence with Bennet between August and November 1650, which means that there is no record of how Cowley took news of Cromwell's victory over the royalists at Dunbar in September. Hyde later observed that Dunbar 'was looked upon, in all places, as the entire conquest of the whole kingdom' (Tuck, 1993, 323). While there may be a touch of *schadenfreude* in Hyde's account of the failure of an enterprise he had opposed from the start, even Buckingham seems to have thought of it as a conclusive defeat, advising Newcastle in December

> to make your peace if it bee possible, in Ingland, for certaynly your Lordship's suffer-
> ing for the K. has been enough to excuse you if you looke a little after your self now,
> when neither he is able to assist you, nor you in a possibility of doing him service. (Tuck,
> 1993, 323)

Nevertheless his dejection must be attributed in part to another setback for the royalists in the interim: the death in November of their Dutch ally, William II, Prince of Orange, who was married to Charles I's daughter, Mary. Cowley regarded this as 'a greater blow than any thing at home can recompence, if we were to have never so good News', because it allowed the Dutch republicans to seize power, which in turn reduced the pressure on their English counterparts (Cowley to Bennet, 18 November 1650; Cowley, 1967, II, 351). Cowley did not despair entirely; however, some promising intelligence the following month, he assured Bennet, 'puts us again into a way of hope' (Cowley to Bennet, 5 December 1650; Cowley, 1967, II, 351). Buckingham rallied also, and was with Charles II at Worcester in September 1651 when a reconstituted royalist army again confronted Cromwell. The outcome was another comprehensive defeat that finally extinguished any realistic hope of restoring the monarchy through force of arms.

Charting the impact of these events is particularly important to any attempt to come to terms with the poems which Marvell wrote during this period: some commendatory verses in the form of a verse epistle 'To His Noble Friend Mr Richard Lovelace, upon His Poems'; the Villiers elegy; another elegy 'Upon the Death of the Lord Hastings', a minor royalist figure who served as a kind of surrogate for the executed king; 'An Horatian Ode'; 'Tom May's Death'; and 'In Legationem Domini Oliveri St John ad Provincias Feoderatas' ('On the Embassy of Lord Oliver St John to the United Provinces'). Commentators have been troubled by the idea of Marvell writing these poems in this sequence to the extent that it seems to them to defy political, and perhaps even psychological, coherence. The conclusion of the Villiers elegy, for example, sounds a rabidly royalist note which is completely at odds with the sober treatment of relations between the sister-republics in the St John poem, while 'Tom May's Death' appears systematically to undermine the classical foundations upon which 'An Horatian Ode' is reared. Rather than continue to be perplexed by these conundrums, some editors have simply cut the Gordian knot and excluded the Villiers elegy and / or 'Tom May's Death' from the canon (see Marvell, 1971, I, 432–5; Marvell, 1984, xxxii–iii; Chernaik, 1983, 206–14, 236–7; Norbrook, 1999, 180; on the history of Marvell attributions, see now von Maltzahn, 1999).

However, such drastic measures may not be needed. These hypomanic swings in political mood are far from incomprehensible given conditions of prolonged uncertainty – as we have just witnessed in the royalist camp between 1647 and 1651. Exactly when was the moment finally to pronounce royalism dead or republicanism triumphant? Was it after the regicide, or after Dunbar, or after Worcester, or after the death of William II? The view from Paris was unclear, but so was it from London too. The tendency to wait on events influenced even the Commonwealth's own propagandists. As Blair Worden has observed, whereas before Worcester they defended the regime largely in terms of *de facto* power, afterwards they felt able to switch from this cautious line of argument to an assertion of republican doctrines (Worden, 1994, 61–2). In Marvell's case, what may finally have persuaded him that it was no longer necessary to keep all his options open was the eclipse of the Orangist party in Holland. Perhaps it was not the execution of Charles I that 'first assured the forcèd power' ('An Horatian Ode', l. 66; Marvell, 1972, 56) but the smallpox which carried off William II.

Another approach may be to ask how royalists read Marvell's 'royalism'. It has been known for some time that Richard Lovelace was interested in 'Tom May's Death', the poem in which Marvell satirically relates an encounter between the ghosts of Tom May, the translator of Lucan and the historian of Parliament who died in November 1650, and of Ben Jonson, who denounces May as a 'Most servile wit, and mercenary pen' (l. 40; Marvell, 1972, 59). Lovelace's satire, 'On *Sanazar's* being honoured with six hundred Duckets by the *Clarissimi* of *Venice*, for composing an *Eligiack Hexastick of* The City', is likewise concerned with misplaced republican literary patronage; mocks suggestions that England is a second Rome; and invokes the ghost of Jonson as the arbiter of literary values (see Rees: 486. Rees also notes that Lovelace like Marvell refers to Vandals and Goths, but this was a commonplace: see, for example, Alexander Brome, 'To Colonel *Lovelace* on his Poems', Lovelace, 1963, lxxxvi.). However, it appears not to have been noticed that 'On *Sanazar's* being honoured' also embodies Lovelace's reading of the commendatory verses by Marvell prefixed to Lovelace's *Lucasta* (1649) – a potentially very revealing arrangement of textual mirrors.

Marvell's poem opens by linking the decline in literary manners to the rise of faction:

> *Our* times are much degenerate from *those*
> Which *your* sweet muse with *your* fair fortune chose,
> And as complexions alter with the climes,
> *Our* wits have drawn the infection of *our* times.
> *That* candid age no other way could tell
> To be ingenious, but by speaking well.

Who best could praise had *then* the greatest praise,
'Twas more esteemed to give than wear the bays:
Modest ambition studied only *then*
To honour not herself but worthy men.
These virtues *now* are banished out of town,
Our Civil Wars have lost the civic crown.
                    (ll. 1–12, Marvell, 1972, 32–3; my emphasis)

However, this is not a straightforward Cavalier diatribe against those responsible for cultural decline, as when Cowley in Cambridge denounces Roundheads in London. It is true that Marvell later singles out the Presbyterians from the

                                    swarms
        Of insects which against you rise in arms:
        Word-peckers, paper-rats, book-scorpions.
                    (ll. 17–19, Marvell, 1972, 33)

But the studied deployment of pronouns, adjectives and adverbs in the opening twelve lines tells a different story. Brick-by-brick ('our', 'those', 'your', 'your', 'our', 'our', 'that', 'then', 'then', 'these', 'now', 'our'), Marvell builds a wall dividing the ways things were from the way they are now – and makes it clear that he is on the other side of it from Lovelace. He is thus to be found with Lovelace's enemies, though he is not one of them (the point being made when Marvell fends off one of Lovelace's female admirers who mistakenly thinks 'that I too of the rout had been' (l. 42)).

Lovelace echoes several of Marvell's images: 'Gnats and Wasps'; 'mist of Insects'; 'Scorpions'; and 'swarms' (ll. 145, 222, 228, 259). He also connects civil war and internecine literary strife:

    Could there nought else this civil war compleat,
    But Poets raging with Poetick heat,
    Tearing themselves and th'endlesse *wreath*.
                    (ll. 155–7, Lovelace, 1963, 197)

Most tellingly of all, he mimics Marvell's lexical technique for differentiating between past and present (in this case ancient Rome and 1650s England):

    A chain or fasces *she* could *then* afford
    The Sons of Phœbus, *we* an Axe, or Cord;
    Sometimes a Coronet was *her* renown,
    And *ours* the dear prerogative of a Crown.
    In marble statu'd walks great Lucan lay,
    And *now we* walk *our own* pale Statua:
    They the whole yeer with roses crownd would dine,
    And *we* in all December know no wine.
                    (ll. 31–8, Lovelace, 1963, 193; my emphasis)

When Lucan is introduced into this Marvellian impromptu, as an emblem of the past-ness of the past despite May's modern renderings, it represents a final tightening of the intertextual knot.

'On *Sanazar*'s being honoured' was first published in *Lucasta. Posthume Poems* (1659) where it was placed immediately after Lovelace's elegiac tribute 'To the Genius of Mr. *John Hall*', the poet and republican propagandist (1627–56). Like Marvell, Hall con-tributed verses to *Lucasta* (1649) and, assuming that the arrangement of *Posthume Poems* embodies Lovelace's intentions, the implication is that the earlier twinning of Hall and Marvell was now being recalled. However, while Lovelace was at liberty to acknowledge his political difference with Hall ('Our *Minds* and *Merits* brake two several ways' (l. 10; Lovelace, 1963, 190)), this was not the case with Marvell. For by the time the poem on Sannazaro was composed in December 1656 (see Duncan-Jones, 1956), Marvell was already established as a supporter of Cromwell's Protectorate. Yet it was precisely this new political and literary establishment that Lovelace wished to satirize: his ostensible target was an instance of sixteenth-century state patronage, but the actual one was the phenomenon of 'Protectoral Augustanism' (see Norbrook, 1999, 299–325, 337–50):

> And now me thinks we ape Augustus state,
> So ugly we his high worth imitate,
> Monkey his Godlike glories; so that we
> Keep light and form, with such deformitie,
> As I have seen an arrogant Baboon
> With a small piece of Glasse Zany the Sun.
> (ll. 19–24, Lovelace, 1963, 193)

As a repository of techniques for satirizing, or merely distancing oneself from, a given literary culture, Marvell's two poems were obviously useful to Lovelace. However, it seems he was not so much enlisting Marvell as attacking him, and that the rework-ing of the poems constituted a critique of him and, by extension, the regime he now supported. This being the case, what must have been significant about these poems, as far as Lovelace was concerned, was that they embodied the commitments from which Marvell had apostasized by throwing in his lot with the Protectorate.

III

One influential early modern handbook for those seeking guidance about how to conduct themselves in times of civil war was *De Constantia* (1584; translated into English as *Two Bookes of Constancie* in 1594), by the Flemish neo-stoic, Justus Lipsius. In one way, Lipsius was quite specific about what could be done when: 'If thou see by certain and infallible tokens that the fatall alteration of the State is come', then 'yeeld to God, and give place to the time' (Langley, 1976, 48). But this advice begged the question of which signs were 'certain and infallible' and which were not. For Thomas Hobbes, Dunbar appears to have signified a 'fatall alteration of the State' just when he was close to completing *Leviathan*. Not only did Hobbes find himself 'with a book supporting a cause already lost', but some of its arguments now 'gave comfort to his enemies more than his friends' (Burgess, 1990, 677, 681; see Hobbes, 1996, xi–i, xliii–v). Anxious to address some of these issues, he appended 'A Review, and Conclusion' to *Leviathan* shortly before its publication in the spring of 1651.

This last-minute addition proved to be highly controversial, above all because of the thoroughness with which Hobbes set out the arguments for submission to the new regime:

> because I find by divers English Books lately printed, that the Civill warres have not yet sufficiently taught men, in what point of time it is, that a Subject becomes obliged to the Conquerour . . . it is then, when the means of his life is within the Guards and Garrisons of the Enemy; for it is then, that he hath no longer Protection from him, but is protected by the adverse party for his Contribution. Seeing therefore such contribution is every where, as a thing inevitable, (not withstanding it be an assistance to the Enemy), esteemed lawfull; a totall Submission, which is but an assistance to the Enemy, cannot be esteemed unlawful. Besides, if a man consider that they who submit, assist the Enemy but with part of their estates, whereas they that refuse, assist him with the whole, there is no reason to call their Submission, or Composition an Assistance; but rather a Detriment to the Enemy. (Hobbes, 1996, 486–7)

Given the relation between protection and obedience, all that is needed to determine the exact 'point of time' at which subjects become obliged to the enemy rather than their former sovereign is a simple judgement about the source of their protection. This was not a particularly original argument, but by 1656 Hobbes (having returned to England himself early in 1652) was claiming that he had 'framed the minds of a thousand gentlemen to a conscientious obedience to present government, which otherwise would have wavered in that point' (Sommerville, 1992, 67). From exile, Hyde beadily noted down that Hobbes 'could not abstain from bragging in a Pamphlet . . . that he alone, and his doctrine, had prevail'd with many to submit to the Government', and filed it away as ammunition for his later indictment of 'the Enormities of Mr. *Hobbes* and his *Leviathan*' (Hyde, 1995, 237, 297).

One of the gentlemen whose minds were framed to obedience was Cowley. Without mentioning Hobbes by name, Cowley's biographer, Thomas Sprat (1635–1713), makes it clear nevertheless that the clinching argument for Cowley was Hobbes's subtle suggestion that resistance actually strengthened the new regime more than submission. When and how Cowley broke his exile is still unclear. He opens the Preface to the 1656 edition of his *Poems* by remarking nonchalantly, 'At my return lately into England. . . .' (Cowley, 1915, 1), but he was in London in the summer of 1654 and was observed at Dover the following March brokering a meeting between Buckingham and one of Cromwell's agents (Nethercot, 1931, 143, 146). Arrested in April in the aftermath of an abortive royalist uprising, he was interviewed by Cromwell personally before eventually being released on bail. In addition, it seems certain that he was expected to make a public avowal of his submission to the Protectorate.

Cowley complied with a flourish in the 1656 Preface:

> Now though in all *Civil Dissentions*, when they break into open hostilities, the *War* of the *Pen* is allowed to accompany that of the *Sword*, and every one is in a maner obliged with his *Tongue*, as well as *Hand*, to serve and assist the side which he engages in; yet when the event of battel, and the unaccountable *Will* of *God* has determined the controversie, and that we have submitted to the conditions of the *Conqueror*, we must lay down our *Pens* as well as *Arms*, we must march out of our *Cause* it self, and *dismantle* that, as well as our *Towns* and *Castles*, of all the *Works* and *Fortifications* of *Wit* and *Reason* by which we defended it. (Cowley, 1915, 9)

It would be fair to say that this sentence hung over the rest of Cowley's life. As editor of the posthumous *Works of Mr Abraham Cowley* (1668), Sprat did everything he could to extenuate the offence. He removed the offending passage from the Preface, and, in the 'Life', insisted that it all boiled down to 'maintaining one false Tenent in the Political Philosophy', and 'the errour of one Paragraph, and a single Metaphor' ('Life', Cowley, 1668a, unpaginated). But the metaphor *is* the problem. For taking the parallel between the pen and the sword to its logical conclusion means that Cowley ends up by endorsing complete and unilateral ideological disarmament. This baffled contemporary observers like David Lloyd who in 1668 voiced his regret that Cowley

> laid down his Pen, when his friends did their Armes; that he marched out of the Cause as they did out of their Garrisons; dismantling the Works and Fortifications of Wit and reason, in his power to keep, when they did the Forts and Castles not so in theirs. (Loxley, 1997, 97)

Why should the royalist surrender what was 'in his power to keep'? Cowley's gesture was supererogatory, his show of submission excessive. However, Cowley never really accepted the force of these objections. Even with the Restoration imminent, and when he was actively seeking to return to royal favour in France, the only error to which he would admit was having written (by a slip of the pen) something that it was possible for others to misconstrue:

> I am fully satisfied in conscience of the uprightness of my own sense in those [two] or three lines which have been received in one so contrary to it . . . yet because it seems they are capable of being misunderstood otherwise than I meant them, I am willing to acknowledge and repent them as an error, hoping that his Majesty . . . will pardon the slip of that man's pen in one expression. (Cowley to Ormonde, 26 December 1659; Nethercot, 1931, 189)

Even using the good offices of Martin Clifford, it appears that no mutually agreeable text could be hammered out. Next, Cowley tried publishing a violent attack on

Cromwell (*A Vision, Concerning his late Pretended Highnesse Cromwell, the Wicked*; London 1651; Cowley, 1915, 45–98). But the real obstacle was the disapproval of Hyde, now Charles II's chief minister and in a position to settle old scores. As with Hobbes, so with Cowley: Hyde kept himself informed. Writing to Ormonde with the news that royalist funds had been sent to Cowley in England, Hyde assured him that 'You will think it strange after you have read the preface to his book' (Hyde to Ormonde, 10 May 1656; Nethercot, 1931, 160).

IV

One of the last glimpses we get of Cowley shows him retrospectively in a very different milieu. In 1689, John Evelyn wrote to Samuel Pepys about the meetings of a committee to improve English, which had been set up in 1664 under the auspices of the Royal Society:

> in order to it three or fowre Meetings were begun at Grey's Inn, by Mr. Cowley, Dr. Sprat, Mr. Waller, the D. of Buckingham, Matt. Clifford, Mr. Dryden, & some other promoters of it. But by the death of the incomparable Mr. Cowley, distance & inconvenience of the place, the Contagion & other circumstances intervening, it crumbled away and came to nothing. (Evelyn to Pepys, 12 August 1689; Jones, 1971, 72)

Through the years, this group had built up a dense network of overlapping affiliations. For example, as we saw, Cowley, Buckingham and Clifford were all at Trinity in the early 1640s; Cowley, Buckingham and Waller shared exile in Paris; Buckingham, his secretary Clifford, and his protégé Sprat were at the centre of a circle of wits (and later collaborated on a play, *The Rehearsal*, satirizing Dryden's heroic drama); and Dryden, Waller and Sprat contributed to *Three Poems Upon the Death of his Late Highnesse Oliver Lord Protector of England, Scotland, and Ireland* (1659).

As Norbrook points out, *Three Poems* 'marks the weary end-point of Protectoral Augustanism, speaking for a generation for which the passions of the Civil War had little meaning' (Norbrook, 1999, 394). All three contributors made the transition to life under the restored monarchy with relative ease (though the Cromwell elegies were cited against them periodically). But if they did have a passion, then it was science rather than politics. This is especially true of Sprat. His elegy for Cromwell (in fact, a Pindaric Ode inspired by the example of Cowley, though 'infinitely below the full and lofty Genius of that excellent Poet') was dedicated to Dr John Wilkins, Warden of Wadham College, Oxford, and brother-in-law of Cromwell (*Three Poems*, 1659, sig. C2). Wadham during the 1650s was the centre of science at Oxford, though not really *because* of its links with the Protectorate. In fact, as Michael Hunter has argued, displaced Anglican clerics were often diverted into science while defeated royalists looked to it for 'new sources of authority and opinion' (Hunter, 1981, 26). Waller, Dryden and Buckingham were all associated closely with the Royal Society, but in many ways Cowley is the best example of the royalist whose interests took a philosophical or scientific turn in the 1650s (or, in his case, perhaps even earlier, during his time in Paris). In 1657, Cowley was incorporated as a Doctor of Physic at Oxford (although he never practised), and in 1661 published *A Proposition for the Advancement of Experimental Philosophy*. Science also featured prominently in his verse. The Ode 'To Mr. Hobbes' considered him exclusively in his capacity as a natural philosopher; 'On the Death of Mr. William Hervey' mourned the discoverer of the circulation of blood; and when Sprat published his *History of the Royal Society* in 1667 another Ode by Cowley was prefixed to it.

In the last stanza of the Ode addressed 'To The Royal Society', Cowley praises Sprat above all for his stylistic achievement:

> So from all modern follies he
> Has vindicated eloquence and wit.
> His candid style like a cleans stream does glide.
> (ll. 174–6, Maclean, 1974, 347)

This was not damning with faint praise because the reform of language was seen as central to the development of science itself. Sprat was especially aware of this since his mentor at Wadham, John Wilkins, was working on *An Essay towards a Real Character, and a Philosophical Language* (1668), which epitomized the drive towards perspicuity. Sprat was also a great admirer of Cowley's prose. One of his most important tasks as Cowley's editor was to see the *Essays* into print for the first time. Remarkably, however, one of the main reasons why he valued the irregularity of Cowley's Pindaric Odes so highly was because of their *prosaic* aspect:

> But that for which I think this inequality of number is chiefly to be preferr'd, is its near affinity with Prose: From which all other kinds of *English* Verse are so far distant, that it very seldom found that the same Man excels in both way. But now this loose, and unconfin'd measure has all the Grace, and Harmony of the most confin'd. And withal, it is so large and free, that the practice of it will only exalt, not corrupt our Prose: which is certainly the most useful kind of Writing of al others: for it is the style of all business and conversation. ('Life', Cowley, 1668a, unpaginated)

Hobbes, notoriously, was not elected to the Royal Society (see Malcolm, 1990). But it is clear that he was in fact working towards an end shared by many of its propagandists – the fashioning of a tone of voice at the furthest possible remove from the enthusiasm and obscurantism of the Interregnum, a tone of voice that came to dominate English philosophical discourse (see Skinner, 1996, 435–7). Cowley like other royalists played a significant part in this process, prompting the thought that perhaps in the long run Cavalier *prose* had its victories too.

References and Further Reading

Achinstein, Sharon (1994). *Milton and the Revolutionary Reader*. Princeton: Princeton University Press.

Burgess, Glenn (1990). 'Contexts for the writing and publication of Hobbes's *Leviathan*'. *History of Political Thought* 11, 675–702.

Chaney, Edward (1985). *The Grand Tour and the Great Rebellion: Richard Lassels and 'The Voyage of Italy' in the Seventeenth Century*. Geneva: Slatkine.

Chernaik, Warren (1983). *The Poet's Time: Politics and Religion in the Work of Andrew Marvell*. Cambridge: Cambridge University Press.

Cowley, Abraham (1650). *The Guardian: A Comedie. Acted before Prince Charls His Highness at Trinity-Colledg in Cambridge, upon the Twelfth of March 1641*. London.

——(1668a). *The Works of Mr Abraham Cowley*. Ed. Thomas Sprat. London.

——(1688b). *Abrahami Couleij Angli, Poemata Latina*. Ed. Thomas Sprat. London.

——(1915). *The Essays and Other Prose Writings*. Ed. A. B. Gough. Oxford: Clarendon Press.

——(1967). *The Complete Works in Verse and Prose of Abraham Cowley*. Ed. A. B. Grosart, 2 vols. Edinburgh (1881). Repr. New York: AMS Press.

Crawford, Patricia (1977). 'Charles Stuart, that man of blood'. *Journal of British Studies* 16, 41–61.

Dryden, John, Thomas Sprat and Edmund Waller, *Three Poems Upon the Death of his Late Highnesse Oliver Lord Protector of England, Scotland, and Ireland*. London.

Duncan-Jones, E. E. (1956). 'Two allusions in Lovelace's Poems'. *Modern Language Review* 51, 407–9.

Dzelzainis, Martin (1989). 'Edward Hyde and Thomas Hobbes's *Elements of Law, Natural and Politic*'. *Historical Journal* 32, 303–17.

——(1990). '"Undouted Realities": Clarendon on sacrilege'. *Historical Journal* 33, 515–40.

——(1999). 'Milton's politics'. In *The Cambridge Companion to Milton*. Ed. Dennis Danielson. 2nd edn. Cambridge: Cambridge University Press, 70–83.

Gardiner, S. R (1979). *Constitutional Documents of the Puritan Revolution 1625–1660*. 3rd edn. Oxford: Clarendon Press.

Griffin, Julia (1998). *Selected Poems of Abraham Cowley, Edmund Waller and John Oldham*. Harmondsworth: Penguin.

Hobbes, Thomas (1990). *Behemoth or the Long Parliament*. Ed. Ferdinand Tönnies, with an introduction by Stephen Holmes. Chicago and London: University of Chicago Press.

——(1996). *Leviathan*. Ed. Richard Tuck. Cambridge: Cambridge University Press.

Hunter, Michael (1981). *Science and Society in Restoration England*. Cambridge: Cambridge University Press.

Hyde, Edward, Earl of Clarendon (1995). 'A survey of Mr Hobbes his *Leviathan*'. In *Leviathan: Contemporary Responses to the Political Theory of Thomas Hobbes*. Ed. G. A. J. Rogers. Bristol: Thoemmes, 180–300.

Jones, R. F. (1971). 'Science and English prose style in the third quarter of the seventeenth century'. In *Seventeenth-century Prose: Modern Essays in Criticism*. Ed. Stanley Fish. New York: Oxford University Press.

Kelliher, Hilton (1978). *Andrew Marvell: Poet & Politician 1621–78*. London: British Museum Publications.

Kenyon, J. P. (1966). *The Stuart Constitution 1603–1688: Documents and Commentary*. Cambridge: Cambridge University Press.

Langley, T. R. (1976). 'Abraham Cowley's "Brutus": Royalist or Republican?', *Yearbook of English Studies* 6, 41–52.

Lovelace, Richard (1963). *Poems of Richard Lovelace*. Ed. C. H. Wilkinson. Oxford: Clarendon Press.

Loxley, James (1997). *Royalism and Poetry in the English Civil Wars: The Drawn Sword*. Basingstoke: Macmillan.

Maclean, Hugh (1974). *Ben Jonson and the Cavalier Poets*. New York and London: W. W. Norton & Company.

Malcolm, Noel (1990). Hobbes and the Royal Society. In *Perspectives on Thomas Hobbes*. Ed. G. A. J. Rogers and Alan Ryan. Oxford: Clarendon Press, 44–66.

Marvell, Andrew (1971). *The Poems and Letters of Andrew Marvell*. Ed. H. M. Margoliouth and revised by Pierre Legouis with the assistance of E. E. Duncan-Jones. 2 vols. Oxford: Clarendon Press.

———(1972). *The Complete Poems*. Ed. Elizabeth Story Donno. Harmondsworth: Penguin.

———(1984). *Complete Poetry*. Ed. George deF. Lord. London: J. M. Dent & Sons.

Morrill, John (1993). *The Nature of the English Revolution*. London and New York: Longman.

Nethercot, Arthur H. (1931). *Abraham Cowley: The Muse's Hannibal*. New York: Russell & Russell.

Norbrook, David (1999). *Writing the English Republic: Poetry, Rhetoric and Politics, 1627–1660*. Cambridge: Cambridge University Press.

Raymond, Joad (1996). *The Invention of the Newspaper, 1641–1649*. Oxford: Clarendon Press.

Rees, Christine (1976). '"Tom May's Death" and Ben Jonson's ghost: a study of Marvell's satiric method'. *Modern Language Review* 71, 481–8.

Russell, Conrad (1991). *The Fall of the British Monarchies 1637–1642*. Oxford: Clarendon Press.

Skinner, Quentin (1996). *Reason and Rhetoric in the Philosophy of Hobbes*. Cambridge: Cambridge University Press.

Smith, Nigel (1994). *Literature and Revolution in England 1640–1660*. New Haven and London: Yale University Press.

Sommerville, Johann P. (1992). *Thomas Hobbes: Political Ideas in Historical Context*. Basingstoke: Macmillan.

Thomas, Peter W. (1991). 'The impact on literature'. In *The Impact of the English Civil War*. Ed. John Morrill. London: Collins & Brown, 123–42.

Trevor-Roper, Hugh (1989). *Catholics, Anglicans, and Puritans: Seventeenth-century Essays*. London: Fontana.

Tuck, Richard (1993). *Philosophy and Government 1572–1651*. Cambridge: Cambridge University Press.

Vickers, Brian (1989). 'Machiavelli and Marvell's "Horatian Ode"'. *Notes and Queries* 234, 32–8.

von Maltzahn, Nicholas (1999). 'Marvell's ghost'. In *Marvell and Liberty*. Ed. Warren Chernaik and Martin Dzelzainis. Basingstoke: Macmillan, 50–74.

Worden, Blair (1994). 'Marchamont Nedham and the beginnings of English Republicanism, 1649–1656'. In *Republicanism, Liberty, and Commerical Society, 1649–1776*. Ed. David Wootton. Stanford: University of California Press, 45–81.

2

Women Writers and Women Readers

Sue Wiseman

I

Now came still evening on, and twilight grey
Had in her sober livery all things clad;
Silence accompanied; for beast and bird,
They to their grassy couch, these to their nests
Were slunk, all but the wakeful nightingale;

So Mary Wollstonecraft quoted Milton's *Paradise Lost* in her anthology of texts dedicated to the education of girls, *The Female Reader* (1789). Why did Wollstonecraft include Milton in her anthology? And why this passage which emphasizes the joys of companionship, concluding with Adam and Eve, 'hand in hand', passing 'On to their blissful bower'? To extend the question, what role did Wollstonecraft think reading ought to play in women's lives, and what roles had it played between the time of the English Civil War and of Wollstonecraft's publication on the eve of the French Revolution? Part of what such use of reading registers is, as in Wollstonecraft's case, a particular author's intellectual trajectory – where *Paradise Lost* offers a vision of pastoral harmony to students of *The Female Reader* Wollstonecraft uses Milton's poem very differently indeed a mere three years later in *A Vindication of the Rights of Woman* (1792). For a writer like Wollstonecraft, her use of Milton illuminates some of the ways in which reading – as registered intertextually in quotation and allusion – illuminates the changing intellectual milieu in which she was writing, as it does for other readers.

During the seventeenth and eighteenth centuries women's relationship to the public sphere – to the sphere of print, politics, opinion – changed substantially. In this chapter, I shall analyse the twin questions of women's writing and women's reading by considering changes in the relationship of women to the overlapping public arenas of literary, political and social debate. It would be problematic, certainly, to chart the shifts in women's participation in the public sphere in terms of simply increased participation. Rather, what we are tracing is a changing print culture repeatedly shaken by political turmoil in the sequential British and European political crises and revolutions of 1640–60, 1688, 1778, 1789 as well as by technological developments in print, changes in the education of women (of which Wollstonecraft's *Reader* is an example), and changes in habits of reading. The effects of these transformations on, say, an elite political writer (like Lady Mary Wortley Montagu, poet, prose writer, social commentator), on a labouring class rural writer (like Mary Collier), or on a poet of African origin (like Phillis Wheatley), are far from the same. Consideration of the place of different kinds of writing, different forms of circulation and, as importantly, the specific circumstances of different women writers and readers illuminates the paradoxical and changing understandings of the 'public' in this period.

For all women writing, however, the strategic use, even display, of reading and learning worked to reinforce the claims they made to enter the sphere of print. As I will suggest, the reading of Milton's texts themselves can act as something of a touchstone for the changes in women's relationship to print, to literature and to political and domestic ideologies. Milton was important to a range of women writers and readers, from Phillis Wheatley to Mary Wollstonecraft, for at least two reasons – his prose and poetry explicitly address both the question of domestic relationships and the interconnections of the private and public spheres, and, importantly, his writing united the English and classical canon of writings which formed the core of the literary canon.

In his divorce tracts of 1643 and 1644 (twenty-five years before he published *Paradise Lost*) Milton explicitly addressed the relationship between the public and the private. Arguing that the man's ability to act virtuously in the public sphere is based on his contentment in the private – out of 'the household estate . . . must flourish forth the vigor and spirit of all publick enterprizes' – he found that when wives are inadequate men are in danger of 'dejection of minde. . . . unprofitable and dangerous to the Common-wealth'. Therefore, divorce should be allowed not only for adultery but for incompatibility. Milton further argues that the man should be allowed to divorce the woman without interference from the courts, according to the statute in the Old Testament book of Deuteronomy (24:1–2), whereby a wife can be with 'a bill of divorcement' sent 'out of [her husband's] house' (*Doctrine and Discipline of Divorce*, 1959). Although Milton implies that women, too, can benefit from divorce he assigns them a place in the private sphere over which men rule: it is the man alone who moves between household and public sphere.

In characterizing public and private in this way Milton is taking up ancient Greek ideas of the public sphere that fit in well with his politics. In Greece men ruled in the *oikos* (household) and went from there into a masculine sphere of debate – the *polis*. Obviously, writing in the England of the Civil War, Milton inhabited a milieu where relations between household and public sphere were much more mediated than in ancient Greece. In England in the seventeenth century, and indeed the eighteenth, access to the public and political sphere was bound not only to gender but to rank, to family, and to literacy. Moreover, at exactly the time when Milton was writing, changes precipitated by the English Civil War meant that women were participating in public debates and particularly in debates based on readings of the Bible impacting on the political sphere. His discussion of women's private place in the divorce tracts and his more complex poetic analysis of Eve's relationship to Adam in *Paradise Lost* (1668) came at a moment when the public sphere was changing.

II

Ancient Greece represented for Milton a model for the exercise of masculine virtue and household government, but the conditions under which he and his female contemporaries were writing worked rather differently. Indeed, the reason that Milton thought that it might be possible to change the law on divorce was that, since 1642, there had been Civil War in England and parliament had assumed control of political processes when Charles I left London. Even before Charles I left London a sequence of events had already begun to change the way print was understood. Two developments were very significant: first, the fall of the court of Star Chamber in 1641 which this meant that there was no overall control over printing and publication and, second, the emergence of weekly newsbooks reporting the deeds of parliament and the progress of the war. David Cressy notes the connection between literacy, education, book production and book ownership and indicates that the bookseller George Thomason was able to collect 680 books and pamphlets per annum between 1640 and 1660 (Cressy, 1980, 45–7). It is disputed how far these changes created a democratic public sphere (Cressy estimates illiteracy in 1641, measured as the inability to make a mark as between 33–9 per cent in four London parishes in London 1641, rising to 74 per cent in two remote Yorkshire parishes) or represented an expansion rather than a qualitative change in the print industry. However, changes in what could be said and by whom were registered by men and women.

Diarists and keepers of commonplace books from a range of social strata recorded their reactions to the war as they read of it in the new newsbooks. For example, in Civil War London the godly Elizabeth Jekyll interpreted God's providences through the reading of newspaper reports. She records parliamentarian triumphs such as the 'great and Wonderfull mercy of God to this kingdome in the delivering of the towne of Plymouth . . . the Enemie came against it, and came so near yt that took their Workes which put the towne into great fear' and set down the royalist defeat at Marston Moor: 'the Earl of Newcastle is . . . fled into Holland, which is the mighty work of God'. Women were involved in the book trade as publishers, printers, vendors, and, as Marcus Nevitt has argued, as writers and publishers of newsbooks.

When he wrote about this period in *The World Turned Upside Down* Christopher Hill noted the presence of women in the gathered churches which were growing up in polemical opposition to the church of England. He was able to notice them because, as well as participating in the oral culture of the gathered churches, the Calvinist emphasis on self-examination led pastors to gather and record testimonies, conversion narratives, stories of men and women finding their way to a God who was no longer bound to a Church hierarchy but who, significantly enough, increasingly had his views and importance canvassed in the sphere of print. In 1641, for example, Katherine Chidley responded in print to a critic of the setting up of churches independent of the established church. Chidley asks 'Whether it be lawfull for such, who are informed of the evills of the Church of *England*, to Separate from it?' Like Milton, she regards the church as still subject to the legacy of Catholicism 'Canon Lawes (the Discipline of Antichrist)' and lacking altogether 'the discipline of *Christ*'. Under such circumstances, separation from the official Church is not a choice, but a duty, whatever persecutions it might bring. The whole of Chidley's tract is an answer to Thomas Edwards. Edwards was a Cambridge educated divine who wrote substantially, attacking those who wished to secede from the Church of England, and his later book, *Gangraena* (1646), which he described as a 'catalogue . . . of the Errours, Heresies, Blasphemies and pernicious practices of the Sectaries of this time' gives a vivid, if extremely hostile, picture of the views of the sectaries – including the women controversialists, like Chidley, who he found particularly repugnant. In attacking Edwards's argument point by point Chidley, like Milton, enters into the modes of seventeenth-century controversial polemic. On the way Chidley makes a point which other women sectaries had made, asking how far a woman had to obey a husband who was not of a similar religious opinion: 'I pray you tell me what authority unbelieving husband hath over the conscience of his believing wife; it is true he hath authority over her in bodily and civil respects, but not to be a lord over her conscience'.

Both a reader and a writer, Chidley engages fully in the sphere of religious controversy. But her writing, though attuned to the aesthetics of argumentation and sharply aware of the telling effect of a good example, does not, any more than Milton's divorce tract, inhabit the terrain of 'literature'. Indeed, one of the characteristics of the sphere of political controversy at the beginning of our period, the 1640s and 1650s, is that one of the effects of the change in licensing laws in 1641 was that a huge range of different kinds of texts jostled together each using rhetorical devices to claim the attention of readers.

Chidley was far from alone in her use of biblical exegesis to challenge the authority of the Church of England. The prophet Anna Trapnel, a member of the Fifth Monarchist sect who anticipated the coming of the millennium, generated six texts, descriptive and prophetic, under (and protesting against) Cromwell's Protectorate. In Trapnel's case the relationship between printed and spoken word is complex as her long poetic prophetic vision, *The Cry of a Stone* (1654) was, it seems, recorded as she spoke it. *Anna Trapnel's Report and Plea* (1654), however, is a narrative of her journey from London to Cornwall, culminating in her arrest for 'aspersing the government' (Graham et al., 1989, 75). This was also the moment at which women began to participate very actively in the politics of the Quaker movement, travelling, preaching and writing as did Elizabeth Hooton, Joan Vokins and Katherine Evans and Sarah Cheevers. The last two, having set off on a voyage to Alexandria, left a record of their interrogation and three-year imprisonment by the Inquisition in Malta. Within the gathered churches many women – such as Hannah Allen, Sarah Davy, Agnes Beaumont – left narratives of their conversions and of God's mercies. While these writings all draw on biblical exegesis and quotation, the sects actually used the Bible in very different ways and different patterns and methods existed.

At the Restoration the role of the sects changed. The Quakers survived into the eighteenth century by substantially changing their organization and politics, including the politics of women's participation and publication. The religious publication of women in the 1640s and 1650s is often regarded as ephemeral and as disappearing at the Restoration. With the exception of the memoir, conversion narrative, and the utopia the specific genres of Civil War publication – the prophecy, the petition, the vision – were less central to the print sphere of the eighteenth century. However, it is clear that the relatively extensive participation of women in the politics of religion during this period, and its effect on public debate influenced, for example, perception of women involved in radical politics throughout the period. As Sharon Achinstein has argued, the period sees women acting in the public sphere – preaching, publishing and interpreting the Bible (Achinstein, 1999). As the nature of the public sphere changed at the Restoration (with particularly harsh implications for writers in the sects) so did women's participation in it. Rather than initiating a simple diminishing of women's participation, the Restoration marks a shift in its nature which marginalized some of the genres used by women radicals.

Writing in modes which contrast with the sectaries, but also in the 1650s and 1660s, Margaret Cavendish, Duchess of Newcastle, is in some ways an exemplary, in others an exceptional, case. Educated only by a decayed gentlewoman, Cavendish's entry into the literary world came when the Duke of Newcastle arrived at the exiled French court of Charles I's queen, Henrietta Maria, and began to woo Margaret Lucas (as she was then), one of Henrietta Maria's ladies in waiting. Still surviving from this moment are the lyrics Newcastle addressed to Margaret and her incisive but semi-literate replies. 'My lord,' she writes 'I have hard thay that have many sutes to prosequt of ther one selddom prefers any other, or if they doe, so slitly as not to be regarded; wherfor I beleuf my lord Jermyn has to many implyments of the Queen's for to desspash yours.' She married Newcastle, shared his exile in Antwerp where they rented Rubens's house, and came to move in the most advanced scientific and philosophical circles. Through her brother in law, Sir Charles Cavendish, Cavendish had contact with the most eminent practitioners of the new science and with political philosophers such as Thomas Hobbes. She engaged with their ideas and *Poems and Fancies* (1653) her first book – a folio volume which, as with all her works, she paid to have published – engaged with the theory of atoms. Yet, as late as 1675 when her *Life* of her husband was published she was aware of the almost crippling lack of education that she brought to these circles and her own endeavours, writing 'Truly, my Lord, I confess, that for want of Scholarship I could not express myself so well as otherwise I might have done, in those Philosophical Writings I published first.' Indeed, she tells us here, that it was not until after the Restoration – by which time she had published just under ten substantial folios of plays, poems, meditations, fiction, letters – that returning to her 'Native Countrey' she 'applied myself to the reading of Philosophical Authors, of purpose to learn those names and words of Art that are used in Schools; which at first were so hard to me, that I could not understand them, but was fain to guess at the sense of them by the whole context'.

Much has been made of the fact that Cavendish's contemporaries were highly critical of her, regarding her as eccentric and self-displaying. Her entry into the sphere of print as an author paying for her own volumes to be printed, and sending off copies to luminaries and the ancient universities, in search of praise, has caused Cavendish to be contrasted by critics from Virginia Woolf onwards with that other writer whose life overlapped with Cavendish's, Aphra Behn. Even her sympathetic biographer noted that she never pursued the project of self-education to its fullest and that she only mentions five poets – Ovid, Shakespeare, Jonson, Donne and Davenant. However, Cavendish's brilliant but partly educated analysis offers an unusual insight, not simply into her times but into the uses she made of patterns of thought, reading, and writing that did reach her. In some ways, Cavendish's lack of education made her into a sponge for the ideas and attitudes that she encountered; it is true that she did not have either systematic intellectual training or training in the genres she wrote in – prose, fiction, poetry, plays and so on.

However, at the same time as imbibing, for example, the conventions of pre- and post-war theatre, and expressing these conventions in her plays, Cavendish also had her own not necessarily consistent but incisive opinions. For instance, as Hilda Smith has recently pointed out, although Cavendish is almost always grouped with royalist poets and certainly shared her husband's life as a faithful servant of the Stuarts, her writings imply a critical attitude to monarchy and, more particularly, the Stuarts. When she came, like Lucy Hutchinson, to write a memoir of her husband, Cavendish dedicates the text to Charles II but goes on to note that the Stuarts left her husband massively out of pocket, made mistakes in conducting the war and even – this is Charles I – at one point actually kept the 'onely Troop of horse' her husband had raised when they were sent to convey arms to the king.

As a writer and reader, Margaret Cavendish's political attitudes, use of genre, engagement with print culture, and reaction to the Restoration, contrast markedly with another royalist poet of the era, Katherine Philips. Where Cavendish was ill-educated Philips was accomplished. Her poetry is highly aware of contemporary and classical models and she translated from the French. Understood by contemporaries as modestly eschewing fame, women's complex relationship to print culture is illuminated by events in Philips's life and by her use of manuscript versus print. Although her earliest printed poem was a commendatory verse in a posthumous volume of the writings of the royalist playwright and soldier, William Cartwright (1651), she did not go on to pursue publication but throughout the 1650s wrote highly charged poetry of friendship which circulated in manuscript.

Drawing on the pastoral personifications of French romance and, as here, on poets
of the previous generation – particularly Donne – Philips's poems elaborate both
royalist politics and highly charged relations with female friends:

> Well! we will doe that rigid thing
>   Which makes Spectators think we part
> Though absence hath for none a sting
>   But those who keep each other's heart.
>
> And when our sence is dispossess'd,
>   Our labouring Souls will heave and pant,
> And gasp for one another's Brest,
>   Since theyr conveyances they want.
>   ('Parting with Lucasia, 13 January
>   1657–8, A Song', Thomas, I, 136–7)

As Kate Lilley has argued, these poems can hardly be understood as a *society* of friendship, in that the women to whom Philips writes – unlike, for example, her fellow-
poet Henry Vaughan – do not write back. Indeed, the one-way dynamic Lilley
describes has a bearing on Philips's overall attitude to control of her texts. Writing
in Wales throughout the 1650s, those writing in Philips's circle – rather than those
who we know only as the recipients of poems of friendship – drew on shared readings which also served political ends, in as Patrick Thomas puts it, 'keeping courtly
values alive' (Thomas, I, p. 9). Platonic love, the ideals of friendship, the association
of romance with court culture, mark Philips's poems as associated with other royalists in her circle, or who like the poets William Cartwright and John Suckling, had
died early in the Civil War. Reading – in the sense of a shared repertoire of authors
and genres valued for both aesthetic and political reasons – was registered by Philips
and her circle as part of a richly self-confirming intertextuality, knitting together the
disparate poets. However, in the 1650s, Philips did not confine herself to poems of
friendship, writing explicitly political poetry, a poem on the Welsh language and
poems extolling the Edenic pleasures of pastoral retirement: 'How sacred and how
innocent / A country life appears, / How free from tumult, discontent / From flat-
terye and feares.'

Highly literary in a self-consciously allusive way that contrasts sharply with
Cavendish's truncated reading and claims to originality, Philips's poetry of the 1650s
was also intended to circulate in manuscript amongst a limited audience between
Wales and London – a kind of circulation which, while not public in the same sense
as print, was not wholly 'private'. Notably, the modes of Philips's circulation changed
at the Restoration when, although she benefited from her status as a royalist, the fate
of her husband who worked for the Protectorate (Cromwellian) administration, hung
in the balance. At this point Philips addressed a sequence of poems praising the newly
restored Stuarts. She also translated an act of Corneille's *La Morte de Pompée*, and then
the full play which found its way into court circles in London. In Dublin, it was performed and then printed, though anonymously. In response to Philips's public profile

in early January 1664 a pirated edition of the poems of the 1650s appeared and Philips's response to this text is suggestive in terms of the relationship between manuscript and public circulation. She wrote to her friend Charles Cotterell ('Poliarchus') of the 'unfortunate Accident of the unworthy publishing of my foolish Rhymes', but noted that another friend has urged her to 'hasten to London and vindicate my self by publishing a true copy'. Accordingly, the publisher was forced to withdraw many copies and Philips's own edition, not very different from the pirated version, appeared in 1667. Philips's reaction to the publication of her poetry, though sometimes interpreted in terms of her eighteenth-century reputation for modesty and obedience, seems less like an aversion to the highly public nature of print (after all she allowed publication of her translation of Corneille, albeit anonymously) than a desire to keep control of her products. This desire, like Cavendish's insistence on her originality, suggests both an emerging conception of the author in relation to texts and a conception of the circulation of literary texts as highly purposive in personal and political terms.

In the eighteenth century Katherine Philips was remembered not only for her excellence as a poet, but for a modesty which contrasted with the flamboyant publicity-seeking of Margaret Cavendish and – particularly – Aphra Behn's successful intervention in the Restoration public sphere. Virginia Woolf contrasts Aphra Behn with her predecessors in terms of status, profession, and writing for money – '[s]he made, by working very hard, enough to live on' (Woolf, 1984, 59). However, examined from the perspective of women's changing relations to the public sphere, we might think of Behn not solely as 'the first professional woman writer' but as participating in a rapidly changing market in words. Behn's lack of a classical education, though contemporaries commented on it, did not stand in her way. She published plays, poetry and fiction and worked successfully for the theatre, switching from theatre to prose when the market in plays collapsed because the two rival London theatre companies amalgamated. Probably Behn's two best known texts are still *The Rover* (1677) and *Oroonoko: or, the Royal Slave* (1688), as well as *Love Letters Between a Nobleman and His Sister* (1684–7), an epistolary novel tracing scandals amongst Whig politicians. But these well-known texts represent a fragment of Behn's output in a career which spanned all the genres and included phases of working for theatre, translation, and prose fiction. *The Rover* draws heavily on a ten-act play by the interregnum playwright, Thomas Killigrew and from such appropriations Behn developed a reputation for putting her reading to work in her writing very directly. However, rather than being significant as plagiarism, what Behn does with Killigrew's play, as well as what she does with the romance form in her shorter fictions (such as *Agnes de Castro*, 'The Dumb Virgin') indicate the ways in which she adapts genres to the new market conditions of late Stuart England. Behn truncates Killigrew's text, emphasizes the interrelationship between the sexes, and shapes it as a comedy for the Restoration stage. In the way Behn writes and reworks we can see an author making her literary abilities and her politics productive in the new Restoration literary marketplace.

III

In her *Reflections on Marriage* (1706) Mary Astell wrote:

> [W]hatever may be said against Passive-Obedience in another case, I suppose there's no
> man but likes it very well in this; how much soever Arbitrary Power may be dislik'd
> on a Throne, not *Milton* himself wou'd cry up Liberty to poor *Female Slaves*, or plead the
> Lawfulness of Resisting a Private Tyranny.

In returning to Milton, Astell (known for her interventions on marriage and on
women's education) reverts to the question of women's place in public and private as
suggested in Milton's divorce writings (Hill, 1986). Although Milton saw divorce as
beneficial to women, his tracts really focus on masculine need for an appropriate help-
meet if he is to be able to function virtuously in the public sphere. Astell's commentary reverses the logic which sees the exercise of power in private and public as
wholly distinct. Assuming that her readers also have access to Milton's ideas, she transfers ideas and vocabulary which were central to the consideration of kings and states
– 'Sovereign Power', 'Rebellious Subject', 'Tyranny', 'Arbitrary Power' – from public
to private realms, inviting the reader to make connections between the excessive exercise of arbitrary power by the tyrant and that power marriage gave the husband.

Astell, writing in the middle of our period, had her writing printed in a public
sphere which was very different from that of the 1640s. The circulation of newspapers
had expanded to become a periodical market, fiction was substantial business, and the
massive changes in the print trade have led some commentators to argue that the
eighteenth century saw a massive shift in the whole way in which people read. Roger
Chartier argues that from reading a few texts intensively (the Bible, commonplace
books), readers came to skim-read a far greater number of texts (Chartier, 1994).
Although this is not proven, it is the case that Astell's text is marked by the context
in which it would be read. Several details of Astell's text respond to the public sphere
in which it was to be published, particularly that the tract itself was circulated in
response to a scandal reported in the public press, and that she is clearly aware that
her writings were to be judged in a public sphere where opinions were important not
necessarily for themselves but according to who held them. She initially published
anonymously, arguing '"Tis a very great Fault to regard rather who it is that Speaks,
than what is Spoken'. Astell's comments indicate an awareness of the position of
women writing on contentious topics within the public arena – that sphere within
which, as Jürgen Habermas puts it, private citizens come together to exercise critical
reason.

Although Habermas's dating of the emergence of the public sphere at the so-called
Glorious Revolution of 1688 has been debated, his understanding of the emergence
of the public sphere as 'the process in which the state-governed public sphere was
appropriated by the public of private people making use of their reason and was established as a sphere of criticism of public authority' has been highly influential.

However, as Astell recognizes, many factors affect the reception of contributions to this notionally free sphere of critical reason including particularly the sex and social status of the author. Within the literary sphere, the genres in which one was writing – prose (including the periodical and fiction), drama, poetry – were also highly significant in relation to sex and status. While poetic production allows us to see the contested boundaries of the public arena throughout the eighteenth century, as women and labouring class poets are printed, if we trace women's writing and reading in the genre of theatre, or novel, or periodical rather different patterns emerge.

The place of women in writing and reading periodicals is significant. One effect of the transformation of the culture of print in the eighteenth century was the consolidation and extension of an idea of women as a specific market of readers, and, simultaneously, the increased participation of women in print as hack writers, literary writers, critics and as social commentators. The invention of women as a market of readers has been associated by literary critics with an intensification of emphasis on women's place in the domestic sphere, something which Nancy Armstrong traces as being presented as desirable to women readers in both fiction and periodicals. Women were the target of periodicals, for which they also wrote. For example, taking up some of the niche marketing of earlier periodicals such as Delariver Manley's *Female Tatler*, John Dunton's *Athenian Mercury*, and of course the early eighteenth-century *Spectator*, under Eliza Haywood's editorial control *The Female Spectator* specifically addressed the female reader and was edited by a woman. As Kathryn Shevelow indicates, the specialization of periodicals such as *The Female Spectator* was a 'logical extension' of the way the earliest periodicals inscribed women as a sub-audience.

Thus, the periodical set up a situation which, based around the idea of actual or imagined exchange between editors, contributors and readers, offered a particular space, theoretically one of free communication yet bounded and arguably domestic, within the public sphere. The stated aim of *The Female Spectator*, 'to *promote the Practice of Virtue* in those who stand in need of such Excitements, by shewing the most amiable Examples of it; and to *reform those Errors in Conduct*, which . . . are productive of the most irreparable Misfortunes', suggests the paradox under which women writers and readers of periodicals entered the public sphere. The first volume indicated that reading, 'universally allowed to be one of the most improving as well as agreeable amusements', needed to be limited to those texts which are 'most conducive to those ends'. Following 'my learned brother' (*The Spectator*) Hayward promises to select material which will allow refined taste to separate itself from 'the vulgar'. Women's potentially promiscuous reading and taste needs to be turned towards virtue, and the purchase of the periodical – itself part of the commercial sphere encouraging such promiscuity – is offered as a solution.

If women readers were both courted and disciplined by the periodical, entry into the public domain as a writer of novels or periodicals brought its own hazards. Alexander Pope, in *The Dunciad* (1728) described Haywood – a novelist as much as an editor of periodicals – in sexual terms, 'her fore-buttocks to the navel bare'. Much read, novels were accorded little aesthetic status – Fanny Burney's reputation was an excep-

tion. As Jane Spencer indicates, while there was no dearth of women writing and publishing novels, their efforts were not likely to bring them literary fame. Within the
eighteenth century public sphere Spencer sees women novelists as using feminine
virtue to negotiate a '"respectable" position'. However, critical opprobrium existed
and in a circular argument the voracious appetite of women readers for novels was
seen as fostering this downmarket genre and the scribblers – including of course
women – who wrote such fiction. Eliza Haywood is once again an example of
commercial success in writing products with assumed low market value. Apparently
left 'depending on my pen' by an 'unfortunate marriage' she had a prolific career in
fiction. Besides working as an actress she edited three periodicals (*The Female Spectator* followed by *The Parrot*, and *The Young Lady*), wrote plays, poems, short fiction and
novels and, following the fashion set by Richardson, impressively adapted her writing
from the erotic style of her earlier novels – like her highly successful *Love in Excess;
or, the Fatal Enquiry* (1719) – to the didactic tastes of the 1740s and 1750s. Linked
to both Behn and Manley, Haywood's career indicates the importance of women
as producers of prose fiction in the early eighteenth century. For all the harsh
denigration of her writing by Pope in the *Dunciad*, Haywood published and sold in
great quantity.

Romance continued to be amongst the genres consistently associated with women
as producers and readers, and it continued to be understood as a feminine genre even
as its nature and modes were internally transformed. Anne Radcliffe, writer of gothic
romance, was brought up in circles that included the bluestocking Elizabeth Montagu
and Hester Piozzi, and her husband, William Radcliffe, was editor and owner of the
English Chronicle. She began publishing in the late 1780s, developing her characteristic use of gothic architecture in *The Sicilian Romance* (1790), *The Romance of the Forest*
(1791) and her amazing success, *The Mysteries of Udolpho* (1794) (for which she was
paid the huge sum of £500) followed by *The Italian* (1797). *The Mysteries of Udolpho*
extends investigation of the imagination of its heroine to a thoroughgoing analysis of
the way in which fantasy operates to render undecidable the borders of true and false.
Although, ultimately, the novel is at pains to resolve its mysteries as part of a 'real'
world rather than supernatural terrors: it offers the reader a seductive account of the
way in which fantasy remakes the world in its own image.

The popularity of romance reading, and its public profile as the reading of women,
indicates as clearly as the emergence of the specialist journal aimed at women the
expansion of the reading public to include women as a category of consumer and
reader. In writing romances Radcliffe participated in a genre which sustained its
popularity and its associations with women over at least two centuries. The novel,
then, was understood as a staple of women's reading and novels were written by
women. Ideologically, however, this did not mean that the novel offered what we
might now understand as a feminist social analysis – rather, that successful writers of
popular fiction captured the issues which motivated their readers. That women participated in the writing of novels did not, as the example of romance fiction makes
clear, transform the genre into a vehicle for what we might understand as feminist
polemic.

The theatre, too, was a sphere in which women participated as writers, players and audiences. The paradox of pleasure and virtue found in the novel is reshaped and accentuated in the theatre, for theatre clearly offered a form in which the audience were both invited to make judgements of taste and to take pleasure in spectacle. Given that women had only acted regularly on the English stage since the Restoration of Charles II in 1660 (though women had appeared in court and other performances before this) it is hardly surprising that debates around theatre crystallize many of the tensions between commerce (availability, circulation, desire, spectacle) and taste (judgement, self-control, politeness). Women writing for the stage in the early eighteenth century included Mary Pix, Catherine Trotter and Susanna Centlivre. A Whig, Centlivre's sixteen plays have political implications (she satirized Tory corruption in *A Gotham Election* (1715)) and she adapts French texts to contemporary taste. *The Gamester* (1705), *The Busy Body* (1709), and *A Bold Stroke for a Wife* (1718) went on being performed for many years. Centlivre's plays conform to early eighteenth-century taste. Much, though not all, of the debate about women's writing for the theatre circulated around the issue of the representation of adultery and sexual transgression (Behn's plays were a target here) and the idea that women, inappropriately, wrote comedies full of sexual innuendo. As Kristina Straub has argued, while the idea of the spectator – watching a performance – is 'a powerful trope for a mode of discursive authority' the spectator's control over the theatrical spectacle and his or her reaction to it was continually tested by sexualized spectacle. The theatre continued to offer a part of public life in which political and sexual instability was built in to the experience – though often projected on to the actors, actresses and writers. For example, a prologue contributed to Mary Pix's *The Innocent Mistress* (1697) read: 'No Bawdy, this can't be a Women's Play. / Nay, I confesse there's Cause enough to doubt, / But, Faith, they say there was a deal cut out.'

As print circulation expanded the question of who might legitimately participate in the sphere of print came to be addressed, explicitly, in several ways as the boundaries of legitimate participation in the cultural sphere proved, in part, permeable. As was the case with women publishing in libertine genres (like Behn) or competing in the periodical market (like Eliza Haywood), participation in print involved complicated negotiations of status – for such writers, lacking entry qualifications, the public sphere did not offer Habermas's ideal of free communication. As the highest of the genres – the one considered most elevating to the reader, and indicating and requiring most skill and knowledge in the writer – poetry is the genre in which we can trace most vividly the question of who might, and might not, appropriately participate in the public sphere.

In 1739 Mary Collier, described on the title page as 'Now a washer-woman, at *Petersfield* in *Hampshire*', published her poem, *The Woman's Labour: An Epistle to Mr Stephen Duck; in Answer to his late Poem, called The Thresher's Labour*. Duck was a labouring class poet who, in the 1730s, was taken up by the elite and given a pension by Queen Caroline. Collier addresses him as 'Immortal Bard', 'Enrich'd by Peers', but besides her praise a strain of rivalry is clear. She asserts, 'No Learning ever was bestow'd on me; / My Life was always spent in Drudgery' and behind Collier's apparent acqui-

escence to masculine primacy in poetry and labour exists a rivalrous assertiveness in
which female labour is repeatedly harder than male:

> The *Washing* is not all we have to do:
> We oft change Work for Work as well as you.
> Our Mistress of her Pewter doth complain,
> And 'tis our Part to make it clean again.

Worse, 'Pots, Kettles, Sauce-pans, Skillets, we may see, / Skimmers and Ladles, and
such Trumpery, / Brought in to make complete our Slavery.' That the existence of
such a poet could seem extraordinary, even exotic, to the elite is as E. P. Thompson
suggests in part 'the almost unbridgeable gap' between 'polite and plebeian cultures'
which existed in the early eighteenth century (Thompson, 1989, v). Yet, as the emergence of Mary Collier and other labouring poets suggests, the 'discovery' of plebeian
poets by the elite inaugurated new and complex patronage relations within the public
sphere as poets and their patrons had common interest in the publication of such
poems, but rather different investments in their reception.

The story of another labouring-class poet, Anne Yearsley, illuminatingly discussed
by Donna Landry, indicates the difficult negotiation of the boundaries of the public
sphere. A milkwoman from Bristol, Yearsley's poetic talent was recognized by Hannah
More, herself author of a wide range of poetry and prose, but especially well known
for her output of *Cheap Repository Tracts*. More used her abilities to encourage a mixture
of obedience and improvement in the lower orders; her educational mission was bound
up with a conservative perception of the proper place of the labouring classes. Beginning as a playwright, More later wrote socially committed poetry, ran a school, promoted women's friendly societies, was a member of the Clapham Sect. Thus her *Village
Politics* (1792), a dialogue she addressed to journeymen and day-labourers under the
name of 'Will Chip' 'a country carpenter', explicitly set out to counter the radicaliz-
ing potential of the French Revolution amongst the English labouring class. In the
tract Tom and Jack dispute on the subject of liberty, in which Tom, who has been
reading Paine's *Rights of Man* asks 'What is *the new Rights of Man?*' and Jack convinces
him it is 'Battle, murder and sudden death' (More, 1792, 19). However, More was
also in favour of the abolition of slavery and wrote 'Slavery, A Poem':

> Perish th'illiberal thought which would debase
> The native genius of the sable race!
> Perish the proud philosophy, which sought
> To rob them of the powers of equal thought!

More met Yearsley in 1784 and helped to edit her work and to arrange for publication by subscription, considering Yearsley's 'wild wood notes' 'extraordinary for a
milker of Cows and a feeder of Hogs, who has never *seen* a Dictionary' (Lonsdale, 1989,
329–3). Yearsley had however read *Paradise Lost*, parts of Pope, Dryden, Spenser and

Prior and the poems indicate that Yearsley used her reading to familiarize herself with poetic convention and to express a melancholy apprehension of the natural world. Thus, the poem 'On Clifton Hill Written in January 1785' opens with a description of a physically and psychologically desolate landscape, 'when angry storms descend, /And the chill'd soul deplores her distant friend' and 'gloomy objects fill the mental eye'. When More decided that she should keep control of the profits from the volume and invested them, Yearsley rebelled and the ensuing struggle was marked by differences in status and perception. More wrote to Mrs Montagu of Yearsley's 'Gauze Bonnets', asking 'Is such a Woman to be trusted with her poor Children's money?' whereas Yearsley's plan was to plough her profits into a circulating library – notoriously the source, amongst other books, of the kind of novels felt to corrupt the female mind. Yearsley eventually got hold of the subscription money and by 1793 had opened the circulating library.

A third example of the way in which entry into the printed sphere was often in the eighteenth century facilitated, limited and shaped – though not wholly controlled – by those in possession of cultural capital is that of the poet Phillis Wheatley. Henry Louis Gates has described the publication of Phillis Wheatley's *Poems on Various Subjects, Religious and Moral* (1773) as the 'birth of the Afro-American literary tradition' (Wheatley, 1988, vii). Wheatley's case, too, illustrates the complexity of entry into the public sphere, not by those to whom (like middle-class women, to whom particular roles were assigned) but of those whose participation directly or indirectly threatened the status of that sphere as delimited, polite, demarcated. Wheatley had failed to get a publisher to take her poems in America but, upon being brought to England in 1773, her poems were published with an endorsement by the leading citizens of Boston who had examined her a year earlier – when she was eighteen – to check that she was truly the author of the poems which indicated knowledge not only of contemporary neo-classical style, but of the classical and English canon, Ovid to Pope. The endorsement, explaining that she was 'but a few Years since, brought an uncultivated Barbarian from *Africa*, and has ever since been, and now is, under the Disadvantage of serving as a Slave', authenticated authorship and, in doing so, ensured the volume's place in the abolitionist literature of the eighteenth and nineteenth centuries, and as a foundational text, addressed by other slave poets. Amongst other topics, Wheatley obliquely addresses her status as a slave brought from Senegal as a child in a poem, 'On being brought from Africa to America', where she asserts ' 'Twas mercy brought me from my *Pagan* land, / Taught my benighted soul to understand / That there's a God, there's a *Saviour* too': concluding 'Remember, *Christians, Negros*, black as *Cain*, / May be refin'd, and join th'angelic train.' Where Wheatley's poems demonstrate her learning, her letters tell us both what it was thought appropriate and improving for a slave-poet to read and hint ambiguously at her own preferences. Writing to a correspondent on her return to Boston in October 1773, she describes her London farewell: 'The Earl of Dartmouth made me a Compliment of 5 guineas, and desired me to get the whole of Mr Pope's Works, as the best he could recommend to my perusal, this I did, also got Hudibrass, Don Quixot, & Gay's Fables. Was presented with a Folio Edition of Milton's Paradise Lost' (Wheatley, 1988, 169–71). Wheatley was encouraged to read, but under direction.

The policing of Wheatley's education and the way in which, for example, Hannah More saw it as her duty to counter revolutionary reading indicate, as James Raven has discussed, a contradiction at the heart of the eighteenth-century public sphere whereby print democratized access to knowledge but many of the people actually involved in the making available of that knowledge had ideological or commercial interests in limiting its circulation. Raven indicates the expansion of access to print by noting that the twenty circulating libraries in London in 1760 had become over two hundred nationally by 1800, and goes on to offer a vivid description of an attempt to limit participation in the reading and writing of books on the grounds of sex and status. This is the *Critical Review* (1772) on the subject of the 'rustic authoress' of the anonymous novel, *Virtue in Distress . . . by a Farmer's Daughter in Gloucestershire*: 'When a farmer's daughter sits down to *read* a novel, she certainly misspends her time . . . : when she sits down to *write* one her friends can have no hope of her.' Raven's research also indicates that libraries, which might be thought of as freely circulating knowledge, also sought to emphasize the respectability of their clientele and actively sought to limit the circulation of their texts (Raven, 1996, 182).

Women readers were the focus of didactic and commercial discourses on print. It is likely that the reading patterns of women changed substantially during the period under discussion. Where in the 1640s the diarist Elizabeth Jekyll combined use of news and the Bible to generate her interpretation of the political and religious significance of the Civil War, John Brewer's study of the recorded reading of Anna Larpent, born in 1758 and the upper middle-class wife of John Larpent, Inspector of Plays in the Office of the Lord Chamberlain, finds her reading 440 titles in the first ten years of her diary, including texts by Spenser, Milton, Gay, Pope, Thomson, Young, Gray. Where Jekyll strives to know God's will, and in doing so grapples with facts and texts which seem to go against her desired interpretation, Larpent, Brewer tells us, struggles to come to her own judgement about texts with which she cannot agree (Brewer, 1994). To characterize Jekyll as an obedient reader of sacred texts, Larpent as a secularized interpreter would be problematically to polarize changes in reading possibilities and patterns. Yet it does seem that the expansion of literacy and print, while it might also bring emphasis on the role of women in the domestic sphere, also gave them access to debates – including those about the nature of private and public, and about the texts that they read.

As Roger Chartier notes, while the traces left by writing are relatively 'conservative, fixed, durable', reading 'rarely leaves traces . . . is scattered in an infinity of singular acts'. Journals, diaries, letters and memoirs bear traces of women's reading. However, texts prepared for publication, as I have been suggesting, use quotation and reading very differently. A final example of the use of reading in a published text is offered by Mary Wollstonecraft (at the end of our period) writing on Milton (who wrote at the beginning). Wollstonecraft's mode of analysis demonstrates vividly the changes wrought in her thinking in response to the French Revolution when, in *A*

Vindication of the Rights of Woman (1792), she addresses the status of women. She writes, 'The conduct and manners of women, in fact, evidently prove that their minds are not in a healthy state; for, like the flowers which are planted in too rich a soil, strength and usefulness are sacrificed to beauty.' Noting that women are treated 'as if they were in a state of perpetual childhood, unable to stand alone', Wollstonecraft returns to *Paradise Lost* with a very different attitude from the one which allowed her to excerpt Milton as the promoter of domestic harmony only three years earlier in her *Female Reader*. Expostulating with those who 'advise us only to render ourselves gentle domestic brutes' Wollstonecraft now finds in Milton a double attitude to the equality and reciprocity of the sexes. First, she finds he patronizes Eve who tells Adam that she is subservient to him: 'God is *thy law, thou mine*: to know no more / Is Woman's *happiest* knowledge and her *praise*.' Yet, elsewhere, she finds 'Milton seems to coincide with me; when he makes Adam expostulate with his Maker' for making him God's own substitute and yet leaving him among 'these inferior far beneath me set?' She quotes Adam's question:

> Among *unequals* what society
> Can sort, what harmony or true delight?
> Which must be mutual, in proportion due
> Giv'n and receiv'd; but in *disparity*
> The one intense, the other still remiss
> Cannot well suit with either, but soon prove
> Tedious alike: of *fellowship* I speak
> Such as I seek, fit to participate
> All rational delight.

Wollstonecraft sees that in *Paradise Lost* Eve presents for Milton an unresolved problem of what the relationship between the sexes is, and what it might be. Are women to be considered subservient, sensual, creatures – in which case they are likely to be '*unequals*' unable to provide '*fellowship*' or is Milton led into contradiction at this point by his own sensuality?

Milton's failure to untangle the dynamic between masculine desire for feminine submissiveness and beauty versus the potential for companionship allows Wollstonecraft to make his problem her own. Where Milton asks, 'Among *unequals* what society / Can sort, what harmony or true delight?' Wollstonecraft offers reason and education. From one whom 'the constitution of civil society has rendered weak, if not vicious', she argues, no virtue can be expected, and 'unless virtue be nursed by liberty, it will never attain due strength'.

Clearly, we cannot generalize about reading from the way in which Wollstonecraft, a polemical and strong interpreter uses Milton to make her own arguments for publication. Yet, equally clearly, the nature of women's writing and reading changed substantially in the period under consideration influenced – as was Wollstonecraft's – by political, social and economic changes. As Denise Riley argues, writing about the problems inherent in taking women as a group, if we take a slice through, say, 1642 and compare women writers they are unlikely to emerge as a group with definition and outline, and if we compare, say, Katherine Chidley with Mary Wollstonecraft the same dissonance is likely to be true. However, precisely because the category women has been imposed so forcefully 'in language, forms of description, and what gets carried out', as Riley further notes, 'feminism has intermittently been as vexed with the urgency of disengaging from the category "women" as it has with laying claim to it' (Riley, 1988, 3–4). In part it is this dynamic we can see at work in Wollstonecraft's writings on Milton.

References and Further Reading

Selected Primary Texts

Astell, Mary (1986). *The First English Feminist Reflections upon Marriage and other Writings*. Ed. Bridget Hill. London: Gower.

Cavendish, Margaret (1675). *The Life of the Thrice Noble, High, and Puissant Prince William Cavendishe*. London.

Chidley, Katherine (1641). *The Justification of the Independant Churches of Christ*. London.

Ferguson, Moira, ed. (1980). *Mary Wollstonecraft: The Female Reader*. Delmar, New York: Scholars' Facsimiles and Reprints.

Firmager, Gabrielle M. (1993). *Eliza Haywood: The Female Spectator*. Bristol: Bristol Classical Press.

Graham, Elspeth, Hilary Hinds, Elain Hobby and Helen Wilcox, eds (1989). *Her Own Life: Autobiographical Writings by Seventeenth-century Englishwomen*. London: Routledge.

Lonsdale, Roger, ed. (1989). *Eighteenth-century Women Poets*. Oxford: Oxford University Press.

Milton, John (1959). *Doctrine and Discipline of Divorce*. In *Complete Prose Works*. New Haven: Yale University Press. Vol. 2.

More, Hannah (1792). *Village Politics*. London: F. & C. Rivington.

Shields, John C. (1988). *The Collected Works of Phillis Wheatley*. Oxford: Oxford University Press.

Thomas, Patrick, ed. (1990). *The Collected Works of Katherine Philips*. Essex: Stump Cross Books. Vols 1 and 2.

Thompson, E. P., ed. (1989). *The Thresher's Labour: The Woman's Labour*. London: Merlin Press.

Todd, Janet, ed. (1993). *Mary Wollstonecraft: Political Writings*. London: William Pickering.

Secondary Reading

Achinstein, Sharon (1999). 'Women on top in the pamphlet literature of the English Revolution'. In *Feminism & Renaissance Studies*. Ed. Lorna Hutson. Oxford: Oxford University Press, 339–72.

Armstrong, Nancy (1987). *Desire and Domestic Fiction*. Oxford: Oxford University Press.

Ballaster, Ros (1992). *Seductive Forms: Women's Amatory Fiction From 1684–1740*. Oxford: Oxford University Press.

Calhoun, Craig, ed. (1992). *Habermas and the Public Sphere*. Cambridge, Mass.: MIT Press.

Brewer, John (1994). 'Reconstructing the reader: prescriptions, texts and strategies in Anna Larpent's reading'. In James Raven et al., eds., 226–45.

Chartier, Roger (1994). *The Order of Books*. Trans. Lydia G. Cochrane. Cambridge: Polity Press.

Cressy, David (1980). *Literacy and the Social Order*. Cambridge: Cambridge University Press.

Ezell, Margaret (1993). *Writing Women's Literary History*. Baltimore and London: Johns Hopkins University Press.

Habermas, Jürgen (1992). *The Structural Transformation of the Public Sphere*. Trans. Thomas Burger. Cambridge: Polity Press.

Hinds, Hilary (1996). *God's Englishwomen: Seventeenth-century Radical Sectarian Writing and Feminist Criticism*. Manchester: Manchester University Press.

Hobby, Elaine (1988). *Virtue of Necessity: English Women's Writing, 1649–1688*. London: Virago.

Landes, Joan B. (1998). *Feminism: The Public & the Private*. Oxford: Oxford University Press.

Landry, Donna (1990). *The Muses of Resistance, Laboring-class Women's Poetry in Britain, 1739–1796.* Cambridge: Cambridge University Press.

Nevitt, Marcus (1999). 'Women in the business of revolutionary news: Elizabeth Alkin, "Parliament Joan", and the Commonwealth Newsbook'. In *News, Newspapers, and Society in Early Modern Britain.* Ed. Joad Raymond. London: Frank Cass, 84–108.

Raven, James (1996). 'From promotion to proscription: arrangements for reading and eighteenth-century libraries'. In James Raven et al., eds., 175–201.

——Naomi Tadmore and Helen Small, eds. (1996). *The Practice and Representation of Reading in England.* Cambridge: Cambridge University Press.

Riley, Denise (1988). *'Am I That Name?' Feminism and the Category of 'Women' in History.* Basingstoke: Macmillan.

Smith, Hilda, L. (1997). '"A general war amongst the men . . . but none amongst the women": political differences between Margaret and William Cavendish'. In *Politics and the Political Imagination in Later Stuart Britain.* Ed. Howard Nenner. New York: University of Rochester Press, 143–60.

Jane Spencer (1986). *The Rise of the Woman Novelist: From Aphra Behn to Jane Austen.* Oxford: Blackwell.

Sharrock, Catherine (1992). 'De-ciphering women and de-scribing authority: the writings of Mary Astell'. In *Women, Writing, History 1640–1740.* Ed. Isobel Grundy and S. Wiseman. London: Batsford, 109–24.

Shevelow, Kathryn (1989). *Women and Print Culture: The Construction of Femininity in the Early Periodical.* London: Routledge.

Smith, Hilda (1982). *Reason's Disciples.* Urbana: University of Illinois Press.

Vickery, Amanda (1993). 'Golden age to separate spheres: a review of the categories and chronology of English women's history'. *Historical Journal* 36.2, 383–414.

Wheatley, Phillis (1988). *The Collected Works of Phillis Wheatley.* Ed. John C. Shields. Oxford: Oxford University Press.

Woolf, Virginia (1984). *A Room of One's Own.* Ed. Hermione Lee. London: Chatto and Windus.

3
Literature and Party, 1675–1760
Brean Hammond

I begin with a song I learned at school in Edinburgh, in many ways a curious choice for a class of lads with galloping hormones:

'Twas on a Monday morning
   Right early in the year,
That Charlie came to our town –
   The young Chevalier!
CHORUS
An' Charlie, he's my darling, my darling, my darling,
Charlie, he's my darling, the young Chevalier! –

As he was walking up the street,
   The city for to view,
O there he spied a bonie lass
   The window looking thro'
An Charlie, etc.

Sae light's he jimped up the stair,
      And tirled at the pin;
   And wha sae ready as hersel
      To let the laddie in.
   An Charlie, etc.

He set his Jenny on his knee,
      All in his Highland dress;
   For brawlie weel he ken'd the way
      To please a bonie lass.
   An Charlie, etc.

It's up yon hethery mountain,
      And down yon scroggy glen,

We daur na gang a milking,
     For Charlie and his men.
An Charlie, etc.

The song is a street ballad probably dating from around 1775, that was revised by Burns (the suggestive third stanza is his addition) and published in James Johnson's famous *Scots Musical Museum* collection in 1796. 'Charlie' is Bonnie Prince Charlie – Charles Edward Stuart, son of the man that many believed was the rightful King James III. The song represents Charles Stuart as a handsome seducer of womenfolk all too willing to succumb to his charms, his Highland dress affording him various kinds of convenience. The girls are afraid to go out milking with the Highland soldiers around, not because they fear violence, but because they dare not trust themselves in the company of such a romantic army. Contrast the song with this sensational and lurid account of anticipated atrocities, cast in the form of a dream-vision, that was published in Henry Fielding's journal *The True Patriot* on 19 November 1745. Since the Highland army was in some quarters invested with considerable romance, as we have seen, Fielding's task as an effective journalist is to represent the enemy as barbaric rapists, playing on his readers' anxieties:

> The first Sight which occurred to me as I past through the Streets . . . was a young Lady of Quality, and the greatest Beauty of this Age, in the Hands of two *Highlanders*, who were struggling with each other for their Booty. The lovely Prize, tho' her Hair was dishevelled and torn, her Eyes swollen with Tears, her Face all pale, and some Marks of Blood both on that and on her Breast, which was all naked and exposed, retained still sufficient Charms to discover herself to me, who have always beheld her with Wonder and Admiration . . . After such a Spectacle as this, the dead Bodies which lay every where in the Streets (for there had been, I was told, a Massacre the Night before) scarce made any Impression: nay, the very Fires in which Protestants were roasting, were, in my Sense, Objects of much less Horror. (Coley, 1987, 132)

It would be too simple, but not entirely distortive, to call those two texts a Scottish view and an English view of the events of 1745–6. When Charles II died in 1685, his brother James succeeded him despite various earlier attempts to exclude him from the throne because he was a Roman Catholic (the 'Exclusion Crisis'). James made a spectacular mess of his reign, and when a son was born to him and his Queen, Mary of Modena, in 1688 (though the rumour was quickly circulated that the baby was actually smuggled into the birthing chamber in a warming-pan!), the political leaders of the nation invited William of Orange, leader of European Protestantism, to come over to England and assume power. That this was accomplished with relatively little bloodshed in England, and that William's assumption of power was followed by legislation that secured Protestant succession and arrived at a compromise between King and Parliament, has led to the events of 1688–9 being termed the 'Glorious Revolution'. Yet many religious and political groups were excluded from the settlement, and one such was the supporters of James III's right to rule, the 'Jacobites'. There were several risings in his support, principally the one he led himself in 1715, and his son Charles's attempt to invade England from the Scottish Highlands in 1745–6, that ended in a bloody slaughter at Culloden Fields. Gaining an understanding of the part played by Jacobitism in British political life is a valuable introduction to the topic of literature and party politics in the period.

I

Fielding's dream-vision was written just before the point of maximum penetration of the Jacobite army into England (Derby, 4 December 1745). A later number of *The True Patriot*, no. 10 published on 7 January 1746, ten days before the Highland army won another battle at Falkirk, has a 'diary' contributed by Fielding's friend James Harris of the events that supposedly follow the Pretender's coming to power. This chronicles the creeping Catholicization of the kingdom, and the destruction of all the institutions of democratic Protestant Englishness. On Fielding the novelist, the impression made by Charles Edward Stuart's invasion was considerable. The events of the '45 form a recurrent backdrop to his most significant novel *Tom Jones* (1749) – Books VII to XII dramatize the events of twelve days in the hero's life in November 1745, so it is entirely plausible that in Book VII Tom should come face to face with soldiers 'marching against the Rebels, and expected to be commanded by the glorious Duke of *Cumberland*'. At times in the novel, attitudes towards Jacobitism assist in organizing the reader's moral perspective. Squire Western's gesture of regularly toasting 'the King over the Water' is seen to be just that: an empty, knee-jerk form of anti-government protest politics. In other places, Jacobite support is figured as a feminized, romantic illusion. What we should really think of Jacobitism as a political cause is most transparently expressed in Jones's conversation with the Man of the Hill, who, in his reclusive ignorance of the two Jacobite rebellions, is a naif deployed to heighten the absurdity of Jacobite politics. His incredulity is constructed as a commonsense, quasi-natural response to the very *idea* of Jacobite pretension:

'it has often struck me, as the most wonderful thing I ever read of in History, that so soon after this convincing Experience, which brought our whole Nation to join so unanimously in expelling King *James*, for the Preservation of our Religion and Liberties, there should be a Party among us mad enough to desire the placing of his Family again on the Throne'. 'You are not in Earnest!' answered the old Man; 'there can be no such Party. As bad an Opinion as I have of Mankind, I cannot believe them infatuated to such a Degree! There may be some hot-headed Papists led by their Priests to engage in this desparate Cause, and think it a Holy War; but that Protestants, that Members of the Church of *England* should be such Apostates, such *Felos de se*, I cannot believe it; no, no, young Man, unacquainted as I am with what has past in the World for these last thirty Years, I cannot be so imposed upon as to credit so foolish a Tale: But I see you have a Mind to sport with my Ignorance. 'Can it be possible,' replied *Jones*, 'that you have lived so much out of the World as not to know, that during that Time there have been two

Rebellions in favour of the Son of King *James*, one of which is now actually raging in the very Heart of this Kingdom?'

What a lesson in Whiggish politics this exchange is! Tom refers, of course, to the events of the so-called Glorious Revolution of 1688. Already by then, the embryonic two-party system that was to be so vitally important in the development of British politics had emerged. King Charles's brother, James Duke of York, had been admitted to the Roman Catholic faith in the late 1660s, shortly after the period during which the monarch had been re-established as head of a national Anglican church. As the 1670s wore on and Charles's efforts to sire a legitimate heir to the throne came to nothing (though his illegitimate efforts were spectacular), the fact of James's Catholicism, public knowledge after 1673, was increasingly troublesome. As anti-Catholic fervour rose in the wake of a so-called 'Popish Plot', spearheaded by Titus Oates (a professional perjurer who had been expelled from more institutions than the King had sired bastards) to the effect that a Jesuit conspiracy intended to replace Charles on the throne by his Catholic brother, three successive parliaments tried to pass legislation to exclude James from the throne. 'Whig' and 'Tory' were initially terms of abuse that, like 'queer' in our own time, were embraced by their intended objects: and the former came to connote those who supported exclusion while the latter referred to those who supported James's hereditary right to rule despite his religion. Looking back at Tom's conversation, we see that he refers to events 'which brought our whole Nation to join so unanimously in expelling King *James*, for the Preservation of our Religion and Liberties'. This begs a very large number of questions, and scarcely represents an objective account of events. The 'whole Nation' never did unanimously endorse the Revolution of 1688. Whig and Tory factions were given good opportunities to solidify into something more permanent by James's way of wielding authority. His use of monarchical special powers in support of Catholics persuaded powerful political leaders that he wanted to promote Catholicism as the state religion. Whatever were his true motives, the action of those leading Whigs who invited William of Orange, as consort of James's daughter Mary, to take the English throne, was not unanimously endorsed. Many stayed loyal to James and his descendants – subsequently named Jacobites. Tom Jones says that James was 'expelled'. Was he? He certainly left the country, but what exactly were the terms upon which the throne of England was said to be vacant? James did not formally abdicate, and of course he mounted a spirited military campaign commencing in Ireland to regain the throne. Those Tories who did not accept the post-1688 Revolution settlement would represent William's takeover as an act of conquest and rape. On the more philosophical plane, Whigs and Tories argued over two different societal models: one that has the monarchy subordinate to parliament as representative of the people (or at least influential sections within it) and according to which a king can be deposed if he breaks an implied contract with the people; another that grants the monarch divine, hereditary and indefeasible right to rule – a right that must be passively obeyed and never resisted. Despite Tom's implication that the political nation was forged in 1688

and that only enthusiasts and fanatics could remain outside it ('hot-headed Papists
led by their Priests to engage in this desparate Cause', in the Man of the Hill's terms),
1688 actually created or underlined several categories of person who might continue
to feel themselves excluded from the polity. Roman Catholics and those extreme
Protestants who refused to accept the Anglican Church and the English Prayer Book
dubbed 'Dissenters' are the most important, but there were still others.

An example might be made of the curious category of Nonjurors. This comprises
the four hundred or so Church of England and Scottish Episcopalian clergymen, and
their senior bishops, who would not swear the required oath of allegiance to William
and Mary. To illustrate an establishment Whig way of representing such people in
imaginative writing, we can turn to Colley Cibber's play staged in 1717 entitled *The
Non-Juror*. The immediate background to the play is the European events that caused
the French to move James III from his Jacobite court in St Germain to papal Avignon
and thereafter to Italy; and the Act of Grace of 1717 that pardoned a number of Jacobite rebels of 1715. The prologue to this play is provided by a prestigious dramatist
and editor of Shakespeare, Nicholas Rowe, and the sheer nastiness of it concentrates
the audience's energies for a virulent piece of scapegoating:

> To-Night, ye Whigs and Tories both be safe,
> Nor hope, at one another's Cost, to laugh:
> We mean to souse old *Satan*, and the *Pope*,
> They've no Relations here, nor Friends, we hope.
> A Tool of theirs supplies the Comick Stage,
> With just Materials for Satirick Rage:
> Nor think our Colours may too strongly paint
> The stiff Non-Juring Separation-Saint.
> Good-Breeding ne'er commands us to be civil
> To those who give the Nation to the Devil;
> Who at our surest, best Foundations, strike,
> And hate our Monarch and our Church alike:
> . . . Why, since a Land of Liberty they hate,
> Still will they linger in this Free-born State?
> Here, ev'ry Hour, fresh hateful Objects rise,
> Peace and Prosperity afflict their Eyes:
> With Anguish, Prince and People they survey,
> Their just Obedience, and His Righteous Sway.
> Ship off, ye Slaves, and seek some Passive Land,
> Where Tyrants after your own Hearts command:
> To your *Transalpine* Master's Rule resort,
> And fill an empty, Abdicated Court:
> Turn your Possessions here to Ready Rhino,
> And buy ye Lands and Lordships at *Urbino*.

If there's one thing that both parties can agree on, the prologue begins, it's anti-
papism. Non-jurors, the prologue argues, are actually Roman Catholic Jacobites who
use the cloak of Anglicanism; and the play that this introduces centres on the exploits

of the hypocritical Dr Wolf, who has wormed his way into the sympathies of a good-hearted if deluded English gentleman, Sir John Woodvil. When Wolf is attempting to seduce Woodvil's wife, the following exchange occurs:

LADY W: you don't take him sure for a *Roman* Catholick?
DOCT: Um – not absolutely – But, poor Soul! He little thinks how near he is one. 'Tis true, name to him but *Rome*, or Popery, he starts, as at a . . .
MONSTER: But gild its grossest Doctrines with the Style of *English Catholick*, he swallows down the Poison like a Cordial. (354)

Wolf turns out to be actually a Roman Catholic priest, as well as a cowardly Jacobite plotter who has deserted his army at the Battle of Preston, and who is now trying to relieve Woodvil of his wife and his estate. Cibber's play, egregiously dedicated to King George I and the House of Hanover, reminds us that one way the period's literature has of representing unincorporated politics is to scapegoat them viciously. Not to swear the loyal Oath is to be a Francophile traitor, engaged in treasonable activities against the state. One wonders what the Roman Catholic poet Alexander Pope made of Cibber's play. Maria Woodvil, Sir John's daughter and the play's love interest, has modelled herself on Pope's coquettish Belinda in *Rape of the Lock*, to the extent of regularly quoting her lines. Even Wolf has been reading Pope: *Eloisa to Abelard*. Despite this concession of Pope's cultural power, Cibber sees no incongruity in using it to fuel an anti-Catholic diatribe. Perhaps this was a deliberate provocation to Pope, who took an appropriate revenge when he made Cibber the King of the Dunces in his 1742–3 *The Dunciad. In Four Books*.

II

We should stay with the earliest phase of party literature, from *c.*1680 to the coronation of King George I, Elector of Hanover in 1714, for some time longer. The first era of party saw publication of the first major piece of party literature, Dryden's 1681 poem *Absalom and Achitophel*. For modern readers, 'great' literature and 'party' literature might seem contradictory notions. Of course politics can, perhaps must, inform literature – the modern sensibility argues – but this should be indirect and as far as possible removed through literary device if art is not to descend into mere propaganda. Seamus Heaney's collection *North* might serve as a model. Dryden's poem, however, engages directly in political polemic. It seeks to persuade us of the rightness of the royalist case against exclusionists and rebels, handling in the process all the key terms of contemporary political philosophy: 'patriarchy, paternity, succession, law, slavery, the state of nature, liberty and freedom' is the list made by Steven Zwicker in his analysis of the poem in the book *Lines of Authority* (Zwicker, 1993, 131). Dryden is writing at the same time as an avalanche of stage plays alluded to and indirectly discussed topical political events like the Exclusion Crisis – adaptations of Shakespeare, English and Roman history plays, Dryden's own version of the French civil wars written in collaboration with Nathaniel Lee, *The Duke of Guise* perhaps the finest of them. (For the best study of such plays, see Owen, 1996.) Scurrilous poems represented the king's lecherous behaviour as directly contrary to the national interest. Philoprogenitive as he was, he was impotent in the one area that mattered, getting a legitimate heir: and so by a bizarre transformation, he could also seem to be effeminate, even homosexual. Poems by John Wilmot, Earl of Rochester, aspersed the king directly and had wide circulation in manuscript, while stageplays such as Wycherley's *The Country Wife* (1675) with its protagonist a supposedly impotent lecher called Horner in hot pursuit of a country innocent, might suggest a hobbled king who chased such a woman in Frances Stuart. (Like Margery Pinchwife, Stuart was often seen in transvestite garb; and she achieved symbolic importance when in 1667 she sat for the figure of Britannia on a specially cast medal.) The modern reader who wishes to be reassured as to the 'art' of Dryden's poem needs only to study the opening passage, in which Dryden attempts to square the circle: a monarch who has several bastards (one of whom, the Duke of Monmouth, is about to cause major political problems when in 1685 he rebels against his king) and who is yet the fountainhead of probity and monogamous legalism! It is a task to defeat the most devious of government spin doctors, but Dryden performs it wonderfully by associating the king's sowing of wild oats with a state of nature that has been since inhibited by 'priestcraft'. Polygamy is sanctioned by the Old Testament: the cursed confinement of monogamy is a recent religious invention. Opening in the manner of a theatrical prologue, the poem sets out at first to jolly along the Restoration courtiers and libertines who attended the louche sex-comedies of the 1670s:

> In pious times, ere priestcraft did begin,
> Before polygamy was made a sin;
> When man on many multiplied his kind,
> Ere one to one was cursedly confined;
> When nature prompted, and no law denied
> Promiscuous use of concubine and bride;
> Then Israel's monarch after Heaven's own heart
> His vigorous warmth did, variously, impart
> To wives and slaves; and, wide as his command,
> Scattered his Maker's image through the land.
> (ll. 1–10)

Priestcraft ('priest-trade' and 'priest-craftiness') is *opposed to* piety, in line 1. Polygamy is of course the standard arrangement in the old Testament. 'Nature' is opposed to 'law'. The monarch is doing God's and nature's own work: notice the pauses that cordon off the words 'cursedly' and 'variously', producing what has been called an 'urbane descent' in the tone almost on a par with an aside in a stage comedy. In a moment reminiscent of Prince Hal's banishment of Falstaff around line 15, however, the poet goes on to argue that, wonderful though these bastard boys are who are the results of such union, they are not legitimate. And 'since like slaves his bed they [the concubines, mothers of the boys] did ascend', (not, of course, a formulation to which Dryden's opponents would subscribe) a responsible monarch simply has to protect legitimate succession. Such poetry gains its excitement from the way in which politics inhabits the imagination – the deft way of dealing with political concepts that frequently depends on finessing rather than on discussing them.

Dryden converted to Roman Catholicism during the reign of James II and was beached by the Revolution of 1688. For the last twelve years of his life, his literary output is a coming to terms with the facts of Protestant ascendancy. All of his later work is suffused with an elegiac and nostalgic atmosphere, but it is not exactly defeatist. Dryden's favoured way of adjusting to the hard facts of the Revolution settlement is to represent ambiguously the competing positions of rival leaders. In his semiopera *King Arthur*, for instance, or his play *Amphitryon*, or in the sonorities of his translation of Virgil's *Aeneid*, Dryden frequently leaves the reader in a position to apply particular roles either to William or to the Stuart line, and the leaders he depicts often have dominantly humane or dominantly political virtues, reserving the preference to the reader. Howard Erskine-Hill (1996, 51) has given exceptionally careful attention to the question of Dryden's enduring Jacobite commitment, and his conclusion is that while there is biographically based evidence for it, in the literary works Dryden's main concern is to 'prompt his readers into an active and compassionate effort to understand the often paradoxical, often tragic, nature of historical process and human endeavour'. This is a position that far transcends the direct partisan engagements of 1681 and perhaps sorts more satisfactorily with a conception of 'great' political writing.

Degree of Jacobite commitment is an issue that affects writers other than John Dryden. In recent years, all of the major male writers in the eighteenth-century canon – Dryden, Pope, Swift and Samuel Johnson – have been considered to be crypto-Jacobites. Their writings have been mined for allegories, codes and dark secrets that reveal their enduring commitments to the House of Stuart. The central metaphor of rape in Pope's *Rape of the Lock*, for instance, and the game of Ombre, have been interpreted by Howard Erskine-Hill (1996) as an allusion to post-Restoration debates over William III's assumption of power – that some pamphleteers represented as a rape of the kingdom. There is not space in a short account such as this to do justice to a topic that has been one of the most controversial in recent scholarship. Perhaps the best way of dealing with this, therefore, is to explain why it has been capable of bringing usually demure scholars to blows, and to set out a position of my own in respect of it.

What is at stake is whether the eighteenth century in Britain was more characterized by continuity or by change, and how true it is that in this period an inclusive sense of British identity was forged. The historian Jonathan Clark has made a charismatic case for the view that England in the eighteenth century remained an *ancien régime*, a stratified, hierarchical society dominated by the established church and by a political oligarchy, not altered significantly by secularization, urbanization or by industrial–agrarian processes that some have considered revolutionary (Clark, 1985;

see also opening pages of Speck, 1998). To show that all of the leading literary figures, at least in the earlier part of this period, were closet Jacobites, is to support this picture of an almost static confessional state. (This is a clear intention where Clark argues that Johnson was a 'Tory, a Nonjuror and a Jacobite': see Clark, 1994, 7.) For others coming from a somewhat different direction, it is to resist the view presented powerfully by Linda Colley, for example, that distinct Scottish, Irish and Welsh allegiances were swallowed up in a pervasive Britishness that saw full legitimization of the Act of Union (1707) and defined itself against France (Colley, 1992). About the narrower question of whether the seminal literary figures of the period were all Jacobites, I would argue that it depends entirely on what one takes a 'Jacobite' to be. If what is meant by that is a person who would rise up in arms to defend the Pretender, then it is patently inappropriate to apply the term to Pope and Johnson, and downright nonsensical to apply it to Swift. Even political figures who are considered to be Jacobites clearly drifted in and out of the commitment, depending on the development of contemporary political events. Given the innate conservatism of all these writers, it is hardly surprising if they held a nostalgic place in their hearts for those who could be regarded as legitimate rulers and victims of history; and it is likely too that Jacobitism did afford them, from its rich thesaurus of politicized symbolism, occasional images and allusions. But Murray Pittock, in his important study of this topic, provides an exquisite formulation of Samuel Johnson's possible attitude towards Jacobitism that should in my view be applicable to all four writers: 'Johnson was a man of Jacobite ideals who distrusted their reality. In this view Jacobitism becomes part of the displaced baggage of human disappointment: the Stuart cause is wise, but every step taken to achieve its ends is vanity' (Pittock, 1994, 132).

Pittock also reminds us that Jacobite commitment generated a literature of its own in ballads and songs and in Scoto-Latin poetry that inscribes a specific view of experience based on loss and eventual return, and recurring images and symbols drawn from the natural world, that are of great beauty. An example is the song 'The Blackbird' that represents allegiance to James (VIII and III) as the lovesong of a young maiden for the loss of her pet. Here are two stanzas:

> Once on a morning of sweet recreation
> I heard a young maiden a-making her moan,
> With such a sighing and sobbing and sad lamentation,
> Crying, 'My blackbird most royal has flown! . . .
>
> O, what if the fowler my blackbird has taken?
> Then sadness and sorrow shall all be my tune,
> But if he is safe, then I'll no be forsaken,
> And hope yet to see him in May or in June.

The lyrical simplicity of this perhaps suggests that there is no need to decode the major poets merely to discover a significance that will never be more than an indistinct vein in the marble.

Before leaving the Jacobites to return to more mainstream partisan activity and literature, there are some other points that we should make. Tory royalism, however ambiguously it informs Dryden's work, certainly is a major determinant factor on women's writing in the later seventeenth century. Some of Aphra Behn's writing, for example, recasts the terms of the Civil War royalist versus parliamentarian conflict into incipiently Whig and Tory allegiances. Her 1677 play, *The Rover*, for example, features a group of cavaliers in exile in Naples who are permitted to behave like latter-day lager louts, whoring and fighting with the locals, and yet be celebrated as the play's heroes; whereas to be 'an English country gentleman' with hankerings for the Good Old Cause like Blunt is to end up crawling down a privy and up through a common sewer! In Behn's *Oroonoko* (1688), the African prince who is the eponymous hero is also a Jacobite sympathizer! In some ways it is inappropriate to call the politically informed writing of such as Aphra Behn, Katherine Philips, Anne Killigrew, Mary Lady Chudleigh, Sarah Fyge Egerton, Jane Barker, Anne Finch and others 'Jacobite'. As Carol Barash's (1994) study argues, the main inspirations behind this group of women writers were actually queens, consort and regnant: Mary of Modena, the second wife of James II, and Queen Anne. The latter, it has been argued, was at best an ambivalent muse, because having failed to bear a child who survived infancy in eighteen pregnancies, she turned to symbolic conceptions of maternity to legitimate her authority, but this 'mother of the nation' posture had the final outcome of equating maternity with failure (Bowers, 1996, 37–89). This group of women writers, Barash argues, saw themselves as part of a female court community, charged with the mission of representing court circles heroically. From the declining divine right model of political authority, the Tory monarchist women writers derived a hope for 'a unified poetic authority that could triumph over the material conflicts of this world' (21), a transcendent ethic that lived in the expectation of otherworldly triumph while leaving everyday life to the authority of men.

III

In the aftermath of 1688, several pieces of legislation were enacted to settle the long struggle between Stuart kings and the parliament that had seen the execution of Charles I in 1649 and a decade of bloody civil war throughout Britain: the Bill of Rights (1689) that made monarchy conditional on the parliamentary will, with the Toleration Act granting religious toleration to all Protestants, the Triennial Act (1694) requiring general elections to be held every three years, and the Act of Settlement of 1701 decreeing that, in default of issue to either William or Anne, the crown would pass to Sophia, Electress of Hanover and to 'the heirs of her body being Protestants'. Such legislation paved the way for a very long period of Whig ascendancy in British politics, to the extent that there was virtually a one-party state after the coronation of King George I in 1714. Before that, nodal events could provoke dramatic collisions between Whigs and Tories, suggesting that there were still considerable differences in principle between them. One such was the trial of the High Church Tory Dr Henry Sacheverell for preaching a sermon in St Paul's in 1709 to the effect that the boundaries of toleration had extended too far, implying that the church and state were not safe in Whig hands. Support for Sacheverell was so strong that a Tory ministry was elected on the back of it, that lasted from 1710 until Queen Anne's death in 1714.

Whether there actually was a separately identifiable Tory party in existence after the General Election slaughter of 1714, and if so what factors identify it, remains a live issue in recent historiography. Going back to the Man of the Hill's conversation with Tom Jones, we read his implication that the consolidation of Protestantism in England has settled all political questions for all time. The prevailing consensus is probably that there continued to be around 130–140 Tories in the House of Commons who mounted a campaign against their own irrelevance, the main platforms of which were, as listed by Ian Christie (1990, 101–22 [104–5]), 'elimination of placement and pensioners in the Commons; "free" (that is, uninfluenced) elections and repeal of the Septennial Act [passed in 1716, decreeing elections every seven years]; a smaller standing army or complete reliance on the militia for defence in time of peace, and lower taxation; repeal of the Riot Act; avoidance of expensive military or diplomatic entanglements on the Continent . . . and full participation for Tory country gentlemen in local government by admission to the commissions of the peace'. And certainly, a strand of Jacobite support was perceptible within this grouping, even if those who supported it would have required of the Pretender a conversion to Protestantism, and even if it was not strong enough to define a party by itself.

Just as controversial as the issue of the continuing existence of an identifiable Tory party is that of the nature of the political opposition to Sir Robert Walpole, who spearheaded the Whig elite in the Commons between 1720 and 1742. For if the Whigs had a monopoly on office during this period, they did not enjoy power unopposed. Before investigating the make up of opposition and of its literary expression, however, we need to confront an extremely important set of cultural and ideological issues. For in many respects, the period leading up to and into the Hanoverian era saw changes much deeper and wider than the gradual triumph of one party over another, the shifting groupings and alliances within that ascendancy, and the relegation of Jacobitism to a recurrent alarm over the threat of foreign invasion. To describe the relationship between literary texts and politics in the eighteenth century, the term 'cultural politics' is much more adequate than the narrower conception of party politics dominated by the labels 'Whig' and 'Tory'. Alexander Pope was one of several writers who disowned such flags of convenience when he wrote: 'In Moderation placing all my Glory, / While Tories call me Whig, and Whigs a Tory'. Pope's claim to eschew conventional party politics is part of a shared sense on the part of several talented writers of the 1730s that an unholy alliance existed between political barons such as the Prime Minister Walpole and an army of venal writers who would do their propagandist dirty work for money. Jonathan Swift, in his 'On Poetry: a Rhapsody' (1733), gives this opinion a characteristically strong expression, satirizing the Poet Laureate Colley Cibber on the way:

Two bordering wits contend for glory;
And one is Whig, and one is Tory.
And this, for epics claims the bays,
And that, for elegiac lays . . .
Harmonious Cibber entertains
The court with annual birthday strains;
Whence Gay was banished in disgrace,
Where Pope will never show his face;
Where Young must torture his invention,
To flatter knaves, or lose his pension.

(ll. 309–12, 321–6)

We should try to understand how this conception of 'culture wars' came about.

It has long been recognized that financing two decades of European war between 1690 and 1710 wrought fundamental changes in the nature of English society. Funding debt on the scale incurred by perpetual mobilization of troops resulted in the creation of new financial institutions (such as the Bank of England and a stock market) and a new financial elite who understood how to manipulate them. Beneficiaries of the 'military-fiscal state' were a new generation of money men who were not affected by high taxation imposed upon landowners and who, as a result, seemed to have a stake in society that was different altogether from the traditional gentry – men whose wealth seemed to be in some respects magical, mere 'paper' assets that bought their way into previously prohibited social strata. Such *nouveau riche* families had value systems that differed from those of traditional landowners. David Womersley (1997, xi–xlvi) has argued powerfully that the 'moneyed interest' and the landed interest developed very different cultural and aesthetic outlooks, that we could designate 'Whig' and 'Tory'. These are not, in this usage, narrow descriptions of voting behaviour or adherences to certain constitutional and religious principles. The contention is that there is a fundamental difference in aesthetic values, literary genres, themes and writing procedures between Whig and Tory writers by the first decade of the eighteenth century, because they are speaking for distinctly different sections of the social elite, who ground their authority with respect to different events – Tories to King Charles's Restoration in 1660 and Whigs to the Glorious Revolution of 1688 – and who require their cultural products to do distinct kinds of ideological work. Whig writing as practised by such as Sir Richard Blackmore, John Dennis, Joseph Addison and others celebrates native and domestic, rather than classical models; identifies with the exploits of William III's reign; and in its admiration for the trading, commercial and financial sectors is likely to applaud military success. It was in this relatively neglected and undervalued strain of Whig writing that early estimation for the 'sublime', biblical poetry, native strains of poetry such as the ballad, and the work of John Milton can be found. In Addison's sequence of *Pleasures of the Imagination*, essays contributed to his periodical *The Spectator*, there is a developing set of beliefs about a conception of beauty that is derivable from the natural world rather than from classical statuary. This aesthetic is more egalitarian, more socially dispersible, than any that had preceded it. Tory writing as embodied by such as Alexander Pope, Jonathan Swift, John Gay and the early theatrical work of Henry Fielding is likely, by contrast, to be classical in allegiance, underpinned by a 'civic humanist' belief in the landowning classes and the duties and obligations that accompany social rank, equivocal about trade and conquest, and condemnatory of the money men. (This grouping is sometimes called 'the Scriblerians' after a literary club that they formed in the reign of Queen Anne, the central satiric endeavour of which was to write the spoof-biography of a mock-learned pedant called Martinus Scriblerus – Martin the Scribbler). With reference to the struggle in allegiance between the 'ancients' and the 'moderns' that divided intellectual life in the later seventeenth century and ramified for decades to come, the Whigs were more likely to support the view that *modern* science and learning had made genuine progress, whereas the Tories would demand veneration of the *ancients*. About modern writing, indeed, both Jonathan Swift in *A Tale of a Tub* (1697–1710) and in later poems, and Alexander Pope in *The Dunciad* (1728–43) were scathing. A major aspect of Scriblerian literary achievement was to construct a myth according to which most modern writing was dull, not worth the paper it was printed on, undertaken purely for mercenary motives, informed by fanaticism, a displacement activity for worthier trades or callings, and finally in *The Dunciad* one of the main contributory factors to the end of civilization as we know it:

> She comes! she comes! the sable Throne behold
> Of *Night* Primaeval, and of *Chaos* old! . . .
> Thus at her felt approach, and secret might,
> *Art* after *Art* goes out, and all is Night . . .
> Lo! thy dread Empire, CHAOS! Is restor'd;
> Light dies before thy uncreating word:
> Thy hand, great Anarch! lets the curtain fall;
> And Universal Darkness buries All.
>   (1743, 4.629–30, 639–40, 653–6)

The lines enact a reverse Creation and a reverse Restoration – a reversal, that is, of two of the foundational guarantors of meaning in a Tory world and in Pope's.

Subsequent literary history has tended to take the Popean cultural map, with its many sectors marked 'here be monsters', at face value. Actually, the Whig aesthetic, if it did not have greater spokesmen, may have had more developmental energy behind it. Many of the socio-economic factors that we can identify as expanding the reading public, creating a demand for professional writing and forming the Whig poetic can also be allied to the promulgation of 'polite' discourse in the period. Much early-century imaginative writing was motivated by the desire to facilitate social intermingling between disparate status groups, in a society rendered increasingly mobile and fluid by the requirements of trade and commerce. Protocols governing behaviour and conversation in recently emergent public spaces were promulgated in the literary periodicals, in sentimental theatre and in the early novel. Although my opening discussion is keyed to the novel, I am conscious that I have had so far comparatively little to say about it. The early novel seldom addressed politics as directly as does Fielding in *Tom Jones*, though a horrific section of Tobias Smollett's *Roderick Random* (1748) is modelled on his experience as a surgeon's second mate on board a Royal Navy ship in combat under Admiral Vernon during the expedition to Cartagena in 1741, and has very clear anti-government implications. Here, we need to address politics of literary *form* more than politics of *content*. To speak of the politics of an entire genre such as the novel – to term it a 'Whig' form – is possibly reductive and unwise. Nevertheless, one can see far more of the Whig agenda behind its development in a writer such as Daniel Defoe, author of that great celebration of trade as the social dynamo of the age, the *Tour through the Whole Island of Great Britain* (1724–6) that Pat Rogers (1998, 199) has called 'truly an epic of the English people', than one can of the Tory. I have written elsewhere of a face-off between *Robinson Crusoe* and Swift's *Gulliver's Travels* that represents the latter as in some respects an anti-novel, opposed to the ideology of trade, economic advancement, scientific progress and modernity that brought the former into being (Hammond, 1997, 268–75).

One final point on the topic of Whig *versus* Tory writing. If the first phase of women's writing was resolutely Royalist and Tory, the Whig vision was increasingly appealing to women writers such as Elizabeth Singer Rowe, one of several poets who celebrated King William's victory over James at the Boyne in fulsome terms; and to the immensely popular playwright Susanna[h] Centlivre. Her play *A Bold Stroke for a Wife* (1718) offers a valuable textual site upon which to observe the clash of Whig and Tory ideologies. Her character Tradelove belongs to the Whig financial interest, and a scene is set in Jonathan's coffee house, centre for the securities market; whereas Sir Philip Modelove is an old beau very much part of the Tory squirearchy. Anne Lovely is a beautiful young fortune closely guarded by Quakers; and in the play's representation of a sect such as the Quakers can be perceived a similar attitude towards dissent (though not as virulent) as in Cibber's *Non-Juror*. Centlivre is behind the Whig low-church consensus that is designed to eliminate religion as a source of conflict. To be sure, women's writing was not *entirely* Whig in the early years of the century. Delarivier Manley's hugely successful *The New Atalantis* of 1709 inscribed a powerful critique of the Whig junto and of Marlborough, the heroic general who was given Blenheim Palace by a nation grateful for his victories over the French in the War of Spanish Succession (1702–13), and she went on to collaborate with Jonathan Swift in the editing of the Tory *Examiner*. Nevertheless, the Whigs had at last found a literary manifesto that seemed capable of appealing to women readers and writers.

IV

We must consider broader issues, then, than those of high partisan politics narrowly conceived. Issues become politicized in cultural circles even when they are not the subject of parliamentary debate or legal dispute: and groups of people can be motivated by attitudes and beliefs, doctrines and myths, that are scarcely at the point of coherent articulation. Perhaps the most significant political development of the decades from the mid-1720s to the mid-1740s was the attempt, commenced by Henry St John, Lord Bolingbroke and William Pulteney, to promote an ideology that was a form of cultural politics in that it was designed to make party politics redundant. For around a decade from 1726, they mounted a campaign, through their organ *The Craftsman* under the editorship of Nicholas Amhurst, to persuade the political nation that a point had been reached at which older distinctions between Whig and Tory no longer existed. There were no longer any actual structural political divisions because everyone barring a few fanatics had now accepted the Revolution settlement, the House of Hanover and the broad, latitudinarian religious solutions that had evolved. The real division, Bolingbroke argues in a succession of historical essays, is between those court Whigs who manipulate political power corruptly in the feathering of their own nests, and those both inside and outside the political establishment whose interest lies in ousting them, referred to by Bolingbroke as the 'Country' interest. Corruption is the problem. A return to the purity of first principles, to a constitution balanced between king, parliament and people that everyone agrees is desirable but that in practice we no longer have because of the greed and deviousness of those in office, is the only political objective. In the 1730s, hopes for the spearheading of such an agenda centred on George's son, Frederick, Prince of Wales, who was represented to be the kind of charismatic, scrupulously principled leader – the 'Patriot King' – that might bring this manifesto to fruition. As Christine Gerrard (1994, ch. 2) has shown, this was never an account of what the political nation *actually* believed. The Whig party was very divided and there was a substantial opposition to those in office from amongst their own ranks, yet these opponents did not accept Bolingbroke's analysis of the anachronism of party. As far as imaginative writers were concerned, however, the normative and utopian elements of Bolingbroke's standpoint were bold, clear and attractive. The period 1726–30 saw an effloration of some of the most outstanding imaginative works in the entire century, appearing almost in competition with one another: Swift's *Gulliver's Travels*, Gay's *The Beggar's Opera*, Pope's *The Dunciad* and Fielding's *Tom Thumb; or The Tragedy of Tragedies*, that were all in some measure affected by the Bolingbrokean analysis of a kingdom in the grip of a corrupt ministerial clique requiring a cleansing of the Augean stable. All relate bad politics to bad art, and find metaphors that ingeniously exchange one for the other. All transcend a merely partisan or Bolingbrokean ideological analysis by borrowing energy from the debased forms of politics and art that they affect to despise. Using parodic and ventriloquial techniques, they let the corrupt and the venal and the dull speak for themselves, condemning themselves, and the social conditions that give rise to such selves, out of their own mouths. *The Beggar's Opera* will furnish an illustration.

To set an opera amongst thieves and whores who live in the shadow of the gallows (a similar *mise en scène* to Defoe's *Moll Flanders*) is already to parody the high plots familiar from Italian opera. To substitute native English songs from many different provenances for Handelian arias is to begin to create a new kind of work that transcends mere parody. To give the thieves and whores a genteel idiom and pretensions to manners, and to equip them with justifications for their actions taken from the sober practices of business and accounting (in the case of the Peachums and Lockit), from seventeenth-century Levelling and military codes of honour (in the case of Macheath's gang of cutpurses), and from heroic tragedy, manners and romantic sensibility (in the case of the Polly–Macheath–Lucy love triangle), is to create a world in which, as the Beggar who is its supposed author says:

> Through the whole Piece you may observe such a similitude of Manners in high and low Life, that it is difficult to determine whether (in the fashionable Vices) the fine Gentlemen imitate the Gentlemen of the Road, or the Gentlemen of the Road the fine Gentlemen. (III.xvi.18–22)

Colin Nicholson's analysis of the *Opera* emphasizes the extent to which *money* creates the series of transformations and commodifications of relationships that confuses values and reduces human beings to beasts of prey (1994, ch. 4). In the terms of this essay, *The Beggar's Opera* is a critique of the military-fiscal state, the inequities of which have worsened during Walpole's corrupt term in office. Alexander Pope's series of imitations of the poet Horace, commenced in 1733 and continuing throughout the 1730s, was more direct and outspoken on the issue of corruption. His *Epilogue to the Satires: Dialogue 1* published in 1738 culminates in an allegorical pageant of the national spirit ('Old England's genius') being dragged through the earth, just as Hector's dead body was contemptuously maltreated by Achilles, while the population at large engages in an orgy of greed. Gay's point that vice is made respectable if owned by the powerful in society (as Peachum says to his wife, 'Money, Wife, is the true Fuller's Earth for Reputation, there is not a Spot or a Stain but what it can take out' [I.ix.8–10]) is taken up by Pope, as the power of gold to destroy values is insisted upon:

> *Vice* is undone, if she forgets her birth,
> And stoops from angels to the dregs of earth:
> But 'tis the *fall* degrades her to a whore;
> Let *Greatness* own her, and she's mean no more:
> Her birth, her beauty, crowds and courts confess,
> Chaste matrons praise her, and grave bishops bless;
> In golden chains the willing world she draws,
> And hers the gospel is, and hers the laws,
> Mounts the tribunal, lifts her scarlet head,
> And sees pale Virtue carted in her stead.
> Lo! at the wheels of her triumphal car,
> Old England's genius, rough with many a scar,
> Dragged in the dust!
>   (ll. 141–53)

By the time this poem appeared, Henry Fielding had already been prevented by the passage of a Licensing Act (1737) from staging any more plays at his subversive venue, the Little Theatre in the Haymarket. Earlier plays like *The Author's Farce* (1730) and *Tom Thumb* (1730) had concentrated on the cultural side of the 'cultural politics' equation, but as he bought further and further into the opposition analysis of Walpolean corruption, plays such as *Don Quixote in England* (1734), *Pasquin* (1735) and *The Historical Register for the Year 1736* (1737) targeted electoral malpractice and ministerial greed directly. By then, the Bolingbrokean analysis had lost its grip, the Opposition having failed to unseat Walpole in the Excise Crisis of 1734, and the nature of opposition politics had dramatically altered.

From 1735 onwards, the most dynamic section of the Whig opposition was the grouping known as 'Cobham's Cubs' or the 'Boy Patriots' – an affiliation of young politicians such as William Pitt, George Lyttelton, the Grenvilles and Hugh Polwarth, third Earl Marchmont, who took their lead from Lord Cobham and other disaffected Whig grandees and who bestowed cult status upon Frederick, Prince of Wales as the 'Patriot King' much desired by Bolingbroke. Even before his death in 1751, such hopes as there could be of Frederick's Leicester House opposition had probably been extinguished. The nature of politics from the fall of Walpole until the accession of George III in 1760 was a shifting sand of family and interest alliances. Leaders of powerful cliques exercised themselves over the question of how to be more inclusive than the binary terms of Whig and Tory, ministry and opposition, or court and country seemed to permit. Much talk, from 1735 onwards, was of a 'broad-bottomed' government that would take disaffected Whigs and even Tories into its ranks; and it was George III's actual willingness to do this in 1760 that finally destroyed any rationale there might have been for the existence of a separate Tory party, with Jacobite hopes having finally ended in the spectacular failure of the French-supported invasion of 1759. The year 1760 therefore offers a clear terminal date for this chapter on the first era of partisan literature. While it lasted, however, the 'Boy Patriot' movement spawned its own forms of literary expression, assuming the mantle of the Bolingbrokean literary resistance movement. Writers such as James Thomson, Henry Brooke, Richard Glover, Gilbert West, George Lillo and, providing continuity with the Whig tradition that began earlier in the century, Aaron Hill, developed an iconography and a poetic that deploys protocols entirely different from the witty, comic-parodic devices of the Scriblerians. Emphases on the natural world, on the sublime and on a more domestic agenda for imaginative writing that we identified in the earlier era of Whig writing are picked up in the 1730s and 1740s. The patriots applied most often to relatively recent British history, to our Saxon or 'gothic' past and the freedoms guaranteed to Englishmen by the first model of a parliament, the witenagemote; and to the reign of Elizabeth, to ground new myths of national identity. Neo-Spenserianism was an aspect of patriot rhetoric observable in, for example, James Thomson's influential peom 'The Castle of Indolence' (1748). And the point is extremely well made by Christine Gerrard that this writing provides continuity with the romantic antiquarianism and literary nationalism of the century's middle decades. On one level, mid-century 'pre-romanticism' can be seen to be an introverted turn away from the public, topical, satirical poetry of Pope. That does not entail, however, that there are no politics in it. In Thomas Gray's 'The Bard' (1757), for instance, there is clearly something at stake for developing conceptions of Britishness. This poem's dramatized narrator is the last of the Welsh bards, who has witnessed his brother-poets being slaughtered at the hands of Edward I's army of conquest, and who, before committing suicide, curses them with the knowledge that a future royal lineage will be Welsh. In the competing accounts of prehistoric Britain that supported Percy's *Reliques* (1765) and the poems that James Macpherson claimed he translated from Gaelic sources and published between 1760 and 1765 as *The Works of Ossian*, Nick Groom (1996, 275–96) has shown cultural politics to be heavily implicated. Were the Goths or the Celts the original inhabitants of Britain, and what hinges on this for our sense of national identity? But these are cultural politics more and more cut adrift from the partisan allegiances that it was the role of earlier writers to widen and popularize. This is so much the case that a writer like Charles Churchill, active between 1761 and 1765, who was a satirist and whose verse tries to revive a directly Popean form of head-on bipartisan conflict between the crypto-Jacobite supporters of Lord Bute and his Caledonian hegemony on the one hand, and the popular supporters of John Wilkes on the other, seems like a throwback. Churchill does not endorse, or cannot resurrect, a sense of the permanently existent and shared norms that gave authenticity to Pope's satirical voice, and his satirical portraits of such as William Hogarth and Samuel Johnson lack authority. One reason for this (among many) is the assimilation of political opposition into a ruling consensus that, when it was threatened by the events surrounding the American and French Revolutions, would be challenged on a far more radical plane than was dreamed of in Churchill's philosophy.

REFERENCES AND FURTHER READING

Barash, Carol (1996). *English Women's Poetry, 1649–1714: Politics, Community and Linguistic Authority*. Oxford: Clarendon.

Bowers, Toni (1996). *The Politics of Motherhood: British Writing and Culture, 1680–1760*. Cambridge: Cambridge University Press.

Christie, Ian R. (1990). 'The changing nature of parliamentary politics, 1742–1789'. In *British Politics and Society from Walpole to Pitt, 1742–1789*. Ed. Jeremy Black. Basingstoke: Macmillan, 101–22.

Clark, J. C. D. (1985). *English Society, 1688–1832*. Cambridge: Cambridge University Press.

——(1994). *Samuel Johnson: Literature, Religion and English Cultural Politics from the Restoration to Romanticism*. Cambridge: Cambridge University Press.

Coley, W. B., ed. (1987). *The True Patriot and Related Writings*. Oxford: Oxford University Press.

Colley, Linda (1992). *Britons: Forging the Nation, 1707–1837*. New Haven: Yale University Press.

Erskine-Hill, Howard (1996). *Poetry of Opposition and Revolution: Dryden to Wordsworth*. Oxford: Clarendon Press.

Gerrard, Christine (1994). *The Patriot Opposition to Walpole: Politics, Poetry and National Myth, 1725–42*. Oxford: Clarendon.

Groom, Nick (1996). 'Celts, Goths and the nature of the literary source'. In *Tradition in Transition: Women Writers, Marginal Texts and the Eighteenth-century Canon*. Ed. S. J. Alvaro Ribeiro and James S. Basker. Oxford: Clarendon, 275–96.

Hammond, Brean S. (1997). *Professional Imaginative Writing in England, 1670–1740: 'Hackney for Bread'*. Oxford: Clarendon.

Nicholson, Colin (1994). *Writing and the Rise of Finance: Capital Satires of the Early Eighteenth*

Century. Cambridge: Cambridge University Press.

Owen, Susan J. (1996). *Restoration Theatre and Crisis*. Oxford: Clarendon Press.

Pittock, Murray (1994). *Poetry and Jacobite Politics in Eighteenth-century Britain and Ireland*. Cambridge: Cambridge University Press.

Rogers, Pat (1998). *The Text of Great Britain: Theme and Design in Defoe's 'Tour'*. Newark and London: University of Delaware Press and Associated University Presses.

Speck, W. A. (1998). *Literature and Society in Eighteenth-century England: Ideology, Politics and Culture*. London and New York: Longman.

Womersley, David (1997). *Augustan Critical Writing*. Harmondsworth: Penguin.

Zwicker, Steven N. (1993). *Lines of Authority: Politics and English Literary Culture, 1649–1689*. Ithaca and London: Cornell University Press.

4

Furnishing the Mind, Creating Social Bonds

Ann Jessie Van Sant

Bella has not a *feeling* heart: The highest joy in this life she is not capable of: But then she saves herself many griefs, by her impenetrableness – Yet, for ten times the pain that such a sensibility is attended with, would I not part with the pleasure it brings with it.'

        (Samuel Richardson, *Clarissa*, 1751, Vol. I, Letter 42, p. 296; hereafter I, 42, 296)

Mrs. *Bilson's* frequent Visits to this afflicted Family became known, and consequently ridiculed, by many of those who esteemed themselves the superior Part of the Company. Lady *Fanny Chlegen* 'greatly wondered, how it was possible for a Woman of any Fashion to go raking into Holes and Corners after every crying Woman . . . if they had any Sensibility, or the least Delicacy of Nerves, they could not be thrusting themselves into Scenes of Distress.'

        (Sarah Fielding, *The Countess of Dellwyn*, 1759, Vol. II, pp. 97–8)

When indulged beyond the bounds of reason, [sensibility] degenerates into weakness; when affected, it is absurd; and when directed to improper objects, extremely dangerous. This word, like *sentiment*, has of late years been often strangely perverted, and applied to gild the violation of the most sacred duties. Excess of sensibility, or a sentimental affection, is often an apology for a young lady's elopement from a harsh father, or that of a wife from a stupid husband. *Delicate feelings* become the substitutes for those of virtue.

        (Review of 'An Essay on Sensibility' (a poem), *Critical Review*, LXVIII, 1789, p. 447)

Sentiment and *sensibility*, as well as *sentimental* (the adjective that can be related to both) are central terms for the study of affective experience in the eighteenth century, and the study of affective experience is a crucial part of the study of the culture. More than fifty years ago, Basil Willey, a historian of ideas, wrote that in the eighteenth century, 'it was discovered that the "Nature" of man was not his "reason" at all, but his instincts, emotions, and "sensibilities"'. Willey further suggested that Rene Descartes' *cogito ergo sum* was 'superseded by the *je sens, donc je suis* associated with Rousseau' (108). Much more recently G. J. Barker-Benfield (1992) has characterized the period with the phrase 'culture of sensibility', and various studies have emphasized the connections rather than the oppositions between sensibility and the prevailing empiricism of the period (Brissenden, 1974; Pinch, 1996) as well as between sensibility and the 'Enlightenment' project as a whole (Denby, 1994). Willey's contrast oversimplifies the relation between feeling and thinking, and Barker-Benfield's term probably suggests too great a degree of cultural coherence, but no serious student of the period can doubt that during the eighteenth century, there is evidence of a wide cultural interest in *feeling* – in the *interior experience of feeling*, in the *physiological structures of feeling*, and in the *social relations grounded in feeling*.

In philosophy, John Locke analysed the source of ideas and the operations of the mind in *The Essay on Human Understanding* (1690). A number of the philosophers who followed Locke wanted to bring to an analysis of the 'affections' the kind of systematic thinking and schematic clarity they found in his *Essay*. David Hume, following his teacher, Francis Hutcheson, emphasized the importance of feeling in moral and aesthetic response, declaring, in what has become a well-known formulation: 'Morality . . . is more properly felt than judg'd of' (III, I, II, 470). Both Hutcheson and Hume argued that while reasoning allows one to choose among methods and strategies for achieving goals, feeling is the basis for choosing those goals. Feeling rather than reason, in other words, accounts for *motivation*. Further, in the work of Hume and Adam Smith, *sympathy* is not only the basis for empathy and pity but is one of the basic operations of the mind. Medical work, too, contributed to this centralizing of feeling – work on brain and nerves made specific not only the pathways of sensation but also the interior system of experience, which was a system of feeling. Both physical and psychological feeling, then, were foregrounded in an explanation of experience.

As indicated by the title, this essay will be concerned centrally with the creation of interior experience and social bonds, but I will begin my examination of this cultural preoccupation with feeling with a close look at two key terms: *sensibility* and *sentiment*. In an early Restoration play, *The Adventures of Five Hours* (1662–3, by Samuel Tuke) well before the 'culture of sensibility' is said to have emerged, two young women characters agree to compare their stories to see which one has greater suffering ('which of us two excells in misery'). After one describes her unbearable situation, her friend replies: 'Your Story I confess is strangely moving; / Yet, if you cou'd my Fortune weigh with yours, / In *Scales of equal sensibility*; / You would not change your Sufferings, for mine' (Act I, 15, 17). Despite the fact that the characters are comparing their sufferings, it is the scales, not the characters, which have sensibility, showing that the central idea in their usage is the fine calibration of the scales. In his *Essay*, Locke uses the term only once – when insisting that arguments about the materiality or immateriality of the soul are of little significance. He finds it evident, he says, 'that he who made us at first begin to subsist here, *sensible* intelligent Beings . . . can and will restore us to the like state of *Sensibility* in another World (IV, 3, 6, 542; emphasis added). In Locke's usage, the term combines *capacity for sensation* with *awareness* and suggests that there is some fusion of sensible and intellectual powers. In 1771, in *The Man of Feeling*, Henry Mackenzie uses the vocabulary of sensibility extensively and once uses the expression 'To people of equal sensibility' (ch. XIX, 23). The capacity for *registering finely* is located in the experiencing being – it is a distinguishing feature of the experiencing being. By this time, knowledge of the nervous system has contributed to making sensibility central to an understanding of what is human.

What helps to make sensibility difficult to define also helps to explain why it could become so culturally pervasive. It drew into its range a number of already existing terms and concepts by supplying a physiology that confirmed and extended them. *Sympathy*, so important in this constellation, though it marginally retained its association with the occult (e.g., sympathy powder) became part of the vocabulary of sensibility. In the *Essay*, Locke uses *Sympathy* – along with *instinct* and *antipathy* – as examples of terms usually used without any meaning (III, XI, 8). But in physiology the more general early use of sympathy to mean 'fellow feeling' between bodily organs (OED) became quite precise in Whytt's mid-eighteenth century physiological treatises: 'Our bodies are, by means of the nerves, not only endowed with feeling, and a power of motion, but with a remarkable sympathy, which is either general, and extended through the whole system, or confined, in a great measure, to certain parts' (492–3). And this more precise technical meaning is the context for its use in philosophy. Although there's always something remarkable, even a little mysterious, in the operation of sympathy, perhaps reflecting its history as an occult term, the nervous system systemized *sympathy*, giving it its modern meaning.

In other cases, sensibility easily mapped onto already existing affective language. The *heart* is an interesting case. In the eighteenth-century language of feeling, the *heart* remains far more prominent than *sensibility*, *sympathy*, *sentiment*(s), *sensible*, etc. combined. In the first edition of *Clarissa* (1747–8), for example, *heart* appears 1,202 times, *sensibility* 12 times (Chadwyck-Healey database for fiction, 1705–80). But like much other affective language, the heart has become an organ of sensibility. It is often 'full of sensibility', and its hardness or softness equates with sensibility. *Heart* was in fact frequently interchangeable with *sensibility* and *sensibility* absorbed the heart's status as *essential centre of the self*.

In the strictest sense, then, physical sensibility is an organic sensitivity dependent on nerve function. Psychological sensibility is based on, continuous with and analogous to physical sensibility. By explaining in a more systematic way than had been available before how both physical and emotional *feeling* work, the idea of sensibility created a scientific and imaginative link between physical structures and 'inward', subjective experience. Its meaning ranges from the receptivity and responsiveness made possible by the nervous system to an ineffable capacity to be affected by one's surroundings. It accounts both for interior, subjective experience and for a capacity for social relation. And further, while accounting for the capacity for sensory experience and thus universally applicable, it is particularly suited to adapt to contemporary ideas about gender and social rank – with a keen capacity for registering translated into the cultural values of delicacy and refinement. And as has been analysed in detail by a number of critics (see especially Mullan, 1988), the delicacy that gives rise both to a highly developed interiority and to sympathy was also the source of nervous disorder. Sensibility was therefore a powerful explanatory concept and a highly paradoxical one.

A brief examination of the term in *Clarissa* can illustrate some of these paradoxes. When Clarissa says of her sister, 'Bella has not a feeling heart . . . Yet, for ten times the pain that such a sensibility is attended with, would I not part with the pleasure it brings with it' her contrast conveys the same commonplace about sensibility that we find in Laurence Sterne's *A Sentimental Journey Through France and Italy* (1768): '– Dear sensibility! source inexhausted of all that's precious in our joys, or costly in our sorrows! . . . – eternal fountain of our feelings!' (277). This close relation of plea- sure and pain characterizes many other uses, including those on the boundary where sensibility informs the method of satirist. 'I love, as I have told you, your pleasantry,' Clarissa writes to Anna.

> Altho' at the time, it may pain one a little; yet on recollection, when I find in it more of the cautioning friend, than of the satirizing observer, I shall be all gratitude upon it. All the business will be This; I shall be *sensible* of the pain in the present Letter perhaps; but I shall thank you in the next, and ever after.
>
> In this way, I hope, my dear, you will account for a little of that *sensibility* which you will find above, and perhaps still more, as I proceed. (I, 38, 258; emphasis added).

By *sensibility*, Clarissa means *sensitivity to psychological pain*. On a similar occasion, Clarissa refers Anna Howe's probing of her sensibility to that of a doctor (in this case closely related to the satirist): 'What patient shall be afraid of a probe in so delicate a hand?' (II, 24, 146).

Anna Howe's test of Clarissa by probing her sensibility reveals a boundary where revelation and exposure come together. But the production of self-revelatory mater- ial concerns another element of the term's meaning, as well. Persisting in her ques- tion of whether Clarissa has developed an affection for Lovelace, Anna Howe writes, 'I would occasion no throb; nor half-throb; no flash of *sensibility*, like lightning darting in, and as soon suppressed, by a discretion that no one of the Sex ever before could give such an example of' (II, 20, 132; emphasis added). Anna Howe here uses the word *sensibility* to mean an involuntary feeling of being animated, thrilled. Lovelace, too, uses it in this sense – to mean a *capacity for desire*. He complains that Clarissa has a 'Youth so blooming: Air so animated – To have an heart so impenetrable' (I, 31, 201). While echoing Clarissa's comment about her sister's 'impenetrableness,' Lovelace here conflates sensibility and heart to mean *the sexual being*, as he does again when he comments on her returning health and spirits: 'My charmer is a little better than she was. Her eyes shew it . . . But yet she has no Love, no Sensibility!' (III, 58, 282). She is susceptible to grief, which means that she is 'penetrable' – but Lovelace has so far not been able to touch her, to 'soften' her heart, to work on her capacity for love and desire. Richardson thus positions the different meanings of sensibility against each other, exploring the psychological complexity of a capacity that identifies wound- ing and penetrating and underlies sympathy, grief, and sexual desire. Although pity and love form a much older alliance, sensibility could explain why they were allied.

Sentiment tells an overlapping but somewhat different story. Like *sensibility*, *sentiment* can mean *refined and delicate feeling*, feeling ranging from grief to sexual excitement. In Mackenzie's *Julia de Roubigne* (1777), Julia says of the man she loves, 'To know such a man; to see his merit; to regret that yoke which Fortune had laid on him – I am bewildered in sentiment again. – In truth, my story is the story of sentiment (Letter X, 51). Although regularly used to mean *feeling*, however, *sentiment* is also widely used to mean *thought* or *opinion*. As reported by Boswell (reporting Hawkins), Samuel Johnson explains why he loves taverns: '"As soon", said he, "as I enter the door of a tavern, I experience an oblivion of care, and a freedom from solicitude . . . wine there exhilarates my spirits, and prompts me to free conversation and an interchange of discourse with those whom I most love: I dogmatise and am contradicted, and in this conflict of opinions and sentiments I find delight"' (697–8, n.). Sentiments are here linked, though not completely identified with, opinions. Clearly belonging in a social setting, they are the ground of agreement and disagreement.

A sentiment in this sense is expressible – and meant to be communicated. Sentiments can be *conveyed, admired, concurred with, declared, contradicted, ridiculed, approved, justified, adopted, examined, explained, displayed, mangled, denied, condemned, published, taken from a book, believed, imbibed,* and *applauded.* For people to be 'of a sentiment' means to be 'of one mind' or 'in agreement'. A mid-century translation of a verse in I Philippians, for example, reads 'Fulfil ye my joy, that you be of one mind, having the same charity, being of one accord, agreeing in sentiment' (Challoner, 1750–2, ch. II, verse 2, 103).

We can again use *Clarissa* to illustrate some of the complexities of this term:

> had I twenty Brother James's, and twenty Sister Bell's, not one of them, nor all of them joined together, would dare to treat me as yours presume to treat you. *The person who will bear much shall have much to bear, all the world thro'*: 'Tis your own *sentiment*, grounded upon the strongest instance that can be given in your own family; though you have so little improved by it. (I, 10, 58; emphasis added)

Anna Howe's sentiment rests on her own experiential certainty that no brother, sister, or combination, would treat her as Clarissa is treated, making it clear that sentiments are closely related to individual experience (Dussinger, 1998). A similar sense of experiential certainty underlies Clarissa's protest to her sister: 'Whose Father, but mine, agrees upon articles, where there is no prospect of a liking? Where the direct contrary is avow'd . . . without the least variation, or *shadow* of a change of sentiment?' (I, 45, 318). She means not just that her answer to Solmes has been an unvarying *No* based on her judgement of his character, but also that her feelings of repugnance and aversion cannot be overcome. Her thinking about Solmes is so closely allied with her feeling that they cannot be separated. This fusion of thought and feeling and the continued pattern of moving from experience to inference make *Clarissa* 'sentimental' in a specialized sense and help to explain why Richardson found it congenial to collect sentiments for separate publication from his characters' statements (*A Collection of the Moral and Instructive Sentiments, Maxims, Cautions, and Reflexions, Contained in the Histories of Pamela, Clarissa, and Sir Charles Grandison* [1755]).

By adopting a sentiment previously voiced by Clarissa (who uttered it in response to seeing her own mother's difficulty increase in proportion to her patience), Anna Howe reveals another important element in 'sentimental' thinking: such distilled or condensed inferences from experience are a social as well as an individual form. They can be seen as a replacement for proverbs in an age that viewed proverbs sceptically. Proverbs are handed down; sentiments are passed around, from one person to another or from poem, letter, or fiction to readers. Sentiments are widely applicable not because they express a collected or traditional authority but because they can be repeatedly confirmed through individual experience (Van Sant, 1998). As proverbs have been tested by time, sentiments move from one scene of testing to another. Lord M., the marginal aristocratic figure in the novel, continually proffers proverbs; Clarissa draws sentiments from her experience. As developed in *Clarissa*, the sentiment is something of a parallel form to the novel, both emerging from experience, both separated from tradition.

In one sense, *Clarissa* might be seen as a struggle between sentiment and sensibility. Clarissa's sensibility provides the material that she works to turn into sentiments. Accepting the vulnerability that characterizes a delicate sensibility, she would nevertheless always subordinate that level of experience to some form of distillation. She enacts the sort of narrative that aims towards the relatively static form of sentiment, and had Richardson put her rather than Lovelace 'in charge' of the story, so to speak, it might have been formally 'sentimental'. But, as I have argued elsewhere, the novel is shaped by the testing, provocative methods it shares with the medical model of sensibility. The continual testing that gives rise to much of the novel is the probing method of the sensibility experiments (Van Sant, 1993). Lovelace enacts that method and therefore dominates the 'shape' of the novel. Richardson's uneasiness about his authorial alliance with Lovelace on this count might be another means of explaining not only Richardson's affinity for collecting sentiments from his characters' statements but also for claiming, as he did, that they were the 'pith and marrow' of his novel.

In general (though with many exceptions), the plural form – *sentiments* – is more likely to be associated with thought while the singular – *sentiment* – is more likely to mean the less definable feeling. Nevertheless, when *sentiment* means feeling, something of the idea of thought often persists, and when it means thought, it is often *thought infused with feeling*. Thus *sentiment*, while an important affective term, also demonstrates that affective experience and thought were not always clearly separated (Brissenden, 1974, 16; Pinch, 1996, 18–19). Various terms used to describe the mind also offer evidence of the period's fusion of interior capacities. The mind is not just a space for ideas. It can be *sensible and tender, benevolent, sordid, sympathetic, ambitious, firm, delicate, susceptible of feeling,* or *agitated.* Traditional contrasts – *body vs. mind, head vs.*

heart, feeling vs. thinking, as well as remnants of the tripartite division of the soul (into nutritive, sensitive, and intellectual principles) – remain functional but share their generalizing power with expressions that imply a unified sense of the self that has experience.

Sentimental Fiction: On the Road for Experience

I feel a damp upon my spirits, as I am going to add, that in my last return through Calais, upon inquiring after Father Lorenzo, I heard he had been dead near three months, and was buried, not in his convent, but, according to his desire, in a little cimetiery belonging to it, about two leagues off: I had a strong desire to see where they had laid him – when, upon pulling out his little horn box, as I sat by his grave, and plucking up a nettle or two at the head of it, which had no business to grow there, they all struck together so forcibly upon my affections, that I burst into a flood of tears – but I am as weak as a woman; and I beg the world not to smile, but pity me. (Sterne, 'The Snuff-Box, Calais', 102–3)

In *A Sentimental Journey*, Sterne moves with complex delicacy towards moments of feeling that stop narrative progress altogether. As Yorick concentrates on his own feeling, readers are invited to pause, to allow their answering feeling to be generated. Henry Mackenzie's *The Man of Feeling* (1771) has a quite similar pattern:

There was an old stone, with the corner broken off, and some letters, half covered with moss, to denote the names of the dead: there was a cyphered R. E. plainer than the rest: it was the tomb they sought. 'Here it is, grandfather,' said the boy. Edwards gazed upon it without uttering a word: the girl, who had only sighed before, now wept outright; her brother sobbed, but he stifled his sobbing. 'I have told sister', said he, 'that she should not take it so to heart; she can knit already, and I shall soon be able to dig: we shall not starve, sister, indeed we shall not, nor shall grandfather neither.' – The girl cried afresh; Harley kissed off her tears as they flowed, and wept between every kiss. (XXXV, 99)

Such structured opportunities for feeling, called 'tableaux', 'vignettes' or 'set pieces' and often, as here, focused on loss, have been seen by many readers, however assessed, as the stylistic signature of the fictions of sensibility (see, e.g., Todd, 1986). What Sterne achieves through digression, Mackenzie achieves through textual fragmentation, but both work against temporal pressure, valuing stasis over progress or continuity.

In a specialized, etymologically based sense, such pause-defined narratives are sentimental. The structured pauses lead from sensation to intensified feeling or to reflection, both of which are examples of 'sentiment'. Rhetorically rather than dramatically organized, such fictions are essentially educative, moving from experience towards contemplation and state-able inference or towards the exercise of the reader's sensibility. In the section above from *A Sentimental Journey*, Sterne creates a sense of psychological depth through a staged stylistic resonance. The reader's attention is sur- prised into memory by the unexpected return of the snuff-box. Sterne's fictions create experience – interior events for readers' pleasure and contemplation, making it pos- sible for readers to do as Locke instructed in the *Essay* – look into their own minds (Van Sant, 1993, ch. 6).

That fictions created experience was widely taken for granted, and the under- standing of how they did so was influenced by Locke. In describing how the mind gains experience or gets ideas, Locke's regular term was 'furnish':

> The Senses at first let in particular *Ideas*, and *furnish* the yet empty cabinet: And the Mind by degrees growing familiar with some of them, they are lodged in the Memory, and Names got to them. Afterwards, the Mind proceeding farther, abstracts them, and by Degrees learns the use of general Names. In this manner the Mind comes to be *fur- nish'd* with *Ideas* and Language, the Materials about which to exercise its discursive Faculty. (I, 1, 15, 55; emphasis added for *furnish*).

Johnson adopts Locke's epistemological use of *furnish* for psychological purposes in *Rambler* no. 4 to talk about the effect of reading novels. (Van Sant, 1998, 419). Novels are usually read by the young, whose minds are 'unfurnished with ideas, and there- fore easily susceptible of impressions' (III, 21). Sterne, to a greater degree, but Mackenzie as well, is furnishing readers' minds with feelings. Locke's spatial metaphors (e.g., 'the mind's presence-room'; an 'empty cabinet') get realized in these fictions, which, in furnishing the mind, also create the imagined space for the furniture.

'"Come, my Emily,"' says the father of the fallen but restored daughter, '"we can never, never recover that happiness we have lost; but time may teach us to remember our misfortunes with patience"' (XXIX, 68). The father's statement – and the daugh- ter's experience leading to it – presumably touch the hearts or exercise the sensibili- ties of readers, creating pity, directly affecting the nervous system and thus creating experience. The statement is therefore sentimental in a double sense: sentimental in creating intensified feeling and sentimental in arriving at a general statement or sen- timent based on deeply felt experience. In both senses, the fiction furnishes the mind.

That novels furnish the mind with feelings was the basis of a contemporary cri- tique of novel reading. On the one hand, a case was often made that such reading was an essential part of education: 'The general plan of modern education, which among the liberal consists of the study of Poets and Sentimental Writers, contributes perhaps more than all other causes to humanise the heart and refine the sentiments' (*Univer- sal Magazine*, LXII, 173). But on the other, such feelings – originating in the fiction and sustained by it – might well not train readers for the moral world but might instead engage them in a closed imaginary world of feeling. And further, furnishing the mind with feelings was equivalent to the older phrase *inflaming the passions*. Thus the sentimental novel was open to the same objections made against romance, justi- fying such phrases as 'lust in disguise'. Interestingly enough, poetry was often distinguished from novels – and recommended, particularly to women readers (Pinch, 56). It was recommended because it was a source of sentiments: 'The mind is thus stored with a lasting treasure of sentiments and ideas' (*The Female Aegis*, quoted in Pinch, 56).

The on-the-road fictions create not only material for the mind but a series of discrete opportunities for establishing social bonds outside the normative framework of the family and outside the niches of the social hierarchy (with no reference to specific, obligation-based relations). The episodes also often turn ordinarily non-sympathetic transactions into sympathetic ones (Harley's visits to Bedlam and to the brothel). They are open to all kinds of criticism (and were satirized by contemporaries), but they are also in a sense experiments in extending social bonds.

Sentimental Fiction: Extending Social Bonds

Sarah Fielding's *The Adventures of David Simple* (1744), together with its sequel *David Simple, Volume the Last* (1753), is a sentimental fiction as it creates opportunities for feeling and as it trains the reader to move towards generalizations from experience. The novel anticipates Johnson's *Rasselas* (and the search for what can't be found) and the man-of-feeling narratives. Without thematizing digression as Sterne does and without entering a pretence of editing fragments as Mackenzie does, Fielding adopts the on-the-road fiction for multiple purposes. And she experiments, as they do not, with the formation of a continuing community.

Fielding's life is less well known and was less publicly intertwined with her fiction than the lives of Richardson and Sterne who enacted for public view some of the problems of their fictions. Fielding was born into gentility, but the provisions for maintaining that gentility were inadequate. After her mother's death, she lived with her maternal grandmother and experienced directly the sort of pressures created by lawsuits, second marriages and the lack of dowries (Bree, 1996). Her life positioned her at the boundaries of the culture's conventional arrangements for families. She was situated to see both the benefit of affective ties and the weakness of the family as a social structure. The novel no doubt reflects her biography, but more important, her biography prepares her to scrutinize affective models.

The formal qualities of *David Simple* have produced a fair amount of critical discussion, much of which was anticipated by Julia Kavanagh in her 1863 essay on Fielding (Bree, 1996). Reminding readers that *David Simple* was published early in the history of the novel ('Richardson's career was but in its dawn; Fielding had only produced his miscellanies and his "Joseph Andrews" when it appeared'), Kavanagh goes on to articulate some of the criticisms of Fielding's style that became common: 'There is a constant struggle going on between narrative and dialogue, without either being able to find its right place; we never know exactly what we are reading, – a sketch of characters or a story.' Further, Fielding's satire 'is better suited to an essay than to a story, and would be more effective in the "Spectator" than in a novel' (56 and 65).

Such uneasiness about the apparent lack of formal control of the novel might call for an analysis like that Kristina Straub provides for Frances Burney's novels in *Divided Fictions*, but it is also possible to see that the multi-faceted quality of Fielding's style reveals its 'sentimental' organization. Her adaptation of the loosely coherent picaresque travel form, which itself tends to be based on a movement from experience to satiric reflection, allows Fielding to be destructive and constructive at the same time. On the one hand, the novel steadily negates through experience what it posits as desirable, thus leading to reductive and satiric sentiments and perhaps by the end of *Volume the Last* alienating its readers from worldly ambitions as it slowly eliminates its characters from the world. On the other hand, it also steadily makes a case for a feeling-based morality and to that end the narrator and characters produce the material for a catalogue of sentiments (both shrewd and affectively appealing) derived from experience: 'There is no Situation so deplorable, no Condition so much to be pitied, as that of a Gentle-woman in real Poverty' (III, II, 132). This generalization invites pity for present misery and offers a social critique. It arises from the experience presented in the narrative (Camilla attempts to support her sick brother; their poverty is ensured by their alienation from the family owing to false charges of incest), but it also brings into view women's economic dependence as an important social problem. Much other material in the novel supports Fielding's 'case' on women's poverty, including such remarkably extended and energetically ironic comments as that about brothers,

> who, by their Fathers having more Concern for the keeping up the Grandeur of their Names, than for the Welfare of their Posterity, having got the Possession of all the Estate of the Family, out of meer Kindness and Good-Nature, allow their Sisters enough out of it to keep them from starving in some Hole in the Country; where their small Subsistence just serves to keep them the longer in their Misery, and prevents them from appearing in the World to disgrace their Brother, by their Poverty, (III, I, 121)

The supportive commentary is itself a wealth of material for 'sentimentizing' (Richardson's term for extracting sentiments from the novel for the *Collection*). The novel frequently reads as if an alternative set of sentiments: alternative, for example to collections of moral sayings, and alternative as well to prevailing opinions about women's experience. And at one point, the novel explicitly endorses the communication of sentiments. Camilla, having moved out of her narrative to 'reflect' on it at some length apologizes slightly to David, who assures her of his interest not only in story but also in sentiment: ' "and, as to her Remarks, he desired her always to tell him what she felt and thought on every Incident that befel her . . . as he was sure . . . her Sentiments were just on all occasions" ' (II, X, 109).

In *David Simple*, what I am calling the sentimental structuring of the narrative allows Fielding's satire to emerge. Men and women of feeling often fare badly in the world, owing to their sympathy and integrity, and thus delineate a standard by which the world is judged. But it isn't just that David's simplicity exposes the duplicity of the world. The sentimental structuring, in creating narrative malleability, lends itself to her feminist critique. That David Simple is a feminized figure has become a commonplace of the commentary on the novel (Bree, 1996; Woodward, 1992), but the novel's feminist stance depends, in my view, less on that feminization than on Fielding's use of this form to articulate and imply the problems of women's experience. My claim is not that such a structuring principle is gendered but that it was accessible to a woman's commentary, and in *David Simple* trains an attentive reader to move toward inferences, often radical ones, from the experience presented.

Fielding's novel deals with issues that, in Kavanagh's words, 'no writer of fiction would [in 1863] venture to introduce' (78), by which Kavanagh means motivating even a step-mother to make accusations of incest. But the generalization can be extended to include the issue of women's cultural marginality and Fielding's interest in the relation between affective ties and property. Fielding is particularly concerned with the *concurrence* of sentiments. Such concurrence coincides with *no division of interests* — specifically no division of property interests. And that is what her 'little society' (which her narrator calls 'our little society') is defined by. Unlike the sibling society with which the novel begins (the 'brotherhood' of David and his brother, Daniel, is destroyed by the latter's property fraud), the 'little society' is structured through what often functions as a utopian-satiric ideal of communal property. Only when Cynthia and Valentine prepare to go to Jamaica, does David 'divid[e] with his friends' 'the small Stock of Money [he] was now possessed of'. And 'this', the narrator emphasizes, 'was the first time the word DIVIDED could, with any Propriety have been used, in relating the Transactions for our Society; for SHARING in common, without any Thought of separate Property, had ever been their friendly Practice, from their first Connection' (VI, I, 265). Only after this use of *divide* does early use of the term seem a matter for scepticism: 'Their Father had left all he had to be divided equally amongst them' (I, VII, 37). Ordinary *division* of property, even when fair, is problematic.

To define a society in which affective bonds displace property bonds requires re-imagining family structures. Fielding was as sceptical of sensibility as later writers, but she had a great interest in imagining powerful affective ties outside the ordinary family but through family structures. Family structures are for the most part a massive failure in the novel (as well as troubled in Fielding's life), and through those failures, she explores something like an ' "affective siblinghood" ', as Terri Nickel argues (239). Though Fielding would have had no sympathy with the political fraternity of the French Revolution, she was imagining social groups outside hereditary ties. The concurrence of sentiments, the meeting of minds, is a marker for the ties not shaped by property interests.

Social Issues and Social Bonds

In modern times, the chief improvement of which we have to boast, is a sense of humanity . . . On general manners, and on several departments of society it has had a considerable influence. It has abated the spirit of persecution: it has even tempered the horrors of war; and man is now more ashamed than he was in some former ages, of acting as a savage to man. (Hugh Blair, Sermon VIII, 'On Sensibility', II, 128)

Humanity, or fellow feeling based on sensibility, was often said to be the distinguishing mark of the age. Humanitarian projects of various sorts proliferated during the period – homes for repentant prostitutes, for poor children, for children abandoned at birth, for disabled mariners. Novels often explicitly featured humanitarian social issues, including prostitution, slavery and other questions more immediately connected to the experience of readers, especially women readers: women's liberty or lack of it to have choice in marriage arrangements, women's poverty relative to men, girls seduced and then abandoned.

In his study, *The Politics of Sensibility*, Markman Ellis investigates the novel's engagement with various social issues. He begins by quoting Frances Burney's response when, at 16, she read Oliver Goldsmith's *The Vicar of Wakefield* (1766). She finds herself moved and surprised that she is so. And then she comments on the opinions Goldsmith presents: 'He advances many very bold and singular opinions – for example, he avers that murder is the sole crime for which death ought to be the punishment, he even goes farther, and ventures to affirm that our laws in regard to penalties and punishments are *all* too severe' (quoted Ellis, 1996, 1). As Ellis indicates, the novels are not all tears. They are opinions, too. And these opinions are what eighteenth-century readers recognized as 'sentiments'. Many novels seem not only to make room for 'sentiments' but to work towards them and to extend them into significant social commentary. Reviewers sometimes comment that a particular novel features sentiments on a certain topic. In its three-page notice of *The History of Emily Montague*, for example, *The Critical Review* makes clear the novel's usefulness as a source of 'tender and delicate sentients on the subject of love and marriage' (quoted McMullen, 1983, 113). And indeed, Brooke's novel is a repository of views on women, men and marriage. A 'sentimentizing' reader would have little (or no) editing to do to arrive at such statements as: 'Women are not obliged in conscience to obey laws they have had no share in making' (Letter 11: 34–5); 'Equality is the soul of friendship'; 'Marriage, to give delight, must join two minds, not devote a slave to the will of an imperious lord'; 'Whatever conveys the idea of subjection necessarily destroys that of love'; 'I have always wished the word OBEY expunged from the marriage ceremony' (Letter 116, 205).

Not all the discussion tends towards radical social improvement. Ellis suggests that novels tend to promote amelioration rather than radical reform. But interestingly enough, they often make space for a critique more radical than the solutions they propose or enact. So much was the novel seen as an appropriate forum for important issues that an acquaintance of Jonas Hanway, a well-known philanthropist, recommended that he use the novel form to write his 'system of ethics' (Taylor, 1943, 14). Hanway was mildly appalled, but the suggestion may show both the novels and Hanway's philosophical reflections were each read as a source of sentiments, despite

the extensive criticism of the novel and despite its being a lower form than philosophical essay.

Another study of great interest for its analysis of the social function of sensibility
is John Mullan's *Sentiment and Sociability* (1988). He examines the work of David
Hume, Samuel Richardson, and Laurence Sterne for their conceptions of 'harmonious
sociability', which rest on 'the communication of passions and sentiments', and which
are 'historically significant' in revealing 'the difficulty which a polite culture was
having in imagining the nature of social relations' (Mullan, 1988, 2). The construction of sociability is more fragile in philosophy than in the novel because philosophy
is under pressure to generalize while novels can delineate persuasive social bonds and
simultaneously acknowledge that they are shared by small communities and exceptional individuals. Mullan argues that while these writers were committed to sensibility, sentiment, and sympathy, they found themselves analysing and dramatizing
the inadequacies, limitations and failures of affective bonds. The displays of feeling
quoted above from *A Sentimental Journey* and *The Man of Feeling* confirm Mullan's
thesis. It is frequently Yorick's and Harley's weaknesses as much as their sympathizing frames to which readers' attention is called. Mullan ends his study with an analysis of the near identity of sensibility as a source of social bonds and sensibility as a
source of nervous disorders, concluding, 'In constructing this pattern of susceptibility, the medical texts dramatize the paradoxes of the vocabulary which elaborates
society as a capacity of the self . . . and, in the end, this capacity can achieve no expression which is not private and exceptional. There is no social space for sensibility. Illness
is its appropriate metaphor' (Mullan, 1988, 239–40).

The paradox that Mullan analyses – that the capacity for 'sociability' is also the
capacity for disease – was frequently recognized by eighteenth-century writers
through a satiric version of sensibility. Fielding, an early critic of sensibility, satirizes
it as a form of cultivated debility: 'Lady *Fanny Chlegen* "greatly wondered, how it was
possible for a Woman of any Fashion to go raking into Holes and Corners after every
crying Woman . . . if they had any Sensibility, or the least Delicacy of Nerves, they
could not be thrusting themselves into Scenes of Distress' (Vol. II, 97–8). Similarly,
in *Evelina*, Frances Burney suggests in her satiric exposure of the sister of Lord Orville
that a claim to being 'nerve all over' is closely allied with self-preoccupation and arrogance. And in *The Wanderer*, Burney extensively satirizes a debilitating irritability in
the figure of Mrs Ireton. (Patricia Meyer Spacks discusses a number of pre-
Wollstonecraft critiques of sensibility by women novelists and argues that women
novelists tended to interrogate sensibility much more than male novelists did.) When
sensibility 'degenerates into weakness', to use the reviewer's phrase, or when it
becomes 'a capricious and irritable delicacy' (Blair, 1802, 129), as it does in the satiric
portrayals, whether the weakness is actual or imagined, it becomes an instrument for
inhibiting generosity to both neighbours and strangers. By analysing and dramatizing forms of self-preoccupation and debility as excessive or affected, periodical writers
and novelists try to separate its diseased from its healthy forms and maintain that self-
love and social meet in acts of benevolence: '[T]o him who is prompted by a virtu-

ous sensibility, every office of beneficence and humanity is a pleasure' (Blair, 1802, 125). The extensive critiques of and apologies for sensibility show that its paradoxical nature though not resolved was continually visible.

What was perhaps less visible as *a problem* was the extent to which sensibility and sentiment were imagined within the existing social order. And this, I think, is a greater cultural limitation than the paradoxical relation of sensibility to disease. On the one hand, the eighteenth-century centralizing of affective bonds reveals an effort to imagine social ties not related to forms of obligation and inheritance, as evidenced in such phrases as 'friend of mankind.' ('The duty to parents is contrasted with the ties of friendship and of love; the virtues of justice, of prudence, of economy, are put in competition with the exertions of generosity, of benevolence, and of compassion' [Mackenzie, *Lounger*, 330].) On the other hand, those deserving of sympathy were often validated by the fact that their gentility showed through their distressed circumstances (objects of sympathy in novels are often said to be above their present condition), or such deserving objects were re-formed (prostitutes were re-made as 'daughters of woe' (Van Sant, 1993, ch. 2). Fielding comes closer than most novelists to examining the gentility divide. The members of her 'little family' of sensibility cheerfully adapt to the necessity of working with their hands to support themselves as they slide down the economic scale (and the pity extended to them for this social dislocation is viewed in the novel with contempt). But at their introduction to David, Camilla and Valentine give evidence even in their rags and misery of not having been 'bred in very Low life' or at least to have risen above it (II, IX, 102). And it is the genteel woman with whose situation Fielding has the greatest sympathy. Her novel could even be used as oblique evidence for the firm boundaries between gentility and non-gentility. When Camilla tells her story (after expressing the opinion, or sentiment, that 'no Condition is so much to be pitied, as that of a Gentle-women in real Poverty'), she describes what happens when women try, by working, to live below their gentility:

> If we were to attempt getting our living by any Trade, People in that Station would think we were endeavouring to take their Bread out of their mouths, and combine together against us; saying, we must certainly deserve our Distress, or our *great Relations* would support us . . . And the lower sort of people use a Person who was born in a higher Station, and is thrown amongst them by any Misfortune, just as I have seen Cows in a Field use one another: for, if by accident any of them falls into a Ditch, the rest all kick against them, and endeavour to keep them down, that they may not get out again. They will not suffer us to be equal with them and get our Bread as they do; if we cannot be above them, they will have the pleasure of casting us down infinitely below them.
>
> (III, II, 132–3)

Such a division, despite what Penelope Corfield calls 'a palpable sense of social mutability' (1991, 105) in the eighteenth century, was deeply entrenched and often reinforced from both sides.

In the second book of the *Treatise* ('Of the Passions'), Hume writes:

> The skin, pores, muscles, and nerves of a day-labourer are different from those of a man
> of quality: So are his sentiments, actions and manners. The different stations of life influ-
> ence the whole fabric, external and internal; and different stations arise necessarily,
> because uniformly, from the necessary and uniform principles of human nature. Men
> cannot live without society, and cannot be associated without government. Government
> makes a distinction of property, and establishes the different ranks of men. This pro-
> duces industry, traffic, manufactures, law-suits, war, leagues, alliances, voyages, travels,
> cities, fleets, ports, and all those other actions and objects, which cause such a diversity,
> and at the same time maintain such an uniformity in human life.
>
>   (II, III, I, 402)

Hume's summary of the history of society is a summary of property and the production of social rank. The social separation between the labourer and the man of quality
is not only visible but acceptable and necessary. Sensibility as a coherent idea was
imagined *within* this social ordering. And people demonstrably more delicate than
predictable by their rank were often moved imaginatively out of it. While ideas of
gentility were fluctuating throughout the century, with a gentility of heart often
standing as a critique of gentility of social rank, gentility itself was reconfirmed. And
sympathy expressed across social ranks reinforced those ranks, with benevolence outlining a paradigm of the benefactor and recipient on different social levels.

Although sympathy could not become a sufficient framework for an extension of
social bonds, it was used as an instrument in social reform both ameliorative and
radical (Van Sant 1993, 1998; Ellis, 1996). I take as my example of the first Hanway's
*A Sentimental History of Chimney Sweepers, in London and Westminster. Shewing the neces-
sity of putting them under Regulations to prevent the grossest Inhumanity to the Climbing Boys.*
In this series of letters excoriating the British public for the deplorable condition of
chimney sweepers, Hanway insists that their misery

> calls for all the relief which can be afforded, to prevent cruelty, and the wasting of the
> human species by a wantonness of inattention. Let any one examine into the merits of
> the cause: With all the laborious efforts which these boys make for a support, their
> bruised bodies, weakened eyes, frequent wounds, lungs stuffed, unwashen, unclothed,
> uncomfortable lodging, and scanty diet irregularly supplied, indeed constitute a
> Sentimental history, equal to any of the miseries which human nature seems capable
> of supporting.
>
>   (pp. xxix–xxx)

His letters are set up not as a continuous narrative or history but as a series of opportunities for feeling and reflection that will move readers towards a distillation of experience – and towards the kind of agreement necessary for regulatory legislation.
Addressing people at a number of social levels ('The magistrate and the legislator,
clergy and laity, sovereign and subject, all in their respective stations, are called on,

as it were by a voice from Heaven, to succour these poor children' [xxx]), he aims for concurrence in sentiment. The second letter expands on a heading, which is the equivalent of a sentiment: '[J]ustice [is] due to every class of the people, on the common principles of mutual protection' (12). Other headings similarly have a 'sentimental' shape: 'Religion and humanity equally concerned in the relief of every object of distress' (37); 'The necessity of regulations for restraining the conduct of master chimney-sweepers towards their climbing-boys' (43). Creating pity and indignation, Hanway aims to dictate public opinion.

For the purposes of this chapter, there are two further points to notice here: First, despite his creation of pity and indignation, and despite pointing to some alternatives to child labour, Hanway actually recommends not that child labour be stopped but that the conditions of the job be improved. His point of view is essentially remedial. His remedies include bigger chimneys, protective clothing (illustrated), and regulated pay. Second, it is legislation that Hanway aims at, not a sustained community of sensibility. His rhetorical task is to extend his audience's experience of those with whom they have affective ties and on the basis of those ties to guide them in arriving at sentiments that allow them to act in the public interest. But it is legislation through which the extension of the community is to be stabilized and guaranteed. Affective bonds are instrumental rather than the source of a coherent or sustaining social model.

The second example – of a radical reform – comes from the debates in the House of Commons on the abolition of the slave trade. In 1791, extended reports of the debates were presented in periodicals. In the *Bee*, a Mr Francis is reported to have insisted on the undeniable injustice of the slave system based on the fact that no slave master had been convicted and punished for the death of a slave. In order to make his case vivid, thereby supporting it emotionally as well as logically, he describes 'some particular instances of brutality of treatment' and ends by asking 'Was there not something in slavery, which debased equally the mind of the master and the slave?' (196)

The Abstract of the Evidence, one of the key texts produced by the abolition movement, displays a diagram of slave ships presented to parliament in the case for abolition. It is a remarkable demonstration of efficiency. Little human figures line the hold of the ship, touching shoulder to shoulder, shackled hand to hand and ankle to ankle (in almost a parody of affective ties). Nothing about the diagram itself is overwrought. It is in fact somewhat understated. But the image of these tiny figures can be extended to include both function and experience (breathing; excreting; terror). Such extension of the image is a move familiar to rhetorical practice. But it was used in 1791 in a context in which words like *sympathy*, *benevolence*, and *humanity* were understood through the concept of sensibility. 'Humanity shudders at the bare idea of it [a slaver crowded enough to be profitable]!' calls into view the motion of the nerves that vibrate and tremble at such a strong image of suffering (200). Mr Fox, arguing in the same debate for the motion to abolish was reported by *Universal Magazine*:

> How [the slaves] were treated, and how the whole of the trade was conducted, it required
> only that they should peruse the evidence on the table to know – and after reading that

evidence, persons who could stand up in that house, and give a vote for its continuance, must have nerves of which he had no conception. (p. 464)

These speakers in parliament attempt to create momentary alliances of sensibility in order to achieve a legislative solution. Moving an audience towards shared sentiment – 'Was there not something in slavery, which debased equally the mind of the master and the slave?' – or toward a community defined by its nerves, makes use of the cultural engagement with feeling but does not count on its stability or continuity.

A final note on Fielding: Fielding's solution to the problem of establishing social bonds allies sensibility with a commitment to 'no separate Property'. In imagining what is essentially a new version of early Christian communal property, she registers a fundamental criticism of contemporary property arrangements (not to mention a dissenting view of the relation between property and society, as established in political theory). But as things worked out historically, some of the problems Fielding exposes through her affectively based critique were to be solved with precisely the opposite sort of strategy – legislation for women's separate property. Fielding's sensibility-based social construction can thus look either deeply conservative, and limited to the exceptional few, or deeply radical, and continually applicable as a critique of social boundaries.

REFERENCES AND FURTHER READING

Barchas, Janine (1996). 'Sarah Fielding's dashing style and eighteenth-century print culture'. *ELH* 63.3, 633–56.

Barker, Gerard A. (1982). '*David Simple*: the novel of sensibility in embryo'. *Modern Language Studies*, 12.2, 69–80.

Barker-Benfield, G. J. (1992). *The Culture of Sensibility: Sex and Society in Eighteenth-century Britain*. Chicago and London: University of Chicago Press.

Blair, Hugh (1802). *Sermons*. 3 vols. New York.

Boswell, James (1904). *Life of Johnson*. London: Oxford University Press. Repr. (1957).

Bree, Linda (1996). *Sarah Fielding*. New York: Twayne.

Brissenden, R. F. (1974). *Virtue in Distress: Studies in the Novel of Sentiment from Richardson to Sade*. New York: Barnes and Noble.

Brooke, Frances Moore (1985). *The History of Emily Montague*. Ed. and intro. Mary Jane Edwards. Centre for Editing Early Canadian Texts: Carleton University Press.

Corfield, Penelope J. (1991). 'Class by name and number in eighteenth-century Britain'. In *Language, History, and Class*. Ed. Penelope J. Corfield. Oxford and Cambridge, Mass.: Blackwell.

Challoner, Richard (1750–2). *The New Testament of our Lord and Saviour Jesus Christ. Translated out of the Latin Vulgat, 1750–2*. Ch. 2, verse 2, p. 103. Text in Chadwyck–Healey Literary Databases 〈*http://lion.chadwyck.co.uk:8080/*〉.

Conger, Syndy McMillen (1990). *Sensibility in Transformation: Creative Resistance to Sentiment from the Augustans to the Romantics: Essays in Honor of Jean H. Hagstrum*. Rutherford: Fairleigh Dickinson University Press; Cranbury, N.J.: Associated University Presses.

Denby, David (1994). *Sentimental Narrative and the Social Order in France, 1760–1820*. Cambridge: Cambridge University Press.

Dussinger, John (1998). 'Richardson and the tradition of moral sentiments'. Intro. to *A Collection of the Moral and Instructive Sentiments, Maxims, Cautions, and Reflexions*. In *Samuel Richardson's Published Commentary on Clarissa*. London: Pickering and Chatto. Vol. 3, vii–l.

'Essay on Sensibility' (a poem). (1789). Review in *Critical Review* 48.

Ellis, Markman (1996). *The Politics of Sensibility: Race, Gender and Commerce in the Sentimental Novel*. Cambridge: Cambridge University Press.

Erickson, Robert A. (1997). *The Language of the Heart, 1600–1750*. Philadelphia: University of Pennsylvania Press.

Fielding, Sarah (1974). *The History of the Countess of Dellwyn*. New York and London: Garland Publishing. Facsimile of London (1759) edn.

——(1998). *The Adventures of David Simple Containing an Account of his Travels Through the Cities of London and Westminster in Search of a Real Friend* and *The Adventures of David Simple, Volume the Last in which his History is Concluded*. Ed. and intro. Peter Sabor. Lexington, Ky.: University Press of Kentucky.

Hanway, Jonas (1785). *A Sentimental History of Chimney Sweepers, in London and Westminster. Shewing the Necessity of Putting Them under Regulations to Prevent the Grossest Inhumanity to the Climbing Boys*. London. Quoted by permission of the Huntington Library.

Hume, David (1975). *A Treatise of Human Nature* (1888). Ed. L. A. Selby-Bigge. Oxford: Clarendon Press.

Johnson, Samuel (1969). *The Rambler*. Ed. W. J. Bate and Albrecht B. Strauss. *The Yale Edition of the Works of Samuel Johnson*. New Haven: Yale University Press.

Jones, Chris (1993). *Radical Sensibility: Literature and Ideas in the 1790s*. London and New York: Routledge.

Jones, Robert W. (1999). Review essay, 'Ruled passions: re-reading the culture of sensibility'. *Eighteenth-century Studies* 32.3, 395–402.

Kavanagh, Julia (1863). *English Women of Letters: Biographical Sketches*. 2 vols. London: Hurst and Blackett.

Locke, John (1975; 1979). *An Essay Concerning Human Understanding*. Ed. and intro. Peter H. Nidditch. Oxford: Clarendon Press.

Mackenzie, Henry (1785). Essay from *The Lounger* 20 (Saturday 18 June). Repr. in *Novel and Romance 1700–1800: A Documentary Record*. Ed. Ioan Williams. New York: Barnes and Noble (1970), 328–31.

——(1970). *The Man of Feeling*. Ed. Brian Vickers. London, Oxford, New York: Oxford University Press.

——(1976). *Julia de Roubigne*. New York: AMS

Press. Repr. of the 1815 edn for R. Scholey, Edinburgh.

McMullen, Lorraine (1983). *An Odd Attempt in a Woman: The Literary Life of Frances Brook*. Vancouver: University of British Columbia Press.

Mullan, John (1988). *Sentiment and Sociability*. Oxford: Clarendon Press.

——(1997). 'Feelings and novels'. In *Rewriting the Self. Histories from the Renaissance to the Present*. Ed. Roy Porter. London and New York: Routledge, 119–31.

Nickel, Terri (1995). '"Ingenious torment": incest, family, and the structure of community in the work of Sarah Fielding'. *The Eighteenth Century, Theory and Interpretation*, 36.3, 234–47.

Pinch, Adela (1996). *Strange Fits of Passion: Epistemologies of Emotion, Hume to Austen*. Stanford: Stanford University Press.

'Proceedings of the first session of the seventeenth parliament of Great Britain' (1791). *Universal Magazine*, June.

'Proceedings in parliament. House of Commons. Abolition of the slave trade' (1791). *Bee*, 6.

Richardson, Samuel (1990). *Clarissa, or the History of a Young Lady: Comprehending The Most Important Concerns of Private Live*. 3rd edn. 8 vols. London (1751). Facsimile edn: New York: AMS Press.

——(1998). *A Collection of the Moral and Instructive Sentiments, Maxims, Cautions, and Reflexions, Contained in the Histories of Pamela, Clarissa, and Sir Charles Grandison* (1755). Facsimile edn in *Samuel Richardson's Published Commentary on Clarissa*. London: Pickering and Chatto. Vol. 3.

Rousseau, G. S. (1966). 'Nerves, spirits, and fibres: towards defining the origins of sensibility'. In *Studies in the Eighteenth Century*. Papers presented at the David Nichol Smith Memorial Seminar, Canberra. Toronto: University of Toronto Press (1968), 137–205.

Skinner, Gillian (1992). '"The price of a tear": economic sense and sensibility in Sarah Fielding's *David Simple*'. *Literature and History* 3rd ser., 1, (spring), 16–28.

Spacks, Patricia Ann Meyer (1994). 'Oscillations of Sensibility'. *New Literary History* 25.3, 505–20.

Sterne, Laurence (1967). *A Sentimental Journey Through France and Italy by Mr. Yorick*. Ed. and intro. Gardner Stout. Berkeley and Los Angeles: University of California Press.

Straub, Kristina (1987). *Divided Fictions: Fanny Burney and Feminine Strategy*. Lexington: University Press of Kentucky.

Taylor, John Tinnon (1943). *Early Opposition to the English Novel: The Popular Reaction from 1760 to 1830*. New York: King's Crown Press.

Todd, Janet (1986). *Sensibility: An Introduction*. London and New York: Methuen.

Tuke, Samuel (1927). *The Adventures of Five Hours*. Ed. B. Van Thal. London: Robert Holden.

Van Sant, Ann Jessie (1993). *Eighteenth-century Sensibility and the Novel: The Senses in Social Context*. Cambridge: Cambridge University Press.

——(1998). 'A dictionary of morality: reading for the sentiment'. Afterword to *A Collection of the Moral and Instructive Sentiments, Maxims, Cautions, and Reflexions* in *Samuel Richardon's Published Commentary on Clarissa*. London: Pickering and Chatto. Vol. 3, 411–37.

Whytt, Robert (1768). 'Observations on the Nature, Causes, and Cure of Those Disorders which are commonly called nervous, hypochondriac, or hysteric, to which are prefixed some Remarks on the Sympathy of the nerves'. In *The Works of Robert Whytt*. London.

Willey, Basil (1961). *The Eighteenth-century Background: Studies on the Idea of Nature in the Thought of the Period*. Boston: Beacon Press. 1st edn (1940). London: Chatto and Windus.

Woodward, Carolyn (1992). 'Sarah Fielding's Self-destructing Utopia: *The Adventures of David Simple*'. In *Living By the Pen: Early British Women Writers*. Ed. Dale Spender. New York and London: Teachers College Press, Columbia University, 65–81.

5

Classical Translation and Imitation

David Hopkins

Evidence of the impact of classical Greek and Roman literature and culture on English poetry between Milton and Blake is ubiquitous and multifarious. The classics pervade the period's poetry at every level, from brief passing references, through the deployment and development of genres and forms established in antiquity (epic, pastoral, elegy, ode, satire, georgic, epigram), to full-dress translations and imitations of the works of the major Greek and Roman poets. Some of the last, moreover – Dryden's translations from Lucretius, Horace, Ovid, Homer and Virgil, Pope's translations and imitations of Homer and Horace, and Johnson's imitations of Juvenal – must be counted, in their own right, among the greatest English poems of the period. And a number of others – Oldham's Horace and Juvenal, Creech's Lucretius, Rowe's Lucan, Garth's Ovid, Francis's Horace, Cowper's Homer, Gifford's Juvenal – follow close behind in historical and aesthetic importance. To 'marginalize' most of the period's classical translations and imitations (in the manner of most modern textbooks, anthologies and academic courses) serves radically to distort our sense of the shape and significance of individual poets' careers and to skew our perception of the larger literary history of the period. 'So much of the poetic vigor of the age', Charles Tomlinson has observed, 'went into great translations. Ignore them, and you get the whole picture out of proportion' (Tomlinson, 1989, 272).

Discussion of classical influence in the period is often conducted in formal and generic terms. In this respect, modern critics are following the precedent of critics of the period, who were much preoccupied with the characteristics and development of particular literary genres, and with categorizing various types of translation and imitation. In his celebrated Preface to *Ovid's Epistles* (1680), John Dryden proposed a tripartite division of translation into 'metaphrase' ('or turning an author word for word, and line by line, from one language into another'), 'paraphrase' ('or translation with latitude, where the author is kept in view by the translator so as never to be lost, but his words are not so strictly followed as his sense, and that, too, is admitted to be amplified but not altered') and 'imitation' ('where the translator – if he has not lost that name – assumes the liberty not only to vary from the words and sense, but to forsake them both as he sees occasion; and taking only some general hints from the original, to run division on the ground-work, as he pleases'). 'Paraphrase' is offered by Dryden as the best option: a *via media* which avoids both the unidiomatic obscurity of extreme literalism, and the unlicensed freedom of versions which give little sense of the quiddity of their originals.

In a categorizing vein similar to Dryden's, modern critics habitually differentiate, in their discussions of classical influence, between 'original' poetry (in which no consistent presence of a classical source is evident), 'translation' (in which the work of an ancient poet is 'rendered' directly into English – with a greater or lesser degree of freedom), 'imitation' (in which the setting of the original is 'transposed' to the present, and modern 'equivalents' found for the ancient characters and situations), 'burlesque' or 'parody' (in which an ancient text is ridiculed by having its style and procedures applied to grossly inappropriate subject matter), and 'mock-heroic' (in which trivial or culpable events or persons in the modern world are ridiculed by being described in an incongruously grand epic style). Commentators also frequently distinguish, at the local level, between 'allusion' (in which a modern poem signals towards a specific classical source which must be recognized if the meaning of the modern text is to be fully understood) and 'echo' (in which material from an ancient text or texts is absorbed less obtrusively into the texture of a modern poem). In a celebrated discussion, Howard D. Weinbrot has further refined the modern definition of 'imitation', distinguishing those examples (such as Oldham's versions of Juvenal) which are, in effect, extremely free translations – in which circumstantial details are 'updated', but the main structure and purport of the original is preserved, and no assumption is made that readers will have independent access to the original – from those (like Pope's *Imitations of Horace*) which operate like extended allusions, in which independent knowledge of the original is required, and in which the reader is expected to move to and fro between the two texts, noting discrepancies and contradictions, as well as more straightforward alignments, between original and 'imitation' (Weinbrot, 1969, 1–58).

In practice, however, such formal, generic, and procedural categories are seldom clear-cut. An 'original' poem, such as Milton's *Paradise Lost*, may contain local passages of close 'translation' or 'imitation'. A 'translation' such as *The Satires of Juvenal and Persius* (1693), which for most of the time leaves the original in its Roman setting, may include local touches of 'imitation', in which features of Restoration political and social life mingle with those of the first century AD. 'Imitations' (of both Weinbrot's types) may include passages which follow their original, for a while, with literal fidelity. 'Burlesque' versions of classical texts may sometimes stimulate genuine insight into, rather than merely encouraging mockery of, their originals: James Scudamore's *Homer à la Mode* (1664), for example, helped Dryden to a positive appreciation of the earthy physicality of Homer's descriptive passages (Sowerby, 1996, 42). The echoes of classical epic in a 'mock heroic' poem may invest the poem's satiric victims with something of the genuine grandeur and dignity of the poem's epic 'originals', as well as subjecting them to satirical mockery. And it is sometimes uncertain whether the perceived presence of a classical original behind an English poem should be thought of as an 'allusion' or an 'echo'. Many of Pope's classical borrowings look at first sight like allusions to particular classical passages (in translations by himself and others), but appear, on closer inspection, to have a more generally evocative quality, 'where a sensitive reader is required to respond to the spirit and tone of the poetry without being precisely aware of its elements or origin' (Rosslyn, 1997, 51–2). And when Dryden, in his version of Horace, *Odes* III. xxix, refers to the goddess Fortune (with no direct prompting from Horace's original) as 'Still various and unconstant still', it is arguable whether we strictly *need* to notice that he is incorporating a reminiscence of *Virgil's* description of woman (*Aeneid* IV. 569) as *varium et mutabile semper* ('always fickle and changeable').

Discussion of seventeenth- and eighteenth-century 'classicism' has sometimes been linked to larger questions of cultural ethos. But here, again, generalization can be dangerous. Textbooks still frequently characterize the literary period from Dryden to Johnson as the English 'Augustan Age', the term (it is said) usefully suggesting the way in which 'the leading writers of the time . . . drew the parallel to the Roman Augustans, and deliberately imitated their literary forms and subjects, their emphasis on social concerns, and their ideals of moderation, decorum and urbanity' (Abrams, 1999, 214). But such descriptions are seriously misleading. The English 'Augustan' period is as notable for its renderings of Homer, Lucretius, Ovid, Lucan, Martial and Juvenal (none of them exactly notable for 'moderation, decorum and urbanity') as for its versions of Virgil and Horace. Moreover, the English 'Augustans'' sense of the 'parallels' between their own culture and that of the Roman Augustans are themselves far more complex and equivocal than the older descriptions imply (Weinbrot, 1978; Erskine-Hill, 1983). Dryden, for example, presents Virgil as a man 'still of republican principles in his heart', and his translation of the *Aeneid* is fully alive to the divided sympathies and melancholy subcurrents which later commentators have detected in Virgil's poem (Burrow, 1997, 28–30). Later eighteenth-century writers frequently either attacked Virgil for his endorsement of Augustus, or defended him as a crypto-republican (Harrison, 1967). And even Horace (whose urbane poise, advocacy of moderation, inner contentment, and retirement, and cultivation of a mean between emotional and philosophical extremes might seem to fit the traditional conception of an 'Augustan poet' more neatly than any other) was more variously received than the earlier accounts suggest. Admired by some as a wise moralist, Horace was suspected by others as a temporizing 'courtier', or even a debauchee. In his *Imitations of Horace* (1733–8), Pope shows his awareness of the full spectrum of contemporary reactions to the Roman poet, using Horace's originals as the basis for an intricate act of intertextual exploration, in which the reader is invited to engage in a complex process of sustained comparison between Horace's texts (printed *en face* in carefully edited versions) and Pope's own. Pope sometimes straightforwardly translates, sometimes freely adapts, and sometimes even subverts Horace's meanings for his own purposes, in an ever-metamorphosing continuum, in which the originals are treated not as 'fixed' or 'known' quantities, but as vehicles for a complex, and often unsettlingly ambiguous play of self-presentation, self-discovery and self-criticism (Stack, 1985).

The classical translations and imitations of the period are sometimes thought of as having been written exclusively by, and for, a narrow élite – gently born, masculine, learned, politically conservative. But their appeal transcended, to a far greater extent than is often acknowledged, the bounds of religion, party, gender, class and educational background. Translations and adaptations of the classics were read avidly both by those who had received a formal classical education and those to whom it had been denied. The most classically saturated 'original' poem of the period, Milton's *Paradise Lost*, was the work of a puritan and revolutionary republican. Nicholas Rowe's version of Lucan's *Pharsalia* (1719) (perhaps the finest large-scale English 'Augustan' verse translation after those of Dryden and Pope) is imbued with its author's passionate Whiggism and admiration for Roman republicanism. The classical translations of Dryden, a Catholic, Tory and (after 1688) a Jacobite, were avidly purchased and warmly praised by his religious and political opponents (there were, in fact, more Whig than Tory subscribers to the first edition of his *Works of Virgil* in 1697). Though the first editions of such works as Dryden's Juvenal and Virgil, Pope's Homer, and Rowe's Lucan were luxury products, affordable only by the wealthy, the poems soon circulated more widely in cheaper reprints. They were received with passionate enthusiasm by the growing body of female readers, and frequently praised by the women poets of the period. They were admired and owned by readers (like Mary Leapor and Robert Burns) well outside the bounds of 'polite society', and feature prominently in the surviving accounts and autobiographies of eighteenth- and early nineteenth-century artisans and working women. The tradition continued: Pope's *Iliad* and *Odyssey*, Francis's Horace, and Dryden's *Ovid's Art of Love* were in the library of John Clare, and, later in the nineteenth century, Dryden's Virgil was one of the first books owned by the eight-year-old Thomas Hardy.

The classically based poetry of the period is by no means of uniform quality or interest. Some of its 'imitations' are ephemeral 'updatings' which evidence no serious engagement with their originals. Classical allusions in the minor poetry of the period are often routine and inert. And many of the complete translations of classical authors produced from the mid-eighteenth century are humdrum productions in a sub-Popeian or sub-Miltonic vernacular, undertaken for pedantic or commercial reasons, in which the ancient poets emerge 'from the mill of decorum in more or less undifferentiated batches or smooth rhyme, or blank verse, and elegant diction' (Wilson, 1982, 80). But at their best, the classically influenced poems of the period present the results of a series of dynamic and creative dialogues with the distant past, designed to enrich the native poetic tradition with a wide variety of imaginative experiences and perspectives not readily available elsewhere. Such engagements assume (as any dealings with an 'alien' culture must, if that culture is to be presumed intelligible) some continuity of human interests, preoccupations, expectations and experiences between present and past. But such an assumption should not be understood as a crude or naive 'essentialism', or as a mere 'appropriation' or 'colonization' by English poets of the classical past. If the English 'Augustans' believed, in Dryden's celebrated formulation, that 'mankind is ever the same, and nothing lost out of nature', they believed, equally, that 'everything is altered'. Pope, who is often accused of 'accommodating' Homer's archaic diction, psychology, morality and theology to models with which his readers were more familiar, asserted passionately the need to register Homer's 'otherness', insisting that Homer's readers should constantly remind themselves 'that they are stepping almost three thousand years back into the remotest antiquity, and entertaining themselves with a clear and surprizing vision of things nowhere else to be found'. Dryden's translation of Virgil's *Aeneid* constantly touches on questions of kingship, usurpation, exile, piety and nationhood in vocabulary which has obvious bearing on the political preoccupations and commitments of a poet who believed that his own rightful king had been driven into exile by an illegal usurper. But that is not to say that Dryden has merely transformed the *Aeneid* into a Jacobite allegory. Readers are invited both to recognize and to resist parallels between Virgil's narrative and characters and the events and personalities of contemporary history. Dryden's own concerns overlap and mingle with Virgil's in an imagined realm neither entirely of the past or of the present, in which the dilemmas of contemporary politics are explored and appraised by being brought into complex conjunction, contrast and overlap with those of ancient Rome (Hammond, 1999, 218–82). In the hands of the 'Augustan' period's greatest practitioners, classical imitation and translation was a way of achieving self-transcendence, self-extension, self-scrutiny, and self-discovery (rather than merely self-confirmation) through imaginative communion and dialogue with distinguished poetic minds, of very different types and temperaments, from the twelve-and-a-half centuries of writing between Homer and Boethius.

My stress so far has been on the hazards of attempting to predict or categorize the uses made of the classics by seventeenth- and eighteenth-century English poets. The rest of the chapter will consist of a brief examination of some of the creative dialogues entered into by poets of the period with three very different classical poets: Homer, Ovid, and Juvenal.

Varieties of Homeric Heroism: Sarpedon, Clarissa, Helen and Satan

Homer's *Iliad* is set in an archaic warrior culture, apparently at the furthest imaginable remove in ethos and values from late seventeenth- and eighteenth-century 'polite' society. From the Renaissance, many critics had felt uneasy about the plain spoken vehemence of Homer's heroes, the quarrelsome immorality of his gods, and the homely bluntness of his descriptions of the natural world. Large stretches of the *Iliad* are taken up with brutally graphic depictions of hand-to-hand fighting. Periodically, however, the narrative is punctuated by episodes in which one or more characters pause to reflect on the significance of the fighting, and its relation to the larger pattern of their life. What, they ask, are the conditions under which human life must be lived? What are the forces (internal and external) which compel and constrain human action? How might the short life allotted to human beings be best deployed? What are the obligations on a warrior, a leader, a husband, a wife? A passage which was frequently felt to focus some of these issues with particular power was the speech (*Iliad* XII. 310–28) made by Sarpedon, the leader of the Lycian contingent fighting on the Trojan side, to his friend Glaucus. The Greeks have retreated behind their fortifications. Sarpedon turns to Glaucus, and exhorts him to join him in an attempt on the Greek fortifications, in a speech which has often been taken to define the privileges and obligations of the Homeric warlord with particular clarity. Why, Sarpedon asks, are they afforded honour (*timé*) above the others in Lycia, with the finest seats, food and wine at banquets, and a great domain (*temenos*) of rich farmland, if they do not take their stand in the forefront of the battle, thereby inspiring the admiration of their fellow Lycians? If they could live for ever, Sarpedon continues, he would neither himself enter the battle where men win *kudos* (the god-given charm that secures victory), nor would he exhort Glaucus to do likewise. But since the demons of death are standing all around them in their thousands, and no man can flee or avoid them, they should go forward, whether this results in their granting some other warrior his victory-wish (*eukhos*) or his granting them theirs.

Sarpedon's appeal rests on certain facts about their present existence: they enjoy rich privileges; they cannot live for ever; they should therefore risk all, in the hope of gaining the glory (*kleos*) which, in their culture, alone gives life true significance and value. There is some disagreement among modern classical scholars about the precise logic of Sarpedon's argument, and the structure of relationships and ethical priorities which it implies. Some maintain that the honour (*timé*) which is owing to the chieftains, and paid in the form of a tribute (*geras*) by their people is their inviolable right, part of the life-lot afforded them by fate (*moira*) or the gods (Benveniste, 1973, 341–2). It has been recently argued that Sarpedon's words should be seen as the expression of a system of 'generalized reciprocity', according to which 'the chieftain should undergo these risks willingly, as a "favour", and not as a determinate (quasi-contractual) quid pro quo for determinate privileges and status' (Gill, 1998, 310–11). On such an interpretation, the aristocrats' willingness to venture their life in battle is felt as an act of gratuitous beneficence, and not, as other scholars have argued, as a 'kind of social contract: valour in exchange for honour' (Hainsworth, 1993, 352).

A similar interpretative division is, interestingly, present in the English renderings of Sarpedon's speech. Sir John Denham's royalist rendering (written in the 1650s, published 1668) presents the heroes' decision to enter the battle almost as an act of aristocratic self-immolation. Denham's Sarpedon addresses his speech to Glaucus 'since he did not find / Others as great in place, as great in mind', and his final resolve is that they should 'tread' 'the noblest path', 'And bravely on, till they, or we, or all, / A common sacrifice to honour fall'. But in Thomas Hobbes's translation (1676), Sarpedon argues that they enjoy their privileges 'because [*sic*] [they] foremost are in fight'. And the Sarpedon depicted by the Whig poet Philip Motteux in 1707 offers an even more thoroughgoing contractual argument, impelling Glaucus to the fight 'for the Common Good', and so that their subjects shall judge them 'Men fit to lead, and worthy to be kngs', rather than 'idle monarchs' and 'luxurious drones', 'The state's disease, or lumber of their thrones; / Resigned to Sloth, and negligent of Fame, / Their neighbours' scorn, and their own country's shame' (Ferraro, 1993, 17–18).

Pope's version of the passage (first published in 1709, and revised for his complete *Iliad* in 1717) draws on all three earlier versions. Why, asks his Sarpedon, should they enjoy their privileges 'unless great acts superior merit prove, / And vindicate the bounteous powers above'? They should, he argues, 'grace' the 'dignity' which the gods have given them by being 'the first in valour, as the first in place'. If they could 'elude the gloomy grave' forever, Sarpedon would not urge Glaucus to the fight:

> But since, alas, ignoble age must come,
> Disease, and death's inexorable doom,
> The life which others pay, let us bestow,
> And give to fame what we to nature owe.
> Brave though we fall, and honoured if we live,
> Or let us glory gain, or glory give!

Pope's rendering of this speech has been criticized for imposing on Homer a self-consciously 'Virgilian' nobility and grandeur, a patterned rhetorical orderliness, and a philosophical abstraction and sententiousness, which are alien to his more concrete and plain-spoken original (Brower, 1959, 108–12; Mason, 1972, 144–9). In this respect, Pope's *Iliad* might seem less obviously 'Homeric' than, for example, Dryden's version of 'The First Book of Homer's *Ilias*' (1700), which renders the fiery impetuosity and plain-spoken directness of Homer's heroes (along with the earthy concreteness of his physical descriptions, and his irreverent handling of the Olympian gods) with more obvious directness and relish (Mason, 1972, 55–60; Sowerby, 1996). What is not so often stressed is the responsiveness and cogency of Pope's engagement with the underlying ethical structure and assumptions of Homer's speech. In his stress on their privileges as gifts of 'the bounteous powers above' which they owe to 'nature', Pope is not (*pace* Brower, 1959, 111) confusing divinely bestowed honour with human tributes, but is observing the Homeric distinction between *timé* and *geras*, as expounded by Benveniste. And in his portrayal of their decision to fight as an act of aristocratic magnanimity ('The life which others pay, let us bestow'), Pope is not (*pace* Brower, 111) merely overlaying Homer with an inappropriately eighteenth-century 'upper-class insolence' or 'Restoration swagger', but anticipating the modern scholarly description of Sarpedon's speech as an expression of 'generalized reciprocity' rather than contractual obligation. Sarpedon's speech, in Pope's rendering, moves beyond the elegiac royalism of Denham and the hard-headed contractualism of Motteux to render the inner workings of an intelligent mind making a conscious heroic decision, in full and sober recognition of the inexorable facts of existence: we all, alas, must die; the challenge which faces us is to decide how best to use such attributes as the gods have given us in the little space afforded, this side of the grave. Pope keeps faith with the underlying assumptions of an 'alien' value-system, while simultaneously conveying the general applicability of Sarpedon's sentiments.

Pope's sense of the larger implications of Sarpedon's reflections lies behind his allusive redeployment of the speech in a very different context. In his final (1717) revision of his 'heroi-comical' poem, *The Rape of the Lock*, Pope added a speech 'to open more clearly the moral of the poem, in a parody of the speech of Sarpedon to Glaucus in Homer'. Towards the end of the poem, Clarissa attempts to persuade Belinda that she should rise above the despair and hysteria to which she has succumbed since the loss of her prized lock to the Baron. The logic of Clarissa's speech closely parallels that of Sarpedon. Why, she asks, are the 'belles' of eighteenth-century high society 'angels called, and angel-like adored' by the 'white-gloved beaux' who pay them tribute, 'unless' their 'good sense' can preserve into later life what their youthful attractions have 'gained' for them? Since they cannot, unfortunately, spend the rest of their days in flirtation and party-going, they must make a valiant resolve:

> But since, alas, frail beauty must decay;
> Curled or uncurled, since locks will turn to grey,
> Since, painted or not painted, all shall fade,
> And she who scorns a man must die a maid;
> What then remains, but well our power to use,
> And keep good humour still, whate'er we lose?
> And trust me, dear, good humour can prevail,
> When airs, and flights, and screams, and scolding fail.
> Beauties in vain their pretty eyes may roll;
> Charms strike the sight, but merit wins the soul.

At first sight, this speech might seem to combine a lesson in providential morality (in which Belinda is counselled to lay aside her frivolous flirtatiousness in order to qualify as a worthy 'housewife') with a textbook exemplification of 'mock-heroic' satire: the debunking application of 'lofty' or 'serious' sentiments to self-evidently trivial subject-matter. But closer inspection reveals that Pope's 'parody' works more complicatedly, to suggest telling parallels, as much as ironic contrasts, between the situation of Belinda and Clarissa and that of Sarpedon and Glaucus. Clarissa offers her advice very much from within the society of 'belles' which she is rebuking: she refers with pride to the 'glories' (the product of 'all our pains') of the young men's adoration of the 'beauties' (among whom she counts herself). As a parallel to Sarpedon's heroic resolve to 'bestow' his life in pursuit of 'glory', Clarissa proposes the need to cultivate 'good humour'. By this key term, it would seem, Clarissa means not a facile jollity, but whatever quality it is (call it 'sanity' or 'balance' or 'poise') which alone will see one through the trials of life, allowing one to keep things in proportion and to avoid emotional hysteria or collapse. It is only such a state that will allow the young girl to retain the affections of a worthy man, even though it may have been her beauty that attracted him in the first place. Thus understood, the effect of the speech is

complex. On one level, Pope is exposing the triviality of the 'belles'' life by contrasting it with life-or-death sacrifices on the Homeric battlefield. But Pope's Homeric
allusion also enables him to show that life for an eighteenth-century 'belle' is as much
a matter of making agonizing (even tragic) decisions as it was for the Homeric warrior.
In the society being portrayed – not one whose values are necessarily endorsed by Pope
– the young girl's powers of attraction will soon fade, and may be even sooner blighted
by 'the smallpox'. She must decide how she can best survive a life governed by the
demands of the marriage market, in which one false move or accident might consign
her to a bad union, to solitary spinsterdom, or to a lifetime of frustration, disappointed
hopes, and the corrupting effects of boredom, backbiting, envy and neglect. The
young girl's plight, though apparently so much less spectacular, is, in its way, as acute
as that of the Homeric warrior, and, like his, centres on the question of how best to
make use of the few years allotted to us.

Pope's awareness of the tragic potential of Belinda's position is perhaps not surprising, in the light of the extremely sympathetic treatment of the female figures
throughout his translation of the *Iliad*. For Pope clearly conceived Homer's epic as
one which is as sensitive to the plight of its heroines as of its heroes. Book III of his
translation contains a notably sympathetic rendering of Homer's portrayal of Helen,
in which Helen emerges not as the culpable *femme fatale* of legend but as a woman of
'repentance and good nature', acutely conscious of the misery which her actions have
caused, but equally aware that she is 'constrained by a superior power', the goddess
Venus, who has given her her spellbinding beauty (rapturously acknowledged even
by the old men of Troy who have suffered so much from its effects), and whose promptings she must obey, if she is not to be rendered by the goddess 'more / The world's
aversion than their love before'.

If it is surprising to find Sarpedon's speech being rearticulated on the lips of an
eighteenth-century 'belle', it is perhaps no less of a shock to find the Greek hero's
words coming from the mouth of the devil. But in Milton's *Paradise Lost* (II. 445–56),
Satan's words, as he offers to make the hazardous journey to earth to corrupt God's
new creation, echo Sarpedon's. 'Wherefore', asks Satan, does he 'assume' his 'imperial
sovereignty' over his fellow angels, unless he is prepared to 'accept as great a share /
Of hazard as of honour', honour which is 'so much to him due / Of hazard more, as
he above the rest / High honoured sits'.

Again it is tempting to see the Homeric allusion as primarily satirical in intention. Satan's heroic offer 'parodies the Son's self-offering in the Atonement, is designed
to aggrandise himself and pre-empts potential rivals in supremacy' (Martindale, 1986,
38). Moreover, in associating Satan with Homeric heroism Milton might be thought
to be asserting the inadequacies of classical (as opposed to Christian) conceptions of
noble action. But an alternative interpretation is possible. Milton, it has been argued,
has conceived of Satan's relations with God within a framework strikingly similar to
the Homeric code of 'honour' (*timé*). God has 'honour' owing to him, by virtue of his
unquestionable status as the ultimate principle of the universe. Satan, feeling himself
'impaired' by the promotion of the Son, has, in a moment of tragic blindness, refused

to pay the 'honour' owing to God, thus breaching his 'fealty' to God and alienating himself permanently from a dispensation in which (as the good angel Abdiel points out) the rest of creation is 'exalted' rather than 'made less' by paying God his due (Mason, 1987, 239–40, 303–41). On such a reading, Milton's use of Sarpedon's speech in Book II need not be seen as merely satirical or debunking in intention. Satan emerges as a genuinely heroic figure, but one who has fatally mistaken his place in the scheme of things, and whose quest for ultimate 'honour' is a demand for a kind of obeisance which should only be paid to God. By imagining Satan's rebellion in Homeric terms, Milton reveals the formidable nature of the threat presented to the 'enormous bliss' which only God's dispensation can guarantee.

Ovidian Wit: Transgressive Exuberance?

If an engagement with Homer allowed poets of the period to explore fundamental questions of heroic choice and tragic necessity, their encounters with Ovid enabled them to deal with taboo subjects which might otherwise have seemed beyond the bounds of civilized discourse, and to write with a fanciful exuberance which might otherwise have been thought to transgress all canons of literary good taste. Ovid had been criticized in antiquity for his supposed trivializing of 'serious' subjects by fanciful playfulness and displays of tastelessly inappropriate wordplay and punning, and such charges were frequently revived during the seventeenth century. Ovid, wrote Dryden in 1680, 'often writ too pointedly for his subject, and made his persons speak more eloquently than the violence of their passion would admit; so that he is frequently witty out of season'. And in the Preface to *Fables* (1700) he elaborated the point: 'Would any man who is ready to die for love', he asked, 'describe his passion like [Ovid's] Narcissus?' 'On these occasions,' Dryden judged, 'the poet should endeavour to raise pity; but instead of this, Ovid is tickling you to laugh'.

But in the act of poetic composition, poets warmed to Ovid's exuberant 'wit out of season' far more than their critical pronouncements would suggest. In his *Spectator* papers on *Paradise Lost*, Joseph Addison noted with approval Milton's pruning of Ovid's 'idle and superfluous wordplay', and pointed out how, when drawing on Ovid's depiction of the flood in Book 1 of the *Metamorphoses*, Milton had omitted the touches with which Ovid had, notoriously, trivialized his description: the wolf swimming among the sheep, the lion carried along by the waves, sea-calves lying where goats formerly browsed. Ovid describes the consequences of the flood with one of his characteristic rhetorical 'turns': *iamque mare et tellus nullum discrimen habebant; / omnia pontus erat, deerant quoque litora ponto* ('now land and sea could not be distinguished; all was sea, and that sea lacked a shore'). Milton compresses Ovid's couplet into six words: 'sea covered sea, / Sea without shore' (*Paradise Lost*, XI. 749–50). However, he preserves Ovid's verbal repetition, reinforcing it with his own pattern of alliteration. And throughout his description of the flood (as elsewhere in *Paradise Lost*) he borrows many salient details from Ovid, to invest his imagined landscapes with touches of the exuberant animism so characteristic of the Latin poet. Thus, Milton's south wind, which 'with black wings/ Wide hovering all the clouds together drove / From under heaven' (*Paradise Lost*, XI. 738–9) is indebted to Ovid's more extended personification of the south wind in the *Metamorphoses* (I. 264–9), and in his depiction of the ordering of Chaos and the six days of Creation (*Paradise Lost*, II. 891–916, III. 708–21, VII. 224–550) Milton's borrowings from Ovid make a vital contribution to his depiction of a universe imbued by God with a mysterious and delightful life of its own (Harding, 1946, 71–8).

The influence of Ovidian habits of mind, in which normal categories and boundaries of existence are constantly blurred or fused by the exercise of puns and fanciful wit, are equally apparent in the very different context of Pope's *The Rape of the Lock* (where the Cave of Spleen contains – in a direct quotation of the opening of the *Metamorphoses* – 'Unnumbered throngs on every side . . . / Of bodies changed to various forms') and in the realm of the Goddess Dulness in *The Dunciad* (where, by the exercise of a characteristically Ovidian pun, 'Maggots half-formed in rhyme exactly meet, / And learn to crawl upon poetic feet' (I. 61–2)).

Ovid's work finds its most extensive reincarnation in the period in the translations of Dryden, who considered the Latin poet to be particularly 'according to [his] genius'. If Dryden's prose criticism repeats the age-old criticisms of Ovid, his translations respond to the Roman poet's 'turns', wordplay and fanciful extravagances with exuberant relish. If Milton had toned down Ovid's personification of the south wind in his depiction of the flood, Dryden entered fully into the spirit of Ovid's passage, enhancing Ovid's fanciful animism with added touches of his own: rain is said, for example, to flow from the south wind's 'robe' and 'heavy mantle', and the wind is imagined as 'squeezing' the clouds 'with his clenched fist', an action which they (being full of water like soaked sponges) 'resist' ('The First Book of Ovid's *Metamorphoses*', ll. 357–66).

In his renderings from Ovid, Dryden discovered the positive artistic effect of the wordplay and turns which Ovid deployed in situations that might have seemed to have demanded more straightforward pathos. In the speech from *Metamorphoses* X, for example, in which Myrrha confesses her incestuous passion for her father, Cinyras, King of Cyprus, Dryden adds 'turns' of his own to enhance the reader's sense of the paradoxical nature of the young girl's plight. Why should her love, Myrrha asks, be thought illicit, when incestuous unions are common in the animal world: 'The hen is free to wed the chick she bore, / And make a husband, whom she hatched before'. The perverseness of her passion for her father, Myrrha observes, is such 'That he's not mine, because he's mine too much'. 'He might be nearer', she muses, 'were he not so nigh'. If she could flee from Cyprus, she says, 'so might I to myself myself restore'. And yet she wants to talk to her father, to kiss him, 'and more, if more I might'. But these touches of studied wordplay do not merely invite mockery of Myrrha, or a complacent sneer at her predicament. The 'turns' and antitheses, rather, create a complex 'distancing' effect whereby readers are allowed to entertain a wider range of emotions than would be possible if they were being drawn more wholeheartedly into Myrrha's predicament, and are alerted to the absurdity and self-delusion of her position, as well as to her agony and frustration.

Dryden responds with equal enthusiasm to Ovid's 'distancing' wit in the very different story of Ceyx and Alcyone, from *Metamorphoses* XI. This episode narrates the fortunes of a married couple divided by the husband's death in a storm at sea, and then re-united in a magical transformation in which both are metamorphosed into sea birds. Ovid's playful animism reaches its height at the moment when the waves mount their final assault on Ceyx's vessel. The decisive 'tenth wave' is likened to a soldier leading an assault on the city. Dryden extends Ovid's conceit (in which the waves had been invested not merely with a human will, but with human competitiveness, envy, vainglory, muscle-power, and tactical skill) with touches of his own, making the waves, explicitly, 'invading billows', evoking their *élan* in the vivid onrush of his verse (the tenth wave 'sweeps all before him with impetuous sway'), and imagining the waves eagerly overcresting each other, 'mounting' on others' 'backs' to enter the city/ship.

Ceyx's drowning is rendered in a way that conveys the near-comic potential of the bobbing motion of his body in the water:

> As oft as he can catch a gulp of air,
> And peep above the seas, he names the fair;
> And ev'n when plunged beneath, on her he raves,
> Murm'ring Alcyone below the waves:

And when Alcyone hears of her husband's death, she is given the most striking piece of Ovidian word-play in the episode, a 'turn' which focuses her sense of loss, while simultaneously distancing the reader from her plight:

> Now I die absent, in the vast profound;
> And me without my self the seas have drowned.

And yet (as with Myrrha) the effect is not merely callous or unfeeling. Throughout the episode numerous details have delicately impressed upon us the couple's *rapport*, as well as allowing us to enjoy the behaviour of the malign or callous powers that have contrived their downfall. Ovid's distinctive combination of playfully distancing wit, exuberant animism, and telling psychological precision allows the reader an unusually inclusive view of the couple's predicament, in which 'sympathy' and 'distance', humour and seriousness, are strangely fused, and which affords equal play to those intuitions which would suggest that the natural world is arbitrarily malign, and those which would imply some mysteriously beneficent ordering in events. The weirdly beautiful moment of Alcyone's transformation into a sea bird epitomizes the blend of involvement and distance, pathos and near-humour, close observation and extravagant fancy, which have characterized the episode throughout:

Headlong from hence to plunge her self she springs,
But shoots along supported on her wings;
A bird new-made about the banks she plies,
Not far from shore, and short excursions tries;
Nor seeks in air her humble flight to raise,
Content to skim the surface of the seas.
Her bill, though slender, sends a creaking noise,
And imitates a lamentable voice.
Now lighting where the bloodless body lies,
She with a funeral note renews her cries;
At all her stretch her little wings she spread,
And with her feathered arms embraced the dead:
Then flickering to his pallid lips, she strove
To print a kiss, the last essay of love.

Juvenal: Hyperbolic Rhetorician or Moral Sage?

The sixteen *Satires* of Juvenal, written in the second and third decades of the second century AD, pillory a variety of vices, strategically located in the recent Roman past. Their targets include the hypocrisy of self-appointed moralists, the miseries of life at Rome, the lusts of women, aristocratic pride, legacy-hunting, the depravities of perverted sexuality, and (in the most famous satire, the tenth) the delusory nature of human wishes. Juvenal writes in an extraordinary blend of vehement declamation, grotesque hyperbole, epic grandeur, epigrammatic wit, withering sarcasm, and out-rageous scurrility, and claims to be denouncing the depravities of modern Rome in the name of older Roman values. English poets inherited two contrasting views of Juvenal from the scholarly tradition. Some commentators had argued that Juvenal's hyperbole and declamatory vehemence were perfect vehicles for his moral 'message' – a view reinforced by their belief in an etymological connection between 'satire' (the genre) and 'satyr' (the mythical figure), with the accompanying conviction that satirists should 'scourge' their victims with the verbal equivalent of a satyr's bacchic staff. Others saw Juvenal as a witty declaimer whose art was more immediately concerned with lurid caricature and fanciful scene-painting than with sincerely felt exhortations to moral reform.

Translators and adapters of Juvenal wanting to be faithful to their original were therefore faced with the problem of what connections they should seek to convey between Juvenal's style and his reformist intentions. Moreover, Juvenal's dense refer-ence to Roman customs, events and personalities faced them with a further challenge: should Juvenal's Roman allusions be left *in situ*, or should an attempt be made to find modern 'equivalents'? In the latter event, should the process of 'imitation' reflect Juvenal's own stance towards his material (whatever that might be thought to be), or 'correct' it, with reference to Christian morality?

No satisfactory solutions to these dilemmas were found in the first two complete English translations of Juvenal, by Sir Robert Stapylton (1647; revised 1660) and Barten Holyday (published 1673, but perhaps written *c.*1640). Stapylton clearly regarded Juvenal primarily as a purveyor of portable moral wisdom (he included an inventory of Juvenalian *sententiae* in his 1660 edition), and his version conveys little sense of Juvenal's onrushing rhetorical dynamism. Holyday translates line for line, almost word for word, producing a contorted syntax that is consistently clumsy, and at times almost unintelligible: his version was mostly admired for its encyclopedic commentary, in which Juvenal's Roman allusions are explained with prodigious learning.

Juvenal fared better in the hands of the Restoration poets John Oldham and Henry Higden. Oldham's versions of *Satires* III and XIII (1683) provide dramatically vivid realizations of Juvenal's satiric *vignettes*, applying them resourcefully to contemporary life, in verse which combines pointed wit with a flexibility and rhythmic verve considerably superior to the flat solemnity of Stapylton and the clotted pedantry of Holyday. Higden's 'modern essays' on *Satires* X and XIII (1686–7) preserve, for the most part, Juvenal's Roman settings, but also incorporate extensive passages of 'imitation', in which the Roman poet's scenes and characters are temporarily transposed to seventeenth-century London. Higden's choice of octosyllabic couplets to make Juvenal English 'in a Modish and Familiar way' sometimes bring the original close to burlesque, but his affably irreverent touch with Juvenal's wit seems to have been a crucial factor in enabling his most illustrious successor, Dryden, to intuit a coherent connection between Juvenal's hyperbolic declamation and what Dryden believed to be the true 'end and scope' of satire: to 'purge the passions' and 'laugh our spleen away', by inflaming our 'concernment' to an exhilarating climax, and finally leaving the mind in a state of satisfied calm.

In his version of Juvenal's tenth satire, Dryden responds with vivid relish to the 'impetuosity' of Juvenal's depiction of the vain wishes (for political power, eloquence, military glory, long life, and good looks) which beset human life. The flavour of his version is well conveyed in the scene in which Juvenal imagines the Roman mob's reaction to the fall of Sejanus, the erstwhile favourite of the emperor Tiberius, who has now denounced him, and ordered his statue to be destroyed. The statue is melted down, and the metal put to ignominious purposes:

> Formed in the forge, the pliant brass is laid
> On anvils; and of head and limbs are made
> Pans, cans, and piss-pots, a whole kitchen trade.

Sejanus' fallen effigy is now made 'the sport and laughter of the the giddy throng':

> 'Good Lord,' they cry, 'what Ethiop lips he has;
> How foul a snout, and what a hanging face!
> By heaven, I never could endure his sight!
> But say, how came his monstrous crimes to light?

What is the charge, and who the evidence?
The saviour of the nation and the prince?'
'Nothing of this; but our old Caesar sent
A noisy letter to his parliament.'
'Nay, sirs, if Caesar writ, I ask no more;
He's guilty, and the question's out of door.'

Without indulging in wholesale 'imitation', Dryden imbues the scene with colourings derived from his observation of the mob violence of Restoration London. The vindictive recklessness of mobs and the thrill of being on the winning side, his treatment suggests, are recurrent and incorrigible features of mob behaviour – and of human beings more generally:

All wish the dire prerogative to kill,
Ev'n they would have the power who want the will.

Juvenal's dismissive scorn is rendered, however, not as mere nihilism, but as an integral part of a proper 'philosophical' response to human folly. A few lines earlier, we have been told of the sage Democritus, who, when contemplating the infinite folly of humanity 'could feed his spleen, and shake / His sides and shoulders, till he felt 'em ache'. Democritus's laughter, however, is to be seen not as mere cynicism or *Schadenfreude*, but as a kind of wisdom which is proof against the vicissitudes of existence, and which, it is suggested, consitutes a possible model of behaviour for us all:

He laughs at all the vulgar cares and fears;
At their vain triumphs, and their vainer tears:
An equal temper in his mind he found,
When Fortune flattered him, and when she frowned.

Such a view is close to Dryden's own imagined ideal of the happy man 'who centring on himself, remains immovable, and smiles at the madness of the dance about him' and who 'will not be higher, because he needs it not; but by the prudence of that choice . . . puts it out of Fortune's power to throw him down' (Epistle Dedicatory to *Don Sebastian* (1690)). It also accords with his rendering of the advice offered by Juvenal at the end of his satire:

Forgive the gods the rest, and stand confined
To health of body, and content of mind;
A soul that can securely death defy,
And count it nature's privilege to die; . . .
    The path to peace is virtue: what I show,
Thyself may freely on thyself bestow:
Fortune was never worshipped by the wise,
But, set aloft by fools, usurps the skies.

A later version of Juvenal's tenth satire saw this ending in strikingly different terms:

> Yet when the sense of sacred presence fires,
> And strong devotion to the skies aspires,
> Pour forth thy fervours for a healthful mind,
> Obedient passions, and a will resigned;
> For love, which scarce collective man can fill;
> For patience, sov'reign o'er transmuted ill;
> For faith that, panting for a happier seat,
> Counts death kind nature's signal of retreat;
> These goods for man the laws of heaven ordain,
> These goods he grants, who grants the power to gain;
> With these celestial wisdom calms the mind,
> And makes the happiness she does not find.

Samuel Johnson's 'imitation' of Juvenal's tenth satire, *The Vanity of Human Wishes* (1749), emphatically reinstates the 'dignity', 'stateliness' and 'declamatory grandeur' which he felt were lacking in Dryden's version. Johnson recasts Juvenal's poem in sternly Christian terms, replacing the insouciant laughter of the Juvenalian/Drydenian Democritus with the sober vision of a sage determined 'Attentive truth and nature to descry, / And pierce each scene with philosophic eye'. In Johnson's rendering of Juvenal's ending, Dryden's tone of heady, self-possessed defiance is replaced by a trembling plea for divine grace and mercy, and muted hopes for 'a happier seat' after death. Earlier in the poem, the breakneck scorn and visual circumstantiality of Juvenal's derisive portraits of human folly have been refashioned as a weighty moral diagnosis of the self-destructive dynamics of human ambition. Johnson replaces Juvenal's Sejanus with Cardinal Wolsey, the favourite of King Henry VIII. Wolsey is evoked poetically as a towering edifice of restless aspiration:

> In full-blown dignity see Wolsey stand,
> Law in his voice, and fortune in his hand;
> To him the church, the realm, their powers consign;
> Through him the rays of regal bounty shine,
> Turned by his nod the stream of honour flows,
> His smile alone security bestows;
> Still to new heights his restless wishes tower,
> Claim leads to claim, and power advances power.

But at his sovereign's sudden change of heart, Wolsey's collapse is equally inexorable:

> At once is lost the pride of awful state,
> The golden canopy, the glitt'ring plate,
> The regal palace, the luxurious board,
> The liveried army, and the menial lord.
> With age, with cares, with maladies oppressed,

He seeks the refuge of monastic rest.
Grief aids disease, remembered folly stings,
And his last sighs reproach the faith of kings.

Commentators on Johnson's poem are divided as to whether such portraits are to be seen as compassionate ('there, but for the grace of God, go I'), or as remorsely stern – even cruel. They also differ on their interpretation of Johnson's conclusion. Is his tone there to be seen as affirmative or despairing? Did he think of himself as extending and developing thoughts which were 'there' in embryo in Juvenal's original? Or was he attempting to 'correct' Juvenal's conclusion in his own, explicitly Christian, ending? However these matters are resolved, it is clear that Juvenal's tenth satire has inspired, in Dryden and Johnson, two very different responses, in each of which the personality and artistic resources of a modern writer are engaged in a complex and fruitful dialogue with those of an ancient author – the result, in each case, being a work which is, simultaneously, a fine English poem in its own right, and a compelling 'reading' of its Latin original.

NOTE

This chapter was completed during research leave
    supported by the Humanities Research Board
    of the British Academy.

REFERENCES AND FURTHER READING

Abrams, M. H. (1999). *A Glossary of Literary Terms*. 7th edn. Fort Worth: Harcourt Brace.

Benveniste, Émile (1973). *Indo-European Language and Society* Trans. Elizabeth Palmer. London: Faber.

Brower, Reuben (1959). *Alexander Pope: The Poetry of Allusion*. Oxford: Clarendon Press.

Burrow, Colin (1997). 'Virgil in English translation'. In *The Cambridge Companion to Virgil*. Ed. Charles Martindale. Cambridge: Cambridge University Press, 21–37.

Erskine-Hill, Howard (1983). *The Augustan Idea in English Literature*. London: Arnold.

Ferraro, Julian (1993). 'Political discourse in Alexander Pope's *Episode of Sarpedon*'. *Modern Language Review* 88, 15–25.

Gill, Christopher (1998). 'Altruism or reciprocity in Greek ethical philosophy?'. In *Reciprocity in Ancient Greece*. Ed. Christopher Gill, Norman Postlethwaite and Richard Seaford. Oxford: Oxford University Press, 303–28.

Hainsworth, Bryan (1993). *The Iliad: A Commentary, Vol. 3: Books 9–12*. Cambridge: Cambridge University Press.

Hammond, Paul (1999). *John Dryden and the Traces of Classical Rome*. Oxford: Oxford University Press.

Harding, Davis P. (1946). *Milton and the Renaissance Ovid*. Urbana: University of Illinois Press.

Harrison, T. W. (1967). 'English Virgil: the *Aeneid* in the eighteenth century'. *Philologica Pragensia* 10, 1–11, 80–91.

Hopkins, David (1985). 'Nature's laws and man's: the story of Cinyras and Myrrha in Ovid and Dryden'. *Modern Language Review* 80, 786–801.

——(1988). 'Dryden and Ovid's "wit out of season"'. In *Ovid Renewed: Ovidian Influences on Literature and Art from the Middle Ages to the*

Twentieth Century. Ed. Charles Martindale. Cambridge: Cambridge University Press, 167–90, 276–9.

——(1995). 'Dryden and the tenth satire of Juvenal'. *Translation and Literature* 4, 31–60.

Martindale, Charles (1986). *John Milton and the Transformation of Ancient Epic*. London and Sydney: Croom Helm.

Martindale, Charles and Hopkins, David, eds (1993). *Horace Made New: Horatian Influences on British Writing from the Renaissance to the Twentieth Century*. Cambridge: Cambridge University Press.

Mason, H. A. (1972). *To Homer through Pope: An Introduction to Homer's 'Iliad' and Pope's Translation*. London: Chatto.

Mason, J. R. (1987). 'To Milton through Dryden and Pope: or god, man, and nature: *Paradise Lost* regained?'. University of Cambridge: unpublished Ph.D. dissertation.

Rosslyn, Felicity (1996–7). 'Heroic couplet translation: a unique solution?'. In *Essays and Studies,*

1997: Translating Literature. Ed. Susan Bassnett. Cambridge: D. S. Brewer, 41–63.

Sowerby, Robin (1996). 'The freedom of Dryden's Homer'. *Translation and Literature* 5, 26–50.

Stack, Frank (1985). *Pope and Horace: Studies in Imitation*. Cambridge: Cambridge University Press.

Tomlinson, Charles (1989). 'The presence of translation: a view of English poetry'. In *The Art of Translation: Voices from the Field*. Ed. Rosanna Warren. Boston: Northeastern University Press.

Weinbrot, Howard D. (1969). *The Formal Strain: Studies in Augustan Imitation and Satire*. Chicago: University of Chicago Press.

——(1978). *Augustus Caesar in 'Augustan' England: The Decline of a Classical Norm*. Princeton: Princeton University Press.

Wilson, Penelope (1982). 'Classical poetry and the eighteenth-century reader'. In *Books and their Readers in Eighteenth-Century England*. Ed. I. Rivers. Leicester: Leicester University Press, 69–96.

6

Forgery and Plagiarism

Nick Groom

Pens can forge, my Friend, that cannot write.

(Alexander Pope, *Epilogue to the Satires: Dialogue II*, 188)

Imitation arises as a scandal,
forgery as a style of genius,
and scholarship as a cure.

(Susan Stewart, *Crimes of Writing*)

The century and a half from 1640 to 1790 witnessed not only the rise of literary property and the establishment of copyright, but a concurrent increase in literary – as well as legal – cases of forgery and plagiarism. The period was obsessed by authenticity and literary theft and produced some of the most renowned literary forgeries: James Macpherson's Ossian and the 'marvellous boy' Thomas Chatterton's Rowley, the fake Formosan George Psalmanazar, William Lauder's interpolated plagiarisms of Milton, and William Henry Ireland's Shakespeare forgeries. Indeed, the entire literary milieu was saturated with these issues through cases of copyright infringement (such as *Pope v. Curll*), pirate printing, and literary property debates (such as the Tonsons' hold over Shakespeare editions). In the field of scholarship too, charges of forgery and plagiarism dogged the development of editorial protocols and historical criticism in literature as diverse as the Bible and old ballads.

Forgery and plagiarism are legal – or at least quasi-legal – terms which carry a powerful literary charge, and this chapter will consider them first as criminal activities, and then as literary and cultural practices. Despite the speed with which copyright and anti-forgery laws multiplied in the period from Milton to Blake, such legislation remained wholly financial: no writer was ever in the dock for forgery or plagiarism, though many booksellers were charged and convicted of copyright infringement and piracy, and many felons were hanged for forging economic bonds. Nevertheless, many writers were compromised by being publicly accused of forgery or plagiarism, and the whole definition of a good author became intimately connected with authenticity. This is apparent in the gradual collapse of theories of imitative composition and the brief but influential displacements of cultural authority by inauthentic writings that ultimately enabled the literary definition of authenticity to evolve.

The Law against Forgery

Forgery (economic, rather than literary forgery) was made a capital offence in 1634, and by the end of the eighteenth century was policed by over 400 separate statutes. These covered specific instances of forgery, such as the forging or altering of bank bills, notes, securities, South Sea bonds, East-India bonds, lottery tickets, legal documents, and wills. Acts of impersonation which resulted in payments to which a person was not entitled, such as military pensions or inheritances, were also classed as forgery and punishable by death. Transportation for fourteen and seven years respectively was reserved for forging stamps and hallmarks, and for using the same stamps more than once. It should be borne in mind that forgery was an offence without benefit of clergy: it is almost by definition a crime of the literate – but it is also worth noting that literary forgery had *not* entered the statute books, although the principle of impersonation and false representation for fraudulently acquiring profit runs very deep in William Blackstone's account in his *Commentaries on the Laws of England* (1765–9). Blackstone defines the forging, counterfeiting, or falsifying of a document as 'the fraudulent making or alteration of a writing to the prejudice of another man's right'. *The Bloody Register* (1764), a compendium of popular trials, includes cases such as Abigail Newstead for coining (sentenced to death but afterwards transported), Frederick Schmidt for forging a banknote for £100 (hanged), William Smith for forging a bill of exchange for £45 (hanged), William Baker for forging a warrant for the delivery of three chests of tea (hanged), and John Rice for forging South Sea shares (hanged).

Why were forgers treated in such an extreme fashion? Forgery was not simply a crime to be punished: it posed a threat to the stability of the entire nation. Historians such as Douglas Hay and Clive Emsley have commented on the severity of forgery statutes, arguing that the expanding capitalist economy at the beginning of the century created a rise in the use of promissory notes, and consequently a sudden increase in statutes against fraud. While there was no immediate evidence that forgery was to become a serious problem, it became an increasingly common offence as the law was deployed to protect commercial interests. Apparently coiners tended to receive much lighter sentences than forgers (life imprisonment or transportation); it was specifically the forgery of economic and legal texts that was so objectionable. Even so, bearing in mind that the law at this stage required specific statutes for every possible offence and was not able to proscribe certain principles of fraud, some offences were not punished. Martin Kayman has argued that Fielding's *Tom Jones* (1749) hinges on Black George's appropriation of the five £100 notes given to Tom by Squire All-worthy, which ultimately being rediscovered help to save Tom from the gallows. And yet Black George escapes prosecution, for there is no crime for which he can be prosecuted. Although Allworthy is able to recognize his own banknotes (the currency is oddly personalized yet remains negotiable), the bills demand their own economic autonomy.

But the dimly recognized principles of fraud are evident in the severity of forgery sentences, and Blackstone indicates that forgery was a crime against the principle of a paper credit economy: in other words it was an ideological crime. And forgery posed, moreover, the biggest single threat to the aristocratic and landowning classes. If rural sabotage such as arson, cattle-maiming, the destruction of trees, and so on had increased to such an extent that it demanded the introduction of the Black Act in 1723, such attacks on authority were actually very localized in effect and served a more symbolic function that hinted at imminent peasant insurgency. Forgery, however, could execute its direst threats against the wealthy and influential and utterly dispossess them: it could deprive the aristocrat of inheritance and the landowner of land. It was theft on a scale that could replot the power structures of the country.

The policing of forgery and the succession of offenders hanged at Tyburn created a new culture of the gallows and indeed a typology of the forger. This was a new class of villain going to the 'fatal tree': educated, respectable, polite, and often dandified. For example, James Boswell described the hanging of the forger Gibson in 1768:

> Mr Gibson was indeed an extraordinary man. He came from Newgate in a coach . . . He was drawn backwards, and looked as calm and easy as ever I saw a man in my life. He was dressed in a full suit of black, wore his own hair round and in a natural curl, and a hat. When he came to the place of execution he was allowed to remain a little in the coach. A signal was then given him that it was time to approach the fatal tree. He took leave of his friends, stepped out of the coach, and walked firmly to the cart . . . When he was upon the cart, he gave his hat to the executioner, who immediately took off Mr Gibson's cravat, unloosed his shirt neck, and fixed the rope. Mr Gibson never once altered his countenance.

Finally, with a stunning demonstration of sang-froid, 'He refreshed his mouth by sucking a sweet orange.'

It is worth emphasizing that the legal record in collections such as *The Bloody Register*, as suggested by Boswell's report, constantly insists on testimony, forensic matter, and confession; in other words, it relies upon the very models of authenticity that forgery mimics and makes inauthentic. As Margreta De Grazia has argued, the concept of the authentic cannot exist without that of the inauthentic, and these paired terms function dialectically. In such a case, the forger is therefore executed in order to assert the authority of the law, as a consequence of Enlightenment definitions of truth. And yet that truth is itself precariously upheld by the very existence of the inauthentic.

In addition to the orange-sucking Mr Gibson, notable forgery cases included Dr Dodd, the Perreau brothers, and James Lyons. Samuel Johnson was only one of many who defended the 'Macaroni Parson' Dr William Dodd against an accusation of forging a promissory note: he wrote speeches and sermons for Dodd, he wrote letters to the Lord Chancellor and other worthies, a petition from Dr Dodd to the King (and one from Mrs Dodd to the Queen), he wrote observations for the newspapers – but all in vain. Amazingly, all the arguments and eloquence of Johnson at the height of his powers could not save Dodd, and the Unfortunate Doctor was executed on 27 June 1777.

The Dodd case, which as Paul Baines has pointed out ran concurrently with the Rowley Controversy (the debate about Thomas Chatterton's forgeries) was considered a national disgrace and helped to swing public opinion against the death penalty for forgery. Moreover, this middle-class identification with the plight of the forger actually obscures a more subtle shift in opinion. Forgers took over from highwaymen as the definitive criminals of the latter part of the eighteenth century: educated and artistic economic individualists. As Lincoln Faller puts it: 'If it had once seemed that anyone might take to the highway, so much more it seemed that anyone, in a pinch, might alter a note or bond.' It was the crime of gentlemen: William Wynne Ryland, engraver to George III and a forger of bills of exchange, was hanged in 1783, and it was only because the law was finally reformed in 1832 that the art critic of the *London Magazine*, Thomas Griffiths Wainewright, was transported to Tasmania rather than hanged in 1837 for forging a Bank of England bill.

The Law against Copying

The first English Copyright Act was passed in 1710 – precisely in the middle of the century and a half covered by this book – but debate about copyright and literary property filled the entire period, from issues concerning the licensing of the press on which John Milton famously wrote *Areopagitica* in 1644, to the ultimate House of Lords ruling in 1774 on the 1710 Queen Anne Copyright Act. Of course, in a sense the very literature of the period was only made possible by copyright laws and the ensuing advent of the professional author, and it is inevitably a subject about which writers became particularly agitated.

In 1667 John Milton, arguably the first professional author, received £20 from Samuel Simmons for *Paradise Lost*: £5 on delivery, £5 when the first edition sold out, and two further payments of £5 for second and third editions. In 1694, John Dryden received £200 in four £50 instalments from Jacob Tonson for his translation of Virgil. Tonson had acquired half rights to *Paradise Lost* in 1683 and in 1695 published *The Poetical Works of Mr John Milton*, in which he had sole rights; in 1697, he published Dryden's *The Works of Virgil*. The Tonsons also had possession of the works of Shakespeare for most of the eighteenth century. In 1715, Alexander Pope made some £3,000 on his translation of Homer's *Iliad*, an extremely ingenious and lucrative deal in which

Pope sold his copyright to Bernard Lintot for 1,200 guineas and made another £1,800 or so from selling subscriptions (an advance payment for each volume in return for which the subscriber's name would be printed in the book). In 1746, Samuel Johnson received £1,575 from five respectable publishers for the *Dictionary of the English Language* (out of which he was to employ his amanuenses; he supplemented his income by writing the *Rambler* and the *Adventurer* in the evenings); thirty years later, and by now in receipt of a pension, he asked for only 200 guineas from a cartel of thirty-six booksellers for the *Lives of the Poets*, although in the event he received twice that amount. If, as Johnson once famously declared, 'No man but a blockhead ever wrote, except for money', he was not positively avaricious.

This trajectory reveals that author–printer relationships shifted in response to the law and the market. Milton's contract, the first such extant, shows that the poet had property in his poem and was able to sell it, and also had some immediate control over reprintings. It is also a complex enough document to suggest that these sort of deals were an established part of the book trade, although he never struck another deal with this particular printer. With Dryden we see the rise of the professional, canon-forming printer investing in long-term profits (Tonson's virtual monopoly over Shakespeare lasted into the 1760s). Pope, however, taking advantage of the recent copyright legislation, was able almost to defraud his printer and position the author as the central market force selling subscriptions, and the rise of the professional writer is confirmed by Johnson's career, in which his major works were sponsored by cartels. This repositioning of the author through five generations was also, we shall see, caused by changing notions of originality and plagiarism.

Since the middle ages, the monopoly of book production (at that stage being the transcription of manuscripts) had been regulated by the Crown and the Stationers' Company, affording some literary protection to authors. But regulation really meant control of the press, and the Stationers' Company was founded in 1556 precisely as a mechanism of censorship to oversee the registering and hence licensing of books: when in 1637 the number of licensed printers was reduced to twenty master printers and books were relicensed, Luther's *Table Talk*, Foxe's *Book of Martyrs*, and the Geneva Bible were all effectively banned by being refused new licences. John Feather has suggested that the whole concept of copyright was an accidental byproduct of such censorship: the crown's need to control the press and consequent establishment of the Stationers' Company and press licensing was seized upon by booksellers for commercial advantage, who could take sole responsibility for printing certain works – and hence reap sole profits. In other words, licensing therefore 'confirmed the idea that a copy was unique and that the right to print it was also unique'. In 1643 it became law that no book could be printed unless it was entered in the Register of the Stationers' Company.

Only members of the Stationers' Company were legally entitled to print, and by the regulations of the company they were required to register themselves as owners of 'copy' (both the manuscript or 'printer's copy' and the right to copy). The company also enjoyed the protection of the crown. Throughout the seventeenth century,

printing was assumed to be a royal prerogative and royal grants were made to printers for the right to print new books. Even after the 1709 Copyright Act it was possible to apply for letters patent for the sole privilege of printing books – usually for
a period of fourteen years (William Warburton, for example, successfully applied for
letters patent for his edition of Pope in 1759). Nevertheless, the Stationers' Company,
like any medieval guild, remained an instrument of regulation which throughout the
seventeenth century became increasingly opposed to possessive individualism.
Although there was the unwritten law that an author's consent was required to publish
a text, printers were almost solely responsible for their books – and were those
who suffered for illegal publishing (ears were cropped) or treason (hanged, drawn, and
quartered).

In 1644, John Milton challenged the printer's monopoly over writers, readers, and
books in *Areopagitica*, published in response to the parliamentary reinstatement of
licensing. In this seminal text, Milton advances the author as rightly responsible for
books, and the reader and reading community as beneficiaries, arguing that the Bill

> will be primely to the discouragement of all learning, and the stop of Truth, not only
> by the disexercising and blunting our abilities in what we know already, but by hin-
> dering and cropping the discovery that might be yet further made both in religious and
> civil Wisdom.

For Milton, all writing carries with it the divinity of the Biblical Word, and the writer,
particularly the good writer and the poet, therefore partakes in this divinity. He
famously warns,

> as good almost kill a Man as kill a good Book; who kills a Man kills a reasonable crea-
> ture, God's Image; but he who destroys a good Book, kills reason it self, kills the Image
> of God, as it were in the eye . . . a good Book is the precious life-blood of a master spirit,
> embalmed and treasured up on purpose to a life beyond life.

Condemned books were, of course, burned by the hangman.

Milton failed to revoke the Licensing Act, however, and such laws, regularly
renewed through the interregnum and Restoration, continued to protect printers and
offered little to authors for the next half-century. The change did not come until 1695,
when both political and philosophical opposition, brewing for some years, prevented
the Act from being renewed. Indeed, John Locke himself fought to end licensing.
Chapter 5, 'Of Property', from 'An Essay Concerning the True Original Extent and
End of Civil Government' in *Two Treatises of Government* (1690; note the exaggerated
anxiety over authenticity in the adjectives 'True Original') is clearly an argument for
authorial rights over their own literary properties:

> every Man has a *Property* in his own *Person*. This no Body has any Right to but himself.
> The *Labour* of his Body, and the *Work* of his Hands, we may say, are properly his. What-
> soever then he removes out of the State that Nature hath provided, and left it in, he

hath mixed his Labour with it, and joined to it something that is his own, and thereby makes it his Property. It being by him removed from the common state Nature placed it in, hath by this labour something annexed to it, that excludes the common right of other Men. For this *labour* being the unquestionable Property of the Labourer, no Man but he can have a right to what that is once joined to, at least where there is enough, and as good left in common for others.

Attempts were made to revive the Licensing Act in 1707, and 1709 – which resulted in the eventual Copyright Act: the 1709 Bill (passed in 1710) was called 'A Bill for the Encouragement of Learning, by Vesting the Copies of Printed Books in the Authors, or Purchasers, of such Copies, during the Times therein Mentioned'. Under this law, which regulated the practices of the Stationers' Company, copyrights belonged to an author, or the bookseller who had bought the right, and lasted for twenty-one years for a book already in print, and fourteen years for a book not yet published. Those rights would return to the author (if still alive) after that term had expired for another opportunity of a fourteen-year term. It was a significant innovation that authors could remain copyright holders, and were entitled to profit from the copying and dissemination of their work, and, as Mark Rose indicates, the Act 'marked the divorce of copyright from censorship and the reestablishment of copyright under the rubric of property rather than regulation'.

Both Daniel Defoe and Joseph Addison published articles during the passage of the bill in defence of author's rights, and compared book pirates to the most savage robbers or kidnappers. For example, Defoe argued in his *Review* (2 February 1710):

> A Book is the Author's Property, 'tis the Child of his Inventions, the Brat of his Brain; if he sells his Property, it then becomes the Right of the Purchaser; if not, 'tis as much his own, as his Wife and Children are his own – But behold in this Christian Nation, these Children of our Heads are seiz'd, captivated, spirited away, and carry'd into Captivity, and there is none to redeem them.

It is worth pointing out that much of Defoe's writing is critically concerned with issues of authenticity: in the veracity and reliability of pseudo-autobiographical characters like Moll Flanders and Robinson Crusoe, the apparition of the ghost of Mrs Veal, and in poems such as 'The True-Born Englishman', which satirizes national purity by describing the genesis of '*That vain ill natured thing, an* Englishman' among an 'Amphibious Ill-born Mob' (ll. 132–3).

Despite the Copyright Act (and the comparable legislation of 'Hogarth's Act' in 1735 protecting copyright in engravings), the precise nature of literary property was debated throughout the eighteenth century in an attempt to establish whether perpetual copyright for printers had survived 1710 as common law. It was not until 1774 that the Act was finally asserted. Tonson, for example, successfully retained his copyright in Milton's *Paradise Lost* in 1736, and, more alarmingly perhaps, declared war on Robert Walker, who had in 1734–5 published a seven-volume edition of *The*

Dramatick Works of William Shakespear in open competition with Tonson's editions. Prices fell from a shilling to a penny a play before Walker was defeated.

Of course, authors could now be equally litigious. In 1741, Pope sued the pirate bookseller Edmund Curll for publishing his correspondence without permission, and in doing so determined that the ownership of letters remained with the writer. Although it transpired that Pope had actually tricked Curll into publishing his correspondence in 1735, as a way of excusing the vanity of an authorial edition, Rose sees the case as a transitional moment in the history of authorship, author's rights, and literary property, arguing that the decision of *Pope* v. *Curll* involved 'an important abstraction of literary property from its physical basis in ink and paper'. Crucially, the author was no longer regarded as the mere inventor of a thing (such as a manuscript), but the producer of meaning. These new rights of literary property were given a philosophical basis by Edward Young's *Conjectures on Original Composition. In a Letter to the Author of Sir Charles Grandison* in 1759. (Interestingly, Pope explained in his preface to the ensuing edition of his correspondence in 1737 that he feared his letters would be forged.)

'The unspeakable Curll' was not the only illegal publisher working in London. Michael Treadwell has researched the twilight world of false imprints, and discovered a small group of specialist publishers who would publish and distribute controversial material in order to disguise or protect authors. Such imprints were particularly expedient around the time of the Popish Plot and the Exclusion Crisis, and consist of spoof names, common names, or false names, coupled with vague geographical locations: 'near the Pall-Mall', 'near Holborn', 'near St Paul's Churchyard', or no address or bookseller's sign. The most notorious use of a false imprint was, again, Alexander Pope, in his first publication of the *Dunciad* (1728). This originally appropriated the name 'A. Dodd' and purported to come from Dublin; another issue exists with 'A. Dod', and a 1729 pirated edition of the work has 'A. Dob' on the title-page: a doubly mendacious claim.

What booksellers feared, though, was not so much the threat of the clandestine London printers as pirate presses in Dublin and Scotland. Dublin, as suggested by Pope's use of the city in his fraudulent imprint, printed with complete impunity works copyrighted in England, and the Scottish book trade too lived by its own laws. Things came to a head in the late 1760s. In 1766, the printer Andrew Millar, to whom James Thomson had sold *The Seasons* (1726–30), and whose copyright had apparently lapsed in 1758 (after two terms of fourteen years), sued Robert Taylor for printing the work in 1763. Thomson's *Seasons* was the best-selling book of poetry of the century and therefore a valuable piece of property. Millar won the case, but the court was not unanimous in its verdict and shortly thereafter, Thomas Becket, who had purchased from Millar's executors the copyright of Thomson's *Seasons*, sued a Scottish printer, Alexander Donaldson, for producing a cheap reprint of the work. Donaldson appealed to the House of Lords, who marginally found in his favour, and the common law right of perpetual copyright was overturned in 1774 (although some university presses were granted perpetual rights to certain books in 1775). The works of dead authors like Shakespeare and Milton and indeed Thomson were now common property – but in response now began appearing in voluminously annotated variora editions to compensate the booksellers for their immediate loss of property.

It is important to note that these were booksellers, not authors, fighting cases of perpetual copyright. Although writers like William Warburton did meddle in the law and produced *A Letter from an Author to a Member of Parliament concerning Literary Property* (1747), the perpetual copyright was broken on an issue of cheap reprints of popular works, which benefited readers rather than authors (who were dead) or booksellers. The question of literary property, which filled journals such as the *Gentleman's Magazine* in the late 1760s, did, however, become a debate about the role and occupation of the writer. Lord Camden, for example, argued that genuine authors did not write for money:

> I speak not of the Scribblers for bread, who teize the Press with their wretched Productions; fourteen Years is too long a Privilege for their perishable Trash. It was not for Gain, that *Bacon, Newton, Milton, Locke,* instructed and delighted the World: it would be unworthy [of] such men to traffic with a dirty Bookseller for so much as a Sheet of Letter-press. When the Bookseller offered *Milton* Five Pounds for his Paradise Lost, he did not reject it, and commit his Poem to the Flames, nor did he accept the miserable Pittance as the Reward of his Labor; he knew that the real Price of his Work was Immortality, and that Posterity would pay it.

It is a revealing passage. Camden, who at this stage was one of the advocates of the authenticity of Thomas Rowley's poetry (Chatterton's medieval forgery), presents the author as a genius necessarily outside, or rather beyond, the market, completely rejecting the model of the professional author.

Despite the fact that, as Thomas Mallon points out, 'The history of copyright actually has more to do with piracy than plagiarism', plagiarism and copyright were intimately connected throughout the period, and issues of literary property were seldom far behind those of lawful printing rights. Although writers accused of plagiarism were never tried under the Copyright Act, it is evident from Defoe's remarks quoted above ('these Children of our Heads are seiz'd, captivated, spirited away, and carry'd into Captivity'), that plagiarism and piracy (what might be called parrots and pirates) were never very distant.

A plagiary (or plagiarist), from the Latin *plagiarius*, is one who forcefully possesses another (it derives from *plagium*, a net to ensnare game). Plagiaries abduct slaves and steal children, disfiguring them to pass them off as their own; plagiaries are man-stealers and press gangsters; plagiaries are kidnappers, seducers, and of course literary thieves. In 1712 John Dennis called a plagiary, 'but a scandalous Creature, a sort of spiritual Outlaw', and in 1751 Richard Hurd described them as: 'those base and abject spirits, who have not the courage or ability to attempt any thing of themselves, and can barely make a shift, as a great poet of our own expresses it, *to creep servilely after the sense of* some other.'

The word first appears in English in 1598 (in John Hall's *Virgidemiarum*), but has a classical source in Martial, and the charge was so frequently made by Greek authors that the investigation of plagiarism was a prominent feature of Alexandrine scholarship, for example in Macrobius's analysis of Virgil's debt to Homer. Anthony Grafton describes Porphyry's account of a dinner party with Nicagoras, Apollonius, Demetrius, and Calietes which degenerates into gossip about plagiarism. Porphyry in fact became a leading authority on forgery and pseudepigrapha (and for his attacks on the Bible was beaten by the early Christians and had his books burnt). And to avoid accusations of plagiarism, dramatists like Plautus and Terence acknowledged their sources in Prologues.

The most influential early use of the concept, however, is Horace's version of Aesop's fable of the borrowed plumage of the crow who disguises himself with peacock's feathers (itself – ironically – an adaptation). The image was deployed repeatedly, for example by Robert Greene who described Shakespeare in 1592 as the 'upstart Crow, beautified with our feathers', and William Wordsworth who criticized Thomas Gray in 1816 for writing 'English Verses, as he and other Eton school-boys wrote Latin; filching a phrase now from one author, and now from another . . . if I were to pluck out of Grays tail all the feathers which, I know, belong to other Birds he would be left very bare indeed.' Anne Killigrew wrote to defend herself against the accusation of plagiarism using the same model, 'Upon the saying my Verses were made by Another' (1686):

> Like *Æsop's* Painted Jay I seemed to all,
> Adorned in Plumes, I not my own could call;
> Rifled like her, each one my Feathers tore,
> And, as they thought, unto the Owner bore.
> (ll. 35–8)

Aesop's image of feathers, and therefore quills, effectively suggesting the vanity of writing and the flightiness of fame and reputation.

Plagiarism was – and probably still is – the severest charge that a critic could lay upon a writer, and it was levelled with particular ferocity by Restoration writers and critics, as if a cultural response to the trauma of rebellion. One of the most idiosyncratic examples of this reinvention is John Wilmot, Earl of Rochester's verse 'Why dost thou shade thy lovely face', for which he simply conflated two of Francis Quarles' poems from *Emblemes* (1635). Situating these meditational verses in the context of a libertine's oeuvre inverts the sinner's call to God to create a lovelorn apostrophe to a mistress: 'The whole object of the exercise', as Anne Barton correctly points out, 'is to change as little as possible of the original while wresting it in a different direction, transforming it into its opposite.' It is a wholesale plagiarism that works as a parody by demonstrating that meaning is reliant upon context.

Rochester escaped any censure as a plagiarist because the text was satirical and in any case only circulated in manuscript. Plagiarism in print, however, was inexcusable.

Aphra Behn was frequently branded a plagiarist, and Dryden's *MacFlecknoe* (which is itself an adaptation of Andrew Marvell's 'Flecknoe') is full of accusations of plagiarism, criticizing Shadwell by comparison with the Jacobean playwrights,

> Where did his [Jonson's] Muse from *Fletcher* scenes purloin,
> As thou whole *Eth'rege* dost transfuse to thine?
>
> (ll. 184–5)

and imagining a literary topography littered with poetic fragments:

> No *Persian* Carpets spread th'Imperial way,
> But scattered Limbs of mangled Poets lay:
> From dusty shops neglected Authors come
> Martyrs of Pies, and Relics of the Bum.
> Much *Heywood*, *Shirley*, *Ogleby* there lay,
> But loads of *Sh——* almost choked the way.
>
> (ll. 98–103)

Dryden was, in turn, castigated by Gerard Langbaine, who in *Momus Triumphans* (1688) offered the most stunning criticism to his contemporaries:

> having read most of our English Plays, as well ancient as those of latter date, I found that our modern Writers had made Incursions into the deceas'd Authors Labours, and robb'd them of their Fame . . . I know that I cannot do a better service to their memory, than by taking notice of the Plagiaries, who have been so free to borrow, and to endeavour to vindicate the Fame of these ancient Authors from whom they took their Spoiles.

Dryden replied that it is the right of the dramatist to adapt and translate, but Langbaine's assault did mean that dramatic sources were increasingly acknowledged by the eighteenth century. Paulina Kewes, who has studied issues of appropriation on the Restoration stage, argues that Langbaine's lists of plays and sources show that he was the earliest proponent of authorship envisaged as intellectual property rights.

Kewes is interested in all 'compromised modes of composition' for the stage – adaptation, appropriation, translation, collaboration, plagiarism, and auto-plagiarism – in order to establish that drama was midwife to the birth of the author before the Copyright Statute of 1710. In doing so, she negotiates a Serbonian bog of seething definitions. Sir William Killigrew's prologue to his play *Zeno*, for example, describes the work as both a translation and adaptation, but the image of plagiarism lurks quite palpably in his apology:

> Though boldly it be here transformed so,
> That Author cannot his own Issue know:
> Like crafty Beggars, when they Children steal,
> Disguise them: lest they should Thefts reveal.

Perhaps most surprisingly, John Bunyan fiercely defended himself in *The Holy War* (1682) against accusations of plagiarism by counter-attacking with a declaration of his author's rights:

Some say the *Pilgrims Progress* is not mine,
Insinuating as if I would shine
In name and fame by the worth of another,
Like some made rich by robbing of their Brother.
Or that so fond I am of being Sire,
I'le father Bastards . . .
    It came from my own heart, so to my head,
And thence into my fingers trickled;
Then to my Pen, from whence immediately
On Paper I did dribble it daintily.
    Manner and matter too was all mine own,
Nor was it unto any mortal known,
'Till I had done it. Nor did any then
By Books, by wits, by tongues, or hand, or pen,
Add five words to it, or wrote half a line
Thereof: the whole, and ev'ry whit is mine.
    Also for *This*, thine eye is now upon,
The matter in this manner came from none
But the same heart, and head, fingers and pen,
As did the other. Witness all good men;
For none in all the world without a lye,
Can say that this is mine, excepting I.

As suggested at the beginning of this essay, plagiarism was beyond the law. It was an ethical rather than a professional issue, and could only attack an author's reputation or person rather than anything more useful, like profits. This was partly because plagiarism is so unruly and ungovernable, and escalates wildly. It dawns on Langbaine (in *Momus Triumphans*) that,

This Art [plagiarism] has reign'd in all Ages, and is as ancient almost as Learning it self. If we take it in its general Acceptation, and according to the extent of the word, we shall find the most Eminent Poets . . . are liable to the charge and imputation of *Plagiary*.

Indeed, this is what Richard Hurd learnt in his 'A Letter to Mr Mason on the Marks of Imitation' (1757). Roger Lonsdale suggests that Hurd is 'baffled' by the extent of his discoveries of poetic borrowing among English writers, and becomes crestfallen at the paucity of the English tradition. Like Langbaine, however, who endeavours to distinguish between classical imitation and modern literary theft, Hurd proposes a category of 'learned *Allusion*' – in which thankfully 'even *Shakespear* himself abounds' – and later scholars such as Thomas Percy made such wholesale borrowing a positive characteristic of his ancient English minstrel tradition.

From a cursory glance at the contents pages of any edition of Alexander Pope's poems, however, it is clear that he felt no anxiety in 'imitating' Chaucer, Spenser, Waller and Cowley, not to mention Horace (explicitly) and Homer, Virgil, and Shakespeare (implicitly). Neither was Pope the only imitator of earlier poets (see, for example, Samuel Jones's Miltonic imitations reprinted in Roger Lonsdale's *New Oxford Book of Eighteenth-Century Verse*). Critics such as Reuben Brower have explained this somewhat generously by presenting Pope as engaging in continual and enriching dialogues with earlier poets. But as Lonsdale argues, the very range of Pope's 'allusion' is troubling: Spenser, Crashaw, Rochester, Denham (as Brower admits), but also Jonson, Suckling, Davenant, Oldham, Roscommon, Dorset, Sedley, Pomfret, Walsh, Fenton, Broome, Addison, Lady Winchilsea . . . Lonsdale puts it bluntly: 'could one, in the early eighteenth century, "allude" to Crashaw?' Furthermore, Roger Lund has also written on Pope's 'poetics of appropriation', and agrees that Pope sometimes concealed his sources (particularly Milton), and his main discovery is Thomas Newcomb's *Bibliotecha: A Poem, Occasioned by the Sight of a Modern Library* (1712), which was evidently a major source for the *Dunciad*. But Lund observes that 'The whole question of his plagiarisms has all but disappeared from modern discussions of Alexander Pope', concluding that this is an 'intertextual logic'. But if plagiarism or piracy was the sort of activity that could land a writer or a bookseller in the pillories of the *Dunciad*, where does the distinction with allusion or imitation lie?

The *Dunciad Variorum* (itself an exuberant rewriting of Dryden's *MacFlecknoe*) appears quite clear on this issue. The poem includes 'the phantom, More' [James Moore-Smythe], a Plagiary, and in a footnote describes the anatomy of the plagiarist thus:

> His case indeed was like that of a man I have heard of, who as he was sitting in company, perceived his next neighbour had stollen his handkerchief. 'Sir' (said the Thief, finding himself detected) 'do not expose me, I did it for mere want: be so good but to take it privately out of my pocket again, and say nothing.' The honest man did so, but the other cry'd out, 'See Gentlemen! What a Thief we have among us! Look he is stealing my handkerchief.'

More's plagiarisms also inspire the epigram:

> M—re *always smiles whenever he recites;*
> He smiles (you think) approving what he writes;
> And yet in this no Vanity is shown;
> A modest man may like what's not his own.

In addition, during the games in Book II, Dulness arranges a booksellers' race for a poet, a 'tall Nothing', which Curll seizes:

> A shapeless shade! It melted from his sight,
> Like forms in clouds, or visions of the night!

To seize his papers, Curl, was next thy care;
His papers light, fly diverse, tost in air;
Songs, sonnets, epigrams the winds uplift,
And whisk 'em back to Evans, Young, and Swift.

(ll. 103–8)

This seems straightforward – except that Pope himself took a couple of lines from Evans for the 1743 *Dunciad*.

Pope had written as early as 1711 in *An Essay on Criticism*:

True Wit is Nature to Advantage drest,
What oft was *Thought*, but ne'er so well *Exprest*.

(ll. 297–8)

And his technique in the *Dunciad* may simply be a re-jigging of these lines: what oft was *writ*, but ne'er so well exprest. Furthermore, Pope's Scriblerian satire casts light on the issue. *Peri Bathos; or, Of the Art of Sinking in Poetry* (1728, penned at the same time as the *Dunciad*), includes a chapter 'Of Imitation, and the Manner of Imitating' which is a parody of Longinus' treatise *On the Sublime*. Longinus, who had considerable influence on eighteenth-century and Romantic literary criticism, argues that *mimesis* (the imitation of other writers) is one of the characteristics of *noesis*, or the instinctive intellectual conception of the artist, which is a way of approaching the sublime. He gives a number of examples – describing, for example, Herodotus and Plato as 'Homeric' – and carefully distinguishes imitation from plagiarism: 'Now this procedure is not plagiarism; rather it is like taking impressions from beautiful pictures or statues or other works of art.' The artist's genius is announced in the ability to copy well. Greek poets and playwrights laid less emphasis on the originality of their material than on the originality (and hence posterity) of their style, and moreover until Aristotle, writers were unwilling to break the flow of their text with references and acknowledgements to other writers. In *Peri Bathos*, however, Pope suggests hack writers as models of perfection (Blackmore, Philips, Welstead, and so forth – those very writers pilloried and parodied in the *Dunciad*), and mischievously proposes that '*Imitation* is of two sorts; the first is when we force to our own purposes the Thoughts of others; the second consists in copying the Imperfections or Blemishes of celebrated authors.' In this context, the *Dunciad* becomes an epic of true copying, in which the genius of Pope is certified by the rich nap of first-rank poets he knits into the text; moreover, by so skilfully imitating them, these allusions also act as a prophylactic against Pope being numbered among the Dunces.

Literary theories of the century tended to follow Renaissance readings of classical authors, seeking authority rather than originality and insisting that imitation is an idealistic activity whereas creative fabrication is somehow dangerous – and of course that all subject matter is common property. Henry Fielding, for example, distinguishes between ancient and modern borrowing in just this way when he defends himself against plagiarism in *Tom Jones*:

The antients may be considered as a rich common, where every person who hath the smallest tenement in Parnassus hath a free right to fatten his muse. Or, to place it in a clearer light, we moderns are to the antients what the poor are to the rich.

He goes on to develop the socio-economic metaphor (which was also current in the Renaissance):

To steal from one another, is indeed highly criminal and indecent; for this may be strictly stiled defrauding the poor (sometimes perhaps those who are poorer than ourselves) or, to see it under the most opprobrious colours, robbing the spittal.

Other popular metaphors included ancient literature imagined as gold ore to be minted, used by the poets John Donne and later William Shenstone, and to distinguish good imitation from bad invention the bee (collecting pollen to make honey) and the spider (spinning flybane out of itself). Both Bacon and Jonson used spider and bee images, as did Jonathan Swift in the *Battle of the Books* (1704), a work which Joseph Levine has characterized precisely as a debate between the classical doctrine of imitation and modern cumulative scholarship.

The imitative or allusive mode of a mid-eighteenth-century poet like Gray, who claimed always to read Spenser before ever sitting down to write verse, was a reaffirmation of Longinian imitation; it is comprehensively analysed by Richard Hurd in his 'Discourse concerning Poetical Imitation', which was appended to his edition of Horace, first published in 1751. Hurd begins:

All *Poetry* . . . is, properly, *imitation* . . . every wondrous *original* . . . but a *copy*, a transcript from some brighter page of this vast volume of the universe. Thus all is *derived*; all is *unoriginal*.

He goes on to define the critical term 'invention' as precisely the philosophical term 'imitation', to defend poets against charges of indebtedness – imitation or allusion is inevitable – and deploys the same image of communality we have just seen above: 'The *objects* of imitation, like the *materials* of human knowledge, are a common stock'.

This was of course the situation in which Samuel Johnson found himself, first, with his *Dictionary of the English Language* (1755–56), and, second, with his compendious variorum edition of Shakespeare, which reprinted the commentaries of previous editors such as Pope. Lexicographers (and editors) are plagiarists of a certain kidney: neither definitions or illustrative quotations are invented for the occasion, but are meticulously gleaned from earlier scholars and writers. Hence Johnson's mild judgement of plagiarism in *Rambler* 143, in which he decides that a preponderance of parallel images is the only proof of the charge, and that chance is always a sure defence.

Ridiculing this with crack-brained vivacity is Laurence Sterne's *Tristram Shandy* (1760–8). Sterne was posthumously attacked first by Hester Thrale and then at length in the 1790s for incessant plagiarism from Robert Burton's *Anatomy of Melancholy* (1621–51), although when one realizes that Sterne's own remarks on plagiarism,

> Shall we for ever make new books, as apothecaries make new mixtures, by pouring only out of one vessel into another?
>
>   Are we forever to be twisting, and untwisting the same rope for ever in the same track – for ever at the same pace?

are plagiarized from Burton, along with most of the rest of this chapter (V. 1), the whole thing begins to look like a typical Shandean joke – made even richer by Sterne instantly wishing that 'every imitator in Great Britain, France, and Ireland, had the farcy for his pains; and that there was a good farcical house, large enough to hold . . . all together'. By the time Sterne wrote this, his novel had been both plagiarized and pirated, and he was signing every copy as it came off the press as an official endorsement to prevent counterfeits and unauthorized continuations.

Literary Forgery

Literary forgeries are perhaps inevitably historical documents. They are either presented as historical finds, or, like Charles I's *Eikon Basilike* (1649; 'the King's image') attempt to intervene in contemporary historical process: *Eikon Basilike*, which went into over forty editions, was in fact properly written by John Gauden. A more sinister example, perhaps, is that of Titus Oates, who masterminded the Popish Plot and attempted to change the course of the succession by forging the 'Windsor Letters' to support his murderous claims.

As suggested above, eighteenth-century history and historiography came into direct conflict with classical learning: it was a part of the debate between the 'ancients' and the 'moderns'. A modernist like Richard Bentley argued that classical works should not be treated as a Parnassian field of universal and decontextualized human wisdom, but needed to be rigorously historicized. Bentley was in fact extraordinarily effective in exploding classical myths, one of his early successes being to demonstrate by a relentless historical logic that the *Epistles of Phalaris*, a mainstay of the 'ancients', was a forged text. It was against Bentley's garrulously digressive and fabulously learned method that Swift's *Tale of a Tub* (1704) was written, and Pope has a Bentleian commentary running throughout the *Dunciad Variorum*. Bentley was also fantastically misguided. His edition of Milton's *Paradise Lost* (1732), for example, was an attempt to apply the techniques of textual transmission he had perfected on classical texts to a modern epic, on the assumption that Milton's amanuensis and printer had miscast the poet's lines, made unsubstantiated revisions, and even interpolated their own lines into the poem. The poor blind poet had obviously been unable to correct his proofs and remained ignorant of the forgery, and it was up to Bentley to retrieve them. In other words, poems written in the last fifty years might be as corrupt as those composed fifty centuries ago.

Bentley was trying to exemplify the role of the modern editor. 'Parallelist' editions of Milton (Thomas Newton), and books on Spenser and Pope (by Thomas and Joseph Warton, respectively) tended to trace references, allusions, borrowings, and imitations – if not plagiarisms. Shakespeare editing, particularly in the hands of Pope, had tended to be bracing and unafraid to meddle with the playtexts of the Bard, and Lewis Theobald's assault on Pope's Shakespeare was very much a Bentleian attack on loosely argued emendation. (It was not until Richard Farmer's *Essay on the Learning of Shakespeare* (1767) that source-hunting became an established feature of Shakespeare editing as well.) Bentley therefore offered his Milton as a model of 'Sagacity and happy Conjecture', in order to create what Marcus Walsh calls 'an ideal Milton, who might and should have written the ideal poem that Bentley's emendations and, at last, rewritings, seek to reconstruct' – and in such a relationship of poet and editor he was echoing the relationship of epic poetry with God's creation. While at one level, Bentley's achievement is laughably inept, William Empson, for one, has used it as a way of mapping potential fault-lines in Milton's poem: reading Bentley can strip away two hundred years of Miltonic veneration, put one in dialogue with an erudite and pugnacious editor, and be forced to justify one's taste.

Oddly, Milton was the victim of another accusation of literary imposture in 1747, when William Lauder (a Jacobite who had managed to lose a leg on a golf course) began publishing essays under the name of 'Zoilus' in the *Gentleman's Magazine*, collected in 1750 as *An Essay on Milton's Use and Imitation of the Moderns, in his Paradise Lost*. Lauder argued that Milton had plagiarized modern Latin poets for *Paradise Lost*, the case being 'proved' by quoting doctored passages from the work of mid-seventeenth-century poets such as Grotius and Andrew Ramsay in which lines from a 1690 Latin translation of *Paradise Lost* had been interpolated. Johnson was sufficiently impressed by Lauder's book to write a preface, but the forged plagiarisms were rapidly exposed.

If Milton was doubly imposed upon, Samuel Johnson appears at the centre of many eighteenth-century debates about literary forgery. He furiously attacked James Macpherson for Ossian and undertook his *Journey to the Western Isles of Scotland* (1775) almost solely to disprove the work. Chatterton's Rowley poetry was read at his Literary Club and he travelled to Bristol to inspect the remains there. He was also devoted to one George Psalmanazar, a cross between a performance artist and a crypto-ethnographer who in 1704 published *An Historical and Geographical Description of Formosa*, as 'a Native of the said Island, now in *London*'.

At least since the time of Herodotus, travel writing and forgery have enjoyed a long relationship, and Psalmanazar exists almost in a tradition of deception. He insisted, by a combination of exotic anecdotes, a gibberish language, a curious alphabet, and an alarming raw diet, that he was a Formosan. It was a performance of otherness that set contemporaries agog: Swift, for example, mentions 'Sallmanaazar' in *A Modest Proposal* (1729) and is clearly indebted to the *Description of Formosa* for *Gulliver's Travels* (1726); it is also inspiring theorists today. Susan Stewart explains the phenomenon of Psalmanazar thus:

The impostor is, of course, self-made. In overthrowing the relation to the rule of the proper name, the impostor becomes his or her own mother and father, and it is the task to the imposture to supply the details of that new, invented genealogy.

And yet there is something even more dazzling in Psalmanazar's work, as when he answers his critics with an elaborate double-bluff in the preface to the second edition of the *Description*:

> You do me more Honour than you are aware of, for then you must think that I forg'd the whole story out of my own Brain . . . he must be a Man of prodigious parts who can invent the Description of a Country, contrive a Religion, frame Laws and Customs, make a Language, and Letters, etc. and these different from all other parts of the world; he must have also more than a humane memory that is always ready to vindicate so many feign'd particulars, and that without e'er so much as once contradicting himself.

As suggested above, cultural history (and in the case of Lauder, a Jacobite, national identity too) was very much at stake in such cases, and antiquarian forgeries, from Shakespearian relics to Richard of Cirencester's map of Roman Britain (published in 1757 and from whence we get the name of the Pennines), were widespread. There seems to have been an almost inevitable relationship between collecting and hoaxing, and antiquarians, such as the fearsome Shakespeare editor George Steevens, were not above forging an Elizabethan letter or a marble memorial to Hardyknute. Forgery haunts the editing of antiquarian texts, such as Percy's *Reliques*. As Stewart says,

> The problem of authenticity [in relation to ballad collecting] arises in situations where there is a self-conscious perception of mediation; a sense of distance between one era and another, one worldview and another; a sense of historical periodization, transformation, and even rupture

– which are precisely the conditions required for forgery.

History was simultaneously material and immaterial – made up of objects and yet in the main unwritten or forgotten. The two most remarkable forgers of the eighteenth century, James Macpherson and Thomas Chatterton, both located their work in an elusive past. Macpherson's Ossian was an oral Celtic epic carried on the breath of the Highlanders for a millennium and a half; Chatterton's Rowley was a fifteenth-century monk whose manuscripts were discovered in a chest in a muniment room of a church in his native Bristol. Both writers provoked intemperate pamphlet wars; both proved to be a major inspiration to the next generation of writers; and while both Macpherson and Chatterton were indisputably described and treated as literary forgers in their time, they are currently being recuperated into the literary tradition in ways that challenge any simplistic dismissal of their work today.

It is tempting to construct a paradigm of eighteenth-century literary forgery, from Psalmanazar to Lauder to Ossian to Rowley: the counterfeit performance text of a fake exotic and his printed testament gives way to a purely textual counterfeit which attacks the native canon; this in turn enables a challenge to the concept of English literature by the oral Ossian, and finally to an affirmation of the English tradition in the lost manuscripts of a medieval monk. The paradigm would continue into the 1790s with William Henry Ireland's 'discovery' of canonical Shakespeare manuscripts. On the other hand, one could note the vacillation between home and abroad, England and Scotland, Metropolis and province, or indeed claim that there is some vast tradition of forgery that stretches back to antiquity.

Such treatments are unhelpfully reductive. The complexity of the terms forgery and plagiarism (and counterfeit, copyright and imitation) within the fugitive contexts of literature and law, resist simple diagnosis. Instead, they shadow other cultural formations – issues of authorship and literary work, freedoms of the press, the transformation of the literary marketplace, theories of originality, inspiration, and authenticity. Forgery and plagiarism are, then, a means of classification: a function of discourse. Although the forger or plagiarist is always in danger of collapsing into an author (as soon as a work is identified as forged or plagiarized, it is stripped of its literary status and its author is exiled to anecdotal literary history), the rehabilitation of forgers and plagiarists needs to situate writing practices both inside and outside orthodox functions of authorship – at any time supporting a culturally specific definition of truth by superseding it.

References and Further Reading

Baines, Paul (1999). *The House of Forgery in the Eighteenth Century*. Aldershot: Ashgate.

Barton, Anne (1988). 'Rochester'. In *John Wilmot, Earl of Rochester: Critical Essays*. Ed. David Vieth. New York: Garland, 1–26.

Brower, Reuben (1959). *Alexander Pope: The Poetry of Illusion*. Oxford: Clarendon.

Clifford, James L. (1975). 'Johnson and Lauder'. *Philological Quarterly* 54, 342–56.

De Grazia, Margreta (1991). *Shakespeare Verbatim*. Oxford: Clarendon Press.

Empson, William (1935). 'Milton and Bentley: the pastoral of the innocence of man and nature'. In *Some Versions of Pastoral*. London: Chatto and Windus, 149–91.

Emsley, Clive (1987). *Crime and Society in England: 1750–1900*. London and New York: Longman.

Faller, Lincoln B. (1987). *Turned to Account: The Forms and Functions of Criminal Biography in Late Seventeenth- and Early Eighteenth-century England*. Cambridge: Cambridge University Press.

Foxon, David (1991). *Pope and the Early Eighteenth-*

century Book Trade. Rev. and ed. James McLaverty. Oxford: Clarendon Press.

Gaskill, Howard and Fiona Stafford, eds (1998). *From Gaelic to Romantic: Ossianic Translations*. Amsterdam: Rodopi.

Grafton, Anthony (1990). *Forgers and Critics: Creativity and Duplicity in Western Scholarship*. Princeton: Princeton University Press.

Groom, Nick, ed. (1993–4). 'Narratives of Forgery', *Angelaki* 1.2.

——(1999). *Thomas Chatterton and Romantic Culture*. London: Macmillan.

——(2001). *The Forger's Shadow*. London: Picador.

Haywood, Ian (1986). *The Making of History: A Study of the Literary Forgeries of James Macpherson and Thomas Chatterton in relation to Eighteenth-century Ideas of History and Fiction*. London: Associated University Press.

——(1987). *Faking It*. Sussex: Harvester.

Jones, Mark, ed. (1998). *Fake: The Art of Deception*. London: British Museum.

Kahan, Jeffrey (1998). *Reforging Shakespeare: The*

Story of a Theatrical Scandal. Bethlehem: Lehigh University Press.

Kayman, Martin (1999). 'The "new sort of specialty" and the "new province of writing": promissory notes, literary property, and the "laws" of the novel'. Paper delivered at BSECS Conference, Oxford, 4–6 January.

Kewes, Paulina (1998). *Authorship and Appropriation: Writing for the Stage in England, 1660–1710*. Oxford: Clarendon Press.

Levine, Joseph M. (1991). *The Battle of the Books: History and Literature in the Augustan Age*. Ithaca: Cornell University Press.

Lonsdale, Roger (1979). 'Gray and "allusion": the poet as debtor'. In *Studies in the Eighteenth Century, Vol. 4*. Papers presented at the Fourth David Nichol Smith Memorial Seminar. Ed. R. F. Brissenden and J. C. Eade. Canberra: Australian National University Press, pp. 31–55.

Mallon, Thomas (1989). *Stolen Words: Forays into the Origins and Ravages of Plagiarism*. New York: Ticknor and Fields.

Momigliano, Arnaldo (1966). *Studies in Historiography*. London: Weidenfeld and Nicolson.

Nichol, Don (1996). 'Warburton (not!) on copyright: clearing up the misattribution of *An Enquiry into the Nature and Origin of Literary Property* (1762)'. *British Journal for Eighteenth-Century Studies* 19, 171–82.

Rose, Mark (1993). *Authors and Owners: The Invention of Copyright*. Cambridge, Mass.: Harvard University Press.

Stewart, Susan (1993). *On Longing: Narratives of the Miniature, the Gigantic, the Souvenir, the Collection*. Durham, N.C. and London: Duke University Press.

——(1994). *Crimes of Literature: Problems in the Containment of Representation*. Durham, N.C. and London: Duke University Press.

Stafford, Fiona J. (1988). *The Sublime Savage: A Study of James Macpherson and the Poems of Ossian*. Edinburgh: Edinburgh University Press.

Walsh, Marcus (1997). *Shakespeare, Milton and Eighteenth-Century Literary Editing: The Beginnings of Interpretative Scholarship*. Cambridge: Cambridge University Press.

White, Harold Ogden (1935). *Plagiarism and Imitation during the English Renaissance*. Cambridge, Mass.: Harvard University Press.

Woodmansee, Martha (1994). *The Author, Art, and the Market: Rereading the History of Aesthetics*. New York: Columbia University Press.

Woodmansee, Martha and Peter Jaszi, eds (1994). *The Construction of Authorship: Textual Appropriation in Law and Literature*. Durham, N.C. Duke University Press.

7

Literature and Nationhood

Murray Pittock

The scholarly debate about the nature of nationality in the eighteenth century and its impact on identity has been slow to gather strength in literary study, however much it is proving itself at the forefront of historical concerns. The idea of neo-classical order and consensus, which has its modern roots in George Saintsbury's *The Peace of the Augustans* (1916), still prevails by stealth in books such as Howard Weinbrot's *Augustus Caesar in Augustan England* (1978) and Paul Korshin's *Typologies in England 1650–1820* (1982), although it has largely given way to the idea of a contested eighteenth century where order is barely maintained, which in turn has released a number of studies of the 'disorderly', based in class and social, or, increasingly, gender premisses. By contrast, the study of nationality in this period remains marginal, particularly in the areas of: (1) the Scottish and Irish literary canon; (2) contested ideas of 'British' nationality, mainly functioning through Jacobite and radical language; and (3) the linkages, rather than the distinctions, between 'popular' and 'high' art in literature, especially noteworthy in their contribution to (1).

To some extent this may be due to a current preference within literary study for sociological theories of nationality rather than historical accounts of it. Benedict Anderson's *Imagined Communities* (1981, 1991) is only the most prominent among a series of studies which highlight the role of 'imagination' and 'invention' in the making of nations, and which suggest that modern nationality itself dates only from the French Revolutionary period. This premiss is normally long on generalities and short on empirical fact, and is brusquely taken to task by, for example, John Cannon in *Samuel Johnson and the Politics of Hanoverian England* (1994) and by the present writer in *Celtic Identities and the British Image* (1999). It does, however, have a certain appeal to a discipline which prioritizes the qualities of imagination, and lends itself to a neo-Romantic overstatement about the influence of creative writers: for example, in Declan Kiberd's contention that Yeats 'invented' Ireland. Such reflection of essentially sociological concepts of 'identity' are currently common in literary study: they marry well to a basic New Historicist concept of the 'thick fact', by enabling the achievement of a single creative writer to stand for a whole period of social and political flux. This is a process which can be seen as re-canonizing the canon in its construction of a 'great tradition' from single figures. Coupled with an unwillingness to project nationalism back beyond 1789 and (in the case of some American critics in particular) with a marked hostility to Jacobite and subsidiary national traditions in eighteenth-century writing, it has, however, failed to lead to a full reassessment.

This is particularly important in the case of Scotland, where in the eighteenth century medieval texts were reprinted and revisited by a patriot Jacobite tradition which saw in the nationalism of Blin Hary's (1440–1493) *Wallace* (1470) and other texts an anticipation of the controversy over Union in their own day. As Susan Reynolds has wisely pointed out to those who would see the term 'nationalism' here as anachronistic:

> The trouble about all this for the medieval historian is not that the idea of the . . . real nation is foreign to the middle ages, as so many historians of nationalism assume, but that it closely resembles the medieval idea of the kingdom as . . . a people with a similarly permanent and objective reality.

Although the term 'nationalism' is first found only in 1836, according to the *OED*, it is cited as if it were already an established term. This should not surprise us: 'nationalist' itself dates to 1715 (much earlier than 1789, note), 'nationality' can be found in 1691. These themselves are arguably only extensions of 'Of Ingland the nacion Es Inglis man thar in commun' (1300) or 'Be cause I am a natyff Scottis man' (Blin Hary). Most famously of course, the Declaration of Arbroath in 1320 mentions not only the English king but also the 'people' of England as adversaries, before going on to state that 'we will never give consent to subject ourselves to the dominion of the English. For . . . it is liberty alone that we fight and contend for . . . to live at peace in that narrow spot of Scotland . . . since we desire nothing but our own'. Scottish national literature in the eighteenth century knew what it was doing when it re-encountered its own medieval period. Nor was this an elite ideology only, for national friction can be found in burgh record, recorded anecdote and the experiences of foreign visitors alike in the medieval and early modern periods.

This is of course only one aspect of the essay which follows, but one mentioned here to allow both particular and general *prima facie* reservations to emerge about the fashionable qualities of 'invention' and 'imagination': a critique which can be found in more detail in William Fergusson's *The Identity of the Scottish Nation* (1998). To evaluate the concepts of literature and nationhood throughout the British Isles in this period, it is important to allow both a greater breadth of eighteenth-century texts to emerge for study, and also to take texts from minority traditions (e.g. Scottish, Irish and Catholic) much more on their own terms than as hostages to a narrative already selected. The re-emergence of James Macpherson (1736/8–1796) in recent years is a good example of how this process is becoming increasingly possible: this, in its turn, has helped to open a closed frontier between anglophone (including Scots) and gaelic literature. This is the kind of development in perspective which can affect unchallengeably canonical writers too: for example, Jonathan Swift's (1667–1745) *Drapier's Letters* (1724–5) have a powerful intertextual presence in Sir Walter Scott's (1771–1832) *Letters of Malachi Malagrowther* (1826), like its forerunner a quasi-nationalist defence of identity built round a currency issue (Scott also incidentally calls 'for a league, offensive and defensive, between Scotland and Ireland in each other's interest'). Close reading, readjusted for national perspective, can have a similar effect. Here Swift castigates Wood in terms anticipatory of *A Modest Proposal* (1729):

> This brings to my Mind the Story of a *Scotch* Man, who receiving Sentence of Death with all the Circumstances of *Hanging, Beheading, Quartering, Embowelling*, and the like; cried out, *What need all this Cookery?* And I think we have Reason to ask the same Question: For if we believe *Wood*, here is a *Dinner* getting ready for us, and you see the *Bill of Fare*; and I am sorry the *Drink* was forgot, which might easily be supplied with *Melted Lead* and *Flaming Pitch*.

Here are familiar Swiftian parameters: feeding as killing, nourishment as starvation, the apparent grounds of life the prelude to death. But if one makes the decision to read the '*Scotch* Man' as a significant example, much more of the passage opens itself out. The 'Sentence of Death' including '*Quartering*' is that of specifically *English* treason law, introduced in Scotland after the Union of 1707 (and arguably in contravention of it). It was also (especially in Jacobite trials) sometimes administered on Scots by English courts for offences which may have been committed in Scotland, in clear contravention of the Union. Like Wood's Halfpence in Ireland, it is an undermining and violating English intrusion into domestic Scottish affairs: and one which is encapsulated in an intimidating and public punishment for disaffection towards the government. Similarly, remembering the Irishness of the compaint, the '*Melted Lead*' image of the last line can encapsulate not only hellishness but also the melting down of the disastrous 'Gunmoney' coinage of the Irish Jacobite war (suggestions of Jacobite war are present not only in the imagery of the last line but in the earlier death of the Scotsman), where even the silver was struck in pewter, with its counterfeits struck in lead: the only time when such base coin circulated so widely anywhere in the British Isles. The imagery thus reinforces ideas of intrusion, oppression, chaos and disorder with their roots in a national question: one of sovereignty in law, over treason in Scotland's case, over currency and the right to mint domestically at the correct weight in Ireland's (Wood's coins were underweight). Ireland, like Scotland, is being served a fatal diet, and those who do the '*Cookery*' are agents of oppression, cannibalizing the domestic rights of Scottish law and the Irish parliament.

To return to the premises defining nationhood in literature outlined above, the awareness of Scottish and Irish distinctiveness is not less important than the ability to identify the presence of dialogue between these national traditions, independent of English literature. One of the key elements here (and an important symbol of the national identity of both countries, in Ireland's case continuing well into this century) is the portrayal of the nation as an oppressed woman. In Ireland, the *aisling* poetry of figures such as Aoghan O Rathaille (*c.*1675–1729) and Eoghan Rua O Suilleabhain (1748–1784) presents a male speaker who encounters a woman, Ireland, in a dream vision. The woman awaits the return of her (Stuart) deliverer from over the sea, the expulsion of those who imprison and rape her, and a fertile renewal based on union with her true lover. As O Rathaille puts it in 'Gile Na Gile' ('Brightness Most Bright'):

> All in derision they tittered – a gang of goblins
> and a bevy of slender maidens with twining tresses.
> They bound me in bonds, denying the slightest comfort,
> and a lumbering brute took hold of my girl by the breasts.

> I said to her then, in words that were full of truth,
> how improper it was to join with that drawn gaunt creature
> when a man the most fine, thrice over, of Scottish blood
> was waiting to take her for his tender bride.
> (trans. Thomas Kinsella)

The *aisling* woman is usually young, but occasionally (as in O Rathaille's 'Mac an Cheannai'/'The Redeemer's Son'), the hope of the poet has become a 'bitter vision', and the woman 'whose name was Eire' memorializes past lovers who will not come again before she dies, a 'dried branch'. This mourning, memorializing, aged woman of the *aisling* tradition can be found again in the *Sean Bhean Bhocht*/ 'Poor Old Woman' of nineteenth- and twentieth-century Irish nationalism: in Yeats's *Cathleen Ni Houlihan* (1902), the prospect of eroticized blood sacrifice renews her youth in the last line of the play.

Scottish royal genealogy had, since medieval times, included a persisting (though decreasing) Irish element in its mythology of origin, and the legitimate claim of the Stuarts to the Irish crown was an important feature in late bardic culture in Ireland. Even more striking, however, is the presentation in both literatures of the nation through the image of a woman, awaiting her lover's return to renew her and restore national order and sovereignty. In the Irish *aisling*, the speaker is male, and the woman-nation the object of his admiring gaze (a tendency which continues in later Irish writing). In Scotland, in contrast, the woman is often the speaker, calling for her own deliverance, in which she sometimes actively participates. In 'Tho Georthie Reigns in Jamie's Stead', which provided the air and some of the imagery for Burns's more enduringly famous 'For a' that and a' that' (an example of cross-cultural influence from popular to print), the woman (Scotland) appeals thus:

> He's far beyond Culbin [Sands – near Elgin] the night
> That has my heart for a that
> He wears the Pistol by his Side
> That'll gar me laugh for a that
> The highland coat the filobeg [philabeg]
> The tartan hoas and a that

He wears that's o'er the hill the night
And will be here for a that.

He wears the broad Sword by his side
Well knows he how to draw it
The Target & the tartan plaid
The Shoulder belt & a that.

The woman-nation, whose 'heart' belongs to the Stuart prince, is aroused to redemptive war in sexual terms: 'the Pistol by his Side / That'll gar me laugh for a that'. In
other songs, 'His Quiver hang down by his thigh' achieves the same effect, or alternatively the sheer excitement of imminent victory:

But to wanton me, but to wanton me
D'ye ken the thing maist wad wanton me ?
To see King James at Edinburgh Cross,
Wi fifty thousand foot and horse.

Similar images and expressions of emotion interpenetrate anglophone and gaelic literature in both Scotland and Ireland, and in the latter country the association of the
feminized nation with the redemptive and eroticized violence required to free her continues through the *Roisin Dubh* (James Clarence Mangan's (1803–1849) 'Dark
Rosaleen') and *Sean Bhean Bhocht* cultural traditions into the political confrontations
of the twentieth century. The Stuart prince's role as both returning lover and warrior
may also be encapsulated in his characterization both in Scotland and Ireland as 'the
Blackbird': traditionally a reference to the dark hair of Charles II and James 'VIII and
III', but also by the implication of restorative and delivering violence to the sword of
Fionn MacCumhail, 'the Blackbird's Son'. Unlike the Arthurianism of Wales, the
Scots-Irish king Fionn and his Fianna were never adopted into central literary or cul-
tural Britishness, despite the somewhat ambivalent efforts of James Macpherson's
Fingal (1761) in this direction. Indeed, heroic swordsmanship was a mark of those
who stood in the tradition of the Fianna in eighteenth-century Jacobite Scotland (as
in Duncan Ban Macintyre's (1724–1812) 'Blar Na H-Eaglaise Brice'/'The Battle of
Falkirk'), while in Ireland the development of the Fenians as a political organization
in the nineteenth century showed the degree of militant life left in the concept.

Leaving aside the later politicizations of these images in Irish tradition, in Scotland the woman-nation image retained a powerful presence in subsequent literature,
from Scott's *Highland Widow* (1832) to John Buchan's *Witch Wood* (1927), J. M. Barrie's
Farewell, Miss Julie Logan (1932) and Neil Gunn's *Butcher's Broom* (1934), while the
heroic symbolism of Fionn is still very much evident in the same author's *Silver Dar-
lings* (1943). Thus a significant part of the literary heritage and imagery of both Scotland and Ireland since the Romantic period derives from their political and cultural
preoccupations and dialogue in the eighteenth century, which surfaced into a high
cultural interest in a rather self-conscious celticism through Macpherson's Ossian
poetry at the end of the Jacobite period in 1760.

A second important issue in any discussion of literature and nationhood is the impact of the vernacular on the conception of literary culture. In the case of Scots or Irish gaelic, the political and cultural differences implicit in the use of the language and its poetic formats and formulae is obvious enough, though there was a dialogue in the sense that Alasdair MacMhaigstir Alasdair's (*c.*1695–1770) writing was influenced by James Thomson's (1700–48) *Seasons* (1730), and in Ireland there is evidence of mixed writing in Irish and English, with a subversive commentary in Irish on the anglophone text: such developments appear to have been rarer in the case of Welsh. One of the most powerful and yet unstable vernaculars however was Scots, the standard language of the Scottish administration since the fifteenth century. Although there were (and are) wide divergences between Scots and standard English in vocabulary, and significant though narrower ones in grammar and syntax, Scots forms had been in decline in print since the Reformation: the dominant vernacular language of Protestantism in the British Isles was English.

English had thus been gaining ground in Scottish written forms for some considerable time before 1700, although spoken Scots retained a hold throughout most of society for a century after this. It was not till the 1760s that there was much sign of elocution in Scotland, and indeed even written Scots of a lightish kind had a presence in published grammars. However, after the Union of 1707, there was a (by no means universal) movement in Scottish writing to revive Scots, led in the first place by Allan Ramsay (1686–1758). Ramsay, in a tradition which also encompassed Robert Fergusson (1750–1774), Robert Burns (1759–1796) and Lady Nairne (1766–1845) among many others, strove to express through Scots verse the spirit of its people. As the high culture of Scotland set its eyes increasingly on the challenge of London's example, the writers of the Vernacular Revival turned to the folk tradition and their interpretation of it as a measure of genuine 'Scottishness'. Ramsay and Fergusson, in poems such as 'Tartana, or the Plaid' and 'Elegy on the Death of Scots Music', also wrote poetry which defended native Scottish industries or cultural traditions against metropolitan or cosmopolitan innovation. Fergusson in particular took a strong politico-economic line: 'Black be the day that e'er to England's ground/ Scotland was eikit by the UNION's bond' ('The Ghaists'). Even Jean Elliot (1727–1805), daughter of such a stout Whig Unionist as Sir Gilbert Elliot of Minto, could write

> Dule and wae for the order sent our lads to the Border;
>   The English, for ance, by guile wan the day:
> The Flowers of the Forest, that foucht aye the foremost,
>   The prime o our land are cauld in the clay.

The increasingly anachronistic nature of the use of Scots vernacular in high cultural print media, combined with its role as the medium for the expression of the sentiments and (as here) the historicity of the ballad/folk tradition, often helped to limit the contemporary political relevance of what were otherwise forthrightly patriotic sentiments. Such contemporary relevance was nonetheless sometimes intended, as will be clear in the discussion of Burns below.

Other writers in this tradition include Alexander Ross (1699–1784), Jean Adam (1710–65), Adam Skirving (1719–1803), father of the portraitist Archibald, John Skinner (1721–1807), Isobel Pagan (1741–1821) and Joanna Baillie (1762–1851). The Vernacular Revival was of crucial importance in the formation and preservation of a separate Scottish tradition in literature. Henceforth, there would be a strong strain in Scottish literature which emphasized the importance of the folk tradition and its themes (Burns, Hogg, Oliphant, Barrie, Buchan, Muir, Gunn, Mitchison, Jenkins, Spark), the nature of Scottishness as essentially tied to the common man (Burns, Gibbon, MacColla, McIlvanney, Welsh, Kelman) and the importance of Scots as a linguistic register of identity (Burns, Scott, Hogg, Stevenson, Douglas Brown, MacDiarmid). The status of writing in Scots in eighteenth-century Scotland is crucial not only to the language, but also to the themes which set apart the literature of nationhood in Scotland.

Neat demarcations in linguistic politics should be resisted, however: James Beattie (1735–1803), who famously compiled a list of Scotticisms to be avoided, also wrote in the vernacular. Being a philosopher of the Common Sense school who believed that premises in argument were ultimately bald claims, he would have recognized the need for caution in generalization. Common Sense itself embodied the paradox of the Scottish Enlightenment: radical change through tradition and continuity. Thomas Reid (1710–96), Beattie and others placed their intellectual endeavours in the tradition of the Scottish medieval university curriculum: but from the Common Sense view that the most extravagant chains of metaphysical reasoning in the end rest on mere assertion ('Principles which must be believed on their own Authority') sprang the Democratic Intellect and the ripening in the Scottish universities of a pattern of general educational enquiry fructified by philosophical methods. Beattie's *The Minstrel* (1771), though a product of the Primitivist revival, was the effusion of a mind far different from James Macpherson's.

By contrast, important writers in English such as Tobias Smollett (1721–1771) could, despite their use of Scottish themes, translate even the simplest Scottish terminology into English for the benefit of their audience. For example, in *Roderick Random* (1748), not only is no attempt made to delineate the hero's accent or idiolect, though his Scottishness is remarked upon by other characters, but Fieldingesque social typology makes a 'squire' and 'parson' stand in for the more natural and accurate 'laird' and 'minister' of the opening chapters. In other words, to adopt English unmodified by Scots could also be to anglicize, and hence deliberately remove oneself from any sign of involvement in a continuing national tradition: Smollett is joining himself to the popular contemporary subgenre of the picaresque which links the medieval quest to the Romantic *bildungsroman*. The 'idea of sentimental education conducted on the road' was one which allied the discovery of self to the discovery of Britishness: thus the novels of Daniel Defoe (1660–1729) and Henry Fielding (1707–1754) share with Smollett a vocabulary and background which illustrates (and indeed overemphasizes) features in common in places which differ. In this, to follow and expand on Ian Watt's *Rise of the Novel* (1957) in terms of more recent socio-historical studies, they delineate aspirations increasingly held in common by a middle class whose values were being created and endorsed by the rapid development of a popular commercial culture in common, visible through the relentless rise of national and local print media, top-heavy with aspirational advertisement (37 per cent of the *Newcastle Courant* in 1725) and effectively distributed through an expanding network of provincial agents.

The importance of Latin as a literary marker of nationality has been long realized in Scotland's case, with the well-documented political conservatism and jacobitical tendencies of the Scoto-Latinists in the north east a marked feature of such studies as Douglas Duncan's *Thomas Ruddiman* (1965). Gavin Douglas, Bishop of Dunkeld's, translation of the *Aeneid* into Scots, with its determination to 'kepand na Suddroun [English], bot our awin langage', had long been a marker of the links made by vernacular patriotism between the two languages: Douglas's text was in fact revived by patriot printers in the eighteenth century. The expression of patriotic sentiments in Latin also had a long tradition, seen as late as James Philp of Almericlose's (1654/5–*c*.1720) *Grameid*, with its celebration, in a fine blend of Lucanian grimness and Vergilian hope, of the deeds of Viscount Dundee in the Jacobite Rising of 1689. Philp writes in a punningly domesticated version of an international tradition: 'Aeneas' (a Jacobite hero) becomes Scotticized as 'Angus', the native version of the name and also the title of Philp's home county! The *Grameid* is the last attempt at a Latin epic in the British Isles, perhaps even the last major Latin poem: at the threshold of the mock-heroic era, it endorsed the subject-matter of a national and religious struggle with unwavering seriousness. Dundee was also celebrated in an elegy by another Scoto-Latinist, Dr Archibald Pitcairne (1652–1713), a friend and associate of Ramsay's.

John Dryden (1631–1700) translated Pitcairne's elegy ('Oh last and best of Scots, who didst maintain / Thy country's freedom from a foreign reign'), and also used the part-translation of the *Aeneid* by the Scottish Jacobite exile Lord Maitland as a basis for his own translation of 1697. Various critics have seen Dryden's version of Vergil as implicitly Jacobite, and here perhaps is an indication of that confluence of a conservative Latinist culture in Scotland and England posited by Jonathan Clark in his 1994 study of Samuel Johnson. This culture, or aspects of it, lies at the heart of the second feature of the literature of nationhood treated in the present essay: that of the idea of a contested British nationality, seen not only through the Jacobite songs and other elements of Stuart culture, but also through the language of high cultural Latinity recently examined in detail by David Money, and earlier the subsidiary subject of a number of studies, beginning with Howard Erskine-Hill's *The Augustan Idea in English Literature* (1983).

As Erskine-Hill points out, Atterbury's preface to Waller, written in 1690, foreshadows the development of a contested 'Augustanism', with its statement that 'I question whether in Charles II's reign English did not come to its full perfection; and whether it has not had its Augustan age as well as the Latin' already outlining a nostalgic and jacobitical premiss for the whole concept. Francis Atterbury's own role in Jacobite affairs only serves to underline such implications. The idea of the Stuart king as an Augustan figure in the character of Horace's *Odes* dated back at least to the Castalian Band poets of James VI's court, and can be found in the Latin poetry with which Scotland welcomed the 1660 Restoration (cf. James Kennedy's 'Aeneas Britannicus'), as well as, of course, its manifest presence in *Astraea Redux* and other work of Dryden's. It fitted other Stuart typology too: the emblem of Fionn was the sun, James VI had been celebrated as an Apollonian sun-king by the Castalians, and Horace's famous 'lucem redde tuae, dux bone, patriae' of *Odes* IV:v made a particularly good coda to these images, particularly in the context of exile and hoped-for return. After 1688, the Augustan image was a contested one, but Stuart Vergilianism and Horatianism persisted into the 1730s at least. Those who sought to distance themselves from its connotations of political disaffection could always rely on the alternative vision of Augustus as an 'infamous' or 'crafty Tyrant', put forward by Henry St John, Viscount Bolingbroke (1678–1751) and Edward Gibbon (1737–1794) among others: though even this was slippery ground, as George II's status as 'Augustus' within Alexander Pope's (1688–1744) *Imitations of Horace* demonstrates. As Pope himself remarked, 'The *Aeneid* was evidently a party piece': he should have known, for the 1743 *Dunciad* is pronounced in its dependence on the darker books of Vergil's epic, particularly Book VI. The 'universal Darkness' of Pope's climax is that of an underworld from which there is no Aenean return to cast light on a Britain where 'Dunce the second reigns like Dunce the first'. Pope is of course explicit in his comparison of his poem with Vergil's: the mock-heroic is one of the discourses through which the reversals of politico-cultural disappointment were expressed. Darkness, Dulness's element, can accompany the mock-heroic moment of climax elsewhere: for example in Canto III of *The Rape of the Lock*.

Pope took some of this material from the controversial pamphlet literature which swamped England in particular in this period of dynastic controversy: for example, the lines 'Thus *Jove* was blest by every grateful *Frog*, / When o're the *Fens* King *Stork* succeeds King *Log*' from *The Anti-Weesils* (1691), appear in *The Dunciad* as 'Loud thunder to its bootom shook the bog, / And the hoarse nation croak'd, 'God save King Log', an allusion apparently also made in a 1737 letter to Swift from Dr William King (1686–1761). In other words, on one level Pope was at one with the level of writing of the Dunces he deplored. A similar interface between popular literature and high culture has been identified by recent research in Dryden's *The Hind and the Panther* (1687). Catholic apologetics and Jacobite Augustanism could of course go best together in the person of Aeneas and his epic: for 'pius Aeneas' foreshadowed Augustus, whose piety was endorsed by his adoption of the title Pontifex Maximus in 12 BC (not to mention his subsequent deification!). This priestly title of the Roman emperors in its turn passed to the papacy; combined with the myth that Brutus, great-grandson of Aeneas, was the founder and begetter of Anglo-British monarchy, it had a powerful attraction as an image to legitimist Jacobitism, often being accompanied by a nostalgic, sacral and intensely traditionalist vision of the crown.

Thus the image of 'British' nationality promoted by Jacobite high cultural classicism was one much more closely interlinked not only with royal power and prerogative, but also with the caesaropapist qualities of the original Anglican settlement, with its essentially medieval descent from the struggles of king and pope. The sacral qualities with which it invested monarchy (such as the royal touch, heavily used by both Charles II and James VII and II) were almost entirely abandoned after 1688; by the 1720s (beginning with the Erastian Benjamin Hoadly's (1676–1761) elevation to Bangor in 1715) its High Anglican counterpart on the bench of bishops was being purged. Besides such 'core' ideological values, Jacobitism was also associated with country politics: hence the Whig tradition of depicting Tory squires as 'boobies', which stretches from the 1690s via Fielding to Macaulay. Such a vision of British culture could also be associated with traditional paternalism (Pope's Man of Ross) or the defence of customary rights, a theme present not only in writers like Pope but also in books such as Henry Fielding's *Joseph Andrews* (1742). The sense that 1688, by so drastically altering the law of primogeniture, marked a watershed in traditional expectations of legal inheritance was a strong one, found in the tapsalteerie world portrayed in John Gay's (1685–1732) *Beggar's Opera* (1728). 'Gentlemen of the road' could indeed be 'fine gentlemen', as 'Captain' Macheath may be: for many of James's army did not serve again after 1688, and some at least turned to highway robbery. When Jemmy Twitcher says 'What we win, gentlemen, is our own by the law of arms and the right of conquest', it can be assumed to indicate to the audience that Macheath's gang takes its example from the regime, whose founder William had already been aligned with his namesake the Conqueror by Gay's friend Pope in *Windsor-Forest* (1713). Jacobites could use such ironies as a badge of pride: the Duke of Wharton 'thought of himself as Macheath', for example. Within the broader context, the decade after George I came to the throne seemed, in manifestations such as the South Sea Bubble and the scandal of Jonathan Wild, afterwards identified with Peachum/Walpole and the conduct of the 'Great Men' of the state in general, to reveal the realities of a world indeed 'turned upside down'. This sense of institutionalized inversion of inherited value is present in a vast range of texts, from Henry Fielding's *Jonathan Wild* (1743) and Swift's *Gulliver's Travels* (1726) to the bawdy and savage satire of Jacobite verse and the cynical note seen in the street literature of chaos and disappointment which greeted the pricking of the South Sea Bubble in 1720:

> So if ye gang near the South Sea Hoose
> The willywhas [rogues] will grip yer gear.
> Syne a the lave [fellow-Scots] maun fare the waur,
> For oor lang biding here.

Just as the crown ('All the dogs o England's Court / They bark and howl in German') and its 'great man' were mocked, so too was London as the centre of the financial revolution, where 'all the world will fare the waur' for 'oor lang biding'. The increasing centralization of power in London and London's government was evident in the

Revolution itself, in Irish policy after Limerick (1691), in Union with Scotland (1707), in the final closure of the Council of Wales and the Marches (1689–94), in the abolition of the Scottish Privy Council (1708) and the suspension of General Convocation after 1717, to name but the most prominent examples. In a world where so much was altering, satire and mock-heroic were natural media of literary response: on a more sophisticated level, Pope's use of zeugma in *The Rape of the Lock* bathetically illustrates the gap between appearance and reality under a regime which 'has no other end but the preservation of property', and yet deprives his co-religionists of it in their tens of thousands. This is not to suggest that all who wrote like this shared a single agenda: but a wide variety of literary discourses at all levels expressed themselves in tones of discontent, dissatisfaction and unease.

This sense of the overturning of an old order and the unpredictability and doubtful legitimacy of the new was strong for many people, and intensified in groups (such as smugglers) who resented the encroachment of taxation on traditional practices. Rural discontent, from the Windsor Blacks to the Irish Whiteboys, drew on aspects of jacobitical symbolism and associations to render their own threat more disturbing to the powers that be. The financial revolution, the enclosure of land and the lack of religious toleration were other elements which sustained a different vision of eighteenth-century Britain from that powerfully purveyed in an increasingly centralized state with aggressive foreign policy aims and a growing commodity industry which through the medium of newspaper advertisement, the mushrooming of provincial titles and improved dissemination, was creating the first homogeneous middle-class audience Britain had known. Against such developments, a Jacobite (or at least jacobitical) note of literary protest can be discerned, blended with other forms of political nostalgia and doubt. It should be stressed that the use of such a discourse does not *necessarily* indicate that the author is a political Jacobite: Swift's is a case in point here. Eventually the nostalgic force of such analyses began to dwindle and attenuate, and the path was open for the reconstituting of an alternative Britain to take place wholly, rather than merely partly, in the imagination. This is the distance which separates the mock-heroic, the 'gloom of the Tory satirists' and the factitious medieval patriot poetry of Allan Ramsay from the development of Primitivism, which forever severs the reality of the British present from the dimensions of the lost past which it celebrates.

Primitivism was perhaps the chief literary manifestation of Britishness in the latter half of the eighteenth century. Aspects of it can be found in the Patriot Whig ideology of the 1730s (which was in some ways constructed to reappropriate imagery tainted with Jacobitism) and in the fascination with the Druids as an ancient British priestly caste, which itself was linked to the rise in gothic particularism (a dedication to liberty regarded as peculiarly Germanic) found for example in William Collins' (1721–1759) *Ode to Liberty* (1746). So popular had the patriot Druids become by mid-century that John Wood's (1704–1754) design for Bath Circus may well have been based on the 'Druid' temple of Stonehenge. In literature, the Druids were accompanied and eventually supplanted by the image of the Bard. In the 1750s, Thomas Gray's

(1716–1771) *The Bard* (1757) was based on information supplied by Ieuan Fardd of the Welsh Cymmrodorion Society, founded in 1751, and thus became a means of supplying an anglophone audience with the 'celtic' spirit, suitably refined for a British readership through the prism of remote nostalgia, a gulf between contemporary and medieval consciousness more evident in British than Scottish or Welsh society. Poets like Robert Southey (1774–1843) and William Wordsworth (1770–1850) felt remote enough from Plantagenet imperialism to find Wallace a fit subject for their poetry: an eighteenth-century Scot might well have more difficulty disassociating himself from the politics of such past struggles.

Such a disassociation was, however, the essence of Primitivism. Its chief ur-texts were James Macpherson's translations and adaptations of gaelic poetry in his immensely influential *Fingal* (1761) and *Temora* (1763). Here the heroic deeds of the Fianna were suitably accommodated within the garb of classical epic and that of the contemporary cult of sentiment which raised agreeable sensations in his British and wider European audience. The demands of politeness ensure that deaths on the battlefield are dealt with by Macpherson with an obliquity unknown to the epic tradition he claims to represent. At the same time, the nostalgic sense of a cause already lost in Macpherson's work portrays the heroic celticism he purports to iconize as a designer accessory of the culture which has superseded it. The addition of implicit anti-Irishness also served to disassociate the Ossian-poetry from its origins.

Macpherson did much to develop the profundity of Primitivism's relationship to the past, and also its vacuity. Just as his own Ossianic endeavour had begun with *Fragments of Ancient Poetry Collected in the Highlands of Scotland* (1760), so Evan Evans published *Specimens of the Poetry of the Ancient Welsh Bards* (1764), Bishop Percy his *Reliques of Ancient English Poetry* in 1765 (an event which 'absolutely redeemed' English poetry according to Wordsworth) and Charlotte Brooke her *Reliques of Irish Poetry* in 1769. This was in its essence a British phenomenon, the acceptance of diversity under the condition of its 'ancientness' in an age where the Enlightenment had, through the teleology of historians such as William Robertson (1721–1793) and sociologists such as Adam Ferguson (1723–1816), helped to commit intellectual society to a paradigm of progress which was not seriously questioned until the First World War. A teleological understanding of history (crudely, 'Whig' history) was crucial in the development of Primitivism, because it allowed the romanticization of what was no longer perceived as a threat: for to categorize something as 'ancient' was to confirm its supersession. The battle of the ancients and moderns of the beginning of the century had turned into a massacre by the latter of the former, symbolized through the interpretation of Culloden (1746) in the Whig historic paradigm. As a result, the way was open to British unity through embracing the 'ancient' through an inclusive, yet subtly patronizing, process of romanticization. George Lyttleton's *Account of a Journey into Wales* (1774) for example, compared the celtic obscurity of Snowdon to the long-vanished mosaic Mount Sinai, while in 1772 Joseph Banks named a cave on Staffa after Fingal, thus beginning a long imaginative colonization of Scotland which reached its apogee under Queen Victoria.

There is a distinction to be drawn of course between the British and the classical 'ancient'. Implicit comparisons of modern civilization with the classical world could still give rise to reservations and cautioning exemplars, as in the work of Edward Gibbon (1737–1794). But even here, the victory of modernity posited in the Enlightenment can be seen: it is not just the gaelic heroic poets, but Homer himself who is being 'civilized' by the discourses through which Macpherson is adapting the epic. Apparently a counterweight to the Enlightenment, Primitivism was in practice its handmaiden: *Ossian* appears to answer Thomas Blackwell's (1701–1757) animadversions on the impossibility of the epic, while in fact confirming them. Although there were undertones of anxiety about social change brought about by increased mobility, the rapid growth of print culture, the creation of a British commodity culture and latterly the Industrial Revolution, such concern usually expressed itself through the prism of nostalgia. Oliver Goldsmith's (1729–1774) 'Deserted Village' is a good example of this, with ruralist idealization taking priority over any critique of social change: 'the tyrant's hand' may have undermined the 'bold peasantry', but the thing that may most affect the speaker is that 'rural mirth and manners are no more'. The 'village preacher' is a memorialized example of rural virtue, like Wordsworth's schoolmaster in *The Prelude* or Pope's Man of Ross: an ultimately Horatian praise of retreat which even in the Jacobite period foreshadowed a politics of disengagement all too manifest in Primitivism. Thus, although Wordsworth makes political points about current social conditions in *The Ruined Cottage, Michael* or 'The Old Cumberland Beggar', the validity of the ancient, traditional way of life they represent is often seen only through an eye which colonizes its choices: 'May never House, misnamed of industry/Make him a captive' Wordsworth says of the beggar, while the Highland lass of 'The Solitary Reaper' is supposed by the uncomprehending poet to voice in her gaelic 'old, unhappy, far-off things, / And battles long ago'. The beggar is more picturesque kept out in the open, while the Highlander's concern is for the 'ancient' space to which she and her speech community have already been relegated by their adoption into British literature. Hence when Highlanders or other members of the dispossessed are given voice by Romantic writers, it is often only so that they can become a mouthpiece for elegy: 'Farewell, farewell dear Caledon, land of the Gael no longer', or the explicitly exilic lament of the famous 'Canadian Boat Song', published in 1829. The moral sentiments of Laurence Sterne (1713–1768) or Henry Mackenzie (1745–1831) are here transposed into the pity an often undefined auditor (and author) feels in conspiracy with his or her readership towards suffering which is usually displayed as a *donnée* of the outsider's condition: 'but we are exiles from our father's land'. In this sense, Wordsworth's 'Highland lass' *is* Macpherson's Ossian: the *raison d'être* of her tongue and culture is to 'sit forlorn at the tombs of my friends'. Politically speaking, such sentiments reinforced 'cultural support for the violent reaction against radicalism': with the interesting exceptions of Joseph Ritson (1752–1803) and James Hogg (1770–1835), the Primitivist world did not welcome a dialogue with the socioeconomic groups whose past it celebrated. Wordsworth's 'Resolution and Independence' in this sense metaphoricizes the priorities of an entire literary movement.

Burns and William Blake (1757–1827) stand out as adapting these priorities in radical redfinitions of literary nationhood which transcended the persisting and obsessive topoi of Primitivism. Although Blake drew on Druidism ('Hear the voice of the Bard!') and the rural/retreat image of true Englishness ('The Ecchoing Green'), he presents the nostalgia inherent in such images as a process of entrapment: the childhood of self or of the race, watched over by the Bard, is a time when (as in 'The Chimney Sweep' or 'London') false consciousness is consolidated: 'White as an angel is the English child: / But I am black as if bereav'd of light'. Blake's vision of the Primitive does not seek to contain its innocence in celebrating it, but to emphasize the corruption of that innocence by the 'mature' polity of its celebrants, and the capability of the 'noble savage' not to subside into pageant but instead to renew itself in revolutionary violence as Orc, spirit of adolescent rebellion and the dissatisfaction of pure infantile passion with its orderly entrapment into guilt, the policing of consciousness by itself so evident in the 'mind-forg'd manacles' of London's citizens. Just as the British state found that the best way to preserve the pageant of Scots patriotism was to submerge it in the British army abroad and in the parade of colourful localism at home, so it also endorses the fossilization of childhood innocence by using evangelical language to convince the oppressed chimney sweep that 'weep, weep' is the cry of an adult trade, not a destroyed childhood. 'So if all do their duty, they need not fear harm' is the voice which itself endorses both the language of Anglo-British identity ('England expects every man will do his duty' – Trafalgar, 1805) and the financial and religious systems which underline its power. Blake mocks the message of the evangelical hymn by using its form to express language which undercuts it: in this and in his 'Primitivist' language and stance he is attacking the British state post-1688 (represented by the Whig-empiricist inheritance of 'Newton & Locke') through the terms used by its own ideologues.

Blake was no 'Jacobite', although his clear inheritance from the spirituality of the Jacobite William Law (1686–1761), with his emphasis on '*Will, Imagination* and *Desires*' is an interesting one. Rather, Blake's use of Milton as an icon is close to that of both Wordsworth and Percy Shelley (1792–1822), while the depth of his dissatisfaction with the state and its agencies in human consciousness was such as to detach him from some of the dominant genres of his age. In this, he was perhaps similar to William Godwin (1756–1836), whose *Caleb Williams* (1794) is arguably the first detective story, and one which centrally places the rural squirearch Falkland (who bears the name of a Stuart hero) at the heart of a web of power and deceit which undercuts the whole worldview of ruralist English ideality. Godwin is attacking Edmund Burke's (1727–1797) *Reflections on the Revolution in France* (1790), just as Jane Austen (1775–1817) later defended them, putting back together in Darcy and Knightley what Godwin had taken apart in Falkland, and in the persiflage of Frank Churchill and Henry Crawford exposing the immorality of French Revolutionary deism. Interestingly, however, even the conservative defenders of ruralist Englishness tend to deeply suspect London and doubt the sincerity of its values: in this Pope, Wordsworth, Blake, Austen and the anonymous street-balladeers of South Sea have much in common. The sheer scale of the expansion of London's consequence in eighteenth-century Britain made it lasting enemies among the literary practitioners of all Britain's identities, in which Primitivism arguably helped to emplace the regionalism and self-conscious sense of locality which so strongly marks English (and in a different way, Scottish) literature from the Romantic period.

Burns of course wrote not simply as a regional or national but as a universal author. The different registers of his Scots and English usage are themselves linguistic signposts round the politics of his world and their expression. In particular, he uses the techniques of the Vernacular Revival not just to venerate the retreating heroic past of his country (a practice wholly compatible with the larger voicings of Primitivism), but also to enter the world of Jacobin radicalism so scorned by the Jean Elliots of this tradition. Burns was not above hallowing Scottish patriotism through a melancholy retrospective: in 'Ye Jacobites by name', 'There'll never be peace till Jamie comes hame' and 'Such a parcel of rogues in a nation' the speaker is a ruined or nostalgic old man overwhelmed by the 'rising sun' of Britain. Yet the core of his achievement as a writer of nationhood lay in another direction: the universalization and radicalization of Scottish language, form, characters and topoi. It is arguable that it is this combination of Scottish language and international radicalism that has excluded Burns from the traditional canonical catalogue of the 'great Romantics': an extraordinary and deeply Anglocentric exclusion, for Burns is one Scottish author whose international appeal, massive range of translation and continuing influence in countries as diverse as Canada and Russia is without question. Generally, appreciation of Burns is based on his vernacular Scottishness in anglophone countries, and on his universalism and radicalism elsewhere: yet it is his greatness that both these work in conjunction.

Burns radicalizes religion, politics and the human condition itself. In 'To a Mouse', 'Man's dominion' which has broken 'Nature's social union' is one which wrecks the human relationship with the mouse by the agricultural development of common land, but which also implies a brutal 'dominion' of economic power, which evicts men as surely as mice: 'thy poor, earth-born companion, / An' *fellow-mortal*!':

> But Mousie, thou art no thy-lane,
> In proving *foresight* may be vain:
> The best laid schemes o' *Mice* an' *Men*,
>   Gang aft agley,
> An' lea'e us nought but grief an' pain,
>   For promis'd joy!

It is power that so often sweeps both aside: the tenant farmer crushes the mouse as the landlord crushes the tenant farmer, though 'A *daimen-icker* in a *thrave* [an ear of corn in two stooks] / 'S a sma' request'. In 'For a' that and a' that', Burns adapts the air and some of the structure of the Jacobite song 'Tho Georthie Reign in Jamie's Stead' to suggest the universality of this desire to despise and mistreat those to whom we feel superior: 'The coward-slave, we pass him by', though 'The rank is but the guinea's stamp'. By using the word 'guinea', the only English coin for which there was no Scottish equivalent, Burns begins to build up a picture of the particularly intense evils of arrogance and exploitation in the English class system, to which he opposes the 'we' of his own community, using also the 'honest man' code of the Jacobite period. By contrast, the 'prince' who 'can mak a belted knight, / A marquis, duke, and a' that' cannot touch the integrity of the true 'honest man' (just as 'English gold' fails to buy and sell the true patriot in Jacobite verse): the 'lord' of class power is abused in vernacular Scots as a 'birkie' and 'coof'. The real 'gree' [prize, reward] is the brotherhood of man of which Scotland is an avatar, implicitly in this poem, more directly in 'Robert Bruce's March to Bannockburn', where the king's address to his soldiers for 'LIBERTY' is an urge to perpetual revolution, the resistance small men and nations owe to tyranny, Blake's Orc in a kilt:

> By Oppression's woes and pains!
> By your Sons in servile chains!
> We will drain our dearest veins,
>   But they *shall* be free!

Burns admitted in a letter to George Thomson that the poem was designed to have a contemporary reference to 'other struggles of the same nature'. Throughout his work (and there is of course the possibility in recent research that the canon of his radical poetry may be expanded), he sought to transform a mode of writing elsewhere sinking into nostalgia to a position where it could bear the weight of contemporary and universal concerns through subtle adaptations of register, form and subject. Burns slyly suggests that Scottish values are (potentially at least) universal ones, and that Scotland is more radical, commonsensical and egalitarian as a society than is England: myths which are still with us.

Any assessment of the idea of literature and nationhood in the eighteenth century must confront the diversity offered by the perspectives, literary communities and strategies of the writers and traditions cited above. What I have wished to outline in a space which could never allow for comprehensive coverage, is the extent to which Britain, Britishness and its component (and indeed oppositional) nationalities in the eighteenth century are defined by perspective to a greater extent than in any other century apart from our own. This essay is about where one stands (or sits) to read literature, and the mind with which one reads it: it has not sought to overemphasize minorities, for one thing that must be understood is that in our period there is no clear *majority*. The population of an England itself politically and religiously divided was barely more than that of Ireland, Wales and Scotland together for much of the eighteenth century, and not least important in any question of standpoint is the realization that neither the demography, the society nor the sociolinguistics of the twentieth century can be imported into it. Even in 1861, interpreters were still being used in London to 'translate' Northumbrian dialect, four hundred years after the first penetration of the region by standard English. Identities change very slowly: for although it may be gratifying to literary critics to believe that writers 'invent' countries, Burns has an answer for them:

> O wad some Pow'r the giftie gie us
> *To see oursels as others see us!*
> It wad frae monie a blunder free us
>   An' foolish notion.

To be successfully 'other' is to know the importance of perspective, and that is what this chapter has been for.

REFERENCES AND FURTHER READING

Anderson, Benedict (1983; 1991). *Imagined Communities*. London: Verso.

Cannon, John (1994). *Samuel Johnson and the Politics of Hanoverian England*. Oxford: Clarendon Press.

Clark, Jonathan (1994). *Samuel Johnson*. Cambridge: Cambridge University Press.

Colley, Linda (1992). *Britons: Forging the Nation 1707–1837*. New Haven: Yale University Press.

Crawford, Robert (1992). *Devolving English Literature*. Oxford: Oxford University Press.

Donaldson, Gordon (1974). *Scottish Historical Documents*. Edinburgh and London: Scottish Academic Press.

Donaldson, William (1988). *The Jacobite Song*. Aberdeen: Aberdeen University Press.

Erskine-Hill, Howard (1983). *The Augustan Idea in English Literature*. London: Edward Arnold.

——(1996). *Poetry and the Realm of Politics: Poetry of Opposition and Revolution*. Oxford: Clarendon Press.

Gerrard, Christine (1994). *The Patriot Opposition to Walpole*. Oxford: Oxford University Press.

Jones, Charles (1996). *A Language Suppressed*. Edinburgh: Edinburgh University Press.

Kidd, Colin (1993). *Subverting Scotland's Past*. Cambridge: Cambridge University Press.

Langford, Paul (1991). *Public Life and the Propertied Englishman 1689–1798*. Oxford: Clarendon Press.

Leersens, Joseph (1986). *Mere Irish and Fior-Ghael*. Amsterdam and Philadelphia: John Benjamines.

Newman, Gerald (1987). *The Rise of English Nationalism: A Cultural History 1740–1830*. London: Weidenfeld and Nicolson.

Ó Tuama, Sean and Kinsella, Thomas (1981; 1994). *An Duanaire 1600–1900: Poems of the Dispossessed*. Portlaoise: Dolmen Press.

Pittock, Murray G. H. (1994). *Poetry and Jacobite Politics in Eighteenth-century Britain and Ireland*. Cambridge: Cambridge University Press.

——(1997). *Inventing and Resisting Britain: Cultural Identities in Britain and Ireland, 1685–1789*. Basingstoke: Macmillan; New York: St Martin's Press.

——(1999). *Celtic Identities and the British Image*. Manchester: Manchester University Press.

Reynolds, Susan (1994). In *Nationalism*. Ed. John Hutchinson and Anthony Smith. Oxford and New York: Oxford University Press, 137–40.

Rogers, Pat (1974; 1978). *The Augustan Vision*. London: Methuen.

Sambrook, James (1986; 1993). *The Eighteenth Century*. London and New York: Longman.

Simpson, Kenneth (1988). *The Protean Scot*. Aberdeen: Aberdeen University Press.

Stafford, Fiona (1986). *The Sublime Savage*. Edinburgh: Edinburgh University Press.

Womack, Peter (1989). *Improvement and Romance: Inventing the Myth of the Highlands*. Basingstoke: Macmillan.

8

The Business of Literature: The Book Trade in England from Milton to Blake

Michael F. Suarez

> Were we to estimate the learning of the English by the number of books that are every day published among them, perhaps no country, not even China itself, could equal them in this particular.
>
> (Oliver Goldsmith, *The Citizen of the World*, 1762)

Authors do not write books. Their toil produces manuscripts, which are then fashioned into books by a network of human labour ranging from the prosperous bookseller-publisher to the journeyman binder earning less than two pence an hour. In the seventeenth and eighteenth centuries, as now, literature was a business because books were a business. Publishers, printers and distributors of books earned their living, either well or ill, by a series of commercial transactions that led step-by-step from the author's manuscript to the book on someone's shelf. Samuel Johnson, the son of a bookseller, was probably exaggerating for effect when he famously opined that, 'No man but a blockhead ever wrote, except for money', but we know that authors as diverse as Behn and Dryden, Defoe and Pope, Goldsmith, Burns, Scott and Johnson himself all took great pride in the fact that they could earn their bread by their wits and their pens. Students of English literature are usually too preoccupied with other concerns to think about the writings of their favourite authors as having to find their way in the marketplace, as commodities which were bought and sold. Yet, that is what they were: if a published poem, novel, essay, or play failed to live up to its price, then most copies of the work might well end up being sold for wastepaper, only to become 'Martyrs of pies, and relics of the bum', as Dryden reminds us.

Consider our own situation today. Is a book published by Gypsy Lane Press likely to be accorded the same reception as a work produced and marketed by Viking Penguin? Is a paperback with a lurid cover on sale in an airport or a supermarket accorded the same cultural status or read in the same way as a hardback displayed in the literature section of Blackwell's or Waterstone's? Who wants to buy and read a novel if the print is too small and the dull paper makes you think you might well go blind before finishing chapter 3? How many readers will purchase the writings of an author, no matter how meritorious, whose work is in print only in an elegant and very expensive edition? In a significant sense, then, who publishes a book, how it is printed, to whom it is marketed, how much it costs, and even whether it is kept in print or not, are all inextricably linked to 'literary' concerns.

Literary critics sometimes write about texts as if there were such a thing as the work 'in itself', abstracted from the signifying materiality and the circumstances of its production. Yet, the idealized text does not exist. There are only real books (and pamphlets, manuscripts and broad-sheets) which bear the traces of their making. The predominantly economic motive of the book trade influenced what writers produced, which writings were published, how books reached readers, and how they were (and are) perceived. The material forms that comprise a book affect meaning and, hence, influence its consumption and reception. Knowledge of book history – of the transmission, production, distribution, and consumption of texts – is not merely a useful adjunct to literary study; it is essential to many of its central concerns, ranging from scholarly editing to theories of reading and of what a text means.

Booksellers and Authors

A bookseller was anyone who engaged in one or more of the following: publishing, wholesale vending of books and/or copyrights to other members of the trade, and retail selling from a shop. Although we may think of these endeavours as generally distinct today, in the seventeenth and eighteenth centuries many booksellers were involved in all three activities. (The modern publisher is an early nineteenth-century phenomenon.) Campbell's *The London Tradesman* (1747) explained that the bookseller's business is 'to purchase original copies from authors, to employ printers to print them, and publish and sell them on their own account . . . but, their chief riches and profit is in the property of valuable copies'. Owning 'copies', or holding the rights to reproduce works that proved to be steady sellers over many years, was often the key to a bookseller's long-term financial success. For more immediate gain, most booksellers also sold stationery; many dealt in patent medicines as well. When, in William Wycherley's *The Plain-Dealer* (1677), a self-important author of a few pamphlets proudly announces that he is about to consult with his bookseller, the widow Blackacre attempts to deflate him by asking if the bookseller will 'sell you lozenges for your cough, or salve for your corns?'

Booksellers ordinarily purchased 'copy', the right to reproduce a writer's work, for a fixed sum. Among his many payments from Jacob Tonson, Dryden earned 250 guineas for the *Fables* (1700) and, according to Pope, £1,200 for his translation of Virgil (1697). Pope literally made his fortune translating Homer. Cleverly inciting a bidding war between Tonson and the rival bookseller Bernard Lintot, Pope made nearly £10,000 for his *Illiad* (1715–20) and *Odyssey* (1725–6). Except for editions of the *Works* of well-known authors, however, poetry generally did not pay very well. Booksellers, being businessmen, did not appraise the worth of an author's copy solely in terms of the likely demand for the text, a difficult judgement based on a combination of the work's subject and genre, the author's reputation and the tenor of the market. Booksellers also calculated the possible worth of a manuscript according to how many printed pages it would make, which largely determined its price when sold to the reading public. If profit margins remained roughly the same, then a bookseller would have to sell three times more copies of a one-shilling poem than a three-shilling novel to make the same profit.

In Fielding's *Amelia* (1752) we learn that, 'A sheet is a sheet with the booksellers; and whether it be in prose or verse, they make no difference; tho' certainly there is as much difference . . . in the work as there is to a tailor between making a plain and a laced suit'. Accordingly, Pope was paid £15 for his *Essay on Criticism* (1711) and £7 for *The Rape of the Lock* (1714). The bookseller Robert Dodsley, who Johnson called 'my patron', gave him 10 guineas for *London* (1738) and 15 guineas for *The Vanity of Human Wishes* (1748). Even when they were lengthy, new poems typically fetched less than popular prose. For *Paradise Lost* (1667) Samuel Simmons paid Milton only £5 down and £5 when the first edition of 1,300 copies had all been sold. Milton's widow subsequently parted with all further rights in the work for £8. Edward Young's *Night Thoughts* (1742–5), a work some 10,000 lines long, earned him 220 guineas, while Goldsmith received £21 for *The Traveller* (1764), a poem of fewer than 450 lines. In 1805, Walter Scott was paid about 700 guineas for *The Lay of the Last Minstrel*. Byron received 600 guineas for *Childe Harold* in 1812.

Needing money while working on the *Dictionary* (1755), Johnson undertook the task of writing *The Rambler* (1750–2) twice each week, for which he was paid 2 guineas per essay. He made nearly £426 directly from his writing and probably at least £100 more from the sale of part or all of the copyright. Authors' remuneration rose faster than inflation as the century progressed, not least because the reading public and, hence, the market for books, was expanding. As the bookseller James Lackington observed, the efflorescence of circulating libraries and reading clubs all over England had increased the demand for books. (Begun *c*.1720, there were some 390 circulating libraries in England by 1800, most of them run by booksellers.) The popularity of the novel, a phenomenon that had a tremendous impact on the book trade, did much to fuel the growth of literature as a major form of popular entertainment. In the first decade of the eighteenth century only about five separate volumes of prose fiction were published in England each year, but in the 1750s more than 40 fictional works, including reprints, were issued annually. By 1800, that number had risen to more than 150. (During the eighteenth century England was becoming a more print-oriented culture. Although the national output of printing, including ephemera, is extremely difficult to determine with exactitude, scholars believe that fewer than 2,000 different items – books, pamphlets, ballads, handbills, catalogues, proclamations, and more – were produced in 1740; by 1800 the number had climbed to about 6,500.)

Prices for fiction varied considerably: Swift was paid £200 for *Gulliver's Travels* (1726), while Fielding received £700 for *Tom Jones* (1749), and £1,000 for *Amelia* (1752). *Rasselas* (1759) earned Johnson £100, which was less than he had hoped for, though Fanny Burney, whose *Evelina* (1778) appeared anonymously, received only £30 from her publisher. Sterne was given more than £1,000 for *A Sentimental Journey* (1768), a little book by an author of enormous reputation. Non-fiction works, especially in multiple volumes, could be highly lucrative. Gibbon commanded two-thirds of the profits for his *Decline and Fall of the Roman Empire* (6 vols, 1776–88), amassing some £6,000. Less sensationally, the first edition of *The Wealth of Nations* (1776) earned £500 for Adam Smith. In light of such figures, it seems scandalous that Johnson received just 300 guineas for *The Lives of the Poets* (1779–81), though that was half again as much as the 200 guineas he had requested. Edmond Malone speculated that Johnson could have set his price at 1,000 or even 1,500 guineas. Of course, some writers did not part with all their rights for a single sum. Pope leased the copyright to his *Essay on Man* in 1733 for £200; some writers sold their copyright for a single edition, while others, like Gibbon, contracted for a profit-sharing scheme.

Booksellers were routinely accused of exploiting writers. In *The Author* (1763), Charles Churchill describes writers as the 'slaves of booksellers'. Robert Burns similarly writes (in 'To Robert Graham of Fintry') of 'Vampyre booksellers' who 'drain' the poor author for their own selfish gain. In Smollett's *Peregrine Pickle* (1751) we read the charge that booksellers are guilty not only of 'limiting men of genius to the wages of a journeyman tailor', but also of 'taking such advantages of their necessities, as were inconsistent with justice and humanity'. Of course, Pope's *Dunciad* (1728, 1743) is the *locus classicus* for indictments against the book trade ranging from unbridled cupidity to gross stupidity, though his little couplet poem on the same theme is less well known: 'What authors lose, their booksellers have won, / So pimps grow rich, while gallants are undone.'

It is certainly true that some booksellers became very wealthy indeed. Thomas Guy, a bookseller (from 1668) dealing chiefly in Bibles, sermons and prayerbooks, amassed a fortune from publishing and clever investments. He is best remembered today for building Guy's hospital in London entirely from his own resources. Guy's success should remind us that, although students of English are understandably most interested in literary books, the largest publishing category in seventeenth- and eighteenth-century England was theology and ecclesiastical affairs. Nevertheless, the two outstanding literary booksellers of Milton's day, Humphrey Mosley and Henry Herringman, earned for themselves a highly respectable prosperity, not least through the copies they held. Their successor, Jacob Tonson, was genuinely affluent. In the latter years of the eighteenth century, Charles Dilly, James Dodsley and Thomas Longman II each left estates of more than £60,000. The publisher-printer William Strahan was worth nearly £100,000 at the time of his death in 1785. These men were among the first English 'media millionaires'; yet, the book trade was a risky business:

surviving records testify that for every bookseller who grew rich there were many who went bankrupt and many more still who earned a decent living, but whose prosperity was hardly noteworthy. In 1797 the typical annual income of most booksellers in London was £200–£600; in York during the same year the average assessed income of booksellers was £180. For comparison, a London glover in 1797 had a typical annual income of £120 and a silversmith could expect to make £300–£500 per annum, a draper £100–£500, a hairdresser £40–£80.

Making a Book: Who, How and How Long?

Working with a marked-up manuscript or an earlier printed edition before him, the typesetter or 'compositor' stood in front of two cases, or wooden trays, divided into many compartments with a supply of letters of the same 'sort' in each compartment. The capital letters were stored in the higher of the two cases and the small letters, more frequently used than the capitals, were located closer to the compositor below the case with the capitals, so he wouldn't have to reach so far for them. This arrangement for ergonomic efficiency is the reason why capital letters are called 'uppercase' and small letters are named 'lowercase'. Selecting the types he needed one-by-one, the compositor arranged them to spell out the words of his text – let's say a novel – in a metal holder called a 'composing stick'. He inserted one or more blank spaces between each word so that every line of type would be justified to the left and the right margins, just as this page is. When the compositor had set, or 'composed', several lines of a page, he would transfer them to an open-ended tray called a 'galley', which could hold at least a whole page of type.

Before the English engraver and type-founder William Caslon began making type according to his own designs in the 1720s, Britain could claim no typographer of real distinction. British printers in the seventeenth and early eighteenth centuries chiefly relied on types manufactured in the Low Countries. From their first appearance, however, Caslon's typefaces were highly successful: most English books produced in the second half of the eighteenth century were set in type from Caslon's foundry.

Books were not printed page by page, but on large sheets of handmade paper, typically measuring 23 × 18 in. (though sizes varied from 27.5 × 19.25 in. to 15.5 × 12.5 in.), which ordinarily had two, four, or eight pages of text arranged in a special order on each side. After printing on both sides, these sheets were subsequently folded once (to form a 'folio'), or twice (to form a 'quarto' consisting of four leaves to make eight pages), or three times (to produce an 'octavo' which has eight leaves comprising sixteen pages). These folded sheets are called 'gatherings' (or 'signatures', or 'quires'). Books were made of the different 'gatherings' assembled in the right order and sewn together. The compositor would therefore set enough pages for an entire sheet, fixing the pages of metal type for printing on each side of the sheet in a pair of iron frames. Each frame full of type, or 'forme', would then be taken to a proofing press where a trial print was made and compared to the typesetter's copy to check for errors.

Once the necessary corrections had been made, each forme was placed on a printing press, which was normally operated by two 'pressmen' – one inking the type by hand for each impression, and the other putting the paper in place, pulling the lever of the press to make the impression, and removing the paper. The two pressmen printed the one side of the sheet as many times as there were to be copies of the edition; then they changed the forme and printed the other side in the same way. Over time, the book was typeset and printed, sheet by sheet, until the whole was finished. Then, the ware-houseman collated all the sheets, making a complete set for each book. These books 'in sheets' were subsequently delivered to booksellers, taken to another workshop for binding, or moved to a warehouse where they were stored for future sale.

Even this schematic summary of typesetting and printing should make it clear that manufacturing a book in the long eighteenth century was a highly labour-intensive process. Let us imagine that we want to publish a novel, *The Adventures of Dorinda Duodecimo*, which, we may suppose, is approximately the same size as *Robinson Crusoe*. How many hours of skilled labour would be required to produce such a work *after* the author had delivered the completed manuscript to the bookseller? If we want to make a 288-page book in octavo, then we shall need 18 sheets (16 pp. $\times$ 18 = 288). Let us assume that the bookseller wants to publish *Dorinda Duodecimo* in the common edition size of 1,000 copies.

First, the text will have to be typeset. A simple calculation will indicate how much work this will entail. Our novel in octavo will have 25 lines per page; each line will consist of 50 'ens' – pieces of type the size of the letter 'n' – including blank types for spaces. Thus, each page will require 1,250 ens of type and the whole book would have roughly 360,000 ens. At a brisk work rate of 800 ens per hour, it would take 450 working hours to set the type for the novel.

If we are printing 1,000 copies of 18 sheets, then the total number of impressions will be $1,000 \times 18 \times 2$ because each sheet has to be printed on both sides. Therefore, the entire edition of the novel will require 36,000 impressions. At a work rate of 200 impressions per hour, the edition will take 180 hours to print. Because the crew con-sists of two pressmen, the total number of hours worked is 360. Therefore, account-ing for typesetting and printing alone, the employees in a print shop would have to labour for 810 (450 + 360) hours in order to produce 1,000 copies of the novel. No wonder then that compositors and pressmen did not attend to one job at a time, but worked on many jobs at once, always giving preference to jobs that would go 'stale' if they were not completed rapidly – a pamphlet on the latest bill before parliament, advertising for a play that was to open in a week's time, a satirical poem on the latest fashion at court, or even a sermon written for the season of Advent.

A substantial book of no particular urgency – a learned translation of a classical author, or a commentary on the Bible, for instance – might take eighteen months or more to produce. Of course, if a printer wanted to speed production, he could have several compositors and several crews of pressmen working on different sheets at the same time, interrupting their work when more urgent business came to the door. It was frequently the case, then, that a printing house would be working on many different jobs during the time that it would take for any single project the size of our fairly typical novel to be completed. This practice of 'concurrent printing', though it may seem chaotic to us, was a practical necessity for the master printer who needed to keep as many of his workmen as fully employed as possible while still being able to respond to the non-book 'jobbing printing' (handbills, invitations, trade cards and the like) that was an essential source of income for his business.

Our calculation to determine how many hours of labour it would take to make 1,000 copies of a novel approximately the size of *Robinson Crusoe* has yet to account for two of the most time-consuming processes necessary for book production: manufacturing the paper on which the book is to be printed, and, much later, folding and binding the printed sheets into a hardback book. Until *c.*1670 almost all the white paper used in England was imported from the continent; paper from French and Dutch mills comprised the majority of the stock used by English printers until *c.*1720. Even after English mills were producing sufficient quantities to supply domestic demand, however, the finest papers still had to be imported until the last quarter of the eighteenth century. A paper mill employing eight workers might typically make 3,000 sheets per day by hand. (Machine-made paper was an early nineteenth-century innovation.) Our novel requires 18,000 sheets or six days' production. Thus, it would require roughly 576 total hours (8 men × 12 hours/day × 6 days) to produce the paper that the printer needs for this one edition. Because binding was an entirely unmechanized process, our figure for the final stage in making a book is staggeringly high. Assuming for the sake of argument that all the copies of our novel were bound most expeditiously in economical 'trade bindings' with a minimum of decoration, then each copy would occupy about three hours to bind and the whole edition would take some 3,000 hours. Thus, to make 1,000 copies of *Dorinda Duodecimo* would require the labour of several kinds of workmen for approximately 4,400 hours.

The Financing, Advertising and Distribution of Books

Before a single copy of a new book was available for sale, the publisher had to invest a great deal of money in its production: buying paper – which in the eighteenth century accounted for 50 per cent of a book's cost – and paying typesetters (called 'compositors') and pressmen. Of course, not all the copies were sold at once, and the edition might not begin to make a profit for a year or two after it was printed. Meanwhile, other manuscripts that the bookseller would like to publish might come along, and he might wish to print new editions of slow-but-steady selling books, each time initiating the same process of heavy investment with delayed profits, straining his financial resources. If one or more of the books did not sell, debts could accumulate. Bankruptcy was common. To address this problem and to facilitate the distribution of books, booksellers frequently joined forces and divided a copy into shares: one bookseller might invest in two-fifths of a copy while three others each might pay for a one-fifth share. Income was proportionate to risk, which was distributed; each bookseller could invest in many different titles, thus diversifying his business. Moreover, the book was more likely to succeed in the market because several booksellers were actively promoting its sale in a variety of London locations. Shares in profitable copies were bought and sold by publishers, sometimes in increments as small as $\frac{1}{64}$. Cuthbert Shaw wrote in 1766 of the booksellers' share-book system: 'Associates in each cause alike they share, / Be it to print a primmer or Voltaire'. Share-books were emblematic of the way in which the eighteenth-century book trade was a fascinating mixture of financial cooperation and competition among its members. The first decades of the nineteenth century, however, witnessed a shift from shareholding arrangements to independently operating publishers with large capital resources and a growing division between wholesale and retail bookselling akin to our situation today.

Another form of financing with implications for distribution was the serial publication of books in 'parts' which began in the 1670s and grew in popularity during the first four decades of the eighteenth century. Serial publication, in which books were usually sold one sheet at a time, most commonly in weekly parts, had distinct advantages for both purchaser and publisher. The customer was able to buy on a kind of 'instalment plan' a work he almost certainly could not afford to purchase outright; the bookseller reached a broader market, received income *while* incurring production costs, could adjust the size of each print run in keeping with recent sales, and charged more per sheet than he would have when selling an ordinary book.

Authors who could not get booksellers to publish their work often resorted to private subscription to finance printing costs, a practice dating back to the mid-sixteenth century. Subscribers, whose names were listed in the front of the work, typically paid half the book's price in advance, half upon delivery of the volume. The practice was particularly popular *c.*1710 to *c.*1745. In the late seventeenth century members of the book trade began financing some of their larger books by commercial subscription – Tonson's 1688 folio *Paradise Lost* is an important early example. Subscription solved many of the problems associated with the financing, distribution and even advertising of books, but grew out of fashion as it came to be regarded as an imposition on the public. Nevertheless, both Fielding and Johnson published in this way.

How did potential customers know what was available for sale? Then, as now, many book-addicts, like Samuel Pepys, could scarcely pass a good bookshop without stopping in to see if anything caught their attention. Booksellers made 'sticking titles' by printing several hundred extra title pages which were then posted as advertisements. These title pages – which often had long descriptive titles and included the name and location of the bookseller – were sometimes called 'claps', because they were stuck (or 'clapped') on walls and on the wooden 'show-boards' and 'rubric posts' set out in front of booksellers' shops. In addition, booksellers advertised to a very promising market by listing a select inventory of their wares, often with prices, on the final pages of the books they published. *The Term Catalogues* (1668–1709) provided a quarterly listing of recently published books, though they were employed chiefly by members of the book trade, rather than the book-buying public. Edward Cave's highly successful monthly, *The Gentleman's Magazine*, founded in 1731, featured a useful list comprising many of the books published in the preceding month. Other periodicals followed suit, most notably *The London Magazine* (1732–85). Between 1773 and 1823 William Bent published a series of catalogues not unlike our *Books in Print* of today.

Advertisements in London and provincial newspapers became the most important means of reaching the reading public. By the end of the 1720s almost every sizeable provincial town had its own local weekly newspaper. Stamp Duty returns indicate that in 1750 total sales of all newspapers in England amounted to some 7.3 million, rising to more than 16 million in 1790. The mutual growth of the periodical press and of the book trade was a synergistic phenomenon. The advent of book reviews had a strong and largely salutary effect on the book trade. *The Monthly Review* (1749–1845), brainchild of the bookseller Ralph Griffiths, became the most important source of book reviews in the eighteenth century. *The Monthly*'s main competitor was *The Critical Review* (1756–90), which Tobias Smollett co-founded in 1756 and edited until 1763. Not surprisingly, reviewers were satirized almost as much as booksellers. 'Peter Pindar' (John Wolcot), for example, describes the tribe of periodical critics as practising their trade 'With hatchets, scalping knives in shape of pens, / To bid, like Mohawks, hapless authors die.'

One key to the distribution of books in London *c*.1675–1750 was the 'publisher'. When the word 'publisher' was used in this period it did not mean one who owns the legal right of reproduction and causes books to be printed and distributed for sale. 'Publishers', sometimes called 'trade publishers', functioned as retail agents for booksellers by selling books, pamphlets and newspapers. When a bookseller did not wish to be identified with what he was publishing, he sometimes used a trade publisher's name instead on the book or pamphlet. Benjamin Tooke, Jr, for example, used a trade publisher's name to distance himself – and the authorities – from Swift's authorship of *A Tale of a Tub* (1704). If no bookseller would publish a would-be author's work, it was a common practice for the writer to pay for the cost of publication and employ a trade publisher to help him sell it: 'Few of the craft [booksellers] will crowd their shelves, / With authors printing for themselves', wrote Samuel Derrick in 1742. (When Robert Dodsley refused to buy the first two volumes of *Tristram Shandy* from Laurence Sterne in 1759 for £50, the clergyman-author had them printed in York at his own expense; they sold so well that Dodsley then paid £350 to secure the copyright for the same volumes.) Sometimes booksellers put the names of one or more trade publishers next to their own names on an imprint because they wanted to advertise wider distribution for a book: Robert Dodsley added 'and sold by M. Cooper at the Globe in Pater Noster Row' to many of his own imprints because Cooper's business was near St Paul's Churchyard in the heart of the book trade, whereas his own premises 'at Tully's Head in Pall Mall' was a good walk to the west.

Below the booksellers and trade publishers in the hierarchy were two other possible links in the network of distribution: 'mercuries' who functioned like trade publishers but were not named in imprints, and 'hawkers', who cried their wares in the street and kept no shop. A pamphlet eventually sold on the street might make its way down the distribution chain from bookseller to trade publisher to mercury to hawker. Many booksellers located near St Paul's relied on trade publishers and mercuries to reach other essential London locations: most especially Temple Bar to supply the Inns of Court and the expanding areas of the metropolis to the west, and the Royal Exchange to supply the City.

The provincial trade, which became prominent only after the lapse of the Licensing Act in 1695 (see below), was primarily a distribution network for books published in London. The income of most provincial printers came chiefly from jobbing printing and newspaper work, rather than from books. Similarly, many provincial booksellers earned much of their living through the sale of stationery. Nevertheless, the dissemination of information and the distribution networks established by local newspaper proprietors and booksellers were vital for the success of the book trade in the provinces.

Edition Quantities and the Number of Editions

In the seventeenth and eighteenth centuries the great majority of editions were made in quantities ranging from 500 to 1,500 copies. Between 1738 and 1785, for example, more than 90 per cent of the books printed in William Strahan's large and successful London printing house were produced in edition sizes of less than 2,000 copies. Editions running fewer than 500 copies generally had a higher unit cost, but press runs over 2,000 most often did not sufficiently reduce the production cost of each book to justify the longer production time, increased financial risk, and the tying up of additional capital in paper and pressmen's wages that they required. A press run of 1,000 copies may be considered typical.

Smollett's controversial *Complete History of England* (1757–8), which generated enormous sales, was first published in an edition of 1,000. Thomas Lowndes, who first published Fanny Burney's *Evelina* (1778), explained to her that 500 was a typical edition size for a work of fiction. Among literary authors, only the most prominent had works printed in editions of 2,000 copies or more. The first volume of Sterne's *Tristram Shandy*, for example, was originally issued in 500 copies, but subsequent volumes of the sensationally popular work saw editions of 4,000 or more. The first two editions of Fielding's *Amelia* (1751) totalled 8,000 copies, while the print run for *Joseph Andrews* (1742) amounted to 6,500 in three editions. Burney's long-awaited *Camilla* (1797) had a first edition of 2,000 copies. These works are unusual exceptions to the general rule that it was rarely in the bookseller's financial interest to invest in a large press run.

Small, inexpensive books such as almanacs, catechisms and primers, however, were often produced in large edition sizes. From 1733 to 1748, for example, Charles Ackers printed 33 editions of Thomas Dyche's school handbook of pronunciation and spelling, *A Guide to the English Tongue* (first published in 1707), in runs ranging from 5,000 to 20,000 copies. Richard Ware, the London bookseller for whom Ackers printed the *Guide*, sold some 275,000 copies in sixteen years. Remarkably, only five of these copies in three editions are known to survive today. Although schoolbooks perish much more readily than most kinds of texts, this example should serve as a strong reminder that the number of surviving copies of a work should not ordinarily be taken as a reliable indication of its contemporary popularity. Indeed, it is often the case that deluxe editions printed in very small edition sizes – and frequently more treasured than read – survive in far greater numbers than do highly popular books that were read to pieces. Moreover, when we compare seventeenth- and eighteenth-century book advertisements and other records with modern enumerative bibliographies, it appears that, even allowing for the advertising of some books that were never actually printed, approximately 30 per cent of published seventeenth-century editions and 20 per cent of eighteenth-century editions do not survive at all. Because many works were only ever printed in a single edition, this means that our record of what was actually published from Milton to Blake is far from complete.

Edition statements on title pages – 'the ninth edition' – are not on their own reliable evidence of how well a book was selling. It was a common trick for a bookseller to take the old title page off the first or second edition of a slow-selling book and try to invigorate public interest by adding a new title page reading 'fifth edition'. Of course, such a book is not really a new edition at all, but merely a reissue: to the naïve reader, whether eighteenth-century or modern, it seems that the book is a best-seller when in fact quite the opposite is true. Booksellers also had a tendency to make sales seem more impressive by skipping numbers when counting editions. It appears that the prominent bookseller James Lackington, for example, tried to make his *Memoirs* (1791) look as if it were more popular than it actually was by publishing a 'seventh edition' immediately after the third. The actor and dramatist Susannah Centlivre pointed out a similar trick in her farce, *The Humours of Elections* (1715). Mallet, a carpenter, brags that one of his sons is

> a bookseller, a notable fellow . . . he is a kind of a Wit . . . he has an admirable knack at quacking titles . . . they tell me, when he gets an old good-for-nothing book, he claps a new title to it, and sells off the whole impression in a week. (I.ii)

It is important to remember that booksellers were not attempting to leave an accurate record for posterity; edition statements, like most other aspects of bookselling, were sometimes exploited in service of the publisher's central purpose: making money. *Caveat lector*: let the reader beware.

Book Prices, Sizes and Bindings

Books were expensive. To understand just how much books cost, consider some of the following prices of common expenditures in London. (It will be useful to recall that 12d (pence) = 1s (shilling); 20s = £1; and 21s = 1 guinea) In 1755 a chicken cost 1s

6d; in 1785 2s 3d; 'coarse beef' in 1779 sold for 3.5d per pound, salt butter 8d per pound, and coal 14d per bushel. Seven pence purchased a pound of sugar in 1779 and in 1795; a pound of good tea went for 12s. The price of a pound of wheat flour in 1786 was 1.75d. One shilling bought admission to the Vauxhall pleasure gardens, or, in 1763, to Mrs Salmon's, the best waxworks in London. An average labourer's annual rent in 1771 was £1 8s 2d with an additional charge for 'firing' (coal fires) of £1 3s 11d. Membership in a circulating library typically cost between a guinea and £2.

For most of the eighteenth century, the price of a pamphlet typically ranged between 6d and 18d (1s 6d), depending upon its length. Early in the eighteenth century most newspapers cost 1.5d (the half-penny paying for the stamp duty), though *The Spectator* sold for 2d. By the 1770s, a thrice-weekly London newspaper such as *The St James Chronicle* was 3d per number. A single play, which was almost always less than 100 pages, cost 1s 6d. Novels and collected essays were generally issued at 2s 6d per volume 'sewn' in paper wrappers and 3s in a generic, trade binding; *Clarissa* (1747–8) and *Humphry Clinker* (1771), for example, were priced in this way. Novels were usually small octavos or duodecimos. The duodecimo, in which each printed sheet was folded to make 24 pages, was highly economical – and thus the favoured format for the novel. Because the smaller page was suited to smaller type, a duodecimo might have almost as many words per page as a large octavo, allowing the bookseller to cut his paper costs considerably because the duodecimo yielded half again as many pages per sheet. Size matters. Large octavos typically cost 5s per volume, sometimes 6s or more if they were quite long. Quartos were still more expensive: Boswell's *Life of Johnson* (1791) was originally published in two quarto volumes for two guineas; the second edition in three ample octavos cost 8s per volume. The price of literature rose in the first decades of the new century: one and a half guineas bought Scott's *Marmion* (1808) in quarto; a guinea purchased Jane Austen's *Emma* (1816) in three rather slender volumes.

Books sold for approximately 2.5d per sheet in the middle decades of the eighteenth century. Naturally, booksellers manipulated the length of the works they sold – by abridging or augmenting the original text, choosing a format (e.g. quarto versus octavo), and selecting a type size – in order to make the book cheaper or more expensive according to the market they were targeting. In his novel *John Buncle* (2 vols, 1756, 1766), Thomas Amory wrote of the notoriously unprincipled bookseller Edmund Curll, 'by filling his translations with wretched notes, forged letters, and bad pictures, he raised the price of a four shilling book to ten'. In contrast, the author of *The London Jilt: or, The Politick Whore* (1683) observed that:

> People now must be very careful that books be not above nine or ten sheets in bulk, [so] that the haunters of taverns and bawdy houses may, by absenting themselves from such places for an evening or two, employ their money to the profit of the bookseller.

As this remark testifies, the printed word had to compete commercially against other forms of entertainment.

The size of books changed considerably from Milton to Blake. Folios (the largest books in which the sheet is folded just once to make two leaves or four pages), which were the proper dress of serious literature until the early 1740s, came to be used primarily for large works of reference – the *Biographia Britannica* (1747–66), or Johnson's *Dictionary* (1755) – or for texts featuring important engravings such as the publisher John Boydell's *Poetical Works of John Milton* (1794–7), and his *Collection of Prints . . . Illustrating the Dramatic Works of Shakespeare* (1803). When Boswell suggested to Malone in 1790 that his great biography be printed in folio, his friend replied that he 'might as well throw it in the Thames, for a folio would not now be read'. Quartos became the most common format for substantial literary works other than novels, though popular quartos were frequently reprinted in less expensive octavo editions to boost sales. Duodecimos became increasingly common as booksellers sought to exploit the demand for more economical books.

Until the 1820s, most books were not offered for sale uniformly bound. A book could be bought in a plain and inexpensive generic 'trade binding' of undecorated brown calf or sheep leather, or it could be purchased entirely unbound 'in sheets', 'sewed', or bound but uncut and undecorated 'in boards'. It would then be taken to a binder who worked independently of the bookseller to be custom-bound in conformity with the owner's particular tastes. The 'forwarder' created the basic binding before the 'finisher' added decoration. A character in Wycherley's *The Plain-Dealer* (1677) makes the common charge that a gentleman's library has been bought merely for ornament: 'your bookseller is properly your upholsterer, / for he furnishes your room, rather than your head'. *Art and Nature* (1738) a comedy by James Miller, takes this commonplace to its logical end: it features a bookseller whose principal business is now selling replicas of the classics 'in wood'. 'My joiner's hard at work', he explains, 'and I have a new edition of 'em coming out shortly – Here is a complete set . . . and as good timber as ever was cut.'

'Edition binding', the uniform binding and covering of an entire edition according to the specifications of the bookseller, made its first appearance in England on a grand scale in the 1760s, when the highly entrepreneurial printer and children's bookseller John Newbery of London sold thousands of books for the juvenile market ready bound in standardized inexpensive covers that were one-quarter leather (the spine) and three-quarters decorated paper boards (the sides). The first decades of the nineteenth century saw important changes in book binding, most notably, the partial mechanization of the binding process and the introduction of the prefabricated 'cloth case' resulting in the widespread introduction of edition bindings in 'publisher's cloth' much like hardbound books of today.

Censorship, Copyright and Regulation of the Trade

The Stationers' Company, granted its royal charter in 1557, played a major role in the conduct of the book trade during the seventeenth and eighteenth centuries. The relationship between the government and the Company, though at times strained, was chiefly symbiotic. The state's interest was political; the Stationers' was financial. Royal patents granted by the Crown in the sixteenth and seventeenth centuries gave members of the Stationers' Company exclusive licence to produce and distribute many of the most popular books in the kingdom, such as the *ABC*, *Catechism*, *Psalms* and almanacs. (This last category was highly remunerative: in the first decade of the eighteenth century almanac sales in Britain were generating some £1,500 in profits each year.) These lucrative patents for perennial sellers became known as the English Stock. Members of the Company were given opportunities, in accordance with their status and seniority, to buy ever larger shares in the Stock – which regularly paid a remarkably high annual dividend exceeding 12 per cent per annum. The English Stock was the financial backbone of the Stationers, not only because of the revenues it generated for its owners, but also because the Company was able to apportion out lucrative contracts to fellow Stationers for the production of these books.

The Stationers' Company was in some respects a government-authorized cartel that limited competition and fostered cooperation among its members, who had strong financial incentives for remaining in the Company. Moreover, many of the government measures to control the press were strongly supported by the Company because they made 'piracy', the unauthorized publishing of a copy held by another, less likely and furthered the Stationers' own business interests. The strictures of the 1662 Licensing Act, for example – limiting the number of apprentices, master printers, and presses, and restricting printing to London, the universities of Oxford and Cambridge, and to York – were beneficial for many of those already well established in the trade. On the other hand the Company was accountable to the authorities for the conduct of the book trade and therefore policed the production and distribution of printed matter in accord with government and Company regulations. The Stationers made it much easier for the state to control the production of print and to discipline those who were in breach of the law. Nevertheless, the censorship of books, either pre- or post-publication, was only fitfully effective in seventeenth- and eighteenth-century England; commercial motives appear repeatedly to have compromised official suppression. James Bramaston's observation in *The Man of Taste* (1733) is telling:

> But to give merit due, though Curll's the fame,
> Are not his brother-booksellers the same?
> Can statutes keep the British press in awe,
> While that sells best, that's most against the Law?

Newspapers, however, were far more susceptible to government censorship and there are many recorded instances of successful state intervention. Moreover, the stamp duties, first imposed on all newspapers in 1712 and remaining in effect throughout the century, were occasionally manipulated to keep periodicals out of the hands of the lower classes and thus sometimes acted as a *de facto* form of censorship.

Unlike the vast majority of statute and common law, the Seditious Societies Act of 1799, passed to suppress those in sympathy with revolutionary France, was highly successful in controlling not only newspapers, but the circulation of books and pamphlets as well. Common law regarding three kinds of libel – obscenity, blasphemy, and sedition – was sometimes used to mete out post-publication penalties and made for famous, if relatively rare, court cases: Edmund Curll, for example, was convicted of obscene libel in 1728 for publishing pornography; Thomas Woolston was successfully prosecuted for blasphemous libel in 1729 for his highly satirical *Discourses on the Miracles of Our Saviour* (1727–9); and in 1764 John Wilkes was found guilty of seditious libel for 'no. 45' of the *North Briton*, which assailed the king.

The widespread notion that the lapse of licensing in 1641 resulted in an explosion of print shows how appearances can be deceiving. Certainly, the number of extant titles increases markedly in 1642, but the total number of sheets printed remains virtually the same. Parliament re-instituted pre-publication licensing in June 1643. Milton's *Areopagitica* (1644), which did not appear until seventeen months afterwards, probably has more to do with the state's reaction against his divorce pamphlets than with the defence of an entirely unlicensed press, as is commonly supposed. Pre-publication censorship in England had perhaps never been greater than under Cromwell and his Commonwealth government, which in 1655 silenced all unofficial periodicals. One of the licensers of the press in 1651–2 was Milton himself.

The Licensing Act of 1662 gave regulatory powers both to the Stationers' Company and to the 'Surveyor of the Imprimery and Printing Presses', a post long occupied by Sir Roger L'Estrange, a pioneering journalist, but no advocate for freedom of the press, and no friend of the Stationers. After 1679 the press was controlled under common law until 1685, when the Licensing Act was renewed until 1694. With the lapse of the Act in 1695 the pre-publication censorship of print in England effectively ended. Although there was still much progress to be made in press freedoms, England had the most liberal policy in eighteenth-century Europe. Though the aim of the Licensing Act was control of the press, it had the additional effect of protecting copyrights since it required the recording of copy ownership in the Stationers' Register. After its lapse, the booksellers lobbied parliament for a new Bill that would once again safeguard their copies.

The 'Act for the Encouragement of Learning' which came into effect in 1710 gave non-renewable protection against piracy to current copy holders for 21 years, and entitled the owner of a new copy to legal redress against infringement for 14 years – and for an additional 14 if he were still alive at the end of the first period. As before, copies had to be entered in the Stationers' Register for proof of ownership. Safeguarding against continental, Scottish and even English piracy was vital for the stability of the Stationer's business, though Fielding's remark in *The Author's Farce* (1730), that '*Grub-Street* harbours as many Pirates as ever *Algiers* did' (III.i), should not be taken seriously. Because the Act did not extend to Ireland, however, Dublin conducted a lively trade in reprints of London publications; these so-called 'moral piracies' were not illegal unless they were offered for sale in England, Scotland or Wales.

Even after a copyright had expired under the 1710 Act, however, mainstream members of the book trade continued to behave as if copyright were perpetual by respecting it as the 'owner's' property and, where appropriate, even buying and selling shares in the copy. The Edinburgh bookseller Alexander Donaldson mounted a legal challenge to the idea of perpetual copyright by publishing and selling in London reprints of works which the London booksellers believed they still owned by virtue of common law, even though the copyrights had expired and were now in the public domain. In *Donaldson* v. *Becket*, the Lords ruled that copyright was not perpetual. Although some booksellers continued to buy and sell old copies, the book trade was compelled to abandon its conservative strategy of concentrating on reprints of long-standing best-sellers and direct its energies instead to discovering, publishing and marketing new books.

The era from Milton to Blake saw England became a culture in which print grew to be indispensable for the conduct of everyday affairs. Inextricably linked to the business of books, literature developed into a form of popular entertainment as never before. Astute students of the period will bear in mind that the book trade was not merely a servant, but a critical and creative agent in the production, distribution and consumption of English literature.

REFERENCES AND FURTHER READING

Belanger, Terry (1977). 'A directory of the London book trade, 1766'. *Publishing History* 1, 7–48.

Blagden, Cyprian (1960). *The Stationers' Company: A History, 1403–1959*. London: George Allen and Unwin Ltd.

Bracken, James K. and Joel Silver, eds (1995). *The British Literary Book Trade, 1700–1820. Dictionary of Literary Biography*. Vol. 154. Detroit: Gale Research Inc.

——(1996). *The British Literary Book Trade, 1475–1700. Dictionary of Literary Biography*. Vol. 170. Detroit: Gale Research Inc.

Darnton, Robert (1990). 'What is the history of books?' In *The Kiss of Lamourette*. Ed. Robert Darnton. London: Faber and Faber, 107–35.

Feather, John (1985). *The Provincial Book Trade in Eighteenth-century England*. Cambridge: Cambridge University Press.

——(1988). *A History of British Publishing*. London: Routledge.

Fergus, Jan (1984). 'Eighteenth-century readers in provincial England: the customers of Samuel Clay's circulating library and bookshop in Warwick, 1770–72'. *Papers of the Bibliographical Society of America* 78, 155–213.

Foxon, David (1991). *Pope and the Early Eighteenth-century Book Trade*. Rev. and ed. James McLaverty. Oxford: Clarendon.

Gaskell, Philip (1985). *A New Introduction to Bibliography*. Oxford: Clarendon.

Hodgson, Norma and Cyprian Blagden, eds (1956). *The Notebook of Thomas Bennet and Henry Clements (1686–1718)*. Oxford Bibliographical Society Publications n.s. 6. Oxford: Oxford University Press.

Maslen, Keith (1993). *An Early London Printing House at Work: Studies in the Bowyer Ledgers*. New York: The Bibliographical Society of America.

McKenzie, D. F. (1974). 'The London book trade in 1668'. *Words: Wai-Te-Ata Studies in Literature* 4, 75–92.

——(1988). 'The London book trade in 1644'. In *Bibliographia: Lectures 1975–1988 by Recipients of the Marc Fitch Prize for Bibliography*. Ed. John Horden. Oxford: Leopard's Head Press, 130–52.

——(1998). 'Trading places? England 1689–France 1789'. In *The Darnton Debate:*

Books and Revolution in the Eighteenth Century. Ed. Hayden T. Mason. Oxford: Voltaire Foundation, 1–24.

All three of the above are in D. F. McKenzie (2001). *Making Meaning: Printers of the Mind and Other Essays*. Ed. Peter D. McDonald and Michael F. Suarez. Boston: University of Massachusetts Press.

Raven, James (1992). *Judging New Wealth: Popular Publishing and Responses to Commerce in England, 1750–1800*. Oxford: Clarendon.

——(1996). 'From promotion to proscription: arrangements for reading and eighteenth-century libraries.' In *The Practice and Representation of Reading in England*. Ed. James Raven, Helen Small and Naomi Taylor. Cambridge: Cambridge University Press, 175–201.

Rivers, Isabel, ed. (1982). *Books and their Readers in Eighteenth-century England*. Leicester: Leicester University Press.

——(2001). *Books and their Readers in Eighteenth-century England: New Essays*. Leicester: Leicester University Press.

Rose, Mark (1993). *Authors and Owners: The Invention of Copyright*. Cambridge, Mass.: Harvard University Press.

Tierney, James E. (1988). *The Correspondence of Robert Dodsley, 1733–1764*. Cambridge: Cambridge University Press.

Treadwell, Michael (1989). 'The English Book Trade.' In *The Age of William III & Mary II: Power, Politics, and Patronage 1688–1702*. Ed. Robert P. Maccubin and Martha Hamilton-Phillips. Williamsburg: The College of William and Mary in Virginia, 358–65.

——(1996). '1695–1995: some tercentenary thoughts on the freedoms of the press'. *Harvard Library Bulletin* 7, 3–19.

Zachs, William (1998). *The First John Murray and the Late Eighteenth-century London Book Trade*. London: Oxford University Press for the British Academy.

PART TWO
Readings

9

John Milton, *Areopagitica*

Martin Dzelzainis

I

Commentators have increasingly converged in their accounts of the literary strategy of *Areopagitica; A Speech of Mr John Milton for the Liberty of Vnlicenc'd Printing, To the Parlament of England* (November 1644). Its potency, they agree, stems from Milton's constant disruption of his own lines of argument, his own sequences of images, and his own rhetorical forms (see Fish, 1988; Cable, 1995, 117–43; Norbrook, 1999, 118–39). But at the same time they have increasingly diverged in their accounts of the tract's ideological identity to the extent that it is now cited in support of flatly opposed positions. Thus a recent textbook on *Free Speech* claims that John Stuart Mill's argument in *On Liberty* (1859) merely 'follows the broad outlines' of *Areopagitica*, as demonstrated by a series of parallel extracts (Haworth, 1998, 120, 224–8; see also Cable, 1995, 129–35). By contrast, Stanley Fish maintains that Milton 'has almost no interest at all in the "freedom of the press"' and even that he 'does not unambiguously value freedom at all' (Fish, 1988, 235). Milton's alleged denial of free speech then becomes the springboard for the yet more startling proposition that 'There's no such thing as free speech, and it's a good thing, too' (Fish, 1994, 102–19). The reason for this lack of consensus is that *Areopagitica*, widely regarded as one of the constitutive texts of modern liberalism, has become a contested site in a larger dispute about liberal values. This essay outlines the more controversial features of the work and then proposes an alternative, republican reading.

II

Half way through *Areopagitica*, Milton changes the angle of his attack on the Licensing Order of June 1643 from 'the no good it can do, to the manifest hurt it causes' (Milton, 1953–82, 2, 530; edition henceforth cited by volume and page number). He focuses on the figure of the licenser, without whose prior consent, according to the Order, no 'Book, Pamphlet, or paper, shall from henceforth be printed, bound, stitched or put to sale' (2, 797). However, Milton complains,

> I know nothing of the licencer but that I have his own hand here for his arrogance; who shall warrant me his judgement? The State Sir, replies the Stationer, but has a quick return, The State shall be my governours, but not my criticks. (2, 533–4)

Milton sometimes refers to critics and criticism in the narrow sense, as when he scorns 'the worme of *Criticisme*' in one pedantic opponent, or mocks *Eikon Basilike* for the 'petty glosses and conceits' yielded by its 'criticism' of divine judgements (1, 916–17; 3, 430). But here Milton is not thinking of critics as commentators upon what is written but as those who choose what is to be read. They are like the connoisseurs of sin who scan 'heathen Writers' on behalf of others and

> instill the poison they suck, first into the Courts of Princes, acquainting them with the choisest delights, and criticisms of sin. As perhaps did that *Petronius* whom *Nero* call'd his *Arbiter*, the Master of his revels; and that notorious ribald of *Arezzo*, dreaded, and yet dear to the Italian Courtiers. (2, 518)

The message of Milton's epigrammatic 'return' to the stationer is thus that those who govern the state will be exceeding their powers if they arrogate to themselves choices 'wherein every mature man might . . . exercise his own leading capacity' (2, 513).

Nevertheless, this attempt to differentiate between governors and critics may appear little better than a verbal sleight of hand. After all, what are our governors for if not to make choices on our behalf? The difficulty deepens when we recall a passage near the start of *Areopagitica*.

> I deny not, but that it is of greatest concernment in the Church and Commonwealth, to have a vigilant eye how Bookes demeane themselves, as well as men; and thereafter to confine, imprison, and do sharpest justice on them as malefactors. (2, 492)

So books as such are not beyond the scope of state surveillance, in which case Milton appears to be asserting simultaneously that the state can and cannot interfere with them, arousing suspicion in turn that the distinction between governors and critics is merely a form of words devised to cover his confusion.

More notorious still is the passage in the peroration that affirms the principle of toleration only to modulate into something harsher:

> if all cannot be of one mind, as who looks they should be? this doubtles is more wholsome, more prudent, and more Christian that many be tolerated, rather then all compell'd. I mean not tolerated Popery, and open superstition, which as it extirpats all religions and civill supremacies, so it self should be extirpat, provided first that all charitable and compassionat means be us'd to win and regain the weak and the misled. (2, 565)

It might be pleaded that Milton is one of many seventeenth-century figures, like John Locke, who argued for toleration but excluded Roman Catholics (see now Coffey, 1998). Furthermore, Milton's expressions appear no more violent than those of Roger Williams, who famously *did* extend toleration to Catholics in his *Bloudy Tenent of Persecution* (1644). For while Williams thinks they should be tolerated, this does not mean, as we might expect, that they are 'to be let alone'. On the contrary, such 'Antichristian idolaters' ought to be 'spiritually stoned to death' (Woodhouse, 1974, 269–70). Even so, there seems no escaping the fact that Milton floats a distinction between governors and critics that he either forgets or disregards.

This crux has become a standard feature of commentaries. David Masson set the pattern when he memorably remarked that *Areopagitica* was a work which 'bites into modern interests and the constitution of the modern intellect' – despite the fact that 'in his theory of Toleration, Milton was decidedly behind some of his contemporaries' (Masson, 1859–94, 4, 288, 302). Likewise, for Catherine Belsey, *Areopagitica* is 'one of the founding and canonical texts of modern liberalism' – even though it offers a 'rather authoritarian version of liberalism' (Belsey, 1988, 77–8). As 'Milton's most inarguably liberal pamphlet', it looms large in Annabel Patterson's account of *Early Modern Liberalism* – notwithstanding 'the exceptions he granted to the ideal of toleration' (Patterson, 1997, 23, 64). Similarly, for Barbara Lewalski its arguments 'have become a cornerstone in the liberal defense of freedom of speech, press and thought' – albeit 'critics have properly taken note' of their qualified nature (Lewalski, 1998, 64). They all insist, that is, on the integrity of Milton's professions of liberal principle while acknowledging that there are exceptions at odds with what he professes – and leave it at that, tacitly conceding that *Areopagitica* 'lacks conceptual coherence' (though, according to Thomas Corns, it is not unique in this respect since it is always a mistake 'to look for philosophical coherence in Milton's controversial prose') (Dobranski, 1998, 146; Corns, 1992, 56).

Others, however, foreground the exceptions in the hope of exposing the emptiness of Milton's professions. Fish welcomes the 'tensions and discontinuities' precisely because they disrupt what is otherwise taken for 'the steady unfolding of a classic liberal vision' (Fish, 1988, 248). Willmoore Kendall argues that we will have 'learned to read the *Areopagitica* only when we can read this passage [about popery] and *not* find in it any inconsistency'. What we must realize is that *Areopagitica*, despite its 'intoxicating rhetoric' of freedom, actually belongs to 'a realm of discourse entirely different from Mill's' and that 'its rightful place' is 'among the political treatises we have all been brought up to deplore' which *oppose* freedom of thought and speech (Kendall, 1960, 440, 446, 453, 461n.). For John Illo too the 'torrential majesty of Milton's prose' and 'the grand libertarian generalities' impede our understanding of *Areopagitica*, which has consistently been read – or rather misread – as if it were the work 'of a Jefferson, not of a Robespierre', whereas the truth is that it was 'not liberal or libertarian even in its own time, but a militant and exclusivist revolutionary pamphlet' (Illo, 1972, 186, 187, 189).

These commentators in short offer a choice between, on the one hand, a tract that is liberal but conceptually incoherent and, on the other, one whose rhetoric of freedom is disconnected from its actually illiberal tendencies. But whichever version you choose, *Areopagitica* is radically inconsistent.

III

My aim is to pick a different route through these issues, guided by the recent work of Philip Pettit and Quentin Skinner on the 'republican' (or, as Skinner prefers to term it, 'neo-roman') theory of freedom which challenges the view of liberty, dominant since the late eighteenth century, as something to be understood purely negatively in terms of the absence of interference or coercion. As Isaiah Berlin, the most influential recent spokesman for the negative concept, puts it, 'being free' is a matter of 'not being interfered with by others. The wider the area of non-interference the wider my freedom'. Liberty is the space within which we are not answerable to others, and, for the purpose of maximizing this space, what matters is not by whom but how much we are governed. Berlin's survey of the extent to which various regimes interfere with us leads him to conclude that liberty 'is not incompatible with some kinds of autocracy, or at any rate with the absence of self-government' since 'it is perfectly conceivable that a liberal-minded despot would allow his subjects a large measure of personal freedom'. This is, moreover, not some hypothesis entertained for the sake of argument but a description of the near-ideal state of affairs that existed in eighteenth-century Prussia or Austria (Berlin, 1969, 123, 129 and n.).

In undoing this knot of liberal beliefs, Pettit and Skinner appeal to several early modern writers – including Milton – who represent a rival tradition of thinking about liberty. Three of the arguments singled out from this tradition are especially relevant to *Areopagitica*. The first is that while the theorists of negative liberty are right in claiming that our liberty will be diminished to the extent that we are interfered with or coerced, this is not the only way in which we can become unfree. We also forfeit our liberty whenever we find ourselves dependent on the goodwill of others for the continued enjoyment of our rights. For even if we are, as it happens, subject to a liberal-minded despot who allows us a large measure of personal freedom, we nevertheless have to live with, and will be constrained in our behaviour by, the danger that this measure of freedom can be taken away at any time. As Skinner remarks, 'it is the mere possibility of your being subjected with impunity to arbitrary coercion, not the fact of your being coerced, that takes away your liberty and reduces you to the condition of a slave' (Skinner, 1998, 72). Accordingly, we can now see that the reason why Milton objects so strongly to the system of pre-publication censorship is that it leaves the author's freedom to publish wholly at the discretion of the licenser. How that discretion happens to be exercised is beside the point. While it is of course deplorable if your work is interfered with, you are no better off if your licenser turns out to be liberal-minded and declines to change one iota of your text because the fact that you are dependent on the will of others, even if they show no inclination at present to exert their powers and may never do so, is enough in and of itself to render you unfree.

Milton's convictions on the topic of freedom and unfreedom were shaped by his reading of Roman law in the early 1640s. The Commonplace book has several entries from Justinian's *Institutes* on 'what lawyers declare concerning liberty and slavery' (1, 470). Just as in the Roman law of persons children and slaves are unfree by virtue of being subject to the will of others (see Skinner, 1998, 40–1), so, according to Milton in *Areopagitica*, to be required to conform to the Licensing Order is to be treated as a child or slave without a will of your own and, in consequence, to be unfree. Even though God did not intend man to be 'captivat under a perpetuall childhood of prescription', Milton observes, those in favour of licensing do not 'count him fit to print his mind without a tutor and examiner' (2, 514, 531). But in this case,

> What advantage is it to be a man over it is to be a boy at school, if we have only scapt the ferular, to come under the fescu of an *Imprimatur*? if serious and elaborat writings, as if they were no more then the theam of a Grammar lad under his Pedagogue must not be utter'd without the cursory eyes of a temporizing and extemporizing licenser. (2, 531)

The author is forced to 'appear in Print like a punie with his guardian'. Nor can any serious reader respect writings produced 'under the tuition, under the correction of his patriarchal licencer' or published 'under the wardship of an overseeing fist'. What the Licensing Order systematically brings about therefore is the infantilization of the author, leaving him in a condition of legal disability which is nothing short of 'servitude like that impos'd by the Philistims', an 'undeserved thraldom upon learning' and a 'second tyranny over' it (2, 532, 533, 536, 539).

The second of the arguments highlighted by Pettit and Skinner concerns law and coercion. This is a topic that those for whom liberty is nothing other than non-interference can exhaust in a few equations. Since all laws are coercive, and since freedom consists in the absence of coercion, freedom is that space upon which the laws have not encroached. And since empty space is empty space wherever you are, the liberty of the subject will not vary from regime to regime, as Hobbes famously insisted: 'Whether a Common-Wealth be Monarchical, or Popular, the Freedome is still the same' (Hobbes, 1996, 149). The reply to Hobbes, as to Berlin earlier, is that in order to remain free it is not enough to avoid being coerced; we must also avoid being dominated by those with arbitrary (even if unexercised) powers. However, this is not quite the last word for, according to Pettit, just as there can be domination without interference (as in the case of the liberal-minded despot), so there can be interference without domination. This is because domination and interference are 'different evils'; whereas the former 'requires only that someone have the capacity to interfere arbitrarily', the latter 'need not involve the exercise of a capacity for arbitrary interference, only the exercise of a much more constrained ability'. The upshot is that 'you can be interfered with by some agency, as in the case of subjection to a suitable form of law and government, without being dominated by anyone' (Pettit, 1997, 23, 80).

This view of state interference as a relatively benign phenomenon helps to make sense of Milton's insistence that the state is properly concerned with 'how bookes demeane themselves'. All the forms of state coercion that Milton is prepared to countenance in fact involve the due process of law and are therefore non-arbitrary. The point of keeping 'a vigilant eye' on books after they have been published is to do 'justice on them as malefactors'. Anyone who publishes their work freely does so 'standing to the hazard of law and penalty' (Milton 2, 492, 531). And when it comes to 'regulating the Press', the most Milton will endorse is the minimal Order of January 1642 which, he reports, required

> that no book be Printed, unlesse the Printers and the Authors name, or at least the Printers be register'd. Those which otherwise come forth, if they be found mischievous and libellous, the fire and the executioner will be the timeliest and most effectuall remedy. (2, 569)

While this sounds draconian, no book would be burnt unless guilty of infractions of the 1642 Order *and* of the existing laws of sedition and libel. As Pettit remarks, 'provided that it is not arbitrary, state interference will not count as a serious loss – as a way of compromising liberty – in the republican's book' (Pettit, 1997, 76n.). Nor does it in Milton's.

The third and final aspect of the republican or neo-roman tradition is statecraft in the literal sense of shaping the state around ideals and values. Here Pettit outlines two possible strategies; the 'first is that the value or good or ideal should serve as a goal for the state to promote, the second that it should serve as a constraint on how the state is to pursue other goals' (Pettit, 1997, 97). So if a state values peace and wishes to promote it, then there are times when the pursuit of this objective may entail going to war. But if peace serves as a constraint, then the state will honour this by behaving peaceably in all its dealings, and will avoid war, even – or especially – war waged in the name of peace.

The classic text in which these statebuilding strategies are played out in tandem is More's *Utopia*. Treating values as constraints to which every part of utopian society must bear witness is what generates much of the fascinating detail in the description of the utopian commonwealth. At times, however, the utopians adopt a consequentialist attitude, promoting their values by whatever means are necessary. Thus they despise war but are ruthless military tacticians. Such paradoxes are, however, a regular feature of the republican tradition. For Machiavelli, freedom is a goal, not a constraint, and, rather than allow citizens who have become corrupt to lose their liberty, he takes the strongly consequentialist line that they must be forced to be free by being coerced into virtue (see Skinner, 1993, 304–6). And, on the eve of the Restoration, it is the line Milton takes in *The Readie and Easie Way* when arguing that it is 'just' for 'a less number [to] compell a greater to retain, which can be no wrong to them, thir libertie' (7, 455). This has been deplored as 'a terrible argument' (7, 212), but it has some claim to be regarded as one of the most characteristically republican utterances in Milton's most republican treatise.

The distinction between goals and constraints helps to explain the charges of conceptual incoherence levelled against *Areopagitica*. For what these assume is that the freedom of speech features in Milton's account of the public sphere not as a goal which the state is to promote but as a constraint by which the state is bound in all its dealings. On this view, nothing that the state does should derogate from, or fail to bear witness to, the ideal of freedom of speech. So when Milton endorses prosecutions for sedition and libel or condones book burning he has evidently forgotten the premise on which his argument is (supposedly) based. But not only does he show no interest in fetishizing freedom of speech, as these commentators require, he also goes out of his way to dismiss statebuilding exercises as such. Plato merely 'fed his fancie with making many edicts to his ayrie Burgomasters' while 'To sequester out of the world into *Atlantick* and *Eutopian* polities, which never can be drawn into use, will not mend our condition' (2, 522, 526). The hostility to mere paper consistency is all of a piece with his consequentialist attitude to the freedom of speech, which the state should promote by whatever means, even if, on occasion, this means suppressing speech (a similar argument applies to the denial of liberty of conscience to Catholics).

My conclusion is that many of our current difficulties with *Areopagitica* are self-created. They arise from a propensity to assess Milton's text in terms of inappropriate, because anachronistic, categories and concepts. One such is negative liberty when, as far as I can see, it is impossible to produce a consistent reading of *Areopagitica* solely in terms of the concept, at least as Hobbes or Mill or Berlin understood it. The republican or neo-roman theory of freedom appears to do much better by the work, above all in effecting a reconciliation between Milton's rhetoric of freedom and the degree of state coercion that he countenances. The slogan 'interference without domination' seems a fair modern rendition of 'The State shall be my governors, but not my criticks'.

REFERENCES AND FURTHER READING

Belsey, Catherine (1988). *John Milton: Language, Gender, Power*. Oxford: Basil Blackwell.

Berlin, Isaiah (1969). *Four Essays on Liberty*. Oxford: Oxford University Press.

Cable, Lana (1995). *Carnal Rhetoric: Milton's Iconoclasm and the Poetics of Desire*. Durham, N.C.: Duke University Press.

Coffey, John (1998). 'Puritanism and liberty revisited: the case for toleration in the English Revolution'. *Historical Journal* 41, 961–85.

Corns, Thomas N. (1992). *Uncloistered Virtue: English Political Literature 1640–1660*. Oxford: Clarendon.

Dobranski, Stephen B. (1998). 'Licensing Milton's heresy'. In *Milton and Heresy*. Ed. Stephen B. Dobranski and John P. Rumrich. Cambridge: Cambridge University Press, 139–58.

Fish, Stanley (1988). 'Driving from the letter: truth and indeterminacy in Milton's *Areopagitica*'. In *Re-membering Milton: Essays on the Texts and Traditions*. Ed. Mary Nyquist and Margaret W. Ferguson. New York and London: Methuen.

——(1994). *There's No Such Thing as Free Speech, and It's a Good Thing, Too*. Oxford: Oxford University Press.

Haworth, Alan (1998). *Free Speech*. London and New York: Routledge.

Hobbes, Thomas (1996). *Leviathan*. Ed. Richard Tuck. Cambridge: Cambridge University Press.

Illo, John (1972). 'The misreading of Milton's *Areopagitica*'. In *Radical Perspectives in the Arts*. Ed. Lee Baxandall. Harmondsworth: Penguin, 179–92.

——(1988). 'Areopagiticas mythic and real'. *Prose Studies* 11, 3–23.

——(1992). 'Euripides, Milton and Thomas Cooper'. *Milton Quarterly* 26, 81–4.

Kendall, Willmoore (1960). 'How to read Milton's *Areopagitica*'. *Journal of Politics* 22, 439–73.

Lewalski, Barbara K. (1998). 'How radical was the young Milton?'. In *Milton and Heresy*. Ed. Stephen B. Dobranski and John P. Rumrich. Cambridge: Cambridge University Press, 49–72.

Masson, David (1859–94). *The Life of John Milton: Narrated in Connexion with the Political, Ecclesiastical, and Literary History of His Time*. 7 vols. London.

Milton, John (1953–82). *Complete Prose Works of John Milton*. Ed. Don M. Wolfe et al. 8 vols. New Haven: Yale University Press.

Norbrook, David (1999). *Writing the English Republic: Poetry, Rhetoric and Politics 1627–1660*. Cambridge: Cambridge University Press.

Patterson, Annabel (1997). *Early Modern Liberalism*. Cambridge: Cambridge University Press.

Pettit, Philip (1997). *Republicanism: A Theory of Freedom and Government*. Oxford: Clarendon Press.

Skinner, Quentin (1993). 'The republican ideal of political liberty'. In *Machiavelli and Republicanism*. Ed. Gisela Bock, Quentin Skinner and Maurizio Viroli. Cambridge: Cambridge University Press, 293–309.

——(1998). *Liberty before Liberalism*. Cambridge: Cambridge University Press.

Woodhouse, A. S. P. (1974). *Puritanism and Liberty: Being the Army Debates (1647–9) from the Clarke Manuscripts with Supplementary Documents*. London: J. M. Dent and Sons Ltd.

10

Robert Herrick, *Hesperides*

Peter Davidson

The 1648 *Hesperides* (in fact two collections published together: the *Hesperides* themselves and a shorter collection of sacred poems, *His Noble Numbers*) seems to be on the
point of vanishing from the canon of seventeenth-century poetry as it is now studied.
Our chief source for the text of Herrick's poems is the *Hesperides* or, to give them their
full title, *Hesperides: or, the works both humane & divine of Robert Herrick Esq*. There are
very few of his authentic poems which are not contained in this one book. We have
every reason to believe that this book (published when the poet was in his fifties)
represents his poems as he wished to see them presented, ordered and laid out. The
clumsily engraved frontispiece, showing Herrick's bust on a monument in front of a
landscape of Parnassus, the hill of the Muses, with the winged horse Pegasus spring-
ing skywards, is an early-modern imagination of an ancient Mediterranean landscape
which succeeds in looking very English. Ill-drawn cherubs dance in a circle in the
middle distance as though they performed a Devonian country dance; two hovering
cherubs carry laurels and scatter flowers. On the pedestal which supports Herrick's
bust, Latin verses praise his mingling of the ancient with the new and the smooth
elegance of his poetic style.

This engraving expresses clearly enough Herrick's intentions for his works: they
are to be elegant within the contemporary definition of elegance and with constant
reference to the Greece and Italy of antiquity. These are the avowed intentions of
almost any poet who came to maturity in the first quarter of the seventeenth century.
The respect for classical antiquity and the immersion in the poetry of Horace and
Ovid in particular, can, obviously, be traced to the titanic classicizing and didactic
figure of Ben Jonson, under whose poetic tutelage Herrick is proud to place himself,
playing dangerously as he does so with the meaning of 'old *religion*' as an acknowledgement of Jonson's intermittent recusancy:

> When I a verse shall make,
> Know I have praid thee,

For old *Religions* sake,
Saint *Ben* to aide me.
Make the way smooth for me,
When I, thy *Herrick*,
Honouring thee, on my knee
Offer my *Lyrick*.

    (*Poems*, ed. L. C. Martin,
    Oxford Standard Authors,
      1965 reprints, 212–13)

Herrick's own description of his intentions in his collection, 'The Argument of his Book' combines with the frontispiece to place Herrick's work in a mode which might be called, in brief, 'antiquarian pastoral'. This 'Argument' is often quoted, as though the summary which it offers is virtually a substitute for reading the works themselves. Apart from the last couplet, the whole argument tends towards limiting the scope of Herrick's work to the rural margins of England. This, combined with the fact of his having been a provincial clergyman, provides a fatally easy opening for sentimental characterization of his work as itself a safe part of 'rural heritage' in all its vagueness.

I sing of *Brooks*, of *Blossoms*, *Birds*, and of *Bowers*:
Of *April*, *May*, of *June*, and *July*-Flowers.
I sing of *May-poles*, *Hock-carts*, *Wassails*, *Wakes*,
Of *Bride-grooms*, *Brides*, and of their *Bridall-cakes* . . .
I write of *Groves*, of *Twilights*, and I sing
The Court of *Mab*, and of the *Fairie-King*.
I write of *Hell*; I sing (and ever shall)
Of *Heaven*, and hope to have it after all.

                    (5)

It must be conceded that Herrick succeeds almost completely in his intentions, too completely for his work to offer any familiar points of contact to a modern reader who is more at ease with the problematic or fragmentary work than with the impermeable surface of Latinate poetry in the tradition of Ben Jonson. This poetic which Herrick inherited from Jonson offers in one sense no difficulties of interpretation in that it concentrates so much on the presentation of a flawless surface, and therefore on transparency of statement. In another sense this type of early-modern writing is insuperably remote from a modern reader when presented, as in the *Hesperides*, in a meditated collection arranged by its author in accordance with a poetic taste which itself can only be recovered by complex acts of historical imagination.

    Indeed, there is no canon of early-modern poetry less fragmentary than Herrick's, and this itself is part of the difficulty of making a reading of his work. It is the experience of many scholars of Caroline poetry to come across poems from the *Hesperides* out of context, perhaps in a manuscript collection of poetry, and to find the poems much more accessible in that context than in the printed form ordained by their author. It might also be true to say that the poems appear much more direct and much more accomplished when read out of context in this way.

The academy of the mid-twentieth century gave Herrick a degree of prominence which was in itself problematic, in that it made him the central poet of a movement which only existed in the mind of literary historians. 'Cavalier Poetry' is a term which has happily fallen out of use together with the old, distorting literary history of the seventeenth century which sidelined the lyric poetry of the 1630s and 1640s as a sterile experiment which had no posterity in the progressive, Augustan era of the Restoration. Within that highly dubious history, Herrick becomes an example of the smoothly accomplished poetic of the Cavaliers, and becomes somehow the central and typical figure of that school. This is to ignore the fact that the greater part of his productive career was spent far from the centres of literary production, a fact which is reflected by the fact that he is well represented in manuscript copies, but not quite to the extent which might be expected. The uncertainties and anxieties embodied in the poetry of Marvell or of the later Richard Lovelace were once seen as a falling away from a standard of control and finish set by Herrick. The converse might now be true and Herrick's pastoral decorum might be read as both trivial and oblique, particularly as an atmosphere of the bellettristic attaches to his work, most probably as a result of the writings of his earlier apologists. Marvell has, rightly, become the central lyric poet by whose complexity and subtlety his contemporaries are, consciously or unconsciously, judged. Such a judgement is never going to restore Herrick to more than a marginal place in the canon, noted for his quinines, his usefulness as an antiquarian recorder of seasonal custom as, for example, that of shouting and firing guns in orchards at midwinter to wake the trees to productivity in the coming year:

> Wassaile the Trees, that they may beare
> You many a Plum, and many a Peare:
> For more or lesse fruits they will bring,
> As you doe give them Wassailing.
> (264)

Despite this, there is much that is instructive (and even a little that is surprising) in his work, if it is given a historically nuanced reading. It can serve, at the least, as a useful example to the modern reader of a collection which is central to the poetic taste of that historically crucial decade, the 1640s. The confident placing of Herrick's bust on the altar of his fame depicted in the frontispiece to the *Hesperides*, could be said to represent a consensus of contemporary opinion: if his book is given careful consideration, at the least some illumination of that vanished aesthetic consensus is likely to emerge.

The *Hesperides* are clearly a collection of work accumulated over a considerable time. There is no reason to suppose that the poems do not span the period from Herrick's Cambridge graduation in 1617 to his ejection from the Church of England living of Dean Prior in Devon in 1647. Indeed, since Herrick was an atypically mature student for the early seventeenth century, graduating at the age of twenty-six after an abandoned apprenticeship in the London merchant and manufacturing community from which he originated, it would be perfectly reasonable to conjecture that the poems collected in the *Hesperides* span an even longer period. Certainly the poems addressed to named patrons and contemporaries would suggest that the collection had slowly come to completion in the tranquil second half of the reign of James and then in the first decade of the reign of Charles I which many contemporaries characterized as England's 'halcyon days' or golden age. It is fair to say that the poetic which Herrick slowly evolved out of the Jonsonian literary continuum served him well throughout twenty years of peaceful half-pagan imagining of the yearly cycle of what then would have been a very remote parish. What is equally clear is that the style which he had evolved became fixed. When, from 1639, the temper of the times became increasingly less accommodating to a traditionalist clergyman more given to imitations of pagan authors than to the composition of work with any devotional content, Herrick's subject-matter mutates sharply, but his manner remains fixed. Unlike, for example, Richard Lovelace whose earlier and more conventional poems transform abruptly into the bitter, disjointed beast-fables which constitute his 'civil war' poems, Herrick's war poetry remains trapped within the pastoral mode. Even when he is forced momentarily into the composition of an immediately political poem such as the speech addressed to the king on his retreat with his army into the west country, there is no alteration of tone or manner to answer the urgencies of the circumstance. What Herrick offers, rather, in his 'To the King, upon his coming with his army into the West' is a reflection of the court poetic of the meridian of Charles's reign, a poem that fits the struggling King into the half-fantasized, half-pagan rural England of the earlier poems, so that he becomes a sort of classical genius of the place, a minor county-god of a Devon still heavily overlaid with the classical landscape of Vergil's pastoral poems.

> Welcome, most welcome to our Vowes and us,
> Most great, and universall *Genius!*
> The drooping west, which hitherto has stood
> As one, in long-lamented-widow-hood;
> Looks like a bride now, or a bed of flowers.
>
>   (25)

In the same way, Herrick in 'The bad season makes the poet sad' is clearly expressing a degree of genuine distress at the condition of the country and at his own poor prospects under the new order, yet he does so in a mode which is so remote from the modes which are recognizable in Marvell or Lovelace as conveying personal sorrow, that the poem as an artefact born of particular circumstances remains in many ways extremely problematic for the modern reader who is trying to understand poetic mode and intention:

> Dull to my selfe, and almost dead to these
> My many fresh and fragrant Mistresses:
> Lost to all Musick now; since every thing

Puts on the semblance here of sorrowing.
Sick is the Land to'th'heart; and doth endure
More dangerous faintings by her desp'rate cure.
But if that golden Age wo'd come again,
And *Charles* here Rule, as he before did Raign . . .
I sho'd delight to have my Curles halfe drown'd
In *Tyrian Dewes*, and Head with Roses crown'd.
And once more yet (ere I am laid out dead)
Knock at a Starre with my exalted Head.

(214)

This is a fair example of the problems which a modern reader is liable to encounter with Herrick: the unexpressive, carefully worked surface of the verse; the almost automatic patterning and balancing of assonance; the determination to remain within a classical-Roman frame of reference. While it is possible that the first six lines quoted above convey an apprehensible melancholy, the conventional intertextuality of the second half is difficult to place, simply too conventionally accomplished to be readable, with its reference to the first Ode of the First Book of Horace, itself something of a cliché of the relation of poet and patron from the high Renaissance onwards. Herrick's response to the disintegration of the England which he had known in the first decades of the seventeenth century is, generally, as polished and as poised as the examples which have been quoted. Herrick seems to have been unable or unwilling to adapt his poetic style to changed circumstances, a reluctance which could be a function of his slight seniority to most of the poets who are thought of as his contemporaries.

To conclude this brief reading of the *Hesperides*, a consideration of Herrick's pre-war subject-matter is essential to an understanding of a poetic achievement, which attempts, and succeeds, in most of the prevailing forms of the 1630s. What will most immediately strike the modern reader reading through the daunting, randomly organized collection, is the preponderance of two-line epigrams, mostly making humorous points which amount to little more than a play on words or the reinforcement of a commonplace. This should alert the reader to the overwhelming popularity of such epigrams with a generation who universally admired the ancient Roman epigrammatist Martial. (Many of Herrick's shorter poems are, in fact, either translations or looser 'imitations' from the Roman lyric poets.) Another numerically significant group within Herrick's collection is formed by poems which take as their subject-matter the customs and ceremonies of the rural year. The wassail poem quoted above is an example of these, but the group also includes one of Herrick's most substantial poems (one of the few on which his future place in the canon may well depend) 'The Hock-cart, or Harvest home', in which the classicizing imagination is happily overlaid on early-modern England:

Come Sons of Summer, by whose toile,
We are the Lords of Wine and Oile:
By whose tough labours, and rough hands,

We rip up first, then reap our lands.
Crown'd with the eares of corne, now come,
And, to the Pipe, sing Harvest home.

(101)

A similarly accomplished description of seasonal custom is the poem 'Corinna's going a Maying' which celebrates the may games which became, in the mid-century, in themselves a symbol of the old rural life which was lost in the parliamentarian victory and in the abolition of the old ceremonial year. It is the end of this poem that sets it amongst a sub-genre – the *carpe diem* or the poem on the swift passage of time – for which Herrick is famous, most of all in his frequently cited 'To the Virgins, to make much of Time' with its first line which has in itself become a clichéd shorthand for Caroline poetry 'Gather ye Rose-buds while ye may'. The end of Herrick's May poem is more carefully nuanced, careful in its echoes of Catullus and translations of Catullus by the English lute-song composer Thomas Campion:

Our life is short; and our dayes run
As fast away as do's the Sunne . . .
All love, all liking, all delight
Lies drown'd with us in endlesse night.
Then while time serves, and we are but decaying;
Come, my *Corinna*, come, let's goe a Maying.

(69)

REFERENCES AND FURTHER READING

Herrick, Robert (1956). *The Poems*. Ed. L. C. Martin. Oxford: Clarendon.
——(1965). *Poems*. Ed. L. C. Martin. Oxford: Oxford Standard Authors. Oxford University Press.

11

Andrew Marvell, 'An Horatian Ode upon Cromwell's Return from Ireland'

Thomas Healy

In May of 1650 Oliver Cromwell returned to England after neutralizing Irish opposition to the new English Republic, a state whose overthrow of tradition had been dramatically demonstrated with the execution of Charles I in early 1649. In July of 1650 Cromwell led an English invasion of Scotland to prevent a royalist regrouping north of the border. Andrew Marvell's 'An Horatian Ode upon Cromwell's Return from Ireland' may be witnessed, therefore, as a specific occasional poem, reflecting the poet's perspective on a few crucial months of 1650 in an England which was undergoing decisive social and cultural transformation. This was a juncture in English history when parliament's victories during the civil wars of the 1640s appeared to signal the commencement of a godly republic, a militant Protestant nation. But such a characterization of this moment was far from secure for contemporaries. As English invasions of Ireland and Scotland indicate, this was not a united nation; nor were continental monarchies happy about events in Britain. The republic's existence needed to be defended militarily and its preservation appeared to rest disproportionately on its most successful general, Oliver Cromwell.

For much of the twentieth century, critical analysis of Marvell's response to these events has, for the most part, proposed that the poet is not partisan in his depiction: that he has sympathies with both Cromwell and Charles I, the republic and the monarchy. However, the gradual acceptance among scholars that Marvell is, like Milton, a defender of parliament and the goals of what is frequently termed the English Revolution has shifted critical opinion to witness the poet as being in favour of Cromwell and republican aims. Two of the most influential accounts of the 'Horatian Ode' in recent years – by David Norbrook and Blair Worden – have convincingly argued that it supports a decisive republican dynamic, a poem in which Marvell is announcing his support for the new English state. Yet, for many readers, the 'Ode' continues to betray a lingering nostalgia for what has been lost. Despite acknowledging Cromwell's elemental vigour and 'industrious Valour', the poem's proclamation that such activity causes the ruin of 'the great work of Time' and has Justice pleading 'the antient Rights in vain' seems to indicate a writer somewhat uncertain about Cromwell's ascendancy (ll. 33–6). Worden, in fact, argues that the 'Ode' marks a decisive turning point in Marvell's own political sympathies: that he was temperamentally royalist before the late 1640s and thereafter a republican (150).

As with so much of Marvell's poetry, 'An Horatian Ode' defies easy categorization. Generically, it appears a public poem, yet it was not published until 1681, after Marvell's death. There is no evidence to indicate that it circulated in manuscript, or that Cromwell saw it. Even its inclusion in the 1681 *Miscellaneous Poems* was short lived as it was cancelled from virtually all copies. The poem did not really become known until it was printed in Thompson's 1776 edition of Marvell's works. Although Marvell did write poetry on Cromwell which was published – *The First Anniversary of the Government under O.C.* which appeared in 1655 – it is not clear whether the *Ode* was similarly designed for circulation but then kept private (and, if so, why?), or whether the poem merely assumes a public mode of address but was always envisaged as a vehicle for private reflection. *The First Anniversary* is atypical of most of Marvell's poetry prior to the Restoration in that it was issued before Marvell's death. Unlike Donne, whose work circulated widely in manuscript, we have little idea of who read Marvell's pre-Restoration work, and, in general, Marvell appears remarkably private in his opinions for a figure who held public offices for many years. The 'Ode''s history is further complicated by recalling that while it may have been written at the time its title announces, it might have been completed later (and if so how much later?) but assumes a contemporary voice; or, if written in 1650, it may be that Marvell revised the poem at a later date (a common feature of Civil War verse), and, if so, when? The closer we scrutinize the text to understand its tone and meanings with precision, the more such questions have significance.

Marvell is a master of the persona. He adopts different voices and plays different parts in his poetry (including that of young women, e.g. 'The Nymph Complaining for the Death of her Faun'). He is also capable of using generic and other literary devices to expose their artifice, allowing him to explore the ways literary language attempts to organize the world. Further, Marvell is also a skilful employer of irony and satire. His attacks on the excesses of the Restoration court, often under the guise of praise, are accomplished exposures of a decadence which threatens the political fabric of the nation. But even in poems which genuinely praise figures or events – such as *Upon Appleton House* which celebrates the family of the parliamentarian general Fairfax, whose daughter Marvell tutored – Marvell's narrator is revealed having his imagery turned around on him in unexpected ways by other figures in the poem (e.g. ll. 385–408), questioning the accuracy of the ostensible poetic vision. The authorial Marvell often playfully exposes the limitations of his poems' narrators, causing the reader to question the veracity of the narrator's view of the world, throwing the integrity of the poetic argument, or at least its apparent argument, into doubt. The poetic voice is never the authorial voice, even if it appears that way. The authorial Marvell seems to stand back from his poetic narrative, critically aware of the instability of language in trying to convey vision, and often deliberately manipulating narrative naiveté to unsettling effect.

'An Horatian Ode', for instance, opens with the announcement that 'The forward Youth that would appear' must now leave languishing in poetry and abandon his books in order to 'oyl th' unused Armours rust'. It is difficult to envisage how a contemporary youth could be described as 'forward' – in the sense of eager and progressive – when he has apparently ignored the five years of civil conflict which have preceded the poem. Of course, one could argue the narrator is aware that the new English state faces far greater conflicts, morally and spiritually as well as militarily, than those confronted in its foundation and is readying himself for these. The narrator, though, apparently disregards his own advice: writing an ode based on a classical Horatian model hardly indicates that his books have been left in dust. As is characteristic of his poetry, Marvell calls the integrity of his narrator, or at least his narrator's poetic control, into question: is he even including himself as a 'forward youth'? This strategy does not annul the poem's capacity to comment seriously on its time; rather, it indicates how Marvell's poetry is never straightforward, and that some degree of self-irony is always present.

Marvell's evocation of Horace is also ironic in a poem which praises a republic. Royalist poets of this period, notably Sir Richard Fanshawe, commonly imitated the Roman poet's elaborate praises of the emperor Augustus to celebrate the Stewart monarchy. Horace's original republican sympathies were transformed into a celebration of imperial Rome as a result of the shifting political and patronage climate of his day. As David Norbrook has forcefully argued, 'Marvell's out-troping poem of return turns royalist Horatianism, and Horace's own monarchism, upside down' in the same way 'the English revolution had turned upside down the monarchical order to return to republican origins' (164). Far from being an exercise in poetic cleverness, this allows Marvell to claim both classical authority and to depict the poem's events as a time of fundamental historical reversal, the advent of something new and magnificent. Blair Worden has noted, too, how the poem celebrates the birth in England of another 'Rome in the west', but one based on godly republican values which would be spread throughout Europe (160–2).

Certainly, much of Marvell's poem promotes Cromwell's energy as a breaker of old moulds, an elemental force whose dynamism cannot be resisted. A common tactic used by parliamentarian writers against their royalist opponents was to accuse them of lethargy. Royalist poetics cultivated a cultural politics of retirement – the only thing the civilized individual could do in times of barbarism was to retreat from the public sphere and try to keep cultural values alive in private until better times returned. In contrast, parliamentarians celebrate their industry, a zeal for constructing anew. In *The First Anniversary of the Government under O.C.*, Marvell celebrates the Commonwealth as a structure erected by having its differing forces organized so that its oppositions can provide the basis of its strength, one enabled by its 'Roofs Protecting weight' (ll. 75–98): a clear reference to Cromwell as Lord Protector. The 'Horatian Ode' also readily employs this republican emphasis on building, suggesting, for instance, that a true understanding of Charles I's severed head is on the model of the Roman Capitol, where a head was discovered in digging the foundations and was correctly prophesied as indicating Rome's coming greatness (ll. 64–72). The cutting off of Charles's head provides the means by which the Commonwealth's true head may arise (Capitol from *caput*, the Latin for head).

This is not to replace Charles by Cromwell – though Cromwell was to be accused of monarchical airs during the Protectorate after 1653. 'An Horatian Ode' makes it clear that Cromwell's power rests in his obedience to the Commonwealth: 'How fit he is to sway / That can so well obey' (ll. 83–4). As Worden notes, there was fear in some quarters that Cromwell did not return as rapidly from Ireland as parliament wished because he was planning his own coup (pp. 154–5). In 1650 these fears were unrealized, Cromwell remained loyal to parliament's commands. Indeed, Marvell never ascribes absolutist ambitions to him even during his Protectorate after 1653. Cromwell may be the roof which unites the Commonwealth in the *First Anniversary*, but he requires its support to sustain his position. In 'An Horatian Ode', it is Cromwell's Christ-like humility – 'He to the *Commons Feet* presents / A Kingdome' (ll. 86–7) – which opposes him to the 'Royal Actor' Charles whose actions at his execution are a further sign that 'He nothing common did or mean' (l. 57): his manners may be fine, but they only serve to point out his distance from the Commonwealth. The accord between state and its true actor, Cromwell – 'So much can one Man do / That does both act and know' (ll. 75–6) – symbolized by the presentation of his Irish victories to parliament, contrasts with the cacophony which surrounds the 'Tragick Scaffold' where the armed bands clap their 'bloody hands' at Charles''s execution. Charles's bowing his head to the axe, 'Down as upon a bed' (ll. 53–64), may note his composure, but it also highlights his inactivity.

Cromwell's subjection of Ireland inflicted terrible carnage on the island. From our different historical perspective it is tempting to claim as pointedly ironic the '*Ode*''s observation that the Irish themselves 'are asham'd / To see themselves in one Year tam'd' (ll. 73–4). However currently distasteful, though, Marvell almost certainly joined with the greater part of parliamentary and Protestant England in seeing the conquest of largely Roman Catholic Ireland as an indication of God's favour toward the new English state. 'An Horatian Ode''s anticipation of victories in Roman Catholic Europe – France (Gaul) and Italy – celebrates Cromwell as a liberating force and further justifies his actions in England. From a militant Protestant perspective, the overthrow of 'papal' Europe would be proof of the new republic as a godly one, fulfilling the designs of the Reformation. That Stuart England, and its Laudian Church, was in similar need of such a Reformation was one of the issues which helped provoke civil division in Britain: Cromwell has already been 'clymacterick' in freeing England. The poem indicates that Cromwell's conquests may be witnessed in terms of the supernatural conflict between the godly and the satanic, with the clear implication that God is on the English side.

There is, though, the problem of Scotland. There was certainly a *realpolitik* involved in the English invasion of Scotland in 1650. During the 1640s, the Scots had been invited south by a then beleaguered parliament and had been instrumental in helping parliament defeat Charles I. The Scots, though, had wished to impose their own Presbyterian religious organization onto England and one of the first actions of Cromwell's new model army had been to force the Scots out of England. The resulting dissatisfaction was making the Scots increasingly sympathetic with the exiled Charles II, and it was to prevent a renewed royalist invasion from the north that the Republic acted. However, while the Scots presence in England in the 1640s had stirred up a traditional mistrust of them, there was not the unanimity of consent about this invasion as there was with Ireland. Scotland was Protestant and recently an ally. Cromwell's military superior, Lord General Fairfax, resigned rather than participate in the action. Further, it had been a design of the Stuarts to effect unification between England and Scotland, to see them as part of a United Kingdom. This had been notably rejected when the Scots had refused to accept Charles's insistence over their conformity to religious observation on the Laudian English Church's model, prompting a disastrous English campaign against Scotland in the late 1630s. It was this event which directly led to civil conflict throughout Britain. Scotland's support for parliament in the 1640s had revived the ideal of a Protestant united island. 'An Horatian Ode', in celebratory mode about Cromwell's Irish victories proclaims 'What may not then our Isle presume / While Victory his Crest does plume!' (ll. 97–8); but it then goes on to disparage the Scots as the same type of prey to Cromwell as the French or Italians, a forceful reminder that 'our Isle' is divided. The republic has not proved a national unifying force any more than the Stuart monarchy. In its concluding section the '*Ode*' reawakens us to its narrator not being able to match his vision to actualities. Marvell is reminding us that the republic's advent does not mark the end of civil conflict.

This, though, does not indicate an implied criticism of Cromwell; rather, the reverse. In *The First Anniversary of the Government under O.C.*, Marvell celebrates Cromwell's achievements, but questions whether the state he governs is worthy of him: 'Thee proof beyond all other Force or Skill, / Our Sins endanger, and shall one day kill' (ll. 173–4). Ironically, at this poem's conclusion, it is the leaders of nations Cromwell opposes who fully acknowledge his power, leading the narrator to apologize: 'Pardon, great Prince, if thus their Fear or Spight / More then our Love and Duty do thee Right' (ll. 395–6). Marvell appears to be displaying similar concerns in 'An Horatian Ode'. The injunction to Cromwell to 'Still keep thy Sword erect' (l. 116) is crucial because of internal as well as external threats. At various points the poem hints that the parliament Cromwell serves may not be his equal. If Charles' severed head foretells the success of the Republic, the poem also implies a parallel between the Roman architects who ran at the discovery of a head beneath the Capitol and (at least some) of the architects of the English state losing their nerve about the nation they are building. Cromwell's energy, the recognition that 'Much to the Man is due' (l. 28) is also an acknowledgement that the Commonwealth's success is disproportionately due to him.

Indeed, Marvell may be using his own narrator as an indication of this. 'The forward youth that would appear' might be the visionary youth of the future, inspired by

Cromwell's industry into abetting the creation of a new state, or he might be the presumptuous youth seeking social success by adapting himself to the Commonwealth's changed cultural parameters. How the republic recognizes its true supporters – writers of genuine odes instead of timely panegyric – in a land where civil divisions are not settled is one of the problems the new state has to confront. While there is no doubt that 'An Horatian Ode' applauds the potentials of its particular historical juncture, those months in 1650 when it seemed that England was at the advent of a momentous historical transformation; it is also true that Marvell is aware of other currents within the nation, even at the heart of the Republic. If Cromwell's 'last effect' is to become the perpetual Protestant soldier with his spiritual armoury at the ready, there is also the recognition that neither Cromwell, nor the forward youth, are likely to have an opportunity to regain their gardens.

REFERENCES AND FURTHER READING

Chernaik, Warren L. (1983). *The Poet's Time: Politics and Religion in the Works of Andrew Marvell.* Cambridge: Cambridge University Press.

Everett, Barbara (1979). 'The shooting of the bears: poetry and politics in Andrew Marvell'. In *Andrew Marvell: Essays on the Tercentenary of his Death.* Ed. R. L. Brett. Oxford: Oxford University Press for the University of Hull, 62–104.

Norbrook, David (1990). 'Marvell's "Horatian Ode" and the politics of genre'. In *Literature and the English Civil War.* Ed. Thomas Healy and Jonathan Sawday. Cambridge: Cambridge University Press, 147–69.

Patterson, Annabel (1978). *Marvell and the Civic Crown.* Princeton: Princeton University Press.

Smith, Nigel (1994). *Literature and Revolution in England.* New Haven and London: Yale University Press.

Stocker, Margarita (1986). *Apocalyptic Marvell: The Second Coming in Seventeenth-century Poetry.* Brighton: Harvester, esp. 257–305.

Wallace, John M. (1968). *Destiny His Choice: The Loyalism of Andrew Marvell.* Cambridge: Cambridge University Press, esp. 69–105.

Wilding, Michael (1987). *Dragons Teeth: Literature in the English Revolution.* Oxford: Clarendon Press, esp. 114–37.

Wilson, A. J. N. (1969). 'Andrew Marvell: "An Horatian Ode upon Cromwell's Return from Ireland": the thread of the poem and its use of classical allusion'. *Critical Quarterly* 11, 325–41.

Worden, Blair (1987). 'Andrew Marvell, Oliver Cromwell, and the Horatian Ode'. In *Politics of Discourse: The Literature and History of Seventeenth-century England.* Ed. Kevin Sharpe and Steven N. Zwicker. Berkeley, Los Angeles and London: University of California Press, 147–80.

Zwicker, Steven N. (1993). *Lines of Authority: Politics and English Literary Culture, 1649–1689.* Ithaca and London: Cornell University Press.

12

Thomas Hobbes, *Leviathan*

David Wootton

Thomas Hobbes (1588–1679) was born as the Spanish Armada threatened the English coast. In his verse autobiography he tells us 'And hereupon it was my mother dear / Did bring forth twins at once, both me and fear.' Fear, we are to understand, was Hobbes's alter ego. After graduating from Oxford he served for thirty years, almost without interruption, first as tutor, and then as secretary for William Cavendish, later second Earl of Devonshire; then as tutor for his son, the third Earl. In this capacity he spent extensive periods in France and Italy, meeting continental philosophers. At first his views were those of a humanist with an interest in reason of state (see his *Discourses*) and history (his translation of Thucydides was published in 1629). But in 1629 Hobbes discovered geometry and began to develop a philosophy which grounded all knowledge in matter and motion. In 1640 his first work of political philosophy, the *Elements*, was in widespread circulation. Since it implied hostility to the claims of parliament, Hobbes thought it wise to flee to France when the Long Parliament was summoned. There he published *De Cive* (1642), served as tutor to the Prince of Wales in exile, and wrote *Leviathan* (1651). Publication of this work in England was followed by Hobbes coming under attack from royalists, Anglicans, and Catholics in France, so that he was forced to flee to England, where he accepted the legitimacy of the parliamentary and Cromwellian regimes, and then of the restored monarchy. In 1668 he completed *Behemoth*, a history of the Civil War. It is worth stressing that Hobbes thought of himself as being as much a mathematician and a scientist as a political philosopher, and that he published as readily in Latin as in English – with the result that he had a European reputation.

From the *Elements* to *Leviathan* and beyond there were minor changes in Hobbes's political philosophy; but the essentials remained the same. Hobbes asked what rational human beings would do if they found themselves outside any framework of law and order. He concluded that in such circumstances there could be no justice or property, and each person would have a right to everything. Since the things that humans desire – food, shelter, prestige – are in limited supply they are naturally in competition with each other. Any success you may have makes it easier for you to attack me, so that if I am rational I will attack you as soon as I can. Thus a war of all against all is inevitable, and life must be 'solitary, poor, nasty, brutish, and short'. Clearly it is to everyone's advantage if they can bring this state of affairs to an end, and this they can do only if they can establish an authority capable of intimidating all who might threaten it. Rational individuals will therefore reach an agreement to establish an all-powerful ruler, and lend him their support in imposing his will upon all and sundry. (Hobbes thought rule by an individual was preferable to rule by a committee, but wanted in any case to insist that subjects were no freer under a representative government than under a despotism.) Hobbes recognized only one limitation on a ruler's power: no individual can give up the right to self-defence (it is significant that Hobbes is the first to use this word, in *Leviathan*), and while I should assist the ruler if he attacks my friend, I must defend myself if he attacks me. Leviathan would thus govern by amassing power in his own hands, while dividing his subjects one from another.

On Hobbes's account, political authority grows out of the consent of individuals, but its prime purpose is to intimidate the individuals who have consented to it. In other words this is, in the first place, a philosophy of fear. Because Hobbes believes fear is pervasive and fruitful he rejects the conventional view that actions carried out under threat of force are involuntary, and that contracts extracted under duress are invalid. If a highwayman offers me the choice between my money and my life, the choice is a free one, as is my decision to establish a government capable of intimidating all and sundry in order to escape intimidation by my neighbours. Second, it is a philosophy concerning rational individuals seeking to pursue their interests: the words selfish (1640) and self-interest (1649) appeared in English while Hobbes was refining his theory, and the first occasion on which 'selfish' was used to designate an ethical theory which regards self-love as the real motive of all human action was in 1663: 'To use the phrase of the time, this Gent. [Hobbes] is very selfish.'

On this account of Hobbes's theory, it would appear to be entirely secular. Out of self-interest, fear, and contractual agreement, rights and duties are constructed, but these rights and duties themselves are dissolved the moment the ruler becomes incapable of instilling fear – hence Hobbes's willingness to abandon the Stuarts and to support parliament in 1651. But Hobbes presented his argument in ambiguous terms, for he maintained that there existed a law of nature, the first duty of which was the duty to seek peace, although this law was ineffectual in the absence of an authority to enforce it. It is thus possible (if perverse) to read him as claiming that rights and duties are established by divine law. Moreover in *Leviathan* (published when there was no religion established by law in England) Hobbes set out to show that his materialist account of human nature (he believed that all life could be explained in mechanical terms, and that all action was motivated by the desire to seek pleasure and flee pain) was compatible with a new reading of the Old and New Testaments – a reading which eliminated the trinity and the soul as traditionally understood, and which grounded Christianity in an obligation to obey the secular ruler, who was to control both state and church, and determine, for example, which texts are to be regarded as sacred. This materialist Christianity, like Hobbes's account of natural law, is open to a number of different readings. Contemporaries tended to believe that Hobbes did not believe in revealed religion, but was merely cynically advocating a religion which would dovetail with his political theory. They freely called him an atheist, although Hobbes seems to have been confident there was a (necessarily material) first cause. More recent interpreters have gone so far as to hold that Hobbes had a genuine, if unorthodox, Christian faith, a view which would have astonished his contemporaries.

Although through most of his life Hobbes claimed to be an orthodox Anglican, *Leviathan* outraged the Anglican clergy and was under systematic attack from the moment of its publication. In addition to making enemies amongst the clergy, Hobbes had attacked the universities. He argued that the humanist curriculum inculcated republican values, while scholasticism fostered a belief in spiritual entities, a belief incompatible with rational calculation of one's interests. In 1666 there was discussion in parliament as to whether Hobbes should be tried for heresy, while in 1683 the University of Oxford condemned and burnt *De Cive* and *Leviathan*. While he himself escaped persecution, anyone espousing his views faced severe consequences, a fact which makes it hard to judge how many admired his work.

Two terms are often used in descriptions of Hobbes but should be avoided. First he is said to be a liberal. In fact, Hobbes wanted to establish a political system in which there was no right to freedom of worship and in which political authority was unchecked by any constitutional constraints. The mere fact that he argued from individualist premises and stressed that each person must pursue their own interests does not make him a liberal. Second, Hobbes is said to be an empiricist. This claim is even harder to understand. The whole point of geometry for Hobbes was that it proceeded by deduction and reached conclusions that were surprising but uncontestable. Hobbes was not interested in how political power is normally established and exercised (any more than a geometer is interested in the best technique for drawing a triangle), but only in how reason required power to be established and exercised: and here he thought he could demonstrate that power must be absolute, subject only to the right to self-defence. In science, Hobbes bitterly attacked the experimental empiricism of Boyle, which claimed to demonstrate the existence of a vacuum, in his *Dialogus* (1661), arguing that experiments were misleading and that the impossibility of a vacuum could both be shown from everyday experience and demonstrated from first principles.

The pursuit of a geometrical or deductive philosophy implied a philosophy of language. In the first place it meant that the meanings of terms must be established by authoritative definition, not by usage. Only if ordinary language was reduced to scientific language, Hobbes believed, would it be possible to escape popular misconceptions regarding free will, limited government, and rights of resistance. Second, it implied that argument should be spare, rigorous and unemotional; the humanist techniques of rhetoric, in which Hobbes had been educated and which he had taught to his pupils, must be jettisoned. Yet, particularly from *Leviathan* onwards, Hobbes's own practice seems to imply a critique of this ideal. Leviathan itself, the great beast of the deep according to the book of Job, is used by Hobbes as a powerful metaphor for his irresistible ruler. If one accepts that Hobbes had no religious beliefs, then half of *Leviathan* is devoted to constructing a set of arguments which are false, but are designed to persuade the average person, incapable of giving up hopes and fears for the next life, that they should adopt Hobbes's political theory, not the teaching of the clergy (which always stressed that true religion was an authority greater than that of any secular ruler). Hobbes therefore appears to have concluded that mere science would never persuade ordinary people, who would learn obedience only through intimidation and rhetorical persuasion; and that the political philosopher would be ineffectual if he did not have the support of the army and the clergy.

The question Hobbes begins with – How would a rational person act if they had only their own reason to guide them? – was derived from the Dutch legal philosopher, Hugo Grotius, and through Hobbes it becomes the defining question for the school of early modern natural law theorists: Locke, Pufendorf, Barbeyrac amongst them. Even Hume, Smith and Rousseau can be read as offering new ways of approaching issues inherited from this tradition. Hobbes is thus a founding figure for traditions which rarely refer to him except to attack him.

REFERENCES AND FURTHER READING

The modern literature on Hobbes is vast. The most useful edition of *Leviathan* is that edited by Edwin Curley (Indianapolis: Hackett, 1994). Jean Hampton, *Hobbes and the Social Contract Tradition* (Cambridge: Cambridge University Press, 1986) provides a fine exposition of Hobbes's argument, drawing on game theory, while Hobbes's philosophy is studied historically by Johann Sommerville in *Thomas Hobbes: Political Ideas in Historical Context* (Basingstoke: Macmillan, 1992). Hobbes's science is best studied through Steven Shapin and Simon Shaffer, *Leviathan and the Air-Pump* (Princeton: Princeton University Press, 1985), and his views on rhetoric and religion through Quentin Skinner, *Reason and Rhetoric in the Philosophy of Hobbes* (Cambridge: Cambridge University Press, 1996). An important newly attributed text is *Hobbes: Three Discourses*, ed. Arlene Saxenhouse and Noel Reynolds (Chicago: University of Chicago Press, 1995). On the response to Hobbes, see Mark Goldie, 'The reception of Hobbes', in J. H. Burns ed., *The Cambridge History of Political Thought 1450–1700* (Cambridge: Cambridge University Press, 1991), 589–615.

13
Katherine Philips, *Poems*
Jane Spencer

Written from the late 1640s to the early 1660s, Katherine Philips's poetry combined the musical beauty of seventeenth-century lyric with the argumentative force of metaphysical poetry. As well as a body of poems (133 in the recent collected edition of her work) and numerous letters, she wrote *Pompey*, a translation from Corneille, performed in 1663, and had nearly completed a translation of Corneille's *Horace* when smallpox cut short her career at the age of thirty-two. Because she addressed her manuscript poems to personal friends and protested vigorously when they were printed without her consent; because she lived much of her time in Cardigan and praised country retirement; and because after her death she was widely celebrated as much for feminine virtue as for writing, she used to be damned with faint praise as a sweet, chaste, essentially private writer, even though she was acknowledged as one of the Cavalier poets. In fact, the public upheavals of her time shaped nearly all her writing, which had a public profile from its manuscript circulation, and through the clear surface harmonies of her poems we can see into some complex political and personal depths. Royalism and passionate female friendship combine in her writing, each being used to express the other, and both emerging as a form of challenge to the world she knew.

Born Katherine Fowler in 1632, her father a London cloth merchant and both her parents from Puritan families, she was educated in a Hackney school run by the Presbyterian Mrs Salmon. At sixteen she married James Philips, nearly forty years her senior and a prominent Welsh supporter of Cromwell. Birth, upbringing, and all the daughterly and wifely duties that were supposed to shape a woman's life 'ought' to have placed her firmly on the side of parliament. At school, however, she developed a close friendship with Mary Aubrey ('Rosania'), from a Welsh Cavalier family. At the age of eighteen, married and separated from her friend, Philips imagined the two women, in death, turning war into peace:

A dew shall dwell upon our tomb
   Of such a quality,

> That fighting armies, thither come,
> Shall reconciled be.
>   (no. 53, ll. 55–8)

However, the union of these 'twin souls' (l. 49) seems to have encouraged not so much a truce between two political viewpoints as the poet's movement towards royalism. Another factor in this was her friendship with Mary Harvey, a pupil of Henry Lawes, the musician whose Cavalier circle was 'concerned to preserve the cultural ideals of the Caroline court' (Thomas, 1990, 6). At school the writer and her friends read the plays of William Cartwright, published by royalists in 1651 with a poem by her among the tributes to the author. After her early marriage she continued to correspond with a growing circle of mainly royalist friends under coterie names, many of them borrowed from Cartwright's work. Deriving their ideals of friendship and civilization from the culture of the French *precieux*, made influential in England by Queen Henrietta Maria, these men and women formed what Sir Edward Dering (Mary Harvey's husband and 'Silvander') later described as a 'societie' intended 'by the bands of friendship to make an alliance more firme than what nature, our countery or equall education can produce' (Thomas, 1990, 11). Friendship's bonds, surpassing the familial ones of 'nature', seem to have combined with the aesthetic appeal of courtly arts to turn the Puritans' daughter into a Cavalier poet.

The conflicting obligations of a wife and a subject resonate within her poems. In 'Upon the double murther of K. Charles, in answer to a libellous rime made by V.P.', Philips performed what royalist poets of the interregnum saw as their duty of resisting the conquering parliamentarians through their writing (Loxley, 1997, 214). Vavasour Powell, a Puritan preacher, had perpetrated a second 'murther' of the king by writing an attack on him after his execution. In her reply Philips, disclaiming any interest in 'the state' (no. 1, l. 1), figures her royalist verse as a filial cry:

> as that sonne whose father's danger nigh
> Did force his native dumbnesse, and untye
> The fettred organs: so here is a cause
> That will excuse the breach of nature's lawes.
> Silence were now a Sin.
>   (ll. 3–7)

The pathos of the son, dumb till passionate concern for the father forces speech, was reinforced by readers' knowledge that this poem was written by 'Orinda': her simile suggests that a daughter is a dumb son, whose silence (traditionally prescribed to women) can only be overcome by the operation of a law even higher than 'nature's'. Devotion to the monarch justifies her speech. At this low point for the royalist cause, when her cry, too late to save the father, can only protect his memory, even a daughter may be allowed to speak as a son.

One J. Jones threatened to publish this poem, which could have been politically damaging to the poet's husband, whose 'moderate Cromwellian views' (Thomas, 1990,

348) made him a target for radical Fifth Monarchists like Powell. The poem to James Philips in response to this situation shows how royalism made it necessary to oppose the biblical notion that husband and wife were one:

> who before
> Lost his repute upon anothers score?
> My love and life I must confesse are thine,
> But not my errours, they are only mine.
> (no. 33, ll. 5–8; Demaria, 1996, 368)

The poet insists that 'Eve's rebellion did not Adam blast, / Untill himselfe forbidden fruit did tast' (ll. 11–12), but the apparent humility of taking on Eve's guilt while exonerating her husband as an unfallen Adam is undermined by the irony that her 'crimes' (l. 1), 'errours' (l. 8), 'faults' (l. 9), 'rebellion' (l. 11) and 'follies' (l. 18) are, from a royalist point of view, the epitome of virtuous action. To suffer punishment for them would be a glorious martyrdom, and there is even a hint of Christ in her self-image: 'if my inke, through malice, prov'd a staine, / My bloud should justly wash it off again' (ll. 23–4). Her poetic voice depends on her asserting her mental and political separation from her husband. Though she implicitly softens his parliamentarian stance by naming him 'Antenor' after the Trojan who tried to reconcile Greece and Troy (Thomas, 1990, 5), her own poetic name has been persuasively presented as a shortening of 'Clorinda', the woman knight in Tasso's *Gerusalemme Liberata* (1581), who opposed her husband in battle (Barash, 1996, 74).

In contrast to this firm separation of Orinda from Antenor, the poet imagines herself fused with Ardelia, with Rosania and, most frequently, with Lucasia (Anne Owen), in poems that celebrate friendship in neoplatonic terms as a mingling of souls. This sense of identity with the beloved is beautifully expressed in the joyful cadences of 'To my excellent Lucasia, on our friendship. 17th. July 1651':

> I did not live untill this time
>   Crown'd my felicity,
> When I could say without a crime,
>   I am not Thine, but Thee.
>   (no. 36, ll. 1–4)

This crown of love is set above the crown of state, and the relationship with Lucasia is placed above marriage:

> Nor Bridegroomes nor crown'd conqu'ror's mirth
>   To mine compar'd can be:
> They have but pieces of this Earth,
>   I've all the world in thee.
>   (ll. 18–21)

The equation of the earth, split in pieces by conquering warriors, with the woman's body possessed by her bridegroom, implies that marriage is a physical violence and a reduction of the bride to her body, in contrast to Orinda's incorporation of Lucasia's soul, which repairs that tearing of the earth to deliver the restored wholeness of 'all the world'. The inclusion of the date in the poem's title is a clue to its political topicality: like other Cavalier poets, Philips imagines friendship as a way of keeping royalist ideals alive in defeat (Miner, 1971, 282–97). Lucasia's soul inspires the writer whose breast has been 'darken'd' (l. 14), as royalist readers would understand, by Charles I's death. In some manuscript versions and in the 1664 and 1667 editions of this poem, the generalized 'crown'd conqu'rors' becomes the more pointed 'Crown-conquerors' (Philips, 1664, 105) in reference to the victorious parliamentarians among whom – intensifying the link between marriage and state oppression – the poet's own bridegroom belonged.

Retirement from the world of 'quarrelling for Crowns', necessary in 'such a scorching Age as this', allows friends to live 'In one another's hearts' and 'Enjoy what princes wish in vain' (no. 22, 'A retir'd friendship, to Ardelia. 23d Augo 1651', ll. 5, 29, 16 and 36). Philips's celebration of friendship operates within the Cavalier circles of the interregnum, an audience tuned to coded political messages, not only as a tribute to Stuart civilization and its neoplatonic ideals, but even as a symbolic protection of the exiled monarchy (Barash, 1996, 77). In a poem addressed to Francis Finch, who had dedicated a treatise in praise of friendship to the fused couple, 'D[ear] noble Orinda-Lucasia' (Thomas, 1990, 8), she speaks in a first person plural that I read as identified with the scattered royalist community, 'undone, wrapt in disguise, / Secure, not happy; cunning, but not wise' (no. 12, 'To the noble Palaemon on his incomparable discourse of Friendship', ll. 1–2). The poem glorifies Cavalier passivity by imagining the king symbolically restored through an idealized friendship. Secretly loyal, uneasily plotting, 'War', their 'design' (l. 3), the royalists are saved (from despair but also from action) by fixing their minds on Finch's ideal. Friendship is a monarch and he 'her great deliverer' (l. 15) who:

> At first discover'd, and then rescu'd her;
> And raising what rude malice had flung down,
> Unvayled her face, and then restor'd her Crown.
> (ll. 16–19)

In 'Friendship's Mysterys, to My Dearest Lucasia', a poem set to music by Henry Lawes, Philips describes the unity of Orinda and Lucasia as a proof to 'the dull, angry world' of the 'religion in our love' (no. 17, ll. 4–5; Demaria, 358). The depiction of their mutual love as a shared imprisonment recalls Lovelace's joy in the liberty of being fettered to his love, and the imagery suggests a similar fusion of the relationship with the beloved and service to the king:

> We court our own captivity,
>   Then Thrones more great and innocent:

'Twere banishment to be set free,
   Since we weare fetters whose intent
Not bondage is, but Ornament.
                    (ll. 16–20)

Orinda and Lucasia are imagined forming in their relationship a reconstituted monarchical state: 'all our titles shuffled so, / Both Princes, and both subjects too' (ll. 24–5).

As the disparagement of bridegrooms' joys and the image of friendship as a female monarch begin to suggest, Philips's friendship poems are significant not just for their covert royalist messages but for their female appropriation of male discourses. The classical models of friendship so important in Elizabethan and seventeenth-century literature assumed as a norm friendship between men, and Jeremy Taylor, in a discourse about friendship addressed to Philips, explicitly endorsed male friendship as the highest type, superior to friendship between man and woman. Friendship between women he ignored (Andreadis, 1989, 50). If classical friendship is understood as male–male, the neoplatonic adaptation of love poetry on which Philips also draws is men's writing about male–female relationships. Her innovation is to write of female friendship in the idioms of heterosexual love poetry, 'usurping the position of the male speaker' (Mermin, 1990, 343). She echoes the combination of passion with metaphysical wit found in Donne's love poems (Andreadis, 1989, 39–42). 'Parting with Lucasia, 13th Janury 1657/8. A song' recalls Donne's 'A Valediction: Forbidding Mourning' with its assurance that the love of united souls can survive physical absence. Orinda and Lucasia cannot really part at all, though they 'will doe that rigid thing / Which makes Spectators think we part' (no. 46, ll. 1–2; Demaria, 367). At the same time, the poem renders its vision of the women's loving souls in insistently physical images of desire that remind us of Donne's dictum in 'The Ecstasy' that 'pure lovers' souls' must 'descend / T'affections, and to faculties' (Donne, 1971, 55):

And when our sence is dispossess'd,
   Our labouring Souls will heave and pant,
And gasp for one another's Brest,
   Since theyr conveyances they want.
                    (ll. 5–8)

In 'Friendship in Emblem, or the Seale, to My Dearest Lucasia', Philips draws on the popular seventeenth-century emblem tradition, describing an emblem of intertwined flaming hearts, signifying passion and friendship, together with a pair of compasses. In her extended discussion of the compasses Philips echoes Donne's use of a similar conceit in 'A Valediction: Forbidding Mourning'. Like him she uses the fixed foot and the moving one as an image of constancy in which 'The steddy part does regulate' the motions of the other (no. 29, l. 31; Demaria, 365); but while Donne's use of this image suggests a heterosexual hierarchy in which the wife's stillness provides anchorage for the active husband, 'who must / Like th'other foot, obliquely run' (Donne, 1971, 85), Philips imagines the friends alternating the roles of wanderer and firm centre between them: 'So friends are onely Two in this, / T'reclaime each other when they misse' (ll. 33–4). The bending of the compasses, too, signifies the mutuality and equality of the relationship:

> And in their posture is express'd
> Friendship's exalted interest:
> Each follows where the other Leanes,
> And what each does, the other meanes.
> (ll. 25–8)

The frequent comparisons her contemporaries made between Philips and Sappho, in spite (or perhaps because) of their insistence on Orinda's greater purity, show an awareness of the eroticism of her writing about love between women. Without reducing the significance of Philips's poetry to biographical speculation, we can see that 'her manipulations of the conventions of male poetic discourse constitute a form of lesbian writing' (Andreadis, 1989, 60).

After the Restoration, when her once-dangerous political allegiances became the source of honourable fame, and 'Upon the double murther' took pride of place in the unauthorized 1664 *Poems*, the tensions between Philips's wifely and royalist duties dissolved. Her known royalism could now be invoked in protection of her husband, a former member of the High Court of Justice under Cromwell who lost his seat in the Commons after the king's return. Philips's poems greeting the Restoration emphasize the king's mercy: 'Revenge to him no pleasure is, / He spar'd their bloud who gap'd for his' ('Arion on a Dolphin to his Majestie in his passadge into England', no. 3, ll. 37–8). In contrast, it has been argued, tensions appeared within her theme of female friendship: once sanctified by its implicit roots in loyalty to the exiled monarchy, it was likely to appear more subversive of sexual norms after the Restoration, so that Philips needed repeatedly to stress the innocence of her love for her friends (Barash, 1996, 92–100). Philips died in 1664, just as she was expanding the range of her work and gaining wider fame, and her correspondent Sir Charles Cotterell (Poliarchus) published her works in 1667. For many years she was remembered as an icon of female virtue, but it is more appropriate to see her as a poet whose verse transformed the tensions and conflicting loyalties of her life and times into a passionate harmony.

References and Further Reading

Andreadis, H. (1989). 'The sapphic-platonics of Katherine Philips, 1632–1664'. *Signs* 15.1, 34–60.

Barash, C. (1996). *English Women's Poetry, 1649–1714: Politics, Community, and Linguistic Authority*. Oxford: Clarendon.

Demaria, R. (1996). *British Literature 1640–1789: An Anthology*. Oxford: Blackwell. Philips's poetry is quoted from Thomas (see below), but page references to poems appearing in this anthology are also included in the text.

De Mourgues, O. (1953). *Metaphysical, Baroque, and Precieux Poetry*. Oxford: Clarendon.

Donaghue, E. (1993). *Passions Between Women: British Lesbian Culture 1668–1801*. London: Scarlet Press.

Donne, J. (1971). *The Complete English Poems*. ed. A. J. Smith. Harmondsworth: Penguin.

Ezell, M. (1993). *Writing Women's Literary History*. Baltimore and London: Johns Hopkins University Press.

Faderman, L. (1981). *Surpassing the Love of Men: Romantic Friendship and Love between Women from the Renaissance to the Present*. New York: Morrow.

Hiscock, W. G. (1939). 'Friendship: Francis Finch's discourse and the social circle of the matchless Orinda'. *Review of English Studies* 15, 466–8.

Hobby, E. (1991). 'Katherine Philips: seventeenth-century lesbian poet'. In *What Lesbians Do in Books*. Ed. E. Hobby and C. White. London: Women's Press.

Jose, N. (1984). *Ideas of the Restoration in English Literature*. Cambridge, Mass.: Harvard University Press.

King, B. (1982). *Seventeenth-century English Literature*. New York: Schocken.

Lilley, K. (1992). 'True state within: women's elegy 1640–1740'. In *Women, Writing, History 1640–1740*. Ed. I. Grundy and S. Wisemen. London: Batsford, 72–92.

Loxley, J. (1997). *Royalism and Poetry in the English Civil Wars: The Drawn Sword*. Basingstoke: Macmillan.

McDowell, P. (1993). 'Consuming women: the life of the "literary lady" as popular culture in eighteenth-century England'. *Genre* 26, 219–52.

Mermin, D. (1990). 'Women becoming poets: Katherine Philips, Aphra Behn, Anne Finch'. *English Literary History* 57.2, 335–56.

Miner, E. (1971). *The Cavalier Mode from Johnson to Cotton*. New Jersey: Princeton University Press.

Moody, E. (1987). 'Orinda, Rosania, Lucasia *et aliae*: towards a new edition of the works of Katherine Philips'. *Philological Quarterly* 66.3, 325–54.

Philips, K. (1664). *Poems by the Incomparable Mrs. K.P.* London.

Pritchard, A. and Thomas P. (1976). 'Orinda, Vaughan, and Watkyns: Anglo-Welsh literary relationships during the Interregnum'. *Anglo-Welsh Review* 26, 96–102.

Pritchard, I. (1983). 'Marvell's "The Garden": a restoration poem?'. *Studies in English Literature* 23, 371–88.

Souers, P. W. (1931). *The Matchless Orinda*. Cambridge, Mass.: Harvard University Press.

Thomas, Patrick, ed. (1990). *The Collected Works of Katherine Philips, The Matchless Orinda, Vol. 1. The Poems*. Essex: Stump Cross Books. Unless otherwise stated all quotations from Philips's poetry are taken from this edition, with poems identified by their number in this volume.

Turner, J. (1979). *The Politics of Landscape: Rural Scenery and Society in English Poetry 1630–1660*. Oxford: Basil Blackwell.

Wilson, K. M., ed. (1987). *Women Writers of the Renaissance and Reformation*. Athens: University of Georgia Press.

14

Lucy Hutchinson, *Memoirs*

David Norbrook

Memoirs of the Life of Colonel Hutchinson is many different things: a love story; a political biography; a war diary; a sociological analysis of English history; and a bitter polemic against the regime of Charles II, with a call to be ready for rebellion when the time comes. This political subversiveness meant that when Lucy Hutchinson wrote the work, soon after her husband had died in prison in 1664, there could be no question of its being printed. The manuscript thereafter fell into the hands of a branch of the family which did not wish to revive memories of republican black sheep, and it was not published until 1806 (when the editor gave it the now-current title). It was immediately recognized as a classic, and has remained more or less continuously in print ever since. The work was early of interest to women writers; in 1861 Jane Williams declared it 'the most perfect piece of biography ever written by a woman' (Williams, 1861, 91).

This Victorian admiration, however, was somewhat double-edged. Lucy Hutchinson was often acclaimed for what was considered a quintessentially female modesty, a readiness to subordinate herself, as wife, to her husband, as man of action. The fact that she addressed the work to her children accentuated this sense of self-limiting domesticity. In the celebrated portrait of her courtship (45–52; Demaria, 331–2), she presents herself as her husband's 'faithful mirror', his 'shadow', her virtues as 'images of his own making'. To recent feminist critics, such qualities are more calculated to alienate than to inspire. In the *Memoirs*, it has been argued, she effaces her own role as a writer.

Hutchinson may adopt the third person to lend her narrative distance; but in fact she very seldom yields up her judgement and narrative control to reported speech or any other mediation, and we are always aware of her informing judgement. The courtship passage – which underwent much revision in manuscript – is a case in point. John Hutchinson has fallen in love with her precisely because she is a writer: on visiting her house in her absence, he has noticed her collection of Latin books, and his interest is quickened when he hears a song she has composed. Lucy Hutchinson is harking back in this passage to the fashionable aesthetic vocabulary of the 1630s. Reflection, in this idiom, is not merely passive. Lucy Hutchinson is her husband's mirror in the act of writing by trying to represent him faithfully; she is composing a 'true history' and is proud that she has more to offer 'than the best romances'. She writes that he polished the virtues which had 'the roughness of the quarry' about them, like a sculptor shaping a statue. Here the husband has the active role; but in declaring that he 'made her more equal to him than he found her', she implies that female qualities are not fixed and natural but are constructs that can be changed (51).

In casting her relationship within aesthetic terms, indeed, she reminds us that she and not her husband was the real artist. And in outlining his family history, she shows why he might have been attracted to a woman writer. The rise of humanist learning in the early modern period did not lead to anything like universal female education, but for some well-to-do households there was prestige in a learned daughter. John Hutchinson's maternal grandmother had 'a high degree of learning and languages, to such an excellency in music and poetry, that she made rare compositions of both kinds' (35). His mother had attended the household of Arabella Stuart, a celebratedly learned royal lady who became a Puritan martyr on her early death (34). Lucy Hutchinson's own father had ensured that she was given an unusually rigorous classical education.

The children for whom she was writing knew that their mother's aspirations as an author were in keeping with those family traditions, and went a long way beyond the *Memoirs.* Though she had eight children, she also found time in her marriage for writing. She had undertaken a translation of Lucretius's atheistic epic, *De rerum natura.* In the humanist tradition, bringing a major classical epic successfully into the vernacular tongue was one of the supreme literary ambitions. When Hutchinson began the project, *De rerum natura* was the last remaining epic, so that her ambitions were high – and overcame the religious scruples which she later felt more intensely. When her portrait was painted jointly with her husband's, she was depicted with a laurel wreath, the emblem of literary composition. After the *Memoirs* she continued writing, perhaps beginning with an account of her own life. (The autobiographical fragment (3–15) is often dated before the *Memoirs;* but the reference to 'my house at Owthorpe' (14) would not have been written before her husband's death, and the *Memoirs* formed her first priority.) The *Memoirs* is in one sense a departure from the literary programme she had set herself; circumstances had forced on her a vindication of her husband, and she subordinated her self-portrayal to that end.

Within that framework, however, her own role as agent and as writer is by no means insignificant. By the end of the story she is negotiating shrewdly with the royalist authorities and putting her case with such vehemence in a letter of protest about prison conditions that the governor relents from 'fear that she would have printed him' (318). In the opening address, she asks to be pardoned for 'drawing an imperfect image' of her husband, also reminding us of her role in the process. And she goes on to complicate the vocabulary of images: her book is merely a 'copy' of him, God being the 'original' of excellence. She admits that she may have 'delighted more than I ought to have done in the mirror that reflected the Creator's excellence, which I should have always admired in its own fountain'. Her husband, 'though one of the best of men, was yet but man, a son of Adam, an inheritor of his corrupted nature'. God's grace alone had 'raised that wretched fallen nature and changed it into such a blessed image of his own glory' (17).

Lucy Hutchinson establishes a powerful tension here between her desire as artist to 'image' her husband and a strong religious awareness that images carry the danger of idolatry. In recounting her courtship, she has allowed nostalgia to push her to the brink of blasphemy. She and her husband were strict Calvinists, committed to the belief that even before humanity's creation, God had decided on the minority who were to be saved and the vast majority who were to be damned. Hutchinson presents her husband's two periods of biblical study which consolidated his beliefs on this point as crucial, heroic stages of spiritual development (54–5, 286–7; Demaria 335–5). This worldview makes virtue in this world a precarious matter: neither high social status nor careful ethical training is any guarantee of ultimate worth. There is thus a kind of spiritual egalitarianism; if the wife images the husband, the husband's virtues too are no more than an image. To write the life of a saint is to try to render a miracle that is ultimately beyond representation, the light beyond the reflection. When describing a battle she writes that if this were a romance she would celebrate the heroes' gallantry, but heroic exploits 'are but the beams of the Almighty' (147). The difficulty for the writer is to hold the worldly action and those transcendental beams in some kind of difficult suspension. The imagery of light and sunshine that pervades the book does some of this work.

Lucy Hutchinson did not repudiate all images. Her husband was a great collector of paintings, and one of the few good points she concedes to Charles I is his love of 'paintings, carvings and engravings' (67). When her husband orders images in a local church to be taken down (76), it is because they have been recently erected as part of a programme to enforce the power and mystique of the Anglican hierarchy, blurring the divisions between the human and the divine.

This problem of idolatry lies at the centre not only of Hutchinson's aesthetic theory but of her theory of history. She situates the life of her husband in a much larger time-scale. Hutchinson draws on the parliamentary historian Thomas May and the republican theorist James Harrington, but she offers a synthesis of her own. History, she believes, is progressing towards a future millennium, in which Christ will rule with his elect saints on earth. Before that day can come, however, earthly kings and the churches which they head must be overthrown.

Kingship is one manifestation of the more general phenomenon of idolatry, of valuing earthly powers and honours above God. Idolatry is strengthened by institutions which place their and their adherents' private interests against the public interest; these include all churches which enforce belief by compulsion. In the middle ages the Catholic church had epitomized idolatry, substituting the worship of images for understanding scripture. The Reformation had 'changed the idol, but left the idolatry still in practice' (59), with princes taking over state churches and appropriating their mystique. Lucy Hutchinson considers the hyperbolical praise of great ladies at court to be part of such idolatry; in praising her husband's love as free from idolatry she is making a political point.

A distinctive feature of Hutchinson's book as opposed to much Puritan apologetic is her consistent counterposing of divine providence to secular 'interest'. Interest is not uniformly evil: God works through secondary, earthly means. Those reformers who want to achieve a kingdom on earth directly, overthrowing all secular authority, will only provoke a tyrannical backlash (59). God's cause is best advanced by a careful re-balancing of secular interests so that the divine interest can best emerge. In this sense, hers is a qualified iconoclasm: she supports the removal of images from churches with parliamentary authority, but would oppose those who take the law into their hands or smash secular images. Following Harrington, she believes that the public interest can best be served by the abolition of the monarchy and the old hereditary nobility. This will open the way to a reformed landed gentry whose wealth will be limited by an 'agrarian law', and who will thus have an interest in political and religious liberty.

Lucy Hutchinson situates John Hutchinson's life in this larger historical pattern. He belongs to a substratum of the Nottinghamshire gentry which has in effect already followed an agrarian law (31), and this helps him to achieve an independence of judgement from court and church. Lacking a vested interest in conformity, he encourages such independence, as his father had done (53; Demaria, 333). While he is head and governor of his household, he readily listens to his wife when she wins him round to a different opinion on a matter crucial to salvation (210–11), and he aims 'rather to convince' his household 'by reason than compel them to obedience' (255).

The *Memoirs* is fundamentally a passionate vindication of her husband, and to that extent it may be thought to err on the side of idolatry; but the narrative eschews some more obvious forms of idealization. We need to remember that at its core are two highly polemical goals. The narrative dealing with the years 1642–5 is based on notes she had taken at the time to defend him against charges of misconduct; the later part of the book aims to vindicate him against charges of cowardice at the Restoration. On each occasion he is presented as infallible in judgement. The description of his period as Governor of Nottingham Castle demonstrates in microcosm the growing divisions that faced the parliamentary party: between those determined to pursue the war to the end and those eager for a compromise settlement; between Presbyterians demanding a disciplined state church and Independents like the Hutchinsons who favoured freedom of Protestant worship. Class animosities between burghers and gentry are never far below the surface: Hutchinson suspects those below as well as those above her in rank. If these sections make flat reading, it is partly because Hutchinson insists that a godly war should not follow the narrative patterns of romance. Conventional heroism is not open to a commander scrupulously trying to reconcile civilian and military obligations, and leading troops who readily claim their own right to decide when to fight (144). There is a striking contrast with a contemporaneous account of the war by a Nottinghamshire neighbour, Margaret Cavendish, Duchess of Newcastle, who presents her husband's exploits as instances of single-handed military genius.

On her husband's actions at the Restoration, Lucy Hutchinson may be guilty of some misrepresentation, in taking all the blame for his recantation on herself. Here too in vindicating his perfection she does not bring him closer to a conventional romance model: rather than joining a military rising he 'thought himself obliged to sit still' and refrain from rebellion (287).

Throughout the book, in fact, Hutchinson has to deal with a career which could be made to look somewhat anti-heroic and to show how his actions take on a new significance in the light of grace. Both cavaliers and the more militant Puritans were ready during the 1640s and 1650s to rush into military action to advance the kingdom of God without considering the effects on secular interests. John Hutchinson's constitutional scruples often place him in a passive role. Disliking the military coup that opens the way to the king's trial, he participates 'very much against his will' (234). When Cromwell usurps power in 1653, he waits for events. He refuses to take up military action against the Restoration of Charles II in 1660, and leaves it to his wife to try to gain his life and estates by forging a letter of recantation. Once his life had been spared, he felt himself obligated to refrain from opposition: thus, ironically, he was finally imprisoned for involvement in a rising in which he had refused to enlist, even at the risk of finding his name dishonoured for cowardice amongst fellow-republicans (287). All these refusals come to prefigure his martyrdom, showing a Christ-like patience and refusal to compromise his principles for the external idols of conventional honour. Lucy Hutchinson is able to add her husband's story to the martyrological literature that had accrued around the regicides who had met their deaths more directly in 1660.

John Hutchinson's passivity is not an end in itself, however. History's iconoclastic momentum has been temporarily stalled but Lucy Hutchinson – lacking the benefit of hindsight – has no doubt that the republican cause will soon revive. At the end of the book, when John Hutchinson gives instructions to his eldest son, he takes it for granted that there will be a further republican rising before long; he should wait to see if it is better managed than the inept 1663 rebellion, and if so he should join it (327).

Lucy Hutchinson's immediate purpose in writing was to control her grief and to remind her children of their father's legacy. She had to construct a vivid verbal 'picture' for her youngest children because they could not even remember what he looked like (18). Her portrayal of her own family members has a warmth lacking elsewhere in the book. The legal details over land transactions, while tedious to us, were of burning interest to the children, as explaining the financial difficulties into which she had been plunged – and which were to lead her before long to sell off all the estates.

These direct addresses to her children, however, do not mean that she did not envisage a wider audience if and when political circumstances changed. She was probably aware that contemporaries like Bulstrode Whitelocke and Edmund Ludlow were working on narratives of the same period. (For general contexts see Royce McGillivray, *Restoration Historians and the English Civil War*, The Hague, 1974.) Her own version is distinguished by its narrative and stylistic concision. Puritan writings favoured extended self-revelation, and this made for diffuseness. Hutchinson's own sentences sometimes wander (the punctuation in modern editions is editorial); but she shows a fondness for terse, epigrammatic effects that perhaps reflects her commitment to classical literature. Very often the terseness is destructive. It has been said that her pen was dipped in vinegar, and she delights in vituperative vignettes, as with the political enemy who 'flung away from the board in a great huff and muttering' (153). When she is relaying a section of narrative composed by her husband, we can easily recognize her own sardonic touch: 'at last, *parturiunt montes*, and out comes Secretary Bennet' (305). Lucy Hutchinson has added the Horatian joke of mountains giving birth to a mouse. A particular favourite is the deflating anticlimax; censure comes so easily to her that it seems hard for her to offer praise without withdrawing it. One parliamentarian defended the regicides 'so generously that it will never be forgotten of him, who indeed hath no other good thing to be remembered' (279).

Classical literature often prescribed a golden mean in life and in writing; Hutchinson's Calvinism instilled a rigid antithesis between a small elect and a huge body of the damned. Her style negotiates these oppositions. She does not accept that Anglicanism was a 'virtuous medium' between Catholicism and Puritanism (58), and ridicules the fence-sitting peer who was 'very often of both parties and advantaged neither' (85). Yet her own and her husband's goal is represented as a more complex middle way, steering a path between the millennialists who rejected all human laws and the authoritarians who reacted against them. In 1648 the radicals became 'as violent in their zeal to pull down, as the others were in their madness, to restore this idol', the king (232). John Hutchinson in the end sides with the radicals but fears that they will provoke a backlash that will undermine their own ends. In her descriptions of Cromwell, we sense Lucy Hutchinson trying to keep a balance by pulling back with some difficulty from a straightforward censure.

The worldview presented in the *Memoirs* will strike many modern readers as repellent. Lucy Hutchinson can relate the slaughter of the unregenerate without any censure or compassion (e.g., 204). Yet the recurrent tension between religious righteousness and political forms or secular interests makes her narrative something more complicated than a conventional chronicle of providences. When dealing with those she considers regenerate, she can move into a more open and lyrical mode of writing; and the book also commands respect for the rigour and strenuousness with which its author tries to vindicate intellectual independence in times of revolutionary uncertainty. The epilogue is a powerful reminder of how hard she found the task. She tells her children: 'however I appear alive in my action I would not have you believe it possible I could survive your late fellow prisoner' (337). She writes as her own ghost. But she had managed to make her cause live.

References and Further Reading

Cavendish, Margaret, Duchess of Newcastle (1906). *The Life of William Cavendish, Duke of Newcastle.* Ed. C. H. Firth. London: Routledge; New York: E. P. Dutton.

Demaria, Robert, Jr (1996). *British Literature 1640–1789: An Anthology.* Oxford, and Cambridge, Mass.: Blackwell.

Hutchinson, Lucy (1906). *Memoirs of the Life of Colonel Hutchinson.* Ed. C. H. Firth. London: Routledge; New York: E. P. Dutton. Still the best edition for historical annotations, and usefully prints extracts from the early drafts; but Firth did not have access to the full manuscript.

——(1973). *Memoirs of the Life of Colonel Hutchinson.* Ed. James Sutherland. London, New York, Toronto: Oxford University Press. Includes sections of the manuscript omitted from the first printed edition of 1806.

——(1995). *Memoirs of the Life of Colonel Hutchinson.* Ed. N. H. Keeble. London: J. M. Dent; Vermont: Charles E. Tuttle. Unless otherwise stated, page numbers in parentheses refer to this modernized edition, the fullest text available to date.

——(forthcoming). *Order and Disorder.* Ed. David Norbrook. Oxford: Blackwell.

Keeble, N. H. (1987). *The Literary Culture of Nonconformity in Later Seventeenth-century England.* Leicester: Leicester University Press.

——(1990). '"But the Colonel's Shadow": Lucy Hutchinson, women's writing, and the Civil War'. In *Literature and the English Civil War.* Ed. Thomas Healy and Jonathan Sawday. Cambridge: Cambridge University Press, 227–47.

McGillivray, Royce (1974). *Restoration Historians and the English Civil War.* The Hague: Martinus Nijhoff. Specialized but acute and informed study.

Norbrook, David (1997). 'Lucy Hutchinson's "Elegies" and the situation of the republican woman writer'. *English Literary Renaissance* 27, 468–521.

Williams, Jane (1861). *The Literary Women of England.* London: Saunders, Otley and Co.

15

John Bunyan, *Grace Abounding*

Anita Pacheco

John Bunyan's *Grace Abounding to the Chief of Sinners* (1666) is the best known of the hundreds of Puritan spiritual autobiographies produced in seventeenth-century England. The word 'Puritan', while notoriously hard to define, refers in its most general sense to all those, whether inside or outside the Church of England, 'who wanted a cleaner break with popery' (Hill, 1964, 20). Yet *Grace Abounding* can also be called a 'Puritan' text in a theological sense, as it is rooted in a particular version of Calvinist orthodoxy that gave enormous weight to the doctrine of predestination: the belief that God before the creation chose a select few for salvation and condemned the majority of human beings to eternal damnation (Stachniewski, 1991, 11–13). For Calvinists of this stamp, the religious life became focused on the quest to discover one's irreversible spiritual identity: was one saved (elect) or damned (reprobate)?

This was not, of course, an easy question to answer. Where could one hope to find conclusive evidence either way? Puritanism, as an experimental (or experiential) religion, told believers that the evidence lay in their own experience. Yet because subjective experience is at best a problematic source of objective, authoritative evidence, Puritan divines like William Perkins identified patterns or stages of elect and reprobate experience. While the elect progressed from conviction of sin through the experience of being called by God to an acceptance of God's saving grace and the imputed righteousness of Christ, the reprobate, after a calling 'not effectual', declined into 'fullness of sin' on the road to perdition. It was through conformity to the elect paradigm that the Christian could gain assurance of salvation. This led logically to prolonged and anxious self-scrutiny, to a search in one's life and states of mind for what were referred to as the 'signs' of election and reprobation.

Grace Abounding and Puritan autobiography generally thus emerged from a religious culture which encouraged habits of introspection and self-examination as well as the narrating of one's experience; admission to a church required the presentation of experiential evidence of conversion and elect identity. The necessity of mapping that experience onto a narrative template accounts for the conventionality of the genre.

Grace Abounding adheres, at least in its broad outline, to the traditional stages of the Puritan conversion narrative: an account of one's unregenerate life, recollections of early signs of God's favour, conviction of sin, calling, conversion, followed by the call to the ministry (Newey, 1988, 191). Yet to discuss *Grace Abounding* in terms of its conformity to a model of elect experience is in fact misleading, for the simple reason that assurance of salvation is a goal that continually eludes Bunyan's grasp. The conversion recounted in *Grace Abounding* is certainly *not* a Pauline one, and even attempts, like that of Anne Hawkins (1982), to trace a more gradual pattern of conversion in the text tend to exaggerate the degree of narrative closure that Bunyan's record makes available (Newey, 1988, 201–3). The first recognizable conversion experience – Bunyan's revelatory encounter with the poor women of Bedford (37) – is followed by a long and gruelling spiritual crisis marked by repeated temptations to doubt, blasphemy and apostasy which appear to confirm a reprobate identity. This narrative of anguish and despair is punctuated by feelings of hope, even elation, but it keeps returning to cast doubt on Bunyan's affirmative religious experiences. Obviously, *Grace Abounding* moves towards an acceptance of the objective truth of the elect narrative and the consequent alleviation of doubt and fear. But this spiritual progress never enables a clear separation of the authorial self from the past selves on which he comments (Nussbaum, 1982, 32; Pooley, 1990, 109). Bunyan's candid admission in the conclusion that he is still prey to atheist thoughts makes it clear that the striving for assurance has no end in this world: 'when this temptation comes, it takes away my girdle from me, and removeth the foundation from under me' (1; Newey, 1988, 205; Nussbaum, 1982, 20).

As the Puritans' supreme religious authority, the Bible is the main channel through which Bunyan seeks to discern his place in God's story. Yet his relationship with the scriptures demonstrates the immense difficulty of translating personal experience into objective evidence of salvation. Bunyan, it has often been noted, accords with other Puritan autobiographers in presenting himself as the passive recipient of biblical texts that 'dart from Heaven into my Soul' (22), 'trample upon all my desires' (58) and fall 'with weight upon my spirit' (62). If, as Peter J. Carlton (1984) has argued, this attribution of agency to biblical texts represents an attempt to give objective authority to subjective experiences, Bunyan seems a less than adept practitioner. Biblical texts that induce despair are regularly countered by others that promise grace and salvation, but the authenticity of these comforting experiences is just as regularly called into question. This circular process is encapsulated in the period of overwhelming despair that follows Bunyan's surrender to the temptation to 'sell Christ' that seizes him after he has received 'blessed evidence from heaven touching my interest in his [God's] love through Christ' (132). Afraid that he has now committed the 'sin unpardonable' (148), Bunyan is tormented for nearly two and a half years by the biblical text denying God's mercy to the reprobate Esau (141). After a more reassuring text ('My grace is sufficient') has 'darted in upon' him (204), he prays that 'both these Scriptures would meet in my heart at once' so that he might see 'which of them would get the better of me' (212). When this textual battle erupts a few days

later and 'this about the sufficiency of Grace' prevails (213), Bunyan reads his experience as the working of God: 'Yet truly I am apt to think it was of God, for the word
of the Law and Wrath, must give place to the Word of Life and Grace' (214). Yet the
language ('apt to think') betrays uncertainty, and the dreaded identification with Esau
soon reasserts itself, albeit with diminished ferocity (see Newey, 1988, 198–200;
Stachniewski, 1991, 137–8).

It is the ephemeral nature of his positive religious experiences that necessitates the
writing of the autobiography, as an earlier episode suggests:

> Wherefore I said in my Soul with much gladness, Well, I would I had a pen and ink
> here, I would write this down before I go any further, for surely I will not forget *this*,
> forty years hence; but alas! within less than forty days I began to question all again. (92)

For Bunyan, as for other Puritan autobiographers, the permanence of a written record
gives textual reality to the moments of optimism. It also enables him to communicate his experience to the godly community (the Bedford Independent church), which
further enhances its objectivity.

The oscillation between hope and despair which characterizes Bunyan's narrative
is in part a measure of the anxiety engendered by a predestinarian theology which
made conformity to the reprobate paradigm a terrifyingly plausible outcome (Stachniewski, 1991, 132–9; Graham, 1990, 120). For Bunyan, confidence in God's favour
constantly confronts the strong possibility of His hostility and rejection. On this level,
Grace Abounding suggests that social factors contributed to the severity of the theological crisis. The narrative opens with a statement of the author's 'pedigree' (1): 'For
my descent then, it was, as is well known by many, of a low and inconsiderable generation; my fathers house being of that rank that is meanest, and most despised of all
the families in the Land' (2). Bunyan immediately goes on to imply that his lowly
origins were in fact a blessing in disguise, giving him a spiritual advantage over those
who 'boast of Noble blood, or of a High-born state according to the flesh' (2). The
passage, however, is less than confident; its implicit equation of the poor with 'spirit'
and the well-born with 'flesh' is coupled with a nervous awareness that in the eyes of
many his 'low and inconsiderable generation' automatically invalidates his claim to
spiritual authority.

This opening passage reminds us that the hierarchical society in which Bunyan
lived was predisposed to identify social lowliness with moral and spiritual unworthiness. John Stachniewski (1991, 63–9) has argued persuasively that Calvinist theology, in the particular historical circumstances of its reception in England, exacerbated
this tendency. Calvinism established its hold over the English imagination during the
late sixteenth and early seventeenth centuries, a period of intense economic instability, when the operation of new and largely unintelligible market forces brought prosperity to some and downward mobility or yet deeper poverty to many. In
Stachniewski's view, this asymmetrical and seemingly arbitrary redistribution of
wealth must have looked like convincing evidence in support of the doctrine of

predestination and encouraged in those who had recently gone down in the world the fear of a reprobate destiny (see also Hill, 1988, 16–20).

Bunyan could certainly number himself among the recently dispossessed, for although he, like his father, worked as a tinker, the Bunyans had been small farmers throughout the sixteenth century (Hill, 1988, 41; Stachniewski, 1991, 139–40). This history of recent family decline may have interacted with the value judgements built into the social hierarchy to turn Bunyan's poverty into a troubling indicator of his spiritual identity. The opening section of *Grace Abounding*, that recounting his unregenerate life, illustrates the way that his feelings of social exclusion fuelled his fear of exclusion from God's grace. The youthful vanities he enumerates in these early paragraphs – his neglect of his literary skills, his swearing, his playing sports on Sundays – are signs at once of social baseness and ungodliness. The shame he feels when a neighbour reproaches him for his swearing reveals his intense sensitivity to social contempt and the way his disreputable social identity induced a despairing conviction of irredeemable sinfulness: 'it is but in vain for me to think of a reformation' (27). This nagging sense of social and spiritual inferiority seems to have intensified as Puritan culture penetrated the village of Elstow, bringing with it an opposition to Sunday sports and recreational bell-ringing – two of the young Bunyan's favourite pastimes, both of which result in guilty expectations of divine punishment: the voice from heaven while he is playing cat and his fears of being crushed by a falling bell.

Bunyan has a go at godly reformation, and admits, with the benefit of hindsight, that his adoption of 'something like a moral life' was undertaken in order 'to be well spoken of by men' (32). The insufficiency to an 'outward Reformation' (30) that was essentially a desperate bid for acceptance into the social mainstream is fully revealed one day in Bedford when Bunyan encounters 'three or four poor women sitting at a door in the Sun and talking about the things of God' (37). This incident marks Bunyan's introduction to the open communion Bedford Baptists, through whom he would enter fully into the world of experimental Calvinism. Part of what Bunyan learns that day is therefore doctrinal: 'convinced of their miserable state by nature', the women show him the futility of his moral reformation and his absolute reliance on God's unmerited grace. But a crucial part of the appeal of the theology is that it is voiced by the poor. As Neil Keeble (1990, 131–3) observes in his astute reading of this episode, the passage traces the movement of the socially marginal to the spiritual centre. These poor women who are too insignificant to have names (even their number is unclear) are by the end of the passage identified as members of the elect: 'they were people that dwelt alone, and were not to be reckoned amongst their Neighbours' (38). Social exclusion is here transformed into a sign of the spiritual elite. Poverty is redefined as the possession of 'a new world' (38), and educational disadvantage transcended by the women's startling, mysterious speech: a 'pleasantness of Scripture language' (38) acquired not at school but from their extensive knowledge of the Bible and their privileged experience of 'a new birth, the work of God on their hearts' (37; Keeble, 1990, 133). What Bunyan found that day in Bedford was a religion that made a spiritual virtue out of poverty, inverting the social values that had insinuated his reprobation. This religion also offered him a new language. While his swearing represented a poor man's vain attempt 'to make my words have authority' (28), speaking the language of the socially respectable felt, Bunyan tells us, like a hollow performance (32). The strange language of the Bedford separatists, invested with the authority of the Scriptures, promises instead a discourse cut loose from the belittling assessments of the social world, through which he might speak as a subject (Graham, 1990, 124–8; Stachniewski, 1991, 146–51).

This episode represents the beginning of the worst of Bunyan's ordeal. It will take him five long years to stabilize a deeply ingrained sense of unworthiness that bolstered his belief in a hostile God who rejects his prayers with contempt: 'it is not for such as thee to have favour with the Highest' (109). But the Bedford Independent church provides a vital social anchor during this period of largely solitary self-scrutiny. And Bunyan's eventual integration into the elect community, accompanied as it was with a new calling as preacher of God's word, is a crucial stage in his construction of a more positive sense of self: 'then I began to conclude it might be so, that God had owned in his Work such a foolish one as I' (274).

The importance to Bunyan of the belief that God's chosen are the poor and oppressed of this world emerges clearly at the end of *Grace Abounding*, in the author's account of his imprisonment, and also in his *A Relation of the Imprisonment of Mr. John Bunyan* (which was not published until 1765). Bunyan was arrested in 1660, soon after the Restoration of monarchy, and charged with refusing to attend services of the established church and with holding a conventicle, or illegal religious meeting. The authorities were suspicious of religious sects, especially after the Fifth Monarchist uprising of 1661, and interpreted religious nonconformity as a reliable indicator of disloyalty to the state. Bunyan could have secured his release had he undertaken not to preach, but he refused to compromise with the authorities and remained in prison for twelve years, during which time he wrote *Grace Abounding*. By this stage of his spiritual journey, he could afford to embrace social exclusion in its most acute form as evidence of election, persecution by the worldly sharpening the conviction of spiritual separateness.

In *A Relation* Bunyan gives a detailed account of his trial, which he dramatizes as a triumphant assertion of his spiritual authority before those who question it on the grounds of his lowly class origins. When the authorities argue that his lack of education disqualifies him from interpreting scripture and that his preaching appeals to 'none but a company of poor simple ignorant people' (104), Bunyan invokes the authority of God's word to discredit their discriminatory discourse: '*That God hides his things from the wise and prudent*, (that is from the learned of the world) *and reveals them to babes and sucklings* . . . that God had rejected the wise, and mighty and noble, and chosen the foolish, and the base' (103).

This demonstration of a biblical knowledge superior to that of his social betters points to an important narrative impulse of *Grace Abounding*: the vindication of Bunyan's claim to pastoral authority. Addressed to his Bedford congregation, the auto-

biography is framed by affirmations of his pastoral role. The first word of the preface
– 'children' – proclaims his position as minister of the spiritual children 'whom God
hath counted him worthy to beget to Faith' (4), and the narrative draws to a close
with Bunyan's account of his call to the ministry. The struggle for discursive authority that has informed the emotional texture of the autobiography works not only to
diminish Bunyan's debilitating sense of exclusion but also to justify his claim to 'a
space in which he can exercise pastoral power' (Pooley, 1990, 114).

In his account of his call to the ministry, in a passage added to the fifth edition
(1680), Bunyan seeks to refute various rumours and slanders intended to tarnish his
reputation as a minister. Rumours that he was 'a Witch, a Jesuit, a High-way-man, and
the like' (307) he dismisses with a shrug, only to go on to devote eight paragraphs to
an impassioned denial of the accusation that 'I had my *Misses*, my *Whores*, my *Bastards*'
(309). The passage seethes with anger towards his detractors – 'what shall I say to those
that have thus bespattered me?' (311) – but in the end it is women themselves who are
the main target (see Keeble, 1990, 139–40; Pooley, 1990, 111):

> And in this I admire the Wisdom of God that he made me shie of women from my first
> Convertion until now . . . it is a rare thing to see me carry it pleasant towards a Woman;
> the common Salutation of women I abhor, 'tis odious to me in whomsoever I see it.
> Their Company alone I cannot away with. I seldom so much as touch a womans
> hand. (315)

Two-thirds of Bunyan's congregation were women, a fact that may help to explain the
anxiety that informs this passage; the charge of womanizing must have represented a
particularly potent threat to his public position (Pooley, 1990, 111; Spargo, 1996,
179). But the passage also shows the ease with which Bunyan is able to 'relocate that
threat within a dangerous female sexuality' (Spargo, 1996, 179).

Tamsin Spargo has discussed the way that Bunyan sought 'to shore up his fragile
authority' as a minister through a textual endorsement of dominant ideologies of
gender, in particular 'the conventional association of the female voice with unruliness'
(Spargo, 1997, 83). Women, of course, played an enormously important role in Puritan
and nonconformist culture. Many congregations had, like Bunyan's, a predominately
female membership. Women sectarians wrote, preached and prophesied, claiming a
public voice that challenged traditional restrictions on women's speech and access to
the public sphere. Bunyan's own arduous quest for discursive authority was, as we have
seen, indebted to the inspiring speech of the poor women of Bedford. But his religion,
though rooted in class consciousness, easily accommodated 'a firm belief in the social
and spiritual inferiority of women' (Thickstun, 1988, 88). Indeed, Bunyan used his
pastoral authority as an instrument to control and silence the women in his church,
opposing their bid to hold separate meetings and denying women's fitness for an active
role in church and public affairs (Keeble, 1990: 146; Spargo, 1997, 77–83).

Yet *Grace Abounding* and *A Relation* attest, in spite of their author, to the centrality of women to nonconformist culture. I refer here not just to the poor women of

Bedford but also to Bunyan's second wife Elizabeth, who appears in *A Relation* in the role of petitioner for her husband's release from prison. Bunyan is careful to present her as properly feminine; Elizabeth comes before the judges 'with a bashed face, and a trembling heart' (117). But the defiant words he attributes to her in this public arena undermine the conservative construction of femininity he sought to authorize and invest her with striking verbal authority as the voice of the poor and oppressed whose spiritual liberation lies at the heart of Bunyan's faith: 'Yes, said she, and because he is a Tinker, and a poor man; therefore he is despised, and cannot have justice' (119).

REFERENCES AND FURTHER READING

Batson, E. B. (1984). *John Bunyan: Allegory and Imagination*. London and Canberra: Croom Helm.

Bell, R. (1977). 'Metamorphoses of spiritual autobiography.' *English Literary History* 44, 108–26.

Camden, V. J. (1989). 'Blasphemy and the problem of the self in *Grace Abounding*'. *Bunyan Studies* 1, 5–19.

Carlton, P. J. (1984). 'Bunyan: language, convention, authority'. *English Literary History* 51, 17–32.

Graham, E. (1990). 'Authority, resistance and loss: gendered difference in the writings of John Bunyan and Hannah Allen'. In *John Bunyan and His England 1628–88*. Ed. Anne Laurence, W. R. Owens and Stuart Sim. London and Ronceverte: The Hambledon Press, 115–30.

Hawkins, A. (1982). 'The double-conversion narrative in Bunyan's *Grace Abounding*'. *Philological Quarterly* 61, 259–76.

Hill, C. (1964). *Society and Puritanism in Pre-Revolutionary England*. London: Secker and Warburg.

——(1988). *A Turbulent, Seditious, and Factious People: John Bunyan and his Church 1628–1688*. Oxford: Clarendon.

——(1991). *Change and Continuity in Seventeenth-century England*. New York and London: Yale University Press.

Keeble, N. H. (1987). *The Literary Culture of Nonconformity in Later Seventeenth-century England*. Leicester: Leicester University Press.

——(1990). '"Here is her Glory, even to be under Him": the feminine in the thought and work of John Bunyan'. In *John Bunyan and His England 1628–88*. Ed. Anne Laurence, W. R. Owens and Stuart Sim. London and Ronceverte: The Hambledon Press, 132–47.

Newey, V. (1988). '"With the eyes of my understanding": Bunyan, experience, and acts of interpretation'. In *John Bunyan: Conventicle and Parnassus*. Ed. N. H. Keeble. Oxford: Clarendon, 189–216.

Nussbaum, F. A. (1982). '"By these words I was sustained": Bunyan and *Grace Abounding*'. *English Literary History* 49, 18–34.

Pooley, R. (1990). '*Grace Abounding* and the new sense of self'. In *John Bunyan and His England 1628–88*. Ed. Anne Laurence, W. R. Owens and Stuart Sim. London and Ronceverte: The Hambledon Press, 105–14.

Spargo, T. (1996). 'Contra-dictions: women as figures of exclusion and resistance in John Bunyan's and Agnes Beaumont's narratives'. In *Voicing Women: Gender and Sexuality in Early-Modern Writing*. Ed. Kate Chedgzoy, Melanie Hansen and Suzanne Trill. Keele: Keele University Press, 173–84.

——(1997). *The Writing of John Bunyan*. Aldershot: Ashgate.

Stachniewski, J. (1991). *The Persecutory Imagination: English Puritanism and the Literature of Religious Despair*. Oxford: Clarendon.

16

John Milton, *Paradise Lost*

Nicholas von Maltzahn

In his epic Milton imagines creation in relation to redemption, in a Christian narration centring in the Fall of man. The poem is designed to draw our worship of the creation toward worship of the creator, as St Paul enjoins (Romans 1:16–25). To do so, however, Milton insists on valuing both. He releases the tensions in the dualism characteristic of the baroque by instead venturing a monist poetry of process. *Paradise Lost* is first of all an epic of choice. The choice offered is by turns an aesthetic, or ethical, or spiritual either/or: a turn toward, or away from what it is to be a creature. Milton focuses on the very point of choice, in a way that enlarges our sense of agency. In the Fall, first of angels, and then of man, he describes the price of self-involvement, and the losses that follow the move from relation to isolation. But the epic also seeks to foster our capacity to choose the offer of grace, and the renewal of relation. The experience of such acceptance is central to Milton's purpose in dramatizing the first chapters of Genesis.

Modern criticism has with great flair questioned the power of language and representation, in ways that erode epic claims to transcendence. Such scepticism, however, invites questioning in turn by an earlier pragmatism. How might the structures of belief, mediated through narration, better equip individuals and societies to live their lives? The complexities of Milton's encyclopedic poem yield some promise also of coherence. Milton, in the English Revolution and after, lived in a time when the relationship of the individual to God was being debated sharply and critically. The sophistications of his narration are allied to a resilient theology, with which he undertakes the two-fold labour 'to assert Eternal Providence' and to 'justify the ways of God to men' (1, 25–6). In its vivid description of heaven, earth and hell, and their inhabitants, the epic describes how the divine proceeds in creation to form of matter both spiritual (angels) and corporeal (e.g. human) beings, animated and free to 'return' to the creator 'If not depraved from good' (5, 469–90). To meet this challenge, Milton quite reinvented mid-seventeenth-century poetics, working to synthesize the wealth of a lifetime's learning. He combined such varied materials as classical epic, contemporary Platonist philosophy, and apocalyptic speculation with the rich legacy of Renaissance poetry, especially from the English and Italian traditions. In his career, his services to individual and society alike included much promotion of the further reformation of church and state. He sought to advance this end by joining in pamphlet controversy as well as in government service during the English Revolution. His tracts by turns expound Christian charity and classical magnanimity, and argue views of faith and citizenship animated by these ideals. In *Paradise Lost* the operation especially of charity is investigated anew as 'the soul / Of all,' capable of creating 'A paradise within' (12, 575–87).

Milton wrote his long-planned epic between 1658 and 1663. Its inception seems to coincide with other expressions of republican dissatisfaction with the monarchist trend of the Cromwellian Protectorate; its conclusion with his dismay at sharpening repression in the Restoration monarchy of Charles II. Only in the winter of 1667, however, did Milton bring the work to the press, with the work finally published that autumn. Now a succession of national calamities favoured the reception of his great religious poem, in a way that might excuse its republican authorship, ineradicable as that was (Norbrook, 1999). Even the recent past might seem another country; they had done things differently there. Milton spoke the republican dialect with a more godly accent than most, however, and this may have helped his work pass the licenser. Early responses indicate that suspicions of the author vied with wonder at his present achievement. The tension naturally led to attempts to reconcile the two, most often through presuming the epic to be some disavowal by Milton of his politics of yesteryear. Then and since, its insistent elegiac note encouraged readers to see *Paradise Lost* as speaking to a more present subject: the history of England in the 1640s and 1650s. But the character of Milton's repudiation of the interregnum invited different constructions. In view of his infamy as a defender of the regicide, it was striking that the epic might read as a very much extended homily against rebellion. Some readers, however, were readier to recognize in the epic a once common, now half-known tongue, insisting on the heavenly kingdom at the expense of human ones, in a politics as old as the biblical books of Judges and of Samuel.

In reaction to Milton's stirring of the collective memory, there was wide agreement about the uncommon learning that marks the poem. This reflects the Restoration habit, common to Milton's friends and enemies alike, of valuing his humanism at the expense of his politics and prophecy. Beyond its allusive classicism, the distinctive diction of *Paradise Lost* and its use of blank verse also found frequent comment. The modest quarto first edition of 1667 was reprinted in 1674, this now in octavo and framed with commendatory poems, one of them a notable response by Andrew Marvell to Milton and his epic. The octavo was reprinted in 1678, but it was in the more imposing fourth edition, the illustrated folio of 1688, that Milton's work received more classic treatment, with further editions and also annotations, biographies and other such marks of cultural status to follow. Milton's influence as a poet develops especially after the Revolution of 1688–9, when a new Whig heroic poetry drew increasingly on his example. Such influence found expression also in the first parodies of Milton, the popularity of which reflects a growing familiarity with Milton's work on the part of a burgeoning English readership. Famously Joseph Addison's essays on *Paradise Lost* in the *Spectator* (1712) celebrated the sublimity of Milton's work, and further prepared Milton's way as the national poet. In the eighteenth and nineteenth centuries especially, Milton's epic made him the major poet, English, learned, and Protestant, whose influence dominates British literary tradition.

Paradise Lost is the most famous of the many biblicist narrative poems and dramas from the European baroque, when Reformed and Counter-Reformation writers alike sought to supply the market for renarrations and dramatizations of salvation history. The epic exhibits many characteristics of baroque grandeur – dynamic contrasts, elaborate stationing, forced perspectives, and the heightening effects of multiplying personages and voices – tempered by a disciplined biblicism. The latter followed from a lifetime of Bible study, apparent also in other of Milton's works, especially in controversy, and in the testimony of his contemporaries, who report his daily reading 'out of the Bible and the best Commentators.' Milton's narrative evolved from his initial plans for a drama, outlined in earlier sketches for biblical tragedies. This projected drama he titled 'Paradise Lost' and then 'Adams Banishment', which he corrected to 'Adam unparadiz'd', with related possibilities of Adam exiled or rather 'in Banishment'. But that Milton soon experienced a pressure back towards narration shows in the successive drafts for this project, especially in the expansion of its explanatory prologue, first given to a strangely preserved Moses, and then to a better placed immortal, the angel Gabriel. Narration solves another difficulty arising in these outlines, in which we are forbidden the sight of 'Adam in the State of innocence by reason of [our] sin'. By contrast, the epic will delight in this prelapsarian perfection, and in the naked beauty and sexuality of Adam and Eve.

Tragedy and epic had long vied in critical estimates of which was the highest of literary modes. Milton himself had wondered in the 1640s which 'shall be found more doctrinal and exemplary to a nation'. With the story of the Fall of man, he chooses finally to forgo the cathartic immediacy of drama, which yields a 'calm of mind all passion spent' (Milton, *Samson Agonistes*, 1758). He came instead to prefer an epic form of biblical narration, with its invitation to interpretation and the plenitude of Christian 'meditation on the happy end' (12, 605). Even so, in the famous close to *Paradise Lost* there is some catharsis as Adam and Eve enter our world with 'Providence their guide'. After the passions raised in the epic, finally by the visions and then narration of human history, and by the expulsion from the Garden, the poem in its ending does promote some calm, despite the incalculable and frightening consequences of the Fall. Michael's assurance that a 'Comforter' will be provided – 'the promise of the Father, who shall dwell, / His Spirit within them' (12, 485–8) – consoles the reader, even in experiencing the human isolation of Adam and Eve at the last, who 'hand in hand with wandring steps and slow, / Through *Eden* took their solitary way' (12, 646–9).

Milton's classicism remains better understood than his biblicism. But the epic as a whole asks a more rational than passionate engagement with its narration, as far as this distinction may be maintained. Having proposed his subject and inspiration in the first invocation (1, 1–26), Milton bids his 'Heav'nly Muse' to 'Say first, for Heav'n hides nothing from thy view, / Nor the deep tract of Hell, say first what *cause*' (1, 27–8; emphasis mine). Reason rejoices in narration as explanation: hence the angelic missions to Adam, whether of Raphael before the Fall, or Michael after it. More especially, the last books of *Paradise Lost* show the accommodation to human limitations of the visions of futurity, which might otherwise overwhelm Adam. These visions in Book 11, which already require mediation, yield to narration and further dialogue in Book 12, as Michael makes allowance for Adam's fallen needs. Plainly Milton invested much in biblical hermeneutics. As yet there is too little intertextual study of Milton's modes of narration in relation to biblical narratives, despite the wealth of secondary materials supporting such investigations, and the obvious merit in reading Milton's biblical allusions more dynamically – as for example in Radzinowicz (1989) on his engagement with Psalms, and in Lewalski (1985) on his prophetic 'transformation of literary forms'.

From the Bible too Milton seems to have gained a greater regard for typological than allegorical means of generating meaning. The chief exception in *Paradise Lost* proves the rule: the unusually Spenserian allegory of Satan, Sin and Death, the anti-trinity of Book 2 (2, 648–814). Neo-classical critics of the stature of Addison and Voltaire decried the peculiarities of this allegory, perhaps overlooking the degree to which its very deformations enact the desolations of pain and death. At first Satan does not recognize his family, these unrelating relations contrasting with the divine communion of Trinity in Book III. That Milton's allegory vividly enacts the connection between his ontology and narration has become plain. As Stephen Fallon explains,

> In the Augustinian conception of evil as the privation of entity lies the ontological rationale for Milton's use of allegory. If Sin and Death embody metaphysical evil, then their 'lesser reality' as allegorical characters fits Milton's ontology of evil. The embodiment is illusory and paradoxical, for metaphysical evil does not exist. (Fallon, 1991, 171)

Putting the being of evil under critique, Milton's allegory indicts self-authorizing subjectivity. Sin here is born of no womb but Satan's mind. The distinction between what is inside and what is outside is further confused in their incest, and then that of Sin raped by their offspring Death, with the resulting birth of Hell Hounds 'hourly conceived / And hourly born' (2, 796–7). Such agonies are represented, spectacularly, as the site not of reality but unreality, a form of torture defiantly self-generated, yielding an allegorical exposition of James I:13–15:

> Let no man say when he is tempted, I am tempted of God . . . But every man is tempted, when he is drawn away of his own lust, and enticed. Then when lust hath conceived, it bringeth forth sin: and sin when it is finished, bringeth forth death.

Where modern investigation has explored 'the conversion of real pain into the fiction of power' (Scarry, 1985), Milton comparably proposed it as a consequence of Satan's extreme subjectivism and incapacity for relation. Eventually inexpressible and enigmatic, the results of privation show in the pre-discursive 'cry of Hell Hounds never ceasing' (2, 654–9). Their 'noise' strangely reveals Satan's fallen loss of agency. Voiced, it might be said, in something like the fourth person plural, this is a violence within and without, at once impossible of dissociation and also held in avoidance, incapable of healing. After the Fall, this grotesque allegory resumes, with Satan enjoining his offspring to take dominion over man: 'Him first make sure your thrall, and lastly kill' (10, 402, 229–414). The violence comes to be written on the human body in the torments of disease envisioned in Book 11, where despair worryingly 'tends' to the sick, while 'over them triumphant Death his Dart, / Shook, but delayed to strike, though oft invoked' (11, 489–93).

The symbolic structures of *Paradise Lost* are more often organized by typology, however. Where Old Testament passages find typological completion in the New, and thus interpretation, Milton's narration draws heavily on both. Enriched by a wealth of biblical commentary, midrash and paraphrase, the narrative is generated through a dense intertextuality. The epic thus sheds light on the Bible, even as it sustains its own complexities by invoking biblical precedent. Passage after passage has for its pretext Old and New Testament example. Whatever the sufficiency of scripture, to which Milton often testifies, he now offers to renarrate it in epic mode with the assistance of the Holy Spirit. This work of prophetic accommodation is justified in his invocations of the Muse (Books 1, 3, 7 and 9), and modelled in the epic by Raphael's own narration, in which he proposes that 'what surmounts the reach / Of human sense, I shall delineate so, / By lik'ning spiritual to corporal forms, / As may express them best' (5, 571–4). More narrowly, the renarration allows Milton to extend the reach of biblical typology through very frequent interpretive glosses. Even one example, from Milton's use of Genesis 18, may indicate how expansively this intertextuality can work. Broadly this text assures his presentation of the 'sociable Spirit' Raphael, drawn otherwise from the apocryphal Tobit (*Paradise Lost*, 5, 221–3; cf. 4, 168–71). The story in Genesis 18 of the presence of the Lord in the visitors to Abraham at Mamre revives the immediacies of Genesis 3, with 'the Lord God walking in the garden in the cool of the day'. In *Paradise Lost*, the biblical promise of a child to the elderly Abraham and Sarah, and their incredulous response, finds prefiguration in Raphael's promise to Adam and Eve of a rich futurity, and their prelapsarian confidence of its truth, which will in some part survive the Fall. But Abraham's subsequent response to the danger of judgement upon Sodom and Gomorrah also catches Milton's eye. Pleading that the righteous within the city may merit its protection from destruction, Abraham moves beyond his own interest to become an advocate for others, and for the mercy within true justice:

> That be far from thee to do after this manner, to slay the righteous with the wicked: and that the righteous should be as the wicked, that be far from thee. (Genesis 18:25)

'That be from thee far, / That far be from thee, Father': so the Son himself urges in a passionate confirmation of the Father's tempering of justice with mercy (*Paradise Lost*, 3, 144–55; cf. Matthew 16:22). In the chronology of the poem, the Son speaks these words long before Abraham does. Through such narrative invention, Milton expands typology, in this case enlarging into Christian principle Abraham's insistent bargaining for social justice.

From the first publication of *Paradise Lost*, its style attracted almost as much comment as its content. The majesty of Milton's oratory gained him many followers in subsequent literary tradition. And later lesser imitations may have come to dull for readers the achievements of the epic itself. In the twentieth century, for example, no less a voice than T. S. Eliot's questioned Milton's rhetoric as hollow, in terms informed by Eliot's revulsion from Milton's republican and anti-episcopal views of state and church, and their American influence. Similar cavils against 'the Grand Style' were expounded by the also influential F. R. Leavis. That these might be the claims of prejudice then appeared from the more discerning readings of *Paradise Lost* by subsequent critics, especially Christopher Ricks, who vividly turned the claims of the 'anti-Miltonists' to better account. Following the example of William Empson, Ricks made searching use of the eighteenth-century critical debates over *Paradise Lost* – where the baroque poem had encountered new prejudices in the age of reason – to argue the sense as well as the sensitivities of the poem. Observing that the interfering eighteenth-century editor Richard Bentley, 'like the anti-Miltonists, had a great gift for getting hold of the right thing – by the wrong end' (Ricks, 1963, 14), Ricks showed the variety of effects in the epic in what remains the best single introduction to its poetry. Much more sympathetic to Milton's talent for paradox and contradiction, he shows the modern reader how the grandeur of this epic is allied to effects of extraordinary subtlety.

But the medium, of course, is finally part of the message, as modern criticism has begun to prove in earnest. Much follows from this recovery of the complexity as well as the coherence of Milton's verse. In particular, the poet's formal innovations are now increasingly understood as a function of his monist worldview, and the poetics that requires. Such an intellectual-historical dimension enriches the critics' descriptions of Milton's densely inflected verse, and its capacities for argument. It adds significance to the blind poet's talent for synaesthesia, that dazzling combination of different senses in which the prelapsarian inhabitants' experience of their world is evoked in terms of 'every lower faculty / Of sense, whereby they hear, see, smell, touch, taste' (5, 410–11). These are subordinate but still integral in even a higher 'intelligential substance'. Likewise, Milton's surprising interest in angelic digestion follows from his investigating how might the 'body up to Spirit work', part of the larger process in which creation 'if not depraved from good' returns to the creator (5, 469–79, 434–43, 464–7; cf. Ricks, 1963, 17). Such ruminations prove integral to Milton's poetics, incarnating the relationship between the sensible and the intelligible.

It is vital for the epic of choice that individual responsibility is thus defined in relation to process. The connection between obedience and being is asserted in the very first human speech that we encounter in the narrative, and shapes its long and complex opening sentence (4, 411–32). At once construing Eve and his relation to her in his initial mode of address, while deducing divine goodness in their created-ness, a goodness understood not to derive from their merit, Adam's first sentence extends to refer also to the condition of their obedience, and the reason of the prohi-bition of the forbidden fruit, a prohibition at once unconstraining, since other fruit is available in plenty, and even constitutive of their dominion, since this 'only sign of our obedience' serves as an ongoing opportunity to confirm their special relation to the creator. In the human realm, a complex poetry works through such implica-tions both to evoke the not quite imaginable prelapsarian world, and also the com-pleteness of tragic consequence after the Fall.

Such effects animate the epic at every turn, not least where Milton moves away from the human sphere. Now the complexity of his poetics can also bring to life the angel hierarchies, the mysteries of which can seem among the less recoverable features of this seventeenth-century poem. Hence, for example, in Raphael's response to Adam's questioning, as delicate an effect as the poet's superb delay over a line-ending can help reenact the sublime 'union of pure with pure / Desiring' peculiar to angelic love:

> Easier than air with air, if spirits embrace,
> Total they mix, union of pure with pure
> Desiring; nor restrained conveyance need
> As flesh to mix with flesh, or soul with soul.
>   (9, 626–9)

Such inflections appear at every level of narration in *Paradise Lost*. Milton uses his dis-tinctive diction, and control of archaism, etymology and allusive naming, in order to charge words with the tension between their possible pre- and postlapsarian meanings. Milton's manipulation of syntax, metaphor and simile yield extraordinary results, as does his structuring of the larger narrative itself. In Book 1, for example, a striking suc-cession of epic similes helps describe the fallen angels in hell, as if to exercise our imag-inations before the still greater challenge in Book 3 of imagining heaven. Milton plays with perspective from simile to simile, and does so even within a single simile, as with the telescopic changes of proportion that complicate the likeness of Satan's shield to the moon, itself proverbially changeable (1, 287–91). And Book 1 ends with one last simile, in which all the grandiose scene of Pandemonium is reduced to lunacy, a 'Moon-struck madness', with the fallen angel forms compared almost whimsically to 'Faerie Elves, / Whose midnight Revels, by a Forest side / Or Fountain some belated Peasant sees, / Or dreams he sees, while over head the Moon / Sits Arbitress' (1, 781–7; 11, 486). With his main narrative, moreover, Milton works still bolder manipulations. In Book 10 especially, the bravura cutting back and forth between earthly, heavenly, and infernal episodes vividly dramatizes the aftermath of the Fall. Constrained to 'process of speech', as he had been with Raphael when recounting 'Almighty works' (7, 112,

178), Milton now joins concurrent episodes – 'Meanwhile . . . Meanwhile . . . Mean while' (10, 1, 229, 585) – in order to link divine judgement and mercy on one hand, and hellish boasting and frustration on the other, with the human experiences of recrimination, despair, dialogue and contrition.

The better appreciation of such features of *Paradise Lost* has led to sophisticated readings of its biblicism, its republicanism and related topics. These in turn have invited the reappraisal of Milton's response to some of the chief issues raised by Genesis 1–3. In recent criticism of the epic, for example, Milton's representation of Eve seems to have found more comment than that of Adam. Feminist investigations have much sharpened our awareness of the gendering of the 'image of God' and its biblical basis. In writing *Paradise Lost*, Milton faced the challenge of reconciling the different accounts of creation, Priestly and Yahwist, in Genesis 1–2:4 and Genesis 2:4–3:24. The former emphasizes the common origin of both sexes on the sixth day of creation, when God creates man in his image: 'male and female created he them' (Genesis 1:27). The Yahwist account, however, describes Adam as formed earlier in creation, with other animals created belatedly, and only then Eve so that Adam might have 'an help meet for him' (Genesis 2:18, 20). Milton's biblicist discipline therefore leads him first to present Adam and Eve in terms of the human features they share:

> Two of far nobler shape erect and tall,
> Godlike erect, with native Honour clad
> In naked majesty seemed Lords of all,
> And worthy seemed, for in their look Divine
> The image of their glorious Maker shone,
> Truth, wisdom, Sanctitude severe and pure,
> Severe but in true filial freedom placed.
>
> (4, 288–94)

Only then does he distinguish further between them as 'Not equal, as their sex not equal seemed', in terms that draw on Paul's anxious advice to the cosmopolitan Corinthians (1 Corinthians 11:2–16), terms as yet unrelieved by Paul's assurance elsewhere that 'there is neither male nor female: for ye are all one in Christ Jesus' (Galatians 3:28). God does not much differentiate between these creatures made in His image, and when He does so it is chiefly for reproductive purposes (3, 93–6; 7, 529–30). And for the modern reader, unlikely to take the story of Adam and Eve literally, Milton's description of their relation still invites our accommodation of the myth to the experience of our own potentials, and their due relation. The poem gives priority to the capacity for 'truth, wisdom, Sanctitude' in each person. But secondarily, in this reading, each person can be given both to 'contemplation . . . and valour', as well to 'softness . . . and sweet attractive Grace' (4, 297–8), with the poem emphasizing the need to experience both of these. In the angelic as well as in the human realm, the resistance to hierarchy is seen as a consequence of the Fall, before which words such as 'submission' and 'subjection' have none of the pejorative associations that they gain in a later world of power politics. The richness of Milton's psychology finds fuller exposition in his narration of Adam and Eve's memories of their birth, where both feminized and masculinized virtues are described as susceptible to narcissism – with Eve too much drawn to her own image (4, 449–91), and Adam to his image in Eve (8, 250–559) – until they are called into a better balance between self and other.

Finally, the modern environmental crisis makes especially topical Milton's theology of nature, and his representation of human responsibility for the world we inhabit. Drawing on the Priestly account of creation in Genesis 1, Milton emphasizes the human creation as continuous with that of other creatures, while at the same time distinct from it because given dominion. Christianity has been faulted for the destructive consequences of its privileging of the human, but the need for human stewardship of creation becomes ever more apparent in our ravaged world. Milton describes a creation 'perfect in that it is destined for perfection' (Gunton 55), and that therefore requires work from its inhabitants, as a form of love. Thus, though it may be inviting for us today to imagine some simpler equality of human and non-human, for Milton such a fantasy of non-dominion leads only to an abdication of our responsibilities. Raphael's description of the days of creation culminates in the presentation of the human as 'the Master work, the end / Of all yet done', the creature who might 'Govern the rest, self-knowing' (7, 510). This purpose for humans seems to define our very creation. Our magnanimity in dominion, as Milton presents it, is to be part of our love of God; our part in creation is through such government to bear witness to Him. After the Fall, this dominion changes into a grim reaping, with Eve ambiguously poised as the 'Harvest Queen' (9, 842), and with Adam soon and fatally joining her. For all other species, and indeed the fabric of the world, must succumb to the effects of human choice. Eve is at once blithe and terrifying when she invites Adam to 'deliver' the 'fear of Death . . . to the Winds' (9, 989), since soon that 'Death' will indeed be distributed far and wide. Responsibilities of stewardship are integral to this epic. Perhaps in this way as much as any other, there is an enduring topicality to the great imagining of creation, choice and destruction in *Paradise Lost*. For Milton insists on our capacity to value our lives as created beings, based on the profound experience of process that can yield. In all its grandeur, the epic encourages us to renew relationship, living more richly in our being, drawn to creator and creation alike.

REFERENCES AND FURTHER READING

Armitage, David, Armand Himy and Quentin Skinner, eds (1995). *Milton and Republicanism*. Cambridge: Cambridge University Press.

Danielson, Dennis (1982). *Milton's Good God: A Study in Literary Theodicy*. Cambridge: Cambridge University Press.

Danielson, Dennis, ed. (1999). *The Cambridge Com-* *panion to Milton*. 2nd edn. Cambridge: Cambridge University Press.

Evans, J. Martin (1996). *Milton's Imperial Epic: Paradise Lost and the Discourse of Colonialism*. Ithaca, N.Y.: Cornell University Press.

Fallon, Stephen M. (1991). *Milton among the Philosophers: Poetry and Materialism in Seventeenth-*

century England. Ithaca, N.Y.: Cornell University Press.

Fish, Stanley (1997). *Surprised by Sin: The Reader in Paradise Lost.* 2nd edn. London: Macmillan.

Frye, Roland Mushat (1978). *Milton's Imagery and the Visual Arts.* Princeton: Princeton University Press.

Gunton, Colin (1998). *The Triune Creator.* Edinburgh: Edinburgh University Press.

Kolbrener, William (1997). *Milton's Warring Angels.* Cambridge: Cambridge University Press.

Leonard, John (1990). *Naming in Paradise: Milton and the Language of Adam and Eve.* Oxford: Clarendon.

Lewalski, Barbara (1985). *Paradise Lost and the Rhetoric of Literary Forms.* Princeton: Princeton University Press.

McColley, Diane (1983). *Milton's Eve.* Urbana: University of Illinois Press.

Milton, John (1953–82). *Complete Prose Works.* Gen. ed. D. M. Wolfe. 8 vols. New Haven: Yale University Press.

——(1998). *Complete Shorter Poems.* 2nd edn. Ed. John Carey. London: Longman.

——(1998). *Paradise Lost.* 2nd edn. Ed. Alastair Fowler. London: Longman.

Newlyn, Lucy (1993). *'Paradise Lost' and the Romantic Reader.* Oxford: Oxford University Press.

Norbrook, David (1999). *Writing the English Republic: Poetry, Rhetoric and Politics 1627–1660.* Cambridge: Cambridge University Press.

Parker, William Riley (1996). *Milton: a Biography.* 2nd rev. edn. Ed. Gordon Campbell. Oxford: Clarendon.

Radzinowicz, Mary Ann (1989). *Milton's Epics and the Book of Psalms.* Princeton: Princeton University Press.

Ricks, Christopher (1963). *Milton's Grand Style.* Oxford: Clarendon Press.

Rogers, John (1996). *The Matter of Revolution: Science, Poetry, and Politics in the Age of Milton.* Ithaca, N.Y.: Cornell University Press.

Sauer, Elizabeth and Balachandra Rajan, eds (1999). *Milton and the Imperial Vision.* Pittsburgh: Duquesne University Press.

Scarry, Elaine (1985). *The Body in Pain.* New York: Oxford University Press.

Shawcross, John (1970–72). *Milton: The Critical Heritage.* 2 vols. London: Routledge.

Stachniewski, J., ed. with Anita Pacheco (1998). *John Bunyan: Grace Abounding with Other Spiritual Autobiographies.* Oxford and New York: Oxford University Press.

Thickstun, M. O. (1988): *Fictions of the Feminine: Puritan Doctrine and the Representation of Women.* Ithaca: Cornell University Press.

Turner, James Grantham (1987). *One Flesh: Paradisal Marriage and Sexual Relations in the Age of Milton.* Oxford: Clarendon.

Watkins, O. C. (1972). *The Puritan Experience.* London: Routledge and Kegan Paul.

17

Aphra Behn, *The Rover*

Ros Ballaster

For Stuart loyalists of the 1660s and 1670s, the genre of comedy provided opportunities for the representation and celebration of a new political order overthrowing an outdated parliamentarianism. Political loyalty to the restored Stuart monarchy was often expressed through the analogy of social and sexual transgression. As Jessica Munns puts it: 'By the late sixties and seventies, many comic heroes express a libertine skepticism with regard to matters social and, above all, matters sexual. Indeed sexual idiom and innuendo often shaped the social and political discourse of loyalty, liberty, rights, and obligations, expressed in terms of family life, personal inclination, potency and impotence' (90). Aphra Behn, as Stuart loyalist and libertine advocate, is no exception to this promotion of a sceptical attitude to sexual and social regulation. However, as one of the few female members of a libertine circle, she also recognized that such licence for men was often won at the expense of women and their reputations. The contrast between Behn's Restoration comedy of *The Rover* (first performed and published in 1677) and its source, Thomas Killigrew's *Thomaso, or The Wanderer*, composed during the Commonwealth years and apparently never produced for the stage, may serve to illustrate both her proto-feminist critique of Restoration libertinism and her Stuart loyalism as well as those points at which the two positions come into tension.

From Wandering to Roving: Thomas Killigrew's Play Adapted

The Rover belongs to the middle period of Behn's dramatic career and is her first really successful play; it is the sixth of her nineteen plays (the majority of them comedies) to have been performed. It and its sequel, *The Second Part of the Rover* (1681) are based on *Thomaso, or the Wanderer*, a closet drama by Thomas Killigrew written in 1654 which Janet Todd suggests Killigrew may have 'given' to Behn for adaptation for the company he ran at Dorset Gardens (*Secret Life*, 214). Killigrew's play has seventy-three scenes organized in two parts over ten acts with some speeches running into two or three hundred words. Behn produces considerable order from this chaos, clearly subordinating sub-plots to the main action involving a 'roving' protagonist, now called Willmore. Despite her contemporary reputation for sexual explicitness, Behn actually cuts much of the vulgarity and bawdry of Killigrew's text. She also gives the play a contemporary twist in associating the figure of Willmore with both Charles II and his young court favourite, John Wilmot, Earl of Rochester, her friend and notorious rakehell; the similarity between the names 'Willmore' and 'Wilmot' would not have been lost on her audience. Edwardo in Killigrew's play, an English friend of Thomaso, becomes Blunt, a turncoat spy for the parliamentarians; when he is asked why parliament has not sequestered his estate because he travels with the Cavaliers in Europe, Blunt responds ' 'Sheartlikins, they know I follow it to do it no good, unless they pick a hole in my Coat for lending you Money now and then, which is a greater Crime to my Conscience, Gentlemen, than to the Commonwealth' (act 1, scene 2, ll. 50–3). Despite its setting in the Commonwealth years, Behn's play becomes a celebration of the restored court in drawing a contrast between the 'free-hearted' behaviour of Willmore and the self-interested viciousness of the Puritan/Commonwealth figure, Blunt. Yet, Behn's Willmore lacks the manipulative ability to plot shown by Killigrew's Thomaso and also by the male rakes in other plays of the 1670s. As Janet Todd points out, Willmore lacks the icy control of Etherege's Dorimant in *The Man of Mode* (1676) and the deep misogyny of Horner in Wycherley's *The Country Wife* (1675) (*Secret Life*, 217). Willmore is a drunk and a rioter, a figure who disrupts rather than engineers plots.

Behn also invents a new 'sober' romance between a pair of lovers, Florinda and Belvile, giving some of Killigrew's 'virtuous' heroine's, Serulina's, more earnest qualities to Florinda. She provides Angellica with a more worthy rival than Killigrew's insipid Serulina for the rover's affections in the shape of the lively Hellena, to whom she transfers a number of lines originally given to men in the Killigrew source. Most striking of all is the dimunition of the role of Angellica Bianca who has more tragic status and more lines in *Thomaso*. The figure of Hellena appropriates some of Angellica's power to 'voice' the position of women. In place of the large and largely disreputable female cast of *Thomaso* (the majority are courtesans), that of *The Rover* is designed to establish a direct and dynamic contrast between three female figures of different estate and type: Angellica (the loving whore), Hellena (the witty lady of quality) and Florinda (the sober mistress). In particular, Behn makes much of the inversion and opposition between the whore and the witty virgin so playfully addressed in the contradiction in their very names of Angellica Bianca ('white Angel' but also the bearer of her creator's initials, AB, just as Killigrew's hero, Thomaso, is 'christened' after his author) and Hellena ('Hell'). Lastly, Behn changes the location of her source, Madrid in Spain, to Naples in Italy. The entire tenor of the play shifts from a critique of repressive ideologies of containment of women, in which Killigrew parallels Spanish Catholicism and English Puritanism, to a celebration of a festive carnival world set in Italy where the shackles of authority are more easily thrown off by the aristocratic 'woman of quality, in parallel with the restored Stuart monarchy displacing the English 'Republic'.

Consuming Passions

Killigrew's original is a black comedy, its language dominated by a metaphor of hunger, in which the exiled cavaliers are driven by both literal and sexual 'starvation' in the depth of Cromwellian supremacy; Behn's play continues to exploit the metaphor of 'consumption', but in terms of a celebration of the indulgence of appetite and the pleasures of greed in the context of a restored Stuart monarchy and a new highly visible opulence at court and capital. The idea that man is a creature driven by appetite rather than a moral being was articulated most clearly by the political and moral philosopher, Thomas Hobbes. Hobbes represents the social contract as one in which figures agree to give power to someone else in order to protect or advance their own property interests. Man is a mere animal in a constant state of competition whose tendencies to aggression can only be held in check by the maintenance of arbitrary authority exercised over them. Hobbes was not necessarily a defender of the Stuart kings and by no means all pro-Stuart writers subscribed to a Hobbesian analysis. However, his writings were popular with the libertine aristocratic circle of men who wrote some of the most influential royalist comedies of the 1670s: William Wycherley, George Etherege and John Wilmot, Earl of Rochester. The heroes of the comedy are 'competitive' – not only as soldiers who earn their living through conflict, but also as lovers and friends, in both heterosexual and homosocial relations. According to Hobbes 'virtue' is not an ideal or abstract term but something to be bartered for and pursued out of self-interest rather than for the good of the state or as a result of 'natural' tendencies to sympathize with others. Behn's heroes exist in just such a competitive world in which 'virtue' lies in the exercise of power to one's own profit or glory. As Hobbes expresses it in the chapter titled 'Of Power' in his 1651 *Leviathan*:

> The *value* or WORTH of a man is, as of all other things, his Price; that is to say, so much as would be given for the use of his Power: and therefore is not absolute; but a thing dependant on the need and judgment of another . . . And as in other things, so in men, not the seller, but the buyer determines the Price. For let a man, as most men do, rate themselves as the highest Value they can; yet their true Value is no more than it is esteemed by others. (part 1, ch. 10, 151–2)

The Rover stages men and women in incessant competition for discursive power; characters compete with each other to gain the upper hand in the dizzying circulation of metaphors of sexual and social exchange. The ostensible winners in this power struggle (Willmore and Hellena) are those who gain 'credit' through their skilful manipulation of rhetoric, yet retain an awareness of the distinction between linguistic and material exchanges; their verbal expenditure is in inverse proportion to their material 'costs' (Hellena retains the most important item of 'credit' for a woman, her virginity, until she has secured marriage, while Willmore acquires food, lodging and sexual gratification despite his empty pockets). These characters recognize the true stakes in the linguistic power games that are at play and in particular the capacity of skilfully deployed language to bring about the fulfilment of desire. Angellica and Blunt are losers because they (differently) mistake the sexual economy in which they find themselves. In claiming to have escaped sexual 'trade', to have entered a realm of affection beyond the duplicitous play of language, they only reveal how deeply cemented are their belief systems in it.

Blunt mistakenly believes he has escaped the circulation/currency of material objects (words or disposable property) in his amour with the common prostitute Lucetta. He thinks that he has found a fine and virtuous woman in Lucetta because she does not ask him for money outright when they first meet, but she later tricks him into removing his clothes, jewellery and all the wealth he has about him. On his first encounter with Lucetta, Blunt responds to Willmore's query as to whether he gave her any money ''sheartlikins, dost think such Creatures are to be bought? Or are we provided for such a purchase? give her quoth ye? Why, she presented me with this Bracelet, for the Toy of a Diamond I us'd to wear' (act 2, scene 1, ll. 48–51).

Likewise, Angellica attempts to differentiate between affective and material or financial exchanges. She explains her rage against Willmore's infidelity in these terms:

> had I given him all
> My Youth has earn'd from Sin,
> I had not lost a thought, nor sigh upon't.
> But I have given him my Eternal rest,
> My whole repose, my future joys, my Heart!
> (act 4, scene 2, ll. 229–33)

If Blunt is treated comically and Angellica's representation verges on tragedy, their error is the same in believing that amatory desire can be separated from other forms of covetousness in which they have engaged and from which they have profited: Angellica as a prostitute, Blunt as a country squire.

Willmore succeeds where Blunt and Angellica fail not by rejecting but by playing the system of exchange. While he appears to be a linguistic as well as financial spendthrift, he makes his words 'count' in that they are used to advance and profit his own interest. Willmore's sexual magnetism and power over language enables him to get something without exchanging anything (the pistole coin he offers Angellica for sex 'wins' her heart – she later translates it into a literal 'pistol' aimed at his head but he easily disarms her as he has easily tricked her with an apparent language of devotion earlier). In recognizing the agency of language, he escapes determination by it and becomes its master rather than its victim. The key to the libertine is this verbal flexibility displayed by a figure who appears to refuse all forms of exchange but in doing so wins 'value' to himself: the figure that Rochester so ably performs in his poetry.

The ambiguity of the libertine figure however lies precisely in this flexibility, indeed hybridity. As James Grantham Turner highlights:

> The libertine is sometimes interchangeable with, and sometimes distinguished from, the Priapean, the spark or ranter, the roaring blade, the jovial atheist, the cavalier, the sensualist, the rake, the murderous upper-class hooligan, the worldly fine gentleman, the debauchee, the beau, the man of pleasure, and even the 'man of sense' . . . With due caution . . . we may establish a maximalist conception of libertinism, in which the rebellious display of illicit sexuality is linked by latent associations and ghostly companionships of language, to the religious and moral systems it purports to reject. (80)

Just such a maximalist concept is evident in Behn's presentation of Willmore in *The Rover*, who is not only a rake but also a festive clown who inverts and desacralizes traditional discourses of religion and morality in the interests of sexual licence. The opening exchange between Willmore and Hellena in act 1, scene 2 sees Hellena countering his use of a blasphemous religious analogy word for word:

HELLENA: Can you storm?

WILLMORE: Oh most furiously.

HELLENA: What think you of a Nunnery Wall? for he that wins me, must gain that first.

WILLMORE: A Nun! Oh how I love thee for't! There's no sinner like a young Saint – nay now there's no denying me, the Old Law had no Curse (to a Woman) like dying a Maid: witness *Jeptha*'s Daughter.

HELLENA: A very good Text this, if well handled; and I perceive Father Captain, you would impose no severe penance on her who were inclin'd to Console her self, before she took Orders.

WILLMORE: If she be Young and Handsome.

HELLENA: Ay, there's it . . . But if she be not—

WILLMORE: By this hand, Child, I have an Implicit Faith, and dare venture on thee with all Faults – besides, 'tis more meritorious to leave the World, when thou hast tasted and prov'd the pleasure on't. Then 'twill be a virtue in thee, which now will be pure Ignorance.

HELLENA: I perceive good Father Captain, you design only to make me fit for Heaven – but if on the contrary, you shou'd quite divert me from it, and bring me back to the World again, I shou'd have a new Man to seek I find; and what a grief that will be – for when I begin, I fancy I shall love like anything; I never try'd yet.

WILLMORE: Egad and that's kind – prithee dear Creature, give me credit for a Heart, for faith, I'm a very honest fellow – Oh, I long to come first to the Banquet of Love! and such a swinging Appetite I bring – Oh I'm impatient. – thy Lodging, sweetheart, thy Lodging, or I'm a dead Man!

HELLENA: Why must we be either guilty of Fornication or Murder if we converse with you Men – and is there no difference between leave to love me, and leave to lye with me? (act 1, scene 2, ll. 161–89)

This exchange sets a pattern that becomes familiar in future encounters between Willmore and Hellena. A blasphemous use of religious metaphor stands for sexual appetite, which is in turn literalized as physical 'consumption' of the love object as food. Yet, Hellena's deftness in handling the 'texts' she is given from Willmore consistently prevents her from being thus 'consumed' by his passion. She sidesteps his attempts to make her 'expend', 'spend' or 'waste' that valuable commodity, her chastity, without the seal of matrimony, refusing to take his promise of love on 'credit'.

In a later encounter in act 3, scene 1, Hellena returns to the theme of physical hunger and suspects that Willmore has sated his appetite elsewhere (as he has with Angellica) when he seeks to see behind her vizard:

HELLENA: I'm afraid, my small acquaintance, you have been staying that swinging Stomach you boasted of this Morning; I then remember my little Collation wou'd have gone down with you, without the Sauce of a handsome Face – is your stomach so queasy now?

WILLMORE: Faith long fasting Child, spoils a Mans Appetite – yet if you durst treat, I cou'd so lay about me still—

HELLENA: And would you fall to, before a Priest says Grace? (ll. 141–7).

In act 5, scene 1, the same metaphors of religious, sexual and gastronomic 'consumption' are being worked on by the pair:

WILLMORE: I love to steal a Dish and a Bottle with a Friend, and hate long Graces – come let's retire and fall too.

HELLENA: 'Tis but getting my consent, and the bus'ness is soon done, let but old Gaffer *Himen* and his Priest, say amen to't, and I dare lay my Mothers daughter by as proper a Fellow as your Father's Son, without fear or blushing.

WILLMORE: Hold, hold, no Bugg words Child, Priest and *Hymen*, prithee add a Hangman to 'em to make up the consort, – no, no, we'l have no vows but Love, Child, nor witness but the Lover, the kind Deity injoyn naught but Love! and injoy! *Himen* and priest wait still upon Portion, and Joynture; Love and Beauty have their own Ceremonies; Marriage is as certain a bane to Love, as lending Money is to Friendship: I'l neither ask nor give a Vow, – tho' I could be content to turn Gipsie, and become a left-handed bridegroom, to have the pleasure of working that great Miracle of making a Maid a Mother, if you durst venture; 'tis upse Gipsie [in the manner of Gipsies] that, and if I miss, I'l lose my Labour.

HELLENA: And if you do not lose, what shall I get? a cradle full of noise and mischief, with a pack of repentance at my back? (ll. 413–31)

Hellena here recognizes that the female 'libertine' needs to transform the terms of the sexual exchange. She cannot operate exactly like a man in that she is vulnerable to pregnancy. In the sexual bargain she may be left with a cost that the man never has to face. Female libertinism must take the form of verbal rather than sexual 'licence', in the playful substitution of fictional versions of the self that pique and maintain the sexual interest of the wayward male's attention, rather than the playful substitution of one love object by another which is the repetitive pattern of the male equivalent. When the lovers confide to each other that they are called 'Hellena the Inconstant' and 'Robert the Constant' (act 5, scene 1, ll. 461 and 456) it may seem another invention given Willmore's serial infidelity and Hellena's steady interest in Willmore alone, but the appellations are to an extent accurate. Willmore is constant in that he is unchanging in his search for sexual pleasure – he only ever appears to us and his fellow-actors in the one 'part' – while Hellena is inconstant in play-acting terms in that she appears in a variety of roles: a gipsy, a lady of quality, a boy.

Thus if The Rover is a celebration of the libertine culture associated with the restored Stuart monarchs, it also recognizes that the essentially asocial vitality of that libertinism requires tempering if it is to serve as a signifier of national unity and a revived sociality. A feminine force, in the shape of Hellena, apparently channels the anarchic priapic ego of the libertine into the healthful social relation of marriage. The play concludes with three penniless Cavaliers who have lost their estates in the recent civil war marrying three aristocratic girls from repressive and devout backgrounds; the men's estates are 'restored' while their wives experience new liberties sexually and relationally to form a new and vital social order.

Yet, the play cannot avoid implying the volatility and reversibility of this comedic 'settlement'. As Turner implies, the libertine tends to resubscribe to the very order he so ostentatiously and publicly rejects. The libertine repeats the religious rhetoric he mocks, turning sensual appetite into a form of worship; in excoriating the practice of prostitution as degrading to 'free love', he becomes himself a prostitute, selling his sexual favours to the highest bidder (Hellena). Blunt and Willmore are not so distant as they first appear: both threaten Florinda with rape and both more or less successfully seek to gratify their sexual appetite for free.

We are left questioning at the end of the play, whether Hellena's bargain is worth it or whether she has merely bought herself a worthless husband, sacrificing her long-term potential for short-term pleasures? Rather than pay Angellica one thousand crowns a month for her sexual favours four days a week, Willmore enjoys a wife who gives him her sexual favours in exchange for her estate of two hundred thousand crowns. Has Hellena really won the battle? Or in winning the battle, lost the war? The implication that the 'bargain' may bring only short-term and illusory stability (like Charles II's own accession) is reinforced when we consider Behn's decisions in writing a sequel, The Second Part of the Rover, performed in 1681. This sequel opens with the news of Hellena's death only a month after the marriage and it goes on to reverse the trajectory of the first part; it is a courtesan, La Nuche, who wins Willmore rather than the virgin prospect, Ariadne, the English Ambassador's daughter. The power of any woman it seems to 'attach' and 'contain' the anarchic energies of the libertine male is only temporary and equivocal. As in all Behn's work, a strong vein of pragmatism undercuts the utopianism and idealism of the text's overt, usually political, message.

REFERENCES AND FURTHER READING

Behn, Aphra (1996). *The Rover, or the Banished Cavaliers.* Ed. Janet Todd. *The Plays. 1671–1677.* Vol. 5 of *The Works of Aphra Behn.* London: Pickering.

——(1996). *The Second Part of the Rover.* Ed. Janet Todd. *The Plays. 1671–1677.* Vol. 5 of *The Works of Aphra Behn.* London: Pickering.

Boebel, Dagny (1996). 'In the carnival world of Adam's garden: roving and rape in Behn's *Rover*'. In *Broken Boundaries: Women and Feminism in Restoration Drama.* Ed. Katherine M. Quinsey. Lincoln, Nebraska: University of Kentucky Press, 54–70.

Canfield, J. Douglas (1997). *Tricksters and Estates: On the Ideology of Restoration Comedy.* Lincoln, Nebraska: University of Kentucky Press.

Copeland, Nancy (1992). '"Once a whore and ever?" whore and virgin in *The Rover* and its antecedents'. *Restoration: Studies in English Literary Culture 1660–1700* 16, 20–7.

De Ritter, Jones (1986). 'The gypsy, *The Rover*, and the wanderer: Aphra Behn's revision of Thomas Killigrew'. *Restoration: Studies in English Literary Culture 1660–1700* 10, 82–92.

Diamond, Elin (1989). '*Gestus* and signature in Aphra Behn's *The Rover*'. *English Literary History* 56, 519–41.

Gallagher, Catherine (1988). 'Who was that masked woman? The prostitute and the playwright in the comedies of Aphra Behn'. *Women's Studies: An Interdisciplinary Journal* 15, 23–52. Rpt (1993) in Heidi Hutner, ed., *Rereading Aphra Behn: History, Theory and Criticism.* Charlottesville and London: University Press of Virginia, 65–87.

Hutner, Heidi (1993). 'Revisioning the female body: Aphra Behn's *The Rover* parts I and II'. In *Rereading Aphra Behn: History, Theory and Criticism.* Ed. Heidi Hutner. Charlottesville and London: University Press of Virginia, 102–20.

Hobbes, Thomas (1968). *Leviathan.* Ed. C. B. Macpherson. London: Pelican.

Killigrew, Thomas (1663). *Thomaso, or the Wanderer: A Comedy.* London.

Lewcock, Dawn (1996). 'More for seeing than hearing: Behn and the use of theatre'. In *Aphra Behn Studies.* Ed. Janet Todd. Cambridge: Cambridge University Press.

Munns, Jessica (1998). 'Theatrical culture 1: politics and theatre'. In *The Cambridge Guide to English Literature 1650–1740.* Ed. Stephen Zwicker. Cambridge: Cambridge University Press.

Owen, Susan (1996). *Restoration Theatre and Crisis.* Oxford: Clarendon.

Payne, Deborah C. (1991). '"And poets shall by patron-princes live": Aphra Behn and patronage'. In *Curtain Calls: British and American Women and the Theatre 1660–1820.* Ed. Mary Ann Schofield and Cecilia Macheski. Athens, Ohio: Ohio University Press, 105–19.

Pearson, Jacqueline (1988). *The Prostituted Muse: Images of Women and Women Dramatists 1642–1737.* London: Harvester Press.

Spencer, Jane (1996). '*The Rover*, and the eighteenth century'. In *Aphra Behn Studies.* Ed. Janet Todd. Cambridge: Cambridge University Press, 84–106.

Todd, Janet (1996). *The Secret Life of Aphra Behn.* London: Andre Deutsch.

Turner, James G. (1987). 'The properties of libertinism'. In *'Tis Natures Fault: Unauthorized Sexuality during the Enlightenment.* Ed. Robert Purks Maccubbin. Cambridge: Cambridge University Press, 75–87.

18

John Wilmot, Second Earl of Rochester, *Satire against Mankind*

Paddy Lyons

'Theirs was the giant race, before the flood' wrote Dryden, extolling playwrights from the pre-Civil War era so as to cast disparagement on his own contemporaries, and thereby voicing the strain of disappointment which is a keynote of late seventeenth-century writing. When asked to join in celebrating the accession of William and Mary to the throne, Aphra Behn took no joy in 'all the Inviting Prospect' and could only deplore 'the Wond'rous Change . . . That makes me Useless and Forlorn'. For Rochester, however, disappointment was not at all so readily articulated in terms of resistance to the shifts of history, but emerges as at once more immediate and more widespread. His poem 'The Imperfect Enjoyment' opens in a frank exultation of sexual enjoyment, only to launch into an outburst of bitter rage as ecstasy is interrupted by premature ejaculation, and then the detumescent penis is berated:

> Thou treacherous, base deserter of my flame,
> False to my passion.

Erectile dysfunction provided Rochester with material for mock-tirades; disappointment takes a less physiological ground and a more analytic tone, as if in resignation to inevitability, when he reflects in a letter to his wife on 'soe great a disproportion t'wixt our desires & what [is] ordained to content them'. His most celebrated poem, his *Satire against Mankind*, presses to its limits this existential turn against the claims of humanism, and offers no remedy.

Behind Rochester's *Satire* are international traditions of sceptical writing, some echoed, and some borrowed on quite directly. For his contemporaries, well-aware of these sources, identifying parallels and drawing comparisons simply highlighted the originality of Rochester's poem. While noting similarities to Boileau's eighth satire (itself loosely based on Juvenal's fifteenth satire) the seventeenth-century critic Thomas Rymer insisted: 'My Lord Rochester gives us another Cast of Thought, another Turn of Expression, a strength, a Spirit, and manly Vigour, which the French are utter strangers to.' And just how it is that the urgent, energetic development of the poem – its movement and its style – give it its extraordinary distinction becomes all the more evident once we consider the relationship of Rochester's *Satire* to its most pervasive source, the writings of the philosopher Thomas Hobbes. From Hobbes the poem derives rhetorical devices that conduct and structure its argument, along with many of the assumptions it entertains. And yet Rochester's poem is very far from re-articulating Hobbist doctrine: the direction it tracks becomes increasingly and bleakly oppositional to Hobbes' positivism, till ultimately it sets Hobbes against Hobbes.

Rochester's poem is most evidently Hobbist at its climax, when it identifies fear as the basic emotion that socializes and civilizes mankind:

> The good he acts, the ill he does endure,
> 'Tis all from fear.
>
> (ll. 155–6)

Hobbes took fear as the primary emotion, and its recognition as crucial to any under- standing of human behaviour. Himself born prematurely in the year of the Spanish Armada, his birth in 1588 brought on by his mother's shock that a foreign fleet had entered English waters, Hobbes wrote wittily in an autobiographical poem that his mother 'did bring forth Twines at once, both Me and Fear'. Hobbes viewed fear as potentially redemptive, as the basic passion which generates the social contract, under- pinning a life-insuring covenant that can benignly contain and combat mankind's destructiveness, and so make human life better and other than that of man to man as wolf to wolf. But in Rochester's *Satire* Hobbes' principle is reiterated only to be turned, savagely, inside-out. While it upholds fear as at once basic and necessary to human socialization, this poem gives no endorsement to fear; but instead, through its actual manifestations in human behaviour fear emerges as at once emotionally repel- lent, and in its effects on mankind, as actively malign:

> For fear he arms, and is of arms afraid:
> From fear, to fear, successively betrayed.
> Base fear, the source from whence his best passions came,
> His boasted honour and his dear-bought fame . . .
> Which makes him generous, affable, and kind.
> For which he takes such pains to be thought wise,
> And screws his actions, in a forced disguise:
> Leads a most tedious life in misery.
>
> (ll. 141–4, 148–51)

Thus, when at its most explicitly Hobbist, Rochester's satire is also virulently anti- Hobbist – and paradoxically so, in that this appalling and anti-Hobbist position is arrived at by advancing from standard Hobbist assumptions through a rigorously

Hobbist methodology. This, then, is a poem which works with and extends tension, a poem in which tension receives no outlet or comforting resolution but, rather, moves into increase and augmentation.

The poem's opening reflects on limitation: 'Were I . . . A spirit free . . .' This initial reflection is poised and balanced in tone, and limitation is allowed, relaxedly and syntactically contained in an easy parenthesis:

> Were I – who to my cost already am
> One of those strange, prodigious creatures, Man –
> A spirit free to choose.
>> (ll. 1–3)

Although the satirist puts forward an outrageously impossible longing – to be

> . . . anything but that vain animal
> Who is so proud of being rational
>> (ll. 6–7)

he does so while acknowledging – rationally and ruefully – the impossibility of occupying any condition other than his own, that of Man. For Hobbes, accepting the limitations of being human was prerequisite to any understanding, and necessary for happiness. When defining 'felicity', Hobbes sharply mocks at the pretensions of scholastic philosophy to speak meaningfully of immortality – which (by definition) is beyond our grasp in our mortal, human state:

> I mean the Felicity of this life . . . What kind of Felicity God hath ordained to them that devoutly honour him, a man shall no sooner know, than enjoy; being joyes that are now as incomprehensible, as the word of Schoole-men *Beatifical Vision* is unintelligible. (*Leviathan*, ch. 6)

Rochester's sardonic treatment of the scholastic clergyman who enters his poem at line 48 to propose 'flight beyond material sense' is a straightforward amplification of Hobbes' sarcasm – which Rochester then summarizes in aphoristic terseness:

> Our sphere of action is life's happiness.
>> (l. 96)

The materialism here and throughout Rochester's poem is that of Hobbes: for Hobbes it was axiomatic that nothing exists except body, 'the whole mass of all things that are . . . is Corporeall, that is to say, Body' (*Leviathan*, ch. 46); and for Rochester's satirist it is a precondition that whatever alternative state he may imagine as potentially more desirable than being human – 'a dog, a monkey, or a bear' – should be, first of all, a corporeal state, one 'of flesh and blood'. From the outset there is precision to Rochester's wording, and for Hobbes 'Perspicuous Words' were 'light of humane minds' (*Leviathan*, ch. 5); yet where Rochester's poem most moves against Hobbes is in perspicuously employing words only to demonstrate an irredeemable misfit between human beings and the linguistic or semiotic domains which we perforce inhabit, and to which Rochester's satire finally depicts mankind as maladapted.

Seeming paradox followed by a telling justification of what might initially appear outrageous is a characteristic device of Hobbes, and Rochester's satirist proceeds to defend his paradox in the way of Hobbes, expounding it both in terms of 'Inference, made from the passions' and 'the same confirmed by Experience'. The satirist first of all justifies mocking the pride mankind takes in rationality by describing the experience of a mind led astray by the light of reason, like a traveller in futile pursuit of a will-o'-the-wisp across unknown, hostile territory:

> the misguided follower climbs with pain
> Mountains of whimseys, heaped in his own brain;
> Stumbling from thought to thought, falls headlong down.
> (ll. 16–18)

No landscape is visible – indeed, in seventeenth- and eighteenth-century poetry, to describe landscape was to designate terrain that had been possessed and mastered, and here that is not at all the case. Instead, effort and physical discomfort are foregrounded. These lines are in this regard an enlargement on Hobbes' pitying evocation of how error swamps

> they which trust to books . . . and not mistrusting their first grounds, know not which way to cleere themselves; but spend time in fluttering over their books; as birds entering by the chimney, and finding themselves inclosed in a chamber, flutter at the false light of a glasse window, for want of wit to consider which way they came in. (*Leviathan*, chapter 4)

Like Hobbes, Rochester here writes as a virtuoso, as if apart from error, and in adroit command of both metaphoric poles, body and mind. But there then appears, briefly, a sudden un-Hobbes-like shift in perspective: knowingness is abruptly demeaned, as an attribute that holds no special dignity, which can be arrived at by the misled as much as by the wise. And the boundary between Rochester's satirist and his target, the foolishly 'reasoning engine' seems about to dissolve:

> old age and experience, hand in hand,
> Lead him to death, make him to understand,
> After a search so painful, and so long,
> That all his life he has been in the wrong:
> Huddled in dirt the reasoning engine lies.
> (ll. 25–9)

Reason is denigrated further, through 'Inference from the Passions', with an assessment of how those who take pride in their wits are likely to fare in everyday living.
The prognosis is despondent:

> wits are treated just like common whores,
> First they're enjoyed, and then kicked out of doors;
> The pleasure past, a threatening doubt remains,
> That frights th' enjoyer with succeeding pains
>
> (ll. 37–40)

And fear has entered the story, corrosively.

Because this is a poem grounded – like Hobbes's writings – in scepticism and unbelief, it has no outside props to rely on, and cannot presuppose or point to some already-
known butt for its satire; it must instead evoke and embody whatever targets it
attacks. To continue his negation of reason the satirist imagines himself accosted by
a clergyman who is through his own words an embodiment of the pride-in-reason
which so far has simply been described. This 'formal band and beard' boasts enthusiastically how reason can:

> Dive into mysteries, then soaringly pierce
> The flaming limits of the universe
>
> (ll. 68–9)

until punctured with the reproof that – for all its lofty claims – his discourse amounts
to nothing more than second-hand stuff, old unfulfilled promises now worthlessly out
of date:

> Hold mighty man, I cry, all this we know,
> From the pathetic pen of Ingelo;
> From Patrick's *Pilgrim*.
>
> (ll. 72–4)

Recovering a perspective to separate the satirist from his target, the aggressive
energies can revive, and the satire continues its Hobbist movement by negating its
negation:

> Thus, whilst against false reasoning I inveigh,
> I own right reason, which I would obey.
>
> (ll. 98–9)

In several respects, the alternative 'right reason' championed here is thoroughly
Hobbist. Like Hobbes it is practical, hedonistic, and in favour of appetite and
desire:

Your reason hinders, mine helps to enjoy,
Renewing appetites yours would destroy.
                              (ll. 104–5)

And it is defined by appealing to imagery which – like that of Hobbes' prose – is drawn from the shared experience of domestic life rather than the deliberate and startling extremes familiar in the metaphysical writings of the early seventeenth century:

Hunger calls out, my reason bids me eat;
Perversely yours your appetite does mock:
This asks for food, that answers, 'what's o'clock?'
                              (ll. 107–9)

But this 'right reason' has, too, an aspect which is alien to Hobbist positivism. Like Rochester's satire, *Leviathan* castigated contemporary universities, branding their teaching of philosophy 'rather a Dream than Science':

Their Morall Philosophy is but a description of their own Passions. For the rule of Manner, without Civil Government, is the Law of Nature; and in it, the Law Civill; that determineth what is *Honest*, and *Dishonest*; what is *Just*, and *Unjust*; and generally what is *Good*, and *Evil*: whereas they make the Rules of *Good* and *Bad*, by their own *Liking* and *Disliking*. (*Leviathan*, ch. 46)

But the very tendency Hobbes disdains is elevated in Rochester's account of 'right reason' as:

That reason which distinguishes by sense,
And gives us rules of good and ill from thence.
                              (ll. 100–1)

And although Hobbes deploringly identified 'the Law of Nature' with the law of the jungle, where there can be only

continuall feare, and danger of violent death; And the life of man, solitary, poore, nasty, brutish, and short. (*Leviathan*, ch. 13)

Rochester's *Satire* has held persistently to sense as the 'light of nature' (line 13); and, in positing sense as itself the direction human actions can best follow, takes a position contrary to Hobbes, for whom 'Reason is not as Sense, and Memory, borne with us . . . but attayned by Industry' (*Leviathan*, chapter 5). For Hobbes, mankind was set apart from beasts through the linguistic capabilities:

There be beasts, that at a year old observe more, and pursue that which is for their good, more prudently, than a child can do at ten . . . For besides Sense, and Thoughts, and the

Traine of thoughts, the mind of man has no other motion; though by the help of Speech,
and Method, the same Facultyes may be improved to such a height, as to distinguish
men from all other living Creatures. (*Leviathan*, ch. 3)

Hobbes' confidence in nurture over nature give an optimism to his post-Saussurean
assertion that '*True* and *False* are attributes of Speech, not of Things' (*Leviathan*,
ch. 4).

From line 114 onwards Rochester's satire develops an account of human behaviour
as seen through the lens of 'reason righted'. 'Right reason', which by definition 'helps
to enjoy', and which emerged as a reliable touchstone by dismissing those modes of
reason that render life wretched, now begins a negation of itself in terms of its own
premisses, advancing a grim account of human conduct under the sway of fear, and –
as Hobbes indeed argued that we should be – entirely governed by fear. It is a further
twist and, in the sharp phrase of Harden Jay, Rochester's poem now takes a shape like
the plays of his contemporary Wycherley, becoming a 'tripartite exercise in negation'.
Any betterment of the human state through civil law – which Hobbes claimed was
the positive outcome of fear – is shockingly absent from life as it is envisaged on the
basis of the satire's 'right reason'.

> Birds feed on birds, beasts on each other prey,
> But savage man alone does man betray:
> Pressed by necessity, they kill for food,
> Man undoes man, to do himself no good.
>   (ll. 129–32)

This indeed develops a democratic vision of mankind, in which without qualification
all are monstrously implicated. It is akin to Hobbes, who saw society – according to
C. B. MacPherson – 'as so necessarily fragmented . . . that all were equal in insecu-
rity'. Driven by fear, man enters the civil realm of language and communication, but
there, instead of achieving happiness

> screws his actions, in a forced disguise;
> Leads a most tedious life in misery,
> Under laborious, mean hypocrisy.
>   (ll. 150–2)

What makes this worse is that language and communicative skills – which Rochester,
like Hobbes, sees as setting mankind apart from and different to beasts – only com-
pound the horror. Language provides the means for malice and treachery, activities
not known among beasts.

> Pressed by necessity, [beasts] kill for food,
> Man undoes man, to do himself no good.
> With teeth and claws, by nature armed, they hunt

Nature's allowance, to supply their want.
But man, with smiles, embraces, friendships, praise,
Inhumanely his fellow's life betrays;
With voluntary pains works his distress,
Not through necessity, but wantonness.

(ll. 131–8)

Most chillingly of all, the sadism which linguistic and semiotic capabilities enable and promote is in itself gratuitous and pointless (wanton), and – thanks to language – it is entered into at once knowingly and joylessly ('With voluntary pains . . .').

From the beginning, this vigorous and lucid poem has been deprecating language. Stumbling, drowning, misled rationality clung vainly to books (line 20); verbal wit was another ruinous manifestation of rationality's pride (line 35); the 'formal band and beard' became ridiculous through his utterances. That right reason 'distinguishes by sense', and not through language, suggests some yearning for a pre-linguistic or extra-linguistic domain. Words which attribute value – such as 'generous, affable, and kind' (line 148) or 'wisdom, power, and glory' (line 154) – are set in frames of relativism, as in Hobbes' analysis. But whereas Hobbes resorted to searching redefinitions so as to reinstate a vocabulary of value, the satire's 'right reason' bluntly cancels out any worth to which words might lay claim. Within language, there is no stability, no master signifier, and in consequence poor hope that enlightenment may ever prevail:

Nor can weak truth your reputation save,
The knaves will all agree to call you knave.
Wronged shall he live, insulted o'er, oppressed,
Who dares be less a villain than the rest.

(ll. 164–7)

If, as the poem alleges and demonstrates, the warp of language draws man inescapably into wretchedness, the poem's own standing is drawn into question – but on this matter it is mute.

It is, however, powerfully insistent. The mode is not that of the opening, where distinctions, limitations and differentiation gave poise and distance, and instead there is repetition, no separation between the satirist and what is under attack, and these containments have given way to a grim and tumbling excess:

   you see what human nature craves:
Most men are cowards, all men should be knaves.
The difference lies, as far as I can see,
Not in the thing itself, but the degree,
And all the subject matter of debate
Is only: Who's knave of the first rate?

(ll. 168–73)

Language can continue its persistent differentiations but, so these lines conclude, to no worthwhile or significant end. Hobbes had deployed eloquence to evoke a painful 'State of Nature' as a departure point, as a horror to be set aside by the efforts of man, a creature endowed with language. But here Hobbes has been put into reverse, and the 'state of nature' reinstated, and as a consequence of mankind's linguistic ability. The poem's ultimate and appalling virtuosity is to reach the outside of language, to have language apprehend and spell out so fully the very absence of distinction and differentiation which language exists to overcome.

Some printings of the poem follow this with pendant lines, which at first seem a backtracking towards comfort. They hypothesize a statesman and then a churchman whose uses of language might improve the lot of their fellow-men. Yet however desirable they might seem, these hypotheses are elaborated in detail ample enough to discredit their very likelihood. Even the standing of these lines is equivocal: they only feature as a continuation of the poem in roughly half the early manuscripts and printings, and otherwise they are absent, or are presented as a separate poem, titled 'The Apology', or simply 'Addition'; they do not appear in either of the two 1679 broadsheet versions of the *Satire* which circulated in print during Rochester's lifetime. Arguments from nineteenth-century aesthetics can sometimes be mobilized to stake out a privileged place for paradox and for excess itself – on the lines of Oscar Wilde's 'All Art is utterly useless' – but such arguments have already been pre-empted and discounted in the course of Rochester's satire:

> thoughts are given for action's government;
> Where action ceases, thought's impertinent.
> (ll. 95–6)

With no space for delighting or glorying in the uplifting brilliance of paradox, or indulging in remorseful abjection, Rochester's poem ends on a blank deadlock, admirable in its vitality and the integrity of its relentless honesty, a defiant non-statement.

REFERENCES AND FURTHER READING

Editions

Rochester left no finished edition of his writings, which come to us from a widely varied range of manuscripts assembled by commercial scribes and casual collectors, and from printers who leave in question every possible concept of respectability. Individual editors have had to devise and declare their approaches and priorities. Keith Walker *The Poems of John Wilmot, Earl of Rochester* (Oxford: Blackwell, 1984) and Harold Love *The Works of John Wilmot, Earl of Rochester* (Oxford; New York: Oxford University Press, 1999) sift and mine manuscript sources for their editions of Rochester's poetry; my edition of Rochester, Paddy Lyons, *Rochester, Complete Poems and Plays* (London: Everyman, 1993) accords relatively more importance to early printings. Jeremy Treglown's edition (Oxford: Blackwell, 1980) of Rochester's *Letters* also includes an incisive survey of biographical material.

Critical Discussion

Rochester's reputation up until the beginning of the twentieth century is documented in *Rochester: The Critical Heritage*. Ed. David Farley-Hills. (London: Routledge and Kegan Paul, 1972).

Three important collections of critical essays on Rochester have appeared: *Spirit of Wit: Reconsiderations of Rochester*. Ed. Jeremy Treglown (Oxford: Blackwell, 1982). *John Wilmot, Earl of Rochester, Critical Essays*. Ed. David M. Veith (New York: Garland, 1988). *Reading Rochester*. Ed. Edward Burns (Liverpool, Liverpool University Press, 1993).

Further helpful studies include: Dustin H. Griffin, *Satires Against Man: The Poems of Rochester* (Berkeley: University of California Press, 1973). David Farley-Hills, *Rochester's Poetry* (London: Bell and Hyman, 1978). Christopher Hill, 'Rochester'. In the first volume of his *Collected Essays: Writing and Revolution in 17th Century England* (Brighton: Harvester, 1985), 298–316. Harden Jay, 'Innocence, Restoration comedy and Mrs Pinchwife'. In *Literature and Learning in Medieval and Renaissance England: essays presented to Fitzroy Pyle*. Ed. John Scattergood (Dublin, Irish Academic Press, 1984). C. B. MacPherson, *The Political Theory of Possessive Individualism, Hobbes to Locke* (Oxford: Clarendon Press, 1962).

19

Aphra Behn, *Poems*

Sarah Prescott

One of the main points of interest about Aphra Behn's literary life is the remarkable range of her work and the versatility of her approach to genre, subject-matter and style. Behn wrote in a variety of modes for the theatre and was a successful and prominent dramatist. Towards the latter end of her career she produced a substantial amount of prose fiction, including the popular *Oroonoko; or, The Royal Slave* (1688) and the three-volume scandal fiction, *Love-Letters Between a Nobleman and His Sister* (1684–7). During her lifetime Aphra Behn was also recognized as a skilful poet who had a good command of the main Restoration poetic styles and forms: pastoral lyrics, sensual baroque, pindarics, free translation of Latin and French sources, satire and public panegyric which commemorated important occasions, such as the death of Charles II and the coronation of James II. Behn produced verse in all these modes and in a variety of contexts, from the coterie circulation of individual poems amongst a close-knit group or 'cabal' of like-minded writers to the publication of collections specifically geared to commercial ends as a way of supplementing her income from the theatre. Behn's literary career exemplifies the rise of the professional writer in the Restoration as a figure who writes for money but who also desires a measure of contemporary and posthumous renown. Unlike her male counterpart John Dryden, however, Behn's sex was always a complicating factor in her literary reputation. Yet Behn repeatedly claimed the right to be considered alongside her male contemporaries; as she states in an address to the laurel from her translation of Abraham Cowley's 'Of Trees' (1688):

> I by a double right thy Bounties claim,
> Both from my Sex, and in Apollo's Name:
> Let me with *Sappho* and *Orinda* be
> Oh ever sacred Nymph, adorn'd by thee;
> And give my Verses Immortality.

The three most significant of Behn's collections of poetry are *Poems Upon Several Occasions: with a Voyage to the Island of Love* (1684), *Miscellany, Being a Collection of Poems By several Hands* (1685) and *Lycidus, or The Lover in Fashion . . . Together with a Miscellany of new Poems By Several Hands* (1688). The versatility and adaptability that Behn displays throughout her work is continued in her poetry where she plays with a number of personae, poetic voices and subject positions. In political terms Behn was a Stuart supporter and her work displays her implicit acceptance of a political system that was hierarchical and based on absolute monarchy. Her public odes to Charles and James – *A Pindarick on the Death of Charles II* and *A Pindarick Poem on the Happy Coronation* – clearly mark her as a Stuart apologist and propagandist; a position that is also apparent in the prologues and epilogues to her plays. However, in her less public poetry Behn's political position is – as we find in much Restoration political poetry and discourse – articulated through the imagery of a 'golden age' or pastoral world which symbolizes loyalty to the Stuart monarchs. Behn's use of a mythical age of prelapsarian social and sexual freedom to denote a celebration of Stuart power is clearly shown in her poem 'The Golden Age'. In this poem, the speaker looks back to an age of undisturbed rural innocence where nature reflects the ideal political state: 'Calm was the Air, no Winds blew fast and loud, / The Skie was dark'ned with no sullen Cloud'. In Behn's fiction broken amatory vows often signify political disloyalty and perfidious lovers suggest deceitful courtiers. In contrast, but by the same token, Behn's 'Golden Age' is a world where there is a constant devotion between swain and nymph. It is a world which sees no shame in sexual passion: 'The Lovers thus, thus uncontroul'd did meet, / Thus all their Joyes and Vowes of Love repeat: / Joyes which were everlasting, ever new / And every Vow inviolably true'. These tropes of Stuart loyalty are continued in 'A Farewell to Celladon, On His Going into Ireland' where Celladon is figured simultaneously as the ideal rural swain and perfect loyal subject: 'The great, the Godlike *Celladon*, / Unlike the base Examples of the times, / Could never be Corrupted, never won, / To stain his blood with Rebel Crimes'. Accordingly, Celladon's loyalty to his king {Caesar/Charles} on his arrival in Ireland is figured in terms of pastoral bliss and the Irish nymphs are enjoined to soothe the anxieties of Celladon's political 'business'. The 'soft tale of Love' whispered by the amorous nymph mingles with the sound of birdsong and the 'distant bleating of the Herds' to create a 'Music far more ravishing and sweet, / Than all the Artful Sounds that please the noisy Great'. Celladon's imagined engagement with these pastoral joys is used as evidence of his political virtue and signifies his status as an exemplar 'Of Honour, Friendship, Loyalty and Love'.

This coded and symbolic representation of political allegiance differs from the open expressions of loyalty found in Behn's public poetry to Charles and James and is more in keeping with Behn's overall poetic practice and her complex negotiation of different voices and subject positions in her work. Towards the end of 'To Celladon' Behn slightly shifts the perspective to suggest a more personal involvement in Celladon's departure, although this more private investment incorporates a collective sense of a loyal public:

And if our Joys were raised to this Excess,
Our Pleasures by thy presence made so great:

Some pitying God help thee to guess
(What Fancy cannot well express)
Our Languishments by thy Retreat.

The use of the amatory language of 'excess', 'pleasure' and 'languishments' suggests
a specifically female engagement with the issues of political loyalty where the female
subject in particular articulates her political position through the discourse of sexual
desire. This use of a gendered poetic voice to authorize political comment is also apparent in Behn's treatment of the potentially delicate topic of the relationship between
Lord Mulgrave and Princess Anne in 'Ovid to Julia. A Letter'. In this poem Behn
employs the familiar amatory language of the ruined female lover which was to
become a commonplace in later fiction by women such as Delarivier Manley and Eliza
Haywood: 'I bring no Forces, but my sighs and tears, / My Languishments, my soft
complaints and Prayers'. However, as Paul Salzman has noted, Behn reverses the usual
gendered subject positions by appropriating the male voice of the poet Ovid
(Mulgrave). Moreover, it is Ovid who becomes the victim of the 'Avenging Deity'
(Julia/Anne) and the woman therefore becomes the active partner in the love affair as
well as acting on behalf of 'all the injured Fair'. By playing with the usual associations of a gendered speaking position, Behn conveys her oblique criticism of 'ambitious' sexual passion – that is, fuelled by the hopes of political advancement. This
general critique then enables her to attack the Duke of Monmouth's revolt against
James II through a continuation of the theme of sexual intrigue as a dangerous and
ill-advised route to political advancement:

The vain young Fool with all his Mother's parts,
(Who wanted wit enough for little Arts,)
With Crowds, and unmatched nonsense, lays a claim
To th' Glorious title of a Sovereign;
And when our Gods such wretched things set up,
Was it so great a crime in me to hope?

Although Aphra Behn was well known for her work as a political poet and Stuart
eulogist, in her time she was primarily recognized as a poet of love. Amatory topics
form a major part of Behn's poetic output, but her emphasis on erotic themes was to
work both for and against Behn's literary and personal reputation. Some commentators used the image of the 'lusty' Astrea to attack Behn by comparing her unfavourably
with the chaste image of Behn's main female counterpart in the Restoration, Katherine Philips, 'the matchless Orinda'. Other writers who supplied the commendatory
verses which prefaced Behn's collections of poetry emphasized Behn's capacity for
amatory subjects from a more positive angle. Charles Cotton's contribution to the
series of verse compliments or 'puffs' which prefaced Behn's 1686 collection, *La
Montre; or, The Lover's Watch*, praises Behn's work in general, but becomes particularly
fulsome when he considers her love poetry: 'But when you write of Love, *Astrea* then

/ Love dips his Arrows, where you wet your Pen: / Such charming Lines did never Paper grace, / Soft as your Sex, and smooth as Beauty's Face'. However, as is the case in commendatory verses to Katherine Philips, whether the aim is to praise or to denigrate Behn, the familiar conflation of a woman writer's personal life with her literary production is suggested. Cotton's hyperbolic compliment draws a deliberate parallel between the beauties of Behn's sex and her poetry: the poems embody the charms of the female poet. However, the association of sensual femininity with women's literary production could always backfire and other, less generous, critics frequently used the prevalence of amatory themes in Behn's work to suggest that her personal life was rather less than respectable. Whatever the tone, the connection between a woman's sexuality and a woman's writing was firmly established.

On reading Behn's amatory poetry it is easy to see why she invited adverse contemporary comments which speculated on her sexuality and it is not difficult to understand the later eighteenth-century reaction against her work in this area. However, part of the reaction against Behn as bawdy and erotic is due to the Restoration genres and discourses in which she worked as well as specific attacks on her sex. In 'The Golden Age', for example, Behn appropriates the male libertine poetic voice who attacks 'honour' in his bid to seduce the pastoral nymph. In addition, her poem 'The Disappointment' – a loose translation or adaptation of a French poem by de Cantenac, 'Sur une Impuissance' – is an intervention into the exclusively male Restoration genre of impotence poetry. It is suggestive of Behn's skill in mimicking a masculinist discourse that her poem was initially thought to be by the famous libertine poet, the Earl of Rochester. 'The Disappointment' was included in Rochester's *Poems on Several Occasions* (1680) and was frequently attributed to him. Nevertheless, despite the obvious similarity in subject matter between Rochester's poem in this mode, 'The Imperfect Enjoyment', and Behn's version of the same theme, it is clear that the two poems differ greatly in terms of perspective and approach.

The titles of the two poems – 'The Imperfect Enjoyment' and 'The Disappointment' – offer an initial clue as to the way in which Behn diverges from the conventions of the impotence genre. Rather than placing emphasis on the man's anger at the loss of sustained sexual enjoyment and his own incapacity, Behn reverses the usual perspective and instead focuses on the sexual frustration experienced by the female character – Cloris – at Lysander's inability to perform. Hints of this reversal of gender positions are offered at an early stage in the poem. In stanza two Behn suggests that Cloris meets Lysander's advances more than half way: 'Her Hands his Bosom softly meet, / But not to put him back designed, / Rather to draw 'em on inclined'. Behn anticipates the eventual outcome by playing with the conventional gender positions of active male and passive female in her description of the supine Lysander who 'lay trembling' at Cloris' feet. At the moment of failed consummation, Behn again uses amatory language usually associated with femininity to refer to a male lover. Lysander is 'o'er-Ravished', his nerves are 'faint' and 'slack' and 'Excess of Love his Love betrayed: / In vain he Toils, in vain Commands; / The Insensible fell weeping in his Hand'. By reversing the usual focus of the impotence poem from the male to the female, Behn also critiques the masculine bias of the genre in particular and discourses of sexuality in general which emphasize male potency and superiority. In stanza eleven, Behn undercuts both generic expectations and gender stereotypes by suggesting that Lysander's failure is not only a personal one but also exposes the false constructions of male sexual power offered by classical sources:

> *Cloris* returning from the Trance
> Which Love and soft Desire had bred,
> Her timorous Hand she gently laid
> (Or guided by Design or Chance)
> Upon that fabulous *Priapus*,
> That Potent God, as Poets feign;
> But never did young *Shepherdess*,
> Gath'ring of Fern upon the Plain,
> More nimbly draw her Fingers back,
> Finding beneath the verdant Leaves a Snake.

Behn continues to subvert classical myth and masculinist poetic bias in her reworking of two Ovidian myths in stanza thirteen of the poem. The narratives of Daphne and Apollo (Daphne flees and turns into a laurel tree to escape Apollo) and Venus and Adonis (Venus hastened to earth on the death of her lover) from Ovid's *Metamorphoses* are both concerned with female sexuality and agency. As Carol Barash has shown, by grafting these two myths together Behn shifts the perspective of the poem 'to the point of view of a disappointed and fearful – but nevertheless desiring – woman' (1996, 124). However, whereas Daphne's fear of Apollo was justified, in Behn's ironic version it is not the fear of rape that spurs Cloris to flee Lysander. In contrast to Apollo's active pursuit, Lysander is passive and 'fainting on the Gloomy Bed'. In effect, then, it is Cloris's frustration with Lysander's inadequacy as a lover, not her fear of male potency, that forces her to fly 'Like Lightening through the Grove . . . Or *Daphne* from the *Delphic God*'. In the final stanza, Behn underlines her use of a female perspective on both male sexuality and the male genre of erotic poetry by drawing a direct analogy between the speaker of the poem and the frustrated Cloris: 'The *Nymph*'s Resentments none but I / Can well imagine or Condole'.

Overall, 'The Disappointment' subverts the hierarchies of gender and genre by focusing attention on the place of the female subject and female sexual desire within a traditionally male form. 'To the Fair Clarinda, Who Made Love to Me, Imagined More Than Woman' has been seen to take Behn's challenge to gender oppositions and poetic conventions even further. In this ambiguous poem Behn recognizes the powerful distinctions that sex offers as a conceptual category by posing her riddle as a question of determinate identity: is the loved object male or female? However, as the poem progresses Behn dismantles this easy opposition by suggesting a hermaphroditic sexual identity which incorporates elements of masculinity and femininity: 'Thou beauteous Wonder of a different kind, / Soft *Cloris* with the dear *Alexis* joined'. The poem has provoked a variety of readings from modern critics. It has been read as an expression of female same-sex desire where the 'real' female form masques the presence of transgressive sexuality:

> In pity to our Sex sure thou wer't sent,
> That we might Love, and yet be Innocent:
> For sure no Crime with thee we can commit;
> Or if we should – thy Form excuses it.

The lines immediately following – 'For who, that gathers fairest Flowers believes / A Snake lies hid beneath the Fragrant Leaves' – have likewise been interpreted as upholding this reading: the snake beneath the leaves being seen as an allusion to the clitoris rather than the penis in an ironic re-working of Behn's own lines from 'The Disappointment'. However, other commentators have taken this as evidence that the addressee is a cross-dressed man. This may refer to the practice of cross-dressing on the Restoration stage and in aristocratic society at large, but it could also be a direct reference to Behn's bisexual lover John Hoyle. Most critics have agreed with Carol Barash that on one level this poem is more rigidly oppositional than Behn's heterosexual erotic verse. Indeed, at the end of the poem Behn appears to make the choice between masculinity and femininity a case of either/or:

> When e'er the Manly part of thee would plead,
> Thou tempts us with the Image of the Maid,
> While we the noblest Passions do extend
> The love to *Hermes*, *Aphrodite* the Friend.

However, as Barash and others have argued, the overall effect of the poem is to unsettle notions of subjectivity and sexuality through the adaptation of Ovidian myth and the complex and ambiguous negotiation of gender identity. Indeed, Behn's ultimate challenge to the conventions of both gender and form was to create a space for the representation of female desire and subjectivity in a predominantly male literary world.

Throughout Behn's work, then, we see her playing with subject positions and different voices, sometimes male but more usually female, in order to deconstruct expectations about both gender and genre. For example, in 'To My Lady *Morland* at *Tunbridge*' the speaker, whose previous lover is now attending Lady Morland, laments the beauty of the man she has lost to her rival: 'How beautiful he looked, with what a Grace; / Whether upon his Head he Plumes did wear; / Or if a Wreath of Bays adorned his Hair'. In a move typical of Behn's use of shifting perspective, however, the superior attractions of the Lady herself are then enumerated and, it is implied, experienced by the female speaker: 'I wished to see, and much a Lover grew / Of so much Beauty, though my Rivals too.' The poem 'A Letter to a Brother of the Pen in Tribulation' offers a rather different example of Behn's manipulation of various poetic voices. Here Behn appropriates the masculine tone of the 'brother of the pen' who is ostensibly sympathizing with Damon's unfortunate contraction of venereal disease but at the same time rather enjoying the spectacle of his uncomfortable cure in the 'sweating-tub': 'Pox on't that you must needs be fooling now, / Just when the Wits had greatest need of you. / Was Summer then so long a-coming on, / That you must make an Artificial one?' However, Behn again subverts expectations by anticipating Damon's curses against the woman who has transmitted the disease. By suggesting that Damon himself must supply the curses and thereby evading any direct comment to the woman in question, the speaker makes Damon the object of ridicule and avoids making this poem into a 'Verse to damn all Woman-kind'.

Despite Behn's skill and range as a poet her work in this area, particularly her love-poetry, contributed to the backlash against her as bawdy and erotic. An example of this reaction against Behn is Thomas Brown's *Letters from the Dead to the Living* (1702) where Behn pens a letter from beyond the grave to the actress Anne Bracegirdle. Brown's fictional Behn is characterized mainly by her crude turn of phrase and her insistence that female virtue is a mere facade masking contrivance, stratagem and lewdness. This image of Behn as a kind of spokeswoman for female immorality was to dog her reputation for almost three centuries. However, in the late twentieth century, Behn's reputation is perhaps higher than it has ever been. Indeed, the distinctive brand of playfulness and subversion that her poetry offers seems particularly suited to recent post-structuralist and postmodern critical constructions of identity and sexuality. In contrast to her previous neglect, Behn is now a widely read and widely taught writer whose work in poetry and prose fiction has received a substantial amount of critical comment and whose plays are beginning to be performed again. It would seem, then, that Aphra Behn has finally achieved the immortality and respect that she wished for in her day, a position which, for many years, must have seemed an impossibility.

REFERENCES AND FURTHER READING

Barash, C. (1990). 'The political possibilities of desire: teaching the erotic poems of Behn'. In *Teaching Eighteenth-century Poetry*. Ed. C. Fox. New York: AMS Press, 164–72.

——(1996). *English Women's Poetry, 1649–1714*. Oxford: Clarendon.

Boehrer, B. T. (1989). 'Behn's "Disappointment" and Nashe's "Choice of Valentines": pornographic poetry and the influence of anxiety'. *Essays in Literature* 16, 172–87.

Duffy, M. (1977). *The Passionate Shepherdess: Aphra Behn 1640–1689*. London: Cape.

Duyfhuizen, B. (1991). '"That which I dare not name": Aphra Behn's "The Willing Mistress"'. *English Literary History* 58, 63–82.

Guibbory, A. (1993). 'Sexual politics/political sex: seventeenth-century love poetry'. In *Renaissance Discourses of Desire*. Ed. C. J. Summers and T. Pebworth. Columbia: University of Missouri Press, 206–22.

Hutner, H., ed. (1993). *Rereading Aphra Behn*. Charlottesville: University of Virginia Press.

Mermin, D. (1990). Women becoming poets: Katherine Philips, Aphra Behn, Anne Finch. *English Literary History* 57, 335–55.

Munns, J. (1996). '"But to the touch were soft": pleasure, power, and impotence in "The Disappointment" and "The Golden Age"'. In *Aphra Behn Studies*. Ed. J. Todd. Cambridge: Cambridge University Press, 178–96.

O'Donnell, M. A. (1986). *Aphra Behn: An Anno-tated Bibliography of Primary and Secondary Sources.* New York: Garland.

Salzman, P. (1996). 'Aphra Behn: poetry and mas-querade'. In *Aphra Behn Studies.* Ed. J. Todd. Cambridge: Cambridge University Press.

Stiebel, A. (1992). 'Not since Sappho: the erotic in poems of Katherine Philips and Aphra Behn'. In *Homosexuality in Renaissance and Enlightenment England: Literary Representations in Historical Context.* Ed. C. J. Summers. New York: Haworth Press.

——(1993). 'Subversive sexuality: masking the erotic in poems by Katherine Philips and Aphra Behn'. In *Renaissance Discourses of Desire.* Ed. C. J. Summers and T. Pebworth. Columbia: Uni-versity of Missouri Press.

Todd, J. (1996). *The Secret Life of Aphra Behn.* London: Andre Deutsch.

——(1998). *The Critical Fortunes of Aphra Behn.* Woodbridge: Boydell and Brewer.

Todd, J., ed. (1992–6). *The Works of Aphra Behn,* 7 vols. London: Pickering.

Young, E. V. (1993). 'Aphra Behn: gender and pastoral'. *Studies in English Literature* 33, 523–43.

——(1995). 'Aphra Behn's elegies'. *Genre* 28, 211–36.

20

John Dryden, *Fables*

David Hopkins

Fables Ancient and Modern, John Dryden's last collection of verse, was published in March 1700, two months before the poet's death at the age of sixty-eight. The volume consists of tales or narrative episodes in verse translated from two classical poets (Homer and Ovid) and two medieval writers (Chaucer and Boccaccio), together with a number of 'original' poems, most notably the St Cecilia's Day ode, 'Alexander's Feast', for long Dryden's most celebrated single poem. *Fables* was widely believed for over a century after the poet's death to be Dryden's crowning achievement, and to constitute proof positive that he had been, in the words of his friend William Congreve, 'an improving Writer to his last; improving even in Fire and Imagination, as well as in Judgement'. The volume was thought to have combined the vitality, daring, exuberance and unsentimental shrewdness of youth, with the sober wisdom, sympathy, and geniality of mellow maturity – a combination all the more remarkable in the light of the political disappointment and ill health under which Dryden had laboured during the period of its composition.

A balanced account of *Fables* must do justice both to the coherent body of recurring concerns which makes the volume more than a mere miscellany, and to the plurality of sentiments, moods, voices, tones, and viewpoints which prevents it from being treated as the expression of any single 'philosophy' (whether political, ethical, or historical), or as the product of any single organizational scheme (whether thematic, architectonic, or dialectical). Dryden's renderings of Chaucer, Ovid, Homer and Boccaccio are, like his other verse translations, detailed acts of 'creative literary criticism' from which readers can derive direct insight into Dryden's originals. But they are, simultaneously, integral parts of Dryden's own *oeuvre*, coloured by his own creative preoccupations, by his reflections on his own life and times, and by his reading of authors other than those whom he is translating. In two of the *Fables* ('To My Honoured Kinsman, John Driden' and 'The Character of a Good Parson') Dryden's principal concern is to express personal commitments and convictions. (He spoke of the former as giving his 'own opinion of what an Englishman in parliament ought to be', and 'as a memorial of [his] own principles to all posterity'; in the latter, he embodied his own ideal of religious conduct in a thinly disguised portrait of the non-juring bishop, Thomas Ken.) But elsewhere Dryden's 'own' voice blends more complicatedly with those of his classical and medieval sources, so that 'his' and 'their' contributions are not easily separable. Each of the poems, moreover, gains some extra resonance from its place in *Fables* as a whole. In his Preface, Dryden clearly invites his readers to share his own pleasure in seeing a recurring set of themes and problems treated in a constantly varied range of tones, and from a constantly shifting set of perspectives.

Dryden equally clearly saw connections between some of the subject-matter of *Fables* and the processes involved in the composition of the volume itself. In his preface he portrays his translating activity as a kind of 'transfusion' or metempsychosis, in which the souls of earlier poets to whom he feels linked by patterns of artistic consanguinity and congeniality have achieved mysterious reincarnation in his mind, and posthumous re-expression through his art. Such thoughts are significantly echoed in his rendering of Pythagoras' great speech on the transmigration of souls from Ovid's *Metamorphoses*, where he responds pointedly to the Greek philosopher's vision of a world animated by continuous processes of decay, transformation, and rebirth – a world in which 'former things / Are set aside, like abdicated kings', and 'our brown locks repine to mix with odious grey', but in which, also, 'All things are altered, nothing is destroyed', since 'Those very elements which we partake / Alive, when dead some other bodies make: / Translated grow, have sense, or can discourse, / But death on deathless substance has no force'. Dryden's vocabulary here clearly signals the applicability of Pythagoras's sentiments to recent political events (the supposed 'abdication' of James II), to the capacity of his own work to endure into the future, and to his own old age and imminent dissolution into the flux of nature (Dryden's 'grey locks' are memorably displayed in Sir Godfrey Kneller's second portait of the poet, painted *c.*1698).

In *Fables*, Dryden treats a number of topics of general human import with which he had been recurrently preoccupied throughout his work: the possibility of human happiness; the nature of personal and civic virtue; the deceitfulness and violence of political debate; the glory, brutality, and absurdity of martial heroism; the nature of true nobility; the affective power of music and poetry; the grandeur, folly, and destructiveness of love; the competing claims of 'human' and 'natural' law; the destructive and creative effects of time and change. Something of the flexible and multi-faceted way in which the volume explores such matters can be seen in a brief survey of the treatment of one of these topics – the power of love – in four poems of very different types and moods.

In 'Palamon and Arcite', Dryden's version of Chaucer's 'Knight's Tale', love (personified in the form of Venus, a figure who combines aspects of the classical love-goddess and the planet of medieval astrology) is depicted as a fearsomely destructive force, one of a family of squabbling deities under whose arbitrary and amoral rule human beings must live their lives. The effects of Venus's power on the two young noblemen, Palamon and Arcite (who both fall in love at first sight with Emily, a woman whom neither of them have ever met) are initially depicted with a diagrammatic stylization which might be felt to border on the comic: 'if that Palamon was wounded sore, / Arcite was hurt as much as he, or more'. But we are soon made aware of the potent destructiveness of the force which has overwhelmed them, when Arcite delivers a memorable speech, asserting love's power to overturn all 'civilized' values: 'Love throws the fences down, and makes a general waste: / Maids, widows, wives, without distinction fall; / The sweeping deluge, love, comes on, and covers all'. The force of Arcite's words is amply confirmed as the poem proceeds. The destructive power of Venus and of her rival Mars (the god/planet presiding, with Pluto, over violence and malignity in all their forms) is confirmed in the person of the wise ruler, Duke Theseus, who acknowledges that he has himself been subject to the influence of both deities, and by the awesome carvings in the gods' temples, where Palamon and Arcite pay their devotions before fighting in the lists for Emily's hand. As expected, their conflict ends in disaster. Arcite is mortally wounded. His dying moments are presented with a clinical directness, and Dryden stresses the young man's shocked incomprehension at his approaching death: it is only just before death that he momentarily rises above his despair to express regrets for his broken faith to Palamon, and to commend his friend as a worthy object of Emily's affection. A year later, Theseus summons Palamon to his court. In a lengthy speech of great wisdom and comprehensiveness (the culmination and resolution of the tale in every sense), he expounds the processes which govern human life from the womb to the grave, giving full weight to those features of human existence which might cause us to despair, while simultaneously insisting on the need to seize the goods of life when they are before us, in heroic defiance of everything that might otherwise overwhelm and confound our efforts. In his rendering, Dryden 'fortifies' Chaucer with a reminiscence of his own earlier translation of Horace's *Odes* III. 29, to invest Theseus's sentiment and tone with a sublime *insouciance* and heady buoyancy in the face of calamity: 'What then remains, but after past annoy, / To take the good vicissitude of joy? / To thank the gracious gods for what they give, / Possess our souls, and while we live, to live?'

If love is seen in 'Palamon and Arcite' as a power of awesome destructiveness, which can only be transcended by heroic effort, in 'The Cock and the Fox' (Dryden's version of Chaucer's 'Nun's Priest's Tale') it is seen as a source of rich comedy. Chaucer's tale is offered, ostensibly, as a cautionary beast fable about the dangers of pride, in which the cock Chanticleer's infatuation with his favourite hen-wife, Pertelote, causes him to forget an ominous dream, and to render himself vulnerable to the flattery of Reynard the fox. A network of subtle intertextual allusions shows that Dryden has seen a larger meaning in Chaucer's tale, reading it as a comic version of the Fall of man, or, more precisely, a comic inversion-before-the-event of Milton's *Paradise Lost* – another celebrated story in which a husband and wife in a secluded sexual paradise succumb, despite advance warnings, to the temptations of a diabolical intruder. Adam and Eve's unashamed sexuality, in harmonious accord with their rational self-knowledge, is central to Milton's conception of their status as the crown of God's creation. Chanticleer's and Pertelote's life is similarly centred on sexual bliss, but of a rather different kind. Chanticleer's powers of sexual endurance are seemingly inexhaustible: 'Ardent in love', we are told, 'outrageous in his play, / He feathered [Pertelote] a hundred times a day'. And, as a cock 'Who true to love, was all for recreation, / And minded not the work of propagation', Chanticleer shows himself to be a singlemindedly 'devoted knight' of Venus. Chaucer's tale, in Dryden's recreation, contains many touches which are sharply satirical of human folly and self-delusion. The language and behaviour of Chanticleer (absurdly self-important and smugly patronizing) and Pertelote (nagging, and peremptorily contemptuous of her husband's fears) are uncomfortably close to home, and are far removed from the dignified exchanges of Milton's Adam and Eve. And Chanticleer's sexual 'freedom' is further mocked by Dryden (in a significant expansion of Chaucer's original) by being compared with the disreputable sexual conduct of monarchs, past and present. Yet the overall effect of the tale, in Dryden's rendering, is far from being a merely bitter, sardonic, or censorious negation of Milton's affirmation of human reason and beauty. If Chanticleer falls through his susceptibility to Reynard's flattery, he is also possessed of an ingenuity or survival instinct which allows him (to every reader's delight) to turn the tempter's flattery on himself, thus escaping from disaster. Without relaxing any of the sharpness of its anatomy of the vanity of cockly/human folly, presumption and self-delusion, Chaucer's tale, in Dryden's rendering, emerges as a comic celebration of humanity, as positive (in its own way) as Milton's radiant assertion of mankind's godlike dignity.

In another of the *Fables*, the story of 'Cinyras and Myrrha' from Ovid's *Metamorphoses*, Dryden explores one of the main themes of 'The Cock and the Fox' – the relation of human and animal sexuality – in a very different context. In this poem, Myrrha, daughter of Cinyras, King of Cyprus, is consumed with an incestuous passion for her father which she eventually (with the assistance of her nurse, and under the cover of darkness) contrives to consummate. When Cinyras discovers the true identity of his young mistress, Myrrha flees, eventually reaching the deserts of Arabia, where she is metamorphosed into a myrrh tree. In his rendering of Ovid's depiction of Myrrha's plight, Dryden exploits the witty puns and verbal 'turns' for which Ovid had so often been criticized, seeing in them a perfect vehicle for exploring Myrrha's intractable dilemma without censoriousness or sentimentality. Are not her feelings for her father, Myrrha asks in a lengthy soliloquy near the beginning of the poem, 'natural'? (Incest is, after all, widespread in the animal world, and practised in some human communities, though not in Cyprus 'where 'tis the country makes the crime'.) Or does her passion transgress 'the sanctions nature has designed', so that the 'sacred quiet' of her mind will be destroyed for ever, if she yields to her desires? Dryden's 'Ovidian' alliteration and wordplay capture the paradoxical nature of her situation: 'The hen', Myrrha asserts, 'is free to wed the chick she bore, / And make a husband, whom she hatched before'. But, as the reader (though not the speaker) can see, Myrrha's argument deconstructs itself: it is only in *human* language and practice that categories like 'wed' and 'husband' are acknowledged. The effect, however, is not merely to deride Myrrha or to milk her situation for prurient titillation. Nor are her incestuous feelings anathematized as 'monstrous', as they had regularly been by earlier commentators on Ovid's episode. The nurse and Cinyras (whose debauchery is stressed in Dryden's version more than in the original) are made to bear their share of the responsibility for the catastrophe, and when Myrrha's metamorphosis finally occurs, it is not depicted as a simple punishment or degradation: she is reassimilated into the 'nature' of which she is so completely and complicatedly a part. Her beauty is preserved in the sweetness of the myrrh tree's resinous gum and her agony in the gnarled shape of its trunk. And the offspring of her 'unnatural' union is not a monster, but the beautiful Adonis, who, by inspiring the love of Venus, 'with her pains, revenged his mother's fires'.

In another of the *Fables*, the tale of 'Sigismonda and Guiscardo' (based on a prose tale from Boccaccio's *Decameron*), love is depicted not as a source of disaster, comic absurdity, or intractable dilemmas, but as a positive force, capable of inspiring heroic eloquence. Sigismonda, a rich young widow, falls in love with Guiscardo, the poor but honourable squire of her possessive father, Tancred. They meet secretly, are married, and continue to hold assignations, until one day Tancred observes them, has Guiscardo arrested, and takes his daughter to task for her association with a person of such ignoble birth. Earlier in the poem, Sigismonda and Guiscardo's secret marriage has been depicted with a buoyant gusto bordering on the comic. But Sigismonda is now transformed into a figure of impressive dignity, responding to her father's accusations in a defiant speech of powerful authority and cogency, in which, aligning herself with the finest traditions of Christian and pagan thought (Dryden's rendering 'fortifies' Boccaccio with echoes of Ovid, Lucretius, Chaucer, Milton, and the Gospels), she defines the nature of true nobility – the quality for which, she claims, she had selected Guiscardo as a lover in the first place. Sigismonda, moreover, boldly defends her sexual conduct, aligning herself in protest with all those women throughout history whose needs and promptings have been frustrated by laws which were none of their making:

> What have I done in this deserving blame?
> State laws may alter; nature's are the same;
> Those are usurped on helpless womankind,
> Made without our consent, and wanting power to bind.

As with the other subjects treated in *Fables*, none of the complementary and contradictory perspectives on the topic of love which emanate from Dryden's imaginative communings with Chaucer, Ovid and Boccaccio, is allowed simply to predominate over, or invalidate, the others. The volume's various 'voices' follow one another in an ever-varying sequence. The result is a uniquely rich and comprehensive portrayal of the forces which exist to ennoble, invigorate, torment, or confound human existence – or to render it delightfully absurd.

NOTE

This chapter was completed during research leave supported by the Humanities Research Board of the British Academy.

REFERENCES AND FURTHER READING

Bates, Richard (1982). 'Dryden's translations from *The Decameron*'. University of Cambridge: unpublished Ph.D. dissertation.

Corse, Taylor (1993). 'Dryden and Milton in "The cock and the fox"'. *Milton Quarterly* 27, 109–18.

Garrison, James D. (1981). 'The universe of Dryden's *Fables*'. *Studies in English Literature* 21, 409–23.

Hopkins, David (1985). 'Nature's laws and man's: the story of Cinyras and Myrrha in Ovid and Dryden'. *Modern Language Review* 80, 786–801.

——(1986). '"An improving writer to his last": the *Fables*'. In *John Dryden*. David Hopkins. Cambridge: Cambridge University Press, 168–200, 209–10.

——(1988). 'Dryden and Ovid's "wit out of season"'. In *Ovid Renewed: Ovidian Influences on Literature and Art from the Middle Ages to the Twentieth Century*. Ed. Charles Martindale. Cambridge: Cambridge University Press, 167–90, 276–9.

Jones, Emrys (1980). 'Dryden's Sigismonda'. In *English Renaissance Studies: Essays Presented to Dame Helen Gardner in Honour of her Seventieth Birthday*. Ed. John Carey. Oxford: Clarendon, 279–90.

Kinsley, James (1952). 'Dryden's character of a good parson and Bishop Ken'. *Review of English Studies* n.s. 3, 155–8.

Levine, Jay Arnold (1964). 'John Dryden's Epistle to John Driden'. *Journal of English and Germanic Philology* 63, 450–74.

Mason, Tom (1975). 'Dryden's version of the "Wife of Bath's Tale"'. *Cambridge Quarterly* 6, 240–56.

——(1977). 'Dryden's Chaucer'. University of Cambridge: unpublished Ph.D. dissertation.

Miner, Earl (1967). 'Thematic variation and structure in *Fables*'. In *Dryden's Poetry*. Earl Miner. Bloomington and London: Indiana University Press, 287–329, 345–6.

——(1967). 'Chaucer in Dryden's *Fables*'. In *Studies in Criticism and Aesthetics, 1660–1800: Essays in Honor of Samuel Holt Monk*. Ed. Howard Anderson and John S. Shea. Minneapolis: University of Minnesota Press, 58–72.

Reverand, Cedric D. II (1988). *Dryden's Final Poetic Mode: The 'Fables'*. Philadelphia: University of Pennsylvania Press.

Smith, Ruth (1978). 'The argument and contexts of Dryden's *Alexander's Feast*'. *Studies in English Literature* 18, 465–90.

Sowerby, Robin (1996). 'The freedom of Dryden's Homer'. *Translation and Literature* 5, 26–50.

Wright, H. G. (1945). 'Some sidelights on the reputation and influence of Dryden's *Fables*'. *Review of English Studies* 21, 23–37.

Zwicker, Steven N. (1984). 'Fables ancient and modern'. In *Politics and Language in Dryden's Poetry: The Arts of Disguise*. Ed. Steven N. Zwicker. Princeton: Princeton University Press, 158–76.

21

William Congreve, *The Way of the World*

Malcolm Kelsall

The ups and downs of Congreve's reputation are a remarkable example of the historic variability of the so-called 'canon' of English literature. At one time he was next to Shakespeare as a symbolic representative of national culture. When the Goodman's Fields playhouse was opened in 1732–3 the theatre was decorated with a statue of George II above the pit attended by images of Peace, Liberty and Justice themselves supported by Congreve, Shakespeare, Dryden and the actor Betterton. The iconography celebrated the triumphalist unity of the Protestant nation and the principles of the Whig revolution of 1688–9. The differences between earlier epochs were obliterated in a celebration of theatrical culture as a transhistorical unificatory force. Yet, in the famous farewell performances of Garrick (1776) Congreve was omitted. Actor and playwright were now separated. Congreve's texts were already becoming subject to radical excisions or revisions in the interests of moral correctness. By the early nineteenth century he was virtually extinct. A few men of letters, like Hazlitt, Lamb and Leigh Hunt still read him with appreciation, but, in common with his fellow dramatists of 'the Restoration', he was dismissed from the nineteenth-century theatre as degrading.

He has had to be rediscovered and reinterpreted, therefore, in the twentieth century. It is a process in which 'literature' and the theatre have been institutionally separated. The plays flickered back to life in revivals by the Stage Society and the Phoenix Society but not until Edith Evans's performance as Millamant in 1924 was the full power of Congreve's theatre revealed. Evans's Millamant was a woman suspended between deep disillusionment with a cruel and shallow world and the ineluctable desire of flesh and spirit to find the security of love. Evans combined the intelligence and provocation of the contemporary theatre of Shaw with a Bradleyan (and Shakespearean) sense of waste. The same year saw the publication of Bonamy Dobrée's seminal *Restoration Comedy 1660–1700*. Congreve had begun to regain something of his original 'classic' status.

Modern scholarship has gone on to reconstitute the history of Congreve's theatre. One of the most important effects of this scholarship has been to destroy early generalizations based on a few (sometimes atypical) texts from the hundreds of new (or revised) plays produced during Congreve's lifetime (1670–1729). Theatrecraft was so diverse and productive that the old commonplace terms 'Restoration' (to describe the stage) and 'comedy of manners' (to define a genre) are inappropriately imprecise. More-over, as the iconography of the Goodman's Fields theatre indicated, contemporaries saw the Tudor to the Georgian period, in theatrical terms, as part of a common move-ment. The closing of the theatres in the Commonwealth was merely a hiatus in the developing continuum of the London stage. Nonetheless, one of the oldest common-places about 'Restoration' theatre has been revitalized by modern (post-feminist) con-cerns with gender issues. The arrival of actresses on the public stage transformed the capabilities of drama as that half of the human race unavailable to Shakespeare became a constructive force in the theatre. *The Way of the World* can handle issues of gender in a naturalistically depicted social world in a manner totally impossible to Shake-speare who had no actors like Elizabeth Barry or Anne Bracegirdle with whom to interact. In comparison, Tudor and Jacobean theatre must have seemed curiously archaic.

Academic scholarship has only just begun to come to terms with post-feminist Con-greve, perhaps because the rediscovered presence of Aphra Behn, as a major woman playwright, is currently recentring the seventeenth-century 'canon'. But perhaps also early academic reading of Congreve was distorted by the massive put down of Con-greve's treatment of sexuality by Leavisism. L. C. Knights (and his followers) weighed Congreve in the scales against the psychic and physical insights to be gained from D. H. Lawrence, or the dark complexities to be found in Henry James, and found the play-wright, like his period, 'gross, trivial and dull'. In contradistinction, academic opposi-tion met Leavisism on its own ground, reading Congreve's comedy as part of a masculine canon possessing a strong moral agenda. The kind of questions posed were of the kind: is *The Way of the World* a 'reformist' comedy in which the witty 'rake' hero of earlier 'Restoration' comedy (Dorimant in *The Man of Mode*, for instance) is sentimentally 'reformed' in Mirabell? The 'rake' hero is associated in this play only with the evil 'false wit' of Fainall who, like a scapegoat figure, carries off with him all the dark associa-tions of predatory libertinism. The social world is controlled ultimately by the 'true wit' of the idealized pairing of generous Mirabell with Millamant. Might Congreve, even, be a Christian allegorist? Do we not see that providence is vindicated by the happy ending in which the virtuous are rewarded and the vicious punished?

These are 'seriously moral' readings of the play. Alternatively *The Way of the World* has been read epistemologically or ideologically as a key text for understanding the intellectual, political or social culture of Congreve's period. Because *The Way of the World* depicts a materialist society engaged in a ruthless struggle for power, its the-matic matter derives from Hobbes, or Hobbes's precursors Machiavelli and Epicurus. Or, because the play raises perplexing questions of knowledge (how do we know the truth about what people say, or about the appearances of things?) Congreve's world relates to the sceptical philosophy of Locke (and his precursors). In the darker read-ings of the play derived from this scepticism, all security of discourse dissolves, so that even the 'ideal' marriage of Mirabell and Millamant becomes shot through with suspicion and uncertainty. Yet, paradoxically, and in contradistinction, it is Locke, as a political apologist for the revolution of 1688–9, who has been seen as providing an ultimately secure underpinning for the society of *The Way of the World*. Contract, as expressed in marriage and in property settlement (Mrs Fainall's deed, for instance), holds fissiparous elements together. From a political viewpoint, this has been described as an expression of a newly emergent 'bourgeois' 'hegemony'. The defeated Fainall stands, by analogy as a 'displaced' signifier of the old Stuart and feudal order, whereas, as members of an emergent middle class, Mirabell and Millamant freely engage in a contractual marriage based on love.

The earnestness of this kind of criticism is remarkable. But *The Way of the World* initially failed to entertain on the stage, and it may well be that the failure was related to the play's complex morality and intellectualism. The plot is desperately difficult to follow (the audience is deliberately misled and confused about 'the black box', for instance) and the familial (and sexual) interrelationships of the characters can be bewildering. Morally, the action turns on the nicest distinctions of social and moral judgement. Initially Mirabell and Fainall are virtually indistinguishable as 'libertines' and are only gradually discriminated by their behaviour to mistress and to wife. But there are other pairings, equally difficult to judge: Mrs Fainall and Marwood, for instance, and Millamant (in her silly moods) and her aunt Lady Wishfort. The aunt is what Millamant might well become when old, ugly and still believing she can 'make' lovers.

The nice distinctions between characters can be deeply disturbing. To take a crucial example: according to 'the way of the world' Mirabell sees it as a considerate act to marry his former mistress to Fainall as a mask for her suspected pregnancy. 'A better man ought not to have been sacrificed to the occasion; a worse had not answered to the purpose. When you are weary of him, you know your remedy' (II. 245–8). That kind of thing had already exposed Congreve to the moral blasts of Jeremy Collier's *A Short View of the Profaneness, and Immorality of the English Stage* (1698). It has been common to dismiss Collier's Puritanism, but his attitude has found modern support in feminist attacks on Congreve as a member of a 'patriarchy' engaged in smutty 'derogation' of threatening women. Whatever one's view of the revival of Puritanism, there is a bleak viciousness in Mirabell's treatment of the Fainalls difficult to reconcile with readings of him as 'a true wit' or 'ideal' gentleman. The biological determinant of his action is gender – it is the woman who carries the baby – and the social determinant is 'reputation' – society condemns the single mother. Thus, a woman, potentially pregnant by one man (who does not want her) must be found a husband. But she is not a helpless commodity passed between males. The 'remedy' to which Mirabell refers is not the resumption of her sexual affairs (as the text implies) but her calling in of her deed of trust which gives her financial control of her matrimonial estate. Money is power. But what sort of basis is this for happy marriage?

Congreve answered Collier's moral objections by claiming that he wrote satire. He stressed he did not demean human kind as a whole. The 'world' of the play is a tiny social group embodying what the social theorist Thorstein Veblen called (in the 1890s) 'the leisure class'. It is a 'world' of consumers rather than of producers, at leisure for pleasure and engaged in useless display. This 'world', in Congreve's dramaturgy, is driven by sexual desire and by the desire for power. 'One's cruelty is one's power', Millamant states (II. 348) rejoicing that her sexual attractiveness gives her the ability to dominate and to hurt others. But artificial manners conceal natural instinct. A mask, real or metaphorical, conceals 'true' identity. Thus Millamant does not speak of herself in the first person here, but objectifies herself as 'one'. But the essential ego, 'I', remains unknown and we see only the social identity. Hence the importance of 'reputation', for one exists as one is perceived.

Congreve's comic target, 'the leisure class', is not specific to his theatre alone. The application of a phrase from the 1890s indicates the strong analogies between Congreve and Wilde. One might equally move back to Shakespeare whose romantic comedy is likewise grounded in unproductive leisure. Accordingly, there are transhistorical generic conventions which operate in this kind of play world. To ignore the generic rules of the game is to misunderstand it. One simple, yet fundamental rule of this kind of comedy is that people behave like this only in plays. One consequence of the separation of the majority of academic criticism from theatre practice is that moral or ideological 'readings' of theatre can become oblivious of even the simplest generic conventions. Only in comic 'play' does a great lady like Olivia marry a Sebastian on first meeting, a bride choose a husband because he learns he is called 'Ernest', or (in Congreve) a servingman (called Waitwell) try to trick an elderly gentlewoman into a bigamous marriage (which would be, in real life, criminal fraud). In short, one of the functions of comedy is to release characters from the ordinary ties of probability and hence of morality. Congreve's satire raises moral issues, but then the 'carnival' of comic theatre tends to dissolve them again. Anything goes in carnival, which means that the usual rules of moral judgement tend to go also. To use one of Millamant's words, one should not be too 'sententious' even about grave issues: witness the Fainalls' marriage.

So 'sententious' has academic criticism become that it might appear mere aesthetic evasion to argue that the really new ground that needs to be broken in the study of Congreve is to be found by working through his theatrecraft. Rather than trying to elaborate on new ways in which plays, somehow, provide a ready and easy way into culture, or cultural theories can be applied to plays, one might begin instead with the simple truism that all writers rewrite other writers (as the case of Shakespeare pre-eminently illustrates). Thus, all playwrights rewrite theatrical tradition and all theatre (even naturalistic forms) is metatheatre, consciously aware, and expectant that the audience knows a common repertory of attitudes, devices, discourses, modes, situations, resolutions. Any modern cinema buff knows this about film, and Congreve's audience was in an analogous position. It knew the conventions of an extensive repertory. The 'meaning' of the text, therefore, exists in the continually shifting interplay of the similarities and differences between this text and the verbal contexts in which it was placed. It is to the play's 'dialogism' that one should look: that is, to the capacity of the playwright's words to enter into new configurations from inherited discourse.

A simple illustration may serve. To return to Millamant's 'One's cruelty is one's power.' The word 'cruelty' has a conventional context which Congreve derived from Renaissance Petrarchanism. In this tradition the male poet's complaint was that his beloved will not grant him his desire and thus she is 'cruel'. But this (male) tradition is revocalized in Congreve because dramatic form allows him to give Millamant the voice (and the wit) to answer the man back. In this world of social appearance, good looks empowers the woman over men, but only if she denies their sexual fulfilment and her own. Once married, as the play makes clear, she will 'dwindle' into motherhood; or, if she does not marry, the ugliness of old age will rob her even of the power of beauty. Therefore, she must be 'cruel'. But the 'dialogism' of words gives to Millamant's speech more than a seventeenth-century resignification. Theatrical tradition is not historically fixed. A modern reader who is aware of Artaud's theories of 'the theatre of cruelty' may recontextualize Congreve's neo-Petrarchan use of the word. Beneath the veneer of wit and manners in Congreve's play there lurks a latent theatre of cruelty (one thinks of Fainall's desire to kill his wife) and a rank animal lust. These cruel forces are masked by social taboos, but these restraints are the thinnest of crusts over volcanic pressures thrusting up from beneath. For a modern audience, knowing in theatre, Congreve, recontextualized in relation to twentieth-century theatre, appears to be a creator of what we call 'black comedy', or even an 'absurdist' writing of a morally nihilistic world.

Hence the importance of the proviso scene, for this is the most complex piece of dialogic metatheatre in the play. It is so complex that no interpretation can exhaust the variables. Although one may readily pick up the signification of Mirabell being able to cap Millamant's verses (which Sir Wilful could not), yet how many even of the original audience would realize that Millamant (when she refers to the aptly designated 'filthy' Suckling) was citing a poem on the jaded pleasures of a rake who having had his sexual fill merely moves on; or that the verses which Mirabell caps describe an attempted rape? Daphne, in the poem, escaped by being changed to a laurel. Millamant, in the play, is locked in a room, and can fly no further. That is a 'cruel' context for a romantic proposal of marriage, and when Millamant ultimately asks, 'Shall I have him? I think I must have him' (with innuendo on 'have') the woman she asks is Mrs Fainall, Mirabell's cast mistress – and we never know if Millamant realizes this. The dialogic ironies are unresolvable.

But the entire proviso scene is an endlessly variable counterpoint on literary commonplaces, originating from Honoré D'Urfé's handbook for gallantry, *L'Astrée* (1607–27), and repeatedly imitated in the theatre, including four variants by Dryden in *The Wild Gallant* (1663), *Secret Love* (1667), *Marriage à la Mode* (1672) and *Amphitryon* (1690). Thus, Congreve's 'modern' (1690s) attitudes exist in dialogue with a century-old concern with the social proprieties of gallantry by which jaded appetite might be kept alive in marriage. Although both partners wish to protect the autonomy of their 'dear liberty', both equally fear liberty may degenerate into libertinism – which is the literary tradition *sotto voce* running through the scene. One remarkable variant in the convention is Mirabell's insistence that his endeavours ('odious' as Millamant finds them) should produce a male heir. Perhaps this reorientates a literary commonplace towards patriarchalism. On the other hand, comic convention determines that the text has nothing to do with real world marriage contracts, nor with the ideology of Christian marriage. Congreve's concern is to rework theatrical conventions already long in the tooth, which is, perhaps, why he gave up writing comedies. *The Way of the World* (1700) marked the end of an epoch and of the century. The play then died with its theatre. It is for us to reinvent it in dialogue with our modern world.

REFERENCES AND FURTHER READING

All quotations are from Lynch, Kathleen M., ed. (1965). *The Way of the World*. London: Edward Arnold.

Birdsall, Virginia Ogden (1970). *Wild Civility: The English Comic Spirit on the Restoration Stage*. Bloomington: Indiana University Press.

Burns, Edward (1987). *Restoration Comedy: Crises of Desire and Identity*. Basingstoke: Macmillan.

Dobrée, Bonamy (1924). *Restoration Comedy, 1660–1700*. London: Oxford University Press.

Donaldson, Ian (1970). *The World Upside Down: Comedy from Jonson to Fielding*. Oxford: Clarendon.

Fujimura, Thomas (1952). *The Restoration Comedy of Wit*. Princeton: Princeton University Press.

Gill, Pat (1994). *Interpreting Ladies: Women, Wit, and Morality in the Restoration Comedy of Manners*. Athens, Georgia: Georgia University Press.

Hawkins, Harriet H. (1972). *Likeness of Truth in Elizabethan and Restoration Drama*. Oxford: Clarendon.

Holland, Norman (1959). *The First Modern Comedies*. Cambridge: Cambridge University Press.

Holland, Peter (1979). *The Ornament of Action: Text and Performance in Restoration Comedy*. Cambridge: Cambridge University Press.

Howe, Elizabeth (1992). *The First English Actresses: Women and Drama 1660–1700*. Cambridge: Cambridge University Press.

Hughes, Derek (1996). *English Drama 1660–1700*. Oxford: Clarendon.

Hume, Robert D. (1976). *The Development of English Drama in the Late Seventeenth Century*. Oxford: Clarendon.

——(1983). *The Rakish Stage: Studies in English Drama, 1660–1800*. Carbondale: Southern Illinois University Press.

Kelsall, Malcolm (1981). *Congreve: The Way of the World*. London: Edward Arnold.

Knights, L. C. (1946). Restoration comedy, In *Explorations*. Ed. L. C. Knights (pp. 131–49). London: Chatto and Windus.

Love, Harold (1974). *Congreve*. Oxford: Basil Blackwell.

Markley, Robert (1988). *Two Edg'd Weapons: Style and Ideology in the Comedies of Etherege, Wycherley, and Congreve*. Oxford: Clarendon.

Morris, Brian, ed. (1972). *William Congreve* London: Ernest Benn.

Mueschke, Paul and Miriam (1958). *A New View of Congreve's 'The Way of the World'*. Michigan: Ann Arbor.

Novak, Maximilian E. (1971). *William Congreve*. New York: Twayne.

Powell, Jocelyn (1984). *Restoration Theatre Production*. London: Routledge and Kegan Paul.

Styan, J. L. (1986). *Restoration Comedy in Performance*. Cambridge: Cambridge University Press.

Van Voris, W. H. (1965). *The Cultivated Stance: The Designs of Congreve's Plays*. Dublin: The Dolmen Press.

Williams. Aubrey L. (1979). *An Approach to Congreve*. New Haven: Yale University Press.

22

Jonathan Swift, *A Tale of a Tub*

Claude Rawson

A Tale of a Tub, with its two appendages, the *Battle of the Books* and the *Discourse Concerning the Mechanical Operation of the Spirit*, is Swift's first important prose work and perhaps his most brilliant. It was written in the 1690s, when Swift was attached to the household of Sir William Temple, published in 1704, and revised for a fifth edition published in 1710 (an amplified version commonly used by readers ever since, containing important additions as well as some emasculation of the original). It appeared anonymously. Indeed, most of Swift's major prose writings, including the *Drapier's Letters*, *Gulliver's Travels*, and *A Modest Proposal*, appeared anonymously or pseudonymously. The reasons doubtless had to do with his temperamental guardedness, his penchant for mystification, and a residual sense that it was ungentlemanly to appear by name in the public prints. But there was also a well-founded anxiety over legal sanctions and career setbacks, since all his works contained elements that might seem politically subversive or personally offensive to powerful interests. But the *Tale* was never publicly acknowledged in any way, and did not in his lifetime appear in authorized editions of his collected works, as *Gulliver's Travels*, for example, did: indeed, the major 1735 edition of his *Works* was used by Swift to bring out a carefully revised and extended version of *Gulliver's Travels*, while retaining the formal pretence of pseudonymity.

The *Tale* was a special case. It was not only left out of the 1735 edition as well as other collected editions, but was the subject of an especially determined, and at the same time regretful, effort of ostentatious concealment. The book, as Swift asserted in the 'Apology' prefixed to the fifth edition of 1710, was partly concerned to attack religious persuasions (Dissenting or Catholic) which Swift saw as inimical to the Anglican Church and which appear as the official targets of his satire, but the sweep and energy of his irony were such that the book was sometimes thought, or represented to be, radically hostile to religion itself. Swift himself felt throughout his life that his failure to secure the highest ecclesiastical promotion to which he aspired was due to influential (including royal) disapproval of the *Tale*'s supposed irreligious tendencies. (On the anonymity of the *Tale*, its occasional ascription to other authors, Swift's mortification at this as well as at the prospect of the disclosure of his authorship, and the aura of scandal surrounding the work, see Ehrenpreis, 1962, 208, 1967 139–40, 326–38.) This may or may not be the only reason for concealment. The *Tale* is a work of exceptional aggressive elusiveness, whose bewilderingly many-sided and versatile manner created a comprehensive atmosphere of diffused irreverence, whose effect (even more than usual in Swift's satire) is to undermine everything it touches, including principles and outlooks to which Swift was intensely loyal. It also has a quality of exuberant and almost 'irresponsible' play, which may at times have seemed inappropriate to Swift's various public roles as priest, as Dean of St Patrick's Cathedral, and as a weighty participant in controversies of church and state in both Ireland and England.

The mercurial and stinging tease of the writing, which leaves the reader permanently unsure as to who exactly is speaking at any given moment, and as to the specific non-ironic point of view which may be thought of as the 'prose sense' of ironic obliquity, is also in its nature not inconsistent with the more pragmatic guardedness of not acknowledging the work at all. The ambivalence of the disavowal is in itself the flip side of Swift's characteristic blending of indirection and forceful attack. At all events, Swift was extremely proud of the *Tale*, and jealously irritated when he saw it, or parts of it, ascribed to others. He is said later in life to have exclaimed: 'Good God! what a genius I had when I wrote that book', a story reported most famously by Sir Walter Scott, which may or may not be factually true, but which reflects a truth of its own both about the book and Swift's feeling for it. (See Guthkelch and Smith, 1958, xix, n. 2, citing Scott's edition of Swift's *Works*, 1824, I.89, Scott having 'got the story from Theophilus Swift'.)

The *Tale*, along with the *Battle of the Books*, which comes after it as a kind of Appendix, was perhaps the most impressive English contribution to the so-called quarrel of the Ancients and Moderns. The history or prehistory of this *querelle* (it is most familiarly referred to in its French form) can be traced back to the Renaissance. The sense of intellectual and cultural liberation generated by the rediscovery and publication of the philosophers and poets of Greece and Rome also engendered a questioning of assumptions about the value of the classical models which helped to bring it about. Were these to be thought of as unsurpassable masterpieces, which modern writers could only hope to imitate from a distance? or were modern achievements capable of excelling them, if they hadn't excelled them already (perhaps by accepting the old models and improving on them, like dwarfs standing on the shoulders of giants, an image often used; or by striking out in new directions, for example in experimental science)?

The debate may now seem dated, but it brought into relief many contested issues which have reappeared in other forms since that time: between science and religion (since scientific enquiry probed into aspects of nature that God chose to keep secret, and since the discourse of scientific causality might seem to challenge a belief in God as creator of all things); between science and poetry, with its traditional links with a humanistic culture steeped in the Graeco-Roman past; between poets whose work failed to live up to or repudiated these associations, and those who, like Swift and Pope, were profoundly attached to them; between 'specialists', technicians, poets who wrote for gain or for party, scholars who delivered pedantic discourses or annotated ancient texts, and, on the other side, a classically schooled patrician elite, including writers who, again like Swift and Pope, did not belong to it by birth but were loyal to its values and aspirations. The gentlemanly tradition of the *honnête homme* prided itself especially on its civilized knowledge 'both of books and humankind', and its freedom from the narrow specialist vision of a Bentley, as portrayed in the *Battle of the Books*. Bentley, one of the towering figures in the history of classical scholarship, might in real life know a great deal more about the classics than any gentleman preening himself on his classical taste, but he was a Modern by virtue of his professional expertise in textual criticism and in ancient history. (For the sake of clarity, I use Ancient and Modern, with capitals, to mean participants in the dispute, and the uncapitalized forms to indicate chronological difference: thus, in the *Battle of the Books*, Virgil is both an Ancient and an ancient, Temple an Ancient and a modern, and Bentley a Modern and a modern).

The English 'Battle of the Books' (Swift's phrase has been appropriated in an important book by Joseph M. Levine as well as in some important essays by John F. Tinkler) reorientated the debate into one more concerned with the antagonistic perspectives of the 'professional scholar and . . . the occasional man of letters' than with 'moderns and ancients' as such. When Swift's patron Temple initiated the English debate in his 'Essay upon the Ancient and Modern Learning' (1690), claiming that the moral and literary superiority of the Ancients was evidenced by the *Epistles of Phalaris* and the *Fables* of Aesop, 'the two most ancient that I know of in prose', Bentley was able to demonstrate that both works were spurious and of a later date. He didn't presume to enter into the debate on the literary merits of these works, though he opined in passing that the high place accorded to their two authors was 'criticism of a peculiar complexion', which 'must proceed from a singularity of palate and judgement'.

Bentley's remark deftly imputes to his patrician opponents the kind of perverse oddity of judgement which the latter would more readily ascribe to him. The English 'Battle' was indeed one which not only pitted literary taste against pedantic expertise but exploited a rhetoric of gentlemanly superiority against boorish positiveness and 'singularity'. On the main scholarly issues, the case of the Ancients was in tatters, but the argument came to be seen as one in which patrician wits, including non-patrician allies like Swift, exposed the vulgarity of low-bred pedants like Bentley and his adjutant, the Anglican clergyman William Wotton. In Swift's *Battle*, the scholar Scaliger (a modern Ancient) berates Bentley for his boorishness: '*Thy* Learning *makes thee more* Barbarous, *thy Study of* Humanity, *more* Inhuman; . . . *All Arts of* civilizing *others, render thee* rude *and* untractable; *Courts have taught thee* Ill Manners, *and* Polite Conversation *has finish'd thee a* Pedant.' The passage is modelled on Odysseus's speech to Thersites in Book II of the *Iliad*, though with variations of extreme interest which cannot be entered into here. (On these differences, see Rawson, 1994, 40–2, 82–9,

92.) In another epic passage, near the end, Wotton hurls a lance at Temple, which hits his belt: but Temple 'neither felt the Weapon touch him, nor heard it fall', a lofty ignoring so absolute that it resolves itself into a withering ignorance, implicitly literalizing the phrase 'people one does not know'.

After the *Tale* appeared in 1704, Wotton published a *Defense of the Reflections upon Ancient and Modern Learning, . . . With Observations upon The Tale of a Tub* (1705). The 'Observations' offered an explication of the story of the three brothers, in the course of arguing that the *Tale* was a work of radical impiety. Swift was sensitive to this charge, which he earnestly sought to rebut in the 'Apology', prefixed for the first time to the fifth edition of 1710. But Swift also impishly took over the explanatory matter in Wotton's attack, printing it in the notes to his own text, turning the *Tale* into an edition of itself, in the guise of a classical text *cum notis variorum* (with the notes of various authorities). Wotton is thus absorbed into the chain of pedantry, as a laboured drudge heavily engaged in explaining the obvious. But he is simultaneously enlisted as an aid to understanding a work he was more concerned to attack than to explain, outwitted by having his aggression read as exegetically helpful, and pilloried afresh by mock-editorial amiability every time his name appears gratefully at the end of a note.

Even before this, though on a smaller scale, the *Tale* had announced itself as a parody of learned editions, with gaps in the manuscript indicated by Latin marginalia and other flippant editorial routines. It was also from the beginning an attack on subliterary or journalistic hack-writing, slipshod, evasive, ignorant, self-consciously digressive, concerned to be up-to-the-minute, fatuously spontaneous in recording the most trivial domestic circumstances of the 'author' and everything that entered his head at the very moment when it did so, including his thoughts on the writing of his thoughts.

Swift purported to be mocking Dryden and other seventeenth-century writers. None of them shows anything like the outrageous textual egotism he ascribes to them, and Swift's manner has much closer analogues in a later literature of self-conscious, self-ironic writing, from Sterne's *Tristram Shandy* to Mailer's *Advertisements for Myself* – works Swift would have detested, and the first of which was expressly composed in the teeth of Swift's derision. This suggests that Swift detected in Dryden and some of his contemporaries incipient elements of a later modernism which do not seem to have been visible to other readers. The use of Swift as a model by Sterne, Joyce and Beckett, all of whom knowingly incorporate his proleptic derision, is a token of his extraordinary prescience as a cultural analyst, as well as of his almost magical inventiveness as a mimic. Although Marcus Walsh, in an important article, has shown that Swift's self-conscious preoccupation with 'textuality', nowadays much discussed, was more widely shared in his lifetime than we previously knew, it was Swift's extraordinary elaboration of a parodic style that paradoxically created new possibilities of self-expression for the very modernism he was resisting.

The *Tale* proceeds on two parallel or alternating tracks, the satire on abuses in religion, and the 'digressions' which form a satire on modern learning. Swift claimed in the Apology to have written in defence of the Anglican Church against its Papist and Puritan enemies. The satire on the latter is probably the most biting. It targets sectarian groups which exalt the individual worshipper or small congregation, with their inner light, private conscience and spontaneous accesses of devotion, unchecked by tradition and institutional authority. Corresponding to them on a secular plane are the journalists, hacks and bad poets satirized in the 'digressions', with their cult of the immediate moment and their sense of the primacy of ego and whim. Both groups are seen as surrendering to the flow of irrational feeling, and the favoured term for this abandonment of rational control is 'enthusiasm', the state described in the Digression on Madness, in which the imagination overwhelms reason, the senses, and the common forms of conduct and thought.

Enthusiastic worship, in this sense, is a principal preoccupation of the *Discourse Concerning the Mechanical Operation of the Spirit*, where it is shown as manipulated by unscrupulous preachers, fanning the devotional excitability of their flock into orgiastic states of sexual lewdness, a frequent accusation against the Puritan sects. The fact that this *Discourse* takes the form of a scientific communication to a member of the '*Academy of the* Beaux Esprits *in* New-Holland' intimates how closely intertwined the religious allegory is with the satire on 'learning', including scientific pretensions. The location of the learned society in New-Holland suggests that modern science and the savages of the South Pacific are more or less on a par: the author's complaint a little later that he has not recently heard from 'the *Literati* of *Topinambou*' is an irony of the same sort, invoking another *locus classicus* of barbaric savagery, the Amerindian tribe of cannibals in whose defence Montaigne had once written (the author also likes to stay in touch with the society of '*Iroquois Virtuosi*'). Scientists, literati and cannibal savages are mad Moderns of the same essential stripe. Modernism is atavistic, perhaps older than the ancients, as old as the unregulated self. It goes back to the beginning of time, like the Modern critics of the Digression Concerning Critics, who descend 'in a direct line from a Celestial Stem, by *Momus* and *Hybris*, who begat *Zoilus*, who begat *Tigellius*, who begat *Etcaetera* the Elder, who begat *Bently*, and *Rymer*, and *Wotton*, and *Perrault*, and *Dennis*, who begat *Etcaetera* the Younger'.

The account of this intellectual riff-raff, in both the *Tale* and the *Mechanical Operation* (which is an addendum to the *Tale*'s religious satire as the *Battle of the Books* is to the satire on learning), is, as I suggested earlier, so inventive, versatile and brilliantly unruly that it risks contaminating the positive values Swift insisted in the Apology that he had been upholding. The sensible, moderate and ecumenical speech Martin (who represents a broadly acceptable form of Christianity largely identifiable with the Anglican Church, while his two brothers Peter and Jack, represent Catholics and Dissenters respectively) makes in section VI is the sanest thing anyone is allowed to say in the *Tale*, but it is deflated both in advance and immediately after by some disconcerting and unruly ridicule, whose exact focus is unclear. It is interesting that Martin, the only representative in the *Tale* of any point of view endorsable by Swift, is given very little to say throughout, presumably because the book's atmosphere of total tear-away irony posed an insoluble dilemma: presenting Martin with the seriousness his views deserve could only introduce an incongruous solemnity; allowing him to be playfully subverted, as in section VI, risked the appearance of impiety which Wotton was in the event quick to seize on. The only way out was to give Martin a low profile. There is no extended treatment of Martin, as there is of Peter and Jack. The lack was noted, and someone tried to make it good by adding a 'History of Martin' to a spurious edition of 1720.

This undercutting, even of a character of point or point of view to whom Swift is undoubtedly loyal, is part of a deep temperamental guardedness, an anxiety about appearing to make 'a figure scurvy' by an undue seriousness of manner, as well as by the various forms of 'lofty style' whose use he 'declined' in the poem 'To a Lady'. (It is interesting that, in the great age of mock-epic satire, this was the one form of parody Swift never attempted, with the single special exception of the *Battle of the Books*, which is flattened by the prose medium and a competing, wholly unepic dimension of mock-journalese, as though the risk of loftiness were to be avoided even in a mock-heroic form.) One of the tendencies of Swift's almost invariable use of parody, even when the main point is not to mock books, is to signal that he must not be thought to have been taken in by styles and modes of writing whose conventions are vulnerable to derision. The immediate effect is to distance or separate Swift, not only in individual passages, but on a structural scale, from any directly identifiable commitment to the things that are said in his writings, or the ways in which they are said.

This impulse to self-distancing, defensive or aggressive or both, ensured that none of Swift's important writings in either verse or prose lacked an element of parodic undercutting. He is probably the most consistently parodic of all eighteenth-century writers. His poems about women, for example, are unremittingly conscious of what he perceived as the routines of post-Petrarchan love-poetry, whether he is violently overturning these routines (as in the scatological poems or 'A Beautiful Young Nymph Going to Bed'), or paying deeply felt compliments to Stella. It is as though nothing seriously evocative of a 'serious' style could be uttered without some parodic deflation of a 'high' alternative. In the prose satires, *Gulliver's Travels* and *A Modest Proposal*, parody functions in a separate and marginal way, providing a vehicle, or an added level of bookish jokerie, in writings whose main satiric energies and concerns (the exposure of human turpitude in *Gulliver's Travels*, the condition of Ireland in *A Modest Proposal*) have little or nothing to do with travel books or economic tracts.

In the *Tale of a Tub*, as in the poems, on the other hand, the texts parodied are for the most part primary embodiments or expressions of the things Swift is attacking (various follies of the intellectual life, stupid attitudes to sexuality). The case of the *Battle of the Books*, the only work in which Swift attempted the quintessentially Augustan genre of mock-heroic, is somewhat different again, since the primary object of the parody is not targeted at the ancient epic writers who are being mimicked, but at various modern pretensions, among which writing modern epics, and believing them to be successful poems, played a relatively minor (though not insignificant) part. It seems likely that Swift's pudeur over mock-heroic involved more than the resistance to residual majesties I have already noted. Whereas Pope and some other contemporaries used mock-heroic as a tribute to epic rather than as a subversion of it, Swift's irony was evidently too corrosive for him to risk deploying it in the vicinity of a genre still regarded in his time as the pinnacle of poetic achievement. As with the character of Martin, that embodiment of a sane Anglicanism, Swift chose the path of minimal exposure, probably for him the safest form of praise.

In all Swift's imaginative works, the narrative or argument is conducted by a speaker, usually derided, whose relationship to Swift is oblique and unstable, and whom (in the case of the *Tale*'s speaker or speakers as in that of the deranged Gulliver or Modest Proposer) it is perilous to separate too radically from the author. It was for a time a fashion in literary criticism, and especially in Swift studies, to discuss texts as though they were written or spoken by a clearly distinguishable 'persona' or 'mask'. The impulse came from various sources: psychological theories of role-playing and defence-mechanisms, poetic doctrines derived from the use of masks in the theatre of ancient Greece or of Japan, and especially from a recognition that ever since classical times, poets have spoken in a formally sanctioned role, as priests of the muses, champions of virtue, courageous opponents of corrupt men in power, rather than in a mode of private disclosure, let alone autobiographical intimacy. In critical practice, persona-criticism was a valuable corrective to an opposite tendency to confuse an author's views with those of his fictive speakers or even his fictional characters.

In the case of a highly self-conscious and defensive ironist like Swift, it seemed especially necessary to issue strenuous reminders that the author should not be mistaken for his speakers, as though that truth had been unavailable to intelligent readers before personae had been wheeled into the seminar room. What began as a valuable refinement soon turned into a mechanical routine as reductive as those it reversed. Painstaking studies identifying the personae of an author, defining the supposed characters of each, positing that an unnamed narrator like that of a *Tale of a Tub* was really a series of distinct characters whose different identities could be successfully charted from sentence to sentence, became commonplace. The habit of writing as though 'persona' meant 'person' rather than 'mask' (or 'role', or 'projection') had the wholly inappropriate effect of treating such figures, whether named and formally identifiable, like Gulliver, or unnamed and too elusive even to characterize, like the 'author' of the *Tale*, as if they were autonomous creations analogous to the characters of a novel or play. It has sometimes been suggested that because the *Tale*'s author, or Lemuel Gulliver, evidently did not closely resemble Swift there must be a total disengagement of the one from the other.

This reductive or rigidified assumption is one of the commonest sources of misunderstanding of Swift, an author in whom it is especially important to recognize he and his speakers are neither the same nor separable, that the one is speaking through the other, sometimes directly, sometimes adversarially, and most often in complex and elusive combinations of the two; that an author who speaks through a mask has in all cases written the script and created the persona, and stands responsible for the result, including the persona's views and the exact attitude to them which may be inferred from the context; that, in other words, authors speak *through* their personae if not always with or in favour of them; and that in Swift, a sense of an aggressive and taunting authorial presence is unusually active. Kurt Vonnegut's remark that 'we are what we pretend to be, so we must be careful about what we pretend to be' offers a salutary warning, provided it is taken to mean not that 'author' equals 'persona' but that authors stand responsible for their inventions in their totality. No criticism of Swift can function usefully without some sense of the complexities which the concept of the persona seeks to come to terms with, but it is nowadays necessary to reaffirm Swift's intimate and elusive manipulation of, and engagement with, even the most derided of his pseudo-voices. The *Tale* is spoken by just such a voice, and once we have recognized how different its 'author' is from its author, it is essential to be aware of their closeness (not resemblance) to each other.

NOTE

Copyright Claude Rawson. Parts of this chapter were included in the introduction to *Jonathan Swift: A Collection of Critical Essays*, ed. Claude Rawson, Prentice-Hall, Englewood Cliffs, NJ, 1994, and appear by permission of the publisher.

MODERN EDITIONS

Prose Works (1939–74). Ed. Herbert Davis and others. 16 vols. Oxford: Blackwell. Vol. 1 includes *Tale of a Tub*.

A Tale of a Tub (1958). Ed. A. C. Guthkelch and D. Nichol Smith. 2nd edn. Oxford: Clarendon Press, 1958. Standard annotated edition, somewhat dated, but still the most reliable.

REFERENCES AND FURTHER READING

Clark, John R. (1970). *Form and Frenzy in Swift's 'Tale of a Tub'*. Ithaca: Cornell University Press.

Ehrenpreis, Irvin (1958). *The Personality of Jonathan Swift*. London: Methuen.

——(1962; 1967; 1983). *Swift: The Man, His Works, and the Age.* Vol. 1: *Mr. Swift and His Contemporaries.* London: Methuen (1962). Vol. 2: *Dr. Swift.* London: Methuen (1967). Vol. 3: *Dean Swift.* London: Methuen (1983).

Elliott, Robert C. (1960). *The Power of Satire.* Princeton: Princeton University Press.

——(1982). *The Literary Persona.* Chicago: University of Chicago Press.

Harth, Phillip (1961). *Swift and Anglican Rationalism: The Religious Background of 'A Tale of a Tub'*. Chicago: University of Chicago Press.

Higgins, Ian (1994). *Swift's Politics: A Study in Disaffection.* Cambridge: Cambridge University Press.

Johnson, Samuel. 'Swift'. In *Lives of the English Poets.*

Leavis, F. R. (1952). 'The irony of Swift'. In *The Common Pursuit.* London: Chatto; Harmondsworth: Penguin (1962). Essay frequently reprinted in collections of critical essays on Swift.

Levine, Joseph M. (1991). *The Battle of the Books: History and Literature in the Augustan Age.* Ithaca and London: Cornell University Press.

——(1977). *Dr. Woodward's Shield: History, Science, and Satire in Augustan England.* Berkeley, Los Angeles and London: University of California Press.

Paulson, Ronald. (1960). *Theme and Structure in Swift's 'Tale of a Tub'*. New Haven: Yale University Press.

Price, Martin (1964). *To the Palace of Wisdom: Studies in Order and Energy from Dryden to Blake*. Garden City, N.Y.: Doubleday.

Quintana, Ricardo (1936). *The Mind and Art of Jonathan Swift*. Rept Glouchester, Mass.: Peter Smith (1965).

——(1955). *Swift: An Introduction*. London: Oxford University Press. The best short introductory book, reliable and lively.

Rawson, Claude (1973). *Gulliver and the Gentle Reader: Studies in Swift and Our Time*. London: Routledge. Paperback, New Jersey and London: Humanities Press (1991).

Rawson, Claude, ed. (1983). *The Character of Swift's Satire: A Revised Focus*. Newark, Del. and London: Associated University Presses. Includes John Traugott, 'A Tale of a Tub'.

Rawson, Claude (1985). *Order from Confusion Sprung: Studies in Eighteenth-Century Literature from Swift to Cowper*. London: Allen and Unwin.

Rawson, Claude, ed. (1994). *Jonathan Swift: A Collection of Critical Essays*. Englewood Cliffs, N.J.: Prentice-Hall. Includes essays by John F. Tinkler and Marcus Walsh referred to above.

Rawson, Claude (1994). *Satire and Sentiment 1660–1830*. Cambridge: Cambridge University Press. Corrected paperback edn, New Haven: Yale University Press (2000).

Rogers, Pat (1972). *Grub Street: Studies in a Subculture*. London: Methuen, 1972. Abridged as *Hacks and Dunces: Pope, Swift, and Grub Street*. London: Methuen (1980).

Rosenheim, Edward W. (1963). *Swift and the Satirist's Art*. Chicago: University of Chicago Press.

Smith, Frederik N. (1979). *Language and Reality in Swift's 'A Tale of a Tub'*. Columbus: Ohio State University Press.

Starkman, Miriam K. (1950). *Swift's Satire on Learning in 'A Tale of a Tub'*. Princeton: Princeton University Press. Reprt New York: Octagon Books (1968).

Williams, Kathleen, ed. (1970). *Swift: The Critical Heritage*. London: Routledge. Collection of early criticism of Swift.

23
Alexander Pope, *Windsor-Forest*
Christine Gerrard

Windsor-Forest (1713) occupies a unique position among Pope's works. His first political poem, it was also his sole attempt at the idealizing mode of panegyric. An early version of the poem existed in manuscript by 1707, predating and thematically linked to his earliest published works, the *Pastorals*. But in early 1712 the approaching Peace Treaty of Utrecht spurred Pope to adapt his youthful 'verses upon Windsor Forest' to a more ambitious theme. The treaty, signed in spring 1713, which Pope's Tory friends Bolingbroke, Swift, Prior and Harley had been instrumental in negotiating, put an end to close on two decades of continental war. Pope was only one of many, and by no means the first, to celebrate the event in verse: Thomas Tickell's *Ode on the Prospect of Peace*, published in October 1712, enjoyed a popularity which *Windsor-Forest* initially failed to achieve. Yet Pope's is a more subtle and complex poem. Windsor Forest, a famous royal hunting ground rich in historical and literary associations, functions as an extended metaphor for the political life of the nation. Pope's family had moved to Binfield, a village in the environs of the forest, in 1700: it was here that the poet spent his teens, and here that he forged his first literary friendships. Thus *Windsor-Forest*'s patriotism is never shallow, rooted as it is in a personal feeling for the landscape, its history and its myths, and permeated by a sober sense of historical awareness. Like Vergil, the Roman poet whom Pope most admired in his youth, Pope's optimistic prophecy of a new Augustan age of domestic prosperity and commercial expansion abroad is qualified by a recognition that the achievements of civilization are often built upon bloody foundations. The upbeat opening and closing scenes frame a far bleaker vision of British history, chequered by periods of tyranny and depredation.

Windsor-Forest is richly and self-consciously allusive. Pope drew on a wide range of literary models, biblical, classical and English. Like Vergil in both the *Aeneid*, and the rural *Georgics*, the poem with which *Windsor-Forest* is most often compared, Pope celebrates the prospect of peace after a period of civil war and political turmoil. The *Georgics*, characterized by sudden tonal and thematic shifts between passages of description, local myth, patriotic emotion, practical agricultural advice, private meditation and public prophecy, offered Pope a model for *Windsor-Forest's* fluid structure and its sharply contrasting scenes of peace and order, ruin and discord. Closer to home was the seventeenth century royalist topographical poem such as Waller's *On St James's Park*, Otway's *Windsor Castle* and especially Sir John Denham's *Cooper's Hill*, to which Pope pays homage in his roll-call of poets associated with the Windsor landscape in ll. 259–315. *Windsor-Forest*, like *Cooper's Hill*, describes Britain's past and her national future from the vantage point of the 'scenes and prospects around Windsor' as well as using as a unifying motif the River Thames, flowing past Windsor through to the port of London and out into the world. Pope's account of Denham's technique could equally apply to his own poem. The 'Descriptions of Places, and Images rais'd by the Poet, are still tending to some Hint, or leading into some Reflection, upon moral Life or political Institution'. Like Denham, Pope creates an allegorical landscape in which natural detail is subordinated to a larger function. Pope expands on Denham's allegorical method (the pursued stag as symbol for the persecuted Charles I) by broadening the range of rural sports (hunting, shooting and fishing) to permit a wider range of political resonances. Hunting can symbolize monarchical tyranny (the biblical King Nimrod who hunted men, William the Conqueror who despoiled his subjects' farms to provide hunting grounds) but also royal paternalism: Anne protects her kingdom just as Diana, the huntress goddess, 'protects the Sylvan reign' (l. 163). Even the river-bed conceals its own micro-constitution, dominated as it is by 'Pykes, the Tyrants of the watry Plains' (l. 146), themselves prey to a larger predator, the angler. Although Pope's description of the Windsor landscape is often vivid and precise, he was not aiming primarily at a faithful or fresh depiction of natural life. His descriptive vocabulary draws heavily upon the visual arts, and his concern with the emblematic is mirrored in his frequent use of the brilliant colours and static postures of heraldry, notable, for example in description of the wounded pheasant with 'glossie, varying Dyes', 'Purple Crest', 'Scarlet-circled eyes', 'painted Wings, and Breast that flames with Gold' (ll. 115–18).

The poem's opening lines celebrate the order and variety of a cosmos governed by God and the peace and plenty of a kingdom governed by a Stuart queen. The balance of light and shade, nature and cultivation in the dappled tones of the Windsor landscape mirrors the *concors discordia*, opposing forces held in an equipoise, emblematic of Anne's reign.

> Not *Chaos*-like together crush'd and bruis'd,
> But as the World, harmoniously confus'd:
> Where Order in Variety we see,
> And where, tho' all things differ, all agree.
>   (ll. 13–16)

From here Pope plunges into a sharply contrasting account of William the Conqueror's depredations of the New Forest and its inhabitants, a dark period in which 'Th' Oppressor rul'd Tyrannick where he *durst*' (l. 74). Contemporary readers, accustomed to the mode of political parallelism by which one historical figure was used to symbolize a more contemporary figure, would have recognized the allusion to William III, also a bellicose hunter and warrior-king. The parallels between the two 'invaders', Norman William and Dutch William, were even clearer in lines (later suppressed) from a 1712 MS draft of the poem: 'Oh may no more a foreign master's rage / With wrongs yet legal, curse a future age!' If Whig minds linked William III with the 'liberty' secured by the Glorious Revolution of 1688, Tory minds linked him with militaristic foreign oppression and the waste of English resources in pursuit of an unprofitable continental war. Pope's ravaged New Forest, a 'dreary Desart and a gloomy Waste' (l. 44), in which pursuit of beasts replaces cultivation of crops, could stand as a trope for Tory fears that England's resources had been wasted in the War of Spanish Succession. Anne's peace would channel national energies into profitable colonial trade rather than profligate war. Through a more positive historical parallel (one which she had herself fostered) Queen Anne is linked to Elizabeth I, protector of the Commons and guardian of commerce, through their likeness to the mythical Diana, 'As bright a Goddess, and as chast a Queen' (l. 162).

Pope's greatest compliment to Anne is more politically tendentious than it first appears: 'Rich Industry sits smiling on the Plains, / And Peace and Plenty tell, a STUART reigns' (ll. 41–2). National prosperity is firmly linked to the Stuart dynasty. Yet Anne was in poor health (she died a year later) and had no surviving progeny. The Stuart line could only be continued through an act of Jacobite rebellion, the restoration of the exiled pretender 'James III', contravening the 1702 Act of Settlement securing the throne for the Hanoverian dynasty. Pope writes from a Tory, even Jacobite perspective, a position belied by the poem's debt to Denham and its dedication to George Granville, Lord Lansdowne, Tory Secretary of State and poet, former panegyrist of James II and his queen Mary of Modena. The poet-philosopher who in ll. 259–326 meditates on English history through the memory of the royalist poets associated with the Windsor landscape (Denham, Cowley, Waller, Granville) invests his vision of recent history with Tory, pro-Stuart emotion. 'What Tears has *Albion* shed?', he asks, for the execution of 'sacred *Charles*' in 1649 and the consequent evils of the Civil War, the Plague and Great Fire of London (in the 1712 MS depicted as punishments for Charles I's execution), culminating in 'A dreadful Series of Intestine Wars, / Inglorious Triumphs, and dishonest Scars' (ll. 319–20, 325–6). It is only Queen Anne, with her Divine fiat ' Let Discord cease!', who restores order from chaos. The Jacobite sentiment may be muted in the published version of 1713, yet the anti-Whig bias remains strong. Whigs had fought strenuously in parliament for the perpetuation of the war: Anne had needed to create twelve new Tory peers (including Lansdowne) to gain the requisite majority. Hence the closing prophecy includes some harsh lines on Marlborough's campaigns, especially the 1710 victory at Saragosa in Spain: 'No more my Sons shall dye with *British* Blood / Red *Iber*'s Sands, or *Ister*'s foaming Flood.'

Images of bloodshed and bleeding, literal and metaphorical, permeate *Windsor-Forest*: William Rufus, bleeding in the forest like a wounded hart; the 'whirring

Pheasant' shot down, who 'Flutters in Blood, and panting beats the Ground' (ll. 111, 114); France destined to 'bleed for ever under *Britain*'s Spear' (l. 310); the river Darent, 'stain'd with *Danish* Blood (l. 348); through to England's sufferings in recent years – 'Heav'ns! what new Wounds, and how her old have bled' (l. 322). Even the Lodona episode in lines 171–210, no mere piece of mythological persiflage, serves to mirror the unremitting aggression. The nymph Lodona, Pope's imaginary *genius loci* of the River Lodon, tributary of the Thames, escapes rape by the lustful pursuing Pan through a desperate metamorphosis into the inanimate – a cold silver stream. One of the poem's strengths is its uneasy recognition that violence is endemic to fallen man's nature and thus inseparable from history. Despite *Windsor-Forest*'s anti-war bias, the poem admits to moments of patriotic pride in British military prowess, notable in the description of Verrio's pageant of Edward III's victories on the walls of St George's Hall at Windsor: 'Monarchs chain'd', '*Cressi*'s glorious Field' and 'vanquished *France*' (ll. 305, 309). The account of the netting of partridges unleashes a disquietingly jingoistic simile, comparing the unsuspecting birds to a 'thoughtless Town' ambushed by British troops: 'Sudden they seize th'amaz'd, defenceless Prize, / And high in Air *Britannia*'s Standard flies' (ll. 107, 109–10). Yet the triumphalist tone is rapidly displaced by the elegiac. Unlike some other English georgics of the period, *Windsor-Forest*'s hunting scenes are memorable less for the robust pleasures of the chase than for the poignant brevity of hunted lives, the pathos of the wounded pheasant ('Short is his Joy!), the brutality of the 'Leaden Death' dealt to the 'clam'rous Lapwings' and the 'mounting Larks' who 'fall, and leave their little Lives in Air' (ll. 113, 132–4). Pope's *Guardian* essay 'Against Barbarity to Animals' (no. 61, 21 May 1713), published weeks after *Windsor-Forest*, is equivocal at best about hunting: the stag, waiting for its throat to be cut, is but 'a helpless, trembling and weeping creature'. *Windsor-Forest* may depict hunting as catharsis, a means of channelling and diverting man's warlike impulses – 'The shady Empire shall retain no Trace / Of War or Blood, but in the Sylvan Chace' (l. 372) – but it is not 'harmless' recreation. Here, as elsewhere, the poem acknowledges victims as well as victors.

In comparison to some of Pope's other poems, *Windsor-Forest* has received relatively little critical attention in recent years, some of it deeply negative. Late twentieth-century anxieties about Britain's imperialist, colonialist past were voiced in Laura Brown's provocative 1985 study (see 'references and further reading') which accuses *Windsor-Forest* of concealing its rapacious imperialism beneath a series of apparently innocent pastoral synechdoches (Windsor oak trees floating down the Thames as a trope for her navy) and lines such as 'For me the Balm shall bleed, and Amber flow' which convert the real bloodshed involved in colonial expansion into an exotic metaphor. Father Thames's swelling prophecy in the closing lines is dismissed as a devious piece of imperialist propaganda. Here Pope, mingling elements from the Book of Isaiah's prophecy of a new Jerusalem with Vergil's prophecy of a new Augustan age of peace and empire, optimistically foresees a time when men's lives will not be wasted in war: swords will become ploughshares. Great public and private buildings, 'glittering Spires', 'the beauteous Works of Peace', will arise: a new Whitehall, sign of a renewed 'Augusta' (Roman name for London) will be built between the cities of London and Westminster (ll. 376–80). The prophecy extends into a fantasy of world domination through Britain's peaceful trade with her colonies.

There is indeed inconsistency within Pope's account of the role of international trade: trade is at once altruistic ('Unbounded *Thames* shall flow for all Mankind', l. 398) and a means of asserting national superiority. A new world order dominated by Britain, in which 'Kings shall sue, and suppliant States be seen, / Once more to bend before a *British* QUEEN' (ll. 383–4), is not entirely compatible with the simultaneous existence of equally prosperous and free nations. Yet it may be over simple to accuse Pope of hypocrisy in his utterance 'Oh stretch thy Reign, fair *Peace*, from Shore to Shore / Till Conquest cease, and Slav'ry be no more' (ll. 407–8). Brown juxtaposes Pope's hope to see the 'freed *Indians* . . . woo their Sable Loves' (ll. 409–10) with the ironic reality of the Utrecht treaty's Asiento clause, granting Great Britain and the South Sea Company the sole right of importing negro slaves into Spanish America. Yet as Howard Erskine-Hill observed in 1998 (see 'references and further reading'), Pope may have been registering his own protest against the implications of the Asiento clause, since no other poet celebrating the Treaty of Utrecht even addresses the issue of slavery. *Windsor-Forest*'s condemnation of Indian and negro slavery is of a piece with its pervasive indictment of other forms of slavery, tyranny and oppression.

Pope never again adopted the laureate voice of *Windsor-Forest*, in which he came closest to Dryden in acting as national poet, voice of the monarch, recorder of Britain's past and prophet of her future. All his future exercises in panegyric were to be mock-panegyric, satirical attacks on a Hanoverian court and a Whig regime from which he felt increasingly alienated. Yet even in *Windsor-Forest*, a poem much concerned with the poet's role, Pope had already perceived a division between the 'happy man' at court and the happy man in virtuous rural retirement 'Whom Nature Charms and whom the Muse inspires' (l. 238). It was from this semi-detached position of moral self-sufficiency that Pope, in the more suburban shade of his Twickenham villa, launched his attacks on the 'new world' of Walpolian England.

REFERENCES AND FURTHER READING

Brower, Reuben A. (1959). *Alexander Pope: The Poetry of Allusion.* Oxford: Oxford University Press.

Brown, Laura (1985). *Alexander Pope.* Oxford: Basil Blackwell.

Carretta, Vincent (1983). *The Snarling Muse: Verbal and Visual Political Satire from Pope to Churchill.* Philadelphia: University of Pennsylvania Press.

Erskine-Hill, Howard (1996). *The Poetry of Opposition and Revolution: Dryden to Wordsworth.* Oxford: Oxford University Press.

——(1998). *Alexander Pope: World and Word. Proceedings of the British Academy 91.* Oxford: Oxford University Press.

Moore, J. R. (1951). '*Windsor-Forest* and William III'. *Modern Language Notes* 66, 451–4.

Morris, David B. (1984). *Alexander Pope: The Genius of Sense.* Cambridge, Mass.: Harvard University Press.

Rogers, Pat (1973). '"The enamelled ground": the language of heraldry and natural description in *Windsor-Forest*'. *Studia Neophilologica* 45, 356–71.

——(1980). '*Windsor-Forest*, *Britannia* and River Poetry', *Studies in Philology* 77, 283–99.

Wasserman, Earl R. (1959). *The Subtler Language: Critical Readings of Neoclassic and Romantic Poems*. Baltimore: Johns Hopkins University Press.

Weinbrot, Howard D. (1993). *Britannia's Issue: The Rise of British Literature from Dryden to Ossian*. Cambridge: Cambridge University Press.

24

John Gay, *Trivia*

David Nokes

In 1715 John Gay was making what, for him, were strenuous efforts to recommend himself to the new Hanoverian monarchy. The Jacobite rebellion earlier that year had been a dismal failure and Tory friends, like Pope and Swift, retreated to the most virtuous obscurity; Pope busily preparing a new translation of the *Iliad*, while Swift buried himself in church affairs as Dean of St Patrick's, Dublin. Gay still had hopes of a court place, though with every month that passed, those hopes became less sanguine. He began *Trivia* (quotations are taken from Dearing and Beckwith, 1974, 134–81) in 1714, and, at the end of that year, sent a sample to a friend, with the comment 'you may easily imagine by this progress, that I have not been interrupted by any Place at Court'. The following month he told another friend that he fully designed 'to pursue the Street Walking with Vigour, & let nothing interfere but a place'. Alas, no such interference occurred, and within a year the poem was finished. It was published on 26 January 1716, and thanks to Pope's efficiency in securing a 'pretty tolerable number' of subscriptions, had a considerable success. His friend, Dr Arbuthnot, commented wittily that 'Gay has gott so much money by his art of walking the streets, that he is ready to set up his equipage' (Burgess, 1966, 15–18).

Like all the best of Gay's writings, *Trivia* resists generic classification. This is not because its literary models are in any way obscure; Gay parades sources from Juvenal, Ned Ward and Swift, and makes clear his basic structure is borrowed from Vergil's *Georgics*. In formal terms the poem is a town georgic; what is elusive is its tone. Some commentators have read its descriptions of the London streets as an exercise in topographical realism; while others regard it as 'a purely literary artifact' claiming 'our experience of it is filtered almost entirely through allusions, recollections, imitations'. Some find a tone of celebration in its description of the busy, dirty town, while others read it as a moral satire. Pat Rogers endeavours to resolve such contradictions by finding in the poem's elusive tone a subtle combination of literary, social and moral themes: '*Trivia* is no more a straightforward mock-heroic than it is straight reportage

. . . the poetry employs . . . moral emblems, such as the Fleet, to state a sociological truth' (see Byrd, 1978, 62; Chalker, 1969, 177–8; Battestin, 1974, 127–40; Rogers, 1972, 162).

These contradictions in the poem derive from the ambiguous status of the georgic form itself. In his influential essay on the *Georgics* (1697) Addison praised Vergil for investing 'the meanest of his precepts with a kind of grandeur'. However, in using a form that celebrated rural labour to describe the commerce of the town, a certain tact was required. 'Virgil's poem of rural labour could not be translated without a certain awkwardness into the terms of an economic system increasingly dependent on capitalism and the city' (Woodman, 1988, 83). Addison found no difficulty in exploiting classical idioms to dignify the claims of commerce, and in *Spectator* 69 he boasted: 'There is no place in the town which I so much love to frequent as the Royal Exchange', celebrating this 'grand scene of business' as the 'Emporium for the whole Earth' (*Spectator*, no. 69, 19 May 1711). But Gay excludes the Royal Exchange from the topography of *Trivia*, and felt no such enthusiasm for identifying stock-jobbers as the modern equivalent of Vergil's sturdy peasantry. Nor, though he offers sympathetic portraits of boot-blacks, sempstresses, apprentices and fruit-sellers, can he adopt the viewpoint of the urban poor. Instead he creates a specific role and status for himself as 'walker', investing the whole business of walking with the mock-earnest seriousness of a practised skill or craft. 'Walking' becomes what agriculture was for Vergil, a purposeful activity, equally beneficent to the individual and his society. In offering advice on the best and safest means of walking the streets of London, Gay often strikes a note of public service: 'Now venture, Muse, from home to range the town, / And for the public safety risk thy own' (2, 5–6).

Throughout the poem he draws a sharp contrast between the public virtues of the walker and the private vices of the aristocrat lolling in his coach or chair. Walking is synonymous with health and honesty: 'Rosie-complexion'd health thy steps attends, / And exercise thy lasting youth defends' (11, 73–4). Coach-riding is a recipe for disease and decay: 'In gilded chariots while they loll, at ease, / And lazily insure a life's disease' (1, 69–74). The walker is openly charitable while the coach-rider is insensitively mean:

> Proud coaches pass, regardless of the moan,
> Of infant orphans, and the widow's groan;
> While charity still moves the walker's mind,
> His lib'ral purse relieves the lame and blind.
>   (2, 451–4)

Rather than ride in such dishonourable pomp, Gay declares: 'O rather give me sweet content on foot, / Wrapt in my virtue, and a good surtout!' (2, 589–90). Coach riding is not only harmful to the individual (leading apparently to rheumatic pains, jaundice, asthma, gout and the stone [2, 505–10]), but pernicious to the public. The poem dwells at length on the traffic hazards of Hanoverian London, with recklessly driven coaches crashing into carts, coach-wheels crushing pedestrians' feet, drivers' whips cutting their eyes, coach-horses mercilessly beaten, and a pile-up in a narrow street leading to a full-scale battle.

> Now oaths grow loud, with coaches coaches jar,
> And the smart blow provokes the sturdy war;
> From the high box they whirl the thong around,
> And with the twining lash their shins resound:
> Their rage ferments, more dang'rous wounds they try,
> And the blood gushes down their painful eye.
>
> (3, 35–40)

Envying even the 'floating town' of Venice (usually itself a symbol of decadence), whose watery thoroughfares preclude such traffic hazards, Gay longs nostalgically for the days when

> Coaches and chariots yet unfashion'd lay,
> Nor late invented chairs perplex'd the way:
> Then the proud lady trip'd along the town,
> And tuck'd up petticoats secur'd her gown;
> Her rosie cheek with distant visits glow'd,
> And exercise unartful charms bestow'd.
>
> (1, 103–8)

Now, all is changed:

> Now gaudy pride corrupts the lavish age,
> And the streets flame with glaring equipage . . .
> In saucy state the griping broker sits,
> And laughs at honesty, and trudging wits.
>
> (1, 113–18)

This contrast between walking and riding is maintained with such consistency throughout the poem, and invested with such a weight of moral significance, that it is impossible to deny that, at some level, it represents an important conviction. At the same time there is considerable irony in the way Gay confers upon his role as 'walker' a kind of heroic dignity. Certainly his Scriblerian colleagues found something richly comic in this assumption, by their corpulent, indolent friend, of such an energetic persona. Arbuthnot's quip that Gay had 'got so much money by his art of walking the streets, that he is ready to set up his equipage' (Burgess, 1966, 27), became a standing joke and many years later Swift was still pointing out the contradictions between Gay's rhetorical and private personas.

> You pretend to preach up riding and walking . . . yet from my knowledge of you after twenty years, you always joined a violent desire of perpetually shifting places and

company, with a rooted laziness, and an utter impatience of fatigue. A coach and six horses is the utmost exercise you can bear. (Sherburn, 1956, 3, 286)

Similar contradictions are easy to find. In Book I of *Trivia* Gay remarks, moralistically: 'While softer chairs the tawdry load convey / To court, to White's, assemblies, or the play' (1, 71–2). White's was a celebrated chocolate house and gambling club in St James's, described by Swift as 'the common rendezvous of infamous sharpers and noble cullies' (*Intelligencer*, no. 9, 1728). Yet by 1721, if not before, Gay was using the club as his London address for correspondence, while his attendances at court, assemblies and the playhouses were even more regular. In other words, in creating this rhetorical persona of the walker, Gay satirizes the very social milieu to which he aspired. One critic puts it well:

> For 'Walking' in this poem is actually the sign of a deliberate non-involvement in the economic system. It is a leisure pursuit as much as a form of labour. The walker has time to remark on all he sees, to stop and browse at bookstalls and to taste oysters . . . Gay cannot find a convincing form of work as the georgic art of living in his period, and it is for this reason that he needs the saving grace of mock georgic. (Woodman, 1988, 88)

Much of this 'mock-georgic' effect is located in a self-conscious irony surrounding the moral attitudes of the walker's claim to be performing a dangerous public duty. Both at the beginning and the end of the poem, Gay offers his work as an enduring monument to his own dedication to public service.

> My youthful bosom burns with thirst of fame,
> From the great theme to build a glorious name,
> To tread in paths to ancient bards unknown,
> And bind my temples with a civic crown;
> But more, my country's love demands the lays,
> My country's be the profit, mine the praise.
>   (1, 17–22)

This is richly ironic. The 'civic crown' refers to the *corona civica*, a Roman honour bestowed on those who saved the lives of fellow-citizens in battle, as Gay here pretends to save his fellow-walkers from the perils of the streets. Gay also purports to offer himself as a candidate for the title of 'city-poet' of London, an office currently held by the truly pedestrian Elkanah Settle and regarded by the Scriblerians as the ultimate badge of literary ineptitude. Even his professed stance of selfless patriotism ('My country's be the profit') parodies the rhetoric of Whig poets whose banging of the patriotic drum was designed more to serve their own interests than the country's.

This ironic camouflage of self-interest as social concern is evident in Gay's mock-heroic presentation of the walker as a latter-day hero, fearlessly risking the dangers of the city streets to serve the public good. Crossing the road becomes a perilous epic adventure.

Now man with utmost fortitude thy soul,
To cross the way where carts and coaches roll; . . .
                              on either hand
Pent round with perils, in the midst you stand,
And call for aid in vain; the coachman swears,
And carmen drive, unmindful of thy prayers.
Where wilt thou turn? ah! whither wilt thou fly?
On ev'ry side the pressing spokes are nigh.
So sailors, while Charybdis' gulf they shun,
Amaz'd, on Scylla's craggy dangers run.
                                    (3, 169–84)

Elsewhere the intrepid walker is compared to Theseus lost in the minotaur's labyrinth (2, 83–6); to Orpheus, charming the powers of hell (1, 204); to Aeneas searching for his bride (3, 92) or bearing his father on his back (3, 368); and to Oedipus at the fatal crossroads (3, 215). There is a knowing and ironic exaggeration about all these epic similes, as Gay playfully presents himself as a latter-day Odysseus and invests the pursuit of sauntering through the London streets with the purposeful aura of a heroic quest.

As in Pope's *Dunciad*, the sense in which the London streets of *Trivia* are both topographically real, and literary metaphors, gives the poem an animation, and vitality of reference which defiantly resists any simple reading. At its best this permeation of the real with the imaginary can acquire a strange visionary and surreal quality which lends satire a disturbing imaginative force. Right at the centre of *Trivia* Gay offers such a vision in his lengthy mock-heroic digression on the birth and life of a boot-black boy. Decoded, this can be read as an extended social reflection on the inequalities of wealth and power in busy streets where aristocrats and urchins are in daily close proximity. But the literary framing of this episode, which has its model in Vergil's account of the art of engendering bees from putrid cattle blood, lends the social satire an additional ironic force (see Dearing and Beckwith, 1974, 2, 557). The episode begins and ends with the street-boy's cry; 'Clean your honour's shoes', echoing along the streets from Charing Cross where he plies his trade. His is the ever-present 'voice of industry', though it is the muse, 'fatigu'd amid the throng', who feels the need for rest.

The boy's story begins, in epic fashion, with the infatuation of a deity for a mortal: 'great Jove (grown fond of change) / Of old was wont this nether world to range / To seek amours' (2, 107–9). In this realistic urban setting Jove's metamorphosis assumes a social colouring and he appears as an aristocratic rake, cruising the alleyways of London for 'rough trade'. Soon there is quite a fashion among the olympians for one-night stands with proletarians: 'ev'n the proudest goddess now and then / Would lodge a night among the sons of men'. Amid all this promiscuity none is more promiscuous than Cloacina '(Goddess of the tide / Whose sable streams beneath the city glide)'. In a footnote Gay informs us that 'Cloacina was a goddess whose image Tatius (a king of the Sabines) found in the common sewer, and not knowing what goddess

it was, he called it Cloacina from the place in which it was found, and paid to it divine
honours.' More prosaically, Cloacina here is the Fleet ditch, the city's main open sewer,
and her 'promiscuity' is thus an appropriate metaphor for the common receptacle for
all the city's refuse. The sewer thus becomes the city's central symbol, a dark, subterranean goddess, receiving her tributes from rich and poor alike. Roving through
the town (the poem accurately traces the sewer's path) the goddess falls in love with
a 'mortal scavenger' or sewage-worker.

> The muddy spots that dried upon his face,
> Like female patches, heighten'd ev'ry grace:
> She gaz'd; she sigh'd. For love can beauties spy
> In what seem faults to ev'ry common eye.
>   (2, 119–22)

Assuming the 'black form of a cinder-wench' the goddess consummates her proletarian amour in a dark alley, and, nine months later 'beneath a bulk she dropt
the boy' (a bulk is a stall in front of a shop). Anxious for the child's future, the
goddess prevails upon her fellow olympians to provide him with the tools of his
trade.

> With the strong bristles of the mighty boar
> Diana forms his brush; the God of day
> A tripod gives, amid the crowded way
> To raise the dirty foot, and ease his toil;
> Kind Neptune fills his vase with fetid oil
> Press'd from th'enormous whale; the God of fire,
> From whose dominions smoky clouds aspire,
> Among these gen'rous presents joins his part,
> And aids with soot the new japanning art:
> Pleas'd she receives the gifts; she downward glides,
> Lights in Fleet-ditch, and shoots beneath the tides.
>   (2, 158–68)

The effect of this richly sensuous vocabulary is to create what Joyce would call an
'epiphany', a literary evocation of divinity within the most humble of human activities. Gay accurately describes the mundane tools of the boot-boy's trade, yet invests
them with all the ritual and mystique of a religious ceremony. Just as Belinda's
toilette-table in the *Rape of the Lock* becomes a mock-sacred display case for the products of the East India Company's commercial exploitation ('Unnumber'd Treasures
ope at once, and here / The various Off'rings of the World appear': 1, 129–30), so the
boot-boy's stand becomes an altar to the spirit of industry. A Mandevillian sense of
irony is at work here, as Gay celebrates the apotheosis of trade not, like Addison, in
the genteel transactions of the Royal Exchange, but in a subterranean world of scav-
enging and begging.

There are, I believe, few people in London, of those that are at any time forc'd to go a-
foot, but what could wish the streets of it much cleaner than generally they are; while
they regard nothing but their own clothes and private conveniency: but when once they
come to consider, that what offends them is the result of the plenty, great traffic and
opulency of that mighty city, if they have any concern in its welfare, they will hardly
ever wish to see the streets of it less dirty. (Kaye, 1924, 1, 10–12, quoted in Copley and
Haywood)

Much of the poem's advice is devoted to instructing his fellow walkers how best
to avoid the filth and refuse that threatens to assail them on all sides. The barber's
apron 'soils the sable dress' (2, 28); chimney-sweeps and small-coals-men smear
clothes with smuts and soot-stains (2, 32–6); fish-stalls leave evil-smelling stains
(3, 106); 'the dustman's cart offends thy clothes and eyes' (2, 37); the chandler's basket
'with tallow spots thy coat' (2, 40); the hooves of dray-horses spatter clothes with mire
and 'muddy blots' (2, 293); mud and rain pose constant threats to hosiery and wigs
alike (1, 200–2). Perhaps the greatest danger to maintaining a cleanly appearance
comes from the open sewers or 'kennels' running down the city streets. After a heavy
downpour he warns,

> you'll hear the sounds
> Of whistling winds, e'er kennels break their bounds;
> Ungrateful odours common sewers diffuse,
> And dropping vaults distil unwholesome dews.
> (1, 169–72)

The most notorious of these open sewers, the Fleet Ditch was described by Defoe in
1722 as a 'nauseous and abominable sink of public nastiness' (Defoe, 1903–4, 5, 29).
But Gay invests this stinking locale, the trysting-place of his dark Goddess, Cloacina,
with a pseudo-mythological dignity, transforming it from a private nuisance into the
topos of Mandeville's consumer society.

> The goddess rose amid the inmost round,
> With wither'd turnip tops her temples crown'd;
> Low reach'd her dripping tresses, lank and black
> As the smooth jet, or glossy raven's back;
> Around her waist a circling eel was twin'd,
> Which bound her robe that hung in rags behind.
> (2, 195–200)

This incongruous deity, herself a kind of literary detritus, made up, like so much
of Augustan 'culture' from wastes and scraps of art and nature, becomes the poem's
animating force. 'Go thrive', she commands (2, 203), bestowing on the boot-boy the
tools of his future trade. Thus happily equipped, the boy, whose street-cry 'Clean your
honour's shoes' resounds from Charing Cross to Whitehall, becomes the symbol of a

society in which the simulacra of classical art provided the acceptable face for an entrepreneurial spirit based on luxury, exploitation and waste. Refuse, in a classical disguise, is the presiding deity of this capital of industry. (The whole Cloacina episode
is to some extent a burlesque parody of the Atistaeus episode in the Fourth Book of
the *Georgics*.)

Gay's ambivalence towards the city's refuse is typical of his stance throughout this
poem. On the one hand he offers fastidious advice for maintaining a cleanly appearance, while on the other he depicts filth and waste as the mythological source for a
flourishing industry. The 'Walker' is neither a plebeian tradesman, nor an aristocrat
lolling in his coach. He is an informed spectator of human affairs and for the most
part appears as a consumer, offering useful advice on the delights and hazards of the
town. But as the author of the poem, he is also a producer, offering his work for sale
for the benefit and entertainment of a discerning public. The poem concludes on a
characteristically ironic note.

> And now compleat my gen'rous labours lie,
> Finish'd, and ripe for immortality.
> Death shall entomb in dust this mould'ring frame
> But never reach th'eternal part, my fame.
>   (3, 407–10)

While his body may become just another waste-product (dust), his 'fame', that is, his
poem, will achieve immortality. Such is the 'classical' commonplace; *ars longa, vita
brevis*. Yet even as he writes this, Gay implicitly subverts it. 'Labours' suggests
an industrial rather than an inspirational process, and the organic metaphor 'ripe'
(for immortality) carries the obvious implication that what is 'ripe' at one time, will
subsequently rot. The final lines make this clearer.

> When critics crazy bandboxes repair,
> And tragedies, turn'd rockets, bounce in air;
> High-rais'd on Fleetstreet posts, consign'd to fame,
> This work shall shine, and walkers bless my name.
>   (3, 413–16)

Literary labours, like any other, have to be brought to market, hawked and advertised
at booksellers' shops, to become part of the consumer life of the capital. And, since
literary works are made of paper, the most distinguished of them, epics and tragedies,
may find the most ignominious end as a commercial waste-product, lining a band-
box, binding a rocket, or by some even more lowly use, be returned to the goddess
Cloacina of Fleet Ditch. Gay's final irony is that in writing a mock-classical poem, he
is actually only bringing another perishable commodity to market; like the boot-black
boy he is a scavenger of the literary sewers and alleyways of Olympus to create a
decorative ornament for his own consumer society. As Gay evokes the boot-boy's
plaintive cry, there is more than a hint of self-portraiture.

But I, alas! hard Fortune's utmost scorn,
Who ne'er knew parent, was an orphan born!
Some boys are rich by birth beyond all wants,
Belov'd by uncles, and kind good old aunts;
When time comes round, a Christmas-box they bear,
And one day makes them rich for all the year.

(2, 181–6)

Though not born an orphan, Gay had become one by the age of ten, and clearly felt himself deprived for fortune's blessings, and the generous favours of indulgent aunts and uncles. Though he had never cleaned the shoes of the wealthy, he had cut and measured their clothes. And even now, as he attended their levees, laughed at their jokes, and flattered them with verses, he felt a certain kinship with the suppliant street-urchins, spattered by the gilded chariots of those who 'loll at ease'.

REFERENCES AND FURTHER READING

Battestin, Martin C. (1974). *The Providence of Wit.* Oxford: Oxford University Press.

Burgess, C. F., ed. (1966). *The Letters of John Gay.* Oxford: Clarendon.

Byrd, Max (1978). *London Transformed.* New Haven: Yale University Press.

Chalker, John (1969). *The English Georgic.* London.

Copley, Stephen and Ian Haywood (1988). 'Luxury, reform and poetry: John Gay's *Trivia*'. In *John Gay and the Scriblerians.* Ed. Peter Lewis and Nigel Wood. London: Vision Press, 62–82.

Dearing, V. A. and Beckwith, C. E., eds (1974). *John Gay: Poetry and Prose.* 2 vols. Oxford: Clarendon Press.

Defoe, Daniel (1903–4). 'Due preparation for the plague'. In *The Works of Daniel Defoe.* 16 vols. Ed. G. H. Maynadier. Boston. Vol. 29.

Kaye, F. B., ed. (1924). Bernard Mandeville: *The Fable of the Bees.* 2 vols. Oxford: Clarendon.

Rogers, Pat (1972). *Grub Street.* London: Methuen.

Woodman, Tom (1988). ' "Vulgar circumstances" and "due civilities": Gay's art of polite living in town'. In *John Gay and the Scriblerians.* Ed. Peter Lewis and Nigel Wood. London: Vision Press.

25

Daniel Defoe, *Journal of the Plague Year*

David Womersley

At the very end of the *Journal of the Plague Year* H.F. compares the surviving Londoners to the Israelites who escaped from captivity in Egypt:

> But I must own that, for the generality of the people, it might too justly be said of them as was said of the children of Israel after their being delivered from the host of Pharaoh, when they passed the Red Sea, and looked back and saw the Egyptians over-whelmed in the water: viz., that they sang His praise, but they soon forgot His works. (256: all quotations from and references to the Penguin edition listed in 'references and further reading')

How should we take this final example from a whole series of comparisons drawn by H.F. between events in London during the 1660s and biblical story? Uncertainty arises when we try exactly to map the flight from Egypt on to the details of the narrative we have just read. The theme of deliverance, of a passage from bondage to freedom, and therefore from a purely negative to a purely positive state, suggests that to have escaped from Egypt is like surviving the plague. However, the detail of the 'Egyptians overwhelmed in the water' surely evokes the culling of Londoners by the plague; together with the emphasis on the ingratitude of the saved ('they sang His praise, but they soon forgot His works'), this makes the connection between biblical Egypt and seventeenth-century London in a slightly different way. In this perspective, the plague is not the period of Egyptian bondage, but, rather, the passage of the Red Sea: deadly to some but salvific to others. The more we study the passage, the more it places us in a dilemma concerning the nature of the plague: was it a punishment, a blessing, or some mixture of the two? In order to answer this question, we must remember Defoe's position as a Dissenter who nevertheless wished to promote closeness between Dissenters and Low Churchmen, and whose belief it was 'that whoever should go about to widen the Difference, or encrease the Misunderstandings between the Church of *England* and the Dissenters, were the real Enemies of both' (*The Shortest Way to Peace and Union*, quoted in Backscheider, 1989, 128).

The *Journal of the Plague Year* purports to be the memoirs of a saddler, 'H.F.', who resided in London throughout the period of the plague and yet remained healthy. H.F.'s evolving understanding of what the plague is, and the language in which he expresses his grasp of its complicated and ambiguous nature, imparts from the outset a dynamic to Defoe's narrative, as different aspects of the plague successively come to the fore. At the outset it is a 'visitation' (e.g. 26 and 39), implying divine retribution. H.F. is tempted to lay the blame for provoking God's anger on the excesses of the court:

> the Court removed early, viz., in the month of June, and went to Oxford, where it pleased God to preserve them; and the distemper did not, as I heard of, so much as touch them, for which I cannot say that I ever saw they showed any great token of thankfulness, and hardly anything of reformation, though they did not want being told that their crying vices might without breach of charity be said to have gone far in bringing that terrible judgement upon the whole nation. (37)

But there are problems with this way of thinking of the plague; for if it was a 'terrible judgement', why were those who had committed the 'crying vices' which brought it into existence preserved? When H.F. once more thinks of the plague as God's instrument of vengeance, it is when he has been insulted by the atheistical revellers at the Pie Tavern:

> I made them some reply, such as I thought proper, but which I found was so far from putting a check to their horrid way of speaking that it made them rail the more, so that I confess it filled me with horror and a kind of rage, and I came away, as I told them, lest the hand of that Judgement which had visited the whole city should glorify His vengeance upon them, and all that were near them. (84)

'Filled me with . . . a kind of rage': when the plague is represented as a pure punishment in this narrowly instrumental way, it seems to be in response to human, rather than divine, resentments.

Gradually the plague reveals some surprising aspects, and generates some unanticipated consequences. As well as physical death to multitudes, it brings to some a vivifying of the spirit:

> Though there might be some stupidity and dulness of the mind (and there was so, a great deal), yet there was a great deal of just alarm sounded into the very inmost soul, if I may so say, of others. Many consciences were awakened; many hard hearts melted into tears; many a penitent confession was made of crimes long concealed. (54)

Under the impact of the plague London becomes spiritually legible. The language of the 'good, religious, and sensible' sexton who at first dissuades and then encourages H.F. to enter the churchyard makes this explicit:

> I told him I had been pressed in my mind to go [into the churchyard], and that perhaps
> it might be an instructing sight, that might not be without its uses. 'Nay,' says the
> good man, 'if you will venture upon that score, name of God go in; for, depend upon
> it, 'twill be a sermon to you, it may be, the best that ever you heard in your life. 'Tis a
> speaking sight,' says he, 'and has a voice with it, and a loud one, to call us all to repen-
> tance'; and with that he opened the door and said, 'Go, if you will.' (79–80)

Under the crushing psychological pressure of the immediacy which the plague
bestows upon death, enabling it to cut through all the elaborate 'culture of death' by
which in a normal state of civilization mortality is softened and accommodated
('Sometimes a man or woman dropped down dead in the very markets, for many people
that had the plague upon them knew nothing of it till the inward gangrene had
affected their vitals, and they died in a few minutes': 96), Christian virtues are released
and strengthened in some – for instance, the 'charitable, well-minded Christians' who
gave 'prodigious sums of money' for the poor (110) – while in others, such as the
impious revellers of the Pie Tavern, it discloses the presence of a shocking spiritual
callousness. As it makes visible the true state of the Londoners' spiritual welfare, so
the plague dispenses with social hierarchy:

> The cart had in it sixteen or seventeen bodies; some were wrapt up in linen sheets, some
> in rags, some little other than naked, or so loose that what covering they had fell from
> them in the shooting out of the cart, and they fell quite naked among the rest; but the
> matter was not much to them, or the indecency much to any one else, seeing they were
> all dead, and were to be huddled together into the common grave of mankind, as we
> may call it, for here was no difference made, but poor and rich went together; there was
> no other way of burials, neither was it possible there should, for coffins were not to
> be had for the prodigious numbers that fell in such a calamity as this. (81)

The punctilios on which such attention was lavished in the habitual worldly state of
spiritual distraction which obtained before the arrival of the plague are now utterly
disregarded. The menace of imminent extinction redirects the attention of the people
away from the trivia by which they had been preoccupied, and towards what is truly,
eternally, important:

> As it [the plague] brought the people into public company, so it was surprising how it
> brought them to crowd into the churches. They inquired no more into whom they sat
> near to or far from, what offensive smells they met with, or what condition the people
> seemed to be in; but, looking upon themselves all as so many dead corpses, they came
> to the churches without the least caution, and crowded together as if their lives were of
> no consequence compared to the work which they came about there. Indeed, the zeal
> which they showed in coming, and the earnestness and affection they showed in their
> attention to what they heard, made it manifest what a value people would all put upon
> the worship of God if they thought every day they attended at the church that it would
> be their last. (187)

Indeed nothing was more strange than to see with what courage the people went to the public service of God, even at that time when they were afraid to stir out of their own houses upon any other occasion. (219)

H.F. increasingly ponders the paradox that, when plague-ridden, London is spiritually healthy. The city has been dichotomized into the hell of the plague-pits and the heaven of enhanced piety. And in that awakened state, people have become as indifferent to the distinction between Dissenter and minister of the church as they now are to the most trifling social detail:

Nor was it [the plague] without other strange effects, for it took away all manner of prejudice at or scruple about the person whom they found in the pulpit when they came to the churches. It cannot be doubted but that many of the ministers of the parish churches were cut off, among others, in so common and dreadful a calamity; and others had not courage enough to stand it, but removed into the country as they found means for escape. As then some parish churches were quite vacant and forsaken, the people made no scruple of desiring such Dissenters as had been a few years before deprived of their livings by virtue of the Act of Parliament called the Act of Uniformity to preach in the churches; nor did the church ministers in that case make any difficulty of accepting their assistance; so that many of those whom they called silenced ministers had their mouths opened on this occasion and preached publicly to the people.

Here we may observe and I hope it will not be amiss to take notice of it that a near view of death would soon reconcile men of good principles one to another, and that it is chiefly owing to our easy situation in life and our putting these things far from us that our breaches are fomented, ill blood continued, prejudices, breach of charity and of Christian union, so much kept and so far carried on among us as it is. Another plague year would reconcile all these differences; a close conversing with death, or with diseases that threaten death, would scum off the gall from our tempers, remove the animosities among us, and bring us to see with differing eyes than those which we looked on things with before. As the people who had been used to join with the Church were reconciled at this time with the admitting the Dissenters to preach to them, so the Dissenters, who with an uncommon prejudice had broken off from the communion of the Church of England, were now content to come to their parish churches and to conform to the worship which they did not approve of before; but as the terror of the infection abated, those things all returned again to their less desirable channel and to the course they were in before.

I mention this but historically. I have no mind to enter into arguments to move either or both sides to a more charitable compliance one with another. I do not see that it is probable such a discourse would be either suitable or successful; the breaches seem rather to widen, and tend to a widening further, than to closing, and who am I that I should think myself able to influence either one side or other? But this I may repeat again, that 'tis evident death will reconcile us all; on the other side the grave we shall be all brethren again. In heaven, whither I hope we may come from all parties and persuasions, we shall find neither prejudice or scruple; there we shall be of one principle and of one opinion. Why we cannot be content to go hand in hand to the place where we shall join heart and hand without the least hesitation, and with the most complete harmony and affec-

tion – I say, whey we cannot do so here I can say nothing to, neither shall I say anything more of it but that it remains to be lamented. (187–9)

London during the plague is heavenly, in that it is free from the 'prejudice and scruple'
which characterize the imperfection of our earthly existence. The city has become a
landscape in which moral and spiritual truth has become visible, palpable and,
through the persona of H.F., traversable.

However, the undogmatic Christian fellowship which H.F. describes flourishing in
London under conditions of adversity, only to be abandoned 'as the terror of the infection abated', is as much an image of what Defoe desired to promote in the 1720s as
of what H.F. experienced in the 1660s. So the question of *persona*, of who is actually
speaking, in that long extract which I have just quoted, is both intricate and of exceptional interest. For it was as much a desideratum for Defoe as for H.F. that 'men of
good principles' should be reconciled to one another, and that the 'gall of our tempers'
should be scummed off. In this perspective H.F. emerges as both an advocate of the
alliance between Low Church and Dissent, and also as an embodiment of the temper
of mind on which such an alliance would depend. Very late in the book H.F. lets
it be known that he himself belongs to the Church of England:

> after the ceasing of the plague in London, when any one that had seen the condition
> which the people had been in, and how they caressed one another at that time, promised
> to have more charity for the future, and to raise no more reproaches; I say, any one that
> had seen them then would have thought they would have come together with another
> spirit at last. But, I say, it could not be obtained. The quarrel remained; the Church and
> the Presbyterians were incompatible. As soon as the plague was removed, the Dissent-
> ing ousted ministers who had supplied the pulpits which were deserted by the incum-
> bents retired; they could expect no other but that they should immediately fall upon
> them and harass them with their penal laws, accept their preaching while they were
> sick, and persecute them as soon as they were recovered again; this even we that were
> of the Church thought was very hard, and could by no means approve of. (243–4)

It is remarkable that H.F.'s acknowledgement of confessional allegiance should be
made in virtually the same breath as his deploring of the ingratitude of the Church
towards the Dissenting ministers who preached in the absence of its own clergymen.
The juxtaposition unfolds a number of distinct, but related, implications. In the first
place, H.F. tacitly repudiates the repeated assertion of the High Church party, that
the Dissenters were a monstrous and seditious brood and to be shunned. The doctrinal differences between the Church of England and the Dissenters are as nothing to
H.F., whose piety is of an undogmatic, practical kind (as is shown by his admiration
for that 'serious, religious, good man' the waterman: 122–7). From H.F.'s standpoint
– a standpoint which Defoe in various ways makes attractive to us – there is no significant distinction to be drawn between Church and Dissent. High Church measures
such as the Schism Act of 1714, which had suppressed the Dissenting academies,
therefore seem less like resolute defences of doctrinal purity than expressions of that

same unregenerate vindictiveness which led to the rejection of the Dissenting ministers after the plague had abated.

In thus making H.F. the mouthpiece for his own desire for a convergence between
Low Church and Dissent Defoe also offers us an embodiment of his own preferred
religious disposition: pious, penetrated by a sense of the divine, but also rational,
unrancorous and undogmatic. He also took implicit issue with the High Church characterization of the Dissenters and their allies, as enthusiastic fanatics averse to all discipline in church and state. Repeatedly, H.F. is distinguished from the credulous
'people':

> I could fill this account with the strange relations such people gave every day of what
> they had seen; and every one was so positive of their having seen what they pretended
> to see, that there was no contradicting them without breach of friendship, or being
> accounted rude and unmannerly on the one hand, and profane and impenetrable on the
> other. One time before the plague was begun (otherwise than as I have said in St Giles's),
> I think it was in March, seeing a crowd of people in the street, I joined with them to
> satisfy my curiosity, and found them all staring up into the air to see what a woman
> told them appeared plain to her, which was an angel clothed in white, with a fiery sword
> in his hand, waving it or brandishing it over his head. She described every part of the
> figure to the life, showed them the motion and the form, and the poor people came into
> it so eagerly, and with so much readiness; 'Yes, I see it all plainly,' says one; 'there's the
> sword as plain as can be.' Another saw the angel. One saw his very face, and cried out
> what a glorious creature he was! One saw one thing, and one another. I looked as
> earnestly as the rest, but perhaps not with so much willingness to be imposed upon;
> and I said, indeed, that I could see nothing but a white cloud, bright on one side by
> the shining of the sun upon the other part. The woman endeavoured to show it me, but
> could not make me confess that I saw it, which, indeed, if I had I must have lied. But
> the woman, turning upon me, looked in my face, and fancied I laughed, in which her
> imagination deceived her too, for I really did not laugh, but was seriously terrified by
> the force of their own imagination. However, she turned from me, called me profane
> fellow, and a scoffer; told me that it was a time of God's anger, and dreadful judgements
> were approaching, and that despisers such as I should wander and perish. (43–4; cf. the
> 'ghost', 44–5)

On the one hand this is almost a textbook resolution of religious enthusiasm into hysteria; on the other, it serves strongly to separate H.F.'s piety from the volatile enthusiasm of which Dissenters and their supporters were suspected. As he moves through
the narrow London alleys, a transit increasingly metonymic of his resolve to thread
his way between the equally unappealing alternatives of seeming 'rude and unman-
nerly on the one hand, and profane and impenetrable on the other', H.F. is as appalled
by the 'force of [the people's] imagination' as any High Churchman could be. But
unlike them he does not make the mistake of crudely confusing Dissent with the
intellectual and emotional waywardness typical of the 'people'. This is in itself an
instance of H.F.'s characteristic scrupulousness, a disciplined and controlled scepti-

cism which distances him from popular credulity, and which marks his language with careful disclaimers, such as 'I know not', 'I will not be positive', 'I do not grant the fact'.

H.F., then, is as much an aspiration as a character. Displaying the piety of Dissent while at the same time being free of the irrationalism of which it was so often accused, he is himself an argument for all that could be gained from a closeness between Low Churchmen and Dissenters. His characteristics are dictated as much by ideological necessity as by psychological probability, as his sustained reflection from towards the end of the novel on the significance of the plague suggests:

> I would be far from lessening the awe of the judgements of God and the reverence to His providence which ought always to be on our minds on such occasions as these. Doubtless the visitation itself is a stroke from Heaven upon a city, or country, or nation where it falls; a messenger of His vengeance, and a loud call to that nation or country or city to humiliation and repentance . . . Now to prompt due impressions of the awe of God on the minds of men on such occasions, and not to lessen them, it is that I have left those minutes upon record.
>
> I say, therefore, I reflect upon no man for putting the reason of those things upon the immediate hand of God, and the appointment and direction of His providence; nay, on the contrary, there were many wonderful deliverances of persons from infection, and deliverances of persons when infected, which intimate singular and remarkable providence in the particular instances to which they refer; and I esteem my own deliverance to be one next to miraculous, and do record it with thankfulness.
>
> But when I am speaking of the plague as a distemper arising from natural causes, we must consider it as it was really propagated by natural means; nor is it at all the less a judgement for its being under the conduct of human causes and effects; for, as the Divine Power has formed the whole scheme of nature and maintains nature in its course, so the same Power thinks fit to let His own actings with men, whether of mercy or judgement, to go on in the ordinary course of natural causes; and He is pleased to act by those natural causes as the ordinary means, excepting and reserving to Himself nevertheless a power to act in a supernatural way when He sees occasion. Now 'tis evident that in the case of an infection there is no apparent extraordinary occasion for supernatural operation, but the ordinary course of things appears sufficiently armed, and made capable of all the effects that heaven usually directs by a contagion. Among these causes and effects, this of the secret conveyance of infection, imperceptible and unavoidable, is more than sufficient to execute the fierceness of Divine vengeance, without putting it upon supernaturals and miracle. (204–5)

This *bricolage* of piety and reasonableness – seen also in H.F.'s equal devotion to the Bible and statistical analysis, to providence and urban geography, as keys to understanding the plague – reveals what Defoe was attempting to do with this book and this character. At the same time, we can look back to Defoe's allusion to the Israelites crossing the Red Sea with which we began, and take a fuller measure of its significance. H.F. embodies Defoe's hopes and desires for a meeting of Church and Dissent: his language, beliefs and demeanour both vindicate the possibility of such a *rapprochement,* and indicate how it might be made to come about. He is the Moses who points the way to, but will not enter, Defoe's promised land of undogmatic Christian fellowship.

REFERENCES AND FURTHER READING

Alkon, Paul, K. (1976). 'Defoe's argument in *The Shortest Way with the Dissenters'. MP,* 73, 13–22.

Armstrong, Katherine (1996). *Defoe: Writer as Agent.* Victoria, B.C.: University of Victoria.

Backscheider, Paula (1986). *Daniel Defoe: Ambition and Innovation.* Lexington: University Press of Kentucky.

——(1989). *Daniel Defoe: His Life.* Baltimore and London: Johns Hopkins University Press.

Bastian, Frank (1965). 'Defoe's *Journal of the Plague Year* reconsidered'. *RES,* 16, 151–73.

Bennett, G. V. (1975). *The Tory Crisis in Church and State, 1688–1730: The Career of Francis Atterbury, Bishop of Rochester.* Oxford: Clarendon Press.

Browning, Reed (1982). *Political and Constitutional Ideas of the Court Whigs.* Baton Rouge and London: Louisiana State University Press.

Clarendon, Edward Hyde, Earl of (1888). *The History of the Rebellion and Civil Wars in England.* Ed. W. Dunn Macray. 6 vols. Oxford: Clarendon.

Clark, J. C. D. (1985). *English Society 1688–1832: Ideology, Social Structure and Political Practice during the Ancien Regime.* Cambridge: Cambridge University Press.

Defoe, Daniel (1966). *A Journal of the Plague Year.* Ed. A. Burgess. Harmondsworth: Penguin.

——(1969). *A Journal of the Plague Year.* Ed. Louis Landa. Oxford: Oxford University Press.

——(1975). *Selected Writings.* Ed. J. T. Boulton. Cambridge: Cambridge University Press.

——(1997). *The True-Born Englishman and Other Writings.* Ed. P. N. Furbank and W. R. Owens. Harmondsworth: Penguin.

——(1955). *The Letters of Daniel Defoe.* Ed. George H. Healey. Oxford: Clarendon.

De Krey, Gary Stuart (1985). *A Fractured Society: The Politics of London in the First Age of Party 1688–1715.* Oxford: Clarendon.

Hunter, J. Paul (1966). *The Reluctant Pilgrim.* Baltimore and London: Johns Hopkins University Press.

Kenyon, John (1977). *Revolution Principles: The Politics of Party 1689–1720.* Cambridge: Cambridge University Press.

Kishlansky, M. (1986). *Parliamentary Selection: Social and Political Choice in Early Modern England.* Cambridge: Cambridge University Press.

Macaree, David (1980). *Daniel Defoe and the Jacobite Movement.* Salzburg: Institut für Anglistik und Amerikanistik.

McKeon, Michael (1975). *Politics and Poetry in Restoration England: The Case of Dryden's Annus Mirabilis.* Cambridge, Mass. and London: Harvard University Press.

McKillop, A. D. (1956). *The Early Masters of English Fiction.* Lawrence, Kansas: University of Kansas Press.

Novak, Maximillian, E. (1977). *Defoe and the Nature of Man.* Oxford: Oxford University Press.

——(1977). 'Defoe and the Disordered City'. *PMLA* 92, 241–52.

——(1983). *Realism, Myth and History in Defoe's Fiction.* Lincoln: University of Nebraska Press.

Oldmixon, John (1742). *Memoirs of the Press.*

Richetti, John J. (1975). *Defoe's Narratives: Situations and Structures.* Oxford: Clarendon.

Rogers, Pat (1985). ' "THIS CALAMITOUS YEAR": *A Journal of the Plague Year* and the South Sea Bubble'. In *Eighteenth-Century Encounters.* Brighton: Harvester, 151–67.

Rupp, E. G. (1986). *Religion in England, 1688–1791.* Oxford: Clarendon.

Schonhorn, Manuel (1968). 'Defoe's *Journal of the Plague Year*: topography and intention'. *RES* 19, 387–402.

Secord, A. W. (1924). *Studies in the Narrative Method of Defoe.* Urbana: University of Illinois Press.

Speck, W. A. (1988). *Reluctant Revolutionaries: Englishmen and the Revolution of 1688.* Oxford: Oxford University Press.

Starr, G. A. (1965). *Defoe and Spiritual Autobiography*. Princeton: Princeton University Press.

——(1971). *Defoe and Casuistry*. Princeton: Princeton University Press.

Watt, Ian (1957). *The Rise of the Novel*. London: Chatto and Windus.

Zimmerman, Everett (1972). 'H.F.'s meditations: a journal of the plague year'. *PMLA* 87, 417–22.

——(1975). *Defoe and the Novel*. Berkeley: University of California Press.

26

Eliza Haywood, *Fantomina*

Sarah Prescott

In traditional accounts of eighteenth-century literature, Eliza Haywood is only mentioned, if at all, because of her inclusion in the second book of Alexander Pope's *Dunciad* where she appears as the prize in a urinating contest between two rival booksellers. Pope's description of Haywood suggests that the type of writing she produced – scandalous intrigue and amatory prose fiction – threatens the literary standards of the day (as defined by Pope) and also implies that Haywood herself is a consummate example of disreputability and sexual promiscuity. Eliza Haywood's prominence as one of Pope's dunces has been one cause of her obscurity in conventional literary histories of the eighteenth century and accounts of the novel as a genre. More recently, however, Haywood's presence as a professional and extremely prolific female author in the increasingly commercial literary marketplace of the early eighteenth century has led to a substantial reassessment of her significance for eighteenth-century literary culture. Haywood is now recognized not only as an innovative writer of fiction but also as a skilful satirist. Furthermore, her proficiency in shaping and adapting to contemporary reading tastes is now seen as an important sign of new conceptions about literature as popular entertainment – and authorship as a professional occupation – that were emerging in the first half of the century.

Eliza Haywood's career began in 1719 and she continued to write until her death in 1756, during which time she worked as an actress, a bookseller, a playwright, a theatre historian, a periodical editor and a translator. However, the majority of her literary output was prose fiction and her fame is mostly due to her success as a novelist: Haywood's first novel *Love in Excess; or, The Fatal Enquiry* (1719–20) is said to have equalled Daniel Defoe's *Robinson Crusoe* (1719) and Jonathan Swift's *Gulliver's Travels* (1726) in sales and popularity. Although Haywood continued to publish fiction into the 1750s the bulk of her novels (over sixty in total) were produced in the 1720s. Indeed, *Love in Excess* began a trend in this decade for short amatory prose fiction by women and Haywood's success prompted a range of other women writers – such as Penelope Aubin and Mary Davys – to capitalize on her work. *Fantomina; or, Love in a*

Maze first appeared in *Secret Histories, Novels and Poems* (1725) and continues the themes of love and intrigue which characterize the majority of Haywood's work. As is the case with many of Haywood's other novellas, *Fantomina* foregrounds a female protagonist who is involved in a series of amatory intrigues which threaten the heroine's virtue and lead to her eventual removal to a monastery.

As Ros Ballaster (1992b) has noted, Haywood typically represents her female characters as one of two types: either as an innocent virgin who falls prey to a perfidious male or as a self-seeking aggressor who mimics the attributes of male vice and is punished at the end of the novel for her unfeminine behaviour. *Fantomina* is unconventional in this respect as the central character, whose real identity the reader never discovers, is both a scheming female plotter and, albeit briefly, an innocent country virgin. Indeed, it is Fantomina's innocence that initially sparks her curiosity as to the behaviour of the men towards the prostitutes who frequent the theatre for sexual trade. As a lady 'of distinguished Birth' (Demaria, 1996, 768; all page nos cited refer to this anthology), Fantomina is accustomed to the respectful attentions of men of fashion and is bemused and shocked at what she sees as the depraved tastes of her male counterparts. In a bid to discover 'in what Manner these Creatures were addressed (768) Fantomina disguises herself as a prostitute and appears the following night in the Gallery, eschewing her socially superior place in a box with the other wealthy theatregoers. As a result of her disguise – which masks her class allegiance as well as her personal identity – Fantomina is enthusiastically approached by the attractive Beauplaisir who pressures her to submit to his proposals in his belief that, as a prostitute, her sexual favours are easily purchased: 'He was transported to find so much beauty and Wit in a Woman, who he doubted not but on very easy Terms he might enjoy' (787).

Despite providing early evidence of Fantomina's skill in deception, the opening of the narrative plays on the reader's expectations concerning the usual trajectory of the seduction plot where the innocent yet desiring woman is seduced by the amorous male. Although she is horrified at the unexpected dilemma she finds herself in because of her disguise, Fantomina displays all the characteristics of the virtuous woman attempting to resist, unsuccessfully, her sexual desire: 'All the Charms of *Beauplaisir* came fresh into her Mind; she languished, she almost died for another Opportunity of conversing with him' (788). Similarly, when she meets Beauplaisir for the second time the seduction scene is couched in the conventional terms of resisting female and demanding male: '*He* was bold; – he was resolute: *She* fearful, – confused, altogether unprepared to resist in such Encounters, and rendered more so, by the extreme Liking she had to him' (789). At this point, despite the fact that Fantomina engineers the meeting herself, Haywood seems to be offering her reader a familiar tale of female ruin: 'In fine, she was undone; and he gained a Victory, so highly rapturous, that had he known over whom, scarce could he have triumphed more' (780). Fantomina's reaction to her seduction seems to confirm the shifted power relations between the lovers where the woman's fate is dependent on the (unlikely) stability of the man's affections: ' "your Love alone can compensate for the Shame you have involved me in; be you sincere and constant, and I hereafter shall, perhaps, be satisfied with my Fate, and forgive myself the Folly that betrayed me to you"' (790).

In the case of Fantomina, however, the shame of the ruined woman is deferred by the heroine's careful concealment of her real identity. Although Fantomina has lost her virtue she maintains her reputation through her use of disguise and is able to mingle freely in polite society despite her sexual misdemeanours. Furthermore, through her continued use of a variety of disguises, Fantomina also circumvents the inevitable waning of Beauplaisir's amorous attentions. In his inconstancy, Beauplaisir is a typical Haywood man, as the narrator's knowing remarks illustrate: 'he varied not so much from his Sex as to be able to prolong Desire, to any great Length after Possession' (791). However, as Beauplaisir's interest in his conquest begins to fade, instead of bemoaning her fate Fantomina plans a series of stratagems to keep Beauplaisir's desire alive and to feed her own passion so that she can constantly relive and relish the moment of her first seduction:

> Her Design was once more to engage him, to hear him sigh, to see him languish, to feel the strenuous Pressures of his eager Arms, to be compelled, to be sweetly forced to what she wished with equal Ardour, was what she wanted, and what she had formed a Stratagem to obtain. (792)

Accordingly, Fantomina adopts a variety of further disguises to trick Beauplaisir and satisfy her own desires. She follows him to Bath where she dresses up as a country serving maid and is employed in the inn where Beauplaisir is lodging. When Beauplaisir inevitably tires of 'the sweet Beauties of the pretty *Celia,* for that was the name she bore in this second Expedition' (793), our heroine reincarnates herself as the Widow Bloomer and intercepts Beauplaisir in his chariot on his journey back to London. Her final appearance is as the domino of eighteenth-century masquerade costume – 'the fair Incognita' – in which disguise she completely masks her face from view. The enterprising plotter is only discovered when she goes into labour at a ball and gives birth to a baby girl, after which event her mother sends her to a French monastery but not before entreating the bemused Beauplaisir (who has been named as the father) to keep the secret of her daughter's shameful ruin.

Haywood's fictional account of Fantomina's adventures is indebted to the practice of masquerade in the eighteenth century, which reached the height of its popularity in the 1720s. Haywood often includes masquerade scenes in her work and she also wrote a novel called *The Masqueraders; or, Fatal Curiosity, Being the Secret History of a Late Amour* (1724). As many critics have pointed out, most notably Terry Castle, in contrast to the restrictions placed on bourgeois women's lives in this period the masquerade was a social space in which it was possible to enact fantasies and assume a different identity while maintaining respectability and reputation through the use of disguise. The parallels between this social practice and Haywood's fictional representation are therefore clear as Fantomina inhabits a range of 'masquerades' in order to trick Beauplaisir, continue her sexual gratification but also keep her good name.

Haywood also alludes to contemporary ideas about the sexuality of actresses when she taps into the anxiety about possible connections between stage acting and female social artifice. Indeed, it is precisely Fantomina's adeptness in assuming different identities that gives her the power over the usually triumphant male:

> She was so admirably skilled in the Art of feigning, that she had the Power of putting on almost what Face she pleased, and knew so exactly how to form her behaviour to the Character she represented, that all the Comedians at both Playhouses are short of her Performances. (795)

Ros Ballaster (1992b), for example, has argued that the practice of masquerade and the writing of amatory fiction are inextricably linked as both provide women with a way in which to avoid the usual social or fictional fates offered to them by giving them the power to take control over their own representation. In terms of fictional plots, this power means that through Haywood's use of shifting disguises for her heroine, the novel *Fantomina* escapes the conventional fictional paradigm which places the woman in the position of passive victim and presents a challenge to normative plot structures. Such a reading of *Fantomina* suggests that through an emphasis on its masquerade qualities the text can be interpreted as positive and empowering in its representation of female desire and female agency.

On one level, then, *Fantomina* can be read as a text which implicitly celebrates female desire by authorizing and enacting women's sexual fantasies through the secret adventures of the protagonist. The aptly named Fantomina is able to act out a series of roles which articulate and embody her passion for Beauplaisir and her constantly shifting identity – as prostitute, maid, widow and domino – means that neither her lover nor the reader is able to categorize or define her. The way in which Beauplaisir moves from woman to woman (or disguise to disguise) also provides the reader with a warning as to the inconstancy of men as well as suggesting the transient nature of desire itself. In this sense, *Fantomina* could also be read as an insider's guide to male perfidy which allows the female reader access to the secret behaviour of men. This effect is especially prominent when Haywood positions letters to the Widow Bloomer and Fantomina next to each other in the text (796), thus exposing Beauplaisir's amatory protestations as mere form. Fantomina's expostulation on receipt of these letters underlines Haywood's point: '"tis thus our silly, fond, believing Sex are served when they put Faith in Man: So had I been deceived and cheated, had I like the rest believed, and sat down mourning in Absence, and vainly waited recovered Tenderness"' (796). In contrast to these foolish women, Fantomina congratulates herself on triumphing over '"even the most Subtle of the deceiving Kind"' (796).

However, it could be argued that *Fantomina* is in fact more conservative in its representation of femininity and its plot trajectory than this assessment suggests. For example, the heroine's various disguises are stereotypes of the different professions available for women in this period and Beauplaisir's particular behaviour to each makes explicit the class and gender assumptions about prostitutes, maids and widows respectively. Without a clear identity of her own, the protagonist can only inhabit other more fixed representations of femininity which, rather than exhibiting the heroine's choice in her role-playing, instead display the narrow range of opportunities that women faced in the early eighteenth century. Fantomina's skill in deception and mimicry also runs perilously close to conventional antifeminist discourse which emphasizes feminine artifice as an adjunct to female vice and inconstancy. Further- more, Fantomina's final incarnation as 'the fair Incognita' could be seen as a complete erasure of identity which, although freeing the heroine from restrictive conceptions of feminine social roles, is a kind of dead end for the protagonist which signals both the futility of her stratagems and the limits of her freedom.

The most deciding factor which upholds this more cautious reading of Haywood's work is the conclusion to Fantomina's story. The heroine's freedom has already been severely curtailed by the appearance of her mother who demands her daughter's return to the social codes of behaviour which her fantasy life has momentarily released her from. Moreover, the intrusion of the material body of the heroine into a narrative based on insubstantiality and a separation of physicality from imaginative fantasy through deception and role-playing, signals the end of Fantomina's 'free-play' of iden- tities and firmly reinscribes her into normative codes of femininity. The birth of Fan- tomina's child takes away her powers of dissimulation and artifice and she can no longer control her own representation. In contrast to her previously skilful manipu- lation of her appearance and manner, when she goes into labour at the ball:

> She could not conceal the sudden Rack which all at once invaded her; or had her Tongue been mute, her wildly rolling Eyes, the Distortion of her Features, and the Convulsions which shook her whole Frame, in spite of her, would have revealed she laboured under some terrible Shock of Nature. (801–2)

Haywood's choice of language to describe Fantomina's plots prefigures the eventual outcome of pregnancy and childbirth when she described her heroine as having 'another Project in *embryo*, which she soon ripened into Action' (797). However, at the close of the text this metaphorical use of motherhood is made literal as Fantom- ina's plots in fact lead directly to the birth of Beauplaisir's child. The mother's words to her wayward daughter emphasize how the text has moved from imaginative inven- tion and the possibility of empowerment to a strict distinction between reality and fantasy: ' "Is this the Gentleman", said she, "to whom you owe your Ruin? or have you deceived me by a fictitious Tale?" ' (802). Just as the heroine's story has to end when she becomes a mother, so too does Haywood's narrative have to succumb to the conventional demands of the amatory plot with Fantomina leaving the country to hide her shame in a French monastery.

As is the case with *Fantomina*, many of Haywood's texts, and novels by other women in the early eighteenth century, seem to offer a mixed message to their readership. On the one hand, amatory fiction such as that practised by Haywood can be read as poten- tially challenging in its emphasis on female desire and experience as the central feature of the narrative. On the other hand, the constant appearance in Haywood's work of women ruined by inconstant men and the blurring of the boundaries between rape and seduction in these texts suggests a rather less than celebratory capitulation to – or a realistic recognition of – social codes which disenfranchise women and limit female experience. This dual effect of amatory fiction is characteristic of its concerns, however, and does not have to be irresolvable or necessarily problematic. The ambiguous mixture of erotic fantasy and didacticism which Haywood's texts offer is precisely their appeal and the popularity of her work testifies to the success of this particular formula.

Despite the interest that Haywood's fiction offers the modern reader, her work and that of her female contemporaries (Penelope Aubin, Jane Barker, Mary Davys and Elizabeth Singer Rowe) has been disregarded as an early example of twentieth-century pulp romances or as primitive versions of the more sophisticated fiction of male writers such as Samuel Richardson and Henry Fielding. While Haywood's early fiction does not involve the reader in the complexities of character motivation, choosing, rather, to rely on a plot-driven narrative, the huge popularity of her work can not be explained away so easily. Recent assessments of Haywood's contribution to the novel have led to a variety of readings of her work and attempts have been made to refigure the evaluative criteria by which to judge early prose fiction by women. Critics such as Ros Ballaster (1992b) emphasize the psychological dimension to her fiction whereas literary historians like Jane Spencer and Janet Todd draw attention to Haywood's place in a tradition of women novelists. More recently, Brean Hammond, Catherine Ingrassia and William Warner see Haywood as part of the changing literary culture in the eighteenth century which was beginning to view writing as a commercial product reliant on increasingly sophisticated modes of marketing authors and their work. Whatever approach is taken, it is no longer possible to ignore Eliza Haywood's presence on the eighteenth-century literary scene. Indeed, a study of her work can stimulate a variety of new perspectives on eighteenth-century culture, the history of the novel and the development of female authorship as a professional occupation.

REFERENCES AND FURTHER READING

Ballaster, R. (1992a). 'Preparatives to love: seduction as fiction in the works of Eliza Haywood'. In *Living by the Pen: Early British Women Writers*. Ed. D. Spender. New York: Teachers College Press.

——(1992b). *Seductive Forms: Women's Amatory Fiction from 1684 to 1740*. Oxford: Clarendon.

Beasley, J. C. (1986). 'Politics and moral idealism: the achievement of some early women novelists'. In *Fetter'd or Free? British Women Novelists, 1670–1815*. Ed. M. A. Schofield and C. Macheski. Athens: Ohio University Press.

Blouch, C. (1991). 'Eliza Haywood and the romance of obscurity'. *Studies in English Literature* 31, 535–52.

Bowers, T. (1994). 'Sex, lies and invisibility: amatory fiction from the Restoration to mid-century'. In *The Columbia History of the British Novel*. Ed. J. J. Richetti. New York: Columbia University Press.

Castle, T. (1986). *Masquerade and Civilisation: The Carnivalesque in Eighteenth-century England*. London: Methuen.

Craft-Fairchild, C. (1993). *Masquerade and Gender:*

Disguise and Female Identity in Eighteenth-century Fictions by Women. University Park: Pennsylvania University Press.

Demaria, R. Jr (1996). *British Literature 1640–1789: An Anthology.* Oxford: Blackwell.

Gonda, C. (1996). *Reading Daughter's Fictions 1709–1834.* Cambridge: Cambridge University Press.

Hammond, B. S. (1997). *Professional Imaginative Writing in England, 1670–1740: 'Hackney for Bread'.* Oxford: Clarendon.

Hollis, K. (1997). 'Eliza Haywood and the Gender of Print'. *The Eighteenth Century* 38, 43–62.

Ingrassia, C. (1998). *Authorship, Commerce, and Gender in Early Eighteenth-century England: A Culture of Paper Credit.* Cambridge: Cambridge University Press.

Langbauer, L. (1990). *Women and Romance: The Consolations of Gender in the English Novel.* New York: Cornell University Press.

Richards, C. (1995). 'The pleasures of complicity: sympathetic identification and the female reader in early eighteenth-century women's amatory fiction'. *The Eighteenth Century* 36.3, 220–33.

Richetti, J. J. (1969; 1992). *Popular Fiction before Richardson: Narrative Patterns 1700–1739.* Oxford: Clarendon.

Rose, M. (1996). *Political Satire and Reforming Vision in Eliza Haywood's Works.* Milan: Europrint Publications.

Ross, D. (1992). *The Excellence of Falsehood: Romance, Realism and Women's Contribution to the* *Novel.* Lexington: University of Kentucky Press.

Schofield, M. A. (1982). *Quiet Rebellion: The Fictional Heroines of Eliza Fowler Haywood.* Washington, D. C.: University Press of America.

——(1985). *Eliza Haywood.* Boston: Twayne Publishers.

——(1990). *Masking and Unmasking the Female Mind: Disguising Romances in Feminine Fiction, 1713–1799.* Newark: University of Delaware Press.

Spencer, J. (1986). *The Rise of the Woman Novelist from Aphra Behn to Jane Austen.* Oxford: Basil Blackwell.

——(1996). 'Women writers and the eighteenth-century novel'. In *The Cambridge Companion to the Eighteenth-Century Novel.* ed. J. J. Richetti. Cambridge: Cambridge University Press, 212–35.

Todd, J. (1989). *The Sign of Angellica: Women, Writing, and Fiction 1660–1800.* London: Virago.

Turner, C. (1992). *Living by the Pen: Women Writers in the Eighteenth Century.* London and New York: Routledge.

Warner, W. B. (1998). *Licensing Entertainment: The Elevation of Novel Reading in Britain, 1684–1750.* Berkeley and Los Angeles: University of California Press.

Whicher, G. F. (1915). *The Life and Romances of Mrs. Eliza Haywood.* New York: Columbia University Press.

27

James Thomson, *The Seasons*

David Fairer

Thomson's *The Seasons* was probably the most widely popular poem of the eighteenth century. It has been calculated that between 1726 and 1820 some 132 editions were published (Havens, 1961, 125–6) and it was an influential favourite throughout the Romantic period. Even in 1818 the critic William Hazlitt could speak of Thomson as 'perhaps, the most popular of all our poets' (*Lectures on the English Poets*, Lecture V 'On Thomson and Cowper'). The ability of *The Seasons* to survive the shifts in literary taste during the century after its publication can be attributed in part to its wide variety of moods and topics, to its memorable (and memorizable) set-piece descriptions and interwoven incidents and stories that were popular with painters, and also to the flexibility of its blank verse which can encompass everything from the sublime and pathetic to the didactic and burlesque. The poem carries the reader through a succession of striking scenes, taking in both horror and amusement, the exotic and familiar, the sentimental and the philosophical.

On 4 June 1726 the *London Journal* celebrated the author of *Winter. A Poem*: 'He has joined with great art the most beautiful imagination and the finest reflection together, adorned with masterly diction and versification . . . He must be allowed to have the genuine spirit of sublime poetry in him, and bids fair to reach at length the heighth of Milton's character'. Being welcomed as the new Milton would bring a surge of confidence to any young poet, and when *Winter* was reissued for a 'second edition' on 16 July it was accompanied by a preface voicing Thomson's lofty ambitions: 'let POETRY, once more, be restored to her antient Truth, and Purity', he wrote, 'let Her be inspired from Heaven, and, in return, her Incense ascend thither; let Her exchange Her low, venal, trifling, Subjects, for such as are fair, useful, and magnificent; and, let Her execute these so as, at once, to please, instruct, surprize, and astonish'. Thomson sees his role as helping poetry to rediscover its primal powers, and in invoking heavenly inspiration he specifically links himself with the poet of *Paradise Lost*, just as his choice of blank verse, rather than the heroic couplet of Dryden and Pope, places him in Milton's line. It is important for modern readers of *The Seasons* to appreciate the fervour with which Thomson's project grew, and how the young poet could redirect the rhetorical power of the presbyterian preacher (his planned vocation) into a very different channel. He wanted his poem to 'please, instruct, surprize, and astonish' his readers.

It is tempting to explain the poem's miscellaneous character by the fact that it grew over the years from small beginnings (the 405-line poem *Winter* published in 1726) to the 1730 subscription edition of *The Seasons* (4,342 lines), expanded finally to 5,423 lines in 1746, with new passages being incorporated into it during several stages of revisal. But it would be misleading to suggest that it somehow lost shape in the process. It is more helpful to consider *The Seasons* as a poem which explores concepts such as order, energy, change, growth, and destruction, and which is repeatedly testing the relations between them. Representing the very world it describes, Thomson's poem confronts the stresses and contradictions that drive 'nature' in all its guises – as the eighteenth century understood it.

That final phrase is important. Criticism of *The Seasons* has found it difficult to free itself from Romantic concepts of poetic language and the natural world. Thomson emphatically does not speak a simple 'language of the heart', but employs a complex and varied style drawing not only on Milton and the classical poets, but on modern science (or 'Natural Philosophy' as it was called); his poem celebrates a nature which embraces human labour and the latest discoveries in geology and botany. Thomson's nature is the world in which everyone lives and works, and which the scientist helps to explain. As we set out into the new millennium, in fact, it is Thomson's nature that we are confronted with: a force which can be exploited for our good, but which can turn against human beings at any moment; something of great beauty and wonder whose laws we meddle with at our peril because we are an integral part of an interdependent system. Rather than being a nature-poet who failed to be Wordsworth, Thomson can be seen as offering a more energetic and all-embracing concept of nature than Wordsworth dared envisage. *The Seasons* is not a failed Romantic poem, but a great eighteenth-century poem. It is characterized throughout by that century's struggle to accommodate the widest possible experiences into an articulate whole.

To understand Thomson's poem we need to catch the excitement of living in an age when the universe was both expanding physically and becoming spiritualized. While the microscope and telescope stretched human perceptions from the infinitely small to the infinitely vast, Newton's discoveries showed that it somehow all made sense. The nation's response to his *Principia* (1687) was a heady mixture of understanding and wonder. Newton brought intellect and spirit together into one equation: his principle of 'gravity' revealed that matter throughout the galaxies was wonderfully organized as if by a controlling mind, so that everything from the motions of planets to the ebb and flow of the tides and the fall of an apple was a manifestation of the same law of nature. For Thomson, Newton was 'our philosophic sun' at the centre of a lucid system, the human equivalent of those stars he had explained, 'the living centre each / Of an harmonious system: all combin'd, / And rul'd unerring by that single Power, / Which draws the stone projected to the ground'. These lines from Thomson's *Poem Sacred to the*

Memory of Sir Isaac Newton (1727) show how gravity could be seen as a divine principle informing our every action: a single equation comprehended both the structure of the universe and the lifting of a teacup.

This idea is at once sublime and witty. It can help us appreciate the way *The Seasons* exploits contrasts between an astronomical and a human scale. The poem ranges through extremes of experience conscious that a single system embraces all:

> With what an awful world-revolving Power,
> Were first th'unwieldy Planets launch'd along
> Th'illimitable Void! Thus to remain,
> Amid the Flux of many thousand Years,
> That oft has swept the toiling Race of Men,
> And all their labour'd Monuments away,
> Firm, unremitting, matchless, in their Course;
> To the kind-temper'd Change of Night and Day,
> And of the Seasons ever stealing round,
> Minutely faithful: Such TH'ALL-PERFECT HAND,
> That pois'd, impels, and rules the steady Whole.
>   (*Summer*, 32–42)

I have chosen to begin with Thomson at his most pompous and inflated in a passage which takes us on a generalized sweep through the solar system. Today we find such grand certainties unsympathetic, perhaps because we see the sublimity without noticing the wit. The easy literalness of 'world-revolving' suddenly shifts to an odd but distinctly human perspective with the word 'unwieldy' – the 'toiling Race of Men' finds everything heavy and difficult, and our 'labour'd' remains are easily swept away. As human beings we are caught between the 'Flux' of human time and the unremittingness of eternity, a contrast nicely caught in the witty half-concealed image of the seasons as a clock, with its hand 'ever stealing round' and keeping 'minutely faithful' (the pun is rich in its implications). The passage ends with three words, *pois'd*, *impels*, and *rules*, which between them express the interrelated principles (a Newtonian trinity) on which the poem is based: tension, dynamism and order.

Thomson's world is not a static system, but one which is forever in motion. Even the stillest moment is poised in a tense anticipation of action:

> Gradual, sinks the Breeze,
> Into a perfect Calm; that not a Breath
> Is heard to quiver thro' the closing Woods,
> Or rustling turn the many-twinkling Leaves
> Of Aspin tall. Th'uncurling Floods, diffus'd
> In glassy Breadth, seem thro' delusive Lapse
> Forgetful of their Course. 'Tis Silence all,
> And pleasing Expectation.
>   (*Spring*, 155–62)

Our imaginations, hardly held in check by the negatives, create an animated scene: we feel the potential for movement and sound ('quiver' and 'rustling') even as they are denied. The motionless water is 'uncurling' and 'diffus'd', but the two words suggest twisting and stretching; the woods close in while we read.

In *The Seasons*, nature is the life-force working through everything, human, animal and vegetable, astronomical and geological. The earth is a living organism whose materials are forever in motion or waiting to have their energies released. In *Spring*, for example, Thomson astonishes us at one point by invoking a 'universal soul' to which he bows down in ecstatic prayer. But at this moment he is not in a church talking to God, but is kneeling surrounded by vegetation as he rapturously contemplates the minute life of plants:

> Hail, SOURCE OF BEINGS! UNIVERSAL SOUL
> Of Heaven and Earth! ESSENTIAL PRESENCE, hail!
> To THEE I bend the Knee; to THEE my Thoughts,
> Continual, climb; who, with a Master-hand,
> Hast the great Whole into Perfection touch'd.
> By THEE the various vegetative Tribes,
> Wrapt in a filmy Net, and clad with Leaves,
> Draw the live Ether, and imbibe the Dew.
> By THEE dispos'd into congenial Soils,
> Stands each attractive Plant, and sucks, and swells
> The juicy Tide; a twining Mass of Tubes.
> At THY Command the vernal Sun awakes
> The torpid Sap, detruded to the Root
> By wintry Winds, that now in fluent Dance,
> And lively Fermentation, mounting, spreads
> All this innumerous-colour'd Scene of things.
>
> *(Spring,* 556–71)

This world in miniature with its air ('live Ether') and ocean ('juicy Tide') bursts into activity, and the reader's imagination is pulled away from a majestically abstract divine spirit to the rising sap of springtime, the true 'essential' element. The tiny fibres of vegetation become the tangible form of life's organic interconnectedness, its 'soul'. Indeed we have just seen the bee 'Cling to the Bud, and, with inserted Tube, / Suck its pure Essence, its ethereal Soul' (511–12).

Though it invokes an all-embracing harmonious system, Thomson's vision is not of a golden age – quite the contrary. His earth is blemished, fallen, subject to terrible destructive forces not only in external nature but inside human beings themselves: his vividly described storms, blizzards or earthquakes in the natural world are paralleled by uncontrolled lusts, fantasies or cruelties in the human world ('all / Is off the Poise within: the Passions all / Have burst their Bounds', *Spring,* 277–9). Accidents and disasters await Thomson's characters: the frantic lover in *Spring* drowns himself; the innocent Celadon and Amelia in *Summer* are killed by lightning; and in *Winter* a shepherd dies in the blizzard. Life is unfair and untidy, and these tragedies are part of the imbalance acted out by the seasons themselves, which since the Flood 'have, with severer Sway, / Oppress'd a broken World: the Winter keen / Shook forth his Waste of Snows; and Summer shot / His pestilential Heats' (*Spring*, 317–20). The earth's sickness is also a human sickness. As a winter storm approaches, Thomson pictures the landscape like a patient unsteady on his feet, alternately pale and flushed, and with spots before his eyes:

> When from the palid Sky the Sun descends,
> With many a Spot, that o'er his glaring Orb
> Uncertain wanders, stain'd; red fiery Streaks
> Begin to flush around. The reeling Clouds
> Stagger with dizzy Poise.
>   (*Winter*, 118–22)

Once again, the word 'poise' becomes tense and uneasy. It is almost a relief when the violence of the storm finally strikes and natural impulses, however terrible, can be released:

> Thro' the black Night that sits immense around,
> Lash'd into Foam, the fierce conflicting Brine
> Seems o'er a thousand raging Waves to burn;
> Meantime the Mountain-Billows, to the Clouds
> In dreadful Tumult swell'd, Surge above Surge,
> Burst into Chaos with tremendous Roar.
>   (*Winter*, 158–63)

It will be a hundred years before such a scene can be captured in paint. Features characteristic of J. M. W. Turner's art are displayed here: the dynamic mingling of the elements (water, fire, earth and air) with waves burning and mountains swirling into clouds; the tension created by conflicting materials superimposed in layers; even the suggestion of a vortex in the swelling and surging. It is no surprise that the two great landscape painters of the early nineteenth century, Turner and Constable, turned to *The Seasons* to provide mottoes for their more dramatic canvases. Both repeatedly quote Thomson in their catalogue descriptions, never Wordsworth.

Many passages in the poem offer visual set-pieces, but they are not composed in a static way. Thomson's fondness for the present participle (-ing) keeps his scenes active, and his sensitivity to colour and texture are palpable. In this description of an autumn twilight the subtle tonalities of the language create a mood-picture in which dark and light are no longer opposing forces but interweaving elements in a living scene:

> But see the fading many-colour'd Woods,
> Shade deepening over Shade, the Country round

Imbrown; a crouded Umbrage, dusk, and dun,
Of every Hue, from wan declining Green
To sooty Dark . . .
    Mean-time, light-shadowing all, a sober Calm
Fleeces unbounded Ether; whose least Wave
Stands tremulous, uncertain where to turn
The gentle Current: while illumin'd wide,
The dewy-skirted Clouds imbibe the Sun,
And thro' their lucid Veil his soften'd Force
Shed o'er the peaceful World.
                                                (*Autumn*, 950–63)

Thomson handles his palette in a painterly way, mixing his pigments ('wan declin-ing Green'), obtaining layered effects ('Shade deepening over Shade'), using soft brush-strokes ('Fleeces'), and all the time conscious of how one colour absorbs another ('imbibe') as air mediates light.

Such descriptive passages in *The Seasons* are not just an atmospheric backdrop. Light and colour are part of the spiritual science of nature, expressive of the universal soul linking human perceptions with the eternal. With the publication of Newton's *Opticks* (1704) the mathematics of refraction made the rainbow more glorious, and the pris-matic colours were shown to come together to form a clear 'white' beam of light, so that like so much of the poem's restless variety, things that appear to take an indi-vidual direction are still part of an all-embracing whole. Light is not some dead fact, but the source of life, and the science (knowledge) of light is suitable for a poet to celebrate. In the eighteenth century, science was not the enemy of imagination, but its inspirer: truth and reason could be sublime and full of wonder.

Thomson's *The Seasons* itself refracts the dynamic cycle of life into its constituent parts, showing us its immense variety. The poem celebrates the tensions and contra-dictions in the world because they are all, however misdirected, part of the energies of life. The truly malign force in the poem is torpor, a diseased, self-pleasing and anti-social malaise which turns away from what life has to offer. Summer, the season of maximum warmth and light, is also the time of plague, seen by Thomson as an evil corruption in which social bonds fall apart and each individual spurns his neighbour ('The sullen Door, / Yet uninfected, on its cautious Hinge / Fearing to turn, abhors Society', 1077–9). In the cycle of the seasons it is winter, when everything is stripped down to its essentials, that is the time of renewal. Throughout the poem, the human spirit is seen as an integral part of the ecological scheme, restoring its energies along with nature:

Close crouds the shining Atmosphere; and binds
Our strengthen'd Bodies in its cold Embrace,
Constringent; feeds, and animates our Blood;
Refines our Spirits, thro' the new-strung Nerves,
In swifter Sallies darting to the Brain;

Where sits the Soul, intense, collected, cool,
Bright as the Skies, and as the Season keen.
                              (*Winter*, 697–703)

REFERENCES AND FURTHER READING

Anderson, David R. (1981). 'Milton's influence on Thomson: the uses of landscape'. *Milton Studies* 15, 107–20.

——(1983). 'Emotive theodicy in *The Seasons*'. *Studies in Eighteenth-century Culture* 12, 59–76.

Barrell, John (1983). *English Literature in History 1730–80: An Equal, Wide Survey*. London: Hutchinson. See pp. 51–109.

Chalker, John (1969). *The English Georgic: A Study in the Development of a Form*. London: Routledge and Kegan Paul. See ch. 4.

Cohen, Ralph (1970). *The Unfolding of 'The Seasons'*. Baltimore: Johns Hopkins University Press.

Fulford, Tim (1996). *Landscape, Liberty and Authority: Poetry, Criticism and Politics from Thomson to Wordsworth*. Cambridge: Cambridge University Press. See pp. 18–38.

Griffin, Dustin (1986). *Regaining Paradise: Milton and the Eighteenth Century*. Cambridge: Cambridge University Press. See pp. 179–202.

Hagstrum, Jean H. (1958). *The Sister Arts: The Tradition of Literary Pictorialism and English Poetry from Dryden to Gray*. Chicago and London: University of Chicago Press.

Havens, R. D. (1961). *The Influence of Milton on English Poetry*. New York: Russell and Russell. First published (1922). See ch. 6.

Inglesfield, Robert (1986). 'Shaftesbury's influence on Thomson's *Seasons*'. *British Journal for Eighteenth-century Studies* 9, 141–56.

McKillop, A. D. (1942). *The Background of Thomson's 'Seasons'*. Minneapolis: University of Minnesota Press.

Nicolson, M. H. (1946). *Newton Demands the Muse: Newton's Opticks and the Eighteenth-century Poets*. Princeton: Princeton University Press.

Price, Martin (1964). *To the Palace of Wisdom: Studies in Order and Energy from Dryden to Blake*. Carbondale and Edwardsville: Southern Illinois University Press. See pp. 352–61, 'The theatre of nature: James Thomson'.

Reid, David (1992). 'Thomson and Wordsworth: a debt with a difference'. *Scottish Literary Journal* 19, 5–17.

Sambrook, James, ed. (1981). *James Thomson: 'The Season'*. Oxford: Clarendon.

——(1991). *James Thomson, 1700–1748: A Life*. Oxford: Clarendon.

Scott, Mary Jane W. (1988). *James Thomson, Anglo-Scot*. Athens and London: University of Georgia Press.

Sitter, John (1982). *Literary Loneliness in Mid-eighteenth-century England*. Ithaca and London: Cornell University Press. See pp. 175–88.

Spacks, P. M. (1967). *The Poetry of Vision: Five Eighteenth-century Poets*. Cambridge, Mass: Harvard University Press.

Terry, Richard (1995). ' "Through nature shedding influence malign": Thomson's *The Seasons* as a theodicy', *Durham University Journal* 87, 257–68.

——*James Thomson: Essays for the Tercentenary*. Liverpool: Liverpool University Press.

Ziff, Jerrold (1964). 'J. M. W. Turner on poetry and painting', *Studies in Romanticism* 3, 193–215.

28
Alexander Pope, The *Dunciads*
Valerie Rumbold

Pope's progressive elaboration of his mock-heroic poem *The Dunciad*, originally published in three books in 1728, spanned the last decade and a half of his life, and marks the culmination of his poetic career.

In its first form *The Dunciad* was a poem satirizing authors whom Pope despised, principally Lewis Theobald (belittled as 'Tibbald' in the poem), who had exasperated him by criticizing his edition of Shakespeare. Book I tells how Tibbald is adopted as son by the goddess Dulness. In Book II his enthronement as king is celebrated by competitive games for bad writers and their publishers, who process westwards through London, enacting a symbolic journey from plebeian to aristocratic districts. In Book III Tibbald descends into the underworld to receive the prophecy that Dulness's empire will overwhelm the whole of human civilization. The epic model most centrally evoked is Vergil's *Aeneid*, whose hero is also son of a divine mother (Venus), destined to take his culture on a westwards journey (from Troy to Italy) in order to found a new empire (Rome). Biblical and Miltonic echoes are also important in suggesting that Dulness inverts the divine order and undoes God's creative word. The first version's conclusion makes the allusion particularly plain:

> *Let there be darkness!* (the dread pow'r shall say)
> All shall be darkness, as it ne'er were Day.
>   (*Dunciad* 1728, III.281–2)

The final lines, however, suggest at least the possibility that the prophecy is no more than a dream: 'He wak'd, and all the Vision mix'd with air' (III.286).

The first stage of elaboration, *The Dunciad Variorum* of 1729, altered the poem slightly, annotated it with extensive footnotes, and surrounded it with prefaces and appendices. The conclusion was expanded to emphasize the metaphysical dimension of the threat posed by Dulness: now she not only destroys the arts and education, but also puts to flight such entities as Truth, Philosophy and religious Mystery. Still, however, there remains the possibility that the vision of her triumph is a delusion: the dream is said to disappear 'thro' the Ivory Gate', alluding to the ancient belief that false dreams came through an ivory gate, and true ones through a gate of horn.

In 1742 *The New Dunciad* presented itself as a sequel to the three-book versions, complete with its own commentary. The sequel depicts Dulness's triumphant enthronement and the homage done her by her disciples, and closes with a reworked version of the previous conclusion to Book III: in the middle of her speech Dulness yawns, and dissolves the whole creation in sleep. Finally, in 1743, the year before Pope's death, he added this sequel, slightly adapted, to a revised version of the original poem and its notes, forming *The Dunciad in Four Books*. This version offered not only elaboration but also surprise, insofar as Tibbald, the original hero, had been displaced in favour of Bays, an easily recognizable caricature of the poet laureate, Colley Cibber. Further adjustments were also made to the conclusion, and it is this final form that is today the most familiar:

> More she had spoke, but yawn'd – All Nature nods:
> What Mortal can resist the Yawn of Gods?
> > (*Dunciad in Four Books* 1743, IV.606–7)

The final lines emphasize the underlying reversal of Genesis:

> Lo! thy dread Empire, CHAOS is restor'd;
> Light dies before thy uncreating word:
> Thy hand, great Anarch! lets the curtain fall;
> And Universal Darkness buries All.
> > (*Dunciad in Four Books* 1743, IV.653–6)

There seems less room than ever for any turning aside of the prospect of terminal disintegration.

Modern work on the *Dunciad*s still draws to a large extent on mid-twentieth-century advances in Pope scholarship, notably James Sutherland's magnificently annotated *Dunciad* volume in the Twickenham Edition, which established the so-called A (1729) and B (1743) texts as a standard form of reference; and Aubrey Williams's *Pope's 'Dunciad': A Study of its Meaning*, which argued for Pope's defence of humane culture in the context of his allusions to the epic texts of Homer, Virgil and Milton. New directions were suggested in 1968 in Emrys Jones's British Academy lecture, 'Pope and Dulness': Jones reminded readers that the *Dunciad*s were a multiplicity, not a simple unity, in regard both to the number of their versions and to the ambiguities of the attitudes they expressed; and he suggested that current appreciations left out of their lofty formulations much of the disruptive energy actually experienced by the reader. Indeed, by the closing decades of the century, the tradition of celebrating the *Dunciad*s as a vindication of universal and unchanging cultural values had become, in the new climate of theoretical, political and gender-based analysis, a problem in itself.

A new consensus developed which took ambivalence and plurality in its stride, often focused on a notion of the onset of modernity. The *Dunciad*s were presented as texts significantly embodied in the material form of their various physical formats, and thus as material commodities within the expanding book trade on which Pope's own material well-being depended – to an extent arguably surprising in a poet who expressed such contempt for the self-generating momentum of the book trade. Feminist theory and the rediscovery of early women writers helped to focus analysis of the *Dunciad*s' construction of women and the feminine as a cultural and historical rather than merely personal or psychological phenomenon. Alongside this turn away from a metaphysical concern with the supposed universality of Pope's concerns came the necessity of taking seriously the multiplicity not only of the texts' versions, but also of their authors and textual components: it became less easy to believe in a poem called *The Dunciad* and more plausible to concede the existence of a sequence of poems inextricably implicated with prose elements not even all necessarily by Pope (since he invited his friends Jonathan Swift, John Gay and John Arbuthnot to contribute in 1729, and William Warburton in 1742 and 1743). By the end of the twentieth century, the *Dunciad*s seemed to be adduced primarily as witnesses to the cultural transformations of modernity.

Pope signals right at the start of the first *Dunciad* his sense that literature is being transformed by a new disregard for conventional boundaries between elite and popular culture:

> BOOKS and the Man I sing, the first who brings
> The Smithfield Muses to the Ear of Kings.
> (*Dunciad Variorum* 1729, correcting the apparent misprint 'BOOK' in *Dunciad* 1728)

Tibbald is blamed for bringing into the realm of elite culture ('the Ear of Kings') what had formerly (and we may understand, properly) been confined to the popular culture of the fairground. The 1729 note comments:

> *Smithfield* is the place where Bartholomew Fair was kept, whose Shews, Machines, and Dramatical Entertainments, formerly agreeable only to the Taste of the Rabble, were, by the hero of this Poem and others of equal Genius, brought to the Theatres of Covent-Garden, Lincolns-inn-Fields, and the Hay-Market, to be the reigning Pleasures of the Court and Town.

The amusements of 'the Rabble' are not, for Pope, part of any kind of culture worth an educated man's attention (the very politeness of our expression 'popular culture' indicates the difference between his assumptions and ours). The problem is, as the *Dunciad*s construct it, that the elite have been seduced by undemanding entertainment; authors, booksellers and playhouse managers have found it profitable; and the powers that be have enlisted it in their project of lulling the public into uncritical acquiescence.

Dulness, the personification on whom Pope focuses his allegory, is to a large extent a goddess of what we would call the media. She is clearly not just the slow and boring stupidity that we would usually call 'dull' (although sending people to sleep is one of her specialities), for she demonstrates Pope's ambiguous sense of the seductive energy of the trends he decries by embodying also stupidity of a perversely active and dangerous kind: in sum she is 'Laborious, heavy, busy, bold, and blind' (*Dunciad* 1728, I.13). In literature she sponsors all that is nonsensical, inconsistent, and contrary to established decorum:

> There motley *Images* her fancy strike,
> *Figures* ill-pair'd, and *Similes* unlike.
> She sees a mob of *Metaphors* advance,
> Pleas'd with the madness of the mazy dance:
> How *Tragedy* and *Comedy* embrace;
> How *Farce* and *Epic* get a jumbled race.
>   (*Dunciad* 1728, I.53–8)

All this is clearly satirical; but what is clear too is the fun that Pope has conceiving it, and the closeness of some of these formulations to experiments which he and his friends (notably Swift and Gay) had made in the mixing of genres and in the disruption of expected harmonies. Recent commentary has made a truism of the conflict between the denunciation evident in passages like these and their tapping into disapproved kinds of transformative energy. The ambivalence seems deeply characteristic of this period's uneasy yet exciting relation both to its past heritage and to the new configuration which we would now call the modern.

The point has often been made that Dulness, the muddled mother who oversees her formless offspring with deluded pride, embodies conflicting assumptions about gender roles, a perception easily connected with the women writers satirized in the *Dunciad*s – who are actually far fewer than is often assumed. Yet to focus on women's writings and the specific challenges they offered to traditional genre boundaries and hierarchies may distort the precise insult actually offered by the *Dunciad*s, for the most striking instances construct their victims more as persons (who happen to have offended Pope, and happen to have done it in a literary context) than as would-be artists, and more as bodies even than as persons. In contrast, manuscript drafts had actually included a competition for women writers which focused explicitly on their alleged artistic failings: the omission of this passage from the published versions, which effectively mutes any direct recognition of women's claims to be considered as active producers of literary art, may in fact be a more effective snub than the lewdness, excrement and innuendo in which he bemires Elizabeth Thomas and Eliza Haywood.

No such problem inhibits Pope's representation of political journalists, another group of writers whose prominence constitutes one of the distinctively new features of the period. Dulness invites them to compete at diving into a sewer:

Here strip my children! here at once leap in!
Here prove who best can dash thro' thick and thin,
And who the most in love of dirt excel,
Or dark dexterity of groping well.
                              (*Dunciad* 1728, II.251–4)

These are writers who in Pope's view will do anything for money – including black-
ening his character and those of his friends (notably the Earl of Oxford, Viscount
Bolingbroke and Bishop Atterbury, all politically compromised, as Tories and potential or actual advocates of the return of the exiled Roman Catholic Stuart line, under
the Whig regime established under the Hanoverian Georges). It is not simply that
Pope is enjoying smearing his antagonists by sending them into places he feels appropriate to their moral squalor, or even that he is giving brilliantly physical realization
to common metaphors like 'gutter press' or 'muck-raking journalism', but that, as
Emrys Jones recognized, at a deeper level he is imaginatively stimulated by these possibilities of fantasy, encroaching as they do on those areas primarily fenced off by the
basic decorums of adult civility. What the journalists and pamphleteers have in
common with Pope, however, is that the expansion of demand for printed matter and
the productive capacity of modern printing enabled them to live on the profits of their
writing.

One factor that might at first sight seem puzzling is the connection between such
notions of modernity and Pope's personal grudge against Lewis Theobald. If Tibbald
is 'the man' who in 1728 and 1729 focuses the transfer of low amusements to elite
consumers that Pope alleges, what is the relation of this claim to the actual cause of
annoyance that prompted Pope to make him the hero of the original poem, namely
Theobald's criticism of Pope's Shakespeare? For although Theobald had also written
poems and plays which Pope considered worthless, it is doubtful that without that
specific offence he would ever have been hero of the *Dunciad*. The answer lies in his
pioneering of a very important strand in the modernization and professionalization of
print culture, one which transformed the way that classic texts are received by their
readers.

Traditionally, elite education since the Renaissance had focused on familiarity with
a canon of Greek and Latin texts assumed to epitomize universal and unchanging standards of taste. By studying them, the student was supposedly enabled to learn both
a rhetoric and a knowledge of men and affairs which would enable him to discharge
the duties of his rank in adult life. Theobald, on the other hand, was an exponent of
a newer kind of literary study which had first impinged on older attitudes in the
person of Richard Bentley, who had at the end of the seventeenth century begun to
elaborate a newly historicist way of reading Greek and Latin. In Bentley's view, the
ancient writers, far from sharing a uniform classicism, were crucially marked by
having lived in different times and in different places. He pioneered the use of tests
based on dated and regionally defined usage to establish whether a particular text
could or could not have come from a particular place and time, and by doing so he

enraged many of Pope's older mentors, and gave impetus to the English branch of the debate known as the Quarrel of the Ancients and the Moderns, which hinged on the relative merits of ancient and modern culture. At issue between Bentley and his opponents were the so-called epistles of Phalaris, routinely praised as being some of the oldest texts extant, and as offering a self-evidently authentic expression of the character of an absolute tyrant; but Bentley showed, by methods now standard in academic textual study, that they could not possibly have been written by anyone who spoke the language of the time and place in which the tyrant Phalaris had lived.

It would be hard to overestimate the scandal that this kind of 'proof' gave to the self-esteem and cultural confidence of an elite trained to regard classic literature as its birthright. Bentley's methods could be directly connected with a newly commercial-izing attitude to literature, for, unlike his opponents, Bentley had a living to make, and made it by pursuing an academic career in which his publications were vital to his status and success. This made him, by traditional standards, a pedant in the literal sense, like the schoolmasters the gentry were accustomed to employ in the education of their sons; but to accept a ruling on the real worth of the classics from such a menial – blinkered, as Bentley's enemies tended to see it, by his grubbing among a litter of ancient scribble and by his preoccupation with detailed variations between texts – was unthinkable.

Theobald had extended Bentley's methods to Shakespeare, and had accused Pope, who had edited the plays from the vantage point of gentlemanly taste, of making a range of mistakes through ignorance of the language, idiom, beliefs and literature of the English Renaissance (see, for example, the contemptuous note attempting to undermine the value of Theobald's medieval scholarship at *Dunciad Variorum* 1729, I.162–6). Theobald, therefore, is satirized in the first two *Dunciad*s as one who makes a trade of literature not simply by writing poems of no particular merit for the com-mercial press and pantomimes offensive to classical taste for the commercial play-house, but also by becoming the kind of pedant who makes a trade of contextualizing the classics of English literature by methods which degrade them in the eyes of a tra-ditional gentlemanly taste. In *The Dunciad in Four Books*, after Theobald has been dropped as hero, the satire against pedantry is refocused back onto the originator of modern textual criticism, Bentley himself. Spoof notes are attributed to 'BENTLEY', and he is also caricatured as Ricardus Aristarchus, who contributes a prefatory essay, offensively dogmatic in tone and dismissive of other critics. In the poem itself, Aristarchus makes a major speech through which Pope satirizes his kind of verbal study as undoing the traditional subordination of word to meaning, and accuses him through his teaching of distracting students from the values enshrined in the classics so that they are left defenceless against Dulness. Aristarchus is made to describe himself as:

Thy mighty Scholiast, whose unweary'd pains
Made Horace dull, and humbled Milton's strains.

Turn what they will to Verse, their toil is vain,
Critics like me shall make it Prose again.
      (*The Dunciad in Four Books* 1743, IV.210–14)

Pope conceives poetry as transcending the words of which it is made; but Aristarchus destroys its transcendence by breaking it down into dead literal fragments. Like the natural scientists also attacked in *The Dunciad in Four Books* he insists on the minute perspective of a 'microscope of Wit' and 'Sees hairs and pores, examines bit by bit': obsessed with the often unattractive detail thus revealed, such observers cannot see 'The body's harmony, the beaming soul'. Such study slights the Creator himself and the poet who, however faintly, echoes his creative power: enthusiasts for detail effectively deny the transcendent values of beauty and significance, and, whether in literature or in life, 'See Nature in some partial narrow shape, /And let the Author of the Whole escape' (IV.455–6).

By unpicking, as Pope saw it, the structure of classical taste and values posited on the texts shared in the education of elite males, Bentley and his successor Theobald were undoing a major element in the hierarchy that made traditional culture workable – and were in effect assisting Dulness in undermining the traditional worldview founded in God as Creator and guarantor of meaning. Once great literature could be deconstructed to the extent that it no longer seemed significantly superior to the products of the gutter press, a levelling of ranks would have been achieved that would threaten the elite roles founded in part on the assumption of superior taste and insight in relation to language and literature. The political implications of such a deconstruction are easy to grasp, but readers who – like us – inherit the consequences of the turn away from universalizing classicism stigmatized by the *Dunciad*s are perhaps in danger of missing another aspect which is, for Pope, overwhelming and obvious. The texts insist that a particular kind of literary beauty is passing away because it is being taught in perversely nitpicking ways, and because its claims to cultural authority and centrality are no longer taken for granted amid the increasing interest of an expanding reading public in consuming newer, less demanding media products. Smithfield culture's transfer from the low associations of the city and its eastern fringes to the more socially distinguished districts of the west end and the court itself is a theme with obvious polemical force, which allows for all sorts of striking juxtapositions; but for those brought up on the classics, its parody of Aeneas's westwards journey to bring his Trojan heritage to Italy, where he will found Rome and its empire, prompts thoughts of loss and decay at the comparison. The games of the writers and booksellers in Book II are hilarious enough and sufficiently plain in their satire even taken alone; but when they are read against the two sets of games in Homer's *Iliad* and Vergil's *Aeneid* to which the notes repeatedly draw our attention, there is both a constant reminder of the artistry and values evoked in the citations, and – to return to the theme of multiplicity and ambivalence – a potentially awkward sense of the similarity between some of the earthy references and ungracious behaviour enshrined in the ancient texts and aspects of modern life caricatured in

Pope's verse. We are told that the originals of Pope's classical allusions have been pointed out in this way 'to gratify those who either never read, or may have forgotten them' (*Dunciad Variorum*, Advertisement, 4). This indicts not only those who presume to engage in literature despite origins too lowly to have furnished them with a classical education, but equally those of privileged background on whom the classics have been wasted.

This perhaps surprising sense that the ruling class is offender as much as victim is strongly pursued. In a surprising turn Pope calls on the social elite (not, as epic precedent demands, on the Muse) to tell the story of the poem:

> Say great Patricians! (since your selves inspire
> These wond'rous works; so Jove and Fate require)
> Say from what cause, in vain decry'd and curst,
> Still Dunce the second reigns like Dunce the first?
> (*Dunciad* 1728, I.3–6)

Repeatedly, the elite have embraced cultural trends they ought to have shunned, the poem claims; so it falls to them, not to the Muse, to explain and account for Dulness's triumph. In their corruption, moreover, they are seconded and supported by the monarchy, the institution traditionally seen as ordering the social world by analogy with and through authority derived from the God whose creative word Dulness has come to undo. The lines quoted above express a very clear disappointment at George II's continuing in the mould set by his father, George I. Of recent years, more and more of the *Dunciads*' satire against the royal family has been brought into critical focus, and we now know that as well as the carefully equivocating sneers in the published texts, Pope had composed, probably in about 1728, a manuscript draft far more personally offensive about George II than anything he ever printed. Even from the evidence of the printed texts alone, it is clear that Pope indicts the king and queen themselves in the collapse of the elite discipline and responsibility that conservative ideology associated with the privileges of rank.

George II had disappointed observers like Pope by reappointing the widely distrusted politician who had dominated his father's administration. Sir Robert Walpole controlled parliament and the king with an effectiveness that contemporaries of a traditional outlook were quick to see as scandalous: with hindsight, this control seems distinctively modern, and Walpole has often been seen as pioneering the role of prime minister, nominally servant of the monarch but in reality the mainspring of government. As a Whig, he was easily aligned by hostile observers with backing for everything commercial and indifference to everything aesthetic or spiritual. Writers resented his pragmatic policy of devoting government money not to art but only to propaganda, a betrayal, in conservative eyes, of the older ideal which placed the poet at the prince's side as celebrant and critic of the values of nation and culture – as Vergil had been under Augustus. In the context of Walpole's long years in office, Cibber (who had, despite his lack of talent, been appointed as poet laureate in 1730, and had published a self-satisfied autobiography in 1740) had by 1743, when he became the new hero of *The Dunciad in Four Books*, assembled an impressive list of qualifications for the role. He was linked with the monarch as his laureate and with Walpole as a supporter of his policies; as a theatrical entrepreneur and an actor who specialized in roles of overweening foppery he was vulnerable to sardonic parallels both with the minister and with his royal master; and his whole career had been about playing to market taste. Although Walpole had, in fact, finally fallen from power by the time *The Dunciad in Four Books* appeared, both Bays and the suppliants to Dulness in Book IV arguably act out Pope's belief that Walpole had been crucially instrumental in estranging the nation from conservative notions of value.

Accounts of the cultural transformations of the eighteenth century regularly produce the *Dunciad*s in evidence: its current status as exemplar of the complications and ambivalences of the onset of modernity seems almost unrivalled. Yet the human mind can only deal with so much at once, and it often seems that as criticism and scholarship shed new light in one area, others recede into darkness. Recent years have seen a hugely important contextualization of the *Dunciad*s in terms of politics, gender, economics, popular culture and the book trade; but the corollary has been a relative neglect of such features as sound, metre, imagery and rhetoric, concerns to an extent compromised in late twentieth-century eyes by their prominence on the discredited agenda of New Criticism. To reconfigure an interpretation of such artistic features within the framework of the new understandings now available, and in time (perhaps) to push at the limits of those approaches, might well be a fruitful project for a new generation of readers.

REFERENCES AND FURTHER READING

Original *Dunciads*

The Dunciad. An Heroic Poem. In Three Books (1728), issued without Pope's name on the title (London). Facsimile in David Vander Meulen (1991), *Pope's Dunciad of 1728: A History and Facsimile* (University Press of Virginia for the Bibliographical Society of the University of Virginia and the New York Public Library, London).

The Dunciad, Variorum. With the Prolegomena of Scriblerus (1729), issued without Pope's name on the title (London). Facsimile in Alexander Pope (1968), *The Dunciad Variorum 1729* (Scholar Press, Menston).

The New Dunciad: As it was Found in the Year 1741 (1742), issued without Pope's name on the title (London).

The Dunciad, in Four Books. Printed according to the complete Copy found in the Year 1742. With the Prolegomena of Scriblerus, and Notes Variorum (1743), issued without Pope's name on the title (London).

Editions

Mack, M., ed. (1984). *The Last and Greatest Art: Some Unpublished Poetical Manuscripts of Alexander Pope*. London: University of Delaware Press.

Rumbold, V., ed. (1999). *Alexander Pope: The Dunciad in Four Books (1743)*. London: Longman Annotated Texts. Addison Wesley Longman.

Sutherland, J., ed. (1943). *The Dunciad*-Revd 1963. Vol 5 of *The Twickenham Edition of the Poems of Alexander Pope*. Ed. J. Butt and others. London: Methuen.

Works Contemporary with the *Dunciads*

Pope, A., ed. (1725). *The Works of Shakespear in Six Volumes, Collated and Corrected by the Former Editions by Mr. Pope*. London.

Popeiana (1974–5). *The Life and Times of Seven Major British Writers*. London: Garland Publishing. 24 vols. Facsimiles of pamphlet attacks on Pope, several relating to *The Dunciads*.

Theobald, L. (1727). *Shakespeare Restored: Or, A Specimen of the Many Errors, as well Committed, as Unamended, by Mr. Pope in his late Edition of this Poet*. London. Facsimile in *Popeiana* above.

Secondary Works

Erskine-Hill, H. E. (1972). *Pope: The Dunciad*. London: Unwin.

Foxon, D. (1991). *Pope and the Early Eighteenth-century Book Trade*. Revd by James McLaverty. Oxford: Clarendon Press.

Francus, M. (1994). The monstrous mother: reproductive anxiety in Swift and Pope'. *English Literary History* 61, 829–51.

Goldgar, B. A. (1976). *Walpole and the Wits: The Relation of Politics to Literature, 1722–1742*. London: University of Nebraska Press.

Hammond, B. (1977). *Professional Imaginative Writing in England, 1670–1740: 'Hackney for Bread'*. Oxford: Clarendon.

Ingrassia, C. (1991). 'Women writing/writing women: Pope, Dulness, and "feminization" in the *Dunciad'*. *Eighteenth-century Life* 14, 40–58.

Jarvis, S. (1995). *Scholars and Gentlemen: Shakespearian Textual Criticism and Representations of Scholarly Labour, 1725–1765*. Oxford: Clarendon.

Jones, E. (1968). 'Pope and dulness'. *Proceedings of the British Academy* 54, 231–63. Repr. in M. Mack and J. A. Winn, eds (1980), *Pope: Recent Essays by Several Hands*. Brighton: Harvester Press, 612–51.

Levine, J. (1991). *The Battle of the Books: History and Literature in the Augustan Age*. London: Cornell University Press.

McLaverty, J. (1984). 'The mode of existence of literary works of art: the case of the *Dunciad Variorum'*. *Studies in Bibliography* 37, 82–105. Partially repr. in B. Hammond, ed. (1996), *Pope*. London: Longman Critical Readers. Addison Wesley Longman.

Rogers, P. (1972). *Grub Street: Studies in a Subculture*. London: Methuen. Abridged in 1980 as *Hacks and Dunces*.

Seary, P. (1990). *Lewis Theobald and the Editing of Shakespeare*. Oxford: Clarendon.

Sitter, J. (1971). *The Poetry of Pope's 'Dunciad'*. London: Oxford University Press.

Williams, A. (1955). *Pope's 'Dunciad': A Study of its Meaning*. London: Methuen.

29

Stephen Duck, *Poems on Several Occasions*

Bridget Keegan

THUS shall Tradition keep my Fame alive;
The *Bard* may die, the *Thresher* still survive.

('A Description of a Journey To Marlborough, Bath, Portsmouth,
&c. To the Right Honourable the Lord Viscount PALMERSTON', 1736)

What is most familiar about Stephen Duck is his compelling biography. An agricultural day-labourer, Duck was rescued from the obscurity of rhyming in a barn and brought to the attention of Queen Caroline who settled an annuity upon him and granted him the post of librarian in her fanciful Merlin's Cave in Richmond Park. Duck spent his remaining years writing occasional verse for the nobility, eventually taking holy orders, and finally (in what transformed his life into a cautionary tale for future labouring-class poets) drowned himself. Such a rags to riches legend invited eighteenth-century readers' curiosity and their animosity – if Swift's 'Quibbling Epigram' against Duck is any indication. The fact that a thresher attracted the attention of the literary and aristocratic elite of the 1730s has continued to prove noteworthy – or at least footnote-worthy – guaranteeing Duck a marginal place in literary history to this day. By and large, however, Duck's poetry, except for 'The Thresher's Labour', has been dismissed or forgotten. Moreover, because Duck's life story has been the focus of critical interest, what is often emphasized about 'The Thresher's Labour' is its documentary and autobiographical authenticity and not its aesthetic or formal achievement.

Such a fate would not have surprised the poet, whose humility proved the greater portion of his charm for his patrons. As his foremost supporter, Oxford Professor of Poetry, Joseph Spence writes in his introduction to Duck's 1736 edition:

He was told this, That he should never speak too highly in Praise of the Poems he had written. He said, 'If that was all, he was safe; that was a Thing he could never do, for he could not think highly of them: Gentlemen indeed, he said, might like 'em because

they were made by a poor fellow in a Barn; but that he knew, as well as any body, that
they were not really good in themselves.'

It is not surprising, given the poet's apparent complicity, that until recently the concluding couplet of the poem to Palmerston (cited above) has accurately summarized
the history of Duck's critical reception.

Later twentieth-century critics have gone beyond remarking upon 'The Thresher's
Labour' because it was produced by 'a poor fellow in a Barn' – though this fact may
be what first draws investigators to study Duck. 'The Thresher's Labour' and its author
have been attracting growing interest as part of the fruitful recovery of works
and authors previously marginalized from the canon. After reviewing the current
critical trends in which Duck's work has been productively reappraised, I wish to
suggest reconsidering Duck as more than a 'one-hit wonder'. Given the importance
of 'The Thresher's Labour' to an ever-widening spectrum of literary historical analyses, it may be time to explore whether any other poems in his corpus broaden an
understanding of Duck's contributions to the varieties and complexities of eighteenth-
century poetry.

There are several critical projects within which Duck's work is a valuable component. These include the following: (1) the excavation of 'labouring-class' or 'plebeian'
writing and the effort to locate a nascent proletarian voice in the early eighteenth
century; (2) the history of literacy and the analysis of the impact of print culture on
all ranks of society; (3) the history of book production and the economics of publishing, most notably the repercussions of the transition from aristocratic patronage to
publishing by subscription to 'free-market' bookselling; (4) the analysis of the concept
of 'genius' as it developed in the eighteenth century and came to shape Romantic
notions of creativity; and (5) developments in the genres of the georgic and pastoral
specifically, and in nature writing in general, and the sociocultural determinants
thereof.

Duck's significance to interpretations of how the socio-economic category of class
(or rank) influence notions of literariness and the literary canon has been the focus
of several Marxist studies. H. Gustav Klaus's *The Literature of Labor* asserts Duck's
significance to 'plebeian poetry' in no uncertain terms. Klaus argues first that
'Possibly Duck's greatest merit is his intuitive recognition that work is a theme
worthy of literary treatment' (11) and second that Duck's true originality can be
seen in the fact that 'never before had there been such a truthful description of
workaday routine in verse' (12). In explicitly Marxist terms, Klaus asserts: 'I know
of nothing else written in the first half of the eighteenth century which comes
anywhere near [Duck's] realistic representation of . . . the relationship between capitalist (landlord) and (agricultural) laborer' (13). Clearly Klaus was not familiar with
Mary Collier.

It is Duck's status as the foil for working-class *women* writers, most notably Mary
Collier, that has produced the most significant political reassessments of his work.
Critics such as Donna Landry, Moira Ferguson, and Richard Greene have acknowl-

edged Duck's place as a significant forebear of labouring women authors throughout the century. In their efforts to resurrect a separate genealogy for women writers of the labouring classes, Landry, Ferguson and others have given Collier pride of place for her powerful response to Duck in 'The Woman's Labour'. Landry sees Collier's poetic rebuttal of Duck's misogynistic comments in 'The Thresher's Labour' as extending the expression of an 'emergent working-class consciousness' well beyond any effort Duck might have made. These Marxist-feminist critics (along with scholars of Romantic self-taught poets such as Robert Bloomfield, Robert Burns and John Clare) regard Duck as the prototype through and against which subsequent writers of the lower ranks defined themselves. Richard Greene notes, 'Whereas prior to [Duck's] success literate elements in the labouring class had been mainly consumers of literature, now they could take on somewhat more confidently the role of producers in that broader market' (108). Duck's poetry prompted a spate of imitators, first in the 1730s, later in the 1750s and again near the turn of the century. In the 1730s alone, Duck inspired not just Mary Collier, but also Robert Tatersal (*The Bricklayer's Miscellany*), John Bancks (*The Weaver's Miscellany*) and more ephemeral productions by miller Henry Frizzle and groom William Hardy. Duck was even influential in the initial literary success of the footman who went on to be the most powerful publisher of the eighteenth century: Robert Dodsley.

Ideologically linked to the studies of Duck's significance to a plebeian or working-class literary history are those which analyse Duck's poem as an example of 'popular culture', including work by E. P. Thompson and Morag Shiach. Shiach details Duck's importance to the history of 'popular culture' and its production by authors whom she labels 'peasant poets'. However, as Shiach points out, paradoxically, Duck and those who wrote because of him aimed not to represent the labouring classes, but to transcend their station and distance themselves from their rank. Nearly all of Duck's poems reveal that he was not writing to articulate a popular oral culture, but to imitate the written language of refined 'high' culture. Even if a 'common' style did seep in, Duck always aspired to the language of Milton and Pope. As Shiach notes, his writing thus signals and mediates a gap in class cultures, marking early eighteenth-century distinctions between vulgar and learned, between rustic and refined, even as it attempts to erase them.

Duck (though never forgetting his humble origins) did all that he could to purge his subject-matter and style of rusticity. After 'The Thresher's Labour' his poems were more often versifications of scripture or classical translations rather than expressions of a nascent working-class position. Precisely what has made his work vexing for Marxist critics who wish to coopt Duck as a decisive predecessor for a proletarian poetics is the rapidity with which he seems to have been mystified by more aristocratic notions of literary propriety. Critics today often anachronistically fault Duck for not consistently speaking for the masses. As Linda Zionkowski notes, 'Duck's verse ratifies elite literary conventions. In fact, Duck adds to the authority of such conventions and practices by ultimately adopting them and by proposing few alternatives derived from his native culture' (95). Duck is described as writing like the poets he admired and not according to how the liberal-minded late twentieth-century critics think he ought to have written. Zionkowski continues that Duck

> may have owed his recognition as an 'Excellent Poet' not to the essential greatness of his poems, but to his skill in adopting a style that sophisticated readers considered 'poetic'. Despite class boundaries, Duck and his patrons shared the same canon and held common beliefs about what constitutes poetry – a coincidence that the commerce in letters had only recently made possible. (93)

Such a claim controverts the notion that Duck had a distinct popular or 'native culture' that he wrote from and about.

Recent criticism discussing the relationship between Duck and his patrons has demonstrated that Duck's allegiance to his high-ranking aristocratic patrons, including Queen Caroline, further troubles Marxist arguments for Duck as a proto-proletariat. The fact that a labourer such as Duck, prior to taking up the pen, would have studied the work of Milton or of Addison might signal a 'democratization' in the realm of literary education (and in literacy demographics in general) and in the book market more specifically. But it did not necessarily indicate the liberalization of the publishing industry.

In *Literary Patronage in England, 1650–1800*, Dustin H. Griffin asserts that 'reports of the decline and death of patronage *c*.1750 are not only highly derivative, but considerably exaggerated' (1996, 247). Griffin reveals that although traditional 'single-source' patronage had begun to erode, for most of the century it coexisted with other forms of financing book production, most notably publishing by subscription. Both methods supported Duck's work; however, the magnanimity of Queen Caroline's gifts to the poet between 1730 and her death in 1737 has led many to assume that Duck's patronage was a vestigial example of traditional patronage by the nobility, and one that, moreover, stood as a last-ditch aristocratic effort to exert control over nascent voices emerging from the lower classes. Zionkowski, for instance, views Caroline's patronage as contributing to the 'containment' of the potential challenge that Duck's writing might have posed to the cultural status quo.

However Caroline's patronage of Duck was more complicated than simple royal condescension or an attempt to limit the incursions of a thresher poet. As Betty Rizzo argues, Caroline's actions may have had more to do with her revenge against the impeccably erudite Alexander Pope (who had impugned her taste in the *Dunciad*) than with an interest in supporting the thresher poet. Rizzo claims that

> Caroline's patronage of Stephen Duck was a rejoinder well-calculated and stinging: natural genius was superior to art and education. Her patronage of Duck, the brilliant exploitation of an accidental opportunity, served both to provide a fashionable model for future patrons and to perpetuate her quarrel with Pope. He was to capitalize upon her taste in poets to establish her dullness; she was to heap benefits on Duck to show how complaisance combined with true genius was rewarded. (1990, 244–5)

As a natural or uneducated writer, Duck was the perfect foil to Pope (who it should be noted, along with Swift, subscribed to Duck's 1736 volume).

Rizzo asserts that patrons such as Queen Caroline manipulated the concept of genius to better market their own aesthetic agenda through the labourer poets. As Jonathan Bate notes, although the OED dates the modern idea of genius from mid-century, the concept finds its first articulation in Addison's *Spectator* no. 160 (an essay it is almost certain that Duck had read, given his externally documented appetite for Addison's essays). Rizzo makes a case for the way in which the idea of genius, which was by definition natural and incapable of being acquired by education, was used by women and bourgeois patrons to assert their taste and their power over a formally educated, male, aristocratic patronage system. Although Duck, in having carefully studied Milton, may have had a better literary education than many twentieth-century undergraduates, the concept of natural genius helped to account for his skill. Because a majority of readers would doubt that a rural 'clown' could produce couplets, natural genius provided a means to justify his unprecedented success. Reading Duck in relation to the aesthetic category of natural genius is thus not merely another way to 'contain' his significance. Instead, it suggests that Duck belongs to another important literary lineage – the heritage of writers contributing to the development of the Romantic aesthetic. M. H. Abrams argues in *The Mirror and the Lamp* that the Enlightenment concepts of poetic genius gave rise to Romantic notions of creativity. These same theories of genius can be seen in contemporary critical discussion of Duck's first volume, making Duck arguably one of the earliest pre-Romantic poets.

It is not merely through the notion of genius that Duck is important to what would later be appropriated as Romantic concerns. With 'The Thresher's Labour', Duck explores the varieties of the human relationship to the natural world. In *The Country and the City*, Raymond Williams has provided one of the strongest reappraisals of Duck's place in the history of writing about the rural environment. Focusing specifically on transformations of the genre of the pastoral as a barometer of the national consensus on the value of rustic life, Williams sees Duck's poem as a part of the tradition of the 'counterpastoral' that reaches its apogee with more powerful poems of rural deracination and destruction such as Goldsmith's 'The Deserted Village', and which continued to find expression in the poetry of John Clare in the 1820s and beyond.

Some of the most significant recent criticism of Duck's work has analysed its place in surveys of the artistic, political and scientific conceptions of rural life in the eighteenth century. John Barrell, for example, has compared Duck's poetic representation of agricultural labour to those found in contemporary visual arts. According to Barrell, 'The Thresher's Labour' is innovative because it refuses to depict rural work as festive and merry (as Thomson had presented it in *The Seasons* and as many painters did as well). Barrell asserts that Duck's realism undermines the arcadian depictions of the efforts of rural labourers 'and repeatedly showed it up as at best wishful thinking on behalf of the polite classes, at worst as a 'Cheat', an instance of how the exploited can imbibe the ideology of their exploiters' (120).

In *Rural Life in Eighteenth-century Poetry*, John Goodridge accords Duck the same degree of creative agency and originality, but reads his poem at an even more productive level of complexity. Goodridge documents Duck's careful accuracy in representing agricultural labour in his poem. Perhaps more significantly, Goodridge argues for Duck's poetic talents – demonstrating, with incontrovertible external evidence, that Duck may have influenced Thomson's *The Seasons* (and not the other way around, as is often asserted). By analysing how Duck vexes the genre categorizations of the pastoral and georgic, Goodridge is further able to support his thesis that Duck's originality is in developing a proletarian anti-pastoral. Emphasizing issues of form (and not merely content), Goodridge succeeds where earlier Marxist critics had failed, establishing Duck's discursive contribution to literary history.

It deserves to be repeated that Duck's relevance to cultural history depends largely on a single poem, 'The Thresher's Labour'. With the significance of this poem determined, critics ought to consider other pieces from *Poems on Several Occasions*. For example, at the time of the collection's publication, Duck's patrons felt his biblically inspired tale 'The Shunamite' was his finest accomplishment. The subject-matter of 'The Shunamite' offers interesting clues into Duck's sense of himself and his literary production, for it is not difficult to surmise that he may have identified with his disempowered heroine. In addition, the poem underscores how Duck, and other self-taught poets after him, were especially fond of versifying scripture. Mary Collier's second best-known poem, 'The Three Wise Sentences of Esdras', drew from a biblical intertext. A survey of the tradition of laboring-class poets from Duck to the nineteenth century reveals that the Hebrew Bible, in particular, was a frequent source of inspiration. This should not be surprising given that it was to read the Bible that early charity schools and later Sunday schools provided literacy education. The Bible was a part of the literary canon open to all ranks of society, regardless of their knowledge of Latin or Greek. Much work remains to be done on the relationship between religious texts (such as the Bible, sermons, and popular conduct books) and labouring-class poetry in the first half of the eighteenth century.

Duck's poems 'On Richmond Park' and 'Royal Gardens' should be re-examined in analyses of poetry devoted to gardens and gardening, alongside works such as Pope's 'Epistle to Burlington' and later garden writings including those of Duck's patron, Joseph Spence and his friend William Shenstone. While neither of these poems express a proletariat anti-pastoral perspective, they deserve to be included among the innumerable topographical and 'prospect' poetry produced throughout the century, all the more so because they prove how all ranks of society actively linked nationalism with landscape and landscape gardening. Finally, poems such as 'A Description of A Journey' should also be considered within that spectrum of art and literature displaying the shifting perspective on rural life in the eighteenth century. Written six years after Duck had been discovered, this poem narrates his return to his native village and marks the distance – physical, intellectual, ideological – that Duck had traversed. Once he had left the countryside for the court, his poetry articulates the separation of the literary and the laborious, allowing the text, more so than 'The

Thresher's Labour', to be read as an early and profound example of the poetry of rural deracination. It is a poem of what would become characteristic nostalgia, commemorating an irreparably lost affiliation with the countryside.

Just as 'The Thresher's Labour' has contributed to expanding an understanding of the dimensions of labouring-class poetry, of the varieties of popular culture, of poetry about labour and about nature, so too can a re-examination of several of Duck's other works (and a reinsertion of them into anthologies of Restoration and eighteenth-century literature) expand our appreciation of Duck as more than just 'a poor fellow in a barn'.

References and Further Reading

Abrams, M. H. (1953). *The Mirror and the Lamp*. New York: Oxford University Press.

Addison, Joseph (1883). *The Works of Joseph Addison*. 6 vols. Philadelphia: J. B. Lippincott and Co.

Bancks, John (1730) *The Weaver's Miscellany: Or, Poems on several Subjects by John Bancks, Now a Poor Weaver in Spittle-Fields*.

Bate, Jonathan (1989). 'Shakespeare and original genius'. In *Genius: The History of an Idea*. Ed. Penelope Murray. Oxford: Blackwell, 76–97.

Collier, Mary (1739). *The Woman's Labour*.

——(1762). *Poems on Several Occasions*.

Davis, Rose Mary (1926). *Stephen Duck: The Thresher Poet*. Orono: University of Maine Press.

Dodsley, Robert (1729). *Servitude: A Poem*.

——(1732). *A Muse in Livery*.

Duck, Stephen (1730). *Poems on Several Subjects Written by Stephen Duck*.

——(1736). *Poems on Several Occasions*.

——(1753). *The Beautiful Works of Stephen Duck*.

Ferguson, Moira (1995). *Eighteenth-century Women Poets: Nation, Class and Gender*. Albany: State University of New York Press.

Goodridge, John (1989). 'Some predecessors of Clare: Stephen Duck'. *The John Clare Society Journal* 8, 5–10.

——(1990). 'Some predecessors of Clare 2: responses to Duck'. *The John Clare Society Journal* 9, 17–26.

——(1995). *Rural Life in Eighteenth-century Poetry*. Cambridge: Cambridge University Press.

Greene, Richard (1993). *Mary Leapor: A Study in Eighteenth-century Women's Poetry*. Oxford: Clarendon Press.

Griffin, Dustin H. (1996). *Literary Patronage in England, 1650–1800*. Cambridge: Cambridge University Press.

Klaus, H. Gustav (1985). *The Literature of Labour: Two Hundred Years of Working-class Writing*. Brighton: Harvester.

Landry, Donna (1990). *The Muses of Resistance: Laboring-class Women's Poetry in Britain, 1739–1796*. Cambridge: Cambridge University Press.

Rizzo, Betty (1990). 'The patron as poet maker: the politics of benefaction'. *Studies in Eighteenth-century Culture* 20, 241–66.

Shiach, Morag (1989). *Discourse on Popular Culture: Class, Gender and History in the Analysis of Popular Culture*. Oxford: Polity Press.

Tatersal, Robert (1734–5). *The Bricklayer's Miscellany: Or Poems on Several Subjects, &c. written by Robert Tatersal, A Poor Country Bricklayer, of Kingston upon Thames, in Allusion to Stephen Duck*.

Thompson, E. P., ed. (1989). *The Thresher's Labour by Stephen Duck/The Woman's Labour by Mary Collier*. London: Merlin Press.

——(1993). *Customs in Common: Studies in Traditional Popular Culture*. New York: New Press.

Williams, Raymond (1975). *The Country and the City*. New York: Oxford University Press.

Zionkowski, Linda (1989). 'Strategies of containment: Stephen Duck, Ann Yearsley, and the problem of polite culture'. *Eighteenth-century Life* 13, 91–108.

30

Mark Akenside, *The Pleasures of Imagination*

David Fairer

During the 1760s Mark Akenside (1721–70), the son of a Newcastle butcher, was at the head of his profession as one of the Queen's doctors and chief physician at St Thomas's Hospital in London. Yet in his spare hours he still worked on endlessly revising *The Pleasures of Imagination*, the poem that had made him a star of the literary world at the age of twenty-two. On seeing the work in manuscript the great Pope is said to have remarked that 'this was no everyday writer', and after its anonymous publication in 1744 it reached a fourth edition by the end of the year. This philosophical poem became much admired, and its wide influence extended to Wordsworth, Coleridge and Keats, each of whom drew from it in different ways. After various stages of revision Akenside decided (according to the advertisement to the posthumous edition of his *Poems*, 1772) to 'write the Poem over anew upon a somewhat different and an enlarged Plan', but this re-structured and substantially rewritten version in five books with its new title *The Pleasures of the Imagination* was never finished. The 1772 *Poems* printed both texts. The poem discussed in this chapter is the original three-book version as revised for the third edition in May 1744.

A philosophical poem nowadays seems a contradiction in terms. Either the delights of the 'poetry' somehow compromise the argument, or 'thought' gains the upper hand and produces a dry theoretical treatise – 'Do not all charms fly / At the mere touch of cold philosophy?' This is Keats's comment in *Lamia* (1820), a poem which stages a confrontation between philosophy's 'truth' and imagination's 'fiction' when the bald-headed philosopher Apollonius destroys Lycius's dream-lover with his chilly gaze. In fact Keats is posing a question which had concerned eighteenth-century philosophers and poets, and which formed the subject of Akenside's *The Pleasures of Imagination*: to what extent is the human imagination compatible with reason (or judgement)? Can the worlds of beauty and of truth be drawn together?

At the end of Keats's 'Ode on a Grecian Urn', the urn famously declares that they can: 'Beauty is truth, truth beauty – that is all / Ye know on earth, and all ye need to know'. This message is specifically a Greek one, and it comes from the world of

Plato's *Symposium*, where 'the Beautiful' (*to kalon*) is the highest truth of all. Through contemplation of physical beauty the human soul can by stages come to know the form of the beautiful itself, the Platonic 'idea' which is the true reality beyond this earthly life. Here below we experience shadowy reflections, a sensual truth of mere appearance. Akenside's poem delivers a similar message to that of Keats's urn:

> Thus was beauty sent from heav'n,
> The lovely ministress of truth and good
> In this dark world: for truth and good are one,
> And beauty dwells in them, and they in her,
> With like participation. Wherefore then,
> O sons of earth! would you dissolve the tye?
>
> (I.372–7)

Both messages are addressed from the Platonic dimension to the 'sons of earth' who are forced to use abstract nouns like 'beauty', 'truth' and 'good' to describe what they think they know. Keats's Greek vase suggests this is all we 'need' to know (his work of art holds a deeper secret), but Akenside's poem, an extended argument rather than a compressed lyric, opens out this enigma in different ways and makes it part of a wider discussion of the faculty of imagination itself.

For Akenside, imagination is the mediator between the internal world of the human mind and the external world, and it draws together the aesthetic order (beauty) and the moral order (truth and virtue). In his preface to the poem, he explains:

> There are certain powers in human nature which seem to hold a middle place between the organs of bodily sense and the faculties of moral perception: They have been call'd by a very general name, THE POWERS OF IMAGINATION . . . the author's aim was not so much to give formal precepts, or enter into the way of direct argumentation, as by exhibiting the most ingaging prospects of nature, to enlarge and harmonize the imagination, and by that means insensibly dispose the minds of men to the same dignity of taste in religion, morals, and civil life.

Akenside's unnamed opponents here are the materialist philosopher Thomas Hobbes and his followers. Hobbes's influential *Leviathan* (1651) argued that imagination is merely 'decaying sense', a store of sense impressions in the memory, which without the guidance of rational judgement is deceptively wayward and can lead to madness. In itself it is certainly not the path to truth (for Hobbes there is no 'higher' truth than observed reality). The importance of reason in guiding imagination had long been part of Renaissance humanist thinking, but a strong neo-platonic tradition also maintained that the imagination could at its highest guide the contemplative 'intellect' (a superior faculty to discursive reason) and bring the *gnosis* or divine vision of the true 'reality'. This dualistic view of human nature (as a paradoxical combination of angelic and bestial) was rejected by Hobbes, whose materialism dispensed with notions of the 'higher' or 'divine' elements of 'the soul'. From the 1660s Hobbes's view became widely accepted.

In striking back, Akenside draws on the writings of several anti-Hobbes philosophers who reasserted imagination's higher powers, especially the Earl of Shaftesbury's *Characteristicks* (1711) and his pupil Francis Hutcheson's *Inquiry into the Original of our Ideas of Beauty and Virtue* (1725). Shaftesbury offered a strongly neo-platonic ideal of 'Virtue' as a state of harmony between the individual and the system of 'Nature', and Hutcheson, working between the material and the ideal, stressed the capacity of the mind to rise from sensual images to intellectual/moral ideas. The opening lines of *The Pleasures of Imagination* put into verse Shaftesbury's concept of the 'frame of nature':

> With what attractive charms this goodly frame
> Of nature touches the consenting hearts
> Of mortal men; and what the pleasing stores
> Which beauteous imitation thence derives
> To deck the poet's, or the painter's toil.
>
> (I.1–5)

In reading Akenside it helps to be aware of the philosophical intricacies of his vocabulary. The Shaftesburian word *frame* implies divine workmanship (we recall Hamlet's 'this goodly frame, the earth'); *attractive* means not only 'lovely', but 'spiritually magnetic, drawing things together'; and *consenting* has the added etymological nuance of 'feeling together, being in harmony with'. Having established the wider 'frame' of his own poem, Akenside quickly moves (lines 3–5) to the importance within this scheme of aesthetic pleasure: his own poem will celebrate the human soul's 'relish' for the beauty and wonder of the natural world and art's ability to capture it.

Here Akenside's model is Joseph Addison, whose extended essay on 'The Pleasures of the Imagination' (published in *The Spectator* 1712) lies behind not just Akenside's title, but much of Book One. In *Spectator* no. 10 Addison had remarked: 'I shall be ambitious to have it said of me, that I have brought Philosophy out of Closets and Libraries, Schools and Colleges, to dwell in Clubs and Assemblies, at Tea-Tables, and in Coffee-Houses', and Akenside's poem shows a similar conviction that philosophical ideas should become part of the sociable public world, and that human pleasure is something deserving study. Addison was a pioneer of eighteenth-century 'aesthetics', that branch of philosophy which is interested in the art-work (especially poetry and the visual arts), its creation/response mechanisms, and the theories of beauty etc. supporting them.

Addison's essay distinguished three categories of imaginative pleasure: the 'great' (the sublime and astonishing), the 'uncommon' (the various and surprising), and the 'beautiful' (colour, symmetry and proportion), and in the first book of *The Pleasures of Imagination* Akenside discusses his equivalent: 'Three sister-graces, whom the painter's hand, / The poet's tongue confesses; the *sublime*. / The *wonderful*, the *fair*' (I.144–6). In considering each of these, however, he tends to move away from Addison's empirically based analysis and explore their transcendent potential. The *sublime*, for example, leads him on a neo-platonic ascent of mind adapted to the more modern concept of intergalactic travel, during which the 'high-born soul'

> Exulting circles the perennial wheel
> Of nature, and looks back on all the stars,
> Whose blended light, as with a milky zone,
> Invests the orient. Now amaz'd she views
> Th'empyreal waste, where happy spirits hold,
> Beyond this concave heav'n, their calm abode;
> And fields of radiance, whose unfading light
> Has travell'd the profound six thousand years,
> Nor yet arrives in sight of mortal things.
>   (I.198–206)

Akenside uses the expansive character of blank verse to convey the range of the human imagination. Whereas Pope in his philosophical poem *An Essay on Man* (1733–4) had exploited the aphoristic tendency of heroic couplets for his philosophical study of human limits, Akenside makes full use of the fluidity of his run-on lines and builds up his argument through long paragraphs. The subject of Akenside's poem is human potential, and he is particularly interested in how ideas and possibilities unfold, in 'what high, capacious pow'rs / Lie folded up in man' (I.222–3). The whole of life grows from the monad, the 'eternal ONE', who 'view'd at large / The uncreated images of things':

>   From the first
> Of days, on them his love divine he fix'd,
> His admiration: till in time compleat,
> What he admir'd and lov'd, his vital smile
> Unfolded into being. Hence the breath
> Of life informing each organic frame,
> Hence the green earth, and wild resounding waves;
> Hence light and shade alternate; warmth and cold.
>   (I.69–76)

The Pleasures of Imagination is particularly concerned with ideas of interconnectedness and organic development, and here the divine *fiat* is not an authoritative declaration of the Word, but a generous and loving awakening to life. Behind Akenside the neo-platonic scholar is the young man who went on to write his doctoral thesis on 'The Origin and Growth of the Human Foetus'.

Akenside's knowledge of ancient Greek literature and philosophy (evident in his many footnotes) was quite precocious, and he draws not only on philosophical writers such as Plato and Aristotle, but on Greek history and politics. This is strategic: *The Pleasures of Imagination* is not purely an aesthetic poem, but one with a sharp political edge in which the democratic freedoms of ancient Greece underpin its philosophic

principles. The young Akenside loudly supported the 'patriot' opposition to Prime
Minister Walpole, and at the age of sixteen published, above the signature 'Britannicus', *The Voice of Liberty; or, a British Philippic*, in which he set out to rouse the
nation's 'public Virtue' by calling for a war with Spain. In the same year as *The Pleasures of Imagination* appeared his *Epistle to Curio*, a satiric attack on William Pulteney
for deserting the opposition cause. It is no surprise, therefore, that in the *Pleasures*
Akenside stresses the union of truth and liberty ('where TRUTH deigns to come, /
Her sister LIBERTY will not be far', I.23–4). Unlike contemporary Britain, Athenian culture knitted society together by noble ideals: 'Genius of ancient Greece! . . .
Bring all thy martial spoils / Thy palms, thy laurels, thy triumphal songs, / Thy
smiling band of arts, thy godlike sires / Of civil wisdom, thy heroic youth / Warm
from the schools of glory' (I.567–90).

Book Two opens by raising the question posed in the last chapter of Longinus's
treatise *On the Sublime*: is liberty essential for a flourishing artistic culture? Akenside
imagines the dawn of a 'radiant æra' in Britain when public virtue and artistic excellence will flourish together as part of 'freedom's ample fabric' ('There shall the Virtues,
there shall Wisdom's train, / Their long-lost friends rejoining, as of old, / Imbrace the
smiling family of arts, / The Muses and the Graces' (II.48–51). The book goes on to
demonstrate how imagination can bring a higher moral truth by giving us an allegorical vision. It consists of a story told by the wise teacher 'Harmodius' (the fact that
he shares his name with the celebrated Athenian freedom-fighter is no coincidence)
in which a youth comes to understand that the virtuous and beautiful need not be
alternatives. Thanks to imagination he is able to reconcile his sublime protectress,
Virtue ('Without whose work divine, in heav'n or earth, / Nought lovely, nought propitious comes to pass', II.383–4), with her beautiful companion, Pleasure ('The fair
Euphrosyné, the gentle queen / Of smiles, and graceful gladness', II.393–4). Unlike
Hercules, who famously had to choose between the two, the young man of imagination can face the pains of life knowing that the ways of heaven are 'just, benevolent
and wise' (II.672).

Book Three juxtaposes the two extremes of imaginative activity: the base imagination which panders to the selfish passions, and the higher vision in which the soul
is ecstatically released through nature and enters into harmony with the eternal world.
The earlier part of the book is a pageant of human folly, reminiscent of Pope's four-
book *Dunciad* published the previous year. Akenside's language takes on a 'sportive'
tone as he pictures an Othello boasting to his naive Desdemona, a plotting courtier,
a haggard former beauty, a resentful cynic, a love-sick romantic, and finally other
groups even more deserving of derision: the timid who compromise with liberty,
honour and virtue, and the ignorant who simply lack moral energy. Akenside's philosophical argument here is that satiric images like these act as a touchstone of true
worth. By a kind of imaginative magnetic attraction, ridicule draws out vice and folly
by capturing its moral deformity: the ridiculous is literally that which can be convincingly ridiculed:

Where'er the pow'r of ridicule displays
Her quaint-ey'd visage, some incongruous form,
Some stubborn dissonance of things combin'd,
Strikes on the quick observer
(III.249–52)

An individual is imprinted with a moral character, 'that secret harmony which blends / Th'æthereal spirit with its mold of clay' (II.280–1), and just as ridicule responds to dissonance, so imagination can draw this harmony out. *The Pleasures of Imagination* closes with a return to that idea. The tone grows more fervent, the verse more buoyant, as we trace the growth of the imaginative individual whose responsiveness to nature becomes increasingly rich and visionary:

Each passing hour sheds tribute from her wings;
And still new beauties meet his lonely walk;
And loves unfelt attract him. Not a breeze
Flies o'er the meadow, not a cloud imbibes
The setting sun's effulgence, not a strain
From all the tenants of the warbling shade
Ascends, but whence his bosom can partake
Fresh pleasure, unreprov'd. Nor thence partakes
Fresh pleasure only: or th'attentive mind,
By this harmonious action on her pow'rs,
Becomes herself harmonious.
(III.591–601)

The responsive human sensibility feels new powers stirring within. For Akenside, the imagination is no mere lumber-room of decaying experience, but an active moral force which delights in its freedom and energy. It would be half a century before Coleridge, in his desperate search for organic unity, would develop the poem's insights into the vital interaction between the imagination and nature.

REFERENCES AND FURTHER READING

Aldridge, A. O. (1945). 'Akenside and Imagination'. *Studies in Philology* 42, 769–92.

——(1949). 'The Eclecticism of Mark Akenside's "The Pleasures of Imagination" '. *Journal of the History of Ideas* 5, 292–314.

Binfield, Clyde (1994). '*The Pleasures of Imagination*: a conundrum and its context'. *Durham University Journal* 55, 227–40.

Dix, Robin (1994). 'Mark Akenside: unpublished manuscripts'. *Durham University Journal* 55, 219–26.

——(ed.) (1996). *The Poetical Works of Mark Akenside*. Madison and Teaneck: Farleigh Dickinson University Press; London: Associated University Presses.

Engell, James (1981). *The Creative Imagination: Enlightenment to Romanticism*. Cambridge, Mass. and London: Harvard University Press. See pp. 42–7, 'Akenside: a cosmic vision'.

Fabel, Kirk M. (1997). 'The location of the aesthetic in Akenside's *Pleasures of Imagination*'. *Philological Quarterly* 76, 47–68.

Griffin, Dustin (1986). *Regaining Paradise: Milton and the Eighteenth Century*. Cambridge: Cambridge University Press. See pp. 110–14.

Hart, Jeffrey (1969). 'Akenside's Revision of *The Pleasures of Imagination*', *PMLA* 74, 67–74.

Houpt, C. T. (1970). *Mark Akenside: A Biographical and Critical Study*. New York: Russell and Russell. First published (1944).

Jump, Harriet Devine (1989). 'High sentiments of liberty: Coleridge's unacknowledged debt to Akenside'. *Studies in Romanticism* 28, 207–24.

Kallich, Martin (1947). 'The association of ideas and Akenside's *Pleasures of Imagination*'. *Modern Language Notes* 62, 166–73.

Marsh, Robert (1961–2). 'Akenside and Addison: the problem of ideational debt'. *Modern Philology* 59, 36–48.

Martin, Philip (1983). 'Keats, Akenside, beauty and truth'. *Notes and Queries* 228, 223–4.

Norton, John (1970). 'Akenside's *The Pleasures of Imagination*: an exercise in poetics'. *Eighteenth-century Studies* 3, (1969–70), 366–83.

Price, Martin (1964). *To the Palace of Wisdom: Studies in Order and Energy from Dryden to Blake*. Carbondale and Edwardsville: Southern Illinois University Press. See pp. 364–6.

Reid, Nicholas (1993). 'Coleridge, Akenside and the Platonic tradition: reading in *The Pleasures of Imagination*'. *Journal of the Australasian Universities Language and Literature Association* 80, 37–56.

Sitter, John (1982). *Literary Loneliness in Mid-eighteenth-century England*. Ithaca and London: Cornell University Press. See pp. 157–75.

Tuveson, E. L. (1960). *The Imagination as a Means of Grace: Locke and the Aesthetics of Romanticism*. Berkeley and Los Angeles: University of California Press.

Wasserman, Earl R. (1953). 'Nature moralized: the divine analogy in the eighteenth century'. *ELH* 20, 39–76.

Whiteley, Paul (1996). '"A manly and rational spirit of thinking": Akenside's *The Pleasures of Imagination* (1744)'. *English* 45, 193–211.

31

William Collins, 'Ode on the Poetical Character'

Katherine Turner

On 20 December 1746 (though bearing the date of 1747 on the title page), a small octavo volume by William Collins, entitled *Odes on Several Descriptive and Allegoric Subjects*, was published by Andrew Millar, one of the most astute and successful London printers of his day. Notwithstanding, Collins's posthumous editor, John Langhorne, in the 1765 edition of the *Poems*, claimed that Collins was so disappointed with the poor reception of his *Odes* that he bought up and burned all the unsold copies from the print-run of 1,000. Collins's frustration was doubtless compounded by the fact that his friend Joseph Warton also published a volume of *Odes* in December 1746, which ran into a second edition in January 1747. Ironically, the two poets, who were friends, had originally planned to publish their odes together, both of them sharing the view expressed by Warton in the 'Advertisement' to his own volume that 'Invention and Imagination [are] the chief faculties of a Poet'. It is unclear why this joint project did not reach fruition, but Roger Lonsdale has suggested that Collins's demand for pre-payment may have encountered resistance from Warton's canny printer, Robert Dodsley, who observed that 'so very few Poems sell, that it is very hazardous purchasing almost any thing' (Lonsdale, 1969, 409).

There is a fitting poignancy in this background to Collins's *Odes* of financial muddle and frustration, given that several of the poems in the volume address the problematic status of poetry and the poet, in an age in which the recent commercialization of literature threatened to destabilize equally recent notions about the sanctity of the poetic imagination. The 'Ode on the Poetical Character' brings into focus these and many other issues. Its seventy-six lines of densely allusive and figurative verse crystallize the literary preoccupations of an age (whether of 'Sensibility', 'anxiety', or innovation) and lay the foundations for later 'Romantic' explorations of poetic genealogy, language and creativity. I propose in this chapter briefly to outline the poem's argument, map out the logic of its allusions, and thereby situate the 'Ode' within a network of contemporary discourses which give the poem its distinctive flavour.

The 'Ode on the Poetical Character', like the other poems in the volume, is a 'Pindaric Ode', a poetic form of dubious lineage and authenticity in Collins's time. Abraham Cowley had first introduced the form into English verse in his stanzaically irregular *Pindarique Odes* (1656), but these were based on a misreading of the Greek poet Pindar (522–442 BC) as simply a passionate disregarder of metrical rules. Collins, a more accomplished classicist, is sensitive to the metre and structure of Pindar's verse, even while he varies it. (Thomas Gray, in 'The Bard' and 'The Progress of Poesy' in 1757, would bring still greater scholarly expertise to bear on the English Pindaric.) The 'Ode on the Poetical Character', like most of the poems in the 1746 volume, alters the Pindaric structure of equally weighted strophe and antistrophe followed by a crisp epode: instead, Collins has a central epode (which has come to be known as a 'mesode', lines 23–54 in this poem) mediating between the strophe (1–22) and antistrophe (55–76). This structure therefore *resists* a sense of climactic closure or resolution, in favour of balanced tension, irresolution, or even (to use Richard Wendorf's phrase), 'structured futility' (Wendorf, 1981, 54). Pindar's odes were generally written for public occasions, such as celebrations of victory in the Greek games, and this declamatory function inheres also in Collins's 'Ode': it is a poem which speaks, albeit obscurely, of shared concerns, not merely of personal anxieties.

The 'Ode' opens with an analogy, introduced by 'As once', which is not finalized until line 17 (a delay which might produce confusion in the innocent reader). In lines 1–16, Collins alludes at length to an episode in Spenser's *Faerie Queene* (Books III and IV), in which Florimel's lost girdle, signifying chastity, is offered as a prize in a competition amongst various ladies: none of them, however, succeeds in wearing it, and their failure obscurely indicates moral disgrace. Within the 'Ode', the 'magic girdle' therefore functions as a symbol for the elusive 'cest' (or belt) of poetic inspiration or 'amplest power': paradoxically, it is both a prize awarded to the true poetical character, and a given attribute that makes true poetic achievement possible. The Spenserian episode is, at line 17, brought into focus as an analogy for the visitation of the poet by 'Fancy', although the syntactical force of 'thus' is vague, and resists any definite sense that this particular poet has actually received the 'godlike gift'.

The mesode (lines 23–54), despite the reference to 'fairy legends' in line 23, moves us into a more robust, Miltonic world: it delineates a myth within which the poet's act of imaginative creation mirrors God's original creation of the universe. This analogy, however, is not straightforward: or, perhaps one should say, analogy overlaps with cause-and-effect, since lines 29–40 re-present the creation of the world as a union between God and Fancy (the 'loved Enthusiast' of line 29), which produces at line 39 the 'rich-haired youth of morn', who may be interpreted as either the sun, or Apollo, or the poet: or indeed all three. The sexual undertones of this passage have been much debated: Richard Wendorf seems closest to the mark when he observes that the imagery of consummation is deliberately open-ended, offering the reader the *option* of comprehending the divine act of creativity through the metaphor of human procreation: the poem thus, again, draws attention to the limitations of poetic representation.

Lines 41–54 describe the creation of the poet's cestus, the 'sainted growing woof'. Although the 'dangerous Passions' are not incorporated into the cestus, the nearness and admiration of 'Wonder' and 'Truth', and in particular of the 'shadowy tribes of Mind' (whose 'braided dance' seems surely to suggest an interweaving into the cestus), blur the distinction between the cestus (and therefore the poet) and these figures, which may well be incorporated into the 'hallowed work'. The mesode, unsettlingly, closes with questions:

> Where is the bard, whose soul can now
> Its high presuming hopes avow?
> Where he who thinks, with rapture blind,
> This hallowed work for him designed?
>   (ll. 51–4)

The following antistrophe flatly refuses to offer an answer, as the scene shifts to Milton's Eden, which is represented (in lines which closely echo *Paradise Lost* IV, 132–8) from the perspective of the would-be invader, Satan. Paul Sherwin observes that even the 'rich-haired youth of morn' of the mesode aligns the poet not with Milton, but with Satan, 'Milton's own antiself and Bloom's archetype of the latecomer poet' (Sherwin, 1977, 32): these alignments, once we reach the antistrophe, suggest that the poet is not only presumptuous and belated, but also – like Satan – filled with despair at his exclusion from bliss.

As the garden is approached, however, this Eden is found to be inhabited not by Adam and Eve, but by relics (or, perhaps, the poetical works) of Milton himself, whose heavenly 'native strains' are favourably contrasted with the amorous poetry of Waller ('myrtle shades' at line 69 denote Venus, to whom that plant was sacred). The traditionally English oak at line 63 on which Milton hung his 'ancient trump' (line 67) represents a native English tradition, whereas Waller's myrtle evokes a spurious and anodyne classicism. The poet's attempts to follow Milton's 'guiding steps' are abruptly and inexplicably nullified:

> In vain – such bliss to one alone
> Of all the sons of soul was known,
> And Heaven and Fancy, kindred powers,
> Have now o'erturned the inspiring bowers,
> Or curtained close such scene from every future view.
>   (ll. 72–6)

The negativity of these closing lines is intense, and may be seen to embody the 'anxiety of influence', the term coined by Harold Bloom with particular reference to later poets' crippling sense of inadequacy in the shadow of Milton. Paradoxically, however, in figuring forth the imaginative landscape of the poet's mind, the 'Ode' has transcended the limitations described in the closing lines. Put another way, the subject matter of poetry has been redefined in the poem: the 'glory' of Milton, and the 'inspiring bowers' of Spenser are no longer available to the poet, but the very nature of poetry, and the newly personified world of 'the shadowy tribes of Mind' have risen to take their place as the preoccupations of modern poetry. John Sitter has suggested that the fall enacted by the 'o'erturned . . . bowers' at line 75 need not be 'any less fortunate than the biblical fall'; it signifies the end of the Edenic stage of English poetry, thus clearing the ground for poetry to assume a redemptive role in modern society (Sitter, 1982, 140). The final image of the closing curtain is suggestive here: most obviously evoking the theatre, it may also be read more positively as an image of domestic enclosure, which signifies the diversion of poetry towards less fanciful, but more grounded and contemporary concerns. Indeed, other Odes in Collins's 1746 volume, far from enacting poetic failure, engage actively with contemporary issues such as the Jacobite rising of 1745–6, the recent war with France and the nature of liberty. Howard Weinbrot has claimed that the five 'patriotic' poems in the volume, which display political engagement and courage, define for us a 'solid poet quite different from the aerial waif now floating in the groves of academe' which the 'Ode on the Poetical Character' would seem to embody (Weinbrot, 1990, 4).

Clearly, though, one would not like to push this upbeat reading of the poem's conclusion too far. There is no doubt that the 'Ode' is deeply concerned with the inaccessibility of true poetic greatness, with (to use Paul Sherwin's phrase), a 'spiritual Calvinism' whereby 'there is a poetic elite and he is unworthy to join it' (Sherwin, 1977, 33). The questions at the end of the mesode ('Where is the bard . . .?') remain unanswered, clearly implying that there is no contemporary poet worthy of the bardic label which Spenser and Milton have sanctified. However, Bloom's paradigm of the 'anxiety of influence', which operates on a psychoanalytical level, can fruitfully be refocused, and the poem shown to embody transitional anxieties of a different, though complementary, nature. It is to these that we now turn.

Deborah Heller has observed that the 'Ode on the Poetical Character' (like the 'Ode to Fear' in the same volume) is 'menaced by a suspicion that where the eyes are active the poetical spirit will not be' (Heller, 1993, 104). Milton's inspired blindness becomes crucial in this context. Heller relates Collins's distrust of the visual to developments in eighteenth-century aesthetics, especially Addison's formulation of the 'Pleasures of Imagination': these essays, published in *The Spectator* during 1712, popularized an empirical model of perception, which could give rise to picturesque or allegoric-descriptive poetry in the manner of Thomson, but which could not aspire to the non-visual, or visionary realm. Blanford Parker's study of *The Triumph of Augustan Poetics* has delineated the political and philosophical backlash, in the wake of the English Civil War, against baroque modes of visionary analogy and imagination, in favour of Augustan naturalism and literalism. For the post-Lockean poet, the figuring forth of an eternal, spiritual order, such as the worlds of Spenser and Milton, was no longer possible, and Collins's 'Ode' gives potent voice to this sense of loss, not only of a poetic epistemology but also of the kind of religious sensibility which was able to visualize the sacred through symbol and metaphor. The same elegiac impulse is evident in the work of Collins's contemporaries, such as Thomas Gray, the Warton brothers, and Edward Young. It may be relevant in this context that during his dying months of madness, Collins, as Johnson recalls, 'had withdrawn from study, and travelled with no other book than an English Testament, such as children carry to the school: when his friend took it into his hand, out of curiosity to see what companion a man of letters had chosen, "I have but one book", said Collins, "but that is the best" (Johnson, II, 315). Thus, the crisis of poetic faith which the ode embodies is also a crisis of religious faith, which has to wait, for resolution, for the reclamation of imagination and vision by early 'Romantic' poets such as Blake and Smart.

If Collins's was a sceptical age philosophically speaking, then this scepticism also extended to the acts of reading and interpretation. The mid-eighteenth century witnessed the rise of criticism and exegesis of native literary texts, activities which had previously been reserved for the Bible and the classics. The editing of Shakespeare had begun in earnest with Pope's erratic edition of 1723–5 – mocked by Lewis Theobald in *Shakespeare Restored* in 1726 – and Theobald's own more rigorous version in 1733. In 1743, Collins himself penned an enthusiastic 'Epistle: Addressed to Sir Thomas Hanmer, on his Edition of Shakespeare's Works'. Arguments about textual variants and possible corruptions began to proliferate, nowhere more bizarrely than in the case of Milton, when the great classical scholar Richard Bentley published his annotated edition of *Paradise Lost* in 1732. Bentley claimed that Milton's reliance on an amanuensis had allowed all manner of errors to creep into the text, many of which had been deliberately inserted. Moreover, 'the friend or Acquaintance, whoever he was, to whom *Milton* committed his copy and the overseeing of the press, did so vilely execute that trust, that *Paradise* under his Ignorance and Audaciousness may be said to be *twice lost*' ('Preface': fonts reversed). Bentley therefore took it upon himself to provide numerous marginal corrections, further elaborated in footnotes. His suggested alterations generally replace Milton's unflinching vigour with an anodyne cheerfulness, and are frequently hilarious, as indeed are his grounds for making them: at Book X, lines 717–18, he simply observes that 'I am at present too much tired, to shew the Faults of this Distich; which will be seen quicker by amending them' (333).

Pope's *Dunciad Variorum* in 1729 parodied the growing rage for annotation and interpretation, which not only created employment for the rising numbers of professional (or 'hack') critics, but also began to undermine notions of textual stability and absolute poetic truth. In this context, Collins's opening lines to the 'Ode', 'As once, if not with light regard / I read aright that gifted bard', take on a playfully sceptical tone. They echo Spenser's own 'Full hard it is (quoth he) to read aright' (*Faerie Queene* I, ix, 6, 6): but Spenser is referring to 'The course of heauenly cause, or . . . / The secret meaning of th'eternall might' (I, ix, 6, 7–8), whereas for Collins uncertainty resides in the meaning of literary texts. The inscrutable symbolism of the 'Ode', and the peculiar use that the poem makes of the Spenserian girdle story, may both be seen as dramatizations of the interpretative difficulties facing the modern reader-poet. Then as now, textual obscurity opens up a wealth of possible meanings, but also runs the risk of confusion and frustration.

Finally, the 'Ode' may be seen to embody another potent mid-eighteenth-century anxiety, which concerns gender. Paul Sherwin has observed that by the end of the poem, 'Collins's original muse, Fancy or the principle of imaginative creation, has been exchanged for Milton: a masculine muse intervening between Collins and Fancy' (Sherwin, 1977, 36). One might take this argument further, and view the hesitancy of the modern poet in terms of his problematic masculinity. The 'blest prophetic loins' (line 21), which may or may not be girded by the heat of poetic inspiration, are more aggressively masculine than the comparable image in the probable source for this line, Akenside's ode 'On the Absence of the Poetic Inclination': 'Where is the bold prophetic heat, / With which my bosom wont to beat?' (ll. 5–6). In Collins's version, a more potent masculinity seems to be a condition of poetic blessedness. This suggestion is reinforced in the poem's closing lines, where the poet is ambivalently positioned between Waller and Milton: Waller's verse was regarded in Collins's time not only as generally amorous (and therefore effeminate), but also as one of the first poetry of Augustan correctness. It is intriguing, then, that the lines immediately following the reference to Waller are redolent of Pope, whose work not only represents the zenith of Augustan correctness but also begins to redefine masculine virtue, incorporating qualities such as feeling, sensibility, even fearfulness into the figure of the good man and poet. As Lonsdale has observed, line 71 of the 'Ode' ('My trembling feet his guiding steps pursue') alludes to the *Essay on Criticism*, where Pope addresses the 'bards triumphant' of 'happier', ancient days:

> Oh may some spark of *your* celestial fire
> The last, the meanest of your sons inspire,
> (That on weak wings, from far, pursues your flights;
> *Glows* while he *reads*, but *trembles* as he *writes* . . .)
>   (ll. 195–8, cited in Lonsdale, 435)

The virtues of sensibility and humility which, with Pope, begin to assert their poetic validity have their own tremulous power, but Collins laments the fact that they cannot hope to achieve Miltonic glory. The final line of the 'Ode' again alludes to Pope, this time to an image of domestic swaddling by the oppressive figure of Dulness – 'Him close she curtains round with vapours blue' (*Dunciad* III, 3) – and enacts a deep uncertainty as to whether the heroic energies of Milton's age can ever be recuperated within the changed social, literary and religious landscape of the mid-eighteenth century. That the 'Ode' can articulate so many of the concerns of Collins's age, however, testifies to its own complex and ambivalent power.

REFERENCES AND FURTHER READING

Akenside, M. (1745). *Odes on Several Subjects*. London: Dodsley.

Bloom, H. (1973). *The Anxiety of Influence*. New York: Oxford University Press.

Heller, D. (1993). 'Seeing but not believing: the problem of vision in Collins's odes'. *Texas Studies in Literature and Language* 35, 103–23.

Johnson, S. (1781). 'William Collins'. In *Lives of the English Poets*. London: J. M. Dent (1964–5). Vol. 2, 313–16.

Lonsdale, R. (1969). *Gray, Collins & Goldsmith: The Complete Poems*. London and New York: Longman.

Parker, B. (1998). *The Triumph of Augustan Poetics: English Literary Culture from Butler to Johnson*. Cambridge: Cambridge University Press.

Sherwin, P. (1977). *Precious Bane: Collins and the Miltonic Legacy*. Austin: University of Texas Press.

Sitter, J. (1982). *Literary Loneliness in Mid-eighteenth-century England*. Ithaca and London: Cornell University Press.

Warton, J. (1746). *Odes on Various Subjects*. London: Dodsley.

Weinbrot, H. (1990). 'William Collins and the mid-century ode: poetry, patriotism, and the influence of context'. In *Context, Influence, and Mid-Eighteenth-Century Poetry*. Ed. H. D. Weinbrot and M. Price. Los Angeles: William Andrews Clark Memorial Library, 3–39.

Wendorf, R. (1981). *William Collins and Eighteenth-Century Poetry*. Minneapolis: University of Minnesota Press.

Woodhouse, A. S. P. (1965). 'The poetry of Collins reconsidered'. In *From Sensibility to Romanticism: Essays Presented to F. A. Pottle*. Ed. F. W. Hilles and H. Bloom. New York: Oxford University Press, 93–137.

32

Samuel Richardson, *Clarissa*

Tom Keymer

There is a startling disproportion of scale between story and discourse in *Clarissa*, between the agonizing simplicity of the novel's plot and the agonized mass of writing that circles around it. Before publication (or in a phase of *Clarissa*'s history that resembles earlier practices of scribal publication), the novel passed among at least a dozen readers in several separate transcriptions, one of which weighed in at thirty manuscript volumes. When Richardson finally went to press in 1747–8, he could limit the text to seven volumes only by switching to smaller type towards the close, and the slow schedule of serialization (which roughly matched the duration of the action) meant that it took the public a year to read the work. By the third edition of 1751, *Clarissa* had been swollen to eight volumes and three thousand pages by Richardson's decision to restore previously deleted passages, insert fresh text, and expand the apparatus to include an amplified preface and postscript, new explanatory footnotes, and two elaborate indexes. Readers of today most often encounter *Clarissa* in a volume built like a telephone directory (Angus Ross's Penguin edition of 1985, to which page-reference is made in this chapter), and it takes 12,763 kilobytes to accommodate the first and third editions in Chadwyck-Healey's website, *Literature Online*. As one of the leading printers of his day, and one whose writing creatively exploits the resources and technologies of his profession, Richardson would have relished this last innovation. Yet the immateriality of electronic text only points up by contrast the daring of *Clarissa*'s original bulk in a culture overwhelmed (according to the Scriblerian analysis) by bales of paper and mass-produced print.

In terms of narrative content, moreover, there can seem little more to all this bulk than to the fugitive amatory fiction of the 1720s (a genre disparaged but also, as Margaret Doody has shown, creatively exploited in Richardson's writing). Some readers have found even less. 'There *is* no Story,' as Hester Piozzi put it sixty years later: 'A Man gets a Girl from her Parents – violates her Free Will, & She dies of a broken heart. That is all the Story' (Smith, 1984, 48). Yet Piozzi could combine this curt summary with a larger view of *Clarissa* as the '*best* of all possible Novels', and she elsewhere records with approval Samuel Johnson's judgement that *Clarissa* was 'a prodigious Work – formed on the stalest of all empty Stories' (Clifford, 1987, 437). How might such paradoxical views be sustained? How might we justify an assessment of *Clarissa* (in one recent restatement) as 'a transformation of the clichés of the amatory pattern into a monumental novel without parallel in English or in European fiction' (Richetti, 1999, 99)?

One way might be to argue that *Clarissa*'s seeming emptiness of plot is only the first of its illusions. Vacuous in itself, the amatory frame was a capacious space in which Richardson could rework and conflate the most powerful of traditions and myths – the Fall of man, the rape of Lucretia, the temptation of Job – while testing their resonance in a rigorously particularized modern world. Moreover, by generating his plot from the stratagems of a villain who also resembles a surrogate artist – Lovelace being 'a great plotter and a great writer' (50), a 'master of metamorphoses' (412) and 'the author of this diffusive mischief' (1,446) – he achieves an ingenious generic reflexiveness that looks forward to Sterne. Another way (which I resume below) would be to look harder at Richardson's handling of the other half of the story/discourse dyad, or at other non-narrative aspects of the work like the encyclopaedic integration of opinion and thought that Johnson also praised. But it is worth beginning with closer study of Piozzi's exact words, for even as they seem to dismiss *Clarissa*'s story, they perfectly catch its richness of implication for the culture in which Richardson wrote.

At first sight, there seems little more to these words than circumlocution and cliché. To talk of violating the free will is to tiptoe decorously past the silent centre – Lovelace's despairing, calamitous rape of Clarissa – around which the text revolves. To talk of broken hearts is to use a phrase that was hackneyed even then, while reductively defining an outcome obscure enough to have generated (like almost everything else in the book) competing explanations. Yet Piozzi's words are better chosen than they seem, and they flow from the text itself. When Johnson sought an illustrative quotation for 'violator' in the sense of rapist for his *Dictionary* of 1755, it was naturally to *Clarissa* that he turned. The will and the heart, moreover, are two of the work's key terms, as the most fine-tuned critical readings have revealed. Tony Tanner has described Clarissa as a character 'assailed by the will in all its forms – written, spoken, physical – against which she can only pit the negating will of her spirit', and he notes the insistence throughout the text of 'four distinct manifestations of this ambiguous word (connoting at least intention, volition, aspiration, and desire)' (Tanner, 1979, 101–2). In similar vein, John Mullan credits *Clarissa* with 'an extraordinary concentration of vocabulary (the property of a text which typically works through repetition and increment)', and he finds in its language of feeling both a dramatized struggle for control of hearts and a literary commitment to their elucidation (Mullan, 1988, 64). In these contexts, the force of Piozzi's summary is more clearly seen. By explaining the plot as a struggle for mastery which generates in turn a fight to the death between wills and hearts, she not only cuts to the centre of the novel's thematization of power but also picks up its most weighted terms.

Hearts and Wills

Clarissa was originally published in three instalments, and the first of these (Letters 1–93 in Ross's edition) subjects the state of its heroine's heart and will to protracted scrutiny. For her family, determined to subject her to a mercenary marriage that will advance their ambitions for land, wealth and a peerage, both should submit to their plan. An early indication of the stakes appears when Clarissa's father forbids her 'the opportunity of corresponding with those who harden your heart against his will' (primarily her confidante Anna), and he goes on to threaten that 'he would break your heart, rather than you should break his' (115). For all its preference for pliability over fracture, her mother's insistence 'that your heart, not your knees, must bend' (89) is only slightly less ominous. But the conflict between Clarissa and her kin is a technical one of rights and duties, and not of sentiments alone, and this dimension is reinforced by her insistence that she has no emotional stake in the clandestine attentions of Lovelace. 'They have grounded their principal argument for my compliance with their will upon my acknowledgements that my heart is free' (136), she complains, counter-arguing for her right to resist 'a command which, if insisted upon, will deprive me of my free will' (148). It is on this desire for autonomy that Lovelace plays, with his wily promise 'to restore me to my own free will' (349).

But it is only after Clarissa's flight with Lovelace from her father's house, in an episode poised ambiguously between elopement and abduction, that the greatest battle of wills begins for real. Richardson had as keen a sense of the cliffhanging serial break as any Victorian novelist, and by suspending the action at moments of unresolved crisis (Clarissa's escape from Harlowe Place in the opening instalment; her first escape from Lovelace in the next) he laid himself open to interventions from readers anxious to mould the story to their own desires. The most tenacious was Lady Bradshaigh, who began after the second instalment (Letters 94–231) to press for a happy ending: most of her letters survive, together with her fascinating annotated copy in which she and Richardson pursue their debate in the margins and endpapers of the text. Yet although the second instalment contrives teasing openings towards compromise and union, it is impossible not to read it in retrospect as an increasingly threatening stalemate. Lovelace's third letter of the instalment describes an alarming new environment in which the heart is now eroticized – 'How near, how sweetly near, the throbbing partners!' (400) – but nastily immune to finer feeling: 'when my heart is soft, and all her own', he boasts, 'I can . . . harden myself at once' (402). The will instead must spearhead a war – 'for a warfare it has truly been; and far, very far, from an amorous warfare too' (401) – in which Lovelace combines obsessive pursuit of power with ill-concealed fears of defeat: 'I will see how *her* will works; and how *my* will leads me on . . . And I find, every time I attend her, that she is less in *my* power – I more in *hers*' (402).

As the action progresses, neither his own campaign to secure Clarissa's corruption, nor hers to secure his reformation, is able to prevail, and in the final instalment

(Letters 232–537) Richardson traces the conflict to the kind of logical outcome from which he had shied in the providentialist ending of his earlier novel, *Pamela*. Lovelace rapes Clarissa, though to do so is only to confess his own defeat, for the rape is a 'mere notional violation' which fails to subdue her will: 'And for what should her heart be broken? Her will is unviolated' (916). Repeatedly he acknowledges that his achievement has only been to 'break her heart, but not incline her will' (960), yet he fails to see the irreparability of the break. Even after her death, he continues to allege her perverseness in his chillingly cynical fable of a miser who, robbed of her gold, deliberately wills her own end: 'the sweet miser would break her heart, and die; and how could I help it?' (1,439). Yet for her part Clarissa cannot 'think of taking the violator to my heart' (1,116), and the temporary loss of sanity which occurs as she tries to make sense of the rape in writing (memorably registered in the original editions by a page of skewed type) marks a more permanent disintegration of the self, together with a loss of the will to live, than Lovelace is able to see. Her death leaves him determined to possess as a physical object what he has failed to gain in spirit. In his deranged response to her death, he demands to have her body opened and embalmed: 'But her heart, to which I have such unquestionable pretensions, in which once I had so large a share, and which I will prize above my own, I *will* have' (1,384). He also demands the executorship of her will, insisting that he must be 'the interpreter of hers' (1,385). Richardson gives the will at length, and in the first edition he switches to scriptorial type at Clarissa's signature, as though to authenticate it as the material resurrection of the faculty she has already mourned when complaining that 'a will of my own has been long denied me' (1,191).

Crucially, the will confers on Anna, and on her executor Belford, the task of assembling from the letters of all the parties involved 'a compilement . . . of all that relates to my story' (1,418). Yet even after Clarissa's death there is a strong sense that the power-struggles of her life, rather than being closed in the multi-voiced history envisaged here, will merely be perpetuated in discursive form. The Harlowes too lay claim to executorship of the will, as though to enforce their insistence that they 'intended not to break her tender heart! – But it was the villainous Lovelace who did that – Not any of us!' (1,396). For his part, Lovelace threatens to write an answer to the proposed history, in which, he complains, he will be 'manifestoed against' (1,437).

Fables of Power

For all its vast bulk, then, there is something very concentrated about the novel's preoccupation with struggles for power between and within its protagonists, and it is no coincidence that one of the most influential (though erratic) modern accounts of *Clarissa* has been the Nietzschian reading of William Beatty Warner. The power-struggles, moreover, have often been held to figure larger conflicts. Marxist critics have looked for socio-historical meaning, typically by contrasting the social ideologies and economic interests of the *parvenu* Harlowes, whose obsessive accumulation of capital and land seems to epitomize the acquisitive ethos of the Walpole years (the text implies a setting of 1732), and the aristocratic Lovelace, who sneers at Harlowe Place as 'sprung up from a dunghill' (161) and disdainfully remembers the stock-market frenzies of the previous decade as 'big with national ruin' (816). There is cogency as well as reductiveness in Terry Eagleton's insistence that Richardson's novels are 'great allegories of class warfare, narratives of alliance and antagonism between a predatory nobility and a pious bourgeoisie', and that they are also active instruments in a cultural shift: 'these novels are an agent, rather than mere account, of the English bourgeoisie's attempt to wrest a degree of ideological hegemony from the aristocracy in the decades which follow the political settlement of 1688' (Eagleton, 1982, 4). Historical-materialist interpretation, however, hardly exhausts the action's larger dimensions. *Clarissa* has been equally important for feminist criticism, not only as 'a frightening relocation of the notion of Christian trial in the sexual combat of this world' (Goldberg, 1984, 23) but also, in its opening phase, as a vexed analysis of the rival claims of female autonomy and patriarchal power. In this guise it resumed and complicated the business of the domestic conduct-book tradition, while also inform-ing debates that were to culminate in Hardwicke's Marriage Act of 1753 (which leg-islated to reinforce parental control). Yet in elaborating his story of authority and disobedience, of free will and temptation, Richardson also invokes the intertext of *Paradise Lost*, and in so doing he points up the larger religious angle of its struggles. The identity implied as Lovelace skulks about the perimeter of Clarissa's garden becomes explicit when he compares himself to 'the devil in Milton' (772), and his eventual success in drawing her into the 'wilderness of doubt and error' beyond the garden walls (556) is one that leaves her 'driven out of my paradise' (393), 'miserably fallen' (479). Given Clarissa's apparent status as an exemplary figure, it is here that her rebellion against authority assumes its most troubling implications.

Yet no single system of equivalence governs the text, which shifts between various and often mutually contradictory patterns of identification. Historically more specific associations emerge when we listen to the novel's earliest readers. One of the most fascinating of the debates that Richardson fostered around his text comes in his cor-respondence on filial obedience with Hester Mulso (later Chapone). Intriguingly, their debate moves seamlessly between the spheres of domestic conduct and political theory, with Mulso enlisting radical authorities like Locke and Algernon Sidney, and Richard-son responding with conservative interrogations: 'suppose the parent or the king exert his authority to the grievance of the child, or the subject; who is to be judge of the reasonableness or unreasonableness of the exertion?' (Chapone, 2, 93). In an age which argued its political theory from domestic models, there can be no doubting the larger scope of *Clarissa*'s vocabulary of power. Where Clarissa's father should gently 'prevent a headstrong child, as a good prince would wish to do disaffected subjects, from running into rebellion and so forfeiting everything' (65), he wields instead 'the tyrant word AUTHORITY' (239). The third edition points up the implications of her fate with an usurper who offers to free her 'from ungenerous and base oppression' (3, 13), but who then insists to the point of rape – the most ancient of metaphors (as in the

Lucretia story) for political tyranny – on 'the rights of his own sovereignty' (5, 238). Nor is theory alone in play here. Written during, and published in the aftermath of, the Jacobite rebellion of 1745–6, *Clarissa* not only invokes earlier parallels – 'as Cromwell said, if it must be my head, or the king's' (402) – but also implies a more urgent, though veiled and intermittent, topicality. When Lovelace speaks of the South Sea Bubble as a Trojan horse, 'big with national ruin', he directly echoes propaganda written by his reported model, the Jacobite Duke of Wharton, and printed by Richardson in Wharton's *True Briton* of 1723. Here is one of many allusions that quietly associate Lovelace with Jacobite ideology and invasion, from his early vow to have the upstart Harlowes 'kneel at the foot-stool of my throne' (145) to his final bloody defeat in the guise of De la Tour's 'dear Chevalier' (1,488).

Writing and Authority

In a novel of the period which gives the '45 rebellion a direct and explicit role, Henry Fielding playfully associates his narrative practice with an anti-Jacobite principle of government by contract: he will principally regard his readers' interests as he writes, he declares, 'for I do not, like a *jure divino* tyrant, imagine that they are my slaves or my commodity' (*Tom Jones*, Book 2, ch. 1). Yet there is a sense in which Richardson's narrative practice constitutes a far more radical devolution of power from author to reader. If his verdict on different aspects of *Clarissa*'s struggles is hard to locate, it is not only because of his own internal contradictions as a zealous upholder of paternal authority who was haunted by visions of its illegitimacy, or as a sometime Jacobite printer who was now close to the centre, both personally and professionally, of a Whiggish political establishment. Characteristically shy of public utterance in a personal voice, he eschewed authorial narration in the Fielding mould, and instead distributed his narrative among the epistolary voices of his protagonists. It is reasonable to speculate, indeed, that it was precisely because of his own divided allegiances that he was able (and perhaps impelled) to create and sustain so wide a range of competing voices, and to use them for the articulation, with equal imaginative conviction, of clashing ideologies and discourses.

Inescapably, the compilation of letters envisaged in *Clarissa*'s will – nowhere declared identical with, yet always strongly suggestive of, the novel we read – is devoid of harmony or coherence. Notwithstanding a prefatory assertion that the narrative is written 'while the hearts of the writers must be supposed to be wholly engaged in their subjects' (35), Richardson progressively interrogates traditional notions of epistolary writing as a radically authentic mode of heartfelt sincerity, and instead represents letters (as Johnson was to do in his 'Life of Pope') as deliberate efforts of the will. Clarissa's uncertainty that her early letters from Lovelace are 'the genuine product of his heart' (269) raises early doubts about the form, as does her reluctant acknowledgement of the representational failures of her own letters: 'The heart is very deceitful', she concedes, when Anna alleges self-serving equivocation.

Her Harlowe accusers put it more strongly. When they threaten to 'search your heart to the bottom; that is to say, if your letter be written from your heart' (154), they challenge the basic truth-claims of her narration. When they complain about her 'power of painting her distresses so as to pierce a stone' (1,156) or her expertise in 'making everyone do what you would when wrote' (1,179), they redefine the act of writing as her most forceful weapon of struggle.

It is not only with Clarissa that such problems arise. Among the most quoted passages of the novel is Lovelace's declaration in the third edition that he 'loved Familiar letter-writing . . . above all the species of writing: It was writing from the heart (without the fetters prescribed by method or study) as the very word *Cor-respondence* implied' (269). But in context the cynicism of Lovelace's remark is plain, and though he later assures Belford that 'as much of my heart as I know of it myself will I tell thee' (915), his theory is that it is not only lack of self-knowledge that interferes between heart and text. From the first his narrative is an expression of desire, rather than some mere plodding transcription of the real: the eroticization of writing is clear enough when he proclaims that 'I never had a more illustrious subject to exercise my pen upon' (399), or when he announces himself regardless in his narrative 'of connexion, accuracy, or of anything but of my own imperial will and pleasure' (403). Writing, above all, is an act of the designing mind. Nor is Clarissa herself at all exempt, as he notes when protesting at one 'whole letter so written as to make herself more admired, me more detested' (1,169), or when complaining that 'tho' the lady will tell the truth, and nothing but the truth, yet perhaps she will not tell the whole truth' (1,095). His own more worldly wise sense is that letter-narration is not representation but rhetoric. 'It is much better . . . to tell your own story, when it must be known, than to have an adversary tell it for you' (1,038), he insists, and courtroom analogies are never far from his thinking: 'But he must be a silly fellow who has not something to say for himself, when every cause has its black and its white side. Westminster-hall, Jack, affords every day as confident defences as mine' (1,031).

It is in this increasingly explicit sense that the letter is not a neutral transcription of the heart but a polemical effort of the will – Lovelace's complaint at Clarissa's power to deceive him 'by the premeditation of writing' (1,269) catches the point to perfection – that one sees the full complication, and the superb appropriateness, of Richardson's narrative form. 'There would hardly be a guilty person in the world, were each suspected or accused person to tell his or her own story, and be allowed any degree of credit' (172), as Clarissa sees at an early stage, yet it is in precisely this dilemma that the novel embroils his readers. The battles of wills and struggles for power that constitute the action of the novel spill over into a narrative form in which the various antagonists of the plot perpetuate their antagonisms in writing. The only access to the story is through a vast labyrinth of pleas and accusations, blackenings and whitenings, which exhaustively replays, in the discourse of the novel, the struggles of its plot. In the end, the opposition between story and discourse simply breaks down, and the struggles for mastery and battles of wills that Piozzi found central to *Clarissa*'s plot reveal themselves as equally a feature of its narrative. By distributing the narrative among his warring characters, Richardson restages their conflicts, through every letter of the text, on a vast discursive scale: power becomes the central concern of story and discourse alike.

By relaying the narrative without authorial mediation, moreover, Richardson effectively delegates to the reader his own authorial prerogative in matters of interpretation and judgement, as though in some kind of gesture to the non-absolutist political principles to which he was simultaneously proclaiming affiliation. The analogy is inherent in the language he uses to describe the relations between author and reader, as when he tells Lady Bradshaigh that he will leave much in his last novel, *Sir Charles Grandison*, to the judgement of his 'Sovereign . . . Readers' (Carroll, 280). The delegation was not without its strains, however, and the more authoritarian side of Richardson's personality came to the fore when public reception of *Clarissa* revealed as many different and extreme judgements among readers as are voiced in the text itself. In the second and third editions he was moved to intervene, contriving a more assertive authorial presence in the text by means of a tendentious summary of the action and a series of footnotes designed to legislate on particular interpretative cruxes. Yet he undertook this reassertion of his own authorial will over readers with an implicit recognition of the arbitrariness of the gesture: the second edition's summary, he privately wrote, was 'a Help to their Recollection, and to their Understanding of it, in the Way I chose to have it understood in' (Carroll, 1964, 126). Moreover, he did so half-heartedly: even in the third edition this new interpretative apparatus remains a tiny proportion of the text, confined to its peripheral spaces. Richardson's genius was for the disposition of his writing in such a way as to register the competing ideologies and discourses of different voices, not to impose a singleness of mind that he manifestly lacked himself (even when separated by several years from the original impetus of *Clarissa*'s creation). His genius, to put it another way, was to activate the hearts and wills of his readers, precisely by concealing his own. In whatever version we read his masterpiece today, it is in the ongoing struggles of its characters and voices, and not in any belated resolution of their antagonisms, that its true power lies.

REFERENCES AND FURTHER READING

Barchas, Janine, with Gordon D. Fulton (1998). *The Annotations in Lady Bradshaigh's Copy of Clarissa.* ELS Monograph Series no. 76. Victoria: University of Victoria.

Beer, Gillian (1989). 'Richardson, Milton, and the status of evil'. In *Arguing with the Past: Essays in Narrative from Woolf to Sidney.* Ed. Gillian Beer. London: Routledge, 62–73.

Bueler, Lois E. (1994). *Clarissa's Plots.* Newark: University of Delaware Press.

Carroll, John (1964). *Selected Letters of Samuel Richardson.* Oxford: Clarendon.

Castle, Terry (1982). *Clarissa's Ciphers: Meaning and Disruption in Richardson's Clarissa.* Ithaca: Cornell University Press.

Clifford, James L. (1987). *Hester Lynch Piozzi (Mrs. Thrale).* 2nd edn. Oxford: Clarendon.

Doody, Margaret Anne (1974). *A Natural Passion: A Study of the Novels of Samuel Richardson.* Oxford: Clarendon.

Dussinger, John A. (1989). 'Truth and storytelling in *Clarissa*'. In *Samuel Richardson: Tercentenary Essays*. Ed. Margaret Anne Doody and Peter Sabor. Cambridge: Cambridge University Press, 40–50.

Eagleton, Terry (1982). *The Rape of Clarissa: Writing, Sexuality and Class Struggle in Samuel Richardson*. Oxford: Basil Blackwell.

Eaves, T. C. Duncan and Ben D. Kimpel (1968). 'The composition of *Clarissa* and its revision before publication'. *PMLA* 83, 416–28.

Goldberg, Rita (1984). *Sex and Enlightenment: Women in Richardson and Diderot*. Cambridge: Cambridge University Press.

Golden, Morris (1985). 'Public context and imagining self in *Clarissa*'. *Studies in English Literature 1500–1900* 25, 575–98.

Gordon, Scott Paul (1997). 'Disinterested selves: *Clarissa* and the tactics of sentiment'. *ELH* 64, 473–502.

Gwilliam, Tassie (1993). *Samuel Richardson's Fictions of Gender*. Stanford: Stanford University Press.

Harris, Jocelyn (1987). *Samuel Richardson*. Cambridge: Cambridge University Press.

Keymer, Tom (1992). *Richardson's Clarissa and the Eighteenth-Century Reader*. Cambridge: Cambridge University Press.

Mullan, John (1988). *Sentiment and Sociability: The Language of Feeling in the Eighteenth Century*. Oxford: Clarendon.

Mulso, Hester (1807). 'Three letters on filial obedience'. In *The Posthumous Works of Mrs. Chapone*. Vol. 1, 19–156.

Richetti, John (1999). *The English Novel in History 1700–1780*. London: Routledge.

Smith, Sarah W. R. (1984). *Samuel Richardson: A Reference Guide*. Boston: G. K. Hall.

Tanner, Tony (1979). *Adultery in the Novel: Contract and Transgression*. Baltimore: Johns Hopkins University Press.

Van Marter, Shirley (1975). 'Richardson's revisions of *Clarissa* in the third and fourth editions'. *Studies in Bibliography* 28, 119–52.

Warner, William Beatty (1979). *Reading Clarissa: The Struggles of Interpretation*. New Haven: Yale University Press.

Weinbrot, Howard D. (1996). '*Clarissa*, Elias Brand, and death by parentheses'. In *New Essays on Samuel Richardson*. Ed. Albert J. Rivero. New York: St Martin's Press, 117–40.

Zimmerman, Everett (1996). *The Boundaries of Fiction: History and the Eighteenth-century British Novel*. Ithaca: Cornell University Press.

33

Samuel Johnson, *The Vanity of Human Wishes*

Thomas Kaminski

When *The Vanity of Human Wishes* was first published in 1749, it bore the following subtitle: *The Tenth Satire of Juvenal, Imitated by Samuel Johnson*. The subtitle provides a great deal of useful information for modern readers wondering how to approach this difficult poem. First, it identifies the primary genre of the work as 'satire'. Second, it suggests that what follows will be in essence a version of a poem by Juvenal, the great Roman satirist of the early second century AD. And, third, the poem will not be precisely a translation, but an 'imitation', a term that in Johnson's day suggested that the poet would allow himself considerable freedom in adapting the original material.

The *Vanity* differs from what modern readers expect from a satire. Rather than ridiculing foolish behaviour or sneering contemptuously at the vices of his fellow men, Johnson offers a tour through the false hopes and empty desires that human beings indulge in. He assumes the pose of a dignified moralist, always sober in his observations on man, sometimes saddened by the foolish choices men make. For Johnson, the essence of satire lay in its moral lessons rather than in the scorn it heaps on the wicked or the foolish. And in Juvenal's Tenth Satire, Johnson chose the ancient poem that best reflected his own moral views.

The most fundamental element of Johnson's moral thought is his conviction that all human beings share the same nature and are thus subject to the same desires and deceptions. As a result, Juvenal could write of the unsatisfying nature of human desires during the reign of the Roman Emperor Hadrian, and Johnson could find the same theme just as relevant sixteen hundred years later. It did not matter that Juvenal had been a pagan, probably a Stoic, and Johnson a Christian. In fact, in his poem Johnson attempted to bring the Judeo-Christian religious tradition together with the classical philosophical tradition. Even the title helped accomplish this. The word 'vanity' derives from the Latin *vanitas*, which means 'emptiness'; thus the title sums up Juvenal's main intent, that the things people desire are 'empty', without real value. Yet to readers of Johnson's day, the title would have called to mind the beginning of the Old Testament book of Ecclesiastes: 'Vanity of vanities, all is vanity.'

For Johnson's Christian audience, then, the poem merges classical wisdom with Judeo-Christian truth, both agreeing that worldly possessions cannot satisfy the deepest human needs.

Johnson was writing an *imitation* of Juvenal's poem, not a translation, and if he maintained the overall theme and structure of the original, he felt free to alter its details in ways that would make it more interesting or more accessible to a modern audience. Numerous English authors had imitated classical poems before, most notably Alexander Pope, who had remade many of Horace's satires during the 1730s. It was Pope's practice in his imitations to substitute contemporary figures for those that Horace had ridiculed. Like Johnson he believed that manners might differ from place to place or from age to age, but human nature remained the same. By pointing out modern, more recognizable examples of the same foolish behaviours, he could bring new life to these ancient works. Johnson followed the same general practice in adapting Juvenal, but with one important difference: he found it necessary to soften the harsh tone of Juvenal's work. Juvenal is often fiercely contemptuous of those he depicts. Although he has filled his satire with moral lessons, he sneers at human folly and its self-inflicted misery. Johnson wanted to instruct, not to sneer; and so he was willing to sacrifice the tone of haughty disdain in order to emphasize the work's moral guidance. In addition, Juvenal drew many of his examples of private conduct from the actions of the upper classes of the Roman empire, a society that could often seem shockingly cruel to modern eyes. Johnson adjusted his examples to fit the temper and behaviour of his own time. As a result, even though the two poems cover the same issues, they often have a very different feel. Juvenal's satire has more bite, Johnson's poem more compassion.

In general, Johnson follows the overall structure of Juvenal's poem. Like Juvenal, he begins by asserting the universality of the human tendency to form empty wishes. Both authors agree that the majority of men live in ignorance of what is good for them, and thus they desire the wrong things. Johnson develops this idea with an elaborate image of man as a wanderer in a maze, endangered by snares that his own passions have set for him. (I shall return to this passage below in my treatment of Johnson's style.) And also like Juvenal, Johnson finds the craving for wealth perhaps the most dangerous of men's desires:

> But scarce observ'd the Knowing and the Bold
> Fall in the gen'ral Massacre of Gold;
> Wide-wasting Pest! That rages unconfin'd,
> And crouds with Crimes the Records of Mankind.
> (ll. 21–4)

Although Johnson was sceptical of other moralists' frequent praise of the benefits of poverty, he yields to Juvenal on this point. The poor man, he tells us, inspires envy in no one; he may sleep soundly in his cottage and whistle carelessly as he passes thieves on the road. Still following Juvenal, Johnson closes the introductory portion of the poem with an address to Democritus, who is said to have laughed uncontrollably whenever he looked on the follies of his contemporaries. Johnson's apostrophe to Democritus, though, is really little more than a nod to Juvenal's authority, for Johnson tends not to laugh at his fellow men in the same manner.

In the main body of the poem, Juvenal examines the various things that men desire, illustrating each category with the stories of famous people whose lives were ruined by getting what they wished for. He first explores the desires for power and for military glory, and then turns to the two personal characteristics that human beings are most likely to wish for, long life and beauty. As he works through these same categories, Johnson tends to broaden or generalize Juvenal's material, as well as to update it for eighteenth-century readers. Thus when Juvenal wishes to demonstrate the madness of seeking power, he dwells at length on the fall of Sejanus, the once-powerful minister of the Emperor Tiberius. Johnson begins this section by personifying 'Preferment', the social influence that members of the English aristocracy possessed by which they might enrich their hangers on. Only after this general introduction does he proceed to his specific examples. For Sejanus Johnson substitutes Cardinal Wolsey, the powerful churchman and Lord Chancellor under Henry VIII, whose fall is no less precipitous than that of Sejanus, but whose end is considerably less violent.

Juvenal next turns to eloquence, which for the Romans represented the primary means of achieving political influence. Although it could bring fame, it was in Juvenal's view just as likely to bring trouble. He points to the fate of Demosthenes and Cicero, each the greatest orator of his day, and each killed by a tyrant he had opposed. Such warnings might have been useful for Juvenal's audience, but they were clearly out of place for readers in Johnson's day. Parliamentary eloquence might raise one to heights from which a fall might be painful, but few would feel their lives threatened by political prominence. So Johnson turns to more personally relevant material. He focuses not on political eloquence but on scholarly renown; the fate he fears is not violent death but public neglect. He invites the hopeful student to examine the lives of those who have lived for learning: 'There mark what Ills the Scholar's Life assail, / Toil, Envy, Want, the Patron, and the Jail' (ll. 159–60). In a single couplet he sums up the grim prospects of the would-be scholar – hard work without reward, the neglect of those who promise help, and even debtors prison. Johnson himself had suffered all of these ills, and many readers find this section the most moving part of the poem.

When he turns to military glory, Johnson follows Juvenal more closely than in any other part of the poem, for the obsession with conquest that haunts some men had not changed in sixteen hundred years. Where Juvenal presents the story of Hannibal, Johnson offers that of Charles XII of Sweden, whose early military successes, disastrous defeat at Pultowa, and exile at a foreign court closely mirror the events that Juvenal relates of the great Carthaginian general. Johnson then appropriates one of Juvenal's own examples, Xerxes, the Persian monarch whose 'invincible' forces were destroyed by the Greeks at the battle of Salamis. Yet Johnson handles Xerxes somewhat differently. Where Juvenal is full of sarcasm, Johnson has a deeper moral point he wishes to make. Xerxes sets forth 'In gay Hostility, and barb'rous Pride'. (The surprising phrase 'gay Hostility' suggests both the lightheartedness of the king and the

colourful outfits of his troops.) He is attended by 'Flattery' and feels himself a match
for the very gods. His surprising defeat, then, is not merely a sign of the unpredictability of fate, but a lesson in the dangers of self-delusion.

Johnson continues to reshape Juvenal's material when he turns to the next topic:
the evils of old age. Juvenal undoubtedly seeks to disgust his reader with his graphic
depictions of physical decrepitude, which include drippy noses, toothless gums, and
flaccid penises. The demands of propriety in Johnson's day prohibited him from
employing the same details, although he suggests the same ideas in less offensive
terms: 'Time hovers o'er, impatient to destroy, / And shuts up all the Passages of Joy'
(ll. 259–60). Who would want long life, both authors suggest, when total physical
debility is so frequently the outcome. And even more tragic is the inevitable decay
of one's mind. Yet both authors also know that some people are vigorous and alert in
old age: for these there are other trials, especially the loss of friends and children
through death. Even here, though, Johnson takes a slightly different approach; he
focuses not just on physical vigour but on virtue. Can moral goodness preserve us
from these ills? The answer, of course, is 'no'. And so death becomes nature's gift of
peace to suffering virtue.

The desire for beauty constitutes the last of the empty wishes that both authors
treat. Once again Juvenal focuses on the physical dangers to which beauty exposes its
possessor, whether male or female: rape, mutilation and the revenge of jealous husbands. Johnson, by contrast, develops the moral dangers that beset beautiful women.
Carried away by the flattery of their admirers and intrigued against by rivals, how
few beauties will heed the call of virtue. In the hopes of imparting his moral injunctions as forcefully as possible, Johnson refuses to paint a hopeful picture:

> The Guardians yield, by Force superior ply'd;
> By Int'rest, Prudence; and by Flatt'ry, Pride.
> Now Beauty falls betray'd, despis'd, distress'd,
> And hissing Infamy proclaims the rest.
>   (ll. 339–42)

In a world of unscrupulous 'lovers' and jealous rivals, beauty places a woman at greater
risk of social disgrace and moral destruction.

If all these desires are empty, and in some cases destructive, what then should
we wish for? Juvenal's answer is simple: quit wishing and leave everything to the will
of the gods; they will provide for you better than you could for yourself. And if
you must wish, wish for a healthy mind in a sound body (*mens sana in corpore sano*).
Johnson's Christian stoicism offers the same answers to the same questions:

> Where then shall Hope and Fear their Objects Find?
> Must dull Suspence corrupt the stagnant Mind? . . .
>
> Enquirer, cease, Petitions yet remain,
> Which Heav'n may hear, nor deem Religion vain.

Still raise for Good the supplicating Voice,
But leave to Heav'n the Measure and the Choice . . .

Implore his Aid, in his Decisions rest,
Secure whate'er he gives, he gives the best.
                    (ll. 343–4, 349–52, 355–6)

For both authors the solution to the human condition is resignation to divine will. Man cannot know what is best for him, but he can trust in Providence. Johnson never directly Christianizes the poem; rather, he suggests the kind of universality that forms the core of his moral thought. The prayer of a wise ancient, especially if he has intuited the existence of a providential divinity, will agree closely with that of a modern Christian; for 'truth' is the same at all times and in all places.

Style

The style of *The Vanity of Human Wishes* is notoriously difficult. Johnson uses many traditional rhetorical and poetic devices with which modern readers often have little familiarity. Even in Johnson's day, though, the difficulty of the couplets was noted: Johnson's friend David Garrick said that the poem was 'as hard as Greek'. The following analysis of selected passages is intended to help inexperienced readers untangle some of the complexities of Johnson's verse.

The most important figure of speech in the poem is *personification*, by which abstract terms or inanimate objects are given human qualities. Johnson generally creates this figure by attaching an active verb to an abstract noun. At the very beginning of the poem, Johnson personifies 'Observation', inviting it to 'survey' human behaviour and report its findings. Johnson develops the findings of 'Observation' in a miniature *allegory* that includes a number of personifications among its constituent elements:

Then say how Hope and Fear, Desire and Hate,   5
O'erspread with Snares the clouded Maze of Fate,
Where wav'ring Man, betrayed by vent'rous Pride,
To tread the dreary Paths without a Guide;
As treach'rous Phantoms in the Mist delude,
Shuns fancied Ills, or chases airy Good.   10

Note that this passage consists of a single complex sentence. Because each couplet is 'closed', that is, ending in a significant pause, an inexperienced reader is liable to treat it as a self-contained syntactic unit; but Johnson often worked in sentences of two, three, four, or more couplets, with each introducing, extending, modifying or clarifying another.

Throughout the passage Johnson personifies human feelings: in lines 5 and 6, we find *hope, fear, desire* and *hate* spreading snares, and in line 7 we are told that man's pride has betrayed him. Modern readers, upon encountering such words as 'hope', 'fear' and 'pride', think in terms of abstractions instead of images; but Johnson's verse requires the reader to visualize an allegorical picture of the real world. The scene is the 'clouded maze of fate', the uncertain world in which we live. Our passions set traps for us around this maze. Man the traveller is uncertain and alone (line 7), for his pride has convinced him to venture forward without a guide. And throughout his wanderings he is beset by illusory visions. Finally, these visions too require interpretation, for the last line of the passage includes some unexpected pairings of adjectives and nouns. We read that 'Man . . . shuns *fancied ills* and chases *airy goods*.' We expect him to shun 'ills', but these ills are only 'fancied', they are not 'ills' at all. And the 'goods' turn out to be 'airy', insubstantial. In other words, man shuns things that will not harm him and chases things of no substance. This is, of course, the essence of the vanity of human wishes.

Johnson's tendency to compress meaning into the tightest units possible can often lead to cryptic couplets difficult for anyone to understand. Consider the following lines: 'Fate wings with ev'ry Wish th' afflictive Dart, / Each Gift of Nature, and each Grace of Art' (ll. 15–16). We once again encounter a personification, but what is 'Fate' doing? From Johnson's *Dictionary* we learn that 'to wing' can mean 'to furnish with wings; to enable to fly'. The meaning of the first line now becomes clear: with every wish we make, fate gives wings to a 'dart', that is, it prepares an arrow to afflict us. Each wish, then, carries with it its own cause of pain. The second line can only be understood by reference to the first. The phrases 'each gift of nature' and 'each grace of art' both stand in parallel with 'every wish', and whatever had been said about that phrase must be applied to the other two. Thus for every gift that nature gives us and for every grace that art can supply our lives, fate has prepared a 'dart' to ruin our joy.

The following couplet, which has already been quoted above, offers another example of how a sensitivity to Johnson's parallel constructions is necessary to untangling a couplet's syntax and grasping its meaning. The attractive woman, Johnson tells us, will have both 'lovers' and 'rivals' plotting against her, and she has only her character to protect her. 'The Guardians yield, by Force superior ply'd; / By Int'rest, Prudence; and by Flatt'ry, Pride.' Two 'guardians' of her virtue are given in the second line of the couplet along with two of the 'forces' that undermine it. The lady's 'prudence', that is, the normal caution one learns from experience, is weakened 'by interest', the belief that she has something to gain from improper behaviour; and her 'pride', her fear of social disgrace, is attacked 'by flattery'. The syntax of the couplet is patterned but precise, and it is only by reference to the first line that we can infer the meaning of the second.

Johnson will sometimes combine personifications with other images, and a reader must visualize the scene in order to understand his ideas. The following quotation begins the section on the desire for power.

> Unnumber'd Suppliants crowd Preferment's Gate,
> Athirst for Wealth, and burning to be great;

Delusive Fortune hears th' incessant Call,
They mount, they shine, evaporate, and fall.

(ll. 73–6)

Johnson here intends for us to see in our mind's eye a great man's estate, its gate thronged with people seeking favours. It is not, though, the estate of any one man, but of 'Preferment' itself. The use of personification makes the point more general: the scene we visualize has symbolic meaning. But the most striking part of the passage is the final line, in which the typical career of the successful place seeker is conveyed through a series of images: 'They mount, they shine, evaporate, and fall.' Most readers see a skyrocket in this progression of images; some consider it a bubble (which was also a derisive term during the eighteenth century for men whose ambition and vanity outstripped their ability and character). In either case the images suggest something short lived, of temporary brilliance but no real substance, and ending in inevitable destruction. Such is the progress of ambition.

Finally, I wish to point out the occasional need for specialized knowledge in order to interpret some of Johnson's lines. Johnson assumes that his readers know something about the figures who represent the different kinds of misdirected desire. His portrait of Xerxes, one of the most famous passages in the poem, offers an excellent example of this need for specialized knowledge. In his depiction of the Persian ruler's growing madness, Johnson says, 'The Waves he lashes, and enchains the Winds.' Johnson assumes that his reader will know the story of Xerxes from either Herodotus or Juvenal. Herodotus tells us that in order to move his army from Persia to Greece, Xerxes built a bridge of boats across the Hellespont. When a storm destroyed the bridge, Xerxes ordered that the waves be whipped and a set of manacles thrown into the water as symbolic punishment. Juvenal embellished the story, asserting that Xerxes whipped the winds and manacled the seas, and Johnson freely adapted Juvenal. To a reader lacking this sort of specialized knowledge, the line has little meaning; to a reader familiar with the sources, it is rich and complex. There are many passages in the *Vanity* that yield richer meaning when their sources are discovered.

Johnson's verse requires various kinds of knowledge if it is to be fully appreciated. First, one should know something of Juvenal and his great Tenth Satire. Next, one must recognize how English syntax can be stretched, bent, and moulded into unaccustomed forms. And, finally, one must respond to personifications not as mere abstractions employed in the service of general assertions, but as the sources of visual imagery and lively descriptions. Johnson is a demanding author, but in this great poem he repays the reader's efforts.

FURTHER READING

The authoritative text of *The Vanity of Human Wishes* is to be found in *The Poems of Samuel Johnson,* ed. D. N. Smith and E. L. McAdam, 2nd edn (Oxford: Clarendon, 1974). The best introduction to Johnson's moral thought remains W. J. Bate, *The Achievement of Samuel Johnson* (NY: Oxford University Press, 1955). For an introduction to Juvenal, see G. Highet, *Juvenal the Satirist* (Oxford: Clarendon, 1954).

N. Rudd provides Juvenal's Latin text, a translation, and extensive commentary on Johnson's poem in *Johnson's Juvenal* (Bristol: Bristol Classical Press, 1981).

34

Henry Fielding, *The History of Tom Jones*

Richard Braverman

'I shall conclude these Papers, with exhorting every Man in this Kingdom to exert himself, not only in his Station, but as far as Health, Strength, and Age will permit him, to leave at present the Calling which he pursues, and however foreign his Way of Life may have been to the Exercise of Arms, to take them up.' These exhortatory words do not come from *Tom Jones* (1749); they appear toward the end of *The History of the Present Rebellion in Scotland*, a pamphlet that Henry Fielding produced in the autumn of 1745 in response to the stunning success of the Highland army led by Prince Charles Edward Stuart. Prince Charles, the legendary 'Bonnie Prince Charlie', had landed in Scotland with the far-flung hope of reclaiming his ancestral crown. His claim dated to 1688, when James II, his grandfather, had fled to France in the face of an invading army led by William of Orange. James never formally abdicated, and his supporters, who came to be known as 'Jacobites', held steadfastly to the belief that the Catholic Stuarts were the rightful claimants to the crown. That belief, grounded in the principle of indefeasible hereditary right, was the bedrock of an underground movement that erupted periodically from the 1690s on.

Bonnie Prince Charlie's invasion, known as the '45 rebellion, turned out to be the final eruption of the Jacobite cause. But if its political aspirations were finally dashed at the battle of Culloden (1746), Jacobitism still had ideological power, and for that reason Fielding drew on the rebellion in *Tom Jones*, setting the events of the novel during the weeks of Prince Charlie's initial success. *Tom Jones* is, of course, a work of fiction, but Fielding thought of it as a species of history, too. Its full title, *The History of Tom Jones, a Foundling*, refers, above all, to the debt that the eighteenth-century novel owed to autobiographical writing, meaning that Tom's story was a personal history as *novel* as those of Robinson Crusoe or Pamela. Yet 'history' in its public sense added more than a layer of background to *Tom Jones*, providing as it did the framework for the conflict at the core of the narrative, the fraternal rivalry of Tom and Blifil.

Tom and Blifil are not brothers but half brothers. Both were borne by Squire Allworthy's sister Bridget, with Blifil the only child of her loveless marriage to Captain

Blifil, and Tom the love-child of her dalliance with one Mr Summer. Though related by blood, Tom and Blifil are, however, utter opposites. A creature of natural benevolence, Tom is warm hearted, sociable and sincere; he radiates the vitality that the cold, scheming and venal Blifil lacks. Blifil, however, knows how to contain his emotions. Tom's, in contrast, get him into trouble, first with Molly Seagram (sex) then with Black George (poaching). So it is only a matter of time before Tom is banished by Squire Allworthy from Paradise Hall.

The rivalry of Tom and Blifil is grounded in the competition for Sophia Western. To the modern reader, the competition appears to be no contest at all, since Sophia is smitten by Tom and repulsed by Blifil. Nonetheless, in the world of the eighteenth-century gentry it is Blifil who has the upper hand, since Tom is of unknown paternity until the novel's end. Blifil has no genuine feelings for Sophia – only sadistic fantasies – but he sees Tom as a threat because the Allworthy estate is without an heir. (When Fielding tells us early in Book I that Squire Allworthy had a loving marriage but no children, he is also telling us that his considerable estate will be up for grabs.) Tom, certainly, is not looking for anything to grab. Nevertheless, he becomes the accidental aspirant because Fielding has a larger design in mind than a family feud, a design that is embedded in the novel's historical framework.

When Bonnie Prince Charlie landed in Scotland in the autumn of 1745, he sparked what would turn out to be the final round of a debate that had been simmering ever since James II fled to France in 1688. The heart of the matter was: who should rule? By the mid-1740s, Britons had been ruled for three decades by a dynasty originally from the German state of Hanover. The beneficiaries of the Act of Settlement (1701) because of their Protestantism, the Hanoverian kings (George I, who reigned from 1714 to 1727, and George II, who would reign until 1760) were far from beloved. Foreigners who lacked the hereditary right of the Stuarts, they came across as bland and plodding while the Stuarts were widely thought to possess the *élan* of kingship. The Stuarts had, from the time of James I and Charles I, worked hard at their image; though tarnished by the sexual escapades of Charles II and the religious machinations of James II, they retained the aura of kingship that was a mainspring of the Jacobite cause. The bedrock of their cause was hereditary right, but the Jacobites also had a powerful claim on the popular imagination, in which Stuart charisma was pitted against Hanoverian dulness.

Fielding scatters references to Stuart mythology throughout *Tom Jones*. Not only are a number of characters – notably Partridge and Squire Western – Jacobite sympathizers; in addition, the innkeeper's wife at Upton mistakenly believes that Sophia Western is the mistress of Prince Charles Stuart; and if no one at Upton ignites the rumour that Tom is the pretender, Fielding links Jones with the latest incarnation of the Stuart mystique. Fielding sets up the association of Tom and the pretender to give the fraternal rivalry with Blifil a historical cast, but he reverses the popular conceptions of Hanoverians and Stuarts to favour the ruling dynasty. As the critic Ronald Paulson points out: 'Fielding has reversed the "popular" characteristics of the Jacobite myth, making Tom the life force which Bonnie Prince Charlie was portrayed as being, while Blifil has all the Hanoverian-Whig traits attributed by the Jacobites – as by many objective Englishmen.' In setting up the fraternal rivalry, Fielding makes Tom the representative of the ruling Hanoverian dynasty and invests him with the charismatic spirit of the Stuarts, while he saddles Blifil with the double negative of Jacobite egotism (e.g., his libertine desire to 'rifle Sophia's charms') and Hanoverian dulness (e.g., his false piety). Their contrast is all the more significant because the novel is set during the early phase of the Jacobite rebellion, when the future is still up for grabs. At that juncture, who will win Sophia is vitally important because the half brothers are nothing less than symbolic rivals for a much bigger prize, England herself.

The depiction of historical struggle as the struggle for a woman and her estate appears with some frequency in seventeenth- and eighteenth-century English litera-ture. In *Tom Jones*, the issue finds eventual resolution through the unification, via the marriage of Tom and Sophia, of the adjoining Western and Allworthy estates. As Western and Allworthy represent conflicting political views – Western is a Jacobite, Allworthy a Whig – the merger of estates is a fitting metaphor for political harmony. Likewise, Tom represents, as a potential husband, a more restrained form of 'govern-ment' than Blifil, whose desire to 'rifle Sophia's charms' is a metaphor of the Jacobite penchant for arbitrary rule.

On one level, then, Tom signals the impending triumph of Hanover over the Jacobite cause. On another, though, he serves as a gentry counterweight to the corrupt values of London and the court. At the end of the novel, Tom returns to Somerset, no longer the non-entity that the name 'Tom Jones' was meant to signify. But neither is he quite a true-born aristocrat in the literary tradition wherein lost children turn out to have aristocratic origins. In that tradition – the romance tradition – the hero's story concludes with the recovery of lost identity, a recovery that restores the hero to his proper station by birth. In *Tom Jones*, this scenario does not quite play out because Tom, to put it bluntly, remains a bastard to the end. He does because, as Hanover's representative, he is a reminder of their bastard claim to the crown, forged as it was in the Act of Settlement. Tom may transfuse cavalier vitality to the Protestant cause, but his appropriation of the persona of the Stuart pretender serves at the same time as a reminder of the fact that Hanover had no comparable figure at the heart of their legitimizing myth.

I have stressed the fraternal rivalry of Blifil and Tom in order to situate the novel within its historical context, a context that requires some elucidation for modern readers. But there is of course a great deal more to the book, as anyone who has even taken a casual look at it can attest. *Tom Jones* runs close to a thousand pages in most editions, and Fielding needs the space because the novel is replete with characters from all walks of life who are set in a complex pattern by a plot that moves from Paradise Hall (Books 1–6) to the road and countryside (Books 7–12) to fashionable London (Books 13–18). The book's scope, to the modern reader, is epic, even though formally it is not an epic. Nevertheless, like epic, it attempts to define the values of an age, much as Homer did archaic honour culture in the *Iliad* or Virgil did Roman *pietas* in the *Aeneid*. It goes without saying that *Tom Jones* is far from the heroic worlds of Homer and Virgil. Yet as the novel traverses English society high and low it shows traditional values – those, more or less, of the Anglican gentry – under pressure from a variety of sources. Part of the pressure was political in nature, as suggested above. But a measure was social, too, and in that regard the novel conveyed some of the tensions between self and society that arose from the new spirit of individualism that suffused the age.

The rise of the novel is generally accepted as a benchmark of the new individualism. Robinson Crusoe probably embodies its spirit as well as any of the fictional heroes of the age. A self-made man, Crusoe creates a society that originates with the individual; and as the island where he is shipwrecked evolves from an unpopulated land to a budding colony, he reverses the time-honoured relationship of self and society by which personal interest (the part) was subordinated to the public good (the whole). Personal interest is naturalized on Crusoe's island because Defoe wants to legitimize an emergent commercial society. Yet in the age the spirit of individualism was by no means limited to the economic sphere. In politics and religion powerful forces associated with it – notably Puritanism and Dissent – had challenged church and state from the seventeenth century on, prompting the portrayal of individualism as a dangerous form of egotism that, if unchecked, would turn the natural order upside down.

In *Tom Jones*, Fielding registered his mistrust of unchecked individualism in several ways. Perhaps least noticed is the choice of narrative form itself – the third person. For Fielding, first-person narrative was the province of the self-centred, confessional mode best exemplified by two novelists with Puritan roots, Defoe and Richardson. By contrast, *Tom Jones* uses first-person narrative just twice – for the interpolated tales of Mrs Fitzpatrick and the Man of the Hill. After her cautionary tale, Mrs Fitzpatrick, who meets Sophia on the road and accompanies her to London, is integrated into the narrative. The Man of the Hill, in contrast, is not. As the critic Leopold Damrosch points out, Fielding leaves him the misfit we find him to connect him to the new, novelistic self of the age:

> The Man of the Hill is a kind of parodic Crusoe, with his animal-skin clothes and retreat from the life of his fellow men. And the story he tells, with its youthful crimes and later disgust with human nature, is a version of the Puritan first-person narrative, imprisoned within the narrowness of an obsessive point of view.

Though committed to the novel form, Fielding, Damrosch implies, was uncomfortable with its confessional side; hence, he stuck to third-person narrative, shunning the egotistical insinuations he pinned on the Man of the Hill. But Fielding's discomfort was broadly thematic, too, and in the remainder of this essay I'll touch upon three issues – social mobility, personal identity, town versus country – that likewise evince underlying tensions between self and society.

As for the first, social mobility, Fielding saw little wrong with the existing class structure. In contrast to *Robinson Crusoe*, there are no self-made men in *Tom Jones*, and the social divide between the world of the gentleman and that of the common lot is quite clear. Eighteenth-century readers would have readily accepted the wealthy estate owner Squire Allworthy as paterfamilias not only to his immediate family but to all those living on his land. Allworthy not only disciplines his own charge, Tom, but when he turns out Black George for poaching, he acts as the local magistrate because in his domain he is the law.

Another small but significant point demonstrates Fielding's resistance to social mobility. When Tom is ejected from Paradise Hall, Allworthy does not send him off empty handed but provides him with a £500 note. By the time Tom gets to Upton, though, he loses it; his 'friend', Black George, is the culprit. The lost note is a small detail in a long novel, but when, much later, it is returned to Tom unnegotiated, it seems that Fielding has used the episode to convey a distrust of credit shared by many of his contemporaries. The note is a symbol of economic growth and social mobility, yet it is not permitted to circulate because Fielding would prefer to keep the Pandora of credit – with its transforming powers – in its box. It was, however, already long out of its box, as a rising commercial society was challenging the supremacy of landed values.

As for the second issue, personal identity, Fielding follows the contemporary practice of naming a novel for its protagonist. But *Tom Jones*, in contrast to *Clarissa*, for example, represents identity less as a personal matter than a social fact. Clarissa is a deeply introspective figure, and her personal identity is a work in progress. Tom is very much the opposite. Though in time he learns the prudential self-control necessary to govern himself and others, he is never given to introspection. (In fact, it could be said that his introspection, if it exists at all, is displaced through the Man of the Hill, whose long narrative registers a progressive alienation from the world.) Instead, Tom is defined, as all the characters in the novel are – with the possible exception of Blifil – by what he does. Plot defines character because to Fielding identity is less a personal than a social matter; people are what they are by virtue of social interactions framed by and large by their station in life. In the end, birth is what matters most, which is why the question of Tom's identity is not so much about something he acquires as about something he recovers. It is all very well that he learns to be prudent, but, in the larger scheme of things, it is essential that he is to the manor born.

As for the final issue, town versus country, Fielding invests the time-honoured trope with ideological significance by making Tom the moral counterweight to the corrupt values of London and the court. Though Tom himself wanders several times from the straight and narrow path, his own brand of egotism – marked by his libertine escapades with Molly Seagram, Mrs Waters and Lady Bellaston – is cured when he returns to Somerset to marry Sophia. His return caps the conflict of town and country, a conflict that takes place by and large through the idiom of sexual mores. Even before the action of the novel reaches London, we get a foretaste of town values when Squire Western's sister counsels a worried Sophia about the double standard: marry Blifil and have Jones. It is fitting that the advice comes from a figure Fielding situates within the moral geography of London and the court. Likewise associated with those precincts is Lady Bellaston, with whom Tom gets entangled in a web of deceit following a chance encounter at a masquerade. To Fielding, as to some of his contemporaries, the corrupt mores at the centre represented a species of over-refinement. Fawning imitators of the French, men like the foppish Lord Fellamar signified the decline of native English virtues; Tom, in contrast, was of sturdier gentry stock. And as Fielding looked to the future, his hero embodied the vision of a leadership grounded in the more home-grown, if somewhat less refined, virtues of the English countryside.

To modern readers who feel more comfortable with the seemingly 'progressive' novels of Defoe and Richardson, Fielding's social conservatism may appear a bit old-fashioned. But it must be remembered that Defoe and Richardson had Puritan roots; both were social outsiders who would have liked to become insiders. Fielding, in contrast, was an insider – by education rather than wealth – and for that reason was less sympathetic than some to the new individualism of the age. His outlook was part pragmatism, part reaction. Cautious about the future in light of the nation's divisive past, he shared with many of his contemporaries a suspicion of movements outside the political or religious fold. It was a wariness, moreover, that did not end with the failure of the Jacobite cause, because in the final pages of the novel the narrator tells us that Blifil (pronounced to rhyme with 'evil') has become a Methodist. The inner light, it would appear, is alive and well, biding the time when it might stir things up once more.

REFERENCES AND FURTHER READING

Battestin, Martin C. and Ruthe R. (1989). *Henry Fielding: a Life*. London: Routledge.

Braverman, Richard (1995). 'Rebellion redux: figuring Whig history in *Tom Jones*'. *Clio* 24, 251–68.

Carlton, Peter (1988). 'Tom Jones and the '45 again'. *Studies in the Novel* 20, 361–73.

Damrosch, Leopold (1985). *God's Plot and Man's Stories*. Chicago: University of Chicago Press.

Jones, Homer (1979). 'Tom Jones: the "bastard" of history'. *Boundary II* 7, 201–33.

McKeon, Michael (1987). *The Origins of the English Novel, 1600–1740*. Baltimore: Johns Hopkins University Press.

Miller, Henry Knight (1976). *Henry Fielding's 'Tom Jones' and the Romance Tradition*. Victoria: University of Victoria Press.

Monod, Paul (1989). *Jacobitism and the English People 1688–1788*. Cambridge: Cambridge University Press.

Paulson, Ronald (1979). *Popular and Polite Art in the Age of Hogarth and Fielding*. Notre Dame, Ind.: University of Notre Dame Press.

Richetti, John (1990). 'The old order and the new novel of the mid-eighteenth century: narrative authority in Fielding and Smollett'. *Eighteenth Century Fiction* 2, 183–96.

Schonhorn, Manuel (1981). 'Fielding's ecphrastic moment: Tom Jones and his Egyptian majesty'. *Studies in Philology* 78, 305–23.

Sherman, Sandra (1998). 'Reading at arm's length: Fielding's contract with the reader in Tom Jones'. *Studies in the Novel* 30, 232–45.

Stevenson, John (1994). 'Tom Jones and the Stuarts'. *ELH* 61, 571–95.

Thompson, James (1990). 'Patterns of property and possession in Fielding's fiction'. *Eighteenth Century Fiction* 3, 21–42.

35

Thomas Gray, *Elegy Written in a Country Churchyard*

Katherine Turner

Few poems have been as well received on their initial publication, and so rapidly assimilated into the canon, as Gray's *Elegy*. Indeed, its very publication came about, so the story goes, because it had already received so much acclaim through its manuscript circulation by Gray's friend Horace Walpole that Gray was forced to publish it before a pirated version was let loose on the world. Less than two weeks after the *Elegy*'s publication (on 15 February 1751), the *Monthly Review* felt that its critical work had already been performed: 'This excellent little piece is so much read, and so much admired by every body, that to say more of it would be superfluous' (*Monthly Review* IV, 309). Within the first year of its publication, five editions had been called for. When, five years later in 1756, Gray was offered the laureateship (which he declined), it was largely thanks to the fame of the *Elegy*, since he had published little else, and nothing of similar public appeal.

Whether popularity is a sign of literary worth was a question which exercised Gray and his contemporaries as much as it does readers and critics today. For Samuel Johnson, the issue was clear: the judgement of the 'common reader' was paramount, and in his 'Life of Gray' Johnson asserted that 'by the common sense of readers uncorrupted with literary prejudices, after all the refinements of subtilty and the dogmatism of learning, must be finally decided all claim to poetical honours' (Johnson, 1781, 392). Although when the 'Life of Gray' was published in 1781, ten years after the poet's death, it created uproar in the literary world for dismissing most of his poetry as mannered and obscure, Johnson made a notable exception for the *Elegy*, pronouncing famously that:

> The *Church-yard* abounds with images which find a mirror in every mind, and with sentiments to which every bosom returns an echo. The four stanzas beginning 'Yet even these bones' are to me original: I have never seen the notions in any other place; yet he that reads them here, persuades himself that he has always felt them. (Johnson, 1781, 392)

Not quite everybody was happy with the *Elegy*'s apparently universal appeal. In 1783, an anonymous and parodic response to Johnson's views was published as 'A Criticism on the Elegy written in a Country Church Yard'. Its author was John Young, Professor of Greek at Glasgow University, and his 'Criticism' expresses anxiety at the equation of popularity and value which Johnson's essay, and the general reception of the *Elegy*, had assumed. Having observed that 'The Elegy . . . has become a *staple* in English poetry. It is even beginning to *get into years*', Young issues the following warning:

> If, in establishing the fortune of literary productions, Popularity established also their worth, Criticism would find herself rid of one of the most unpleasing, as well as unprofitable, of her tasks. But this is not the case. The maxim 'Vox Populi, &c.' taken in its full range, is not more destructive to good government, than hurtful to sound criticism. To examine the *Elegy written in a Country Church Yard*, so as to rest its merits upon firm ground, its popularity should be kept out of view. (1793, 4)

For Young – a professional guardian of classical learning – the accessibility, emotion and sentiment which made the *Elegy* so popular were precisely its failings. It is worth noting at this point that Gray himself (also a classical scholar) was bemused and slightly aghast at the poem's rapturous reception, remarking to a friend in 1765 that it 'owed its popularity entirely to the subject' – so-called 'graveyard poetry' being then extremely popular – and that 'the public would have received it as well if it had been written in prose' (Lonsdale, 1969, 113). The poems he published next, 'The Bard' and 'The Progress of Poesy' in 1757, were by contrast deliberately obscure and intellectually elitist: indeed, a quotation from Pindar on their title page (they were issued together, as *Odes*) proclaims – in Greek! – that they are 'vocal to the intelligent alone'. No doubt disingenuously, Gray writes to his friend William Mason in September 1757 that 'nobody understands me, & I am perfectly satisfied' (*Correspondence* II, 522). In the allusive density of the *Odes*, Gray is trying to wrest control of poetry back from the proliferating and anonymous reading public who had enthusiastically taken the *Elegy* to their bosom. He was too late, of course, to save the *Elegy* from its own popularity, and from its unique status within a historical moment which required just such a poem, to form the core of what John Guillory has described as the new 'vernacular curriculum' of eighteenth-century bourgeois culture. Guillory observes that the poem's popularity was 'an effect of its very successful "translation" of classical literacy into an anthology of quotable vernacular phrases' (Guillory, 1993, x). For the 'middling sort' in the eighteenth century, the *Elegy* represented precisely the sense of a shared literary language and set of moral values which the emerging bourgeois public sphere demanded, and through which, indeed, the middle class was coming culturally to define itself. The remaining part of this chapter will delineate the features of the *Elegy* which made it so peculiarly congenial to the 'common reader' of its time, and to the canon of 'English Literature' thereafter; it will then briefly consider changing critical attitudes to the poem within the twentieth-century academy.

The broad accessibility of the *Elegy* in the eighteenth century owed much to Gray's apparently effortless yet highly sophisticated blending of poetic sources and allusions. The poem's distinctive poetic texture is richly suggestive yet rarely obscure. Paul Williamson has described the mixture of classical and Christian elegiac traditions which co-exist within the poem (Williamson, 1993). An early draft of the poem, known as the Eton College MS, was much briefer, and offered a more straightforwardly Christian consolation to the 'unhonour'd Dead', to mankind in general, and indeed to the poet, who is invited to rest content with the 'cool sequester'd Vale of Life'. This aspect of the poem ties it into a popular sub-genre of writing from the preceding thirty years or so, including Blair's *The Grave* (1743), Young's *Night Thoughts* (1742–6), and Parnell's 'A Night Piece on Death' (1721), in which the spectacle of a graveyard moves the speaker to reflect that 'Time was, like thee they life possessed, / And time shall be, that thou shalt rest' (ll. 27–8). As Williamson notes, and as such poems demonstrate, the notion of Christian elegy is in fact a contradiction in terms, since the Christian emphasis on the life hereafter undermines the grief of the truly elegiac (whether this be a lament for an individual, as in 'Lycidas', or for a more nebulously sad state of affairs, as in *The Vanity of Human Wishes*, for example). The revised and published version of the *Elegy* recognizes and indeed embodies this paradox: Gray removes the four stanzas of Christian moralizing – which amounts to consolation – and instead highlights the classical tradition of elegiac lament (from sources such as Virgil's Fifth *Eclogue* and Moschus's *Lament for Bion*) and the neoplatonic strand of melancholy mysticism embodied in Milton's 'Il Penseroso'. Roger Lonsdale has observed that although the early form of the *Elegy* was 'in some ways more balanced and lucid than in its final version', Gray probably came to feel that 'its very symmetry and order represented an over-simplification of his own predicament' (Lonsdale, 1969, 114–15). This sense of personal crisis, Lonsdale argues, is dramatized in the melancholic youth introduced into the poem's closing stanzas and 'epitaph', which crystallize and intensify the web of allusion to 'Il Penseroso'. Offering a broader, cultural rather than a biographical reading, Williamson (1993, 49) suggests that Milton's poem is a crucial adumbration of the 'melancholy man of genius' who haunts the mid-eighteenth century, and whose melancholia becomes a sensuous and aesthetic form of subjectivity even while it pays lip service to a sense of Christian morality.

Much critical ink has been spilt on the identity of the melancholic youth within the *Elegy*: is he Gray himself? Or a fictional narrator-poet? Or a hitherto invisible tombstone-engraver? (this rather daft 'Stonecutter' controversy was finally quashed in 1957 by John Sutherland). Curiously, eighteenth-century readers and critics seem not to have been troubled by these questions: they appear to have been content to rest with a mysterious and shadowy relationship between narrator, poet and melancholy youth. The question of precise identity was perhaps less important than the general feeling. In this, the *Elegy* is symptomatic of a broader shift in sensibility, of which one finds evidence in much fiction of the period: the self is represented not only as a product of a network of cultural traditions and signs, but also, and in reaction against this recognition, as a fragile, unique and unknowable entity who exists in a precarious relationship to modern society.

If the poem's enactment of sensibility struck a chord in 1751, its choice of diction and use of allusion were similarly congenial: it is worth exploring these aspects in more detail. In the 'Preface' to *Lyrical Ballads* of 1805, Wordsworth was infamously (and misguidedly) to attack the 'poetic diction' of Gray's 'Sonnet' on the death of Richard West, and, by extension, the artificiality and pretentiousness of mid-eighteenth-century poetry as a whole; and T. S. Eliot was to continue the assault, complaining that the poetry of this period ('an age of retired country clergymen and schoolmasters') was 'intolerably poetic' (Eliot, 1930, 14). Gray himself wrote privately to his closest friend Richard West on 8 April 1742 that 'the language of the age is never the language of poetry' (*Correspondence*, 1, 192). But the *Elegy* is peculiarly free from excessive poetic diction: in general, its vocabulary is just sufficiently elevated, and its syntax inverted just enough (as in 'Yet even these bones from insult to protect') to convince its readers that they are reading 'poetry', without seeming strained or unnatural. As Guillory puts it, 'the very pressure of the common language on the language of the poem' means that it 'failed to be perceived, in Gray's own terms, as "the language of poetry"' (121). Hence, ironically, its popularity.

Similarly, the poem's deployment of allusion is pitched at a level which pleases the reader without intimidating. In this respect, it differs not only from Pope's and Swift's high 'Augustan' use of allusion, which Martin Price has characterized as 'complex, urbane, and deliberate' (Price, 1990, 46), but also from Gray's own consciously challenging mode in 'The Bard' and 'The Progress of Poesy' of 1757. To these poems, Gray provided a few curmudgeonly footnotes which serve only to deepen the reader's sense of ignorance. The allusive mode of the *Elegy* by contrast may be described as 'involuntary', as Price explains:

> The borrowings may be allusions, but often they are not. We need not trace them to a source. We recognise that the terms have had some earlier life in literature; they have an aura. (Price, 1990, 49)

As Lonsdale's absorbing annotations reveal, the *Elegy* is chock-full of possible allusions not only to the works of Virgil and Horace; Milton, Spenser and Shakespeare; Pope and Thomson; but also to many more contemporary poems, by Thomas Warton and Mark Akenside as well as the 'graveyard school' mentioned earlier. Recognition of such allusions may enhance a reading of the poem, emotionally or intellectually: however, such recognition is almost never essential to the poem's basic 'meaning'. Hence the *Elegy*'s appeal to a range of readers with a range of literary knowledge (or indeed very little), and hence its peculiar status as a distillation and convergence of classical and vernacular traditions: within the poem, the canon is condensed and naturalized, apparently without effort.

The poem also contains several moments of – for want of a better term – 'private' allusion: echoes of Gray's own works or those of his close friend Richard West, whose sudden death in 1742 lurks beneath the generalizing surface of the *Elegy*. For example, lines 33–6 seem to recall four lines from West's 'Monody on the Death of Queen Caroline' (published in 1748 but probably written in 1736–7):

> Ah me! what boots us all our boasted power,
> Our golden treasure, and our purpled state,
> They cannot ward th'inevitable hour,
> Nor stay the fearful violence of fate.
> (Dodsley, 1748, II, 289)

Similarly, Robert Gleckner has detected in the closing scenario of the *Elegy* (ll. 106–14) a recollection of Gray's own translation of Propertius's *Elegy* 2:1, which he had sent to West a month before his death:

> Today the lover walks, tomorrow is no more;
> A train of mourning friends attend his pall,
> And wonder at the sudden funeral.
> (lines 96–8: cited in Gleckner, 1997, 132)

Obviously, the general reader in 1751 could have had no inkling of this last example of private allusion: rather, the idea of 'aura' identified by Price informs the poem in an almost indefinable way, contributing to its sense of poignant inevitability without irritating with the search for precise sources.

The discussion so far has explored the qualities which constituted the *Elegy*'s centrality to the literary arena of its day, and which to some extent account for its continuing popularity over the next two hundred years or so. Perhaps predictably, twentieth-century criticism, whether hostile or sympathetic, has consistently discovered complexity and ambivalence both within the poem and in its relationship to historical context. Ambiguity at the most basic level, concerning the identity of 'thee' at line 93, prompted the 'Stonecutter' controversy which was discussed briefly above. Other debates have been more ideologically inflected and have reflected differing critical schools of thought. An important reassessment of the *Elegy* began in 1935 with Empson's historically informed critique of the repressive politics which lurk beneath the poem's pastoral nostalgia. The lines to which Empson most objected were 53–6:

> Full many a gem of purest ray serene
> The dark unfathomed caves of ocean bear:
> Full many a flower is born to blush unseen,
> And waste its sweetness on the desert air.

Here, he argues, Gray by 'comparing the social arrangement to Nature' makes it 'seem inevitable, which it was not, and gives it a dignity which was undeserved' (Empson, 1935, 4). His point might seem incontrovertible, but Cleanth Brooks for one (in 1947) argued against Empson, pointing to the limitations of judging the 'poetry of the past' significant merely as 'cultural anthropology' (Brooks, 1947, x), and urging instead the universalizing pathos of the poem. Brooks's argument depends on a close reading of the poem which emphasizes its aesthetic self-sufficiency: the *Elegy* mimics the 'storied urn' of line 41, becoming a 'poetic structure' (112) outside history.

This new critical emphasis on the transcendental qualities of poetry is disingenuous since Brooks assumes a continuously stable Christian worldview. Not surprisingly, Empson's approach has had more inheritors. In a historical fleshing out of Empson's basic objection, Richard Sha has placed the critique of Gray's 'patronizing attitude towards the poor' within a detailed context of eighteenth-century attitudes towards poor relief and class structure: Gray, like others of his class, bases his sympathy for the poor on their 'cheerful industry' and 'their acceptance of their place' (Sha, 1990, 338–9). Addressing the question of historical context more broadly, others have teased out the political complexities within the poem's view of history. James Steele in 1974 explored Gray's broadly Whiggish sympathies, while Suvir Kaul in 1992 offered a more problematic reading of Gray's politics as conflicted and anxious. In the context of such questions, the implications of the references in lines 57–60 to the English Civil War figures of Hampden, Milton and Cromwell (which replaced first-draft references to Cato, Tully and Caesar) have become more ambivalent.

The gothicizing of the landscape within the poem, with its ivy-clad ruins, has also provoked debate: does it enact aesthetic or political nostalgia? W. C. Dowling (1992) argues that such uses of the past (by Thomas Warton and William Collins as well as Gray) in mid-eighteenth-century poetry represent a radical transformation of the meaning of history, such that the myth of Britain's gothic past of benevolent feudalism becomes an imaginative rather than a political ideal. John Sitter (1988) developed the more defeatist implications of this kind of approach, arguing that the focus on the isolated artist in mid-eighteenth-century poetry embodied a new sense that poetry would henceforward disengage itself from politics and focus instead (rather narcissistically) on the predicament of the poet. David Fairer (1993) has elegantly fused the poem's textual self-consciousness with a broader sense of cultural disablement, observing that:

> There is a surfeit of holy texts in Gray's *Elegy* – storied urns, frail memorials, artless tales, and uncouth rhymes – strewn around and begging to be read, imploring the passing tribute of a sigh. But the effect of Gray's speaker is not to recover and reanimate them. Instead he builds up a sense of frustration of indignant possibility left interred and repressed, however much the turf heaves about him. (155)

More recently still, Robert Gleckner (1997) has adopted a psychoanalytic approach to the *Elegy*'s projection of a poetic self, seeing the poem as a suppressed lament for West, and a covert exploration of Gray's own repressed sexuality, which is the prime factor in his social marginalization and sense of poetic emasculation ('Full many a flower is born to blush unseen / And waste its sweetness on the desert air' becomes, in this reading, an image of masturbatory loneliness). Working from a post-structuralist perspective in 1987, Stephen Bygrave saw the poem as a precursor of the Romantic 'conversation poem', which 'moves from the single first-person singular into a kind of repressed dialectic of self and society, finally withdrawing from an assertion of the reintegration of the self at a higher level' (Bygrave, 1987, 173); while Henry Weinfield, addressing the 'problem of history' in 1991, pronounced that 'If the *Elegy* has a subject, this is perhaps nothing less than the problem of locating meaning and value in human existence generally' (Weinfield, 1991, xix). Weinfield's qualifier here – 'If the *Elegy* has a subject' – would have astonished Gray's contemporaries. Yet, given the proliferation of critical approaches to the poem in recent years, Weinfield's hesitancy seems fair enough. Celebrated in its own day for its apparently universal appeal to the emotions, the *Elegy*'s place at the centre of critical dispute in our own time is predicated upon a precisely opposite quality, the intellectual challenge posed by its alleged evasiveness. It becomes a textbook illustration of Derrida's claim that 'the absence of the transcendental signified extends the domain and the play of signification infinitely' (Derrida, 1978, 110).

The *Elegy* has functioned as a hostage in the central critical debates of our time, over interpretation, value, and the canon. In a sense, however, the poem has the last laugh in every debate, simply because the continual cycle of re-reading and reinterpretation serves only to confirm its centrality to the canon. In the changing critical status of the *Elegy*, we witness not so much a dramatic refashioning of the canon – Gray's poem may be being supplemented by recently rediscovered eighteenth-century poems, but has not so far been displaced by them – as a redefinition of what makes a poem interesting, worth reading, and worth studying. Bosoms are no longer supposed to return echoes to the poem: rather, sceptical minds continue to find interest, complexity and difficulty therein. Gray might now be able to declare of the *Elegy* rather than the 1757 *Odes* that 'nobody understands me, & I am perfectly satisfied'.

REFERENCES AND FURTHER READING

Brooks, C. (1947). *The Well Wrought Urn: Studies in the Structure of Poetry*. New York: Cornwall Press.

Bygrave, S. (1987). 'Gray's "Elegy": inscribing the twilight'. In *Post-Structuralist Readings of English Poetry*. Ed. R. Machin and C. Norris. Cambridge: Cambridge University Press, 162–75.

Derrida, J. (1978). 'Structure, sign and play in the discourse of the human sciences'. In *Modern Criticism and Theory* (1988). Ed. D. Lodge. London and New York: Longman, 108–23.

Dodsley, R. (1748). *A Collection of Poems by Several Hands*. Vol. 2. London: Dodsley.

Dowling, W. C. (1992). 'Ideology and the flight from history in eighteenth-century poetry'. In *The Profession of Eighteenth-Century Literature: Reflections on an Institution*. Ed. L. Damrosch. Madison: University of Wisconsin Press, 135–53.

Eliot, T. S. (1930). 'Introductory essay to S. Johnson'. *London: A Poem and The Vanity of Human Wishes*. London: Haslewood.

Empson, W. (1935). *Some Versions of Pastoral*. London: Chatto and Windus.

Fairer, D. (1993). 'Thomas Warton, Thomas Gray, and the recovery of the past'. In *Thomas Gray:*

Contemporary Essays. Ed. W. B. Hutchings and W. Ruddick. Liverpool: Liverpool University Press, 146–70.

Gleckner, R. F. (1997). *Gray Agonistes: Thomas Gray and Masculine Friendship*. Baltimore: Johns Hopkins University Press.

Gray, T. (1971). Ed. P. Toynbee and L. Whibley. *Correspondence of Thomas Gray*. 3 vols. Oxford: Oxford University Press.

Guillory, J. (1993). *Cultural Capital: The Problem of Literary Canon Formation*. Chicago and London: University of Chicago Press.

Johnson, S. (1781). Thomas Gray. In *Lives of the English Poets*. London: J. M. Dent (1964–5). Vol. 2, 383–92.

Lonsdale, R., ed. (1969). *Gray, Collins & Goldsmith: The Complete Poems*. London and New York: Longman.

Price, M. (1990). 'Sacred to secular: Thomas Gray and the cultivation of the literary'. In *Context, Influence, and Mid-eighteenth-century Poetry*. Ed. H. D. Weinbrot and M. Price. Los Angeles: William Andrews Clark Memorial Library.

Sha, R. (1990). 'Gray's political elegy: poetry as the burial of history'. *Philological Quarterly* 69, 337–57.

Sitter, J. (1982). *Literary Loneliness in Mid-eighteenth-century England*. Ithaca and London: Cornell University Press.

Steele, J. (1974). 'Thomas Gray and the season for triumph'. In *Fearful Joy: Papers from the Thomas Gray Bicentenary Conference at Carleton University*. Ed. J. Downey and B. Jones. Montreal and London: McGill-Queen's University Press.

Sutherland, J. H. (1957). 'The stonecutter in Gray's "Elegy"'. In *Twentieth Century Interpretations of Gray's Elegy: A Collection of Critical Essays* (1968). Ed. H. Starr. Englewood Cliffs: Prentice-Hall.

Weinfield, H. (1991). *The Poet without a Name: Gray's Elegy and the Problem of History*. Carbondale: Southern Illinois University Press.

Williamson, P. (1993). 'Gray's "Elegy" and the logic of expression'. In *Thomas Gray: Contemporary Essays*. Ed. W. B. Hutchings and W. Ruddick. Liverpool: Liverpool University Press.

Young, Mr (1793). *A Criticism of the Elegy Written in a Country Churchyard. Being a Continuation of Dr J——n's Criticism on the Poems of Gray*. London: G. Wilkie.

36

Samuel Johnson, *Dictionary*

Anne McDermott

The eighteenth-century concept of knowledge tends to lay an emphasis on ordering what is already known rather than on discovering new things (though the century did make many new discoveries). Learning is seen as a series of repeated acts rather than one intuitive grasp. This difference is evident in the works of scholarship and learning which the century produced – they are typically lists or tables – and the most typical of all are the many dictionaries and encyclopedias that were produced in the course of the century. Carolus Linnaeus, a Swedish botanist of the period, devised a system of taxonomy (i.e. classification) for all living organisms, with the purpose of being able to name them all reliably and consistently and establish the relationships between them. Isaac Newton had traced the motions of all the planets and transformed these apparently random movements into the solar *system*, thus creating order out of chaos. It became the ambition of many scholars and thinkers to do the same for their own areas of expertise. The opening words of the Preface to Johnson's *Dictionary* make it clear that he thought of his dictionary as doing for the language what scientists and thinkers had done for other areas of knowledge:

> When I took the first survey of my undertaking, I found our speech copious without order, and energetick without rules; wherever I turned my view, there was perplexity to be disentangled, and confusion to be regulated.

He describes the state of the language in his time as being like a cultivated but overgrown garden, 'suffered to spread, under the direction of chance, into wild exuberance'. Johnson sees his role as like that of the gardener: pruning a bit here, lopping a bit there and generally straightening things up.

Other countries had already apparently succeeded in ordering and regulating their language, with a result that was envied by Britain. France had long had a *Dictionnaire*, produced by the Académie Française, which refined and regulated the language, proclaiming correct usage and excluding 'barbarisms', and Italy had its own dictio-

nary, produced by the Accademia della Crusca, which celebrated its national literature. Britain, by contrast, had nothing to compare with these efforts. Though there
were many dictionaries, and Johnson's was by no means the first as has sometimes
been claimed, these tended to be aimed at schoolboys or the uneducated classes
(including women) and contained mostly explanations of 'hard' or technical terms,
Latinate expressions and obscure scientific terms. What many felt was needed was a
dictionary which would describe the *whole* language and unreservedly celebrate its
glory while, at the same time, purifying it and preserving it from decay. Johnson's
dictionary was thus intended to be a monument to linguistic nationalism, to
bring the English language up to the level of Italian and particularly French, so
that 'we may no longer yield the palm of philology without a contest to the
nations of the continent' (preface). But, paradoxically, the aim was also to purify the
language of the influence of other languages such as French. Johnson was very strongly
opposed to the influence of French on English, which he thought was causing it to
'gradually depart from its original Teutonick character, and deviat[e] towards a *Gallick*
structure and phraseology', and would end by 'reduc[ing] us to babble a dialect
of France'.

Johnson's *Dictionary* grew out of a long campaign for a standard authority for
English. In the seventeenth century there had been many voices raised in favour of a
linguistic academy which would make pronouncements on correct usage in just the
same way as the Académie Française. One of the most famous of these was Jonathan
Swift's, whose *Proposal for Correcting, Improving and Ascertaining the English Tongue*
appeared in 1712. Alexander Pope had also frequently expressed the need for an
authoritative English dictionary and had even gone as far as compiling a list of 'authorities' (writers whose works would be used to 'authorize' a particular usage). Johnson
somehow inherited this list from Pope and includes many of those on the list among
the writers whose works he quotes in the dictionary. The background of expectation
surrounding Johnson's dictionary was that it would be authoritative, that it would
provide a standard against which to measure English usage, that it would embody
and encapsulate the purity of the language, and that it would make pronouncements
on matters of correctness.

This expectation was bolstered by the fact that Johnson's patron for the initial
project was the Earl of Chesterfield, a man noted for his views on linguistic purity.
With typical flourish, Chesterfield announced that he would regard all authority on
matters of usage as resting in Johnson himself: 'I will not only obey him, like an old
Roman, as my dictator, but like a modern Roman [i.e. Catholic], I will implicitly
believe in him as my pope, and hold him to be infallible while in the chair.' Some
felt uneasy at this investment of authority in one man, and Johnson himself, writing
in the *Plan* (1747) displaced this authority on the one hand onto Chesterfield, declaring that he was 'exercising a kind of vicarious jurisdiction' on his behalf, and, on the
other, onto the writers ('authorities') whose works he quoted, and through them onto
Pope who had chosen them. However, he does make some authoritative pronouncements, stating his intention to 'secure our language from being over-run with *cant*',

to 'brand with some note of infamy' barbarous or impure words, 'as they are carefully to be eradicated wherever they are found' (and he notes that 'they occur too frequently even in the best writers'), and, finally, to hope that his dictionary may preserve the purity of the language. In a telling metaphor, he compares himself to one of Caesar's soldiers, newly arrived in Britain, and expresses his hope that 'though I should not complete the conquest, I shall at least discover the coast, civilize part of the inhabitants, and make it easy for some other adventurer to proceed farther, to reduce them wholly to subjection and settle them under laws'.

In the course of compiling the dictionary, however, Johnson somehow lost his patron. Whether Chesterfield neglected him or Johnson neglected to pursue Chesterfield assiduously enough is unclear (and maybe it was a bit of both), but what is certain is that when the *Dictionary* was finally ready and just about to be published, Chesterfield wrote two essays for a magazine called *The World* which appeared to lay claim to the whole enterprise, as though he had been a supportive patron throughout, and Johnson responded by sending Chesterfield a famous letter of rebuke. The letter has come to be regarded as a turning point in literary history as the world of letters moved from one dominated by patronage to one based on professional writers earning their own living by dealing directly with booksellers (i.e. publishers). This overstates the case somewhat, since it was Robert Dodsley, a bookseller, who suggested Chesterfield as an appropriate patron, and Johnson himself was not averse to dealings with patrons, as his many subsequent dedications testify. But the letter was unambiguous in its rejection of Chesterfield: 'Is not a Patron, My Lord, one who looks with unconcern on a Man struggling for Life in the Water and when he has reached ground encumbers him with help?' Johnson took his revenge by defining the word 'patron' in his dictionary as 'One who countenances, supports or protects. Commonly a wretch who supports with insolence, and is paid with flattery'.

Alone, then, with the help of just a few amanuenses (i.e. scribes), of which he had only a maximum of four at the peak of the project, Johnson set about compiling this massive work. He had decided early on that he would follow the example of the Italian *Vocabolario* (1623) and include quotations from notable writers to illustrate and authorize the usage of the word he was defining, and so he set out on a vast reading project which encompassed many more than the writers identified by Pope. His method was to mark the books with a pencil, putting short vertical lines at the beginning and end of the passage he wished to quote, underlining the word it was illustrating in the passage, and writing the initial letter in the margin. Thirteen of these books have survived and this methodology can be clearly seen. The amanuenses then transcribed the passages and crossed out the initial letter in the margin when they had done so.

This methodology evidently worked well, but Johnson seems to have got it wrong initially when it came to compiling the entries for the *Dictionary* itself. He got the amanuenses to transcribe the passages directly into notebooks, using a copy of Nathan Bailey's revised dictionary, *Dictionarium Britannicum* (1736) as a guide for the word list and the alphabetical order of the words, and leaving space between the quotations for Johnson to add later the etymologies, definitions and grammatical information. He soon found that this method did not work, since he could not know in advance how much space he would need for each entry and the framework of quotations already written down must have become like a straitjacket, forcing him to write his entries in a particular way. Expensive as it was, involving the waste of a great deal of paper and effort, Johnson abandoned this method and started more or less from scratch (the letters A–C still bear some signs of his early attempt). This time, he had the amanuenses transcribe the passages onto slips of paper which could be cut and pasted into the text in a much more flexible way.

This new methodology allowed him to carry out, in some degree, his intention, announced in the *Plan*, of ordering the entries in such a way that the various senses of each word could be arranged by starting with the 'natural or primitive signification' (that which was closest to its etymology, so *to arrive* means to reach the shore in a voyage – Latin *riva* = shore), moving next to its extended or 'consequential' meaning (so, 'He arrived at his country seat'), then to its metaphorical meaning (so, 'He arrived at a peerage'). After having gone through the natural and figurative senses of the word, Johnson stated that he would append the poetical sense, if there was one, 'where it differs from that which is in common use', and follow it with the familiar, the burlesque and any peculiar (i.e. unique) sense 'in which a word is found in any great author'. This accords with his aim to order the language according to regular principles, and he does sometimes succeed in arranging entries in this way. The senses of the verb 'to eclipse', for example, are ordered as follows:

1. To darken a luminary.
2. To extinguish; to put out.
3. To cloud; to obscure.
4. To disgrace.

But he found, in the end, that the language was not rational or regular enough to allow all the entries to be arranged in this way, and he confessed his failure in the preface: 'kindred senses may be so interwoven, that the perplexity cannot be disentangled, nor any reason assigned why one should be ranged before the other'. However, despite the fact that he noticed that 'the shades of meaning pass imperceptibly into each other', Johnson's discrimination of several different senses of the same word, subtly nuanced to discriminate them from one another, is what principally sets his dictionary apart from those which preceded it. He broke each entry down into numbered senses and included features such as phrasal verbs (e.g. *to set up*), which had not been systematically treated before, with the result that many of his definitions have found their way unchanged into what is still the most complete dictionary of modern English, *The Oxford English Dictionary*.

Unlike *The Oxford English Dictionary*, Johnson does not try to organize his dictionary on historical principles. He is not concerned to try to plot the historical development of the language from its roots through all the changes which have happened to it. This historical aspect is dealt with in the (rather inadequate) History of the English Language printed in the prefatory material. On the other hand, Johnson is not presenting current contemporary English as it was in 1755 when he first published the *Dictionary*. The texts he uses to illustrate and authorize usage are mostly taken from the period 1590–1700 and represent what Johnson thought of as a golden age of literature, what he called 'the wells of English undefiled'. There is some irony in the fact that this phrase was used by Spenser, a poet writing in Johnson's supposed golden age, to describe the language of Chaucer who was writing two hundred years earlier. Johnson shows some recognition in the preface that to pursue perfection in the form of idealist linguistic designs, is 'like the inhabitants of Arcadia [an ideal landscape], to chase the sun, which when they had reached the hill where he seemed to rest, was still beheld at the same distance from them'.

The kinds of writers Johnson includes are fairly predictable: Shakespeare, Dryden, Milton, Addison, Swift, Pope, Hooker, Tillotson, Clarendon, Locke, the Bible (Authorized Version), Bacon, Spenser and many others, all notable for their literary and stylistic excellence. These are supplemented by many sources which are 'encyclopedic' in the sense that they give the latest information on aspects of knowledge which we would now expect to find in an encyclopedia. He also uses short-cuts such as concordances, indexes, miscellanies and glossaries which had lists of quotations, or 'sentiments', ready for him to cull. Another technique he uses is to extract quotations which appear in footnotes in the texts he was marking up. Despite these short-cuts, Johnson did an immense amount of reading for the *Dictionary*, and though he describes this reading as 'fortuitous and unguided excursions into books', most of the texts he quotes are similar in exhibiting fairly orthodox and mainstream political and religious opinions.

Johnson was criticized when his *Dictionary* appeared for filling it full of Jacobite and 'high-flying' (high-church Tory) tenets. Certainly, he makes his own political allegiance clear in the respective definitions of 'Whig' and 'Tory', but, in general, his dictionary is not explicitly or primarily political. Writers are more likely to be included or excluded for their religious views, rather than their political views. Hobbes is excluded because of his deterministic and mechanistic views, verging on Calvinism, and, significantly, John Bramhall's essay refuting Hobbes is heavily quoted. Samuel Clarke's sermons are excluded, despite Johnson's admiration of their style, because Clarke was unorthodox on one point: he was a Unitarian who did not believe in the Trinity. Several physico-theologists (writers who found the evidence for God's existence and reasons to admire him in nature), such as Boyle, Bentley, Ray and Burnet, seem to be quoted for no other reason than their religious views, and many well-known sermon writers, such as South and Tillotson, are included for similar reasons.

Clearly, Johnson thought his quotations would do more than simply illustrate the meanings of words. In the preface he acknowledges that his first endeavours were thwarted because, to keep the size of the volumes manageable, he had to expunge many passages and edit the rest, so that 'by hasty detruncation . . . the general tendency of the sentence may be changed'. In spite of this disclaimer, Johnson's editing is generally very skilful: he forms pithy statements and maxims out of diffuse prose without changing the sense of the sentence. A quotation from Hooker under 'law' reduces the original passage from 'Laws politique, ordeined for externall order and regiment amongst men, are never framed as they should be, unlesse presuming the will of man to be inwardly obstinate, rebellious, and averse from all obedience unto the sacred lawes of his nature' to 'Laws politique among men presuming man to be rebellious'. There is, conversely, not much evidence of Johnson manipulating a text to serve his own propagandist purposes. When Johnson revised the *Dictionary* in 1773, however, there is some evidence that he tried to include even more texts of a moral and politically conservative nature.

One of Johnson's express aims in the *Dictionary* had been to fix the language, to preserve its purity and prevent it from decaying, but this is an area in which he has to concede failure in the end. Some anomalies of spelling 'must be tolerated among the imperfections of human things', and though he declares his intent of trying where possible to keep spelling as close as possible to the root of the word, he confesses that he has been 'often obliged to sacrifice uniformity to custom' (preface). An example of the difficulty facing him is the fact that the spellings 'centre'/'center' were used almost interchangeably in the eighteenth century, and though he chooses the spelling 'centre' for the headword, the alternative spelling appears very frequently in the *Dictionary*, including in Johnson's own prose.

Some parts of the language, which he calls 'fugitive cant' (technical words or terms of trade or commerce) can, he thinks, change without regret and be 'suffered to perish', but the more durable parts of the language – those words which appear in the great works of literature – he is more concerned to retain. But this desire for permanence becomes, in the end, an example of the vanity (i.e. futility) of human wishes. A dictionary that promises to fix the language is like 'the elixir that promises to prolong life to a thousand years'. It is not possible, he concludes, in a living language which is changing at every moment, to prevent words from changing their meanings or to fix spelling to an agreed standard that everyone will follow: 'words are hourly shifting their relations and can no more be ascertained in a dictionary, than a grove, in the agitation of a storm, can be accurately delineated from its picture in the water'. The change of metaphor from a soldier attempting to subdue a new colony in the *Plan* to a painter trying desperately to depict a changing natural scene in the preface gives a vivid sense of Johnson's change of view of his role as a lexicographer. His comment about the difficulty in discriminating shades of meaning might be made about his whole enterprise in the *Dictionary*: 'this uncertainty is not to be imputed to me, who do not form, but register the language; who do not teach men how they should think, but relate how they have hitherto expressed their thoughts'. It is one of the ironies of the history of language, then, that Johnson's *Dictionary* should have come to be regarded as the epitome of authoritarian, prescriptive lexicographic practice. Perhaps this has more to do with the fact that, though he disclaimed authority, Johnson's *Dictionary* was regarded as the standard for English for the next hundred and fifty years or so.

References and Further Reading

Demaria, Robert, Jr (1987). *Johnson's Dictionary and the Language of Learning*. Chapel Hill, N.C. and London: University of North Carolina Press.

——(1986). 'The theory of language in Johnson's *Dictionary*'. In *Johnson After Two Hundred Years*. Ed. Paul Korshin. Philadelphia: University of Pennsylvania Press, 159–74.

De Vries, Catharina M. (1994). *In the Tracks of a Lexicographer: Secondary Documentation in Samuel Johnson's Dictionary of the English Language (1755)*. Utrecht: LEd.

Kolb, Gwin J. and Kolb, Ruth A. (1972). 'The selection and use of illustrative quotations in Dr. Johnson's *Dictionary*'. In *New Aspects of Lexicography*. Ed. Howard D. Weinbrot. Carbondale, Ill.: University of Illinois Press, 61–72.

Reddick, Allen (1990). *The Making of Johnson's Dictionary 1746–1773*. Rev. edn (1996). Cambridge: Cambridge University Press.

Sledd, James H. and Kolb, Gwin J. (1955). *Dr. Johnson's Dictionary: Essays in the Biography of a Book*. Chicago: University of Chicago Press.

Thomas, Eugene J. (1974). 'A bibliographical and critical analysis of Johnson's *Dictionary* with special reference to twentieth-century scholarship'. Unpublished doctoral thesis, University of Aberystwyth.

Weinbrot, Howard D. (1972). 'Samuel Johnson's *Plan* and the preface to the *Dictionary*: the growth of a lexicographer's mind'. In *New Aspects of Lexicography*. Ed. Howard D. Weinbrot. Carbondale, Ill.: University of Illinois Press, 73–94.

37

Samuel Johnson, *Rasselas*

Anne McDermott

It is difficult to say what *Rasselas* is. Like a novel it has characters and a discernible narrative, but the focus of the text is not on the characters and their emotional or intellectual development, nor on the specific events of the narrative and their consequences, but on the development of ideas about human nature and happiness. For this reason it has sometimes been called a philosophic tale. It has something of the form of a parable or an allegory, since the narrative is not linear and progressive, but circular – the characters ending up more or less where they began.

It also bears a strong resemblance to the oriental tale, which was an extremely popular genre in the eighteenth century, the most famous example being the translation of the Arabian Nights into French (and subsequently from French into English) in 1704–17. Johnson himself had written some oriental tales for his journal *The Rambler* (*Ramblers* 204 and 205), giving the history of Seged, lord of Ethiopia. Seged resolves to retire from the cares of high office for ten days and to fill his time with enjoyment and pleasure. His quest, however, like that of Rasselas, is unsuccessful: the people he gathers into his 'house of pleasure' are riven by jealous anxieties, and he finds that he cannot banish disquiet, envy or petty fears. Death, too, is beyond his control and, like the Stoic philosopher in *Rasselas*, his daughter dies, leaving him grief-stricken.

Rasselas is, to some extent, also based on historical and geographical descriptions of Abyssinia (modern-day Ethiopia). Johnson's first book had been a translation into English of the French version by Joachim Le Grand's of the account of his travels in Abyssinia by Fr. Jerome Lobo, a Portuguese missionary. The topographical details and some of the description of the paradise-prison, the Happy Valley, could well have come from this and other accounts of travellers' explorations. Abyssinia was probably chosen as a location because, as well as being exotic and culturally different, it was also a Christian country. But *Rasselas* is clearly more than just a fictionalized account of travellers' tales. Johnson does not wish to show how exotic and strange Abyssinia is, but rather how much it is like anywhere else. He believes that human nature is the same everywhere and so, to a great extent, the setting is largely irrelevant.

There was a strong tradition in the eighteenth century of tales told by a detached observer of his (they were usually male) encounter with a strange culture. This could work in either of two ways: either the observer travels to strange lands and comments on the manners and customs there, comparing them, usually unfavourably, with his own (as in *Gulliver's Travels*), or a traveller from a strange land arrives in Britain and is puzzled by many of the manners and customs he finds here (as in many of the *Spectator* essays). Both of these forms may be used effectively for social commentary and satire on contemporary society. This is clearly not Johnson's purpose, however: he does not wish to comment on his own particular society and culture in mid-eighteenth-century England, so much as on *all* human societies and manners everywhere.

In terms of the issues it deals with, the tale bears strong affinities with the 'wisdom' literature of the Bible: the Book of Proverbs, the Book of Job and Ecclesiastes. These books of the Bible deal with the nature of the world of human experience – its difficulties, its apparent injustices, and the undeniable fact that there is no easy equation between merit and reward. Like the Book of Proverbs, *Rasselas* contains many statements of aphoristic wisdom: 'Example is always more efficacious than precept' (ch. 30, 74); 'Man cannot so far know the connexion of causes and events, as that he may venture to do wrong in order to do right' (ch. 34, 82); 'He does nothing who endeavours to do more than is allowed to humanity' (ch. 29, 72). Many of these maxims are stated by Imlac, the sage, and in this respect he occupies a similar role to that of 'the wise' in the Book of Proverbs and the Preacher in Ecclesiastes. He is prevented from sounding too hortatory or portentous, however, by having any pretensions to wisdom undercut by his companions: 'Imlac now felt the enthusiastic fit, and was proceeding to aggrandize his own profession, when the prince cried out, "Enough! Thou hast convinced me, that no human being can ever be a poet"' (ch. 11, 28). Imlac himself is aware that the teachers of wisdom are no better able to cope with the difficulties of life than are ordinary people: 'Be not too hasty . . . to trust, or to admire, the teachers of morality: they discourse like angels, but they live like men' (ch. 18, 47).

Most of the books of the Bible, while perfectly aware that innocent people sometimes suffer, do, nevertheless, seem to equate suffering with wickedness and reward with virtue. They concern a God who is intimately involved in a people's history and will save them from oppression. The Book of Job and Ecclesiastes question this easy assumption. Job has inflicted upon him a great and undeserved suffering in order to test his faith and to test whether human beings only do good for the sake of reward. He loses all of the things that are associated with happiness: health, great wealth, and his wife and children. Not surprisingly, he rails against a God who could allow him to suffer in this way, but ultimately maintains his integrity and is rewarded by having his wealth restored to him and new children born to him to replace those he has lost.

Ecclesiastes is probably closer in tone to *Rasselas*, being concerned not so much with the unjust distribution of rewards and punishments as with the ultimate unsatisfactoriness of 'rewards'. Life is depicted as monotonous and repetitive and a state of being in which all is vanity (i.e. futility):

> I made me great works; I builded me houses; I planted me vineyards: I made me gardens and orchards . . . Then I looked on all the works that my hands had wrought and on the labour that I had laboured to do, and behold, all was vanity and vexation of spirit, and there was no profit under the sun. (Ecclesiastes 2:4–5; 11)

There is a cynical, pessimistic aspect to this viewpoint, but, like *Rasselas*, one of the issues it deals with is how we as humans cope with the fact that most of what we do brings with it some sort of disappointment, vexation, frustration, anxiety or even simple boredom, and how, despite all that, we can make the most of human life.

The tale of *Rasselas* works like a kind of reversed utopia: Rasselas and his companions travel away from the Happy Valley in search of the miseries of the world, 'since the sight of them is necessary to happiness'. The ending of many utopian visions is here only the beginning. The satisfaction of every material want in this earthly paradise does not bring fulfilment partly because it is in the nature of human beings to need something to strive for, and if material wants are satisfied, they will simply be replaced by other wants and desires. This perception puzzles Rasselas at first until he realizes that it is a feeling shared by everyone else in the Happy Valley: 'I am hungry and thirsty like him [the beast], but when thirst and hunger cease I am not at rest . . . I long again to be hungry that I may again quicken my attention' (ch. 2, 5–6). What Rasselas is, without realizing it, is profoundly bored. He tires of luxury and forgoes the 'dainties' and the musical entertainments that are intended to please him, but he does not yet know what he is searching for. Chapter 3 is ironically entitled 'The Wants of Him that Wants Nothing', pointing up the paradox that even the supply of every want (i.e. need) does not satisfy us because to want (i.e. desire) is part of what it is to be human. As Imlac later puts it, 'some desire is necessary to keep life in motion, and he, whose real wants are supplied, must admit those of fancy'.

The other reason why unhappiness exists in this earthly paradise, despite the fact that discord has been banished, is that, as Seged discovered, it is impossible to banish negative human emotions such as envy. Even in a place where it is impossible to compete for power because the power of the king is absolute ('impotence precludes malice') and there is no need to compete for material goods because they are held in common ('envy is repressed by community of enjoyments'), there will still he malice and envy because, as Imlac perceives, 'there may be community of material possessions, but there can never be community of love or esteem. It must happen that one will please more than another [and] he that knows himself despised will always be envious'.

Rasselas's encounter with the aeronautical engineer lays down a pattern that is repeated throughout the narrative. The engineer is engaged in a project which, to Johnson and his contemporaries, would have seemed utterly futile. The attempt at human flight, though rational, is doomed to failure, and the bathos of the engineer's rapid descent into the lake is typical of all human endeavours and aspirations.

The story of Imlac, the sage, also prefigures the remaining narrative. His father, a wealthy merchant, aspires to nothing more than the increase of wealth, and, though Imlac does not share this aspiration, he recognizes that his own desire for increase of knowledge does not bring him unalloyed happiness. Knowledge is 'certainly one of the means of pleasure', and ignorance is 'a vacuity in which the soul sits motionless and torpid for want of attraction', but the possession of knowledge does not prevent loss of friends; nor does it bring status, wealth or attention. In the end, all it teaches is that 'Human life is every where a state in which much is to be endured, and little to be enjoyed'.

The rest of the narrative is a series of illustrations of this truth. The four companions, Rasselas, Imlac, Nekayah and Pekuah, reach Cairo and discover that the young men whose life seems to be one long round of parties have chosen a course which is empty, transient and lacking in anything solid or durable. If these young men place too much emphasis on the pleasures of the senses, Rasselas next meets a philosopher who places too much emphasis on the capacity of human reason. He has adopted the Stoic philosophy of dealing with the miseries of the world by training his mind to be indifferent to both pain and pleasure. But the theory proves inadequate when tested by real human sorrow and Rasselas discovers on his next visit that the philosopher is broken by grief at the loss of his daughter.

The party next visit a group of shepherds to experience the pastoral life, in which they expect to find 'innocence and quiet', but instead they find the shepherds 'rude [i.e. uncivilized] and ignorant', 'cankered with discontent' and preoccupied with 'stupid [i.e. vacuous] malevolence'. As a contrast they next visit a stately palace where they meet a wealthy and apparently happy man, but his happiness is destroyed by lack of security against his enemy, and they learn that he must soon flee his home for fear of invasion. When the party encounter a hermit, they discover that his retirement from the world has produced a 'mind disturbed with a thousand perplexities of doubt, and vanities of imagination'. He tells them that 'the life of a solitary man will be certainly miserable, but not certainly devout'. Rasselas goes to an assembly of learned men and meets a natural philosopher who tells him that the way to be happy is 'to live according to nature'. What he means by this is not clear and Rasselas concludes that he is 'one of those sages whom he should understand less as he heard him longer'.

Rasselas and Nekayah then divide and Rasselas investigates the life of people at court, at the centre of power and influence. He finds that 'their lives were a continual succession of plots and detections, stratagems and escapes'. Nekayah, who investigates humble life, has fared no better: family life is riven by disagreements, marriage is a source of discord because 'some husbands are imperious, and some wives perverse', yet single people are peevish and malevolent ('Marriage has many pains, but celibacy has no pleasures'). Domestic discord, she concludes, is not easily avoided. As if to prove this point, Rasselas and Nekayah then fall into disagreement about the results of their investigations until reprimanded by Imlac: 'while you are making the choice of life, you neglect to live'.

Their visit to the pyramids, one of the greatest works of human ingenuity, shows only that the enormous labour of constructing them was without purpose, except that it satisfied 'that hunger of imagination which preys upon life, and must always be appeased by some employment'. The kidnapping of Pekuah teaches Nekayah the lesson that grief, too, can only be assuaged by activity. Imlac advises her: 'Do not suffer life to stagnate; it will grow muddy for want of motion: commit yourself again to the current of the world'. Pekuah, meanwhile, learns that stagnation can be caused by living in the seraglio, in the society of women who, because they have no knowledge and unvaried experience, could have nothing to talk about and nothing to do except fill the time with trivial activity.

Back in Cairo, the companions meet an astronomer, a man of deep learning and integrity, who is convinced that he has gained the power to control the weather. This is not a simple portrait of a megalomaniac meteorologist – rather than glorying in his power, the astronomer is made anxious by his responsibilities. The cause of his predicament is his solitude (both social and intellectual) and the cure is to persuade him gradually to 'take delight in sublunary pleasures' by re-establishing social contact. This episode is particularly powerful because the astronomer has many of the qualities most associated with happiness: he has great wisdom, benevolence, generosity and charm, yet his devotion to learning – no great sin, after all – has led to the worst of human predicaments: madness. The distance between merit and reward is at its largest here: 'Few can attain this man's knowledge, and few practise his virtues; but all may suffer his calamity' (ch. 43, 104). *Rasselas* is at its bleakest at this point in the narrative. Interpolated into the tale of the astronomer is a discourse with an old man. This man, like the astronomer, has found that age does not alleviate, but rather intensifies, the disappointments and vexations of life, and that his only hope is 'to possess in a better state that happiness which here I could not find, and that virtue which here I have not attained' (ch. 45, 109).

A visit to the catacombs gives rise to a meditation on the nature of human mortality and the immortality of the human soul. This seems to turn the tale into a traditional Christian apologue – 'by showing the unsatisfactory nature of things temporal, to direct the hopes of man to things eternal', as Boswell puts it in his *Life of Johnson*. One of the consolations traditionally offered by Christianity is the compensation of the life hereafter. In Heaven, Johnson writes elsewhere, we will find 'a state more constant and permanent, of which the objects may be more proportioned to our wishes, and the enjoyments to our capacities'. Johnson's poem, *The Vanity of Human Wishes* (1749), which also deals with the illusory prospects of happiness held out by human wishes and pursuits, offers the traditional Christian advice of relying on patience (i.e. forbearance) in this world while hoping for a better life in the next. That hope which impels us forward is, itself, our best source of happiness in this world and is provided by 'celestial wisdom', together with love and faith, to 'calm the mind'.

But the final chapter of *Rasselas*, 'The conclusion, in which nothing is concluded', suggests a continuation of the irony and lack of definitive answers to the human predicament that are present in the rest of the tale. Rasselas and his companions finally make their choice of life. They have learned to be sceptical about easy answers to the problem of human happiness, and though each of them forms a 'scheme of happiness', 'of these wishes that they had formed they well knew that none could be obtained', and so they return to Abyssinia. Though Nekayah concentrates her mind on the 'choice of eternity' and Pekuah forms her 'scheme of happiness' around the convent of St Anthony, yet the choices of the characters suggest an engagement with the world rather than a retreat from it, and the return to Abyssinia is not an acceptance of defeat, but a recognition that no one place is more favourable to happiness than any other.

There is no facile moralizing here. We are not being urged to forgo the temptations of the flesh and the pleasures of this world as a way of ensuring eternal happiness in the next. Nekayah learns that 'what satisfaction this world can afford, must arise from the conjunction of wealth, knowledge and goodness': rather than suggesting that an ascetic denial of earthly pleasures is the best life for a Christian, the lessons of the tale suggest that happiness, both earthly and eternal, is best achieved by a moderation of expectations combined with a determination to strive and be active, and a willingness to find happiness in any situation. One can and should enjoy the limited pleasures this world offers and 'palliate what we cannot cure', as Johnson puts it in the preface to his *Dictionary*. The tale ends as neither wholly Christian (in its traditional formulations), nor wholly secular. It is a guide to life based on hope, temperance and wisdom which is yet committed to an engagement with the world: 'Of the blessings set before you make your choice, and be content' (ch. 29, 72).

REFERENCES AND FURTHER READING

Ehrenpreis, Irvin (1981). '*Rasselas* and some meanings of "structure" in literary criticism'. *Novel* 14, 101–17.

Jones, Emrys (1967). 'The artistic form of *Rasselas*'. *Review of English Studies*, n.s. 18, 387–401.

Kolb, Gwin J. (1951). 'The structure of *Rasselas*'. *Publications of the Modern Language Association* 66, 698–717.

Lascelles, Mary (1951). '*Rasselas* reconsidered'. *Essays and Studies by Members of the English Association*, n.s. 4, 37–52.

Lockhart, Donald M. (1963). ' "The fourth son of the mighty emperor": the Ethiopian background of Johnson's *Rasselas*'. *Publications of the Modern Language Association* 78, 516–28.

Preston, Thomas R. (1969). 'The biblical context of Johnson's *Rasselas*'. *Publications of the Modern Language Association* 84, 274–81.

Rees, Christine (1996). *Utopian Imagination and Eighteenth-century Fiction*. Harlow, Essex: Longman. Ch. 8: 'Utopia and the philosophical tale: *Rasselas*'.

Tomarken, Edward (1989). *Johnson, 'Rasselas', and the Choice of Criticism*. Lexington, Ky.: University Press of Kentucky.

Walker, Robert G. (1977). *Eighteenth-century Arguments for Immortality and Johnson's 'Rasselas'*. ELS Monograph Series, 9. Victoria, B.C.: University of Victoria.

Weinbrot, Howard D. (1971). 'The reader, the general, and the particular: Johnson and Imlac in Chapter Ten of *Rasselas*', *Eighteenth-century Studies* 5, 80–96.

Wimsatt, W. K. (1968). 'In praise of *Rasselas*: four notes (converging)'. In *Imagined Worlds: Essays on Some English Novels and Novelists in Honor of John Butt*. Ed. Maynard Mack and Ian Gregor. London: Methuen.

38

Christopher Smart,
Jubilate Agno
Alun David

Jubilate Agno was written by the poet Christopher Smart between 1758–9 and 1763. Since its publication in 1939 it has become one of Smart's best-known works. Research since then has considerably illuminated its intrinsic qualities and its sources. The following discussion gives a brief account of the author's life, and offers critical comment on the poem's structure, motivation, language and style. All references in parentheses are to the Clarendon edition, listed in the References and Further Reading.

Christopher Smart and *Jubilate Agno*

Smart was born in Kent in 1722; his father was steward to the estates of William, Viscount Vane. He was educated at Durham School and Pembroke Hall, Cambridge, where he was highly regarded as a scholar and a poet. In 1742 he won the title 'Scholar of the University', and in 1745 became a Fellow of Pembroke Hall. After moving to London in 1749 he retained his fellowship, and was therefore able to compete in the University's annual Seatonian competition in the composition of religious poetry, which he won five times between 1750 and 1755.

In London, Smart joined John Newberry's stable of professional authors, contributing to the editing and writing of numerous periodicals. He wrote occasional verse and became a public performer, appearing in a series of tavern entertainments under the title 'Mother Midnight's Oratory'. In 1752, he married Anna Maria Carnan, Newberry's Catholic stepdaughter. Their daughters, Marianne and Elizabeth, were born in 1753 and 1754 respectively.

Smart never enjoyed financial security – partly as a result of his spendthrift habits – and on more than one occasion suffered physical and mental illness. At some juncture around early 1756 he underwent a medical crisis; in his *Hymn to the Supreme Being on Recovery from a Dangerous Fit of Illness*, published later that year, he celebrated his recovery and reinvigorated Christian faith. However, in May 1757 he was admitted to St Luke's Hospital for the insane, and the following year to a private madhouse in Bethnal Green, where he would remain until 1763; it was in this latter period of enforced restraint that he wrote *Jubilate Agno.* He began writing it at some point between June 1758 and April 1759, and continued at the rate of between one and three lines a day until his release.

The main justification for Smart's confinement was his habit of breaking into prayer at any time, regardless of conventional notions of propriety, and encouraging others to join him. His own words in *Jubilate Agno* suggest that his behaviour could become disruptive: 'For I blessed God in St James's Park til I routed all the company' (B89). By contemporary standards, he was treated with relative humanity in the asylum: he had access to books, journals and a garden, he received visitors, and enjoyed the company of a pet cat. He had occasion in *Jubilate Agno* to express his gratitude for small mercies: 'For I bless God that I am not in a dungeon, but am allowed the light of the Sun' (B147). Nevertheless, he vehemently denied the justice of his confinement, and initiated legal proceedings against those he held responsible for it after his release in 1763. The circumstances of his discharge, officially uncured, remain something of a mystery, but it is possible that the intervention of friends may have played an important part in it.

After his release Smart attempted to resume a literary career. He undertook a number of ambitious publishing projects, and produced substantial works such as *A Translation of the Psalms of David* (1765), *The Works of Horace, Translated into Verse* (1767), and *A Song to David* (1763), which he considered to be his best poem. Despite the support of numerous friends and patrons, these ventures did not enable him to secure his subsistence. He was arrested and placed in custody for debt default in 1770. He died in prison in 1771.

Although he describes himself in *Jubilate Agno* as a public writer with a national constituency – 'For by the grace of GOD I am the reviver of ADORATION among ENGLISH-MEN' (B332) – there is no evidence that Smart considered completing or publishing the work. Some passages of *Jubilate Agno* anticipate Smart's later writings: for instance, lines B601-13, which associate 'twelve cardinal virtues' with the tribes of Israel, are echoed in *A Song to David.* The manuscript of *Jubilate Agno* remained in private hands until its publication by W. F. Stead in 1939. It is now held at Harvard University's Houghton Library.

Structure

Twelve years after *Jubilate Agno*'s first appearance, W. H. Bond's edition (1951) offered a radical reappraisal of the poem's organization. Bond's rearrangement of the manuscript into four fragments based on the relationship of the two main kinds of verse in *Jubilate Agno* is universally accepted by modern scholars as an accurate representation of the work's structure. *Jubilate Agno* is written in 'free' verse. Apart from the invocation (A1–2), every line begins with either the word 'Let' or 'For': every page of the manuscript's sixteen folio leaves contains verses belonging to one category rather than the other. The two categories of verse are generically distinct. In each 'Let' verse, a biblical personage or the 'house' of a modern individual is summoned to worship or praise with a living creature, animal or vegetable. The 'For' verses exhibit more variety in their style and content; they refer to topical events, scientific propositions, and Smart's deteriorating relationship with his family, amongst other matters. Noting the numbering of the folios, and the parallel dating and verbal correspondences of many verses, Bond argued that *Jubilate Agno* was conceived as an 'antiphonal' text, with 'For' verses offering responses to 'Let' versicles. (Some verses, however, cannot be married off in this manner, and it is not uncommon for the degree of verbal correspondence within 'Let'-'For' pairings to fall to zero, particularly in fragment C. It should also be noted that other structural motifs have been discerned: for instance, the names in the 'Let' verses often replicate scriptural genealogies and catalogues.)

Bond's view of the structure of *Jubilate Agno* affects the interpretation of the work's meaning. In particular, it emphasizes the poem's close relationship with Christian liturgical tradition, discussed in the next section. It also bears on the local analysis of the poem's verbal texture. Consider the following passage (B123–4):

> LET PETER rejoice with the MOON FISH who keeps up the life in the waters by night.
>> *FOR I pray the Lord JESUS that cured the LUNATICK to be merciful to*
>> *my brethren and sisters in these houses.*
> Let Andrew rejoice with the Whale, who is array'd in beauteous blue and is a combination of bulk and activity.
>> *For they work me with their harping-irons, which is a barbarous*
>> *instrument, because I am more unguarded than others.*

Without the benefit of Bond's reordering, Stead interpreted the second 'For' verse as a reference to some kind of physical maltreatment allegedly suffered by Smart at the hands of the asylum staff, a reading supported in context by the first 'For' verse. But when the antiphonal structure is recognized, the reference to 'harping-irons' (harpoons) clearly provides a correspondence with the parallel 'Let' verse. Smart lends the whale the first person pronoun (as he did to other animals; see B640), thereby giving voice to the suffering 'dumb creature' (B183) with an implicit contrast between the violent 'work' of the whalers and the poet's sympathetic artifice. Self-reference may also be intended in B124, but such a reading is more difficult than a literal interpretation of the 'For' verse, based on its correspondence with the 'Let' versicle.

Motivation

The primary motivation for writing *Jubilate Agno* was devotional; the work is presented as an act of worship. Smart considered himself a loyal member of the Church of England, and *Jubilate Agno* may have begun as an imitation, or even revision, of the Benedicite, the canticle which calls on the whole of the creation to join in praise of God. *Jubilate Agno* is also an evangelical work, in the sense that it insists on the truth of Christian teaching, and the centrality of the Bible to the Christian faith. At many points, Smart represents himself as a modern martyr, imitating the sufferings of Christ, or a prophet, heralding the end of the world and exhorting the nation to reform its ways. The poet vigorously asserts the authority of the Bible ('the philosophy of the scriptures' B130) over spheres of intellectual and cultural activity that were becoming more likely to be regarded in a secular light (see, for instance, the scientific propositions of B158–B224, or the discussion of national origins in B433–61).

Apart from its religious purposes, it has been argued that *Jubilate Agno* came to serve Smart as a commonplace book and a journal, especially in fragment D. In the latter regard, it should be noted that *Jubilate Agno* not only records day-to-day events in Smart's life, but also offers self-analytical reflection, for instance on his practice as a poet:

For my talent is to give an impression upon words by punching, that when the reader casts his eye upon 'em, he takes up the image from the mould which I have made.

(B404)

Language and Style

It must be avowed that the language and style of *Jubilate Agno* can present considerable difficulties, even for specialist readers. Much of the poem's vocabulary derives from recondite or technical sources. Smart was, moreover, much given to multilingual homonyms and other forms of word-play. The reader is not only faced with references to hundreds of biblical personages, but also with possible puns on the Hebrew etymologies of their names. The style is often elliptical and allusive, and in these respects may owe something to the analysis of classical Hebrew poetry proposed in Robert Lowth's *Lectures on the Sacred Poetry of the Hebrews* (1753), which Smart read in the original Latin and greatly admired. Fortunately, modern scholarship has shed light on many of *Jubilate Agno*'s sources that might otherwise have remained obscure. The bibliography lists a number of illuminating studies, of which the foremost is the commentary to the Clarendon edition by Karina Williamson.

The difficulties of *Jubilate Agno* have sometimes led critics to characterize its style as 'mad writing', the unintelligible acting out of the author's psychosis. Opponents of this view have sometimes asserted that Smart was an essentially sane eccentric; more recently, it has been proposed by Clement Hawes that *Jubilate Agno* is very much concerned to counter the mentality that would stigmatize certain forms of religious, political, and literary self-expression as madness. These positions are not altogether mutually exclusive; readers will draw their own conclusions.

It is important, however, to keep the difficulty of *Jubilate Agno* in perspective; it contains many lines and passages of extraordinary directness and intimacy. The poem is best known as the source for the passage, 'For I will consider my Cat Jeoffrey'

(B695–768), which, although not without idiosyncrasy, is renowned for the simplicity of its colloquial, observational manner, and its freedom from conventional diction and sentiment. Furthermore, notwithstanding its originality, *Jubilate Agno* was by no means hermetically sealed against the literary culture of eighteenth-century England. Consider the following:

> Let Rizpah rejoice with the Eyed Moth who is beautiful in corruption.
> *For the piety of Rizpah is imitable in the Lord – wherefore I pray for the dead.*
> (B93)

These verses exemplify *Jubilate Agno*'s intimacy with the Bible: they cannot be understood without the knowledge that Rizpah is mentioned in 2 Samuel 21 as a concubine of Saul, whose mourning for her sons persuades David to arrange their burial. Christ's connection with mourning was proverbial – Smart refers to him as the 'Man of Melancholy' in connection with the recently bereaved Jacob Grieve (D67), and elsewhere. The language is somewhat antique; 'corruption' is used in its older sense, meaning physical decay. Nonetheless, these verses offer an unusually vivid instance of melancholic or 'graveyard' poetry, a popular mid-eighteenth-century genre to which Smart had contributed early in his career, and to which he would return: compare 'On the Sudden Death of a Clergyman', published in 1750, and 'Melancholy', which appeared in his last volume, *Hymns for the Amusement of Children* (1771). This rendering of the 'beautiful in corruption' connects *Jubilate Agno* more closely to the mainstream of eighteenth-century poetry than has often been acknowledged.

References and Further Reading

Bond, W. H. (1950). 'Christopher Smart's *Jubilate Agno*', *Harvard Library Bulletin* 4, 39–52.

Dearnley, Moira (1968). *The Poetry of Christopher Smart*. London: Routledge and Kegan Paul.

Guest, Harriet (1989). *A Form of Sound Words: The Religious Poetry of Christopher Smart*. Oxford: Clarendon Press.

Hawes, Clement (1996). *Mania and Literary Style: The Rhetoric of Enthusiasm from the Ranters to Christopher Smart*. Cambridge: Cambridge University Press.

——(1999). *Christopher Smart and the Enlightenment*. New York: St Martin's Press.

Keymer, Tom (1995). 'Presenting jeopardy: language, authority, and the voice of Smart in *Jubilate Agno*'. In *Presenting Poetry: Composition, Publication, Reception*. Ed. Howard Erskine-Hill and Richard McCabe. Cambridge: Cambridge University Press, 97–116.

Mahony, Robert and Betty Rizzo (1984). *Christopher Smart: An Annotated Bibliography 1743–1983*. New York: Garland Publishing.

Parrish, Charles C. (1961). 'Christopher Smart's knowledge of Hebrew'. *Studies in Philology* 58, 516–32.

Sherbo, Arthur (1967). *Christopher Smart: Scholar of the University*. East Lansing: State University of Michigan Press.

Stead, William Force (1939). *Rejoice in the Lamb: A Song from Bedlam*. London: Jonathan Cape.

Walsh, Marcus and Karina Williamson (1980–96). *The Poetical Works of Christopher Smart*. 6 vols. Oxford: Clarendon Press.

Williamson, Karina. 'Smart's *Principia*: science and anti-science in *Jubilate Agno*'. *Review of English Studies* n.s., 30, 409–22.

39

Laurence Sterne, *Tristram Shandy*

David Fairer

Though in one sense, our family was certainly a simple machine, as it consisted of a few wheels; yet there was thus much to be said for it, that these wheels were set in motion by so many different springs, and acted one upon the other from such a variety of strange principles and impulses, – that though it was a simple machine, it had all the honour and advantages of a complex one, – and a number of as odd movements within it, as ever were beheld in the inside of a Dutch silk-mill.

(V.6)

Sterne's *Tristram Shandy* offers the reader many different models of itself – the game, the journey, the hobby-horse, the joke, the doodle, the humorous seduction, the *coitus interruptus*. But this spinning-machine is a helpful way to begin thinking about some of the intricacies of a novel which on first acquaintance might seem to be little more than inconsequential chatter, or a vehicle heading nowhere (and of course it is both of those as well). Tristram here offers us an image of his family, the Shandys (*shandy*, a northern dialect word, meant 'wild' or 'crack-brained'), an odd assortment of characters who jostle along together like mixed items in a basket. Two of them are returned adventurers: Walter Shandy, a former Turkey-merchant (trader with the Ottoman empire), the theorist who has a new plan for everything, seeking patterns and precedents in each obscure treatise he has looked into, forever hoping to solve difficulties and direct life to a desired end; and Uncle Toby, a former army Captain wounded in the groin by a fragment of parapet dislodged by a cannon-ball at the siege of Namur, re-enacting the traumatic scene on the bowling green outside, so that his whole being, physical and mental, is fixed on one idea: the centrifugal and the centripetal. Walter is left clutching at thin air as life outruns all his plans to shape the future (his elaborate educational treatise, *Tristra-paedia*, always lags behind his growing son); Toby's consciousness pulls everything towards his fortifications and implacements where all his meanings are centred. Walter longs to straighten out the future, Toby to straighten out the past. Unfortunately they are both living in a world where nothing runs straight.

Just as the spinning machine has to tease out its threads and avoid knots, so the novel's garrulous narrative spins its individual threads of thought and incident, conscious of the frequent 'cross accidents' when they intersect or the troublesome knots when they become entangled. The paragraph quoted above occurs at a moment when Tristram is carefully keeping his threads separate; to do this he has just suspended his mother in an awkward twisting posture (and holding her breath) evesdropping at the parlour door ('I am determined to let her stand for five minutes') while he brings us up to date with parallel events in the kitchen: 'whatever motion, debate, harangue, dialogue, project, or dissertation, was going forwards in the parlour, there was generally another at the same time, and upon the same subject, running parallel along with it in the kitchen'. In both places the news of Bobby Shandy's death has broken: in the parlour, his father Walter is stoically invoking classical precedents for an oration on the inevitability of death ('Where is Troy and Mycenae, and Thebes and Delos . . . ?') while Toby's innocent questions 'break the thread' of his speech; simultaneously in the kitchen each of the servants gives the news a personal spin, before Corporal Trim achieves a moment of epiphany by 'dropping his hat plumb upon the ground' (V.7): while others verbally 'wind and turn the passions' Trim captures the very 'sentiment of mortality' in a single eloquent, perpendicular, gesture.

This is a rare and precious moment when entanglement gives way to unexpected simplicity. It is paralleled by a similar moment of grace at the very end of volume VII, a volume of fits and starts and narrow escapes in which Tristram has been fleeing from death. He finally comes across some French peasants celebrating the vintage, and as he joins in their dance, his partner Nannette's hair unknots itself before him ('the whole knot fell down') – suddenly life becomes simple and wonderful: 'She looked amiable! – Why could I not live, and end my days thus? Just disposer of our joys and sorrows, cried I, why could not a man sit down in the lap of contentment here – and dance, and sing, and say his prayers, and go to heaven with this nut-brown maid?' (VII.43).

But in Tristram's life the threads of narrative are so often entangled. What should ideally run parallel or perpendicular, tends to twist or deviate. In the following chapter (VIII.1) he starts off his new volume by facing this fact. A man trying to be true to the sensations and experiences of his life only falsifies by straightening them out:

> every step that's taken, the judgment is surprised by the imagination. I defy, notwithstanding all that has been said upon *straight lines* in sundry pages of my book – I defy the best cabbage planter that ever existed, whether he plants backwards or forwards, it makes little difference in the account . . . I defy him to go on coolly, critically, and canonically, planting his cabbages one by one, in straight lines, and stoical distances . . . without ever and anon straddling out, or sidling into some bastardly digression. (VIII.1)

In this novel the lines of narrative accelerate or linger, leap ahead or repeatedly return to the same point (the story of the King of Bohemia and his seven castles never gets told); sometimes we have to wait for the connection as various threads are followed until the point is finally explained. In VI.40 Tristram offers his readers a kind of narrative tachograph of his progress through the first four volumes ('these were the four lines I moved in') where we can see the straight threads jerk and shudder from the horizontal, inscribing a series of kinks, balloons, arabesques, squiggles and giddy projections backwards and forwards. 'What a journey!', he exclaims.

Indeed. We have come to know our hero from the moment of his first desperate journey as a 'homunculus', a tiny little gentleman-sperm threading his way to the egg, whose direct progress is interrupted by his mother's sudden thought about winding the clock. He is forced to spend his next nine months recovering from exhaustion and disordered nerves, 'a prey to sudden starts or a series of melancholy dreams and fancies' (I.2). Along with the grandfather clock, which had interposed so significantly in his early life, the mechanism of the novel and the mechanism of Tristram's life have been simultaneously set going. Both share the spinning machine's 'odd movements' and 'different springs . . . [acting] one upon the other from such a variety of strange principles and impulses', and they each spin out like a consciousness expanding itself before our eyes as the fabric of the book grows.

The mechanisms of Sterne's novel are the mechanisms of the modern mind. By the early eighteenth century the age-old 'humoral pathology' (the healthy body keeping the 'four humors' in balance) and 'faculty psychology' (the mind compartmentalized into higher and lower faculties, with rational judgement controlling imagination) were being replaced by more unified accounts that grew out of early discoveries of the nervous system. Thomas Willis's explanation (in *A Discourse Concerning the Souls of Brutes*, 1684) of how the 'animal spirits' moved through the brain-vessels, or Nicholas Robinson's theory of the nerve fibres (*A New System of the Spleen*, 1729), saw the mental state as dependent on the health of the communicating medium: the animal spirits might deviate into unusual channels, or the nerves could become too tight or too flaccid. Mind and body were being thought of as interdependent. In *The Natural Method of Cureing the Diseases of the Body, and the Disorders of the Mind Depending on the Body* (1742) George Cheyne offered his latest findings in a long explication worthy of Walter Shandy:

> I conceive [the mind] acts on the Organs by means of the *Mechanism* of the Brain and its *Nerves*, which are an Infinity of differently situated, complicated and stretch'd little *Filaments* or *Fibrils*, fill'd with a soft *milky* cellular Substance, (like a *Rush* with its *Pith*) contain'd in small *membranous* extremely *elastic* Sacks or *Tubuli*, all whose *elastic* and *energic* Virtue consists in the proper *Tension* or *Vibrations* of these Sacks or *membranous* Coats, spread over all the *Solids* of the Body. (94)

How precarious human health and sanity could seem – and how dependent on the intricate network of minute channels by which life circulated. At the moment of conception Tristram's 'animal spirits' are 'ruffled beyond description', and his future physical and mental journey through the novel will be no less subject to upset. As

Tristram remarks: 'A man's body and his mind . . . are exactly like a jerkin, and a jerkin's lining; rumple the one – you rumple the other' (III.4).

Tristram Shandy also engages repeatedly with the philosophical implications of the new physiology, and especially with the work of John Locke, whose concept of the mind as a network of thought-paths (the equivalent of the wires in a primitive computer) emphasized the tendency in a person's animal spirits to wander off the road and find a congenial path for themselves:

> Custom settles habits of thinking in the understanding, as well as of determining in the will, and of motions in the body; all which seems to be but trains of motions in the animal spirits, which, once set a-going, continue in the same steps they have been used to, which, by often treading, are worn into a smooth path. (*An Essay Concerning Human Understanding*, 1690, II.xxxiii.6)

Locke's image explains how two very different ideas can be associated within the mind, which becomes used to stepping from one to another. That *Tristram Shandy* is going to be full of this kind of mental path-making is clear from the opening page where Tristram explains the significance of his seminal deviation:

> You have all, I dare say, heard of the animal spirits . . . Well, you may take my word, that nine parts in ten of a man's sense or his nonsense, his successes and miscarriages in this world depend upon their motions and activity, and the different tracts and trains you put them into, so that when they are once set a-going, whether right or wrong, 'tis not a halfpenny matter, – away they go cluttering like hey-go-mad; and by treading the same steps over and over again, they presently make a road of it, as plain and smooth as a garden-walk. (I.1)

Generically, 'Lockean man' is an individual. Having no innate ideas, every person begins as a blank sheet on which experience writes its increasingly complex programme; the billions of ideas running through the mind help to form its network of connections (the sensorium), but are also channelled by it into habits of thought and 'associated' images. In Locke, oddness and 'extravagance' (literally 'wandering out of the common path') become explicable by 'chance or custom'. He begins his chapter on the association of ideas (II.xxxiii) with the heading 'Something unreasonable in most Men', and continues: 'There is scarce anyone that does not observe something that seems odd to him, and is in itself really extravagant, in the opinions, reasonings, and actions of other men.' The necessary corollary to Locke's associationist theory is therefore his stress on the importance of clear communication between these dissimilar individuals and each person's complete understanding of the other's meaning ('When a man speaks to another, it is that he may be understood'). For Locke, words are arbitrary signs of ideas (III.ii.1) and are effective only when speaker and hearer agree on their precise signification – not only that, but 'unless a man's words excite the same ideas in the hearer which he makes them stand for in speaking, he does not

speak intelligibly' (III.ii.8). Hence Tristram's fastidious need to communicate explanatory material to his readers. We have to see and know as much about his world as
possible, and in order to explain the meaning of an event or the nuance of a remark,
other incidents must be introduced. In the end, the only way to overcome this comic
Lockean nightmare is for us to share every experience, each idea, singly and in combination, that has shaped Tristram's being. In Sterne's version of the Lockean individual '– Endless is the Search for Truth' (II.3). Tristram becomes desperate at how
the materials for his life are accumulating faster than he can sort and explain them to
us: even before he emerges from the womb (in volume 3) his mind and body have
been shaped by the world waiting to receive him. Add in the Shandy household, and
the task of following each thread becomes impossible:

> My mother, you must know, – but I have fifty things more necessary to let you know
> first. – I have a hundred difficulties which I have promised to clear up, and a thousand
> distresses and domestic misadventures crowding in upon me thick and threefold, one
> upon the neck of another . . . I have left my father lying across his bed, and my uncle
> Toby in his old fringed chair, sitting beside him, and promised I would go back to them
> in half an hour, and five-and-thirty minutes are lapsed already. (III.38)

Tristram plays a game with the 'now' of writing and the 'now' of reading, attempting at various moments to bring them together ('And here am I sitting, this 12th day
of August, 1766, in a purple jerkin and yellow pair of slippers, without either wig
or cap on', IX.1). At other points the author's 'now' is humorously aligned to the
reader's schedule: 'Lay down the book', he tells us, 'and I will allow you half a day to
give a probable guess' (I.10). When in I.20 he sends an inattentive female reader back
to re-examine a passage, she returns a paragraph later to face the author's questions,
while we have moved on with the narrative.

The novel throughout plays games with the reader's awareness of 'duration'. This is
part of its Lockean obsession with trains of ideas and mental perception. Tristram even
patronizingly explains that Locke's *Essay* is really a version of his own project: 'It is a
history-book, Sir . . . of what passes in a man's own mind' (II.2). In the *Essay* Locke distinguishes 'duration' from 'time' ('Time is Duration set out by Measures', II.xiv.17) and
he argues that our sense of duration is our awareness of 'a train of ideas which constantly
succeed one another' in the mind (II.xiv.3. This is discussed by Walter and Toby in
III.18). To that extent duration is subjective, time objective. Sometimes, however,
things move faster than the mind can perceive them, so it is possible for an extremely
rapid series of events to form in effect a single idea, what he terms an 'instant'. Locke's
example of this is, appropriately for *Tristram Shandy*, the flight of a cannon-ball. If the
cannon is fired through a room and the ball 'take[s] with it any limb or fleshy parts of
a man', it must hit the two walls and the man's flesh in succession, 'yet' comments
Locke, 'I believe, nobody who ever felt the pain of such a shot, or heard the blow against
the two distant walls, could perceive any succession' (II.xiv.10). Such an 'instant' strikes
the mind, says Locke, as a single idea.

For Uncle Toby, his own experience with a cannon-ball constitutes a single idea in these terms, an instant made eternity, to which he obsessively returns. Though Toby is a simple soul with only a single 'here' and 'now' to recover, his mental/physical landscape is fraught with intricacies: 'the ground was cut and cross-cut with such a multitude of dykes, drains, rivulets, and sluices, on all sides, – and he would get so sadly bewildered, and set fast amongst them, that frequently he could neither get backwards or forwards to save his life' (II.1). When his struggle to re-enact is transferred to the bowling-green at Shandy Hall, things are little better. Such a location is, after all, a physical symbol of his own mind, across which his ideas, like bowls across the greensward, curve always to one side. Toby's mental bias, forever pulling him back to the bowling-green, makes verbal communication with his brother virtually impossible.

Walter Shandy too is conscious that the accidents of life are forever pulling his schemes out of line. Tristram invites us to pity his perpetual self-defeat: 'inoffensive in his notions, – so played upon in them by cross purposes; – to look down upon the stage, and see him baffled and overthrown in all his little systems and wishes; to behold a train of events perpetually falling out against him' (I.19). As if parodying the Lockean train of ideas, physical events and objects often form an unstoppable procession, as they do for the unfortunate Dr Slop when he is ambling on his frail pony to help with Tristram's birth while Obadiah is speeding 'the adverse way' along the narrow lane astride a galloping coach-horse towards him. Walter has urgently dispatched Obadiah to fetch the man-midwife, and his wishes are about to be met – head on. As Tristram later remarks: 'When the precipitancy of a man's wishes hurries on his ideas ninety times faster than the vehicle he rides in . . . woe be to the vehicle and its tackling' (VII.8). The opposite unequal forces encounter each other at a sharp bend in the lane, with disastrous results:

> What could Dr Slop do? – He crossed himself + – Pugh! – but the doctor, Sir, was a Papist. – No matter; he had better have kept hold of the pummel . . . for in crossing himself he let go his whip, – and in attempting to save his whip . . . he lost his stirrup, – in losing which, he lost his seat; – and in the multitude of all these losses (which, by the bye, shews what little advantages there is in crossing) the unfortunate doctor lost his presence of mind . . . tumbling off [his pony] diagonally, something in the stile and manner of a pack of wool. (II.9)

Dr Slop falls off his horse because he is a Roman Catholic.

It is Tristram who is the ultimate victim, not only of this concatenation but of many other seemingly disconnected incidents which finally converge on him – or more precisely, bear down on his nose and groin. Walter's anxiety that everything should turn out right for his child-to-be, thanks to the novel's inverse principle, ensures disaster. One such thread is through the well-meaning Obadiah who liked to whistle while on horseback, and who consequently knotted up Dr Slop's bag to stop its contents jingling: 'he tied and cross-tied them all . . . with such a multiplicity of round-abouts and intricate cross turns, with a hard knot at every intersection or point where the strings met' (III.8). Faced with this embodiment of the novel's tangled lines, Slop cuts his way through – and also painfully through his thumb. If we factor in the awkward forceps and Slop's increasing harassment, we can appreciate the weight that Tristram's nose finally has to bear. 'Sport of small accidents, Tristram Shandy! that thou art, and ever will be!' (III.8). As readers, we are encouraged to use our imaginations to trace out the many threads of fate that interweave through his story:

> You may conjecture upon it, if you please, – and whilst your imagination is in motion, you may encourage it to go on, and discover by what causes and effects in nature it could come to pass, that my uncle Toby got his modesty by the wound he received upon his groin. – You may raise a system to account for the loss of my nose by marriage-articles, – and shew the world how it could happen, that I should have the misfortune to be called TRISTRAM, in opposition to my father's hypothesis . . . These, with fifty other points left yet unravelled, you may endeavour to solve if you have time. (II.19)

In defiance of this world of fate and chance, Walter Shandy asserts an odd combination of talismanic texts and the human will, 'that great and elastic power within us of counterbalancing evil' (IV.8). To counter the damage to his son's nose, he therefore exploits the 'magic bias' of the name Trismegistus ('as the greatest evil has befallen him – I must counteract and undo it with the greatest good'), but yet again human agency fails him (this time Susannah) and turns his plan awry. In contrast, Uncle Toby has a simple faith which tends to let things beyond the bowling-green take their natural course while he whistles *Lillabullero*. When Walter mentions the 'secret spring' which will redeem his son, Toby takes it to be religion: 'Will that set my child's nose on? cried my father . . . It makes every thing straight for us, answered my uncle Toby'. But in this novel neither Walter's interventionism nor Toby's *laissez faire* can stop life's mechanism from running its course. Toby's sense that things will straighten themselves out is all very well, but he too becomes an instrument for irreversibly shaping Tristram's mind and body.

Both incidents (benign and malign) involve a sash window. The benign moment is Toby's sparing of the fly: 'Go, says he, lifting up the sash, and opening his hand as he spoke, to let it escape; – go, poor devil, get thee gone, why should I hurt thee?' (II.12). This gesture forever imprints an image of benevolence on Tristram's mind and gives him a 'vibration of most pleasurable sensation'. But Toby, who would not hurt a fly, is also responsible for another 'accidental impression' on his nephew, this time a physical one, when the five-year-old is circumcised by the sash window in the nursery (V.17) whose counterbalancing mechanism of pulleys and weights Trim has dismantled. Toby's wish for a pair of cannons for his battlefield finally draws a connective thread from his wound to young Tristram's. Well might Walter Shandy lament: 'Unhappy Tristram! child of wrath! child of decrepitude! interruption! mistake! and discontent! What one misfortune or disaster in the book of embryotic evils, that could unmechanize thy frame, or entangle thy filaments! which has not fallen upon thy head' (IV.19).

This novel of spider's webs, thread papers, cross-purposes, puzzled skeins, knots and entangled filaments, is acutely conscious of how 'texts' are (as etymology tells us) woven together. Our modern critical concern with a separate 'context' splits apart two words which had once meant the same thing. In 1642 Milton spoke of the Christian Bible as a 'sacred context' within which 'all wisdome is infolded', and it is useful to think of Sterne's fiction as a 'context' in that sense. Tristram repeatedly teases us with the hidden meanings and cross references that abound in his book, and with the inter-connectedness of its 'odd' textual parts. It is an organic work, and from its first page we watch things germinate and grow: we see ideas implanted, impressions received, sensations communicated, and these in turn make links with other experiences, until a full fictional cerebellum develops. Through all the confusion and folly the life-force threads its way, even down to the 'fat, foolish scullion' struggling with her dropsy, who announces while she scours the fish-kettle in the kitchen that she is 'alive' (V.7) – it is her one big simple idea, her private triumph over mortality, and she is on her knees while saying it. Let her not be forgotten.

Tristram's own machine, and that of the novel, will eventually stop like the clock – with disconcerting suddenness. The machine of criticism must do the same, with so much unsaid and so many threads not followed. But that is not the end of reading. In I.20 Tristram rebukes the 'vicious taste . . . of reading straight forwards'. Getting to know *Tristram Shandy* involves thinking spatially, and working backwards as well:

> from the beginning of this, you see, I have constructed the main work and the adventitious parts of it with such intersections, and have so complicated and involved the digressive and progressive movements, one wheel within another, that the whole machine, in general, has been kept a-going. (I.22)

REFERENCES AND FURTHER READING

Anderson, Howard (1971). '*Tristram Shandy* and the reader's imagination'. *PMLA* 86, 966–73.

Booth, Wayne C. (1952). 'The self-conscious narrator in comic fiction before *Tristram Shandy*'. *PMLA* 67, 163–85.

Brady, Frank (1970–1). '*Tristram Shandy*: sexuality, morality, and sensibility'. *Eighteenth-century Studies* 4, 41–56.

Briggs, Peter M. (1985). 'Locke's *Essay* and the tentativeness of *Tristram Shandy*'. *Studies in Philology* 82, 493–520.

Brooks, Douglas (1973). *Number and Pattern in the Eighteenth-century Novel*. London and Boston: Routledge and Kegan Paul. See ch. 8.

Cash, Arthur H. and John M. Stedmond, eds

(1971). *The Winged Skull: Papers from the Laurence Sterne Bicentenary Conference*. London: Methuen.

Conrad, Peter (1978). *Shandyism: The Character of Romantic Irony*. Oxford: Basil Blackwell.

DePorte, Michael V. (1974). *Nightmares and Hobbyhorses: Swift, Sterne, and Augustan Ideas of Madness*. San Marino: The Huntington Library.

Ehlers, Leigh A. (1981). 'Mrs. Shandy's "Lint and Basilicon": the importance of women in *Tristram Shandy*', *South Atlantic Review* 46, 61–75.

Harries, Elizabeth W. (1982). 'Sterne's novels: gathering up the fragments'. *ELH* 49, 35–49.

Hawley, Judith (1991). '"Hints and Documents" 1: a bibliography for *Tristram Shandy*'. *The Shandean* 3, 9–36.

Howes, Alan B. (ed.) (1974). *Sterne: The Critical Heritage.* London and Boston: Routledge and Kegan Paul.

Lanham, Richard A. (1973). *Tristram Shandy: The Games of Pleasure.* Berkeley: University of California Press.

Mullan, John (1988). *Sentiment and Sociability: The Language of Feeling in the Eighteenth Century.* Oxford: Clarendon Press. See ch. 4.

New, Melvyn (1969). *Laurence Sterne as Satirist.* Gainesville: University of Florida Press.

New, Melvyn (ed.) (1992). *New Casebooks: Tristram Shandy.* Houndmills: Macmillan.

New, Melvyn and Joan (1978). Laurence Sterne, *The Life and Opinions of Tristram Shandy, Gentleman: The Text.* 2 vols. Gainesville: University of Florida Press. *The Notes.* Ed. Melvyn New, with Richard A. Davies and W. G. Day. Gainesville: University of Florida Press (1984).

Preston, John (1970). *The Created Self: The Reader's Role in Eighteenth-century Fiction.* London: Heinemann.

Rothstein, Eric (1975). *Systems of Order and Inquiry in Later Eighteenth-century Fiction.* Berkeley: University of California Press. See pp. 62–108.

Seidel, Michael (1979). *Satiric Inheritance: Rabelais to Sterne.* Princeton: Princeton University Press, see ch. 9.

Stedmond, John M. (1967). *The Comic Art of Laurence Sterne.* Toronto: University of Toronto Press.

Traugott, John (1970). *Tristram Shandy's World: Sterne's Philosophical Rhetoric.* New York: Russell & Russell. First pub. (1954).

Tuveson, Ernest (1962). 'Locke and Sterne'. In *Reason and Imagination: Studies in the History of Ideas 1600–1800.* Ed. J. A. Mazzeo. New York: Columbia University Press, 255–77.

Zimmerman, Everett (1987). '*Tristram Shandy* and narrative representation'. *The Eighteenth Century: Theory and Interpretation* 28, 127–47.

40

James Macpherson, *Fingal* and Other Poems

Dafydd Moore

The facts concerning the production and reception of James Macpherson's *Poems of Ossian* have been established and argued over frequently enough since the 23-year-old Macpherson met the dramatist John Home in the Scottish spa town of Moffat in 1759. The evidence and results of these debates and investigations are to be found in the bibliography to this article. For this reason, and because I want to signal my sense of the importance of actually reading *Ossian*, this chapter will concentrate on suggesting some ways in which the evolution, form, and feel of the poems can be interpreted in terms of the conditions and motivating forces behind their appearance. Within the constraints of space I also want to indicate in passing how Macpherson could be seen as a vital part of the story of British literature from Milton to Blake, and how writing about *Ossian* involves thinking about fundamental issues of cultural identity both in a historical and in a theoretical or methodological sense. It goes without saying of course that in the present context such comments will be selective and brief (rightly or wrongly I have little to say, for example, about the sublime), but that I hope they will stand as a representative introduction to the field.

The Poems of Ossian appeared in three separate volumes. Subsequent to meeting Home in 1759, Macpherson was prevailed upon to publish translations of a small selection of gaelic poems he claimed to have collected in the Highlands. These appeared in June 1760 as *The Fragments of Ancient Poetry*, with a preface by the eminent Hugh Blair (who was soon to be appointed the first Regius Professor of Literature at Edinburgh University). The *Fragments* introduced a new world and a new note to mainstream literature, a misty celtic past of noble warriors and beautiful maidens which would have a profound effect on the artistic output – in literature, painting and music – of every European country for the next sixty years, and arguably longer. The central thematic and stylistic elements of the complete Ossianic vision were present from the very first of the *Fragments*. Fragment I represents a dramatic exchange between Vinvela and her love Shilric bemoaning the departure of the latter 'to the wars of Fingal'. Fragment II opens with a solitary figure sitting by a 'mossy fountain':

Dark waves roll over the heath . . . It is mid-day: but all is silent. Sad are my
thoughts alone. Didst thou but appear, O my love, a wanderer on the heath! . . . thee
I would comfort, my love, and bring thee to thy father's house . . .
But is it she that appears, like a beam of light on the heath? bright as the moon in
autumn, as the sun in a summer-storm, comest thou lovely maid over the rocks, over
the mountains to me? – She speaks: but how weak her voice! like the breeze in the
reeds of the pool. Hark!

Returnest thou safe from the war? Where are thy friends my love? I heard of thy
death on the hill; I heard and mourned thee, Shilric!

Yes my fair I return; but I alone of my race. Thou shalt see them no more: their
graves I raised on the plain. But why art thou on the desert hill? why on the heath
alone?

Alone I am, O Shilric! alone in the winter-house. With grief for thee I expired.
Shilric, I am placed in the tomb.

(PO, 9)

The *Fragments* establish the innovative prose-poem style of *Ossian,* a style which reflects
both the gaelic ballads Macpherson had read and current primitivist theory about the
structure of early poetry (thinking influenced by Robert Lowth's work on Hebrew
verse earlier in the eighteenth century). It should be noted that this style was also
hugely influential, for example on Blake and Whitman to name but two. Key features include the paratactic, incantatory quality; the definite yet strangely anonymous
characters (whose names, according to Macpherson, have significant meanings in
gaelic, a fact which both particularizes and generalizes them); the overall vagueness
and confusion, which encourages the imaginative engagement of the reader with the
words. To a world accustomed to the rigid formality of neo-classical verse, the *Fragments* were a shock to the system, but at the same time the haunting style of *Ossian*
owes much to a strange familiarity created through echoes and approximations of Classical, Miltonic and, particularly here, Old Testament verse. If Macpherson's prosody
is established here, then so is the rest of the Ossianic mode: the sublime desolation
of graves on a hillside; the vague watery ghosts; the setting of mountain, moor and
heath; the alignment of scenery, atmosphere and lyric mood; a dead beauty and the
bloody, terrible and obscure wars of Fingal. The *Fragments* also lay out the central
theme of *Ossian*: death, misfortune and a seemingly wilful dysfunction; for example
here in the perverse twist seemingly motivated by nothing other than the workings
of a malevolently ordered Ossianic universe.

Missing from the *Fragments* was a central and coherent cast of characters, most
notably Fingal, and the single controlling consciousness of Ossian himself. These features were introduced, along with copious notes and dissertations filling in the details
of the ancient Caledonian world in order to give the whole production weight, in the
second and third volumes of poems, *Fingal* (December 1761) and *Temora* (March
1763). These publications represent the fruits of trips made to the Highlands by
Macpherson in late summer of 1760 and the summer of 1761, trips funded by the
so-called Scottish literati who were excited by the possibility of ancient epic

material extant in the wilds of the Highlands (contributors included David Hume, Adam Smith, Hugh Blair, Adam Ferguson and Henry Home, Lord Kames). The volumes (each containing the title poem and various shorter pieces) were presented as the poetic remains of Ossian, a third-century gaelic prince, warrior and bard, a claim which was the source of a bitter controversy. In fact they represent loose translations of gaelic ballads and prose tales concerning the heroes Fionn and Cuchulain, combined with (increasingly) generous contributions from Macpherson's own imagination as he sought to build disparate gaelic traditions into a substantial and coherent legendary matter which would answer to not only his own needs, as he sought to champion gaelic culture, but also those of his Edinburgh sponsors. The rest of this chapter suggests some textual evidence for those agendas.

Interest in the *Fragments* had been intense because they held out the possibility of an ancient national literature comparable with those of other countries. The lack of such a (neo-classically recognized) literature was felt acutely by a Scottish intelligentsia increasingly self-confident in most other cultural fields (for example, history and philosophy). But ancient national literature, by mid-eighteenth-century standards at least, was understood in terms of identifiable stories and identifiable poets. Thus in the case of *Fingal* Macpherson adapted and greatly embellished – 'completed' as it were – the 'invasion narratives' of gaelic legend (which date from the sixth century) in order to create a neo-classical epic, which, since it was standard literary theory to assume a single poet behind great epic documents, he provided with an author figure Ossian. But Macpherson goes beyond merely positing an author:

> Many a voice . . . in tuneful sounds arose. Of Fingal's noble deeds they sung, and of the noble race of the hero. And sometimes . . . was heard the name of the now mournful Ossian.
>
> Often have I fought, and often won in battles of the spear. But blind, and tearful, and forlorn I now walk with little men. O Fingal, with thy race of battle I now behold thee not. The wild roes feed upon the green tomb of the mighty king of Morven.
>
> (*PO*, 79)

From this point on the poem is punctuated with such editorial comments and with digressions, some of which explain events in the main narrative, some of which seem the self-indulgent musings of an old man. This emphasis on Ossian represents the logical conclusion of the cult of the primitive poet to which *Ossian* owes much, and to which it would itself contribute massively. This theory of poetry, developed by (to name just two of particular relevance to Macpherson) Thomas Blackwell of Marischal College Aberdeen (whose theories on classical poetry Macpherson would have been taught while at the Aberdeen universities in the mid-1750s) and Blair himself, held that earliest states of society – which they associated with simplicity and vigour – were most likely to produce heroic epic poetry. Primitive 'noble savage' poets encountered a raw life in the raw, and wrote with the immediacy only direct experience brings. Thus as the ideal primitive poet Ossian is closely associated with the actions he describes and he narrates them, and reflects on the process of narration, as felt experience.

At the same time, if Ossian represents an influential enactment of the primitivist theory of the twenty years prior to his appearance, he also foreshadows developments we have come to associate with the Romantic movement. Features of Romantic poetry such as the emphasis on poet as (troubled) hero for example, and the development of lyric memoir epics, are both present in Ossian. Indeed the narrative situation of old Ossian is precisely the 'spontaneous overflow of powerful feelings recollected in tranquillity' which Wordsworth would hold as an ideal in poetry.

The dual perspective of then and now encapsulated in this passage is a central feature of *Ossian*, and a major source of the Ossianic melancholy which surfaces in the *Fragments*, continues through the later volumes, and for which Macpherson's work is primarily known. Ossian narrates his tales from a perspective which has seen the greatness pass, and even his depictions of the Fingalian world in its pomp are tinged with the shadow of a more profound future defeat. Ossian even invests the representation of his characters with this awareness, as Fingal puts it after his conclusive victory at the end of *Fingal*:

> to-day our fame is greatest. We shall pass away like a dream. No sound will be in the fields of our battles. Our tombs will be lost in the heath. The hunter shall not know the place of our rest. Our names may be heard in song, but the strength of our arms will cease.
>
> (*PO*, 101)

Again this cross-fertilization between (notional) creative and created sensibility could be seen as a proto-Romantic trait. However, having considered aspects of the evolution and form of *Ossian* in terms of certain of the motivating forces behind *Ossian*, I want to end by considering this sense of foredoomed defeat in a similar way. In doing so we are eluctably drawn into questions of the politics of cultural representation too involved to consider in the present context in anything more than the broadest of outlines.

Ossian is, I have suggested, a work of cultural nationalism, an attempt to aggrandize Scottish culture in the eyes of the world by the discovery of a 'Northern Homer'. But the Lowland literati who sponsored this project had little desire for the wished-for national epic to stir nationalist feeling of a separatist nature, or to further alienate an already resentful and suspicious English cultural establishment. At the same time they wanted the Scottish epic to be expressive of the values and ideals they believed would best serve Scotland, and Britain, in the modern world. The stakes were even higher than usual at the beginning of the 1760s since from the outbreak of the Seven Years War the literati had been agitating for a Scottish militia, which involved – however paradoxical this may sound – downplaying the strident (or 'disloyal' from an Anglo-British point of view) militarism of the Scottish past within its call for a Scottish military identity (after all it was less than twenty years since a Scottish army had threatened the internal security of Britain and the throne itself). *Ossian* inscribes this double agenda: as an epic of martial adventuring it represents a pro-militia statement by positing a fighting spirit as an integral part of Scottish national identity, while its sense of doom, its nostalgic implication that all this was long ago and over for good, ensures that the poems are not only a source of the melancholy reflection considered morally valuable by the literati but also that they are not a call to arms for an independent Scottish nation. Both these imperatives are served in the insistent message of *Ossian* that 'the fame of my former actions is ceased; and I sit forlorn at the tombs of my friends' (*PO*, 104).

The sense that Macpherson's gaelic epic might ultimately valorize as a national quality a tearful resignation to the 'facts' of existence ties *Ossian* to the sort of stoic sentimentalism promoted by Adam Smith's *Theory of Moral Sentiments* (1758), and by Blair in his sermons and literary criticism. In the final analysis, the national epic *Ossian* mythologizes the new cultural values of sentimentalism and sensibility within its portrayal of traditional heroic virtue. Critics have deconstructed this in terms of the creation of a sentimental and sentimentalized Scottish – and wider celtic – cultural identity of glorious defeat heroically borne. By inscribing the celt as a natural outsider and loser, such an identity, it is claimed, operates as an assimilative strategy to mythologize Anglo-Saxon hegemony: according to this narrative historical movements and a genetic predisposition to defeat, not English policy, are responsible for the ever greater marginalization of the celt. Accordingly *Ossian* stands accused of cultural bad faith, transforming a vibrant gaelic cultural identity into a melancholy mulling over a defeat it inscribes as inevitable. Heroic celticism is evoked only for the emotional charge realized by acknowledging its passing.

This line has much to recommend it, but some other things also need to be considered. First of all, that a reprioritization of the mental over the physical – of, say, stoic endurance to memory over stoic endurance in battle – is a concern of wider mid-eighteenth-century cultural discourse. *Ossian*'s stoic sentimental resignation can be interpreted as being – wittingly or otherwise – a tool of Anglo-British cultural ideology by defusing protest into nostalgia, but it also encapsulates and foreshadows other responses to the fact that an increasingly urbanized, commercialized, and industrialized society was eroding the traditional grounds for action and virtue. The challenges of redefining national identity in terms other than active political participation came early to a Scotland denied self-government from 1707, and *Ossian* can be seen as part of an ongoing attempt to answer the question implied above by Fingal: what is the relationship between strength and song? This may make us view *Ossian* in a more favourable light, and *Ossian*'s reception helps sharpen the point.

First, English guardians of cultural values did not see *Ossian* as an assimilative manoeuvre working to cement their own stranglehold on British cultural identity. They saw celtic impertinence, a brazen attempt to appropriate the cultural values of sensibility for Scotland. The vehemence of the dispute over *Ossian*'s authenticity (unknown beyond the British Isles, where the stakes were not so high) was, arguably, one result of this perception. Second, we should not discount the fact that *Ossian* was a great favourite of later Romantic writers such as Herder, who, for example, was to emphasize cultural heritage – the *kulturstaat* – over tangible legislative form as the locus of national identity. To insist that the only valid forms of national conscious-ness are those which explicitly encourage people to mount barricades is not only naive, but plays into the hands of the hegemonic forces we are supposedly debunking. In short we should not overlook the fact that the Ossianic condition would speak pow-erfully to several generations confronting the cultural and spiritual uncertainties and fears of late eighteenth- and nineteenth-century Europe.

One final point on reading Macpherson's sentiment. It would also be a mistake to associate Macpherson too completely with the Anglo-British patrons who encouraged and assisted him. Of particular relevance here is Macpherson's Jacobite heritage, as a member of a clan which was 'out' in 1745–6 and viciously 'pacified' subsequently (events Macpherson lived through as a child), and as a student in Aberdeen exposed to the final flourishings of the Jacobite high culture of the Episcopal north east. Jaco-bitism is a fraught issue in modern eighteenth-century studies but suffice it to say for our purposes that Stuart mythology, and latterly martyrology, derived much of its power of critique and protest through its evocation of defeat, of the passing of an older, nobler way of life. *Ossian*, which contains Jacobite echoes in its image struc-tures, systematic allusion and narrative tropes, may, in a celebration of defeat and loss which is becoming increasingly sentimental and vicarious, nevertheless still be articu-lating a voice of genuine cultural protest against the passing of an entire culture. In other words, *Ossian* may be both an elegy for nationalism and a nationalist elegy, and we ignore the ambiguity at our peril.

This brief overview offers but an introduction to *Ossian*'s connections and to some of the issues at stake when thinking about Macpherson. What I hope emerges is a sense that *Ossian* stands on diverse cultural, aesthetic and national boundaries, and that, because such places are often neither comfortable nor uncomplicated places to find oneself, the poems are not only multi-faceted, but challenging, fraught and not a little difficult.

References and Further Reading

Donaldson, William (1988). *The Jacobite Song: Political Myth and National Identity*. Aberdeen: Aberdeen University Press.

Gaskill, Howard (1986). 'Ossian Macpherson: towards a rehabilitation'. *Comparative Criticism* 8, 113–46.

Gaskill, Howard, ed. (1991). *Ossian Revisited*. Edinburgh: Edinburgh University Press.

Gibbons, Luke (1996). 'The sympathetic bond: Ossian, celticism and colonialism'. In *Celticism*. Ed. Terence Brown. Amsterdam: Rodopi, 273–92.

Hook, Andrew (1988). 'Scotland and Romanti-cism: the international scene'. In *The History of Scottish Literature; Volume 2 1660–1800*. Ed. Andrew Hook. Aberdeen: Aberdeen University Press, 307–23.

Kidd, Colin (1993). *Subverting Scotland's Past: Scottish Whig Historians and the Creation of an Anglo-British Identity, 1689–c.1830*. Cambridge: Cambridge University Press.

MacGann, Jerome (1996). *The Poetics of Sensibility: A Revolution in Literary Style*. Oxford: Clarendon Press.

Macpherson, James (1996). *The Poems of Ossian and Related Works*. Ed. Howard Gaskill with an introduction by Fiona Stafford. Edinburgh: Edinburgh University Press.

Pittock, Murray (1997). *Inventing and Resisting Britain: Cultural Identities in Britain and Ireland, 1685–1789*. Basingstoke: Macmillan.

Potkay, Adam (1992). *The Fate of Eloquence in the Age of Hume*. Ithaca: Cornell University Press.

Robertson, John (1985). *The Scottish Enlightenment and the Militia Issue*. Edinburgh: Edinburgh University Press.

Sher, Richard (1985). *Church and University in the Scottish Enlightenment*. Edinburgh: Edinburgh University Press.

Simpson, Kenneth (1988). *The Protean Scot: The Crisis of Identity in Eighteenth-century Scottish Literature*. Aberdeen: Aberdeen University Press.

Stafford, Fiona (1988). *The Sublime Savage: James Macpherson and the Poems of Ossian*. Edinburgh: Edinburgh University Press.

——(1996). 'Primitivism and the "primitive poet": a cultural context for Macpherson's Ossian'. In *Celticism*. Ed. Terence Brown. Amsterdam: Rodopi, 79–96.

Stafford, Fiona and Howard Gaskill, eds (1998). *From Gaelic to Romantic: Ossianic Translations*. Amsterdam: Rodopi.

Stewart, Larry L. (1971). 'Ossian in the polished age: the critical reception of James Macpherson's *Ossian*'. Unpublished Ph.D. thesis, University of Michigan.

Thomson, D. S. (1952). *The Gaelic Sources of Macpherson's Ossian*. Edinburgh: Aberdeen University Press

Trumpener, Katie (1997). *Bardic Nationalism: The Romantic Novel and the British Empire*. Princeton: Princeton University Press.

Weinbrot, Howard (1992). *Britannia's Issue: The Rise of British Literature from Dryden to Ossian*. Cambridge: Cambridge University Press.

Womack, Peter (1989). *Improvement and Romance: Constructing the Myth of the Highlands*. Basingstoke: Macmillan.

41

Henry Mackenzie,
The Man of Feeling
David Womersley

Towards the beginning of his *Enquiry Concerning the Principles of Morals* (1751), David
Hume drew his reader's attention to a recent disagreement between philosophers:

> There has been a controversy started of late . . . concerning the general foundation of
> Morals; whether they be derived from Reason, or from Sentiment; whether we attain
> the knowledge of them by a chain of argument and induction, or by an immediate
> feeling and finer internal sense; whether, like all sound judgement of truth and false-
> hood, they should be the same to every rational intelligent being; or whether, like the
> perception of beauty and deformity, they be founded entirely on the particular fabric
> and constitution of the human species. (170)

The exploration of the notion that our moral ideas might arise from sense rather than
reason had begun with the third Earl of Shaftesbury, Anthony Ashley Cooper. From
his writings, first collected in 1711 as *Characteristicks*, sprang what came to be called
the 'moral sense school', in which a trio of Scottish philosophers were pre-eminent:
Francis Hutcheson, David Hume and Adam Smith. There were, to be sure, important variations of emphasis between the work of these three later philosophers. Nevertheless, if they had been obliged to choose between the two positions outlined
schematically by Hume above, they would have agreed with him that morality is more
properly felt than judged of, and that therefore to have a sense of virtue is nothing
but to feel satisfaction of a particular kind.

Although the interest in moral feeling arose first amongst philosophers, it quickly
influenced more imaginative literary forms. Works of both eighteenth-century drama
and poetry displayed the lineaments of the man or woman of feeling, in whom the
moral sense was embodied and dramatized in action. It was however in Henry
Mackenzie's novel of 1771, *The Man of Feeling*, that the 'moral sense' school of thought
received its most intriguing literary expression. This fragmentary account of events
in the life of a man, Harley, who possesses a moral sensibility to an extreme degree,

enjoyed an intense but brief popularity. Nevertheless, it has a permanent importance, as the work which both epitomized sentiment most precisely and presciently (although silently and at the level of implication) indicated the contradictions and limitations of the sentimental philosophy.

In the middle of the novel, Harley reflects on the moral temper of his age:

> 'Perhaps,' said Harley, 'we now-a-days discourage the romantic turn a little too much. Our boys are prudent too soon. Mistake me not, I do not mean to blame them for want of levity or dissipation; but their pleasures are those of hackneyed vice, blunted to every finer emotion by the repetition of debauch; and their desire of pleasure is warped to the desire of wealth, as the means of procuring it. . . . This I hold to be an alarming crisis in the corruption of a state; when not only is virtue declined, and vice prevailing, but when the praises of virtue are forgotten, and the infamy of vice unfelt.' (82–3)

There is nothing remarkable about the substance of Harley's analysis of the ethical corruption of Hanoverian England; such gloomy diagnoses had been commonplace since the mid-century writings of Dr John 'Estimate' Brown. But it takes on interest in the light of what it suggests about the relation between the values of Mackenzie's novel and the society within which it was published. For it implies that Mackenzie is aware that his book is belated – that the public may have already begun to forsake the values and attitudes which it celebrates. It is of course not unusual for a book to encapsulate a phase of taste then on the cusp of decline. What gives the phenomenon significance in the case of *The Man of Feeling* is the fact that 'moral sense' philosophy conceals important implications for how society is held together. For although the moral sense is a question of feeling – and hence is intimate and private – as the ground of morality, it governs our relations with others, and hence acquires a public and social aspect. This paradox of something at once private and public is reflected in Harley himself, who is in fact almost constituted out of a series of paradoxes. Prone to 'aukward blunders' as a result of being 'entirely occupied by the ideal' (17), he is nevertheless intensely physical, and registers his ineffable emotions in an eloquent language of sighs, tears, gestures and flushes. His moral refinement expresses itself partly in a noble indifference to practical consequences (his carelessness of financial gain is a characteristic on which Mackenzie touches more than once) and in an attachment to 'goodness for its own sake' (54), yet his independent evaluations of experience are sometimes decidedly consequentialist in character, as when he reflects that 'he was perhaps as well entertained, and instructed too, by this same modest gauger, as he should have been by such a man as he had thought proper to personate' (29). Harley is a 'child in the drama of the world' (17), but his sensibility performs the very adult function of holding society together. His success in doing that depends on his success in preserving his feelings 'untinctured with the world' (60); and he himself is aware that the socially indispensable 'feelings . . . that applaud benevolence, and censure humanity' are most often to be found, and assume their strongest and purest form, in those who 'live sequestered from the noise of the multitude' (104). So the sentimentalist philosophy confronts us with this challenge: how can the feelings, on which society depends for its cohesion, be introduced into society without thereby losing the quality on which they rely for their social potency? Mackenzie's novel displays for us the moral beauty and affectingness of Harley's sympathy, but Harley's virtue cannot be generalized. A society of Harleys, even a society organized on his principles, is inconceivable. He is an isolated figure, unable to reproduce himself (his sexual timidity is of significance here), wandering through a society which in general proceeds on quite other principles: principles of acquisition, of selfishness and of callousness to others. Even the formal fragmentariness which Mackenzie chose for his novel contributes to our sense of Harley as at once central and peripheral, anomalous and indispensable: for just as Harley's virtues cannot be generalized throughout society, so they cannot be given expression within a coherent novel structure.

The conceit of the discovered document is not unique to *The Man of Feeling*; for instance, in 1765 Walpole had used it for the first edition of *The Castle of Otranto*. Mackenzie ingeniously refines on the notion, however, by having his manuscript fall into the hands of an unsentimental curate, fond of hunting, who exploited the quality of the paper as 'excellent wadding' (5). When it comes into the possession of the narrator, the random removal by the curate of material here and there has produced an incomplete and interrupted narrative. The implications unfold themselves in a number of directions. In the first place, the resulting frustration of our narrative curiosity (the question 'What happens next?', which we pose to ourselves as we read) obliges us to attend to the particularity of the episode before us. Mackenzie thus engenders in us a form of reading which is akin to the sentimental morality of the man of feeling himself in its focus on singularity and heedlessness as to consequences. (Although in fact the disruption of the narrative is more apparent than substantial: it takes no very great power of inference to discern the thread of events lying behind the novel.) He suggests that such was his purpose in a letter of 1769, explaining the attractions to him of this fragmentary form:

> I have seldom been in use to write any prose, except what consisted of observations (such as I could make) on men and manners. The way of introducing these by narrative, I had fallen into in some detached essays, from the notion of its interesting both the memory and the affections deeper than mere argument or moral reasoning. In this way I was somehow led to think of introducing a man of sensibility into different scenes where his feelings might be seen in their effects, and his sentiments occasionally delivered without the stiffness of regular deduction. (Thompson, 1931, 107–11)

Furthermore, Mackenzie at certain points makes the narrative refer to, and assume in us knowledge of, passages which have been lost:

> Peter stood at the door. We have mentioned this faithful fellow formerly. (18)

> We have related, in a former chapter, the little success of his first visit to the great man. (23)

The effect of this is again to align us at least figuratively with Harley: to make us in a mild way childish readers, just as he is a child in the theatre of the world.

However, although the framing device is an ingenious ploy on Mackenzie's part to secure for his novel a sympathetic readership, there is no question that an appropriate audience can be taken for granted. After all, the manuscript fell into the unresponsive, indifferent, hands of the curate, and within the story itself Coke upon Lyttelton, the legal primer with which one of Harley's guardians attempts to lure him into a legal career, is put to quite foreign uses:

> He profited but little by the perusal; but it was not without its use in the family: for his maiden aunt applied it commonly to the laudable purpose of pressing her rebellious linens to the folds she had allotted them. (12)

Books may commonly be misapplied, and thus fail of their intended effect. But failure and impotence are placed in an equivocal light by Mackenzie, to the point where they are not easily distinguishable from success and influence. Harley expires at the point of eliciting a declaration of love from Miss Walton, whose wealth would have remedied the genteel poverty into which his family have fallen: it is a complicated moment which fuses triumph and futility. To have married would inevitably have entailed compromise for Harley – if nothing else, he would have had to enter the realm of adult sexuality, the ardours of which would have been fatal to sentimental delicacy. Slipping out of life on the brink of being summoned to do justice to the affections aroused in himself and Miss Walton is thus for Harley at once an evasion and a consummation, in which the essential paradoxes of sentiment – that it is potent only when ineffectual, healthy only when sickly – receive vivid expression.

It is in the domain of politics that the paradoxical character of sentiment operates most strikingly. When Harley says to the school-mistress who had taken pity on Edwards's grandchildren 'let us never forget that we are all relations' (97), it is easy to see how the sense of filiation on which moral sense philosophy is predicated might become the ground for an egalitarian vision of society in which the man of feeling's indifference to social rank and outward respectability would assume a political colouring. For it is noticeable that *The Man of Feeling* has many points of contact with the radical literature of the 1790s. The story of old Edwards shares many ingredients with 'Michael', or *The Ruined Cottage*, or *Adventures on Salisbury Plain*. The story of the domestic oppression of Count Respino, related in 'The Pupil. A Fragment', foreshadows the despotic behaviour of Godwin's Tyrrel in *Caleb Williams*, only transposed into an Italian setting. The repeated pattern of the novel, in which characters relate the history of their sufferings to a sympathetic audience, is here primarily a device for displaying and eliciting sentiment, but later in the century in a novel such as Mary Wollstonecraft's *Maria* it is a means whereby those who have suffered oppression learn of the extensiveness of the wrongs they have endured, and resolve to resist them. In *The Man of Feeling*, then, we can see a potential for radicalism which is not as yet fully realized. Even the language in which Harley describes the situation of those with moral sensitivity is pungently political:

'Let me intreat you, Sir,' said he, 'to hope better things. The world is ever tyrannical; it warps our sorrows to edge them with keener affliction: let us not be slaves to the names it affixes to motive or to action. I know an ingenuous mind cannot help feeling when they sting: but there are considerations by which it may be overcome; its fantastic ideas vanish as they rise; they teach us − to look beyond it.' (73)

But the political language in *The Man of Feeling* is necessarily tethered to metaphor, for to take political action would be to have elected to be moved, rather than merely touched. The closing words of the novel show pity being elevated above hatred by the anonymous narrator in whom Harley's virtues have become re-embodied:

I sometimes visit his grave; I sit in the hollow of the tree. It is worth a thousand homilies! Every nobler feeling rises within me! every beat of my heart awakens a virtue! − but it will make you hate the world − No: there is such an air of gentleness around, that I can hate nothing; but, as to the world − I pity the men of it. (132−3)

The utmost of which the man of feeling is capable without compromising his moral standing are local, discrete acts of charitable relief. Anything more systematic or far reaching would require just those human qualities which he has forsaken. It is notable that when in the 1790s the acute local insights of the man of feeling are elaborated into a coherent vision of social injustice, sentiment will have been reinforced by reason.

REFERENCES AND FURTHER READING

Braudy, Leo (1973). 'The form of the sentimental novel'. *Novel* 7, 5–13.

Brown, John (1758). *An Estimate of the Manners and Principles of the Times.*

Cooper, Anthony Ashley, third Earl of Shaftesbury (1711). *Characteristicks.*

Crane, R. S. (1935). 'Suggestions toward a genealogy of the *Man of Feeling*'. *ELH* 1, 205–30.

Friedman, Arthur (1970). 'Aspects of sentimentalism in eighteenth-century literature'. In *The Augustan Milieu: Essays Presented to Louis A. Landa.* Ed. H. K. Miller, E. Rothstein and G. S. Rousseau. Oxford: Clarendon.

Frye, Northrop (1956). 'Towards defining an Age of Sensibility'. *ELH* 23, 144–52.

Hagstrum, J. H. (1980). *Sex and Sensibility: Ideal and Erotic Love from Milton to Mozart.* Chicago: Chicago University Press.

Hilles, F. W. and H. Bloom, eds (1965). *From Sensibility to Romanticism.* New York: Oxford University Press.

Hume, David (1975). *An Enquiry Concerning the Principles of Morals* (1751). In David Hume, *Enquiries concerning Human Understanding and concerning the Principles of Morals.* 3rd edn. Ed. P. H. Nidditch. Oxford: Clarendon.

Humphreys, A. R. (1948). 'The friend of mankind'. *RES* 24, 203–18.

Hutcheson, Francis (1725). *An Enquiry into the Origin of our Ideas of Beauty and Virtue.*

Mackenzie, Henry (1970). *The Man of Feeling.* Ed. Brian Vickers. Oxford: Oxford University Press.

Mullan, John (1988). *Sentiment and Sociability: The Language of Feeling in the Eighteenth Century*. Oxford: Clarendon.

Parnell, Paul E. (1963). 'The sentimental mask'. *PMLA* 78, 529–35.

Smith, Adam (1759). *The Theory of Moral Sentiments*.

Starr, G. A. (1977). '"Only a boy": notes on sentimental novels'. *Genre* 10, 501–27.

Thompson, H. W. (1931). *The Scottish Man of Feeling*. London.

Todd, Janet (1986). *Sensibility: An Introduction*. London and New York: Methuen.

Willey, Basil (1940). *The Eighteenth-century Background*. London: Chatto and Windus.

42

James Boswell, *The Life of Johnson*

Bruce Redford

Boswell's *Life of Johnson* is the pre-eminent example in English biography of the art that disguises art. This irresistible but elusive masterpiece exists in two distinct versions: the original manuscript (which allows us to reconstruct every stage of composition) and the published text of 1791 (which Boswell revised twice before his death in 1795). Close study of the work in its successive stages confirms what many readers have intuited from the final version alone: that Boswell was a sophisticated craftsman, but that in commenting on his craft he failed to do it justice. The work and not the author is our most eloquent, reliable, and convincing witness to the multiple uses of 'the fact imagined' (Wimsatt, 1965, 165).

To take Boswell's initial declarations at face value is to interpret the *Life* as faithfully Johnsonian in manner as well as matter. The biography's opening sentence, for example, ventriloquizes its subject:

> To write the Life of him who excelled all mankind in writing the lives of others, and who, whether we consider his extraordinary endowments, or his various works, has been equalled by few in any age, is an arduous, and may be reckoned in me a presumptuous task. (Chapman and Fleeman, 1970, 19)

In this preliminary flourish, Boswell adopts a Ramblerian periodic structure, complete with inversion and suspension, to capture His Master's Voice. At the same time, he makes use of the 'mock humility topos' (a stylized gesture of unworthiness) to emphasize the difficulties of his undertaking. This pattern – a gesture of self-deprecation complicated by a massing of credentials – continues throughout the introduction. On the one hand, Boswell suggests, he and he alone is equipped for the 'arduous . . . task'; on the other, he is inadequate to it. The same rhetorical tactic directs the reader's attention away from the biographer's art to the biographer's industry, considerations of 'scrupulous authenticity' displacing those of 'literary ability'. Over and over again Boswell presents himself as a faithful practitioner of Johnson's biographical methods and a trustworthy compiler of facts: 'Let me only observe, as a specimen of my trouble, that I have sometimes been obliged to run half over London, in order to fix a date correctly.' An innovative, even a revolutionary text thereby enters the world in a posture of ancestor worship: 'If authority be required, let us appeal to Plutarch, the prince of ancient biographers . . . To this may be added the sentiments of the very man whose life I am about to exhibit' (19–24).

Scrupulous rereading, however, supplemented by the evidence of the manuscript, helps us to locate in Boswell's exordium a different story about the work it introduces. This story is bolder and more eclectic than the biographer's own account; it reaches out to epic, theatrical and visual models for precedents and paradigms. Central to these models is the idea of display. Boswell 'exhibits' Johnson in three modes or guises – as a classical hero, a pictorial subject, and a dramatic protagonist. Let us consider all three separately before assessing their combined effect.

The *Life* as Epic

From start to finish, Boswell compares Johnson to figures from classical epic. Johnson's appearance alone aligns him with heroic models: 'His figure was large and well formed, and his countenance of the cast of an ancient statue' (Chapman and Fleeman, 1970, 1,398). Furthermore, the earliest witnesses attest that he behaved like a hero – a composite of Agamemnon, Achilles and Odysseus – even in childhood. According to Boswell, 'the boy is the man in miniature,' and that boy deserves the epithet assigned by Homer to Agamemnon: 'From his earliest years his superiority was perceived and acknowledged. He was from the beginning *Anax andron*, a king of men' (355). Like Achilles, Johnson seethed with an anger that boiled over into violent words and deeds. This violence most often took the form of verbal 'tossing and goring'. Yet Boswell insists as well on Johnson's physical prowess:

> One day, at Mr Beauclerk's house in the country, when two large dogs were fighting, he went up to them, and beat them till they separated . . . He told me himself that one night he was attacked in the street by four men, to whom he would not yield, but kept them all at bay, till the watch came up. (579)

As such accounts make clear, the *agon* waged by Johnson *agonistes* manifested itself in a surprising number of ways. And when the verbal and the physical were united, the result was unforgettable – witness the letter that responds to threats from James Macpherson, whose Ossianic poems Johnson had called into question: 'I hope I shall never be deterred from detecting what I think a cheat, by the menaces of a Ruffian' (579).

In general, however, battlefield epithets and exploits take second place to feats of intellect. Like Odysseus, Boswell's Johnson is *polutropos*, a 'man of many turns' whose deeds never cease to astonish and to teach:

It seems to me . . . that this extensive biographical work . . . may in one respect be assimilated to the ODYSSEY. Amidst a thousand entertaining and instructive episodes the HERO is never long out of sight; for they are all in some degree connected with him; and HE, in the whole course of the History, is exhibited by the Author for the best advantage of his readers. (7)

Boswell's comparison of his epic designs to Homer's reveals as much about his narrative method as it does about his conception of Johnsonian heroism. To 'assimilate' the *Life* to the *Odyssey* is to focus on several key features: the sheer scope of the work, which tracks its central character through a densely and diversely populated landscape; its stringing of episodes along a slender chronological thread; its sustained testing of the hero. Like Odysseus, moreover, Johnson is essentially the same at the end of the story as he was at the beginning. Different facets are exhibited at different stages of the narrative, but the epic protagonist does not, in contrast to a novelistic character or a post-Freudian biographical subject, grow and change. In short, the *Life*, like the classical epic, tells a non-developmental tale. There are surprises en route, but they derive from the shock of recognition, from the experience of getting to know a hero who is astonishingly diverse but fundamentally consistent.

This epic blend of dynamism and stasis is best illustrated by a conversation (26 October 1769) that enriches the biography but strains the friendship. It does so by importing a *bête noire*, the cheerful atheism of David Hume:

When we were alone, I introduced the subject of death, and endeavoured to maintain that the fear of it might be got over. I told him that David Hume said to me, he was not more uneasy to think he should *not be* after this life, than that he *had not been* before he began to exist. JOHNSON. 'Sir, if he really thinks so, his perceptions are disturbed; he is mad: if he does think so, he lies. He may tell you, he holds his finger in the flame of a candle, without feeling pain; would you believe him? When he dies, he at least gives up all he has.' BOSWELL. 'Foote, Sir, told me, that when he was very ill he was not afraid to die.' JOHNSON. 'It is not true, Sir. Hold a pistol to Foote's breast, or to Hume's breast, and threaten to kill them, and you'll see how they behave.' BOSWELL. 'But may we not fortify our minds for the approach of death?' Here I am sensible I was in the wrong, to bring before his view what he ever looked upon with horrour; for although when in a celestial frame, in his 'Vanity of Human Wishes,' he has supposed death to be 'kind Nature's signal of retreat,' from this state of being to 'a happier seat,' his thoughts upon this aweful change were in general full of dismal apprehensions. His mind resembled the vast amphitheatre, the Colisaeum at Rome. In the centre stood his judgement, which, like a mighty gladiator, combated those apprehensions that, like the wild beasts of the *Arena*, were all around in cells, ready to be let out upon him. After a conflict, he drove them back into their dens; but not killing them, they were still assailing him. (426–7)

This haunting conversation is one of the most thoroughly worked over in the entire *Life*. Boswell revises the manuscript to add details that heighten the tension of the intimate encounter and emphasize its revelatory significance. But he lavishes most of his care on the extended or epic simile – the only one of its kind in the biography. Like the similes in Homer, this comparison takes us away from the scene while quickening our 'aweful' awareness of it. Boswell narrates a battle that never changes and never ends: 'After a conflict, he drove them back into their dens; but not killing them, they were still assailing him.' Johnson spends his life, and the reader spends Boswell's *Life*, in an arena where the wild animals are always bested but always besieging. Only at the close of the biographical narrative do witnesses intimate a final victory: 'Mr Strahan has given me the agreeable assurance, that, after being in much agitation, Johnson became quite composed, and continued so till his death' (1,391). The heroic gladiator quits the arena with calm of mind, all 'apprehensions' spent.

Boswell tells an Odyssean tale in another respect: though it does not begin *in medias res*, the *Life* follows classical precedent in stressing the linear design of the narrative. Boswell strives to create an almost subliminal impression of temporal flow as he narrates Johnson's epic journey. It goes almost without saying that the biography's sheer length helps to instil in the reader this sense of duration. In addition, the ostentatious chronological signposting, a species of biographical time-line, guarantees that we keep track of *our* progress as well as the hero's: at the top of every page Boswell supplies a double marker, as in 'Sunday, 27 November 1774' reinforced by 'Aetat. 65'. The two odysseys – the one of living, the other of reading – measure themselves out simultaneously.

The *Life* as Portrait

Yet while it emphasizes time passing, the biography also seeks to decelerate temporal flow. Boswell's control of chronology and topography is such that, for most of the *Life*, we never leave London – and in London it almost always seems to be spring. Consequently we feel ourselves burrowing deeply into a single, suspended, archetypal moment (Alkon, 1973, 249–50). By emphasizing Johnson's unchanging nature, moreover, Boswell also slows or even suspends time. In place of a developmental study, he supplies a full-length portrait – a portrait that is static yet vibrant, fundamentally consistent yet constantly surprising.

In his important essay, 'Literary Form in Factual Narrative: The Example of Boswell's *Johnson*', Ralph Rader identifies what he calls 'the creative secret of Boswell's art: he had within his mind not a series of disjunctive photographic impressions but a single dynamic image of Johnson' (Rader, 1985, 28). The biographer-painter builds up this image by applying innumerable, exact brushstrokes – those 'minute particulars' that compose what Boswell himself calls 'the Flemish picture which I give of my friend' (Chapman and Fleeman, 1970, 869). By 'Flemish', Boswell appears to mean 'closely observed' or 'minutely detailed'. A 'Flemish' aesthetic is one that resolutely documents unflattering data – not only wrinkles, veins and moles but inner flaws as well – in the pursuit of a convincing likeness.

The 'Flemish' model manifests itself in various ways. For example, the eighteenth-century reader of the *Life* would have encountered Johnson first not in textual but in pictorial form: Boswell took special pains to supply a frontispiece that reproduced Reynolds's portrait of the great lexicographer. This portrait not only introduces the subject; it also supplies a visual reference point, as in Boswell's account of their first meeting:

> I found that I had a very perfect idea of Johnson's figure, from the portrait of him painted by Sir Joshua Reynolds soon after he had published his *Dictionary*, in the attitude of sitting in his easy chair in deep meditation, which was the first picture his friend did for him, which Sir Joshua very kindly presented to me, and from which an engraving has been made for this work. (277)

In addition to furnishing Boswell with 'a very perfect idea of Johnson's figure', the painter also influenced the biographer's technique. Reynolds composed for Boswell's use an eloquent 'sketch' of Johnson, a word-portrait whose effect can be traced in the opening dedication and the concluding 'Character' (Hilles, 1952, 69–70). Implicitly but unmistakably, the dedication associates the enterprise of the biographer with that of the portrait-painter in terms that anticipate Boswell's metaphor of the 'Flemish picture':

> You, my dear Sir, studied him, and knew him well: you venerated and admired him. Yet, luminous as he was upon the whole, you perceived all the shades which mingled in the grand composition; all the little peculiarities and slight blemishes which marked the literary Colossus. (Chapman and Fleeman, 1970, 2)

Inspired by Reynolds, Boswell inserts multiple cameo portraits within the 'grand composition' that is the *Life*; each one of these cameos (such as the recreation of Bennet Langton's first view of Johnson) subsumes 'peculiarities and slight blemishes' into an aura of irresistible magnetism. And at the very end of the *Life* – after he has unveiled, interpreted, and then buried the 'Colossus' – Boswell resurrects him by 'collect[ing] into one view the capital and distinguishing features of this extra-ordinary man' (Chapman and Fleeman, 1970, 1,398). This daring endgame, by which we *see* Johnson with a fresh and final intensity, matches portrait with portrait. Images bookend the biography.

Boswell begins to alert the reader and to create an interpretative context for the Character by tallying up the existing portraits of Johnson in an extended footnote. This mini-catalogue speaks obliquely of Boswell's own project: 'As no inconsiderable circumstance of his fame, we must reckon the extraordinary zeal of the artists to extend and perpetuate his [Johnson's] image' (1,395). In order 'to extend and perpetuate' his version of that image, Boswell proceeds to delete the subdivisions ('religious, moral, political, and literary') he had taken over from the Character that introduces his *Journal of a Tour to the Hebrides*: these categories intrude an arbitrary schema that works against

the unity of the portrait. He refines the key verb in the introductory paragraph –
starting with 'sum up', combining it with 'collect', discarding both in favour of 'bring
together', and settling finally on 'collect into one view'. He adds two sentences that
describe Johnson in motion:

> but when he walked, it was like the struggling gait of one in fetters; when he rode he
> had no command or direction of his horse, but was carried as if in a balloon. That with
> his constitution and habits of life he should have lived seventy-five years, is a proof that
> an inherent *vivida vis* ['lively power'] is a powerful preservative of the human frame.
> (1,398–9)

These sentences complete the description of Johnson by conveying a sense of his
massive, ungainly, but vigorous body – a body that is as scarred yet as heroic as his
mind.

It is the final sentence of the Character, however, that drives home the full import
of Boswell's picture-making tactics. That sentence acquires an epitaphic force from
being separately paragraphed. It acquires an epigrammatic force from a dense cluster
of puns: 'the more that we consider his character, we shall be the more disposed to
regard him with admiration and reverence'. Here Boswell activates the multiple meanings of 'character', 'consider', and 'regard', as defined in Johnson's *Dictionary*. The most
important of these three words is the biography's final verb, 'regard'. All but one of
Johnson's seven definitions apply: 'to value', 'to observe', 'to pay attention to', 'to
respect', 'to look towards', and 'to observe religiously'. We complete the Character
and close the biography understanding that our regard *for* Johnson depends upon our
regard *of* him – that vision has led to veneration.

The *Life* as Drama

Four years before Johnson's death, Boswell told his friend Andrew Erskine that he had
decided 'to write Dr Johnson's *Life* in Scenes' (Waingrow, 1969, liii). After beginning
to compose the biography, he wrote to Thomas Percy: 'it appears to me that mine is
the best plan of Biography that can be conceived; for my Readers will, as near as may
be, accompany Johnson in his progress, and as it were see each scene as it happened'
(Waingrow, lxiii). This statement adumbrates the promise that Boswell makes at the
beginning of the biography, a promise that connects the iconic model we have just
been exploring to the conception of the *Life* as theatre-piece:

> Indeed I cannot conceive a more perfect mode of writing any man's life, than not only
> relating all the most important events of it in their order, but interweaving what he
> privately wrote, and said, and thought; by which mankind are enabled as it were to see
> him live, and to 'live o'er each scene' with him . . . And he will be seen as he really was;
> for I profess to write, not his panegyrick, which must be all praise, but his Life . . . To
> be as he was, is indeed subject of panegyrick enough to any man in this state of being;

but in every picture there should be shade as well as light, and when I delineate him without reserve, I do what he himself recommended, both by his precept and his example. (Chapman and Fleeman, 1970, 22)

Boswell 'delineates' Johnson and causes us to 'see him live' not only by pictorializing but by dramatizing — by setting his protagonist in motion within a sequence of carefully scripted playlets. He signals his intention by quoting part of a couplet from Pope's prologue to Addison's *Cato,* one of the most popular of eighteenth-century dramas: 'To make mankind in conscious virtue bold, / Live o'er each scene and be what they behold.' This couplet not only exhorts the audience to emulate the worthy protagonist; it also suggests that the key to the didactic exercise ('to make mankind in conscious virtue bold') is the absorption of spectator into spectacle ('live o'er each scene and be what they behold'). For Boswell's purposes these lines are ideal, since they legitimate a model for biography that is at once kinetic and static. Such a model seeks to visualize the subject and to set it in motion, thereby turning the reader into a spectator.

As Boswell understood, Johnson, for all his strictures against players and play-acting, was himself a consummate performer. He practised, perfected, and strove to institutionalize through the Literary Club a highly theatrical kind of conversation. Always inclined to abstract from the particular, Johnson had thought carefully about the theory behind his practice:

Talking of conversation, he said, 'There must, in the first place, be knowledge, there must be materials; — in the second place, there must be a command of words; — in the third place, there must be imagination, to place things in such views as they are not commonly seen in; — and in the fourth place, there must be presence of mind, and a resolution not to be overcome by failures. (1,195)

The greatest conversational set-pieces in the *Life* are precisely those that fulfil these Johnsonian prerequisites. The talk is substantive, fluent, and competitive; it exhibits a conscious virtuosity that never lapses into preciosity. In order to recreate the aura as well as the substance of such talk, Boswell shapes his raw materials (which include notes, memoranda and journal entries) into a succession of dramatic arcs. These arcs are designed to shrink or even to dissolve the barrier between spectator and *dramatis personae.* Vicarious participation is only one of Boswell's goals, however. His final purpose is to make us 'be what [we] behold' by emulating the virtues of the protagonist.

Perhaps the most theatrical of all the conversations in the *Life* is Boswell's account of the first meeting between Johnson and Wilkes. Here life and art interpenetrate: the participants are aware of playing parts in a Boswellian script, while the report of their role-playing is itself elaborately scripted. In fact, Boswell contrives a perfect fit between the arts of social management that create the encounter and the arts of biographical management that do it full justice. Although journal entries underlie most of the extended conversations in the *Life*, in this instance the original notes generate the narrative in the manuscript, which Boswell revises several times over and continues to fine-tune in proof. The original record, which he described elsewhere as his 'cake of portable soup', preserves the core of the dialogue but little in the way of vivid or circumstantial detail. When Boswell expands the dehydrated 'cake' into biographical broth, he translates theatrical metaphor ('live o'er each scene') into structural practice with complete success. The result is a miniature play, which moves from prologue through rising action and blocking action to climax and epilogue (Molin, 1963, 314).

The prologue emphasizes the difficulty of Boswell's self-appointed enterprise: to 'bring . . . together' men 'more different' than could be imagined. The two key verbs are 'negotiate' and 'manage'. Boswell tells Edward Dilly, his prospective host, 'if you'll let me negotiate for you I will be answerable that all shall go well'. 'How to manage' this negotiation is 'a nice and difficult matter' (Chapman and Fleeman, 1970, 764–5). Even more emphatically than the first edition, the manuscript describes Johnson and Wilkes as aggressive enemies, and Boswell as a resourceful mediator between warring parties.

The blocking action begins when Boswell discovers on the afternoon of the dinner that Johnson has completely forgotten (or says that he has forgotten) about the engagement at Dilly's, and has promised Anna Williams to dine at home. Boswell emphasizes the theatrical significance of the moment by describing Johnson's state of mind through yet another allusion to *Cato*: the hero of Addison's play is 'indiff'rent in his choice to sleep or die'; the hero of Boswell's playlet is 'indifferent in his choice to go or stay'. Boswell himself plays the role of rakish fortune-hunter, a composite of Sheridan's Jack Absolute and Sir Lucius O'Trigger: his 'solicitations' to Anna Williams 'were certainly as earnest as most entreaties to ladies upon any occasion', and when he and Johnson are finally on their way, he 'exulted as much as a fortune-hunter who has got an heiress into a postchaise with him to set out for Gretna-Green' (767).

Boswell's notes suggest that the conversation at Dilly's did not progress in a clear sequence, but rather moved by fits and starts. As he expands the notes, Boswell repositions blocks of dialogue, achieving a crescendo, a sense of growing cordiality. After the climax, when Johnson and Wilkes collaborate in turning their puppeteer into a puppet, the improbable 'bond of union' is consolidated via anecdotes of Mrs Macaulay and the Attorney General – anecdotes that occur piecemeal in the notes. Boswell completes the theatrical structure of the whole by adding a one-sentence epilogue. This epilogue reintroduces the idea of 'management' and crowns Boswell's achievement with the accolade of a theatrical politician: 'Mr Burke gave me much credit for this successful *negociation*; and pleasantly said, that "there was nothing to equal it in the whole history of the *Corps Diplomatique*" ' (776).

In his opening statement of intention and method, Boswell declares forthrightly, 'What I consider as the peculiar value of the following Work, is the quantity that it contains of Johnson's conversation.' He goes on to say, in a sentence reworked at proof stage, 'the conversation of a celebrated man, if his talents have been exerted in conversation, will best display his character' (23). The commitment to displaying Johnson unites the epic, the pictorial and the dramatic aspects of Boswell's enterprise. As an epic hero à la Odysseus, Johnson is 'never long out of sight'. As the sitter for a full-length 'Flemish' portrait, he is painted in 'shade as well as light'. As a dramatic protagonist, he 'advance[s] through', as well as upon, 'the several stages of his life' (22). In adapting and combining all three models, Boswell aims to be 'entertaining and instructive', to elicit and sustain our 'regard'. The ultimate paradox of the *Life* is that its strikingly un-Johnsonian innovations in biographical method triumphantly confirm the premise that launches *Rambler* no. 60: 'All joy or sorrow for the happiness or calamities of others is produced by an act of the imagination.'

REFERENCES AND FURTHER READING

Alkon, Paul K. (1973). 'Boswellian Time'. *Studies in Burke and his Time* 14, 239–56.

Brady, Frank (1984). *James Boswell: The Later Years, 1769–1795*. New York, Toronto and London: McGraw-Hill.

Chapman, R. W. and J. D. Fleeman, eds (1970). *Boswell's* Life of Johnson. London, Oxford and New York: Oxford University Press.

Hill, G. B. and L. F. Powell, eds (1934–64). *Boswell's 'Life of Johnson'*. Oxford: Clarendon Press. 6 vols.

Hilles, F. W., ed. (1952). *Portraits by Sir Joshua Reynolds*. New York, London, Toronto: McGraw-Hill.

Molin, Sven Eric (1963). 'Boswell's account of the Johnson–Wilkes Meeting'. *Studies in English Literature* 3, 307–22.

Rader, Ralph W. (1985). 'Literary form in factual narrative: the example of Boswell's *Johnson*'. In *Boswell's 'Life of Johnson': New Questions, New Answers*. Ed. John A. Vance. Athens: The University of Georgia Press.

Redford, Bruce, ed., with Elizabeth Goldring (1998). *James Boswell's 'Life of Johnson': An Edition of the Original Manuscript*. Vol. 2. Edinburgh: Edinburgh University Press; New Haven: Yale University Press.

Waingrow, Marshall, ed. (1969). *The Correspondence and Other Papers of James Boswell Relating to the Making of the 'Life of Johnson'*. New York and Toronto: McGraw-Hill.

——(1994). *James Boswell's 'Life of Johnson': An Edition of the Original Manuscript*. Vol. 1. Edinburgh: Edinburgh University Press; New Haven: Yale University Press.

Wendorf, Richard (1990). *The Elements of Life: Biography and Portrait-painting in Stuart and Georgian England*. Oxford: Clarendon.

Wimsatt, W. K. (1965). 'The fact imagined: James Boswell'. In *Hateful Contraries: Studies in Literature and Criticism*. Lexington: University of Kentucky Press, 165–83.

43

William Blake, *Songs of Innocence and Experience*

Jon Mee

William Blake's *Songs of Innocence and of Experience* certainly ranks among the most distinctive and individual collections of poetry in a century obsessed with originality and genius. It was not even published in a conventional way. *Songs* began life as an exercise in self-publishing, and never reached an audience in Blake's lifetime beyond those few collectors who bought copies printed by the author himself. Without mentioning Blake, the successful bookseller James Lackington noted in his 1792 *Memoirs* (224) that several authors had tried to sell their own works in order to by-pass the book trade. Blake went further than most and attempted to exploit the expanding market for illustrated books – to which he had contributed both as a designer and copy engraver – by combining his genius as a writer and artist into the form of an illuminated book. For all their originality, however, the songs often work by mimicking familiar forms and arousing expectations which they go on to frustrate. Playing on generic conventions only in order to leave the reader in an uncomfortable quandary, they seem to practise 'the infernal method' recommended by Blake in *The Marriage of Heaven and Hell*, 'melting apparent surfaces away, and displaying the infinite which was hid' (see *The Complete Poetry and Prose*, ed. Erdman, p. 39, cited hereafter as E).

Although *Songs* remains Blake's best-known work, printing the books was a small-scale operation probably intended originally to showcase his talents as a visual artist (Viscomi, *Blake and the Idea of the Book*). Only twenty-four copies of the combined *Songs* survive, along with four separate copies of *Experience* and twenty-six copies of the separate *Innocence* (although more may be discovered, and have been very recently). The combination of the visual and verbal arts in the collection remains one of its most exciting dimensions. Critics have long pointed out that the designs which accompany the poems cannot simply be regarded as illustrations, that is, few of them simply show what the poems they accompany tell. On several of the pages, in fact, the visual dominates the verbal. Certainly any reader intending to read the poems seriously needs to look at them alongside the designs with which they were originally published by Blake.

Innocence and Experience both seem to have been available to buyers separately as well as in a combined volume. Together they illustrate 'the Two Contrary States of the Human Soul' (title page: E7). Although Blake wrote in *The Marriage of Heaven and Hell* that 'Without Contraries there is no progression' (E34), there is no straightforward journey from innocence to experience in the combined version of *Songs*. Poems do echo each other across the divide between the two parts of the collection, but despite critical attempts to establish a pattern of correspondences no single set of relationships structures the collection. In fact Blake altered the contents and order for different editions. 'The Little Girl Lost' and 'The Little Girl Found', for instance, along with 'The School Boy' and 'The Voice of the Ancient Bard', all appeared first in *Songs of Innocence*, but were more often placed by Blake in the Experience section of the joint collection. Not that seeking echoes between the poems is irrelevant. Blake always wrote in a way which 'rouzes the faculties to act' (E702). The collection seems to encourage its readers to find echoes, but ultimately frustrates any attempt to reify them into an overarching system. A playful open-endedness is a feature of the patterning of correspondences between the poems, the relationship between text and design on individual pages, and the texts of the poems themselves.

This open-endedness makes a particularly striking contrast between the poems and the children's verses to which many critics have pointed as their source (see, for instance, Glen, *Vision and Disenchantment* and Leader, *Reading Blake's Songs*). Children's literature was a growth industry in the eighteenth century. The publisher Joseph Johnson, for whom Blake did most of his copy engraving work in the 1780s and early 1790s, was closely involved with this part of the book trade. Blake himself provided illustrations for Johnson's edition of Mary Wollstonecraft's *Original Stories from Real Life* (1791). Earlier children's literature, such as Isaac Watts's *Divine Songs* (1715), hugely popular throughout the century and beyond, was usually baldly moralistic, often threatening divine retribution for very minor misdemeanours, but even the more liberal children's literature of the kind published by Johnson, influenced by the educational theories of Rousseau, tended to be didactic in its recommendations of Reason and Nature. Neither left much room for spontaneous play or the imaginative exploration of the world. Neither allowed the perspectives of Innocence seriously to challenge the perspectives of Experience. They certainly did not concur with Blake's view that 'the innocence of a child' could be superior to 'the errors of acquired folly' (E600). The divinity of play, in contrast, is a major theme of poems such as the 'Nurse's Song' of Innocence where the nurse seems to be educated out of ignorance by the children in her charge. In the design which accompanies the poem, she is invited to join in the play by filling the space left in the circle of dancing children. Other poems present the suppression of such instinctual pleasure as an almost ungodly denial of human divinity. 'Holy Thursday' of Innocence even hints that divine retribution awaits those who would regiment desire and drive away the presence which serves to protect them: 'Then cherish pity, lest you drive an angel from your door.' Several of the poems are almost parodies of children's literature in that they end, like 'Holy Thursday', with lines that can easily be mistaken for traditional moral sentiments. These lines on closer inspection prove to be difficult to square with the rest of the poem in anything like a conventional sense. The most discussed example is probably 'The Chimney Sweeper' in Innocence. Its closing line, 'So if all do their duty, they need not fear harm', places a great deal of pressure on eighteenth-century ideas of what 'duty' might entail. Betrayed by his father and mother, exploited by his master, only the sweep himself tries to do his duty by creating a Heaven from this Hell for his friend Tom. Rather than educating the child, the poem asks its adult readers whether they are doing their duty to the sweeps.

This poem highlights another generic connection for *Songs* in the flood of poetry published in newspapers and periodicals in the 1770s and 1780s which again and again addressed humanitarian issues such as slavery, prostitution and child labourers such as Blake's sweeps (see Glen). While these poems sometimes reflected genuine concerns, and could be connected to real reform movements, such as John Howard's work in the prisons, they often represented little more than opportunities for the polite reader to exercise his or her sensibility. A good example, which provides a direct analogy for Blake's Chimney Sweep poems, is Mary Alcock's 'The Chimney-Sweeper's Complaint' (*Poems*, 22–4):

A CHIMNEY-sweeper's boy am I;
Pity my wretched fate!
Ah, turn your eyes; 'twould draw a tear,
Knew you my helpless state.

Far from my home, no parents I
Am ever doom'd to see;
My master, should I sue to him,
He'd flog the skin from me.

Ah, dearest Madam, dearest Sir,
Have pity on my youth;
Tho' black, and cover'd o'er with rags,
I tell you nought but truth.

My feeble limbs, benumb'd with cold,
Totter beneath the sack,
Which ere the morning dawn appears
Is loaded on my back.

My legs you see are burnt and bruis'd,
My feet are gall'd by stones,
My flesh for lack of food is gone,
I'm little else but bones.

Yet still my master makes me work,
Nor spares me day or night;
His 'prentice boy he says I am,
And he will have his right.

'Up to the highest top', he cries,
'there call out chimney-sweep!'
With panting heart and weeping eyes,
Trembling I upwards creep.

But stop! no more – I see him come;
Kind Sir, remember me!
Oh, could I hide me under ground,
How thankful should I be!

Alcock's poem is not to be lightly dismissed as sentimentalism. It has a directness and energy often lacking in the magazine verse of the period. Where it differs from Blake is in the way it privileges the polite reader for whom the sweep exists entirely as a victim. Alcock's sweeper is incapable of conceiving of his own freedom in any positive sense and wishes only to hide himself from oppression. It is never suggested that such children, no less than the reader of sensibility, might have aspirations and imaginative capacities of their own. The smooth easy rhythms of the poem seem made for ease-of-consumption rather than any fundamental challenge to the assumptions of the reader. Blake's poem with its stuttering internal rhymes, echoes and repetitions is much more difficult to read smoothly. Alcock's reader is outside of the problem. It is only the master who oppresses the child. The reader is not called upon to consider his or her role in the system of child labour. Blake's reader is directly implicated in what is happening: 'So your chimneys I sweep & in soot I sleep.' For all that he may not be entirely able to perceive the causes of his suffering, Blake's sweep retains an imaginative autonomy and a sense of active human sympathy in the midst of suffering and degradation. He is not simply a victim. Although the last line of the poem has often been read ironically, to regard the sweep's dream merely as the product of false consciousness would be to miss this dimension of the poem. Blake's sweep is not entirely deluding himself about duty. He may not be able to alleviate the suffering and pain, but he has found a creative way to comfort his friend in their immediate circumstance. The poem throws the question of duty back on to its readers, asking them to examine their role in what has been revealed, and denies them the comforts of mere spectatorship.

The experience of seeing something familiar like the moral at the end of 'The Chimney Sweep' transmute into a strangely different alternative is an integral part of the experience of reading *Songs*. Many of the poems, for instance, make use of traditional Christian symbolism, a poem like 'The Lamb' is a case in point, but these symbols are frequently used in ways which seem at odds with the Christian orthodoxy of Blake's time. Partly this is a culminative effect. 'The Lamb' could be read as a conventional statement of the immanence of Christ, but, placed in the context of the collection overall, it seems typical in having little room for any other conception of divinity than the Divine-in-the-Human. No less than the more obviously polemical *The Marriage of Heaven and Hell*, *Songs* implies that 'All deities reside in the human breast' (E38). Both texts are also equally concerned with the pain brought about by forgetting this fact. Blake was involved in the Swedenborgian movement when the

Songs were being contemplated, but institutionalized religion is presented as a painful blight on natural energies in poems such as 'The Garden of Love' and 'London'. The anger articulated in such poems may reflect the revolutionary sympathies expressed more overtly in Blake's unpublished poem *The French Revolution* (1790). Certainly the trinity of 'God & his Priest & King' indicted by the Chimney Sweeper in the Experience version was a common target in the radical literature of the period (see Mee, 1992, 181–2). Recent critics of the poems, however, have suggested that the voice of Experience is often being presented as deliberately limited in its view of oppression and suffering, in a kind of parody of poems such as Alcock's, cut off from the Innocence it should be seeking to liberate (see Glen, 1983, 222). From this perspective, the speaker of 'London', for instance, could be seen as trapped within and perpetuating 'mind-forg'd manacles' in his despair. He fails to see any redemptive possibilities in the city that so oppressively surrounds him. The difficulty for the reader and critic is to register this limitation while taking seriously the anger and frustration vented in that most powerful of poems.

Perhaps the most famous poem in the whole collection is 'The Tyger'. Here too the relationship of the speaker to what is described is far from straightforward. If the energy of the tiger echoes contemporary descriptions of the French revolutionary crowd as several critics have suggested (see Erdman, 1977, 195; Crehan, 1984, 127–8), then the speaker seems both appalled and fascinated by its tremendous energy. The tiger refuses to accommodate its interrogator, who finishes simply by restating the question, but now with less conviction. The move from 'Could' to 'Dare' seems to mark the impossibility of any 'frame' for this fearful symmetry. Where it is framed, is on the page, by its creator Blake. In this respect Blake's human 'hand or eye' seems superior to the 'immortal'. Or is it that immortality is being offered to any human hand turning the page or eye reading the poem that will claim for itself the power of the tiger? Certainly the poem seems to end with a challenge, a 'Dare', to see who will enter into, take on and perhaps take over the energy of the tiger in 'Mental Fight' (E95).

The 'Bard' who welcomes the reader in the 'Introduction' to Experience suggests Blake's relationship with eighteenth-century primitivists such as Thomas Gray and James Macpherson, but, when compared to the nostalgia which permeates their writing, Blake's poetry has a much stronger sense of the possibility of recuperating the energies of Innocence for the present. In this respect Innocence and Experience are not opposed in the collection, but shown to permeate in different ways every aspect of existence. 'The Lamb' and 'The Tyger' exist as productive contraries in the same collection. Indeed the latter was engraved on the back of the copper plate on which the former was etched. Innocence can be reborn at any point in time to provide an alternative to the bitterness and oppression which Experience critiques. Without perceiving the barren world of oppression the potentiality of Innocence cannot fully be grasped. Without a sense of the utopian possibilities of Innocence, the perspectives of Experience are simply affirmations of despair. For unredeemed Experience 'The Tyger' is simply a poem about 'dread'. From the perspective of the contraries of the combined collection, however, it challenges the reader to think of a way in which the tiger can lie down with the lamb.

WRITINGS

Blake, William (1991). *Songs of Innocence and of Experience.* Ed. Andrew Lincoln. London and Princeton: Princeton University Press.

Erdman, David V., ed. (1988). *The Complete Poetry and Prose of William Blake.* New York: Doubleday.

REFERENCES AND FURTHER READING

Ackroyd, Peter (1995). *Blake.* London: Sinclair-Stevenson.

Alcock, Mary (1799). *Poems.* London.

Crehan, Stewart (1984). *Blake in Context.* Dublin: Gill and Macmillan Humanities Press.

Erdman, David V. (1977). *Blake: Prophet Against Empire.* 3rd edn, Princeton: Princeton University Press.

Gardner, Stanley (1986). *Blake's 'Innocence and Experience' Retraced.* London: Athlone Press; New York: St Martin's Press.

Gillham, D. G. (1966). *Blake's Contrary States: 'The Songs of Innocence and of Experience' as Dramatic Poems.* Cambridge: Cambridge University Press.

Gleckner, Robert (1959). *The Piper and the Bard: A Study of William Blake.* Detroit: Wayne State University Press.

Glen, Heather (1983). *Vision and Disenchantment: Blake's 'Songs' and Wordsworth's 'Lyrical Ballads'.* Cambridge: Cambridge University Press.

Holloway, John (1968). *Blake: The Lyric Poetry.* London: Edward Arnold.

Lackington, James (1792). *Memoirs of the First Forty Five Years of the Life of James Lackington.* 2nd edn. London.

Larrissy, Edward (1985). *William Blake.* Preface by Terry Eagleton. Oxford: Blackwell.

Leader, Zachery (1981). *Reading Blake's Songs.* Boston: Routledge and Kegan Paul.

Mee, Jon (1992). *Dangerous Enthusiasm: Blake and the Culture of Radicalism in the 1790s.* Oxford: Oxford University Press.

Shrimpton, Nick (1976). 'Hell's hymnbook: Blake's *Songs of Innocence and of Experience* and their models'. In *Literature of the Romantic Period, 1750–1850.* Ed. R. T. Davies and B. G. Beatty. New York: Barnes and Noble, 19–35.

Thompson, E. P. (1993). *Witness Against the Beast: William Blake and the Moral Law.* Cambridge: Cambridge University Press.

Viscomi, Joseph (1993). *Blake and the Idea of the Book.* Princeton: Princeton University Press.

Watts, Isaac (1715). *Divine and Moral Songs for Children.* London.

PART THREE
Periods

44

Literature, 1681–1688

Abigail Williams

Introduction

The period 1681 to 1688 spans seven years of enormous political upheaval, covering the climax of the Exclusion Crisis, the formation of the first recognizable political parties, and the arrival of William of Orange at Torbay in November 1688. One of the most striking aspects of the literature of the 1680s is its engagement with the issues generated by these events – this, after all, is the period that saw the birth of party-political literature. Over the course of the decade, the press, released by the lapse of the Licensing Act in 1679, pumped out thousands of pamphlets, poems and news-sheets as Whigs and Tories, Anglicans and Dissenters tried to justify their political and religious positions.

However, for all this diversity of opinion, there has been a tendency in many accounts of the literature of this period to concentrate almost exclusively on the works of the Tory writers who responded to the Exclusion Crisis and its aftermath. In particular, the Stuart laureate John Dryden is accorded a degree of authority as a spokesperson for contemporary events that he was unable to secure at the time. This has meant that, for example, his satire on the politics of the Exclusion Crisis in *Absalom and Achitophel* has tended to dominate accounts of the literature produced by the crisis. The problem with constructing a narrative around Dryden, or his political allies such as Roger L'Estrange and John Oldham, is that it obscures the political debate that characterizes the literature of the 1680s. Tory propaganda on the events of the Exclusion Crisis and its aftermath was matched by Whig writing. Opposition poets such as Thomas Shadwell, who Dryden satirized at such length in *MacFlecknoe*, produced poems and plays throughout this period which offer an alternative perspective on contemporary events and literature. The intention of this chapter is to juxtapose Whig and Tory writing in order to restore this sense of debate and contest to the literature produced between 1681 and 1688. The chapter will explore the way writers from opposite ends of the political spectrum responded to the changing events of the decade by developing their own distinct sets of images and arguments about public life.

1681–1682: Responses to the Exclusion Crisis

The Popish Plot, and the Exclusion Crisis that followed it, were started with a rumour. In October 1678 the Privy Council began investigating the fictional allegations of Titus Oates, a discredited Jesuit novice, who had claimed that he knew of a popish plot to assassinate the king. His tale was given credibility by the sudden murder of Sir Edmund Berry Godfrey, the Justice of the Peace to whom he had made his depositions about the plot, and it was immediately assumed that the murder was the work of papists. This fear of Catholic conspiracy was increased by the discovery that the seized papers of Edward Coleman, the Duke of York's former secretary, contained treasonable letters to Louis XIV's confessors about a plot to overthrow the Church of England and re-establish Catholicism as the national faith.

The apparent confirmation of the plot aroused concern about the future safety of the Protestant religion, which had been growing over the course of the 1670s. Fears were focused on the political and religious implications of the eventual succession of Charles's brother and heir, James, Duke of York, whose Catholicism had been evident since 1673, and who was married to a Catholic Italian princess, Mary of Modena. Out of the hysteria over the Catholic threat a pressure group emerged, who believed that the only way to safeguard the national religion was to pass a Bill of Exclusion to prevent James from ever acceding to the throne. This group was soon to be known as the Whigs, a name derived from 'Whiggamores', fanatical Scottish Covenanters, while those who opposed them became known as the 'Tories', from a name for Irish brigands.

Images of Party

One of the most confusing aspects of the literature of the Exclusion Crisis is that many writers are anxious to distance themselves from affiliation with either Whig or Tory parties. Authors from both sides often present themselves as moderates who are steering a careful middle way through the troubled waters of political partisanship. Thus Andrew Marvell's attack on the government in *An Account of the Growth of Popery and Arbitrary Government* (1677) gives an impression of impartiality and moderation at the same time as mounting the politically inflammatory claim that 'There has now for diverse Years, a design been carried on, to change the lawfull Government of England into an Absolute Tyranny, and to convert the established Protestant Religion into down-right Popery' (Marvell, 1677, 3).

One way in which writers show themselves transcending party allegiance is by presenting party politics as factionalism, so that their own political agenda appears to be neutral. We find this strategy employed in the Tory writer Thomas Otway's popular tragedy *Venice Preserv'd* (1682), in which Otway depicts a conspiracy to overthrow the republican government of Venice. Although Otway clearly directs the play's application towards contemporary politics in the prologue and epilogue, where he refers to the Whigs as 'the rebel tribe', it is hard to pin down the tragedy as a simple fable. By simultaneously demonizing rebellion and revealing the corruption of the senate that the conspirators seek to displace, he creates a fable about revolution and bad governance that resists identification as Tory propaganda. The general context of political uncertainty and instability in the play, which depicts a city 'Upon the very brink of a gaping ruin', seems to gesture towards the whole range of political extremity that had been generated by the Plot and Exclusion debate.

To complicate further the question of political allegiance, there were also writers and politicians who described themselves as 'Trimmers', and who formalized the rhetoric of moderation that we have seen in Marvell and Otway into a distinct political category. The most famous of these was the Marquis of Halifax, whose *Character of a Trimmer* was circulating in manuscript from 1685. Although Trimmers were attacked with the same fury as those within the party-political arena – in his epilogue to *The Duke of Guise*, Dryden describes the Trimmer as 'A Twilight Animal; true to neither Cause, / With Tory Wings, but Whiggish Teeth and Claws' (Dryden, 1958, I, ll. 43–4) – Trimmers claimed that they offered a third way, beyond partisanship. In the *Character*, Halifax explained that

> This innocent word Trimmer signifieth no more than this, that if men are together in a boat, and one part of the company would weigh it down on one side, another would make it lean as much to the contrary, it happeneth there is a third opinion, of those who conceive it would do as well, if the boat went even, without endangering the passengers. (Halifax, 1989, I, 179)

Yet for all this rhetoric of moderation, it is also possible to identify more clearly defined party polemic in contemporary writing. There is a growing consensus among historians of this period that the most significant issue underlying the question of the exclusion of the Duke of York was that of religion. While both Whig and Tory writers were quick to draw on a thriving tradition of anti-Catholic rhetoric in response to the Plot, as in the Tory poet John Oldham's *Satires on the Jesuits* (1681) or the Whig dramatist Elkanah Settle's anti-popery in *The Female Prelate* (1680), they were more commonly divided by their differing interpretations of the religious implications of the crisis. On the whole, loyalist Tories saw the threat to national stability as coming from the assault of Dissenters on the Anglican Church and the monarchy. Whig Exclusionists, on the other hand, many of whom were Dissenters, were worried about the harsh laws against religious nonconformists, and the royal encouragement of Catholicism, which was believed to come hand in hand with political absolutism.

Tory writers attacked the opposition by stressing its religious diversity, and emphasizing its links with republicanism. Many of the First Whigs had either been republicans, or had come from families that had supported Cromwell, and thus their opponents suggested that what they really aimed at was a reprise of the events of the 1640s and 1650s. In his satirical poem, *The Ghost of the Old House of Commons*, the Tory politician and writer the Earl of Roscommon accuses the Whig leader the Earl of Shaftesbury of 'driving Eighty back to Forty-Eight' (Roscommon, 1965, l. 48). Similarly, in *The Medal* (1682), Dryden describes the way in which the rivalry among the assorted groups of nonconformists within the opposition will end in the sort of radical disunity last seen at the mid-century:

> The swelling Poyson of the sev'ral Sects,
> Which, wanting vent, the Nation's Health infects
> Shall burst its Bag; and fighting out their way
> The various Venoms on each other prey.
> (Dryden, 1958, I, ll. 294–7)

We find the same emphasis in Tory plays – in his comedy, *City Politiques* (1683) the dramatist John Crowne suggests that the real aims of the Dissenters are to attack church and state, and bring a return of civil war chaos. The Whigs pose a more serious threat than the Catholics, since they 'have a worse design on religion, to make her a bawd to carry on some lewd project' (Crowne, 1967, I, i, 103). He derides their claim to be 'true Protestants':

> There is in every true Protestant breast
> A Heraclitus Ridens, his contest,
> A knave in earnest and a saint in jest.
> The saint looks up to heaven, the knave that while
> Your pocket picks, and at the cheat does smile. (I, i, 152–3)

As Crowne's ridiculing of the 'true Protestant' suggests, one way in which Whig writers represented their relationship with the dissenting community was by drawing on the rhetoric of Protestant nationalism. This was useful because it not only focused on the central issue of the crisis – the threat of a Catholic plot and succession – but it also implied a sense of unity between the Anglicans and the various groups of dissenters and nonconformists that made up a large section of the Whig supporters.

Opposition writers connected the cause of 1678–82 to earlier phases of English Protestant history, and in particular, to a narrative of Catholic threats to the national religion that could be traced back to the advent of the Armada. In his pamphlet *Sion in Distress. Or, the Groans of the Protestant Church* (1681) the Baptist Benjamin Keach writes of a history of Protestant oppression which connects the 'present threat' to 'martyr'd Pride under Mary, / Spanish Armada, Powder treason' (Keach, 1681, 101). The fiercely Protestant Elizabeth I was particularly important in the anti-Catholic narrative developed by Whig polemicists, partly because her Treasons Act of 1571, designed to exclude possible Catholic successors to the throne, was often cited as a precedent for the Bill of Exclusion.

The Tudor queen was the centrepiece of the Whigs' popular pope burning processions, held on the anniversary of her accession, where her statue appeared bearing a shield saying 'Magna Charta et Religio Protestantium'. In Whig drama, she is often invoked nostalgically, as a representative of all that is compromised by the current crisis. Thomas Shadwell's heavily censored comedy *The Lancashire Witches* (1682) centres on the figure of the country gentleman Sir Edward Hartfort, who lives like the gentry of 'the Golden Days of Queen Elizabeth' (Shadwell, 1927, IV, III, 136). His principles of hospitality, kindness to his servants and toleration of Dissenters make him a representative of a traditional political order, which is threatened by a tyranny of superstition and Francophilia. Similarly, the populist Whig farce *The Coronation of Queen Elizabeth* (1680) draws parallels between contemporary events and the fate of beleaguered Elizabethan Protestants threatened by a pope and cardinals who are plotting to murder the queen. The comparison between Elizabeth and Charles is implicitly critical of the Stuart king: she dealt with the threat to the national faith the right way, having 'maugred all the Plots and dire Conspiracies of Rome', and showed proper gratitude to her loyal Protestant subjects (*The Coronation of Queen Elizabeth*, 1680, sig. a2r).

The figure of Elizabeth was important in Whig propaganda because she enabled opposition writers to realign Exclusionist politics with a history of earlier Protestant nationalism. She enabled Whig writers to write the history of their cause in a way that could exclude the dangerous precedents of mid-century republican rebellion. The extent to which the first Whigs were concerned to distance themselves from earlier civil war radicals is demonstrated by the publication of Andrew Marvell's *Miscellaneous Poems* in 1681. Marvell could be appropriated as a proto-Whig on the basis of his Restoration prose writings – in his attack on the archdeacon of Canterbury, Samuel Parker, in *The Rehearsal Transpos'd*, he seemed to have anticipated contemporary concerns about the Anglican church and toleration, while his *Account of Popery and Arbitrary Government* (1677) had provided a cogent case for the country opposition. Yet the former MP for Hull had also occupied a prominent position under Cromwell, and had written a series of poems in support of the Commonwealth. When the Whig bookseller Robert Boulter published his posthumous *Miscellaneous Poems* in 1681, they contained none of the Cromwell poems, which were not reprinted until 1776. Instead of revealing a dangerous revolutionary, a careful editorial selection ensured that their author was presented as a moderate Whig. Marvell's satire on the Catholic priest of 'Flecknoe, an English Priest at Rome', and his country house poem 'Upon Appleton House' revealed an anti-Catholicism very appropriate to the issues of the current crisis.

One important way in which Tory propagandists emphasized the links between the first Whigs and Civil War republicans was by focusing on the populist nature of the Exclusionists' support. They portrayed Whig activists as nothing more than 'rabble-rousers', and a series of poems and plays of the early 1680s harped on parallels with the incitement of popular unrest in 1641. In Tom D'Urfey's *The Whigs' Exaltation*, a reworking of a ballad that the Royalist poet Francis Quarles had used in the 1640s to satirize extreme Puritans, D'Urfey's parody of a Whig claims that he will

        teach the Nobles how to bow,
And keep their Gentry down.
Good manners has a bad repute,
And tends to pride, we see;
We'll therefore cry all breeding down,
And hey boys up go we.
                    (D'Urfey, 1968, ll. 11–16)

Although the Whigs did indeed have a substantial following among 'the people', demonstrated in their monster petitioning campaigns and pope burning rituals, they had to be careful to downplay this populism, since their electoral success depended on appeasing country gentry voters, who were likely to run scared at the prospect of popular uprising.

Absalom and Achitophel

Absalom and Achitophel, perhaps the most famous text to have been generated by the political crisis, is clearly deeply engaged with these arguments that we have seen growing out of the Exclusion debate. It was published in November 1681, immediately before the Earl of Shaftesbury was due to be tried for treason. In the mock-biblical poem, Dryden uses the story of Absalom's rebellion against King David, taken from the book of Samuel, as a parallel to Monmouth's rebellion against Charles. The poem is a tissue of allusions to a wide range of literary and biblical texts – to the Old and New Testaments, to Vergil, Ovid and even Miltonic epic. Yet *Absalom and Achitophel* was also a product of contemporary political pamphleteering. One way in which it obviously borrows from earlier Tory arguments about the crisis is by portraying the plot and Exclusionist cause as a continuation of Republican agitation: Dryden explains that 'The Good Old Cause revived a plot requires; / Plots, true or false, are necessary things / To raise up commonwealths and ruin kings' (Dryden, 1958, I, ll. 82–4). He also engages with the Whig use of the term 'patriot'. For opposition writers, Whig 'patriots' such as Shaftesbury or Thomas Thynne were those fighting for their country's interests against those of France or Rome, which were being furthered by Catholic conspirators. Thus in Shadwell's *The Lancashire Witches*, Sir Edward Hartfort's definition of his Whiggish political agenda: 'I am a true English-man, I love the Princes Rights and Peoples Liberties, and will defend them both with the last penny in my purse, and the last drop in my veins, and dare defy the witless plots of papists', is said to be 'Spoken like a Noble Patriot' (Shadwell, 1927, IV, III, 137). Dryden attacks this type of rhetoric in his poem, where he claims that the Duke of Monmouth was

        Gull'd with a Patriot's name, whose Modern sense
Is one that would by Law supplant his Prince;
The People's Brave, the Politician's Tool;
Never was Patriot yet but was a Fool.
                    (Dryden, 1958, I, ll. 965–8)

Responses to *Absalom and Achitophel* took on Dryden's Tory propaganda point by point, revealing just how clearly the poem was situated in an ongoing battle of political rhetoric and counter-claim. Whig poets attempted to rescue the rhetoric of patriotism for their leaders, and the anonymous author of *Directions to Fame, about an Elegy on the late deceased Thomas Thynn* . . . (1682), an elegy on the murdered Whig magnate Thomas Thynne, describes the Whig lords as

> Fam'd Patriots, not in late Poets sense,
> As those who would by Law supplant their Prince;
> But such, whose wishes are to have Charles great,
> That he might ever fill his Father's seat.
>   (*Directions to Fame*, 1975, 18)

Similarly, in the mock-biblical *Azaria and Hushai*, Samuel Pordage qualifies and modifies the depiction of Whig popular support found in Dryden's poem. Where the laureate had described Monmouth as 'On each side bowing popularly low' (Dryden, 1958, I, l. 689) Pordage presents Monmouth's followers as aristocratic:

> Not factious Sects, the Rabble, or the rude
> Erring, unthinking, vulgar Multitude:
> But the chief Tribes and Princes of the Land,
> Who durst for Moses's ancient Statutes stand.
> The pious, just, religious and the good,
> Men of great Riches, and of greater Bloud.
>   (Pordage, 1682, 23)

Images of London

If *Absalom and Achitophel* was intended to influence the outcome of Shaftesbury's trial, it failed. The Whig leader was acquitted at the end of November 1681 by a carefully selected grand jury of London Whigs, who refused to accept the charges against him, and returned an 'ignoramus' verdict. Their supporters celebrated with bonfires and congratulatory poems, while Tories were outraged at the decision, which confirmed their fears that the city was out of control. Following the trial, the king determined to step in and regain control of the city's legal and political machinery. In the summer of 1682 he used his newly elected Tory Lord Mayor, John Moore, to nullify the election of two Whig candidates who had recently been elected as city sheriffs, prompting a huge controversy about the city's self-governance.

This sequence of events focused attention even more clearly on the status of the city of London. There were already existing debates between Whigs and Tories over the validity of city politics – London was the home of one-tenth of the national population, and of the most easily mobilized body of popular support. It was here that the Whigs organized their petitions and pope burnings, and here that the Tories saw the most visible signs of the populist politics that they feared so much. Thus much of the contest between Whig and Tory in the early 1680s involved competing images of the city itself: was it, as Tory propagandists suggested, a hotbed of unruly radicalism, or as Whig writers claimed, the loyal capital of Protestantism?

The events of late 1681 and 1682 only served to magnify these tensions. Out of the turmoil of municipal politics came a spate of Tory comedies, such as John Crowne's *City Politiques* (1683) Aphra Behn's *The City Heiress* (1682) and Tom D'Urfey's *Sir Barnaby Whigg* (1681) all of which parodied the archetypal prosperous City Whig. In Behn's play, the satire centres on Sir Timothy Treat-all, a hypocritical Whig Dissenter who is a composite of the Earl of Shaftesbury, Sir Patience Ward, the Whig Lord Mayor, and Sir Thomas Player, an old and notoriously lecherous City alderman. From the beginning of the play, Behn foregrounds Sir Timothy's greed and lack of political integrity, as he declares

> my Integrity has been known ever since Forty-One; I bought three thousand a year in Bishops Land, as 'tis well known, and lost it at the Kings return; for which I'm honour'd by the City. (Behn, 1996, I, i, 97–100)

There is a similar ambivalence about merchants and trade in Tory poetry – in *The Medal*, his satire on the coining of a medal to celebrate Shaftesbury's acquittal, Dryden presents the affluence brought by the port of London as a corrupting evil:

> I call'd thee [the Thames] Nile; the parallel will stand;
> Thy tides of Wealth o'rflow the fatten'd Land;
> Yet Monsters from thy Large increase we find;
> Engender'd on the Slyme thou leav'st behind.
> (Dryden, 1958, I, ll. 171–4)

It is an image very far from that at the end of his earlier account of the city in *Annus Mirabilis* (1667), where he had described London with her 'silver Thames, her own domestick Floud' who 'shall bear her Vessels, like a sweeping Train' (Dryden, 1958, I, ll. 1, 189–90). By the early 1680s it was Whig writers who were the biggest supporters of trade. A considerable section of the Whig following in the city came from its mercantile population, who had long been hostile to Charles II's foreign policies, partly for economic, and partly for ideological reasons. Thus Whig poets appropriated the tradition of imperial poetry typified by *Annus Mirabilis*, as in Thomas Thompson's long poem on the shrieval elections, *Midsummer Moon: Or the Liveryman's Complaint* (1682):

> The stately Nereids, with the swelling tide,
> Rich freights from all the universe provide:
> Whate'er of rarities the East can shew,
> With all the glittering entrails of Peru

Cargoes of myrrh and frankincense they bring,
And pearls and diamonds for an offering.
                    (Thompson, 1968, ll. 351–6)

Thompson's passage, with its nereids, naiads, and Thames mythology signals backwards to earlier poetic models, not only to Dryden's London of *Annus Mirabilis*, but also to John Denham's *Cooper's Hill*, and Edmund Waller's *To My Lord Protector*. However, there is an important difference from these poems, since trade for Thompson and other Whig writers is inflected with Protestant, anti-French sentiment. In *Midsummer Moon*, London's imperial prowess is wholly connected to her defence of Protestantism: 'For wealth without our liberties would be / But painted chains and gilded slavery' (ll. 363–4).

The debate about the status of the city of London and its citizens was central to the hugely contentious publication of Dryden and Nathaniel Lee's tragedy *The Duke of Guise* (1683). In the play, which was initially banned because of its reflections on the Duke of Monmouth, Dryden and Lee developed a clear parallel between the sedition of the Catholic League against Henri III of France, and that of the Whigs against Charles. They used the analogy to warn of the potential disloyalty and sedition of a capital city, and the danger of allowing a parliamentary body to oppose royal policies. In the prologue, Dryden made it very clear how specifically he held the City Whigs to blame for the assault on royal authority, claiming that their true intention was to 'Make London independent of the Crown: / A Realm apart; the Kingdom of the Town' (Dryden, 1958, I, ll. 41–2). He was answered by a battery of Whigs defending the city. In *A Defence of the Charter and Municipal Rights of the City of London* (1683) the Whig lawyer Thomas Hunt claimed that Dryden and Lee had 'executed the Magistrates in Effigie upon the Stage' (Hunt, 1683, 24). Two months later, the author of the pamphlet *Some Reflections upon . . . the Duke of Guise*, possibly Thomas Shadwell, again took issue with the laureate's charges of disloyalty, emphasizing that the city

> was so mainly Instrumental in his Happy Restauration which has been his back ever since when he has needed it, which has not suffered so much as a Riot to pass unpunished during his Government. (Shadwell, 1927, V, 389)

The Tory Reaction

By the end of 1682 the crisis had moved into a new phase. Charles's Oxford parliament in October 1681, at which he insisted on his intention to reject Exclusion, prompted the beginnings of a reassertion of royal authority that became known as the Tory reaction period. The interruption of the shrieval elections in the summer of 1682 was one sign of this change in policy. Other punitive measures were also taken, as the government clamped down on political opposition in the localities, suppressed

demonstrations and persecuted the religious dissenters who had been closely allied
with the Whig cause. While some of the more radical Whig activists such as Algernon Sidney and William Russell were to continue in their active opposition to the
court, most of the Exclusionists either made their peace with the king, or went into
exile on their country estates.

There is a marked shift in literature from the years of the Exclusion Crisis to the
mid-1680s. Fewer new plays were produced in these years, partly because of the
closure of the King's Company in 1683, and its merging with the Duke's Company,
which created a monopoly for the next thirteen years. The absence of commercial
rivalry meant that the theatre was dominated by new productions of older works. In
addition, many of the older playwrights like Etherege and Wycherley had stopped
writing, while Otway and Lee were at the end of their careers. There were also fewer
satires in circulation, due to the enforcement of government restrictions on 'seditious'
publications. Some radical Whig writers were even silenced permanently, such as the
'Protestant joiner' Stephen College, author of the highly critical satire 'A Raree Show',
who was executed shortly after the Oxford parliament of 1681. The newly rigorous
censorship was compounded by the renewal of the Licensing Act in 1685, and the
reinstatement of Roger L'Estrange as its enforcer.

Tory Victory

Tory writers were quick to celebrate the declining political fortunes of their opponents. The years between 1682 and 1687 are marked by a series of satires on Whig
defeats. The death of the Earl of Shaftesbury in October 1682 produced a flurry of
attacks on stock themes, as Tory satirists crowed over the demise of the opposition
leader who was said to have coveted the throne of Poland, and who, they claimed,
planned to bring in a new commonwealth under cover of the Plot. These posthumous
attacks on Shaftesbury were followed by jubilation over the revelation of the 'Rye
House Plot' in 1683, which prompted more triumphalism, as Tory writers rejoiced
over the apparent confirmation and defeat of the Whigs' republican conspiracy. The
execution of Algernon Sidney, and the suicide of the Earl of Essex might have created
martyrs for later Whigs, but in the 1680s their deaths were predominantly the subject
matter of Tory satire. In the anonymous *Algernon Sidney's Farewell*, Sidney celebrates
his arrival in hell, where he will sit at the right hand of Shaftesbury, and display the
gory scars of his republicanism to the devil, while the author of the mock *Elegy on the
Earl of Essex* claims that the Earl of Essex killed himself 'Lest thy false tongue should
through thy throat impart / The bloody treasons that oppress'd thy heart' (*Elegy on
the Earl of Essex*, 1968, ll. 39–40).

Tory triumphalism can also be found in the theatre. Dryden's opera, *Albion and
Albanius* (1685), was a straightforward celebration of the newly asserted Tory hegemony: whereas Dryden's heroic tragedies of the 1670s had explored the complexities
and instabilities of power and monarchy, the opera, as its author explained in his

preface, 'plainly represents the double restoration of his Sacred Majesty' (Dryden, 1956, XV, l. 300). Dryden drew on Restoration iconography, featuring triumphal arches and figures of Justice and Democracy, in a coupling of the political and the lyric based on the past two decades of English history. However, this celebration of the king's achievements was suddenly rendered invalid, after only two or three performances by Charles's death. Dryden doctored the opera so that it included James's accession, and Venus's prophecy that he would be

> Ador'd and fear'd, and lov'd no less;
> In War Victorious, mild in Peace,
> The joy of men, and *Jove's* increase.
>> (Dryden, 1956, XV, III, i, 223–5)

The Whig Response

The change in political climate after 1682, and the Tory backlash at former Exclusionists, meant that Whig writers had to find alternative ways of voicing their political agenda. One of the interesting literary phenomena of this period is the way in which former Exclusionist writers drew on older literary tropes to characterize their continuing opposition to the government. Although it was dangerous to write, or print seditious material during the 1680s, there were underground publishing networks, largely run by nonconformist booksellers and printers, which enabled opposition writers to circulate their unlicensed propaganda.

Many moderate Whig activists avoided the fate of more radical Whigs by adopting a life of quiet retirement, from which they tended to articulate a different perspective on public affairs. Similarly, Whig poets drew on a tradition of the Horatian retirement poem to characterize their exile during the 1680s, in the same way that royalist poets such as Lovelace, Herrick and Cowley had described their responses to the events of the 1640s. The Whig journalist John Tutchin's 'Discourse of Life' finishes with such a paean to an idealized life of gentle retreat:

> Grant me, good God! a Melancholy Seat
> Free from the Noise and Tumults of the Great:
> Like some Blest Man, who his Retinue sees,
> A tall and sprightly Grove of servile Trees.
>> (Tutchin, 1685, 147)

In this poem Tutchin, like other Whig poets, aspires towards a moral, rather than a political perspective on contemporary public life. Whereas the poems of the Exclusion Crisis deal with the details of the revelation of the plot, the passage of the Exclusion Bills or the shrieval elections, later Whig poems tend to situate themselves beyond local issues. Once it became clear that the Whigs had no further hope of constitutional political success, poets drew more heavily on satire to provide a moral victory, as a substitute for a material victory. This tied in with the use of 'country' rhetoric as an expression of their political grievances. This country rhetoric, used by opposition writers in the early 1670s, was based around a resentment of the executive, a mistrust of the court, and a suspicion that the power and wealth of courts corrupted all who entered them. By 1682 it was again an ideal idiom for the apparently passive Whig supporters forced into retirement on their estates, eschewing both the possession and the pursuit of executive power. Thomas Shadwell's translation of *The Tenth Satire of Juvenal* (1687) makes a classic statement about the relationship between virtue and public life. In his formulation of 'Cato's answer to Labienus' from Lucan's *Pharsalia*, Shadwell propounds the heroism of principled failure, as Cato asks Labienus

> If any *violence* can depress the *brave?*
> Or *Fortune's* threats force against *Vertue* have.
> Are great attempts by not succeeding less?
> Does a brave act grow braver by success?
> We of these truths such full conviction find,
> *Heav'n* cannot fix them deeper in the mind.
> (Shadwell, 1927, V, ll. 8–13)

Ironically, many of the arguments found in these Whig poems were to reappear in the following decade, this time used by Jacobite authors such as Dryden and George Granville, who drew on the classical humanist tradition to describe their own political alienation and dispossession.

The State of the Art

Another way in which Whig and Tory writers continued to play out their differences in the mid-1680s was through their very different representations of contemporary poetic achievement. In 1685 the Earl of Roscommon published his influential *Essay on Translated Verse*, in which he traced the progress of poesy through from classical Rome to a new heyday in Restoration England. The *Essay* was partly a celebration of the fruits of Roscommon's informal literary academy, formed during the early 1680s, which included Dryden, the Earl of Halifax and the Earl of Dorset. Although the group was initially founded to reform the English language, the most significant evidence of its activity was a series of translations of classical texts, such as John Oldham's translation of Horace's *Ars Poetica* in 1681, and Thomas Creech's translation of Lucretius in 1682. The translations made classical texts available for the first time to many contemporary readers, particularly women, who had not been educated in Latin and Greek. However, although the academy was intended to be non-partisan, and above contemporary political difference, Roscommon's *Essay* clearly followed an established tradition of Tory criticism, dating from the Restoration, which had tended to associate the return of the king in 1660 with a renewal of national culture. In *An Essay of Dramatic Poesy* (1668) Dryden had famously claimed that 'with the restoration of our happiness, we see revived poesy lifting up its head, and already shaking off the rubbish which lay so heavy on it' (Dryden, 1956, XVII, 63). Similarly, Roscommon identified the revival of the muses with the fortunes of the Stuart monarchy:

> By secret influence of Indulgent Skyes,
> *Empire*, and *Poesy Together* rise . . .
>   Now that *Phoebus* and the *sacred Nine*,
> With all their Beams on our blest Island shine,
> Why should not *We* their *ancient Rites restore*
> And *be*, what *Rome* or *Athens* were *Before?*
>   (Roscommon, 1997, ll. 354–5, 372–5)

In the 1680s we find Whig poets countering these Tory images of restoration and revival with their own alternative narrative of the moral decline of the national literature. John Cutts, the soldier-poet who was later to become Baron Cutts, the Williamite war hero, constructs his 'Musarum Origo: or the Original and Excellence of the Muses' around a very different teleology:

> In dissolute, and undiscerning times,
> When Vice unmasks, and Vertues pass for Crimes,
> The sacred Gift of charming Poetry,
> Is look'd on with a slight, and scornful Eye;
> But if we trace the steps of former Years,
> It's high Descent, and Dignity appears.
>   (Cutts, 1687, ll. 9–14)

Anticipating the arguments of the Whig critic John Dennis, Cutts traces his muses not through the classics and France, as Roscommon and Dryden had done, but through David and Solomon and the sacred origins of poetry in the Bible. He implies that until contemporary poetry regains its moral and Christian function, the current literary scene is destined to languish. John Tutchin uses the image of Augusta in his 'A Satire against Vice' to make a similar point. Where Dryden had used Augusta in his Restoration panegyrics to suggest an age of unprecedented literary and political triumphs in post-Restoration England, Tutchin argues that the failure of writers to use their work to safeguard morality has led to a state where

> Our fair Augusta, once the nations pride
> To whom new honours brought each flowing Tide
> Now, by its peoples crimes, a Desart made
> And though a well-built town, a very shade.
>   (Tutchin, 1685, 9)

Tutchin argues in his preface that to achieve a meaningful restoration of the city, contemporary writers must address moral issues, since although poetry 'may be, like bitter drinks disgustful to the Palate, yet it is good for the health of the whole. And tho' it may be airy in the Expression, it ought to be good and solid in the Moral' (Tutchin, 1685, sig. a4v).

The rejection or suspicion of the moral laxity of Restoration culture found in these poems is mirrored in the drama of the mid-1680s. From 1682 onwards there is an increasing sense of disapproval of the sex comedy that had been so popular in the 1670s, and a shift towards 'purer' forms of comedy. The former Restoration rake Sir Charles Sedley observed the change of literary climate in his prologue to *Bellamira, or the Mistress* (1687), which begins:

> Is it not strange to see in such an Age
> The Pulpit get the better of the Stage?
> Not through Rebellion as in former days,
> But Zeal for Sermons and neglect for Plays.
> Here's as good Ogling yet, and fewer Spies.
> For Godly Parents watch with whites of Eyes.
> (Sedley, 1928, II, ll. 1–6)

The dedication to Aphra Behn's *The Luckey Chance, or an Alderman's Bargain* (1686) is another testament to the changing expectations of contemporaries. Behn defends the theatre on the same grounds on which her plays had traditionally been attacked, arguing that 'publick Pleasures and Divertisements' are 'the Schools of Vertue, where Vice is always either punish't, or disdain'd' (Behn, 1996, ll. 10–12). Behn's attempt to claim a moral high ground for her play can be compared with the changing perspective on rake-culture that we find in her *Love Letters between a Nobleman and His Sister* (1684–7). The sensational romance fiction, which tells the story of the hypocritical lovers Sylvia and Philander, is based on the story of the abduction of Lady Henrietta Berkeley by Lord Grey of Werke, one of Monmouth's supporters in the rebellion of 1685. Monmouth appears in the fiction as Cesario, while Shaftesbury is resurrected as Tomaso. In earlier works, Behn had compared her own time to a mythic golden age, in which sexual desires could be freely expressed. But by the late 1680s her tale of rakes and sexual opportunism is not a celebration of sexual libertinism, but an allegory about the political double-dealing and unscrupulousness of the Whig rebels.

The changing perspective on the world of Restoration libertinism and sex comedy that we see demonstrated in these texts was confirmed by the enormous success of Shadwell's overtly didactic comedy *The Squire of Alsatia* (1688). The play is structured around a contrast between two systems of education: Sir William Belfond brings up his elder son severely, educated only in estate management, while his brother, Sir Edward, brings up his younger son more indulgently, giving him the benefits of a liberal, 'gentlemanlike' education, which includes foreign travel, and education in classical authors. The older cousin, Belfond Senior, grows up to be boorish and uneducated, and soon falls into the hands of London low-life cheats and gulls. Belfond Junior, on the other hand, is essentially a man of principle, whose education enables him to turn his back on the temptations of the life of the city rake. Unlike many earlier comedies, which had often ended with the superficial reform of a rake, in the *Squire of Alsatia* there is an insistence on the central didactic design throughout the play, which culminates in Belfond Junior's final unequivocal assertion:

> Farewell for ever all the Vices of the Age.
> There is no peace but in a Virtuous Life,
> No lasting Joy but in a tender Wife.
>   (Shadwell, 1927, V, V, i)

James's Reign

When James II ascended the throne following Charles's sudden death in 1685, he began his reign with the goodwill of the many Tory Anglicans who had supported his succession during the Exclusion Crisis. However, it was not long before he began to alienate his subjects. As he started to appoint Catholic peers as Privy Councillors, and staff his army with Catholic officers, the Anglican majority began to resent having to share power with the King's Catholic confederates. In April 1687 the king issued a Declaration of Indulgence, which set aside the penal code for Catholics and Dissenters, and in doing so he finally drove the Anglicans into active opposition. Most of the bishops did not support the Declaration, and encouraged their clergy to dissent from the king's instructions. When James issued a second Declaration in April 1688, and instructed the bishops to order their clergy to read the declaration from the pulpit, the crisis came to a head. Seven Anglican bishops signed a petition to explain their refusal to obey the king's order, and were subsequently taken to trial in June 1688, when James made a criminal complaint of seditious libel against them. Shortly after the trial, Mary of Modena gave birth to a son, apparently consigning the nation to a Catholic succession. On the day that the bishops were acquitted, a group of seven statesmen signed a letter of invitation to the staunchly Calvinist William of Orange, James's Dutch son in law, in which they offered him their support if he brought a force to England against James.

The Catholicism of the court of James II and his wife, Mary of Modena, had created a literary culture very different from that of the court of Charles II. Mary's circle formed a community of women, amongst whom were the poets Anne Killigrew, Jane Barker and Anne Kingsmill, later the Countess of Winchilsea. Killigrew, who had a position as maid of honour to the queen, was from a family that had attended on and lived with royalty for several generations. Several of her aunts had been royal maids, while her uncles were the popular royalist dramatists Thomas and William Killigrew. Killigrew's pious poetry, published the year after her death from smallpox, reveals the extent to which these family ties gave her both an intimacy with public figures, and a sense of herself as a participant in wider historical change. Service to the royal family is configured as a spiritual friendship that undercuts class differences, as in the poem 'On My Aunt Mrs A. K. Drown'd under London-bridge', in which she describes her aunt as 'The highest Saint in all the Heav'n of Court. / So Noble was her Aire, so Great her Meen, / She seem'd a Friend, not Servant to the Queen' (Killigrew, 1686, ll. 11–13). But the poem also reveals the way in which family traditions such as the Killigrews' were political allegiances. It becomes clear that there is no clear division between the private and the public, as she interprets her virtuous aunt's death as a sign of the forthcoming civil wars:

> When angry Heav'n extinguisht her fair Light,
> It seem'd to say, Nought's Precious in my sight;
> As I in Waves this Paragon have drown'd,
> The Nation next, and King I will confound.
> (ll. 16–19)

Out of the Catholic court also came Dryden's *The Hind and the Panther* (1687). Dryden was one of a handful who had converted from Anglicanism to Catholicism under the new king. In *The Hind and the Panther* he offered his defence of the Roman Catholic faith. He characterized the various denominations as animals – the Presbyterian Wolf, the Baptist Boar, the Anglican Panther and the Catholic Hind – and used the allegories and prophecies of the beast fable to produce a poem that was part spiritual meditation, part theological debate. He also used the poem to defend his conversion, answering the criticism that his new faith was the product of political expediency by reminding his detractors of the penalties still endured by Roman Catholics:

> Your bloudy Comet-laws hang blazing o're their head.
> The respite they enjoy but onely lent,
> The best they have to hope, protracted punishment.
> (Dryden, 1958, II, pt III, ll. 381–3)

The conversion and the poem prompted many satirical responses. The laureate's critics accused him of converting for political interest, attacking *The Hind and the Panther* as the most transparent piece of government hack-work he had yet produced. One of the most influential of all the attacks on the poem was the young Charles Montagu and Matthew Prior's joint effort in *The Hind and the Panther Transvers'd to the Story of the Country Mouse and the City Mouse* (1687). In their short parody, Montagu and Prior satirized the use of the fable as a vehicle for doctrinal debate, by telling Horace's fable of the city mouse and the country mouse in the same manner. They introduced their version by asking:

> is it not as easy to imagine two Mice bilking coachmen and supping at the Devil, as to suppose a Hind entertaining the Panther at a hermit's cell, discussing the greatest mysteries of religion . . . ? (Montagu and Prior, 1968, 119)

While the poem may not have endeared its authors to Dryden or the court, both poets were to be handsomely rewarded by William III's Whig ministers. Meanwhile, there were other opposition poets waiting in the wings. As the discontent with James's reign increased, and concern grew over royal domestic policy, there was a revival of the type of topical opposition satire found during the Exclusion Crisis. James's Declaration of Indulgence was answered by critics such as the anonymous author of *Doctor Wild's Ghost*, who attacked the hypocrisy of those willing to convert to secure their own political advantage:

> Soon as they found their church was i' th'wrong box,
> Fled from her faster than from whore with pox –
> So rats by instinct quit a falling house,
> So dying beggar's left by every louse.
> (*Doctor Wild's Ghost*, 1968, ll. 18–21)

The satirical pace continued to quicken, and early in 1688 the former Restoration rake, Charles Sackville, Earl of Dorset, began to circulate his scathing *A Faithful Catalogue of Our Most Eminent Ninnies* (1688). The *Catalogue* presented a very different image of the Stuart court from that found in Killigrew, or Dryden. James and his courtiers were reduced to crudely sexualized caricatures, as Dorset mounted a Juvenalian attack on the profligacy of the Stuart brothers, in which he set out to describe

> The vicious lives and long detested fame
> Of scoundrel lords, and their lewd wives' amours,
> Pimp-statesmen, bugg'ring priests, court bawds, and whores.
> (Dorset, 1968, ll. 12–14)

Like Andrew Marvell in his *Last Instructions to a Painter* (1667) written two decades before, Dorset conflated sexual vice and political corruption to present an image of a court incapable of seeing beyond its own desires. However, unlike his brother, James II was not to outweather this political storm. By the autumn of 1688 Thomas Wharton's ballad 'Lilli Burlero', originally written against the Earl of Tyrconnel's administration in Ireland, was widely circulating, its cod-Irish brogue mocking the Irish troops that James had recruited in support of his rapidly weakening position. The opening lines of the poem prophesied the now inevitable invasion of the Dutch stadtholder:

> Ho, brother Teague, dost hear de decree,
> Lilli burlero, bullen a-la;
> Dat we shall have a new debittie [deputy]
> Lilli burlero bullen a-la.
> (Wharton, 1968, ll. 1–4)

Wharton's ballad celebrated the 'Protestant wind' that had faced Tyrconnel in 1687: it was again appropriate for the Dutch invasion of 1688, when the English fleet was prevented from setting sail to attack the Dutch forces by winds that blew William safely to shore at Torbay in Devon on 5 November. William set up camp with his troops in Exeter, but before there was any conflict with James's forces, the news arrived that the king had tried to flee the country, and had been ignominiously caught by a group of Kentish fishermen. This effectively destroyed any hope that a settlement might be reached to enable James to keep the throne.

When he returned to London he was greeted by an order from William commanding him to vacate the city under an armed escort. He escaped for a second time, and made his way to France, where he was to remain. Meanwhile, William and Mary set about formalizing their accession. The Convention parliament of January 1689 hammered out the terms of the transfer, in which James was declared to have 'abdicated', leaving the throne to his daughter and her husband. By the end of April 1689 William and Mary had been crowned king and queen of England.

Conclusion

For the new king's followers, 1688 marked the end of a decade of political turmoil and the beginning of a reign from which they, and many later Whigs, were to date the birth of modern political liberty. Former opposition writers were rewarded by the new regime: Dryden lost his position as poet laureate to his adversary Shadwell, and satirists such as Montagu, Prior and Dorset were given government appointments that were to make them some of the most influential men in the country. Yet for others, the accession signalled the unlawful end of a century of Stuart rule, and the disruption of dynastic tradition. It drove James's supporters into political exile, and inspired a series of Jacobite writers that would continue to articulate images of their dispossession and nostalgia well into the following century. Thus the party divisions that we see instituted in this period continued to inform English literary culture. While the constituencies of the Whig and Tory parties were to alter over the following decades, the creation of a party-political arena in the 1680s had changed the way that writers viewed themselves in relation to public life for ever.

KEY READINGS

Ashcraft, Richard (1986). *Revolutionary Politics and Locke's 'Two Treatises of Government'*. Princeton: Princeton University Press.

Barash, Carol (1996). *English Women's Poetry, 1649–1714: Politics, Community and Linguistic Authority*. Oxford: Clarendon Press.

Braverman, Richard (1993). 'The plots thicken:

dogma and its discontents through Exclusion'. In *Plots and Counterplots: Sexual Politics and the Body Politic in English Literature, 1660–1730*. Cambridge: Cambridge University Press.

Corns, T. N., Speck, W. A. and Downie, J. A. (1982). 'Archetypal mystification: polemic and reality in English political literature,

1640–1750'. *Eighteenth-Century Literature* 7, 7–11.

Directions to Fame (1975). *Directions to Fame, about an Elegy on the Late Deceased Thomas Thynn esq.* (1682). In *Drydeniana*, 14 vols. New York: Garland (1974–5), Vol. 6.

Hammond, Paul (1983). *John Oldham and the Renewal of Classical Culture*. Cambridge: Cambridge University Press.

Harris, Tim (1987). *London Crowds in the Reign of Charles II: Propaganda and Politics from the Restoration until the Exclusion Crisis*. Cambridge: Cambridge University Press.

——(1993). *Politics under the Later Stuarts: Party Conflict in a Divided Society*. London: Longman.

Harth, Phillip (1993). *Pen for a Party: Dryden's Tory Propaganda in its Contexts*. Princeton: Princeton University Press.

Hughes, Derek (1996). *English Drama 1660–1700*. Oxford: Clarendon Press.

Hume, Robert D. (1976). *The Development of English Drama in the Late Seventeenth Century*. Oxford: Clarendon Press.

Keeble, N. H. (1987). *The Literary Culture of Non-conformity in Later Seventeenth-century England*. Leicester: Leicester University Press.

Knights, Mark (1994). *Politics and Opinion in Crisis, 1678–81*. Cambridge: Cambridge University Press.

Owen, Susan J. (1996). *Restoration Theatre and Crisis*. Oxford: Clarendon.

Special issue on Thomas Shadwell (1996). In *Restoration: Studies in English Literary Culture 1660–1700* 20.

Todd, Janet (1996). *The Secret Life of Aphra Behn*. London: Andre Deutsch.

Winn, James A. (1997). *John Dryden and his World*. New Haven and London: Yale University Press.

Womersley, David (1997). *Augustan Critical Writing*. London: Penguin.

Zwicker, Steven N. (1993). 'Paternity, patriarchy, and the "noise of divine right": *Absalom and Achitophel* and *Two Treatises of Government*'. In *Lines of Authority: Politics and English Literary Culture 1649–1689*. Ithaca and London: Cornell University Press.

——(1998). *The Cambridge Companion to English Literature 1650–1740*. Cambridge: Cambridge University Press.

REFERENCES AND FURTHER READING

Behn, Aphra (1992–6). *The Works of Aphra Behn*. Ed. Janet Todd. 7 vols. London: Pickering.

The Coronation of Queen Elizabeth (1680). *The Coronation of Queen Elizabeth, With the Restauration of the Protestant Religion: Or, the Downfal of the Pope*. London.

Crowne, John (1967). *City Politiques* (1683). Ed. John H. Wilson. London: Edward Arnold.

Cutts, John (1687). *Poetical Exercises Written upon Several Occasions*. London.

Doctor Wild's Ghost (1968). *Doctor Wild's Ghost. On his Majesty's Gracious Declaration for Liberty of Conscience* (1687). In *Poems on Affairs of State: Augustan Satirical Verse 1660–1714*. Ed. George deF. Lord. 7 vols. New Haven: Yale University Press (1963–75). Vol. 4. Ed. Galbraith M. Crump.

Dorset, Charles Sackville, Earl of (1968). *A Faithful Catalogue of Our Most Eminent Ninnies* (1688). In *Poems on Affairs of State: Augustan Satirical Verse 1660–1714*. Ed. George deF. Lord. 7 vols.

New Haven: Yale University Press (1963–75). Vol. 4. Ed. Galbraith M. Crump.

Dryden, John (1958). *The Poems of John Dryden*. Ed. James Kinsley. 4 vols. Oxford: Clarendon.

——(1956). *The Works of John Dryden*. Ed. E. N. Hooker et al. 20 vols. Berkeley and Los Angeles: University of California Press (1956–).

D'Urfey, Thomas (1968). *The Whigs' Exaltation* (1682). In *Poems on Affairs of State: Augustan Satirical Verse 1660–1714*. Ed. George deF. Lord. 7 vols. New Haven: Yale University Press (1963–75). Vol. 3. Ed. Howard H. Schless.

Elegy on the Earl of Essex (1968). *An Elegy on the Earl of Essex* (1683). In *Poems on Affairs of State: Augustan Satirical Verse 1660–1714*. Ed. George deF. Lord. 7 vols. New Haven: Yale University Press (1963–75). Vol. 3. Ed. Howard H. Schless.

Halifax, George Savile, Marquis of (1989). *The*

Works of George Savile, Marquis of Halifax. Ed. Mark N. Brown. 2 vols. Oxford: Clarendon.

Hunt, Thomas (1683). *A Defence of the Charter, and Municipal Rights of the City of London*. London.

Keach, Benjamin (1681). *Sion in Distress. Or, the Groans of the Protestant Church*. 2nd edn. London.

Killigrew, Anne (1686). *Poems by Mrs. Anne Killigrew*. London.

Marvell, Andrew (1677). *An Account of the Growth of Popery, and Arbitrary Government in England, More Particularly, from the long Prorogation of November, 1675*. London.

Montagu, Charles and Matthew Prior (1968). *The Hind and the Panther Transvers'd to the Story of the Country Mouse and The City Mouse* (1687). In *Poems on Affairs of State: Augustan Satirical Verse 1660–1714*. Ed. George deF. Lord. 7 vols. New Haven: Yale University Press (1963–75). Vol. 4. Ed. Galbraith M. Crump.

Pordage, Samuel (1682). *Azaria and Hushai, A Poem*. London.

Roscommon, Wentworth Dillon, Earl of (1965). *The Ghost of the Old House of Commons* (1681). In *Poems on Affairs of State: Augustan Satirical Verse 1660–1714*. Ed. George deF. Lord. 7 vols. New Haven: Yale University Press (1963–75). Vol. 2. Ed. Elias F. Mengel.

——(1997). *Essay on Translated Verse* (1685). In *Augustan Critical Writing*. Ed. David Womersley. London: Penguin.

Sedley, Charles (1928). *The Poetical and Dramatic Works of Sir Charles Sedley*. Ed. V de Sola Pinto. 2 vols. London: Constable.

Shadwell, Thomas (1927). *The Works of Thomas Shadwell*. Ed. Montague Summers. 5 vols., London: Fortune Press.

Thompson, Thomas (1968). *Midsummer Moon: Or the Liveryman's Complaint* (1682). In *Poems on Affairs of State: Augustan Satirical Verse 1660–1714*. Ed. George deF. Lord. 7 vols. New Haven: Yale University Press (1963–75). Vol. 3. Ed. Howard H. Schless.

Tutchin, John (1685). *Poems on Several Occasions*. London.

Wharton, Thomas (1968). *A New Song* (1688). In *Poems on Affairs of State: Augustan Satirical Verse 1660–1714*. Ed. George deF. Lord. 7 vols. New Haven: Yale University Press (1963–75). Vol. 4. Ed. Galbraith M. Crump.

45
Literature, 1701–1713
Stuart Sherman

One of the newest things in early eighteenth-century Britain was the pace of news itself. On 11 March 1702, there appeared a new paper named *The Daily Courant*, whose title announced its innovation. Its editor-publisher, Samuel Buckley, was the first in England to put out a paper every day (except for Sunday, which would have no paper of its own until the 1770s); before now, papers had appeared thrice weekly at most. The title also pinpointed the purpose of this ambitious new schedule. A few earlier newspapers had called themselves *Courants*. The word derives from the Latin for *to run* (*currere*); on a paper's masthead, it implied the speed, diligence, and energy necessary in tracking current events. By his bold new rate of publication, Buckley undertook to keep his readers *au courant*, literally up-to-date, as no English newspaper had before.

The *Daily Courant* proved both profitable (it ran for thirty-three years) and, in its way, prophetic. In the decades following its debut, readers witnessed a mighty increase in the sheer quantity of printed matter available for consumption, and in its innovative variety as well. In the *Courant*'s first number, Buckley drew a useful distinction. He announced that he would print 'only Matter of Fact; supposing other People to have Sense enough to make Reflections [i.e., to form opinions] for themselves'. Readers, though, manifested a near-insatiable appetite for both modes, for opinion as well as fact. Alongside the thriving newspapers there developed new periodicals of 'Reflection', which offered a running commentary on politics (*The Review*, *The Medley*, *The Examiner*), literature, and the ways of the world (*The Tatler*, *The Female Tatler*, *The Spectator*). For all their growing number and variety, the periodicals provided only the metronomic pulse (monthly, weekly, daily) in an ever-thickening cacophony of print. Pamphlets, poems, ballads and pictures (ranging from woodcuts to engravings) cropped up copiously *ad hoc*, in response to every breaking news story and running controversy. Perhaps nothing better illustrates the new possibilities of print than the career of one writer who seized upon almost all of them – Richard Steele. Moralist, pamphleteer and playwright, he became in 1707 the editor of the government's official newspaper *The London Gazette*. In 1709 he created *The Tatler*, a thrice-weekly paper

audaciously and often comically committed to a wide range of matters: news, literature, theatre, morals. And in 1711, he and his longtime friend Joseph Addison created
The Spectator, Britain's second daily paper, printed by the same Sam Buckley who was
still busily producing the *Courant*. The *Spectator* presented itself almost as an anti-
newspaper, teaching its readers to reflect attentively on the conduct of their own lives
rather than distracting them with 'Matter of Fact' about distant, transitory events. 'Is
it not much better', Addison famously enquired, early in the paper's run, 'to be let
into the Knowledge of ones-self, than to hear what passes in *Muscovy* or *Poland*' (no.
10). Yet the question itself suggests the anxiety of competition, of jockeying for position in the unprecedentedly dense and variegated world of print.

So great was the new print profusion that it prompted graphic artists to devise a new
kind of picture in response. The 'medley' emerged in the century's first decade as a genre
of engraving closely related to the older 'still life'. But in place of slain animals and cut
fruits, it showed a surface bestrewn with the various ephemera of the press: newspapers, pamphlets, essays, engravings, portraits, poems, maps, playing cards, etc. 'The
whole thing', wrote one of the genre's pioneers, is 'a Deceptio Visus' – an optical illusion, meant to trick viewers into momentarily believing that they are looking not at a
picture, but at a heap of actual printed materials: 'for at a small distance, they appear
like so many single pieces promiscuously thrown one upon another' (quoted in Hallett,
1997, 214). The promiscuity was the point. The artist depicts, with painstaking
realism, all those printed genres which themselves conjure up, each in its own way, elements of the actual world – the games played with the cards, the countries delineated
in the maps, the famous faces displayed in the portraits, the facts narrated by the newspapers, the controversies debated in the pamphlets. Amid these layers 'thrown one upon
another', the medley makes a double claim about Britain at the turn of the century. Not
only is it a place of copious, seemingly chaotic variety, abounding in things to do and
see and read and buy. It has also produced more ways of representing that variety by
ink on paper than at any time heretofore. The medley displays the promiscuous double
plenitude – realities and representations – of the present tense.

It does so without explicit commentary. It depicts the fact of present plenitude,
and invites the viewer's reflection. Is the abundance here displayed to be understood
as auspicious – as the augury of a new age in which Britons will rightly rejoice in the
abundance of their acquisitions, their information, and interactions? Or does the
medley instead depict *too* much, a looming glut, a print-fostered state of confusion,
distraction, and indulgence? Is the plenitude here displayed a reason for celebration,
or for suspicion?

Your answer, in 1701–13, would depend partly on your politics.

The Politics of Profusion

The *Courant* debuted at a news-rich moment. Three days earlier, a horse-riding
accident had ended the life of William III, the Dutch-born stadtholder who, in that

invasion-by-invitation dubbed the Glorious Revolution, had sustained the Protestant succession by driving his Catholic father-in-law James II from the English throne, and ruling there in tandem with his wife Mary, James's eldest daughter. Mary had died in 1692. Now, at her husband's death, the crown passed to her younger sister Anne, her father's second daughter by his first (and Protestant) marriage.

Byzantine in its politics, superabundant in its literature, the reign of Anne (1702–14) nonetheless lends itself readily enough to a simple preliminary sketch. It was framed by a question and punctuated by a merger, spanned by a war abroad and shaped by party conflict at home. The question was that of succession: how was Protestant rule to be sustained after the death of the queen, whose own children had all perished in infancy or youth? The merger was the Act of Union (1707), which melded Scotland with England and Wales to form the new nation of Great Britain. The war was the War of the Spanish Succession (1702–13), waged against the French to forestall their fusion with Spain, and prevent thereby the expansion of Catholic empire. The parties, who raged over all these issues, were the Tories and the Whigs.

The question of succession was settled in theory just before Anne's reign began, and in practice just after it ended. In 1701, parliament passed the Act of Settlement, by which the British crown was to pass to the German House of Hanover, directly descended from Anne's great-grandfather James I. The succession would thus by-pass that alarming nearer claimant, Anne's Catholic half-brother James Edward, her father's son by his second wife. (It was the announcement of this prince's birth, and the prospect of a Catholic succession, that had spurred William's Bloodless Revolution.) The Act of Settlement was fulfilled when, at Anne's death, her remote German cousin George assumed the British throne, indifferent to his subjects and unschooled in their language.

Still, the fear of an attempted insurrection by James's supporters (dubbed Jacobites, from Latin *Jacobus*, James) was sufficient to propel major policies during Anne's reign, and long after. The queen and her ministers pursued the Act of Union in part to secure Scots participation in the war against France, but mostly to control and contain the threat posed by the intense Scots allegiance to James Edward. The war itself was entwined with the question of the British succession, as well as the Spanish. Before William's death, the French king Louis XIV had declared his support for James Edward's claim to the throne. To restrain Louis's imperial ambitions abroad was to sustain the prospect of a Protestant succession at home. The British victory, sealed by the Treaty of Utrecht in 1713, helped to smooth the transition of power at Anne's death a year later.

The war brought Britons other benefits. As they watched themselves winning (for the first time in more than three hundred years) a massive conflict on the continent, Britons began to reconceive themselves as a nation capable of almost anything. For this pleasing new self-image, the press provided, throughout the war, a broad and gleaming mirror. In reams of celebratory verse and in pages of partisan prose, readers ardently tracked the progress of distant campaigns, and gloried in the successes of the English general John Churchill, whom Anne made Duke of Marlborough as an expression of her own favour and the nation's gratitude. Marlborough's doings sustained a whole print industry. Each victory prompted fresh paeans from the poets, and filled long columns in the newspapers. During a momentary lull in the conflict, Steele announced, in jest, a famine among the journalists, and proposed the founding of a veteran's hospital 'for the Relief of such decayed News-Writers as have served their Country in the Wars'. The details of the conflict had fed their pages and their coffers fat, he implied; in peace they might well starve.

Steele was mostly joking. The news-supply might momentarily run low, but the national self-conception, so deftly fostered by the wartime press, was one not of starvation but of surfeit, of present plenitude and future possibility. This exhilaration derived partly from the economic arrangements that made the war possible. In order to fund his ambitious assaults on France, Anne's predecessor William had fostered a new institution – the Bank of England – and a new system of finance. The scheme made Marlborough's victories possible; it also made London merchants rich beyond any previous measure, and underwrote new, immensely profitable ventures in international trade. In private homes and public places, the proof of this burgeoning commerce lay pleasingly close at hand. Tea from China, tobacco from Virginia, coffee and sugar from the Caribbean – all were relatively new, comparatively inexpensive, and enormously popular.

Within this cluster of commodities, newspapers and other periodicals played a multiple and crucial role, as advocates, practitioners, and embodiments of the new commerce. They reported on trade (listing, for example, the merchant ships recently arrived from foreign ports). They abetted trade, in their commerce-celebrating copy, and in the advertisements that filled their columns and underwrote their costs. And they constituted, of course, a commodity in themselves, proffering their prose bounty at the rate of about a penny a sheet. In these ways also, the periodicals contributed to Great Britain's growing self-satisfaction. One of the favoured forms of leisure, particularly among members of the middling, mercantile class who made up the core of the papers' readership, was to sit comfortably in public coffee-houses, and at domestic tea-tables, reading the news of foreign victories while savouring the comestibles of foreign countries. So situated, amid their drinks and their papers, the men and women of Great Britain imbibed and pondered a sense of their global reach, their pleasing new position near the centre of a planet increasingly commercialized.

It can seem paradoxical that a nation unified by triumphs abroad was at the same time riven by party conflict at home. In parliament, in the press, in conversations private and public, Whigs and Tories waged a war of words which could sometimes seem to match the fierceness of foreign combat. In fact the two conflicts were fundamentally linked. The War of the Spanish Succession, with its high successes and enormous expense, helped heighten differences long brewing between the parties. At stake was the question of how the nation should see and shape itself in the new century. The rage of party was in part a tug-of-war between two visions of history.

Half a century later, Samuel Johnson sketched the vectors. 'The prejudice of the Tory', he remarked, 'is for establishment; the prejudice of the Whig is for innovation.'

The parties traced their origins to the Exclusion Crisis of the early 1680s, when Tories upheld the established continuity of the Stuart line and Whigs advocated an innovative disruption of it, struggling to bar Charles II's Catholic brother from the throne. Later that same decade, many Tories reluctantly colluded with the Whigs in that definitive innovation, the supplanting of English James with Dutch-born William (some Tories, though, remained Jacobites for life). Party cooperation, always tenuous, soon collapsed, and by the early eighteenth century, the words *Tory* and *Whig* crystallized two clusters of allegiances and concerns, often fiercely opposed. The Tory taste for establishment dictated a devotion to monarchic prerogatives, to the Church of England, and to the interests of the landed gentry, that small cluster with large wealth who had for centuries wielded, virtually unchallenged, a power grounded in extensive estates and in the rents they yielded. Whig 'innovation' entailed enthusiastic support for the Glorious Revolution, for policies of religious tolerance, and for all measures that advanced the interests of the newly prosperous and powerful merchant class. Tory establishment traced its roots to the country, the rural world where the estates lay. Whig innovation centred in the City, that teeming sector of London where merchants and manufacturers (many of them members of the dissenting religious communities whom the Tories despised) launched and sustained their ever-expanding ventures.

For the Tories, the symbiosis between new commerce and foreign battle posed a serious threat. One of the war's chief effects at home was the transfer of wealth from the country to the City, in the form of a land tax by which the monarchs subsidized their armies and paid interest on the national debt. The gentry now watched what seemed to them unwarrantably large portions of their tenants' rents travel not into their own hands, but ultimately into the hands of the merchants who had loaned the government war money in the first place. As the war's costs mounted, Tories agitated for its speedy resolution; they had come to think of the conflict as an immeasurably lucrative scam on the part of London merchants. The political pivot-point in Anne's reign came in the general election of 1710, when, aided by a sudden surge of feeling against religious dissent, the Tories won a huge majority in parliament. They promptly supplanted Anne's Whig ministers with their own men, hobbled Marlborough's command and then dismissed him from his post, and in three years brought the long war to its largely prosperous conclusion. The Treaty of Utrecht brought Britain new territories and new trading privileges, but it did nothing to dissolve the Tories' long-standing difficulties with new methods of war, wealth and worship. Their brief time in power ended a year later, when Anne's death and George's accession ushered in a stretch of Whig dominion that lasted decades. Ever since 1688, the Whigs had been able to stake the firmest claims to the new plenitudes of the present. Tory models for how the world should work resided in the established but ever-receding past. Johnson's distinction, between 'establishment' and 'innovation', makes a larger point: what sundered the parties was partly a difference in their sense of time, in the way they weighed the claims of the past against the pull of the present and the future.

That difference mattered enormously, in literature as well as politics. 'We have *Parties*, both in Wit and State', Alexander Pope would later remark (Womersley, 1997, xxxix). The political struggles between Tories and Whigs were played out also as a 'battle of the books' which pitted the Ancients against the Moderns, in a contest to determine whether British literature and British life should be shaped in accordance with classical models or must be reconceived under the auspices of new science and new commerce. The rage of party produced reams of print. The difference in political arguments begot differences too in literary form, in the ways the writers treated their topics, in the ways their texts conceived and moved through time. The differences are encapsulated in two vehemently opposed political papers that began to appear just after the Tory takeover of 1710: the Whig *Medley*, edited by Arthur Mainwaring, and the Tory *Examiner*, written for a while by Jonathan Swift. In the *Medley*'s first number, Mainwaring explained that he had chosen the title because under its auspices, 'I can properly make use of any matter whatsoever . . . the more various the subject is, or the more different sorts there are of it, the more likely will it be to make what we mean by a medley . . . I have declared against form and order, and at first assum'd a liberty to ramble as I pleased' (quoted in Hallett, 1997, 222). 'Liberty' had been the Whig watchword ever since the Revolution, when parliament enacted British freedom by the singular innovation of choosing and establishing its own new king. Mainwaring here takes that political term as warrant for literary form: for the freedom 'to ramble' at pleasure, for the value of variety and improvisation. Like many of the pictorial medleys, Mainwaring's verbal *Medley* construes plenitude and disorder, impressions 'promiscuously thrown upon one another', as a useful and fascinating way of representing the wide world. The *Examiner*, by its very title, took issue with this outlook, declaring itself deliberate where the *Medley* was improvisatory, proudly selective and focused where its rival was indiscriminate. The contrast continued just below the titles, where Mainwaring presented a plain table of contents, listing the number's 'different sorts' of topics, while the *Examiner* would commence with a Latin epigraph, a short quotation from an ancient author appropriate to the single topic of that day's essay. Again, establishment confronts innovation: the Tory looks back to what has been, the Whig proclaims the plenitude in the present, and to come.

The *Medley* and the *Examiner* were overtly partisan, but the differences they embody, in their forms and textures, operated throughout the writing of this period, even when it was less blatantly political. The Whig vision found an exhilarating and inexhaustible abundance in the present moment, in the range of wares that trade distributes, in the varieties of worship that toleration endorses, in the array of print genres that innovation produces, and in the diversity of the consumers who read the papers and debate them. The Tory programme looked askance at the same phenomena. It warned that the opacities of presentism would eclipse a more luminous past, both recent (the Restoration) and ancient (Greece and Rome); and that the new cornucopia of commerce, print and conversation teemed with trivia rather than real wealth. The running contest between these two responses animates much of the writing in Anne's reign, making it fierce or funny, and often (in the period's many brilliant satires) both.

In order to get at both the pleasure and the point of this writing, it pays to read closely for the ways each author shapes time, and pictures plenitude.

This is not quite the same thing as affixing a party label – Whig or Tory, Ancient or Modern – to every passing text. In both wit and state, party affiliations could seem at times remarkably supple. Some of the period's most important politicians – Robert Harley, Marlborough himself – deemed themselves Whig at one time and Tory at another. So did some of the major writers. Over the next few pages, the contest between Whig celebration and Tory suspicion will be played out mostly as a dialogue between Addison and Steele on the one side, Swift and Pope on the other (with other voices occasionally joining in). Addison and Steele were lifelong Whigs and brilliant propagandists for their cause. Swift turned Tory during the pivot-year 1710, when he began writing the *Examiner* in the service of Harley's new administration. Pope kept the extent of his Tory sympathies more covert. Yet for a time, Addison and Steele were friendly with both Swift and Pope, publishing their writing and praising their work. Gradually, what Swift once called the 'Curse of Party' (*Journal to Stella*, 27 December 1712) eroded most of these friendships (only the one between Swift and Pope remained intact to the end of life). Yet even at the moments of convergence – when Swift's work appears in the *Tatler*, Pope's in the *Spectator* – it is possible to detect the tensions that would sever these connections, and shape the age.

Mighty Contests, Trivial Things

In Whig poetry as in Whig politics, the present generally outshines the past. Near the start of his poem *The Campaign* (1705), Joseph Addison celebrates Marlborough's latest victory by comparing it favourably with ancient epic. As the poet conjures up the battle in his mind's eye,

> sieges and storms appear,
> And wars and conquests fill th'important year,
> Rivers of blood I see, and hills of slain,
> An Iliad rising out of One campaign.
>
> (ll. 9–12)

Homer's *Iliad* rose out of the Trojan War, which took ten years. Marlborough's triumphant 'One campaign' had required only three months (May–August 1704). Addison gauges the difference in glory partly as a difference in sheer speed. In *Advice to the Poets* (1706), a poem celebrating a later victory, the Whig encomiast Richard Blackmore makes the same point, more explicitly. He begins with a plea on his own behalf:

> OH! let the Conqueror stop his swift Career,
> A while the Foe, a while the Poet spare.

What Muse can follow with an equal Pace,
Thro' the bright Stages of his rapid Race?
                              (ll. 1–4)

Marlborough's triumphs are so many and so quick that the poets can't keep up: 'He Conquers faster, than our Bards can Write' (12) – and more gloriously than any soldier about whom bards have written before. At one point in the poem, Blackmore suggests that his fellow poets might use Achilles as a possible prototype for Marlborough's merits. A few lines later, though, he sets the notion aside:

But by this famous *Greek*'s, ye Poets know,
The *Briton*'s Courage you imperfect show.
Fierce is the *Greek*, and rugged as the Age,
And too near Brutal is his Martial Rage.
The *Briton* is courageous and serene.
                              (ll. 346–50)

To compare Marlborough with Achilles is to diminish Marlborough. The rapid present in every way surpasses the lumbering past.

At a time when ancient languages, ancient authors, and ancient heroes had held sway for centuries as embodying the heights of human achievement, this Whig stance was iconoclastic, and problematic. The Whig poets were proposing a new kind of epic, grounded firmly in the present, overgoing old heroes and old authors. In a verse *Epistle to Richard Blackmore* (1706), an anonymous (but certainly Tory) satirist took the poet to task for one of his earlier efforts along these lines, an epic called *Eliza* in which Blackmore compared Queen Anne's accomplishments to those of Queen Elizabeth more than a century before:

In *ANNA*'s Reign thou has *ELIZA*'s grac't,
The *Present Age* out-shining far the *Past*.
For, whate'er Fame to *Her* [Elizabeth's] advantage tells,
The *Copy* the *Original* excells.
                              (Anon., 1975, ll. 23–6)

The lines are pointedly preposterous. At the time *Eliza* appeared, Anne's reign had run only three years; Elizabeth's, forty-five years long, was perhaps the most celebrated in British history. The writer is not so much belittling Anne's accomplishments as he is ridiculing the assumption underlying Blackmore's praise, that anything in the Whiggish present surpasses everything in the pre-Revolutionary past. Elsewhere in the same piece, the satirist lumps Blackmore's epic aspirations with the more craven practices of a notorious versifying journalist, whose sole ambition (so the satire argues) is to be the first to publish a poem on any breaking news story:

De Foe, as ever, execrably bad,
Throws out a hasty *Poem*, wrote like Mad.

'Twas the first-born, and welcome in *our Mirth*,
Tho' not *One Muse* assisted at its birth.
(ll. 47–50)

The critique of Whig poetics comes through with caustic clarity. To assume the intrinsic superiority of present events is to court self-deception on a grand scale. To set aside established models of poetry for frantic innovations, to trade old *Iliad*s for new, is to debase art into a branch of journalism, and to fill the world with mad and execrable ephemera. To ignore ancient models is to abjure indispensable ancient aid. At literary births so doggedly modern, not one Muse will act as midwife.

The period's most enduring articulation of this critique came from one of the Ancients' youngest advocates. Alexander Pope had launched his career with a quartet of proudly Virgilian pastorals, published when he was twenty. At twenty-two he enlarged his reputation with *An Essay on Criticism* (1711), a long poem in which he urged his readers to judge modern writing by ancient standards. At one point, Pope launches a kind of prayer before the still-burning altars of the ancient authors, imploring 'some Spark' of their 'Coelestial Fire' so that he may teach 'vain Wits' (empty, self-enamoured modern writers and critics) 'that Science *little known*, / T'admire Superior Sense, and *doubt* their own!' (ll. 202–3). The prayer is precarious. Pope has already made clear that the capacity of his contemporaries for such such fruitful self-doubt is strictly limited. The couplet's last words echo those of another near the beginning of the *Essay*, where Pope, in a famous analogy, draws a connection between overweening modern self-confidence and the overwhelming modern obsession with the present moment: ''Tis with our *Judgments* as our *Watches*, none / Go just *alike*, yet each believes his own' (ll. 9–10). In 1711, pocket watches were new and faulty mechanisms. Losing or gaining a few minutes a day, they worked just well enough to make clear (when compared with someone else's timepiece) that they did not work perfectly. In Pope's witty construction, watches are Whiggish things, exclusively and therefore unreliably committed to tracking present time. Like 'our *Judgments*', they stand in sore need of a corrective.

For watch-wearers, that corrective was the sun. Sundials, carefully placed and precisely calibrated, still told time more accurately than any mechanism yet invented. Accordingly, Pope turns his imagery towards the sun. As watch-wearers must adjust their instruments, so 'true genius' and 'true taste' – the good poet and the good critic – must both 'alike from Heav'n derive their Light' (l. 13). The sun presides throughout the *Essay* as the recurrent image for those values by which poets and critics should steer their course, in their turn away from the erroneous arrogance embodied in modern clockwork. As our central source of illumination, 'still divinely bright, / One *clear*, *unchang'd*, and *Universal* Light' (ll. 70–1), the sun serves as emblem for both 'Unerring Nature' and for its greatest poet – since 'Nature and Homer' are in fact 'the same' (l. 36).

The sun is perhaps the most commonplace of all metaphors, and remarkably adaptable as a means of figuring time. The poet can either emphasize (as Pope does) the orb's fixity and permanence ('still divinely bright . . . *unchang'd* . . . *Universal*') or depict it as reappearing from morn to morn – as an image of successiveness and flux. Sun-imagery is therefore peculiarly commodious to both the Whig and Tory sense of time, and is worth tracking through several works on both sides. In *The Rape of the Lock* (1711, 1714), his next great success, Pope again plays the sun against the watch. Here he is describing the delayed dawn of London's fashionable world, whose denizens like to sleep late in their well-draped beds.

> *Sol* thro' white Curtains shot a tim'rous Ray,
> And op'd those Eyes that must eclipse the Day;
> Now Lapdogs give themselves the rowzing Shake,
> And sleepless Lovers, just at Twelve, awake:
> Thrice rung the Bell, the Slipper knock'd the Ground,
> And the press'd Watch return'd a silver Sound.
>
> (ll. 13–18)

The pressed watch was an often elegant instrument whose small bells rang the time (hours and minutes) at the push of a button; its chief use was for telling time at night, when darkness made the dial invisible. Pope's just-waking beauties, shrouded still in sun-excluding curtains, ignore the daylight and behave as though it's still nighttime; in his comic account, they manage to 'eclipse the Day' not only by outdoing the sun in lustre, but also by overlooking it altogether. Here as in the *Essay*, the watch abets an oblivion to brighter realities and richer values. Pope has already introduced such values in his opening invocation just a few lines earlier:

> What dire Offence from am'rous Causes springs,
> What mighty Contests rise from trivial Things,
> I sing –
>
> (ll. 1–3)

In twenty-two syllables, Pope manages to echo the *Iliad, Odyssey, Aeneid* and *Paradise Lost*, and thus to establish the epic vantage from which, pitched, like his sylphs, above the fray, he will observe, enjoy, and laugh at the sublunary doings down below. Pope's *Rape* is, in many respects, the argument of his *Essay* enacted as comedy, paralleled down to its opening gambit (the two sun/watch passages appear in identical positions, at the start of the second verse paragraph). In both works, watches delude and distract. Sunlight and epic are, we find, the same.

Two years earlier, Swift too had staged a sunrise, in a short poem called 'A Description of the Morning', first published in one of the early numbers of Steele's *Tatler*. Here are the opening couplets:

> Now hardly here and there an Hackney-Coach
> Appearing, show'd the Ruddy Morn's Approach.
> Now *Betty* from her Master's Bed had flown,
> And softly stole to discompose her own.
>
> (ll. 1–4)

The sun here shines upon a different sector of the social register from that illumi-nated in the *Rape*. The hackney-coaches (the horse-drawn, eighteenth-century equiva-lent of buses or taxis) lurch violently ('hardly') into motion, while the serving-woman Betty tries, by rumpling her unslept-in bed, to conceal last night's liaison with her master. Introducing the poem to readers of the *Tatler*, Steele, in his Whig way, extolled its innovative accuracy. The poet, he wrote, has 'run into a Way [of writing] perfectly new, and describ'd Things exactly as they happen'; his lines are not just a description of *any* morning, 'but of the Morning in Town; nay of the Morning at this End of the Town, where [the writer] at present lodges' (no. 9). Steele's own praise increases in specificity as it proceeds, zooming in on the particular place and time ('*this* End', 'at *present*') where both the poet and his praiser dwell. Introducing the poem this way, Steele effectually *Tatler*izes it. He makes it seem deliberately, ostentatiously local and present-tense – an inventive form of verse journalism.

Many of Swift's readers would recognize with pleasure (as did Steele himself) that the poem was not so simple – that it was, instead, doubled, entwining past and present, ancient and modern, at every turn. The coaches call to mind the chariot of Phoebus Apollo, whose daily advent, in ancient myth and ancient poetry, declared the dawn. Betty, departing from her master's couch, reincarnates Aurora, goddess of dawn, who on numberless Homeric mornings leaves the couch of her still-slumbering husband in order to go and light the day. Like Pope in the *Rape*, Swift here draws on ancient conventions as a means of shedding (sun)light on modern conduct. *Now* is his first word, and his milieu (it will appear four times in the poem's sixteen lines). But he imbues this *now* with an abiding sense of *then*, of ancient poets and the even more ancient Arcadias that they conjured up in pastoral verse (significantly, he works also in the past tense – *show'd* – and even in the doubled past of the pluperfect – *had flown*). Swift, like Pope, deals in a doubled sun, one that shines right now on watch-wearers and on four-post beds, but one that also images the ancient light, that 'Coelestial Fire', by which alone modern authors can see and write the world aright.

As it happens, admirers of the *Tatler* and the *Spectator* sometimes compared those papers with the morning sun. But they conducted their comparison with a difference. Late in the *Spectator*'s run, the paper published a poem in its own praise by the ardent Whig playwright Nahum Tate. The poem looks back on that moment, early in 1711, when Steele brought the thrice-weekly *Tatler* to a close, only to supplant it, three months later, with the daily *Spectator*. Tate compares the *Tatler* to the sun gone down, and describes Great Britain's distress at the ensuing darkness:

> Robb'd of his sprightly Beams she wept the Night,
> Till the *Spectator* rose, and blaz'd as bright.
> So the first Man the Sun's first setting view'd,
> And sigh'd, till circling Day his Joys renew'd.
> (no. 488)

What stuns and satisfies the speaker here is the *Spectator*'s successiveness, the sun-like rhythmic sequence of its return, as it 'rises' anew with every 'circling Day', at a rate more rapid and more reassuring than that of the vanished *Tatler*. A year earlier, when the *Spectator* was new, John Gay had voiced the same sense of wonder by means of the same implicit image. British readers, he asserts, 'had at first no manner of Notion how a Diurnal [i.e., daily] Paper could be continu'd in the Spirit and Stile of our present SPECTATORS; but to our no small Surprize, we find them still rising upon us' (*The Present State of Wit* [1711], 6). It is instructive to compare Gay's solar image, of the papers 'still rising', with the passage already quoted from the *Essay* in which Pope describes Nature as a sun that is 'still divinely bright'. In Pope's line, *still* means *always*; Pope is describing a permanence, an actual *still*ness, an illumination that is always up there whether we manage to see it or not. In Gay's phrase, by contrast, *still* means something closer to *continually, repeatedly*: even as we sit here marvelling, new *Spectator* papers keep on coming. Pope's sun figures permanence, Gay's sun figures process. The difference between the two encapsulates the fervent dialectic, during Anne's reign and after, between the Ancient and Modern conceptions of literary time: one the time of the sundial, in which the glorious past functions as a fixed point of reference, the light by which the present is seen, measured, judged; the other the time of the pocket-watch, which rapidly and busily tracks the present by its own means and on its own terms.

From the Tory point of view, the Whig taste for successiveness was a source of cultural malaise. In the world and on the page, it fostered an approach too random, too unselective, too much a matter of one thing after another. For purposes of this critique, the favourite target was the newspaper, an enterprise in which the Whigs predominated (as editors, writers, publishers) for most of Anne's reign. In August 1712, the *Spectator* published a letter by Pope, in which he satirically announced his plans for 'Publishing a daily Paper, which shall comprehend in it all the most remarkable Occurrences in every little Town, Village and Hamlet, that lie within ten Miles of *London*' (no. 452). Describing this mock-project, Pope makes clear that the pointless comprehensiveness of the information ('all the . . . Occurrences' in 'every little Town') will follow as a direct result from the compulsion to gather and distribute it every day. The daily paper virtually demands this descent into triviality because there is not worthwhile matter sufficient to meet so insistent a schedule of publication. In a follow-up letter a few days later, Pope proposed a parallel project, 'a *News-Letter of Whispers*' – that is, of local gossip (no. 457). From both enterprises Pope jokingly promises himself big profits. He thereby makes his point: the newspapers purvey fresh data at such a rapid rate that they have fostered in their readers a frantic appetite for information, coupled with an utter incapacity to distinguish between the news that matters and the news that doesn't. They are 'pleased with every thing that is Matter of Fact, so it be what they have not heard before'. In one respect, this is nothing new. Every 'little Town, Village and Hamlet', and every city too, has always enjoyed its daily round of whispers. Until recently, though, such traffic was confined to talk rather than paper (whispers are evanescent; they vanish soon as spoken). Print has changed the patterns of distribution and consumption. In order to succeed as a commodity, the newspapers must accord unsorted trivialities the permanence of ink and paper. It makes them the basis of a corrupt and corrupting commerce in indiscriminate information – a waste of the too-willing reader's time.

In the end, then, what was at stake in the tug of war between past and present, between Ancient and Modern, was – to echo Pope's invocation in the *Rape* – a 'mighty contest' over what to do about 'trivial things' – how to assess them, how to use them, whether to banish them, assimilate them, or even celebrate them in the writing of the present age. Pope's poem itself constitutes perhaps the period's single most dazzlingly intricate response. By writing up what is essentially the story of a card-playing-party gone wrong as though it were also an epic and a fairy tale rolled into one, Pope achieves an array of effects ranging from the comic and satiric to the tender and the almost-tragic. At the end of the poem, when the cut curl (the 'raped lock') of the heroine's hair becomes a constellation shining above fashionable Pall Mall, Pope makes clear his confidence that he has engineered the apotheosis of the trivial, while still critiquing its triviality all the while.

Swift played a similar game in a lower register. At the end of his 'Description of a City Shower', the second poem he published in the *Tatler*, he lists the debris that clots a rain-swelled urban gutter after a storm: 'Sweepings from Butchers Stalls, Dung, Guts, and Blood, / Drown'd Puppies, stinking Sprats, all drench'd in Mud, / Dead Cats and Turnip-Tops come tumbling down the Flood' (ll. 61–3). What could be more plentiful, and more trivial? Even the metre acts out overflow: the rhyme runs for three lines instead of the usual two; the last line runs twelve syllables instead of ten. Swift claimed to detest such devices in the work of his contemporaries, yet he deploys them here with satiric brilliance and, at the time of the poem's publication, he deemed it the best thing he had ever written. To this day it remains deliciously unclear whether he prided himself more on the way in which he decries modern decay (ancient pastoral rainshowers were much prettier), or on the almost loving exactitude with which he evokes its odoriferous details. In his short prose piece *The Battle of the Books* (1704), Swift staged one of the most adroit, straightforward defences of Ancient merits over Modern follies. But in his poetic practice and in Pope's, the satiric horror at present glut, at certain modes of modern surfeit, often shades over into a fascination with, even an attraction to, the very trivia being satirized.

In the essays of Addison and Steele, the treatment of trivia is less ironic, and more forthrightly favourable. At the top of many *Tatlers*, Steele quoted a line from the Roman satirist Juvenal: *Quicquid agunt Homines nostri Farrago Libelli*: 'anything that mortals do [will supply] the medley of our little book'. By quoting the line, Steele invokes the authority of an ancient to endorse what had now come to be seen as a patently modern and particularly Whiggish procedure: the making of an ongoing textual medley (*farrago*) from the ingredients of the promiscuous present. In the *Tatler* and especially in the *Spectator*, Addison and Steele gave the line from Juvenal a turn well-calculated to flatter their enormous audience. Taking as their papers' core topic 'the working of one's own Mind', they were implicitly assuring their readers that anything *you* do will be of interest to *us*. By this reckoning, nearly nothing could be dismissed as merely trivial. With proper 'Reflection', any 'Matter of Fact' might be turned to worthy use. The everyday medley, so distasteful to the Tory palate, might be offered up as a magnificent feast.

Conversation and Commerce

In the satire on the newspapers that he sent in to the *Spectator*, Pope traces the current taste for trivia to two sources: to conversation (those whispers full of fallacy, that gossip which fails to distinguish the 'remarkable' from the unremarkable) and to commerce: the new print media which are obliged by their very frequency to place such trifles before a reading public increasingly debased. In its purposeful capaciousness, the *Spectator* made room for such critiques, but it also embodied a running response to them. It too, after all, was a 'daily Paper', and it made conversation and commerce not only its reigning topics, but its mode of being: it conducted conversations in its pages, and perpetuated commerce in its advertising columns and its own prodigiously profitable circulation. Yet by the very act of publishing Pope's letter, Addison and Steele make clear that they deem themselves innocent of the triviality it satirizes. They have supplied plausible arguments for thinking so throughout the paper's run. From the start, the paper's putative author Mr Spectator has presented himself as an insatiable but very useful snoop, who constantly monitors British conversations and commerce, in order to elevate their quality and celebrate their effects. He proposes to cultivate them in ways that will help his readers prosper, as talkers, thinkers, sellers, shoppers. Rightly practised, he argues, conversation and commerce are not the font of trivia, but the source of power.

Three days after Pope's first letter appeared in its pages, the *Spectator* presented an essay by Steele (no. 454) that encapsulates the ways the paper sustained its celebration. The piece begins with Mr Spectator lying awake 'one Night last Week' in Richmond, a Thames-side village west of London. Restless in Richmond, Mr Spectator rises at four in the morning and heads downriver towards the city, resolving 'to rove by Boat and Coach for the next Four and twenty Hours, till the many different Objects I must needs meet with should tire my Imagination, and give me an Inclination to a Repose more profound than I was at that Time capable of'. The 'many different objects' he meets with during these twenty-four hours fall readily into two categories: people (widely diverse), and the material goods (mostly commercial) with which they engage themselves and each other. In the course of the essay, Mr Spectator encounters and describes, in ways inflected by his own deep pleasure and idiosyncrasy, a variety of mortals: coachmen, grocers, chimney sweeps, women of fashion, beggars, ballad-singers, shop-girls, merchants, night owls. And he enumerates the things they buy, sell, and consume: apricots, melons, coach-rides, clothes, songs, cosmetics, 'patches, pins, wires', soup, steaks, ale, and (at the very end of the day), the candlelight by which Mr Spectator makes his way home. Once there, he finds himself wondering what to make of what he calls this 'trivial Day', and professes himself momentarily 'at a Loss what Instruction I should propose to my Reader

from the Enumeration of so many insignificant Matters and Occurrences'. Their significance, though, has become clear in the course of their enumeration: London (and
by extension Britain) now teems with persons and with products, in matchless abundance and variety. Their plenitude is a source of pleasure. Earlier in the essay, Mr
Spectator paused to sum up his delight: 'It was a pleasing Reflection to see the
World so prettily cheqer'd since I left *Richmond*, and the Scene still filling with Children of [each] new Hour' – that is, with people going about their business in its
proper time and place. In Steele's sentence, as in John Gay's earlier praise of the *Spectator* itself, the adverb *still* means *continually, persistently*. It celebrates, in Whig mode,
a ceaselessly productive process. The constant 'filling' with fresh data is the essay's
point.

Fullness, in the world and on the page, is in effect the point of every *Spectator* essay.
It is implicit even in the paper's plan of publication, as enunciated by Mr Spectator
at his very first appearance:

> since I have neither Time nor Inclination to communicate the *Fulness* of my heart in
> Speech, I am resolved to do it in Writing; . . . For this Reason therefore, I shall publish
> a Sheet-*full* of Thoughts every Morning, for the Benefit of my Contemporaries. (no. 1;
> italics added)

As Addison and Steele repeatedly make clear, fullness is a defining feature not only
of the paper's author and of its schedule, but of its audience as well. They never tire
of enumerating (often at deliberately comic length) the various factions among their
multitudinous readership:

> all manner of Persons, whether Scholars, Citizens, Courtiers, Gentlemen, of the Town
> or of Country, and all Beaux, Rakes, Smarts, Prudes, Coquets, Housewives, and all sorts
> of Wits, whether Male or Female . . . Contented or Miserable, Happy or Unfortunate,
> High or Low, Rich or Poor . . . Healthy or Sick, Married or Single . . . and of what Trade,
> Occupation, Profession, Station, Country, Faction, Party, Perswasion, Quality, Age or
> Condition soever. (no. 125)

Here, Steele is not merely listing the *Spectator*'s several audiences; he is inviting all
the parties listed to write letters for publication in the paper. He is asking them to
send stuff in, to talk back, to sustain the *Spectator* with their own thought and prose.
The exchange thus imagined was hardly confined to ink and paper. The conversation
among the *Spectator* and its readers was notably audible: the papers were very often
read aloud, their contents discussed and debated, in public gathering places and household circles. The *Spectator* embodied, to an extent unmatched by any previous paper,
the Whig commitment to the idea of a public sphere, in which conversation begat
consensus, and consensus helped to shape the state.

Such a programme, of course, provoked scepticism as well as celebration. We have
seen one such response already, couched in Pope's analogy between our judgements
and our watches. If 'each believes his own', then the chances of consensus will be slim

indeed. What is needed, Pope argues, is not conversation but authority (Nature, Homer, the blazing sun itself). Addison and Steele, too, deal extensively in authority. The *Tatler*'s fictitious author Isaac Bickerstaff repeatedly proclaimed himself 'the Censor of Great Britain', and his successor Mr Spectator willingly assumes that same moral role (though not the grandiose title). Unlike Pope, though, Addison and Steele take care to present their authority as deriving as much from their readers as from themselves; the letters, in which readers take over the paper's columns to voice their own views, implicitly enforce this claim. When Pope's *Essay* first appeared, Addison praised it in the pages of the *Spectator*, commending it to his audience for the instruction it might offer them: 'If the Reader would see how the best of the *Latin* Criticks writ, he may find their manner very beautifully described . . . in the *Essay* of which I am now speaking' (no. 253). Addison admires Pope the popularizer, the teacher who makes ancient achievements accessible to a new readership potentially as wide-ranging as the *Spectator*'s. He tends to overlook Pope the elitist, eager to mock 'our *Judgments*' and to form them for us. His oversight partly indexes the cunning of Pope's own tactics – the way his offhand tone, as of a casual conversation already in progress ('’Tis with our *Judgments* as our *Watches*') partly camouflages his contempt for those 'vain Wits' who, indulging a delusion of their own 'superior Sense', set so much store by modern conversation (Womersley, 1997, xxxv). Addison, praising the *Essay*, responds more to its genial surface than to its caustic substance.

Geniality is the *Spectator*'s own mode, the medium in which it conducts its celebrations. In the course of his 'trivial Day' in London, for example, Mr Spectator revels in the medley-like conversation (on 'Cards, Dice, Love, Learning and Politicks') that he overhears in a coffee-house. But he reserves his highest praise for the satisfactions of commerce. He finds them everywhere: on the Thames, where farmers transport their produce, radiating cheerful confidence in 'the Sale of their Goods' and in the profits they'll secure; in the coffee-houses, where men of business conduct transactions that involve staggering sums; and at the Royal Exchange, a large and elegant building filled with shops, which Mr Spectator dubs 'Centre of the World of Trade'. There he pauses on a balcony and listens with pleasure to the sounds rising 'from the Area below, where all the several voices lost their Distinction, and rose up in a confused Humming', consisting in equal measures of conversation and commerce. The moment recalls an earlier *Spectator* essay (no. 69), which Addison had devoted wholly to the Exchange, where he found proof of Britain's new commercial reach, of its centrality in the globe-wide 'World of Trade':

> Our Ships are laden with the Harvest of every Climate: Our Tables are stored with Spices, and Oils, and Wines: Our Rooms are filled with Pyramids of *China*, and adorned with the Workmanship of *Japan*: Our Morning's-Draught [i.e., drink] comes to us from the remotest Corners of the Earth: We repair our Bodies by the Drugs of *America*, and repose our selves under *Indian* Canopies . . . Nature indeed furnishes us with the bare necessaries of Life, but Traffick [trade] gives us a great Variety of what is Useful, and at the same time supplies us with every thing that is Convenient and Ornamental.

Once again, Pope provides instructive counterpoint to Addison's Whiggish confidence. In the second version of his *Rape of the Lock* (greatly expanded from the first), the dressing table of the heroine Belinda teems with 'every thing' (to borrow Addison's phrasing) 'that is Convenient and Ornamental' – and international. Unlike Addison, though, Pope seizes the opportunity for a comedy of scale, describing jewelry, perfume, and hair care in epic terms:

> This Casket *India*'s glowing Gems unlocks,
> And all *Arabia* breathes from yonder Box.
> The Tortoise here and Elephant unite.
> Transform'd to *Combs*, the speckled and the white.
>   (ll. 133–6)

There is humour here (an entire continent distilled into a fragrance) but there is grandeur too. In the *Iliad*, Achilles's wondrous shield, fashioned by the divine blacksmith Hephaistos, depicts and encompasses all the activities of the world. Pope here suggests, Addison-like, that Britain's international trade (as compassed in Belinda's cosmetic arsenal) accomplishes a comparable wonder, and may even amount to a modern equivalent for epic attainment. But the next couplet hints at trouble on the table, and in the world it represents:

> Here files of Pins extend their shining Rows,
> Puffs, Powders, Patches, Bibles, Billet-doux [love letters].
>   (ll. 137–8)

What are Bibles doing here, in this lustrous alliterative list of fashion accessories? They now serve as accessory too. Fashionable women sometimes carried small bibles as a stylish adornment, a dress accent on the order of a brooch or necklace. In his letter to the *Spectator*, Pope had argued that the newspaper's glut of information had fostered a corresponding failure to discriminate between the important and the trivial; here, the glut of goods fosters the same failure. Trade produces too much trivia: caught in its midst, even scripture becomes (in Addison's words) a 'Convenience and an Ornament' rather than an oracle. Pope's list is not too far in spirit from Swift's at the end of 'City Shower', where all those items of urban debris 'come tumbling down the flood'. This time, though, the inundation consists not of floating garbage but of fancy goods.

It may be therefore all the more dangerous. Amid the modern flood of print and products, must Britons drown? Or might they learn to navigate it for their own good? With increasing fervour over the course of their careers, Swift and Pope insisted on the first and bleaker likelihood: in the Tory-toned pessimism of *Gulliver's Travels*, where long lists (of foolish experiments, of deadly weapons) index the sheer quantity of modern folly; and in the closing apocalypse of the *Dunciad*, where the 'Universal Darkness' unleashed by the inchoate medley of print culture occludes forever the '*Universal* Light', that ancient 'Coelestial Fire' that Pope had hoped to propagate, decades earlier, in his *Essay on Criticism*. Addison and Steele, by contrast, affirmed the nation's prospects for navigation, encouraging their readers to embark upon a scheme of self-cultivation, couched as a carefully considered programme of acquisition. In paper after paper, they urged their audience to pursue not just those lustrous conveniences and ornaments available at the Exchange (which, if misused, might well distract them from more important matters), but also those habits of conduct and of mind that will regulate their consumption and refine their minds: politeness and taste, enacted in the art of spectatorship itself. During his day out in London, Mr Spectator repeats an argument he has made often elsewhere: that to *see* something wholly and imaginatively is in a sense to take possession of it – to enter into an immaterial but very profitable visual commerce. Looking out over the Royal Exchange, watching 'the Crowds about me . . . with their Hopes and Bargains', Mr Spectator slips, chameleon-like, into their commercial idiom: 'I found my Account' – that is, I secured my profits –

> in Attention to their several Interests. I, indeed, look'd upon my self as the richest Man that walk'd the *Exchange* that Day; for my Benevolence made me share the Gains of every Bargain that was made.

The *Spectator* offers itself in part as a handbook for this mysteriously cashless mode of acquisition, in which the intangibility of the exchange helps make commerce seem not crass but generous. In one of the paper's earliest numbers, Addison had voiced the hope that his readers, too, would 'find their Account in the Speculation' – i.e., the *Spectator* essay – 'of the Day' (no. 10). Now, 444 papers later, at the end of his 'trivial Day' amid the commerce and conversation of London, Mr Spectator tries again to help them do so. Though stymied for a moment as to the proper value 'of so many insignificant Matters and Occurrences', he nonetheless hits quickly upon a familiar solution: 'I thought it of great use, if [my readers] could learn with me to keep their Minds open to Gratification, and ready to receive it from any thing it meets with.' In the *Spectator*'s system of moral, aesthetic, and perceptual bookkeeping, the seemingly 'insignificant Matters and Occurrences' of a 'trivial Day' end up mattering enormously. They are the stuff of commerce and of conversation; rightly observed, carefully recorded, they become a form of wealth, a means of profit – an object not of suspicion but of celebration.

REFERENCES AND FURTHER READING

Anonymous (1975). An Epistle to Sir Richard Blackmore, Kt., On Occasion of the Late Great Victory in Brabant. In *Poems on Affairs of State, Vol. 7*. Ed. Frank H. Ellis. New Haven, Conn.: Yale University Press, 197–200.

Brewer, John (1997). *The Pleasures of the Imagina-tion: English Culture in the Eighteenth Century*. New York: Farrar Straus Giroux.

Colley, Linda (1992). *Britons: Forging the Nation 1707–1837*. New Haven: Yale University Press.

Glendinning, Victoria (1998). *Jonathan Swift: A Portrait*. New York: Henry Holt.

Hallett, Mark (1997). 'The medley print in early eighteenth-century London'. *Art History* 20, 214–37.

Harris, Tim (1993). *Politics under the Later Stuarts: Party Conflict in a Divided Society 1660–1715*. London: Longman.

Holmes, Geoffrey (1993). *The Making of a Great Power: Late Stuart and Early Georgian Britain, 1660–1722*. London: Longman.

Ketcham, Michael (1985). *Transparent Designs: Reading, Performance, and Form in the 'Spectator' Papers*. Athens: University of Georgia Press.

Levine, Joseph M. (1991). *The Battle of the Books: History and Literature in the Augustan Age*. Ithaca: Cornell University Press.

Mack, Maynard (1986). *Alexander Pope: A Life*. New York: W. W. Norton.

Mackie, Erin (1997). *Market à la Mode: Fashion, Commodity, and Gender in* The Tatler *and* The Spectator. Baltimore: Johns Hopkins University Press.

Morison, Stanley (1932). *The English Newspaper*. Cambridge: Cambridge University Press.

Pocock, J. G. A. (1985). *Virtue, Commerce, and History: Essays on Political Thought and History, Chiefly in the Eighteenth Century*. Cambridge: Cambridge University Press.

Rawson, Claude (1985). *Order from Confusion Sprung: Studies in Eighteenth-century Literature from Swift to Cowper*. London: George Allen and Unwin.

Sherman, Stuart (1996). *Telling Time: Clocks, Diaries, and English Diurnal Form, 1660–1785*. Chicago: University of Chicago Press.

Speck, W. A. (1998). *Literature and Society in Eighteenth-century England: Ideology, Politics and Culture, 1680–1820*. London: Addison Wesley Longman.

Sutherland, James (1986). *The Restoration Newspaper and its Development*. Cambridge: Cambridge University Press.

Weinbrot, Howard (1993). *Britannia's Issue: The Rise of British Literature from Dryden to Ossian*. Cambridge: Cambridge University Press.

Womersley, David (1997). *Augustan Critical Writing*. London: Penguin.

46
Literature, 1733–1742

Christine Gerrard

By 1733, Robert Walpole, the most powerful Whig premier since the accession of the Hanoverians in 1714 and the onset of single-party government, was well into his second decade of office. Through a combination of political ability, opportunism and sheer tenacity he had forged for himself a prime ministerial role from his combined offices of Chancellor of the Exchequer, Leader of the Commons, and King's adviser. Since the mid-1720s Walpole had faced mounting opposition from Tory backbenchers and dissident Whigs dissatisfied with his principles and policies. But it was only in the last nine years of the 'Robinocracy' – the period 1733 to 1742 – that parliamentary pressure, reinforced by popular opinion, made any major impact on his policies. In 1733 widespread national hostility forced Walpole to abandon his plan for a general excise tax on imported goods. The threat of itinerant customs officers with the right to enter and inspect smacked to many of arbitrary ministerial power and intolerable interference in the nation's daily life. Although the Excise Crisis failed to dent significantly Walpole's parliamentary majority in the general election of 1734, it revealed his vulnerability to public opinion. The years between 1733 and 1739 were marked by steadily escalating pressure for Britain to go to war with Spain over trading rights in the Spanish colonies. Spain had originally declared war on Britain in 1727: in 1729, Walpole, who believed that Britain's trade interests were best advanced through peace, negotiated the Treaty of Seville: but this served only to fan rather than quench war fever. Relations between Britain and Spain continued to deteriorate as pressure mounted from the mercantile communities. In October 1739 Walpole reluctantly declared war. After the initial victory at Porto Bello that year was followed by a series of reversals, including the disastrous siege of Cartagena of 1741, Walpole's perceived mishandling of the war led to loss of parliamentary confidence and his resignation in January 1742.

Walpole and the 'Literary Opposition'

In a period in which literature and politics were inseparable (it is hard to think of any authors in this period whose work remained untouched by political debate), writers played a key role in intensifying public hostility to Walpole. Yet not all the literary talent was ranged against the administration: Edward Young, John, Lord Hervey, Lady Mary Wortley Montagu and Sir Charles Hanbury Williams all remained staunch court Whigs. More significantly, Walpole hired from government funds a considerable number of competent political journalists, such as William Arnall, Matthew Concanen and James Ralph, to defend his policies in the ministerial press. Any broader account of this period which focuses only on opposition writers will fail to convey the sense of dialogue, of daily debate conducted in the ministerial and opposition press over such key themes as liberty, corruption, and most especially the debate over the English past. But the ministerial press – papers such as the government-funded *Daily Gazetteer*, the *Daily Courant*, the *London Journal* and Orator Henley's eccentric *Hyp-Doctor* – rarely matched the literary standard of the leading opposition journals. The most important of these was *The Craftsman* (1726–35), co-founded by the former min-isterial Whig William Pulteney and the High Church Tory cum Jacobite Henry St John, Viscount Bolingbroke, followed by *Mist's Weekly Journal* (1725–8) and its suc-cessor *Fog's* (1728–37), and *Common Sense* (1737–43), to which two leading literary peers, George Lyttelton and Philip Stanhope, Lord Chesterfield, contributed. It is almost a truism to point out that Walpole succeeded in alienating most of the liter-ary talent of his day. Writers as politically diverse as Swift, Pope, Samuel Johnson, James Thomson, John Gay, Henry Fielding, Mark Akenside, Richard Glover and Richard Savage, attacked Walpole's regime in plays, poems and prose. Their hostil-ity stemmed in part from Walpole's self-proclaimed indifference to letters. Although by no means an uncultured man, Walpole believed that poetry and politics did not mix. He refused to offer political patronage or government sinecures to promising authors, a situation compounded by Hanoverian royals' own indifference to English literary culture. During a period in which few writers, barring Pope, were successful in managing their own career in the new commercial literary marketplace, many – including Pope – looked back nostalgically to a former heyday of courtly letters. Recent research would suggest that Walpole had indeed broken a tradition of Whig political patronage which had flourished in the reigns of William and Anne, when authors such as Prior, Congreve, Addison, Steele and Philips had occupied official posts. The relations between the minister and his hired 'hacks' was rather more prag-matic. As Swift remarked in his *On Poetry: A Rhapsody* (1733), a cynical guide on how to succeed as a writer in the modern age, 'A Pamphlet in Sir *Bob*'s Defence / Will never fail to bring in Pence; / Nor be concern'd about the Sale, / He pays his Workmen on the Nail' (ll. 187–90).

Swift's poem echoes Pope's *Dunciad* (1728) in its ironic account of Grub Street hackery and the decline of letters under Walpole and the Hanoverians. A common

complaint in oppositional writing was that vulgar, mindless or foreign forms of entertainment – farce, Italian opera, pantomime shows – had encroached upon the foothills
of Parnassus: the invasion of the high by the low, symbolized by the appointment to
the poet laureateship in 1730 of Colley Cibber, showman, stage manager and comic
actor, whose flashy egotism (captured in the comically self-aggrandizing *Apology for
the Life of Mr Colley Cibber*, 1740) seemed to epitomize the spirit of the age. As
Bertrand Goldgar (1976) argued in a classic account of this period, writers did not
necessarily oppose Walpole because he personally failed to give them patronage but
because they believed, rightly or wrongly, that the commercial values driving society
under Walpole had depressed literary standards. Yet the neglect of literature was only
part of a broader spectrum of Walpolian policies which alienated writers. Equally
widespread was the denunciation of corruption in public affairs: Walpole had became
notorious for doing business by political backhanders and bribes. He acquired his
nickname 'The Screen of Brass' from both his broad, florid countenance, apparently
incapable of a blush, and from his highly efficient 'screening' of the government and
royal family's involvement in the South Sea Bubble fiasco of the early 1720s. Walpole's
pragmatic political management stood in sharp contrast to an ideal of civic virtue
enshrined in the writings of the seventeenth-century Commonwealthmen such as
James Harrington, recently revived by Bolingbroke and drawn on pervasively in oppositional journalism. Other writers, such as the low church Scottish Whig James
Thomson, who had initially supported Walpole, turned against him in the stinging
Britannia of 1729 less for his political corruption and indifference to letters than for
his pusillanimous 'peace at any price' foreign policy, and subsequently for his religious policy (his ecclesiastical manager was the high church Bishop Gibson). As
Alexander Pettit has emphasized (1997) there was no such thing as a monolithic 'literary opposition to Walpole', but individual writers and fluid groupings of authors
motivated by often quite disparate concerns.

Whig and Tory, Court and Country

This diversity reflects the composition of the 'opposition to Walpole' within
parliament. For many years political historians asserted that political labels such as
'Whig' and 'Tory' were irrelevant during the decades of Whig rule between 1714
and 1760: instead one should talk about the 'country' opposition to the court, since
by the 1730s, dissident Whigs and Tories shared the same principles. Any study of
parliamentary conduct in the Walpole period reveals a fissured opposition. The intransigence of Walpole's opponents in parliament proved a near insuperable barrier to
an effective challenge to his policies – one of the reasons Walpole remained in power
for as long as he did. High church Tories, especially those with latent Jacobite
sympathies, often found little ground for consensus with 'turncoat' Hanoverian
Whigs who had only recently baled out of the government. The need for unity

was the driving force behind *The Craftsman*. The paper drew heavily on the civic-humanist tradition of thought which had supplied a platform for country oppositions to the court since the 1670s, calling for a burial of party labels in the interests of patriotism, an ideal of selfless public activity which found its noblest embodiment in the Roman republican hero Cato. This was also the refrain of Bolingbroke's 1734 *Dissertation on Parties* which attempted to explode traditional party distinctions. It was only in the late 1730s, under the aegis of Frederick Prince of Wales, the new figurehead of the opposition, that such attempts at rallying Whigs and Tories in a 'Broad-Bottom' opposition met with any degree of success.

The Politicization of Pope

Recent scholarship has recovered a far wider range of writing from the Walpole period than that produced by the 'Tory wits', Swift, Gay and Pope. Gay died in 1732, and Swift, by this time living permanently in Ireland, contributed little to the opposition campaign in the 1730s save a few satirical squibs. The 1734 publication of a quarto pamphlet of his so-called 'scatological' poems, *Strephon and Chloe, Cassinus and Peter* and *A Beautiful Young Nymph Going to Bed*, courted a rather different kind of controversy. His ironic 'autobiography', *Verses on the Death of Dr Swift* (written in 1731, published 1738–9), defined his role more clearly as that of an Irish patriot. Pope must, however, remain central to any narrative of this period, less on grounds of intrinsic literary superiority, but because by the early 1730s he was so considerable a public figure that his literary career, and his personal friendships, were constantly held up to political scrutiny, debate, censure and praise. During his early years under Queen Anne, Pope had attempted to maintain political neutrality, despite his close friendship with the Tory leaders Bolingbroke and Harley. After Anne's death in 1714, the fall of the Tories and the subsequent Whig persecution of his Jacobite friend Atterbury kept Pope away from politics. The years spent translating Homer were followed by *The Dunciad* (1728), primarily a satire on bad writing and a riposte to his critics, but by implication a slur on the Walpole ministry and the Hanoverian dynasty, with its sly dig at the recent succession of George II: 'Still Dunce the second reigns like Dunce the first' (i, 6). The period 1733 to 1738 was the most fertile of Pope's entire career. Between 1733 and 1734 he was almost certainly pulled in several different directions. On the one hand he was attempting to construct a coherent theodicy for the age in his *Essay on Man*, published between 1733 and 1734. On the other hand, under the influence of Bolingbroke, his closest friend and mentor, the *Essay on Man*'s 'Guide, Philosopher, and Friend' (iv, 390), he was becoming drawn into a world of oppositional politics. The four *Epistles to Several Persons*, later known as the 'Moral Essays' (three of which were published in this period) contain an uneasy blend of philosophical generalization and sharply satirical social and political commentary. The most pointed of these was the January 1733 *Epistle to Bathurst*, 'On the Use of Riches', with its satire on Balaam, product and ultimate victim of nouveau-riche aspiration, its ironic praise of Whig-engineered schemes of paper-credit ('That lends corruption lighter wings to fly!' (40)) and its condemnation of Walpole's cronies – Peter Walter, a crooked financier, Dennis Bond, expelled from the Commons for embezzling Charitable Corporation funds, Sir John Blount, a director of the South Sea Company, and Francis Charteris, whose moral turpitude (twice pardoned for rape) had become notorious. The next month, February 1733, witnessed the first of the *Imitations of Horace*, *Satire II.i*, more daring in its satire on court and government than anything that he had published so far. Pope had perhaps been emboldened into attack by Walpole's imminent defeat in the Excise Crisis. In proclaiming himself 'To VIRTUE ONLY and HER FRIENDS, A FRIEND' (one of whom is named as Bolingbroke) and exploring the moral freedom of the satirist 'Hear this, and tremble! you, who 'scape the Laws' (121, 118) its oppositional tenor was unmistakable. It provoked an attack in the pro-government *Daily Courant* and a spin-off poem, *The State Dunces*, dedicated to Pope from another opposition satirist Paul Whitehead. *Satire II.i* also contained a slur on Lord Hervey, Queen Caroline's close confidant, and Lady Mary Wortley Montagu, both staunch court Whigs, which provoked the vicious jointly penned *Verses Address'd to the Imitator of . . . Horace* (1734).

That same year Pope published his *Epistle to Cobham*, 'Of the Knowledge and Characters of Men'. A poem not overtly political in orientation was made so by its dedicatee and its closing compliment, Cobham's imagined deathbed wish: 'Oh, save my country, Heav'n!' (265). In spring 1733 Pope's friend Richard Temple, Viscount Cobham, a highly distinguished soldier and a loyal supporter of Walpole, had criticized the ministry for its cover-up of the inquiry into the South Sea Company: for this perceived piece of political treachery he had lost both his place and his regiment. The cashiering of Cobham became a *cause célèbre*, and was undoubtedly a ministerial mistake, since Cobham went into opposition taking with him a significant body of Whig supporters, including the seasoned political veteran and writer Lord Chesterfield, and his own young nephews, whose political careers he launched with his personal wealth. Pope's dedication to the patriotism of a publicly disgraced man was pointed. In 1735, shortly before his friend Arbuthnot's death, Pope rushed into print his *Epistle to Arbuthnot*, the product of their discussion over the appropriateness of lashing 'General Vice' when the times deserve it, as well as Pope's most sustained defence of his '*person, morals* and *family*' in the wake of recent public attacks. The most daring and tendentious of the *Imitations of Horace* appeared in 1737, the *Epistle to Augustus*, a critically informed survey of English cultural history concluding with an ironic mock-panegyric to George Augustus, a very un-Augustan figure in terms of his 'disdain' for verse, and for a universal peace bought at the expense of British pride: 'Your country's peace, how oft, how dearly bought' (397). By 1738, the year in which Pope published his outspoken *Epilogues to the Satires*, he had come to define his public identity predominantly as a good man and a satirist, morally independent of court and government.

The Patriot Opposition

Yet by no means all oppositionial writers practised or even approved of satire. The chorus of ministerial scepticism which greeted Pope's self-proclaimed role as reformer of the age was swelled by the voices of Pope's friends and admirers who considered satire at best a negative, at worst a deeply flawed genre. In 1730 and 1731 Aaron Hill and George Lyttelton addressed poems to Pope advising him to give up 'meaner' satire in favour of 'a lasting Column to thy Country's Praise'. George Lyttelton was Lord Cobham's young nephew. By 1735, along with his relatives Richard Grenville, Thomas Pitt and William Pitt, he had entered parliament and moved straight into opposition. This group of 'Boy Patriots' or 'Cobham's Cubs', as they were nicknamed by ministerial hacks, represented a new and significant force within the opposition. They were young and inexperienced but unlike other dissident Whigs could boast a past untainted by former ministerial association as well as the energy of youth. They are particularly important from a literary perspective. Lyttelton, leader of this group, was a very capable writer himself – to his youthful love poems he added a considerable range of political pamphlets and the highly popular oppositional *Persian Letters* (1735) – and other members of his circle, including his cousin Gilbert West, boasted literary talents. More importantly, Lyttelton saw himself as a patron of letters, and attempted to extend his circle to accommodate writers such as James Thomson, Thomson's friend David Mallet and Richard Glover. The chief card which they had to play was the favour of Frederick Prince of Wales, eldest son of George II and Caroline, who had become increasingly alienated from his parents and from Walpole since his arrival in Britain in 1728. In 1734 Frederick signalled his growing closeness to the patriot circle by appointing Lyttelton as his equerry. Lyttelton drew talented writers to the attention of the prince: this group of dissident Whig poets and playwrights came closer to approximating the ideal of royal patronage lamented by Pope and his friends.

Patriot poetry is very different in tone and form from the satirical writings of Pope or Whitehead. The patriots' repudiation of satire was part of a larger literary-political agenda which favoured the hortatory over the critical: 'uplifting' and less narrowly topical genres, such as the historical or epic poem, and the blank verse tragedy. Typical of these were Thomson's *Liberty*, published in two parts in 1735–6, a five-book blank verse poem tracing the progress of the goddess Liberty through a now fallen Greece and Rome to Britain's shores, with the warning of her imminent departure, or John Dyer's similar *The Ruins of Rome*, first written in 1729 and published in 1740. The patriot poets' patriotism was not born out of a misplaced nostalgia for an irrecoverable past. They frequently invoked former periods of British national glory, less to inspire a sense of gloom at current degeneration than to rouse a spirit of national pride. The Saxon or 'gothic' past had given Britons their rugged sense of political independence, and the reign of Elizabeth I pride in British mercantile prowess. In this they echoed the patriotism constantly voiced by Bolingbroke in

The Craftsman: 'I feel a secret pride in thinking I was born a Briton', as one essay had begun. Other works recalled the self-abnegation of classical patriotism: Richard Glover's epic *Leonidas* (1737), which promoted the 'love of liberty' epitomized by the Spartan's stand at the battle of Thermopylae, attained a popularity well beyond its intrinsic literary merit. Glover was also the author of *London: Or The Progress of Commerce* (1739), an allegorical blank-verse tribute to commerce, and the stirring *Admiral Hosier's Ghost* of 1740. A successful merchant and 'City poet', Glover represented a continuation of the tradition of city poets turned epicists initiated by the much derided Richard Blackmore, William III's physician. The strains of mercantilism which had been associated with Whig writing since the late 1710s, and with the Walpole administration up to around 1728, had by now become firmly opposition property. The writings of Glover, and especially George Lillo, also part of this circle, reflected extra-parliamentary activities. Much of the pressure placed on Walpole over both the Excise Crisis and war with Spain came from the petitions raised by the commercial and mercantile communities in large cities such as Liverpool, London and Bristol. In 1736, Lillo, a former city jeweller, author of the 1731 *George Barnwell, or The Merchant's Tragedy*, produced his *The Fatal Curiosity*, a play set in Elizabethan Cornwall. Young Wilmot, who has recently returned, disguised and sunburnt, from the voyage to Guyana with Raleigh, dies with tragic irony at the hands of his parents, decayed gentry greedy for gold, but not before this representative of the freewheeling mercantile spirit of the age has uttered a patriotic rallying cry to the audience.

> Turn then thy eyes to the prolific ocean
> Whose spacious bosom open to thy view.
> There deathless honour and unenvied wealth
> Have often crowned the brave adventurer's toils.
> This is the native uncontested right,
> The fair inheritance of ev'ry Briton
> That dares put in his claim.
>
> (II.ii, 8–14)

Political Drama and the Stage Licensing Act of 1737

By March 1737, the month in which Henry Fielding chose to stage Lillo's *Fatal Curiosity* as the 'afterpiece' of his own highly provocative *Historical Register for the Year 1736*, Walpole's government was making serious moves to clamp down on the freedom of the stage. During the preceding decade drama had proved a potent vehicle for attacking the administration. Since the late 1720s the two patent theatres (Drury Lane and Lincoln's Inn Fields) had staged a number of original or revamped historical tragedies which could enjoy a topical application: the 'historical parallel' play, such as Ralph's *The Fall of the Earl of Essex* or the anonymous *The Fall of Mortimer* (both 1731) aimed dangerously high at Walpole. One of the most audacious of these 'application' plays, William Harvard's 1737 *King Charles I, or Majesty Misled*, implied that

George II was being 'misled' by his minister in ways that might lead to fatal consequences. Although tragedy depicted the affairs of monarchs in remote times and places and avoided literal social comment, it could, through veiled allusion and innuendo, prove far more subversive than satirical comedy. Other dramatists such as Henry Fielding took advantage of the unauthorized expansion of the London theatres following the success of Gay's *Beggar's Opera* in the late 1720s, to stage plays at new venues such as Goodman's Fields, in London's east end. During his early years as a dramatist, Fielding's burlesques were not predominantly targeted at Walpole: comedies such as *Don Quixote in England* (1734) or burlesques such as *The Author's Farce* 1734 (initiating a pattern for Fielding's 'rehearsal' plays, or plays within plays) are fairly even handed in their hits at both government and opposition. It was only after the creation of his own theatre company, the 'Great Mogul's Company' at the Little Theatre at the Haymarket, that Fielding came out openly against the ministry. *Pasquin* of 1736 was mildly satirical, the *Historical Register for the Year 1736* (1737), a sequence of revue-style sketches, was bitingly so. As Lord Egmont observed, it was 'an allegory on the loss of the Excise Bill. The whole was a satire on Sir Robert Walpole'. As recent evidence has shown, Fielding followed the political fortunes of his erstwhile school friend and literary patron George Lyttelton. Between the time of *Pasquin* and the *Historical Register* the Prince of Wales had gone into open opposition to his parents (appointing Lyttelton as his secretary) and opposition forces had regrouped. Other dramatists took advantage of this newly combative mood. Between the end of January and late May 1737 Robert Hume estimates that approximately one hundred performances of plays openly hostile to the ministry were staged at three of London's four theatres (Hume, 1988, 240). In the spring of 1737 the ministry made determined moves to grasp control of the stage. Walpole had already managed to silence some of the more outspoken political drama. In the absence of any official censorship methods, the authorities had used other means to close down productions – in the case of the controversial 1731 *Fall of Mortimer* at the Little Haymarket, the harassment of actors, with warrants for their arrest. But Walpole had already explored official avenues, in 1735 attempting to capitalize on a far broader movement for the moral reformation and regulation of the stage. In 1735 Sir John Barnard, a leading city alderman with opposition sympathies, introduced into parliament the Barnard Playhouse Bill, designed to 'restrain the Number and scandalous Abuses of the Play-Houses'. This Bill's real purpose was to shut down Goodman's Fields (it was purportedly corrupting the morals of apprentices and servants) and to prevent the erection of any new theatres in or near the City of London. The Barnard Bill had received widespread approval and would probably have been passed had Walpole not attempted to add an amendment giving the Lord Chamberlain the power to censor plays. Barnard and his followers had no intention of handing over regulatory powers to the ministry and the Bill failed. In February 1737 the ministry attempted another Bill, which did not proceed, then in May a Bill for the Stage Licensing Act which rapidly sailed through the Commons by the end of June without significant resistance. The Stage Licensing Act contained two central provisions – the limiting of theatres to the two patent theatres and the legal requirement to submit all plays to the Lord Chamberlain for approval at least two weeks prior to performance. It effectively removed political controversy from the British stage.

The long-term consequences to British drama were deeply damaging – Drury Lane and Covent Garden, facing no competition, settled into a rut of stale productions. The immediate consequence for the opposition was not entirely negative. Fielding had already shut up shop at the Little Haymarket, possibly silenced by a large bribe from Walpole: the end of his career as a dramatist led first to him training as a lawyer, then to writing novels. For the ministry, censorship proved a two-edged sword. The first play to be banned was the patriot dramatist Henry Brooke's *Gustavus Vasa: or, the Deliverer of His Country*, set in sixteenth-century Sweden and dramatizing the heroic efforts of the exiled Gustavus, rightful heir to the throne, to lead his people against a usurping king and an evil minister. The play had Jacobite as well as Whiggish over-tones, though Brooke of course asserted his political innocence by proclaiming, in his preface to the printed edition (1739), that he was only motivated by love for his country and for liberty (itself a politically loaded word). This subscription edition proved a sell-out success, as opposition followers greeted each other with an adapta-tion of the play's catch-phrase, 'Britain, O my country, yet I'll save thee'. Other early banned plays were of a similar historical-allegorical, Patriot cast – Thomson's *Edward and Eleanora* (1738) and William Paterson's 'Gothic' *Arminius* (1740). In parliament the Licensing Act had been opposed in the Commons by William Pulteney, in the Lords in a famous speech by Lord Chesterfield. It was also attacked in opposition news-papers and political pamphlets, the most famous of which, the young Samuel Johnson's *A Compleat Vindication of the Licensers of the Stage* (1739) was a masterpiece of Swiftian irony. Johnson adopted the voice of a ministerial spokesman to ridicule the Patriot love of liberty embodied in Brooke's banned play, thereby implicitly indicting Walpole's government for its self-serving and cynical policies. Johnson's defence here of every man's 'sacred unalienable birthright' against royal and minis-terial tyranny shows him in a surprising radical, proto-Paine mood.

The Year 1738

The year 1738 represented a high water mark of opposition activity, in parliament, the provinces and the press. In September 1737 Prince Frederick had moved into open opposition (the final rift had occurred after a row over the christening of his first child) and had set up a separate court in Leicester House. Increasing extra-parliamentary support for the campaign pressing for war with Spain seemed to weaken Walpole's position: the summer and autumn saw a revival of opposition hopes and a stepped-up campaign which the patriots centred on the prince. Bolingbroke, now back in England, was urging the prince to become 'a centre of union . . . under whose influ-ence men of different characters and different views will be brought better together'. Cobham's patriot supporters were working hard to forge a new 'Broad-Bottom' alliance with the Tories centred on Frederick. The prince was certainly willing to act in this role, courting public popularity in a series of well-timed royal progresses in the provinces as well as making himself very visible in the London theatres. Many patriot plays, with their portrait of an ideal prince come to save the nation, were aimed directly at Frederick, sitting in the royal box. A more thoroughgoing attempt to instil in the prince the 'Idea of a Patriot King' was Bolingbroke's famous work of that title, circulated in manuscript among the prince's followers in 1738, though not published until 1749. Here Bolingbroke painted an idealized portrait of a ruler operating above political party (a dig at the 'Whig' King George II), one who had the interests of his people and nation at heart, who refused to be led by royal favourites, who embodied both royal charisma and observed Whig principles of government (an ingenious synthesis of Whig and Tory elements). Although impractical as a political nostrum, the *Idea of a Patriot King* proved imaginatively potent to a number of Frederick's supporters and opposition poets, a legacy evident in its revival during subsequent decades of Hanoverian rule. Pope thought highly enough of his friend's work to print a secret copy of it in 1740–1 lest it be lost to posterity. Bolingbroke had returned to England in the spring of 1738 (ostensibly to sell his house, in reality to involve himself in opposition politics) and for much of the year lived with Pope at Twickenham.

The year 1738 also represented the most intense period of Pope's involvement with opposition politics, initiated by the controversial *Epistle to Bolingbroke*, one of his last Horatian imitations, published in March. In May and July that year he also published Dialogues I and II of the *Epilogue to the Satires*, also known by the year of their publication, *One Thousand Seven Hundred and Thirty-Eight*. In these two poems Pope moves beyond Horatian good humour and moderation, single-handedly lashing out at vice and corruption with his 'sacred weapon! left for Truth's defence' (ii, 212). Dialogue I ends with a magnificently sombre cavalcade, the Progress of Vice steadily moving through the nation: only the poet himself remains aloof and contemptuous. Never had Pope been so lofty or outspoken in his defence of the satirist's high calling – nor so clear in his support for opposition leaders and his indictment of the ministry. The second Dialogue reads like a roll-call of opposition names, many of the young Whig patriots whom Pope had befriended. Pope was never more than ambivalent about Prince Frederick, however, always mistrustful as he was of Hanoverian royalty. This was the last political poem which Pope published until his *New Dunciad* of 1742. Pope may have been in some way silenced by the ministry, perhaps 'warned off' by the highly publicized arrest in 1739 of Paul Whitehead for his *Manners*, an imitation of the *Epilogue to the Satires*. Another controversial work published in 1738 was the anonymous *London*, an imitation of Juvenal's third Satire with pointed contemporary and political application. Pope admired the poem, and determined to discover the author – as it turned out, Samuel Johnson. During his early years in London Johnson was a virulent supporter of the opposition: *London*, followed by the virtually simultaneous *Compleat Vindication* and *Marmor Norfolciense* (1739), all contained seditious material. *Marmor*, a mock-prophecy deciphered from a runic stone, has an unmistakably Jacobite thrust. Lines in *London* hinting at the 'ropes' needed to 'rig another convoy for the k—g' (246–7) point to both George II's much criticized trips to visit his German mistress as well as another sort of rope – a noose. Yet *London* as a whole represents a broader mood of opposition feeling than the narrowly Jacobite. The corruption of London replaces the corruption of Juvenal's Rome: Johnson's indictment of a society in which bribery and backhanders prove a better route to ascent than merit also has a personal ring – 'SLOW RISES WORTH, BY POVERTY DEPRESS'D' (177). The opening lines, nostalgic in their evocation of 'Britannia's glories' in the days of Elizabeth I or Alfred's 'golden reign', a time before 'English honour grew a standing jest' (26, 248, 30), combine the heady mood of indignation and patriotic jingoism characteristic of the closing years of the decade and embodied in a number of other pieces published that year, including Pope's *Epilogue to the Satires* and Mark Akenside's stirring *Voice of Liberty: A British Philippic*. It is scarcely any wonder that the rather general satire on party politics found in Gay's second series of *Fables*, posthumously published in 1738, was almost totally ignored.

War with Spain and the Fall of Walpole

By the summer of 1738 Walpole was faced by a formidable pressure group of Atlantic merchants and backed by parliamentary opposition, demanding a parliamentary review of the rights of British merchants to freedom of navigation. Walpole's attempts to negotiate the Treaty of Pardo with Spain broke down when the South Sea Company withdrew its support, and in October 1739 he was forced to declare war. It is hard to estimate what role poetry played in whipping up war fever. However, in this period – unlike the Excise Crisis – the worlds of 'high' culture (Miltonic blank verse) and 'low' culture (popular ballads, prints, and plays) were seamlessly intertwined. Verses from Akenside's *Voice of Liberty* were appended to an inflammatory print of 1738 which depicted British sailors imprisoned and tortured by 'insulting' Spaniards (shades of the Spanish inquisition) while Elizabethan naval heroes looked down horrified from the heavens. Richard Glover's *Admiral Hosier's Ghost* (1740), a rousing ballad recalling the fate of Hosier and his crew, who perished of fever in 1726 while waiting in vain for ministerial permission to strike down a Spanish gold fleet in the West Indies, proved highly popular. So too, of course, did James Thomson and Thomas Arne's famous lyric, 'Rule, Britannia', first sung in 1740 at a performance of the *Masque of Alfred* written for Prince Frederick.

Alfred capitalized on the mood of triumphalism which followed Admiral Vernon's seizure of Porto Bello. Vernon, by this stage a national hero, whose form appeared everywhere in prints, commemorative poems, ballads and chinaware, was also an opposition MP: his successes fuelled a nationalist ardour that was also anti-government in orientation. Patriot writers, notably George Lyttelton, contributed pamphlets to the campaign demanding an expansion of Britain's trading empire. Yet British victories in the War of Jenkins' ear (so named after a captain whose ear had been sliced off by Spanish costaguardas) proved few. The government's failure to send out sufficient land forces was blamed for Admiral Haddock's setbacks in the Mediterranean and for Vernon's slow progress in the West Indies after Porto Bello. In February 1741 the opposition Whig MP Samuel Sandys proposed a famous motion to remove Walpole 'from the king's counsel and presence for ever'. The failure of this motion (Tories were reluctant to challenge the royal prerogative or add their votes to the 'discontented Whigs') proves that even at this stage, attempts to create a 'Broad-Bottom' opposition from Tories and Dissident Whigs proved difficult. In the new parliamentary session of January 1742 Walpole was finally unable to command a working majority and was forced to resign office.

The Demise of Patriotism

Walpole was not, however, replaced by a new kind of ministry, a 'Broad-Bottom' administration drawn from the best men of both parties, as the *Craftsman* and *Common Sense* had promised. The Whig administration remained virtually intact: the former patriot Whig William Pulteney replaced Walpole, and in subsequent months other former opposition Whigs took government places. Prince Frederick was reconciled to his father (albeit temporarily) in return for a raise in his allowance. Widespread political cynicism followed. Even by 1740, Pope had detached himself from some of his former opposition patriot friends: his unpublished gloomy satire *One Thousand Seven Hundred and Forty*, 'O wretched B[ritain], jealous now of all', cast doubt on the motives of all politicians, both patriot and ministerial. Henry Fielding's cynical *Opposition: A Vision* of 1741, an extended allegory of a divided and untrustworthy opposition, revealed his new-found support for Walpole. By early 1743, even Johnson was beginning to distance himself from his former patriot zeal: sympathy for Walpole permeates his parliamentary report on Sandy's 1741 motion published in the *Gentleman's Magazine*. In 1744 Mark Akenside's bitter *Epistle to Curio* lambasted Pulteney's calculated desertion of his patriot principles. It was only after the fall of Walpole that in March 1742 Pope published his *New Dunciad*, effectively a fourth book to add to his three-book *Dunciad* of 1728–9 – a fulfilment of the prophecy of Queen Dulness's reign in Book III of the original version. *The New Dunciad* was far more political in intent and range than the original poem. Pope was looking critically at 'wretched [B]ritain' after twenty years of Walpole's administration. 'Dullness' is no longer confined to bad writers: it is an infectious malaise, a moral and spiritual torpor spreading through the length and breadth of the kingdom. Pope here moves through an extraordinary range of subjects – the decay of theatres, schools, universities, the arts and sciences, the church, philosophy, young men on foreign tours, the rise of political bribery and more insidious forms of corruption. One of the pivotal figures in *The New Dunciad* is the 'Wizard Old' (an opposition figure for Walpole) whose magical 'Cup' is glossed as the 'cup of Self-Love' or self-interest, which has poisoned the nation. The next year, Pope revised the entire poem, adding the fourth book: it was published as *The Dunciad in Four Books* (1743), starring Colley Cibber, rather than the original

Lewis Theobald, as 'hero' of the poem – a fitting final epitaph to Walpolian England before Pope's death the next year.

New Directions

The fall of Walpole marked a number of new directions in literature. The succession of Whig administrations which followed in his wake failed to throw up any leader as personally distinctive and charismatic as Walpole. During the twenty years of the 'Robinocracy' political and visual satire had slowly developed around Walpole a whole network of satirical correspondences, described by Mack as 'the extensive vocabulary of disaffection minted by the writers of the *Craftsman* and kept bright by continual rubbing' (Mack, 1969, 128). Walpole's fall, and the subsequent cynicism about patriotism, led many poets and writers not only away from satire but from all politics. This was most true of the mid-century poets, Gray, Collins and the Warton brothers, who were beginning to explore themes such as the Gothic past (in part inspired by the political rehearsal of these ideas in the 1730s), the imagination, nature and more remote locations. William Collins's anonymously published *Persian Eclogues* of 1742 were a new departure in the exotic, an attempt to recreate the 'elegancy and wildness of thought' of Persian poetry which in his preface he contrasts with the 'cold' and more prosaic Augustan manner. During the Walpole years the taste for the 'primitive' characteristic of the mid-century poets had already revealed itself in the vogue for 'untutored genius'. The self-educated farm labourer Stephen Duck had become a cult figure: his 'Thresher's Labour', pirated in 1730 but first published with Duck's authorial approval in his *Poems on Several Occasions* of 1736, was a vigorous and frankly anti-pastoral account of the labourer's life from the labourer's perspective. In 1739 Mary Collier, the 'washer-woman' poet, produced her *Woman's Labour*, a trenchant riposte to Duck's dismissive account of his fellow female labourers. Yet even a writer like Duck, not addressing political themes, became caught up in the political crosscurrents of the Walpole years. Lionized by Queen Caroline and turned into a kind of tame hermit, the keeper of her rustic 'Merlin's Cave' in Richmond Gardens, Duck was second only to Cibber in opposition satire as a symbol for the nadir to which literary standards had plummeted in the period. As Swift scathingly remarked, 'From *threshing* Corn he turns to *thresh* his Brains / For which Her *Majesty* allows him *Grains*' ('On Stephen Duck, the Thresher and Favourite Poet' *c*.1730, l. 3).

The most significant new developments in literature in the closing years of the Walpole era were the novels of Richardson and Fielding. Richardson's *Pamela; Or, Virtue Rewarded* of 1741, the product of the successful middle-aged printer responsible for, among other things, the ministerial *Daily Gazetteer*, turned into a national cult. Richardson's tale of the serving maid 'rewarded' for her virtue provoked Fielding's first exercises in creative writing since the Licensing Act ended his career as a playwright. His dramatic talent for burlesque shaped the sharply satirical *Shamela*, an expose of the thinly veiled social climbing which he believed to be the hidden recipe for *Pamela's* success. But *Joseph Andrews*, published in 1742, proved more than another Richardson spin-off. Joseph, Pamela's burly fictitious brother, may be absurd in his Pamelistic defence of his 'chastity', but the work as a whole develops a moral sensibility, a notion of generosity, good humour and active charity, which came to characterize his subsequent masterpiece *Tom Jones*.

REFERENCES AND FURTHER READING

Browning, Reed (1982). *The Political and Constitutional Ideas of the Court Whigs*. Baton Rouge, La.: University of Louisiana Press.

Carretta, Vincent (1983). *The Snarling Muse: Verbal and Visual Political Satire from Pope to Churchill*. Philadelphia: Philadelphia University Press.

Dickinson, H. T. (1988). 'The politics of Pope'. In *Alexander Pope: Essays for the Tercentenary*. Ed. Colin Nicholson. Aberdeen: Aberdeen University Press.

Erskine-Hill, Howard (1981–2). 'Alexander Pope: the political poet in his time'. *Eighteenth-century Studies* 15, 123–48.

——(1984). 'The political character of Samuel Johnson'. In *Samuel Johnson: New Critical Essays*. Ed. Isobel Grundy. London: Vision.

——(1996). *Poetry of Opposition and Revolution: Dryden to Wordsworth*. Oxford: Clarendon Press.

Gerrard, Christine H. (1994). *The Patriot Opposition to Walpole: Poetry, Politics, and National Myth, 1725–1742*. Oxford: Oxford University Press.

Goldgar, Bertrand A. (1976). *Walpole and the Wits: The Relation of Politics to Literature, 1722–1742*. Lincoln, Nebr.: University of Nebraska Press.

Hammond, Brean (1984). *Pope and Bolingbroke: A Study of Friendship and Influence*. Columbia, Mo.: University of Missouri Press.

Holmes, Geoffrey and Daniel Szechi (1993). *The Age of Oligarchy: Pre-industrial Britain, 1722–83*. London and New York: Longman.

Hume, Robert D. (1988). *Henry Fielding and the London Theatre 1728–1737*. Oxford: Oxford University Press.

Kaminski, Thomas (1987). *The Early Career of Samuel Johnson*. New York: Oxford University Press.

Kramnick, Isaac (1968). *Bolingbroke and His Circle: The Politics of Nostalgia in the Age of Walpole*. Cambridge, Mass.: Harvard University Press.

Langford, Paul (1975). *The Excise Crisis*. Oxford: Oxford University Press.

Mack, Maynard (1969). *The Garden and the City: Retirement and Politics in the Later Poetry of Pope, 1731–1743*. Toronto: University of Toronto Press.

Nicholson, Colin (1994). *Writing and the Rise of Finance: Capital Satires of the Early Eighteenth Century*. Cambridge: Cambridge University Press.

Pettit, Alexander (1997). *Illusory Consensus: Bolingbroke and the Polemical Response to Walpole, 1730–1737*. Newark, Del.: University of Delaware Press.

Rogers, Nicholas (1989). *Whigs and Cities: Popular Politics in the Age of Walpole and Pitt*. Oxford: Oxford University Press.

Skinner, Quentin (1974). 'The principles and practice of opposition: the case of Bolingbroke versus Walpole'. In *Historical Perspectives: Studies in English Thought and Society in Honour of J. H. Plumb*. Ed. Neil McKendrick. London: Europa.

Wilson, Kathleen (1995). *The Sense of the People: Politics, Culture and Imperialism in England, 1715–1785*. Cambridge: Cambridge University Press.

47
Literature, 1757–1776
Nick Groom
Adam Rounce*

I

Literature in the two decades between 1757 and 1776 is remarkable more for its vivacious diversity than the defining stature of a single writer or conformity to a particular style. From *Ossian* to *Tristram Shandy*, Kit Smart's *Jubilate Agno* to Samuel
Johnson's edition of Shakespeare, we are faced with an extraordinary range of writing
that belies attempts to explain it within a single cultural field – and it may be that
the comparative failure of critics to identify a dominant strain among these writers is
precisely what has kept this period so excitingly fluid.

Johnson figures as a microcosm of these problems: a lexicographer, editor, essayist,
novelist, polemicist, poet and travel writer, of whose conversation, habits, and diet
we have, from 1763, a minuscule account in James Boswell's *Life of Johnson* (for
example, on Easter Sunday 1773 they dined upon 'a very good soup, a boiled leg of
lamb and spinach, a veal pye, and a rice pudding'). By 1757 Johnson had completed
the great *Dictionary* (1755–6), he wrote *The Idler* essays 1758–60 and in 1759 the
novel *Rasselas*. His edition of the plays of Shakespeare appeared in 1765, he published
four political pamphlets and a few poems and dramatic prologues, and *A Journey to
the Western Islands of Scotland* (1775). In 1777, Johnson accepted the commission to
write *The Lives of the English Poets* (1779–81).

What characterizes Johnson's literary oeuvre in this period? Certainly not 'literary
loneliness' or that ghastly term 'pre-romanticism'; perhaps it is a model of professional authorship that shapes his output (save that he was in receipt of a pension of
£300 from 1762), perhaps it is an ever-inquisitive and companionable Enlightenment
scepticism (he launched his literary 'Club' in 1764), perhaps it is a vigilant morality
that unceasingly polices the infinite variety of human experience. One prominent
theme does, however, tie Johnson's major work to that of his contemporaries, and
will give some shape to this essay: the formation of a recognizable tradition of English
literature.

* Adam Rounce is Leverhulme Special Research Fellow at the University of Bristol.

Johnson's *Dictionary* not only imposed a pragmatic order upon the English language, it was also a compendium of English writers, deploying the best part of a quarter of a million illustrative quotations – and of course the fifty-two *Lives of the English Poets* was a canon-building enterprise par excellence. His edition of Shakespeare likewise collected the remarks made by earlier editors in a running commentary of footnotes that doubled as both elucidatory annotation and a history of Shakespeare editing – in particular he was keen to preserve every one of Pope's notes, 'that no fragment of so great a writer may be lost'. But it is especially worth noting that Johnson's prefatory essay on Shakespeare's particular qualities emphasizes his naturalness: 'Shakespeare is above all writers, at least above all modern writers, the poet of nature; the poet that holds up to his readers a faithful model of manners and of life', and in doing so creates characters as types (what he calls 'species') of human nature, rather than describing eccentric or exaggerated individuals.

> This therefore is the praise of Shakespeare, that his drama is the mirror of life; that he who has mazed his imagination, in following the phantoms which other writers raise up before him, may here be cured of his delirious ecstasies, by reading human sentiments in human language; by scenes from which a hermit may estimate the transactions of the world, and a confessor predict the progress of the passions.

Lest we forget, this is the Johnson who as a child reading the Ghost's speech in *Hamlet*, fled out into the street in terror, and who noted in his concluding remarks to *King Lear*, 'I was many years ago so shocked by Cordelia's death, that I know not whether I ever endured to read again the last scenes of the play till I undertook to revise them as an editor'.

So it is possible to see Johnson as part of a developing project of the humanities, through historical reorganization and revaluation, and literary anthologization. The momentum of this cultural reassessment is also apparent in such popular and successful ventures as Robert Dodsley's *Collection of Poems, by Several Hands* (1748–58), Thomas Percy's *Reliques of Ancient English Poetry* (1765), and even William Blackstone's *Commentaries on the Laws of England* (1765–9). Dodsley's *Collection* was the essential touchstone of contemporary poetry (including by its sixth edition of 1782 at least 130 poets), and Percy, despite his insistence on presenting 'ancient English poetry', also included several contemporaries among his collection, placing current poetic practice in a context of an identifiable literary tradition. Moreover, anthologies were of course communal activities, involving many poets and scholars – from the leader of taste and fashionable gardener William Shenstone to the Oxford Professor of Poetry Thomas Warton. (This growing interest in social mechanics would also eventually inspire Adam Smith's *The Wealth of Nations*, 1776.) But while Johnson and the publishing firm of Robert and James Dodsley constituted perhaps the most powerful axis around which this emergent cultural awareness formed, there were others: Horace Walpole and Thomas Gray, for example, were similarly engaged in compiling and composing antiquarian literature, in the shape of Walpole's *Catalogue of the Royal and Noble Authors of England* (1758) and Gray's attempt at his own history of English poetry.

These antiquarian scholars and aesthetes also had a profound impact upon the poetry and prose of the period – most obviously in their own writing, such as Walpole's *The Castle of Otranto* (1764), Gray's spectacular poem *The Bard* (1757) and his succession of translations from Norse and Welsh poetry, and Percy's ballad *The Hermit of Warkworth* (1774), but also discernible in popular novels like Tobias Smollett's *Life and Adventures of Sir Launcelot Greaves* (1762), in which a mad protagonist becomes a quixotic knight errant. An examination therefore of this new spirit of medievalism and tradition allows a considered reassessment of the work of the major poets of the period – poets who all too often receive scant attention.

The publication of Thomas Gray's two Pindarick Odes in 1757 (*The Bard* and the poem later entitled *The Progress of Poesy*) has often been seen as the turning point of his poetic career. The enormous public success of his *Elegy Written in a Country Churchyard* (1751) had been founded upon the extent to which Gray had appeared to tap a very general nerve: the aphoristic, homiletic qualities of the *Elegy* were seen to be, in Johnson's phrase, 'sentiments to which every bosom returns an echo'. The nostalgic melancholy of the *Ode on a Distant Prospect of Eton College* (written in 1742, but not published until 1747), had similarly evinced accessibility. The epigraph from Pindar attached to the 1757 Odes Gray himself translated as 'vocal to the intelligent alone'. *The Bard* and *The Progress of Poesy* questioned the intelligence of their readers most effectively; their obscurity became a byword, and they soon represented an extreme poetic modernity that was rooted in a vision of the inspirations of the remote past. The Odes were seen either as the height of a poetic sublimity, or as an example of mere pretentiousness, in a controversy that lingered on beyond the end of the century.

These general responses to the Pindarick Odes are representative of much subsequent criticism of mid-eighteenth-century poetry, which is neither wholly condemnatory, nor unequivocal in its praise; something always mitigates the achievements of this poetry, and the separation of supposed qualities from perceived weaknesses and limitations never shows any awareness of how dependent such perception is on the subjectivity of the critic. As mentioned above, it is the contention of this chapter that the literature of this period cannot easily be shoe-horned into a homogeneous series of simple dichotomies, just as Gray's Pindarick Odes are neither as fully revolutionary and ground-breaking, nor as merely fashionable, as their original supporters and opponents claimed.

Indeed, Gray is another useful example of why the period from 1757 to 1776 has often proved elusive to critics and literary historians. Gray's attitude towards his poetry is in itself a very complex question: his life of almost total scholarly seclusion has suggested a diffidence towards his artistry at odds with the vigorous attempts of the two odes to suggest something of a primitive, bardic form of inspiration, like the opening invocation of *The Progress of Poesy*,

> Awake, Æolian lyre, awake,
> And give to rapture all thy trembling strings.

From Helicon's harmonious springs
A thousand rills their mazy progress take.
                    (ll. 1–4)

The awakening of the Greek lyre, with its onrush of music down the streams from the haunt of the Muses, sees Gray asserting his relationship with Pindar, the Greek poet of similarly inspired music, in his own lofty (and often obscure) odes. The Pindaric was the model of the Great Ode in English poetry from the seventeenth century onwards, yet its specific qualities (other than rhyme and metre replicating each other in a tripartite structure of stanzas) were not especially fixed. Gray catches the expected fervent, inspired tone: 'The subject and simile, as is usual with Pindar, are united' as a footnote he added in 1768 testifies; the poetry describes and enacts its own subject.

Yet such confidence is harder to locate in the poem's ending, as the story of the art form's 'progress' has brought us from the home of the Muses to Shakespeare, Milton and Dryden. But what lies beyond? 'O lyre divine, what daring spirit / Wakes thee now?' (ll. 111–12), a question that is only mutedly answered by the speaker's self-positioning in the poetic pantheon:

Yet shall he mount, and keep his distant way
Beyond the limits of a vulgar fate,
Beneath the Good how far – but far above the Great.
                    (ll. 121–3)

The rays of poetic inspiration have shined before the eyes of the young poet, but the extent of such inspiration is limited. Gray's projected poetic authority is circumscribed: he cannot fully accept and uphold the poetic responsibility of the 'lyre divine', nor can he wholly reject its allure.

Recent criticism of Gray has centred this need for (and yet partial rejection of) poetic authority around Gray's difficulties with achieving a role, both in his lack of any clear function in society, and in his (at least potential) homosexuality. Such criticism differs not in spirit from most accounts of Gray through the years; he has always been seen as a tentative poet, resigned to not quite being able to reach his desires. Just as the potential of the poet is left hanging at the end of *The Progress of Poesy*, so *The Bard* can be seen as an extension of this concern with literary fame, as the monologue of the Welsh bard, in defiance of Edward I's destruction of the oral tradition to which he belongs, is also a thinly veiled questioning of the future of contemporary poetic modes. The ambiguity in its ending comes from the paradoxical joy of its speaker as he annihilates himself:

'To triumph, and to die, are mine.'
He spoke, and headlong from the mountain's height
Deep in the roaring tide he plung'd to endless night.
                    (ll. 139–44)

This 'triumph' of authentic poetic inspiration is as close as Gray comes to full poetic authority. As it is tempered by the death of his speaker (and of the tradition he represents), it is an ending typical of Gray, with poetic inspiration both reaffirmed and destroyed.

The Pindarick Odes embody Gray's characteristic combination of bardic confidence and scholarly reticence. Their influence in the second half of the eighteenth century was pervasive, serving as a belated example of the kind of poetry that Joseph Warton had advocated in the oft-quoted 'Advertisement' to his *Odes on Various Subjects* (1746). Claiming that 'the fashion of moralizing in verse has been carried too far' and that 'Invention and Imagination' are 'the chief faculties of a Poet', Warton calls his odes 'an attempt to bring back Poetry into its right channel'. Warton's ambition set his poetry larger tasks than it could achieve; his prose speaks more boldly for his ideas than his actual poetry could ever do. Thus the earlier *The Enthusiast: or the Lover of Nature* (1744) ostensibly shows his attempt 'To lift my soul above this little earth, / This folly-fetter'd world' (ll. 207–8), yet worldly matters (in the form of literary criticism) inevitably creep in: 'What are the lays of artful Addison, / Coldly correct, to Shakespeare's warblings wild?' (168–9). This anticipates the later argument of the 'Advertisement': Warton's poetry never quite stops being a manifesto.

Joseph's brother Thomas Warton published a similar, but more successful, youth-fully exuberant poem: *The Pleasures of Melancholy* (1747, but written in 1745 at the age of seventeen), regarded today as an adjunct to his later critical endeavours. It is heavily influenced by Mark Akenside's enormously popular didactic poem, *The Pleasures of Imagination* (1744) and by the shorter poems of Milton, especially 'Il Penseroso' and 'L'Allegro' – Warton would later produce an edition of Milton's shorter poems in 1785. The other author promoted is Spenser (prefiguring Warton's influential literary-antiquarian essay *Observations on the Faerie Queene* of 1754), in a passage strikingly similar to his brother's attack on Addison, moving away from Pope and towards the greater imaginative freedom of 'magic SPENSER'S wildly-warbled song' (l. 157). Neither brother could fully support their ideas for a new channel of poetry through their own verses; instead, they made their mark through criticism. Thomas's later verse shows an interesting conflict between his antiquarian interests and a perceived increasing domination by the powers of reason over ancient sources of inspiration; in Warton's later poetry, 'gothic' ruins free the latent powers of the enthusiast to connect imaginatively with the primitive past, whilst meditating on the implications of such decay for the present. Such a double perspective was utilized more effectively in his critical work. His eventual *History of English Poetry* (1774–81), which in its copious quotation doubled as a compendium of English poetry as well as a history, made generous use of unpublished manuscripts of medieval verse, and yet also recognized the ruinous state of the archive. Warton's *History* effectively set a new agenda in antiquarian history because it embraced a more chaotic version of history, as indeed Edward Gibbon's *History of the Decline and Fall of the Roman Empire* (1776–88) symbolically marked the collapse of great systems of society and modes of thought, and Gibbon's exemplary organization of his material was itself eloquent of that fall. If

Warton's scholarship survives in importance far above his poetry, that does not mean that the latter deserves to be left to moulder away. The sparse attention paid to his poems has, however, ensured that criticism has looked elsewhere for a more fully achieved example of the kind of poetry that the Wartons endorsed from the 1740s onwards.

II

Such an example has often been found in the poetry of William Collins, friend (and schoolmate, at Winchester) of the Wartons. Collins planned to publish his 1746 *Odes on Several Descriptive and Allegorical Subjects* jointly with Joseph's *Odes on Various Subjects*. In the event, the volumes were published separately, but this has not prevented Collins from being closely associated with the views of Joseph Warton's 'Advertisement' as if they were his own. Indeed, this sort of assumption has typified Collins's posthumous reputation, which has seen him portrayed as a divinely inspired madman and as a 'pre-romantic' in his 'alien' genius. Collins is thus made to fit into a hegemonic model of mid-eighteenth-century poetry which obscures his individual values.

Collins lacked any real readership until after his death in 1759, when the imaginative qualities of his *Odes* attracted a slightly younger generation in the 1760s. The Miltonic and Spenserian echoes in the *Odes* have often been seen as Collins's imaginative anticipation of Romanticism, yet there is at least an equal amount of material taken from the couplet poetics of Dryden and Pope, the two poets who stand more directly behind Collins's early couplet work, the *Persian Eclogues* (1742). Making this side of Collins's influences antithetical to the tradition of Milton and Spenser is an example of the tendency in much nineteenth- and twentieth-century criticism of the period to see influences, genre and movements in exclusive terms, without understanding the artistic complexities and ambiguities behind such issues. Collins's most difficult poem, the 'Ode on the Poetical Character', is thus usually read as Collins's dramatic rendering of artistic 'anxiety' in the face of Milton's achievement, as Collins views Milton's Edenic poetic sanctuary:

> My trembling Feet his guiding Steps pursue;
> In vain – Such Bliss to One alone,
> Of all the Sons of soul was known,
> And Heav'n, and Fancy, kindred Pow'rs,
> Have now o'er turn'd th' inspiring Bow'rs,
> Or curtain'd close such Scene from ev'ry future View.
>
> (ll. 71–6)

This view of Collins, running ineffectually after the gigantic achievement of Milton, has been made the perfect example, chronologically, of what lay between Milton and the Romantics, and so Collins's lack of complete artistic achievement became a symbol

of the supposedly muted poetic possibilities of his era. Yet this reading does little justice to the sophistication of the poem, or for the familiarity of its final sentiment,
which is as much a traditional trope as a statement of belatedness. Collins is a complex
and original figure working within a variety of traditions, whose work defies easy
categorization.

One of Collins's most influential poems is the posthumously discovered and incomplete 'Ode on the Popular Superstitions of the Highlands of Scotland', first published
in 1788. This ode is addressed to the playwright John Home, telling him of the inspiration to be found in the subjects of his native land:

> Even yet preserved, how often may'st thou hear,
> Where to the pole the Boreal mountains run,
>   Taught by the father to his listening son
> Strange lays, whose power had charmed a Spenser's ear.
> At every pause, before thy mind possessed,
>   Old Runic bards shall seem to rise around.
>   (ll. 36–41)

Collins anticipates the interest in the 'Runic bards' that would result in the publication of the poems of 'Ossian' from 1760, and Thomas Percy's *Five Pieces of Runic
Poetry* (1763) and subsequent *Reliques of Ancient English Poetry* in 1765. Collins's
anticipation is grounded in a literary and oral tradition: these 'lays' had previously
charmed Edmund Spenser. Significantly, this combination of a written tradition
accompanying more primitive forms of inspiration can also be found in an equally
influential unfinished poem, James Beattie's *The Minstrel* (1771–4), which blends
the education of the young minstrel Edwin with folk-tales, myths, and natural
'sublime' experiences, and the poetical and historical inspirations of Homer, Virgil
and Plutarch.

An increasing adherence to primitive forms of inspiration is also evident in Joseph
Warton's amplification of his critical position, *An Essay on the Genius and Writings of
Pope* (1756), where he debates whether the kind of poetry written by Pope makes him
belong to the 'first class' of poets, along with Shakespeare, Milton and Spenser. Warton
was soon followed by Edward Young (and subsequently William Duff and Alexander
Gerard), who theorized and more importantly eulogized this 'original genius' that
dispenses with the poetic practice of imitation for an energetic, fertile, and natural
creativity: 'The pen of an Original Writer, like Armida's wand, out of a barren waste
calls a blooming spring' (*Conjectures on Original Composition*, 1759). Young's own pantheon included Shakespeare, Ben Jonson, Dryden and Addison.

By the conclusion to the second volume of his *Essay* (delayed until 1782), Joseph
Warton claims that '[Pope] has written nothing in a strain so truly sublime as *The
Bard* of Gray' – a comment that shows Gray's works to have become a critical benchmark. *The Bard* has become Warton's exemplum, and yet Warton is somewhat
peremptory in making Gray a figure of such centrality. Gray's poetry after the

Pindarick Odes shows his increasing attraction to the emergent poetic primitivism exemplified by Edmund Burke's *Philosophical Enquiry into the Origin of Our Ideas of the Sublime and Beautiful* (1757), James Macpherson's Ossianic *Fragments*, and by his own scholarly interest in Icelandic and Norse poetry.

Gray had been sent a pre-publication copy of *Fragments of Ancient Poetry, collected in the Highlands of Scotland, and translated from the Galic or Erse Language* in 1760, and, like so many other readers, was thrown into ecstasies by their brooding and windswept visions:

> Autumn is dark on the mountains; grey mist rests on the hills. The whirlwind is heard on the heath. Dark rolls the river thro' the narrow plain. A tree stands alone on the hill, and marks the grave of Connal. The leaves whirl round with the wind, and strew the grave of the dead. At times are seen here the ghosts of the deceased, when the musing hunter alone stalks slowly over the heath. Appear in thy armour of light, thou ghost of the mighty Connal! Shine, near thy tomb, Crimora! like a moon-beam from a cloud. (Fragment V)

Macpherson attributed the *Fragments* to 'Ossian', a third-century bard and the last of the Celts, and thereby inaugurated a Celtic revival on which the sun has never since set. (Currently, the tradition is invoked most enthusiastically by the poet Robert Crawford, but it is worth noting that it has only been in the past few years that Macpherson has received any serious and sustained critical attention.) The *Fragments* were rapidly augmented and re-edited into two Homeric epics: *Fingal* (1761) and *Temora* (1763). They are wild and desolate verses, echoing back through the centuries like the ghost of a disinherited Scottish identity, and so in Macpherson too one perceives the lineaments of national renewal and a recognition and restoration of a lost heritage, as part of a Scottish cultural revival. But the *Fragments* was also a strikingly fashionable collection, not least as it gave an almost immediate proof of Burke's aesthetic treatise on the sublime, in which sublimity was defined as an encounter with obscurity, whether gothic ruins hinting at the abyss of history, or a vast mountain shrouded in mist.

Walpole too, whose main occupation in these years as in nearly every year was in writing letters and turning his mansion Strawberry Hill into an extravagant gothic confection, was inspired by his devotion to antiquarian pursuits and the dreamlike moodiness of *Ossian* to publish his own 'discovery': *The Castle of Otranto* (1764). This short book, arguably the founding Gothic novel (though that distinction, it has been argued, properly belongs to Thomas Leland's *Longsword* of 1762), is a bizarre, uncanny, and preposterous melodrama of the middle ages, literally dreamt up from the furniture that stuffed Walpole's preposterous gothic house: 'I gave rein to my imagination', he declared, 'visions and passions choked me'. The plot creaks along awfully, like some prodigiously rusty suit of armour animated by the keening spirit of a monstrous bagpipe, but despite passages of absurdity and indeed hilarity, the book has a peculiarly claustrophobic quality to it, and has maintained its interest among critics, especially those of a psychoanalytic bent. *The Castle of Otranto* escalates Warton's desire for 'Invention and Imagination' to a dizzying extreme, and the book becomes an intoxicating succession of puzzling portents, riddling symbols, and obsessive Shakespearean allusion, conducted in a sort of pantomimic torture chamber. The novel also exhibits a very modern anxiety over its own production, and the first edition had an elaborate preface claiming that the story was a translation from the sixteenth-century Italian, and attributing it to one William Marshal. As with *Ossian*, it was impossible to separate the inspirational qualities of the past from questions of authenticity.

III

Examining the figures normally associated with the Wartons' desires for a new poetic shows how hard it is to uphold the traditional view of the period, although a number of writers can be gathered together as seamlessly sharing the poetics of 'sensibility' or 'sentimentality'. Laurence Sterne's idiosyncratic *Life and Opinions of Tristram Shandy, Gent* (1759–67), a justly famous and delightful romp stretching over nine volumes, is not, in the context of sensibility, quite as idiosyncratic as one might be led to believe, but still provides some of the most dazzling experiments with narrative and authorial presence seen in the century. *Tristram Shandy* is a book that is determinedly digressive, perpetually drawing attention to its own bookish conventions and to the opacity of the printed medium, and is written in a crack-brained ludic prose that perpetually spirals out of itself. The novel is full of little jokes and conceits that were not likely to appeal to critics like Johnson – a black page to indicate mourning, displaced chapters, a page of marbled paper, blank pages and lines of dashes and asterisks, and so forth – although Johnson did declare rather wittily (bearing in mind the games Sterne plays with novelistic time and the fact that Sterne himself is a character in the book who dies in the first volume), 'Nothing odd will do long. "Tristram Shandy" did not last'.

Because of its playfulness and knowing formal chaos, *Tristram Shandy* has, rather lamely, been repeatedly named of late as the first 'postmodern' novel in its preoccupation with the mechanics of meaning, the endless succession of signs, the lack of a master-code, and so forth. This sort of belated theorizing is as insidious as theories of pre-romanticism: both approaches treat a text as only being critically accommodated years, centuries even, after publication. Books are wrenched from their context, and the context remains denuded (which is another reason for the relative neglect of this immediate period). In fact, as indicated above, *Tristram Shandy* does not need the anachronistic justification of postmodernism, for it not only makes much better sense in the 1760s, it also crucially allows us to understand the 1760s better. The novel is in the tradition of Robert Burton's *Anatomy of Melancholy* (1621–51) and Jonathan Swift's *Tale of a Tub* (1704); it emphasizes the mid-century's concern over epistemology and literary form, the booktrade and the materiality of the world, over the relationship between author and work and reader, the mixed media of print, and, of

course, the uses of history and the definition of English literature and a national tradition. *Tristram Shandy* is stuffed with allusions and citations, but in a way that
ridicules the utopianism inherent in writing a dictionary or compiling histories or
anthologies of English literature (as mentioned elsewhere, Sterne's comments on plagiarism are themselves plagiarized from Burton).

But Sterne is most significant in terms of the 'sentimental' vogue – which again he
appears to be satirizing almost before it has got off the ground. Sentimentality in the
eighteenth century meant enjoying a minute sensitivity to the ebbs and flows of feelings and having a finely tuned sensibility able to read the emotions of others through
fleeting gestures or looks – as evinced most powerfully in Samuel Richardson's *Clarissa*
(1747–8). But through the 1760s it became arch, over-sophisticated, and self-conscious: an artificial, if occasionally histrionic, pose. The genre is typified by Frances
Brooke's translation *Letters from Juliet Lady Catesby* (1760), and her own *Lady Julia Mandeville* (1763), Henry Brooke's (no relation) *The Fool of Quality* (1765–70) – a digressive, self-reflexive tear-jerker, derived in part from Rousseau's *Émile* (1762) – and Henry
Mackenzie's *The Man of Feeling* (1771), of which Mackenzie is the ostensible editor of
fragments of a manuscript that has been in part consumed by being used as gun
wadding. Thus Sterne's Scriblerian satire of sentimentality in *Tristram Shandy* consists
in staging properly 'affecting moments' (such as my uncle Toby rescuing the fly) while
glorying in double entendres, cross-purposes, and non sequiturs; underscoring how
little knowledge is got by 'mere words', and yet how susceptible the human body is to
the depredations of language. In *A Sentimental Journey* (1768) too, Sterne (specifically
parodying Smollett's *Travels through France and Italy* of 1766), lightly analyses the 'har-
monic vibrations' of the senses and their concomitant emotional effects in a series of
episodes by turns sensitive and salacious: ' "Tis sweet to feel by what fine-spun threads
our emotions are drawn together.'

John Butt concludes his magisterial volume on *The Mid-eighteenth Century* in the
Oxford History of English Literature by arguing that the period was characterized by
a thirst for strong sensations, such as original genius, the sentimental, the sublime,
the supernatural, and the exotic, and that writers were uninhibited in their physiological responses. Certainly one might agree with this assessment if turning from the
sentimental to James Boswell's scandalous seduction of Louisa Digges on 12 January
1762: 'A more voluptuous night I never enjoyed. Five times was I fairly lost in
supreme rapture . . . I surely may be styled a Man of Pleasure.' But despite the prevalence of sentimental literature and sentimental engravings (often of pivotal scenes in
ballads, plays, or popular novels) it becomes difficult to argue for a movement of 'sensibility' on an individual level except in the most general terms, since so many writers
seem to be working as exceptions to most rules.

If a poetry of 'sensibility' exists, its general qualities are most easily found negatively in the relatively neglected satires of Charles Churchill, whose contempt for most
mid-eighteenth-century poetry serves at least one useful purpose in indicating what
was fashionable. Churchill's work has often been described as that of an ersatz Pope

or Dryden, and his topicality of reference has proved his undoing. Much of his satire was written in the cause of John Wilkes's controversies of 1763, and therefore has a strong political flavour. But there is much to be said for Churchill's work, despite its unevenness and tendencies to erupt into polemic; his star burned briefly, but brightly, and for the three years of his career, from 1761 until his untimely death in 1764, his popularity was immensely greater than that of any other mid-century poet. The level of Churchill's invective never weakened during his brief career, but his technical sophistication grew immensely. By his last poems, he had developed a loose, colloquial form of the heroic couplet that could be devastating. His last work, the 'Dedication to the Sermons' is a virtuoso denunciation of William Warburton, friend (and literary executor) of Pope, Bishop of Gloucester, and perpetual controversialist:

> HEALTH to great GLOSTER – from a man unknown,
> Who holds thy health as dearly as his own,
> Accept this greeting – nor let modest fear
> Call up one maiden blush – I mean not here
> To wound with flatt'ry – 'tis a Villain's art,
> And suits not with the frankness of my heart.
>
> (ll. 1–6)

The register of Churchill's address is deliberately complicated by its extremely flexible syntax. The whole poem is a succession of double-edged remarks, insults disguised as compliments, and criticisms of Warburton's moral probity. The accepting of the greeting, and the blush that follow imply a bribe (reinforced by the double syntax of 'I mean not here', showing the difference between Warburton's public and private behaviour). The poem literally does 'wound with flatt'ry', as the ostensible address to Warburton's health becomes a devastating exposure of the underside of his achievements. As a model of satiric involvement, Churchill would later influence Byron, and at his best, he counters the familiar argument that all couplet verse in the century after Pope is monotonous and derivative. His school friend and fellow member of the 'Nonsense Club', Robert Lloyd, mined a similar satiric vein (though often using Swiftian octosyllabics), attacking the pretensions of dunces and the nouveau riche in poems like 'The Cit's Country Box' (1756) and *The Actor* (1760).

The other outstanding writer of couplet poetics in the period is Oliver Goldsmith. Goldsmith's innovations in his greatest poem, *The Deserted Village* (1770), are of subject, rather than form, linking the mid-eighteenth-century pastoral elegy with a sense of implicit social protest. Goldsmith stands as a corrective to the peculiar nationalist Georgic of John Dyer's *The Fleece* (1757), where the didactic purpose of the poem (the care and products of sheep) is used as a springboard for a Whiggish sense of liberty. This demands productivity as a unifying social force which, the poem suggests, is the only measure of national health: 'But chief by numbers of industrious hands / A nation's wealth is counted' (Book III, ll. 531–2). The brash social optimism of *The Fleece* exists on an uneasy truce between its recommended economic 'progress', and the way that such progress has damaged rural communities that are supposedly its beneficiaries. Hence Dyer's (to modern minds) facile identification of the workhouse as a vehicle for public good: such 'seats of kind constraint' (III, l. 235) are merely a way of ensuring that the welfare of the community is upheld, in proportion (as always) to its level of production. Such an analysis of deep-rooted social problems is attacked directly by Goldsmith in *The Deserted Village*, contrasting the 'innocence and health' (l. 67) of idyllic rural life in the village of Auburn, with the ruinous present:

> But times are altered; trade's unfeeling train
> Usurp the land and dispossess the swain;
> Along the lawn, where scattered hamlets rose,
> Unwieldy wealth and cumbrous pomp repose;
> And every want to opulence allied,
> And every pang that folly pays to pride.
>
> (ll. 63–74)

The mixture of radicalism and paternalism in the poem continues to attract debate: the 'Golden Age' of Goldsmith's village, with its 'wholesome' and 'light' labour is unlike that of any labouring community in the eighteenth century – does this overdetermine the poem's protests against enclosure and 'trade's unfeeling train'? Furthermore, it has been argued that the village in its former glory is also a place of fixed social boundaries and limits to material and intellectual improvement. Yet such criticisms do not always do justice to Goldsmith's use in the poem of the disordered and ruined rural space as a metaphor for the questioning of the 'progress' – both capital and imperial – that Dyer had so encouraged. The poem's influence, in both a positive and negative sense, was both deep and wide. It inspired George Crabbe to attack what he saw as the absence of its naturalism in *The Village* (1781); William Cowper had to negotiate his view of British progress around the poem in his great 'domestic' epic, *The Task* (1782); and it also asserted pastoral as a model for radical social protest, such as in the later works of Robert Bloomfield and John Clare. Furthermore, Goldsmith's contemporary John Langhorne (erstwhile editor of William Collins and translator of Plutarch) produced in *The Country Justice* (1774–5) a poem which, in its prosaic presentation of the sufferings of the rural poor, influenced the young Wordsworth. But while Goldsmith's influence is far-reaching and important, his diverse use of literary forms tends to diffuse his overall achievement. In *The Vicar of Wakefield* (1766), Goldsmith created an enduringly popular tale which managed to join the sentimental novel whilst simultaneously mocking it, and the equally successful *She Stoops to Conquer* (1773), joined Richard Brinsley Sheridan's *The Rivals* (1775) and *The School for Scandal* (1777) in attacking and parodying the high-spun morality of the then prevalent sentimental comedy. These three plays remain the most popular of eighteenth-century dramas.

IV

The year 1771 marked the death of Thomas Gray and Christopher Smart, two poets not often yoked together. The end of Gray's scholarly travails contrasts greatly with Smart, whose years of penury and intermittent insanity ended in a debtor's prison, and whose reputation is based largely around two poems, *A Song to David* (1763) and *Jubilate Agno* (written between 1758 and 1763, but not published until 1939). The intense religiosity of these poems (and Smart's legendary incarceration after his compulsive need for public prayer), have tended to distance him from his contemporaries, yet his work shares a lot of the characteristics of the period, not least in his working in a wide variety of genres.

Smart's first substantial work, the so-called 'Seatonian' poems, anticipate his later themes, such as the opening of *On the Goodness of the Supreme Being* (1756), with its address to 'Orpheus, for so the Gentiles call'd thy name, / Israel's sweet Psalmist' (ll. 1–2). King David, Israel's bard, and the key figure of Smart's poetry, is identified as the classical poetic archetype. The formal orthodoxy of the Seatonian poems gives way to the antiphonal verse of *Jubilate Agno*, Smart's 'magnificat' or song of praise, written from a lunatic asylum. In the *Jubilate* the imitation of Hebrew verse structures (related by the scholarship of Smart's friend Robert Lowth, and his influential 1753 lectures *De Sacra Poesi Hebraeorum*) allows Smart to develop an extremely flexible form of free verse, based around the form of statement and reply:

> Let Shobi rejoice with the Kastrel – blessed be the name JESUS in falconry and in the MALL.
> For I blessed God in St James's Park till I routed all the company.
>
> Let Elkanah rejoice with Cymindis – the Lord illuminate us against the powers of darkness.
>
> For the officers of the peace are at variance with me, and the watchman smites me with his staff.
>
> (Fragment B, 89–90)

The poem is thus a unique mixture of biblical prophecy and celebration, and an account of Smart's spiritual progress. Smart describes his aesthetic in the following terms: 'For my talent is to give an impression upon words by punching, that when the reader casts his eye upon 'em, he takes up the image from the mould which I have made' (Fragment B, 404). Smart's 'mould' imprints the image in the reader's mind because the divine truth of his poem, its rejoicing in the fecundity of the created world and its maker and saviour, cannot be questioned. Smart sees form not merely as a means of expression – to aspire to the level of the divine Psalmist David, form has to become the expression of its subject. The intricately plotted stanzas of *A Song to David* subordinate form to a complex function to realize this: it is a 'Great Ode', a poem which attempts (as much as Gray and Collins's Pindaricks) to invoke the sublime inspiration of ancient poetry. The only difference is in Smart's use of biblical, rather than classical, precedents. The careful structuring of numbers of stanzas for each theme (12 virtues, 10 commandments, 7 pillars, 4 seasons, 5 senses) and the equally precise syntactical parallelism of key phrases, is a different version of the metrical symmetries of the English Pindaric's tripartite structure. The result is a unique example of a poem that has to be both equal to, and more than, the sum of its parts (containing as it does the creation of the world, all earthly wisdom, and the ten commandments), as Smart exalts, in his conclusion:

> Thou at stupendous truth believ'd,
> And now the matchless deed's atchiev'd,
>   DETERMINED, DARED, and DONE.
>   (ll. 514–16)

Smart has succeeded in celebrating David's 'matchless' achievements, and in doing so his own achievement should stand as matchless in its own right (just as the creation of the world is matchless).

Smart's progression to the bardic tones of the *Song* and the primitivism of the *Jubilate*, via biblical scholarship, does not give a complete understanding of his career. As well as his translations of the Psalms, he translated Horace in the 1760s, using a variety of forms, many of which revert to a poetic orthodoxy. Smart's versions of Horace look back to Pope and Dryden, just as his free verse experiments in the *Jubilate* connect with the prose poems of *Ossian* and the later fourteeners of William Blake. Smart's interest in free verse is an attempt to perceive revelation. The emergent interest in ballad forms similarly praises the old English ballads for their ability to turn on a moment of mystery and revelation; this represents their primitive identification with an authentic source of inspiration, the numinous that Smart is also looking for. In his search for poetic authenticity, Smart symbolizes a wider need in the period to rediscover authentic sources of art, whether through scholarship or divine inspiration; the relative neglect of the full body of his oeuvre has prevented it being seen just how much he relates to his own time, whilst still managing to appear ahead of it.

The extreme diversity of Smart's work shows the greater diversity of the period, and how this has often been ignored and misunderstood through over-consideration of generalizations like 'sensibility'. The most significant literature of the years 1757 to 1776 is too complex to fit into notions of canon formation, and the less significant ranges from Chinese miscellanies to conduct literature and hymns, the first 'Mother Goose' collection to murder trial transcripts, and at the edges of literary culture we have such 'texts' as souvenir 'Tristram Shandy' soup. Yet the idea of a canon was growing ever more influential throughout the period, and paradoxically it would be fair to say that the growth of canon formation is matched commensurately by the questioning of such formations by contemporary literature. The diversity of the period ultimately repudiates the need for such definitions, formations, groups and genres, beyond the most generalized examples.

This situation is perhaps most compellingly apparent in the case of Thomas Chatterton, equally misunderstood through the condemnatory term 'forgery' as Christopher Smart was through supposed lunacy. But the gradual compilation of Chatterton's complete works has revealed the amazing range of literary opportunities open to an energetic young writer of the mid-century. Chatterton composed in a stunning array of styles and voices – elegies, Churchillian satire, political letters, African eclogues, Saxon Ossianics, and medieval verse – and under many different pseudonyms. His writing can only be characterized by sheer diversity, and stupendous energy – such as in the searing attack of 'Kew Gardens':

> Rest Johnson hapless Spirit rest and drink,
> No more defile thy Claret Glass with Ink;
> In quiet sleep repose thy heavy head;
> Kenrick disdains to piss upon the dead.
> Administration will defend thy fame,
> And Pensions add Importance to thy name.
> (ll. 917–21)

He is most notorious, however, for his 'Rowley' poems, poems that describe and re-enact the literary and antiquarian culture of fifteenth-century Bristol. This tale of forgery, partly because it is so extraordinary (charity-educated teenager forges reams of medieval literature), partly because it has such a spectacular denouement (he commits suicide in poverty, aged seventeen – though this myth has now been exploded, with potentially enormous consequences for Romanticism and Pre-Raphaelitism that have yet to be properly understood), has traditionally obliterated Chatterton's stunning achievement. It is not that he wrote fifteenth-century verse that remains convincing today, it is that he summoned into existence an entire medieval world, populated by poets, politicians, and antiquarians. Whether providing a literary context for the execution of Sir Charles Bawdin, or describing little flowers in such a way that would inspire Keats and Clare fifty years later, Chatterton had what can only be described as the 'poetic faculty' in making the mundane sing, and sing such songs as had never been heard before.

> In Virgyne the sweltrie sun gan sheene,
> And hotte upon the mees[1] did caste his raie;
> The apple rodded[2] from its palie greene,
> And the mole[3] peare did bende the leafy spraie;
> The peede chelandri[4] sunge the livelong daie;
> 'Twas nowe the pride, the manhode of the yeare,
> And eke the grounde was dighte[5] in its mose defte aumere.[6]
> ('An Excelente Balade of Charitie', ll. 1–7)

Notes: [1] meads [Chatterton's note, as are the following]; [2] reddened, ripened; [3] soft; [4] pied goldfinch; [5] drest, arrayed; [6] neat, ornamental.

At one level, one is tempted to accept that this is a gorgeous vision of England and Englishness measured through the fantastical archaism of an invented language. And indeed along with everything else, Chatterton was actually commissioned to write a history of England (confirming David Hume's remark on 28 March 1769 that 'History, I think, is the Favourite Reading'). But in this essay we have argued against seeing in history (or nation, or canon, or sensibility – or of course forgery, for that matter) a key to Chatterton's, or any other writer's, work. His 'African Eclogues', for instance, offer a remarkable perspective on colonialism that blasts any simple comprehension of national identity (and flattens verses such as the imbecilic *Sugar-Cane* (1764) of James Grainger). They literally summon another world:

> Three times the virgin swimming on the breeze,
> Danc'd in the shadow of the mystic trees:
> When like a dark cloud spreading to the view,
> The first-born sons of war and blood pursue;
> Swift as the elk they pour along the plain;
> Swift as the flying clouds distilling rain.
> Swift as the boundlings of the youthful roe,
> They course around, and lengthen as they go.
> ('Narva and Mored', ll. 23–30)

This is not mere 'exoticism', it is not even a reading of African otherness; rather, it proposes a new cultural economy of racial power relations that places the European invader in such dislocation that he becomes almost invisible: a debilitating disease that spirits away the real living:

> Where the pale children of the feeble sun,
> In search of gold, thro' every climate run:
> From burning heat, to freezing torments go,
> And live in all vicissitudes of woe.
> ('Narva and Mored', ll. 55–8)

Primitivism is exposed as an ideological conceit, history is indeed a catalogue of crimes. It is perhaps no surprise that Chatterton has been most conveniently parcelled away as a precocious forger (he was only seventeen when he wrote these lines shortly before his untimely death), the 'African Eclogues' are barely read, and critics have been unwilling – or incapable – of accommodating Chatterton as an anti-type of the Johnsonian writer.

REFERENCES AND FURTHER READING

Barker-Benfield, G. J. (1992). *The Culture of Sensibility: Sex and Society in Eighteenth-century Britain.* Chicago and London: University of Chicago Press.

Bertelsen, Lance (1986). *The Nonsense Club: Literature and Popular Culture, 1749–1764.* Oxford: Clarendon.

Bogel, Frederic V. (1984). *Literature and Insubstantiality in Later Eighteenth-century England.* Princeton: Princeton University Press.

Brown, Marshall (1991). *Preromanticism.* Stanford: Stanford University Press.

Butt, John and Geoffrey Carnall (1969). *Oxford History of English Literature, Vol. 8: The Mid-Eighteenth Century.* Oxford: Clarendon.

Cox, Stephen (1980). *'The Stranger Within Thee': Concepts of the Self in Late Eighteenth-century Literature.* Pittsburgh: Pittsburgh University Press.

Gleckner, Robert (1997). *Gray Agonistes: Thomas Gray and Masculine Friendship.* Baltimore and London: Johns Hopkins University Press.

Griffin, Robert (1995). *Wordsworth's Pope: A Study in Literary Historiography.* Cambridge: Cambridge University Press.

Groom, Nick, ed. (1999). *Thomas Chatterton and Romantic Culture.* London: Macmillan; New York: St Martin's.

Hudson, Nicholas (1990). *Samuel Johnson and Eighteenth-century Thought.* Oxford: Clarendon.

Kaul, Suvir (1992). *Thomas Gray and Literary Authority: Ideology and Poetics in Eighteenth-century England.* Oxford: Oxford University Press.

Kernan, Alvin (1989). *Samuel Johnson and the Impact of Print.* Princeton: Princeton University Press.

Lipking, Lawrence (1970). *The Ordering of the Arts in Eighteenth-century England.* Princeton: Princeton University Press.

Lonsdale, Roger (1969). *The Poems of Thomas Gray, William Collins, Oliver Goldsmith.* London and New York: Longman.

McGann, Jerome (1996). *The Poetics of Sensibility: A Revolution in Literary Style.* Oxford: Clarendon.

Pittock, Joan (1973). *The Ascendancy of Taste: The Achievement of Joseph and Thomas Warton.* London: Routledge.

Riberio, Alvaro and James Basker, eds (1996). *Tradition in Transition: Marginal Texts, Women Writers and the Eighteenth-century Canon.* Oxford: Clarendon Press.

Sitter, John (1982). *Literary Loneliness in Mid-eighteenth-century England.* Ithaca: Cornell University Press.

Todd, Janet (1986). *Sensibility: An Introduction.* London and New York: Methuen.

Wendorf, Richard (1981). *William Collins and Eighteenth-century British Poetry.* Minneapolis: University of Minnesota Press.

Woodman, Thomas, ed. (1998). *The Early Romantics: Perspectives in British Poetry from Pope to Wordsworth.* London: Macmillan.

PART FOUR
Genres and Modes

48

Pamphlets and News

Joad Raymond

a wise man will make better use of an idle pamphlet, than a fool will do of sacred
Scripture.

(Milton, *Areopagitica*, 1644)

Grubstreet! thy fall should men and Gods conspire.

(Pope, *The Dunciad*, 1742, 3, 311)

Not all of the denizens of 'Grub Street' were pot-poets or limping hacks. Probably the
most famous controversial pamphlet of the seventeenth century is *Areopagitica*, Milton's
redoubtable defence of the liberty of reading and therefore of liberty of the press from
pre-publication censorship. It was printed in small quarto and retailed at 4d. For Milton
the path to spiritual enlightenment needed no protection or authorization by an *impri-
matur*, and his evocation of a marketplace of print underscores the importance of pamphlets as a forum for the free and open encounter between truth and falsehood.

The experience of this marketplace, browsing through a bookseller's stall, or examining the wares of a hawker or mercury-woman, gave the word 'pamphlet' a more
concrete and tangible meaning than it retains today, when an abstract definition is
necessary. A pamphlet was a small vernacular book of a few sheets folded in quarto,
costing a few pennies, dealing with some topical or controversial subject in an accessible style, addressed to a broad readership and thus intended to have a popular effect.
A contemporary would have known a pamphlet by sight and touch, by the rough
paper, bold and simple title-page, crude typography and simple stitching; the sight
would have excited the itch of news. Newspapers initially assumed the same form as
pamphlets, served the same purpose and fed the same appetites, before diverging
through the later seventeenth and eighteenth centuries. Pamphlets, news and newspapers were closely associated, for which reason their history and nature are treated
together in this section.

The pamphlet format had first been developed for topical materials during the
1580s, and by the mid-seventeenth century a range of stylistic modes and typo-

graphical conventions had evolved with which even the barely literate might feel comfortable. All Hell broke loose in the summer of 1641, when incipient political conflict and instability in government control over stationers resulted in an outbreak of sensational political pamphlets. Speeches and proceedings in parliament, formerly jealously guarded, became increasingly available to the reading public, alongside other news and squibs on current affairs. Some pamphlets were soberly presented, if not always reliable; others were undisguised propaganda, and exploited the language of conflict and a diversity of literary forms, from the simple dialogue to Lucianic satire. In November 1641 the first printed weekly account of parliamentary news appeared; soon a London consumer could choose one of a dozen of these newspapers, or newsbooks as contemporaries described them, according to preference, availability and day of the week. Editors developed increasingly sophisticated ways of presenting the news, and within a decade advertising had joined news and editorials as a regular element of a newsbook. The modern trade in news had begun.

The shifting political culture of the seventeenth century was clearly reflected in, and perhaps amplified by, the novel prominence of pamphlets and news publications. The verbal energy of seventeenth-century pamphleteering, and the political tensions of civil war, pressured traditional literary writing into similar engagements, influencing style and subject matter. The polite and disciplined aesthetic of Caroline art was displaced by fiercer modes inclined to satire. Literary writing had become not just political, but often polemical.

Anxieties about change amplified scorn of the news culture. Satire of cheap print emerged with the Elizabethan pamphlet, but from the 1640s onwards 'Grub Street' became a powerful and enduring metaphor for the abuses of the printing press, a metaphor anchored in metropolitan geography and in popular fears of social upheaval and the decline of intellectual culture. It received its fullest exposition in Pope's mock-epic *The Dunciad* (1728–43), which maps out a literary and political topography, ridiculing critics, journalists, prolix versifiers and all varieties of hacks who live from hand to mouth in the parish of St Giles and worship the goddess Dulness.

Nonetheless, pamphlets and newspapers are not to be dismissed as worthless and ephemeral. Much satire of them is ambivalent, and praises, or offers thoughtful critique, while relying on the formulae of denunciation; and not without reason. The poetry of Andrew Marvell and John Dryden is inflected with the languages of journalism, and the early novelists of the eighteenth century were indebted not just to the markets for reading that these new modes of writing had generated, but to the plain prose styles, sense of time, interest in the details of contemporary daily life, and even to the techniques of reporting and narrative strategies developed in political pamphleteering and journalism. Many accomplished writers, including Henry Fielding, Tobias Smollett, Jonathan Swift, Daniel Defoe and Samuel Johnson, were involved in the periodical business. Pamphlets and news should be taken seriously as part of the literary culture of their day.

Pamphlets were heterogeneous in subject matter. Once the form had acquired its conventions anything could be squeezed into it. Many pamphlets were concerned with

politics in the traditional sense: parliamentary proceedings, speeches, royal proclamations, political manifestos, articles of agreement, proposals and counter-proposals,
character-sketches, accounts of military encounters at home and abroad. Some
extended to abstract political theory; others railed against the abuses of the times; and
yet more explored every shade between these contrasts. Pornographic writings, commercial proposals, complaints of the decay of manners and rise in wantonness, remarks
on fashions, reports of crimes, their punishments, scaffold speeches, tales of monstrous
births, and miracle cures were all published as pamphlets. The format of the brief,
small quarto was also used for sermons, many of which were conscious of the same
time-bound stories as news pamphlets; though perhaps diminished by the rise of the
pamphlet, the pulpit also served as a means of distributing news. The contents of
pamphlets reflected the preoccupations of seventeenth-century readers: news, politics
and religion.

For most of the late seventeenth and eighteenth centuries pamphlets were viewed
with a mixture of idealism and suspicion. Thus *Fog's Weekly Journal* (1729):

> Political Pamphlets are generally written for one or other of the following Purposes.
>
> *First*, In order to disabuse the Publick in Respect to some false Notions with which
> the People by the Artifices of designing Men may be possess'd, in prejudice to the *True
> Interest* of their *Country*, and then it is a *laudable, honest,* and *virtuous Occupation;*
>
> Or, *Secondly*, For the Service of some *Party, Faction*, or *particular Set of Men*, in which
> Case, they generally have a Tendency toward the deceiving and imposing upon Mankind,
> and then all the Cunning of which the *Author* is Master, is employ'd.

By 1641 the pamphlet was a thermometer of political temperature. Examinations of
press output for the seventeenth century suggest that in years of heightened political
expectations, such as 1641–2, 1648, 1659–60 and 1679–81, the number of items
produced by the press increased markedly. More modest fluctuations can be detected
in 1620, 1628 and 1630. It is probable that during these years fewer substantial folios
were produced, making way for more small and often short quarto books. The Popish
Plot of 1679–81, a period of relaxed press controls, witnessed a flood of pamphlets,
spreading fear of Catholic conspiracy on the one hand, and fear of a Puritan attempt
on the monarchy on the other. The Revolution of 1688 produced a surge of justifications and condemnations of the legitimacy of the new rulers. There were also some
smaller and more localized skirmishes, such as the controversy over standing armies
in 1697–9. The political arena had a developing annex in the marketplace of print.
Contemporaries recognized the pamphlet as a vehicle for the conduct of debate and
the expression and manipulation of public opinion.

The newspaper developed in parallel with the pamphlet, sharing commercial, social
and political concerns. During the eighteenth century pamphlets were increasingly
printed in a smaller, octavo format, though in other respects they remained more or
less the same in appearance between the 1640s and 1790s. Newspapers, on the
other hand, underwent a significant transformation from weekly quartos to multi-

columned, daily folios, similar to those with which we are familiar today. The news-books of the civil war were eight-page, numbered and dated pamphlets. They com-bined news (domestic and foreign), editorial and advertising in varying degrees; in this respect little changed for many decades. A formal alteration occurred with the appearance of the *London Gazette* (initially the *Oxford Gazette*) late in 1665, which was a bi-weekly news*paper*: a half sheet of paper printed in two columns on each side. It was an official publication and its near-monopoly position assisted its editors in their endeavour to manipulate readers according to government interests. Sales of the *Gazette*, reaching thousands, were accordingly higher than those of individual news-books in preceding years. The closed market persisted until 1679, when the Printing Act of 1662 lapsed, and popular rumour gave impetus to the news market.

Newspapers were internally heterogeneous, and so a reader would glean from one what she or he might gather from a number of pamphlets. Their editors or authors culled together, under pressures of time and deadlines, what copy they could from their sources: correspondence, oral report, personal observation and other publications. The demands of periodicity and the limitations of the printing press and distribution mechanisms shaped the form and the content of the newspaper. Some editors created room for literary self-consciousness, however, and the editorials of newsbooks and newspapers often sounded in a more powerful, theatrical voice than was found in most pamphlets. Newspapers covered the full breadth of the subjects treated in occasional pamphlets; other contents included advertisements offering goods and services for sale and noting lost property, and, occasionally, features such as puzzles and question-and-answer sections. A few periodicals were specialized: *The Philosophi-cal Transactions*, founded in 1666 by the London Royal Society, presented the latest discoveries in natural philosophy; *The Publick Adviser*, established in 1657, consisted entirely of advertisements, and operated in conjunction with a series of London information offices. Most, however, were more general and juxtaposed a diversity of materials.

This miscellaneousness, which was an effect of the exigencies of periodicity, had far-reaching implications: the periodical created a space which could be exploited for all manner of news and non-news related items. The title of John Dunton's *The Night-Walker; or, Evening Rambles in search after lewd Women* (1696–7) is self-explanatory; *The English Lucian* (1698) also offered essays on titbits, the city and its vices. *The Athen-ian Mercury*, which appeared weekly between 1691 and 1697, invited and answered questions on any subject, from '*Whether there is a Philosophers Stone?*', through '*How many Angels fell in the Rebellion?*' to '*Why do you trouble yourselves and the World with answering so many silly Questions?*'. These questions, presented anonymously, were answered by an 'Athenian society', a glamorous mask disguising a committee con-sisting of the bookseller Dunton and a handful of friends. *The Athenian Mercury* looked forward to the literary periodicals and monthly reviews of the eighteenth century, which took advantage of the periodical form for new purposes. In 1691 Dunton set aside one issue per month to answer only questions asked by women. He thus antici-pated his own *Ladies Mercury* (1693) in providing a space exclusively (in practice probably not) for women, implying that there might be a discrepancy in the abilities or needs of the sexes. This then paved the way for *The Female Tatler* (1709–10), *The Young Ladies' Miscellany* (1723), *The Female Spectator* (1744–6) and *The Lady's Magazine* (1770–1832), periodicals which envisaged a set of interests for women discrete from those of male readers. Women had long been involved in the book trade, as printers, publishers, mercury-women, readers and authors. The emergence of a press apparently specifying women as an audience may reflect the general expansion of the book trade to a point at which a journal for women was commercially viable; or the changing place of women in the spheres of business and public life; or it may reflect shifting expectations of gender roles.

The Athenian Mercury solicited its questions through coffee-houses. Pamphlets and newspapers were linked to other social spaces in which news was gathered and disseminated: including coffee-houses, the Exchange, St Paul's, marketplaces, bookseller's stalls, alehouses, and, later, newsrooms, where papers could be read or borrowed for a fee. Visitors to these spaces would exchange news and opinion, fostering interest in current affairs, sometimes generating copy for pamphlets and papers. Oral, printed and manuscript exchange worked in concert. A 1647 pamphlet reported suggestively: 'When I was lately in *London*, as I passed by *Pauls* churchyard, I spyed a friend in a Stationer's Shop, who, after salutes passed, with some briefe discourse of the times, informed mee of some late newes out of Italy arrived at his hands in a Letter from a friend.' Coffee-houses, which rose to prominence in the second half of the seventeenth century, were intimately linked with the fortunes of the newspaper. The two-way relationship was indicated in *The Weekly Comedy. As it is Dayly Acted at Most Coffee-houses in London* (1699), and in the peripatetic essays in Ned Ward's monthly *The London Spy* (1698–1700). Mr Spectator, the voice of the eponymous literary periodical, presented himself as a frequenter of coffee-houses. Their busy, gossipy atmosphere was evoked, usually satirically, in many pamphlets and poems. They became 'the Schools of Town Politics', instructing talkative 'coffee-house politicians' in the news and politics of their day.

Another external force shaping the evolution of the press was licensing legislation. The final expiration of the 1662 Printing Act in 1695 loosened the formal controls on the press, though its consequences have been greatly exaggerated, along with the efficacy of pre-publication licensing. During 1681–5 Charles II was able to keep a tight rein on the press while the licensing laws remained inactive because other forms of supervision and the threat of post-publication prosecution were effective as a means of curbing the press. Legal and economic constraints did not cease in 1695. Obscenity and libel laws, open to political application, exerted an influence out of proportion to their infrequent use. In 1707 a new Treason Act was introduced; in 1719 it took its only victim, the journeyman printer of a Jacobite pamphlet. Many other stationers were arrested for their role in publishing and distributing the pamphlet. In 1726 a system for monitoring the contents of the provincial press was introduced. Licensing was only one aspect of government control of the press, and the parliament who let the Printing Act lapse had no intention of permitting unconditional liberty of printing. Jacobitism and, later, Jacobinism were focuses of subsequent government interventions, interventions which often proved successful.

Economic restrictions also influenced the press, and these did not end in 1695. Many journals were run at a small profit, and the transience of many titles indicates the vulnerability of the enterprise. Publishing newspapers became an increasingly specialized area of the book trade, and stationers collaborated in syndicates or 'congers' in order to pool resources. From the stationers' perspective the situation worsened when the Stamp Act of 1712 imposed duties on each copy of a newspaper sold, on each advertisement, and on each edition of a pamphlet. A loophole in the Act was revised in 1725; a second Act doubled the duties in 1757, and its application was refined in 1773. Stamp Duty struck hard upon the precarious economics of the newspaper: Swift mourned ambivalently 'the Parliament has killed all the Muses of Grubstreet'. He exaggerated, but the duty ensured that subsidies would play an important part in the future of newspapers.

The 1690s did, however, see the beginning of the most important changes to the newspaper since the 1640s, in a gradually expanding market, a differentiation between products, increasing frequency and geographical diversification. In 1695 three tri-weeklies appeared, supplementing the bi-weekly *London Gazette*: these were *The Post-Man* (–1730), *The Post-Boy* (–1736) and *The Flying Post* (–1735). The first successful daily paper, *The Daily Courant*, appeared in 1702 (a near-daily newsbook had appeared for just over three weeks in 1660). In 1706 the first evening paper, the *Evening Post*, appeared; it was soon supplemented by others. A greater variety of periodicity entered into the trade: soon there were dailies, morning and evening, bi-weeklies, tri-weeklies, fortnightlies and monthlies. The first Sunday paper appeared in 1779, prompting further recriminations against the profanation of the Sabbath. Many papers recycled materials from other papers; the *Daily Journal* commented in 1721, 'whoever has seen two or three of 'em has seen them all'. Newspapers offered a diversity of products, from plain news to weekly essays on cultural concerns. Most offered a recipe with three ingredients: news (foreign and/or domestic), editorial and advertising. Dailies tended not to offer essays, and increasingly lost the front-page editorial; and the weekly essay papers offered neither news nor advertising. In general, increasing space was devoted to advertising. The eighteenth century also saw the introduction of more sports news, especially racing, cricket and boxing. Specialist periodicals developed from this: *The Historical List of all Horse-Matches Run* (1733) and *The Racing Calendar* (1769).

Notwithstanding such product differentiation, political parties played an increasing role in the editing and financing of the press. In the 1700s Robert Harley established a propaganda machine which instead of simply repressing the opposition, systematically employed the press for his own ends. Sir Robert Walpole further developed this approach, and during the 1730s the key to controlling the press became not prosecutions but the allocation of subsidies, pensions and bribes. When Walpole fell from power it was found that he had spent £50,000 managing the press between 1731 and 1741. Contemporaries had anticipated that the figure would be higher.

The expansion of the press was also reflected in the appearance of the first provincial newspaper, the *Norwich Post* in 1701 (though Oxford-centred 'national' newsbooks were published in Oxford during the 1640s). Other cities soon followed, indicating that the flow of newspapers from London into the provinces had laid sound foundations for local enterprise. Fifteen weekly provincial newspapers had been established by 1712, though economic precariousness and the impact of the Stamp Act left just four remaining at the end of that year. The provincial papers repeated news and editorials from the London press, but they also purveyed local news, became involved in local disputes, and were sensitive to the needs of local readers. London remained the centre of news and the news trade, as it was the nexus of trade routes and the focus of politics and fashion, but this probably supported as much as it challenged regionalism. London coffee-houses soon stocked provincial papers. The mutual trade in news enhanced the sense of belonging to a nation.

Scotland and Ireland already had an indigenous news trade. *The Irish Monthly Mercury* was printed by the invading English at Cork in December 1649 and January 1650. *An Account of the Chief Occurrences of Ireland* followed in Dublin in 1660, then *Mercurius Hibernicus* in 1663. A handful of others ensued, some reprints of English and Scottish texts; the trade gained pace with *The News-Letter* (1685–6), and by the turn of the century Dublin readers had a choice of titles. Limerick, Cork, Waterford, Belfast and Derry followed hesitantly through the next century. Between the 1720s and the 1740s the Irish periodical press developed literary and controversial journals, along the lines of the English.

The newspaper in Scotland began as Edinburgh reprints of London newsbooks of the 1640s. The first London newsbook, *Heads of Severall Proceedings* of 22–9 November 1641, was reprinted at Edinburgh, and was followed by others, more numerous than long-lived. *Mercurius Scoticus*, edited and printed in Leith, appeared briefly in 1651; the first long-lived Scottish newsbook was a reprint of London's *Mercurius Politicus*, printed at Edinburgh and Leith between 1653 and 1660. The first durable Scottish paper with distinctly Scottish interest was the bi-weekly *Edinburgh Gazette*, founded in 1699. By the middle of the eighteenth century Edinburgh, Glasgow and Aberdeen had an established news trade, with the *Edinburgh Evening Courant* (1718–1886) and *Caledonian Mercury* (1720–1867), the *Glasgow Journal* (1741–?1841) and *Glasgow Courant* (1745–60), and the *Aberdeen Intelligencer* (1752–7) and *Aberdeen Journal* (1748–). Edinburgh also produced literary magazines, including the patriotic *Scots Magazine* (1739–1826), offering a Scottish perspective on British writers. Dundee, Perth, Dumfries, Kelso and Berwick also produced long-lived periodicals.

Curiously Wales did not follow this pattern. The first Welsh periodical was *Tlysau yr hen oesoedd* ('Gems of Past Ages'), printed in Holyhead in 1735. This was followed in 1770 by *Trysorfa gwybodaeth, neu eurgrawn Cymraeg* ('Treasury of Knowledge, or Welsh Magazine'), then in 1793 by *Y Cylchgrawn Cymraeg* ('The Welsh Magazine'). The first, and apparently premature, English-language periodical in Wales was *The Cambrian Magazine*, two issues of which were printed at Llandovery in 1773. In

contrast to Ireland and Scotland, the indigenous Welsh-language periodical preceded
the English-language press, and the literary magazine arrived before the newspaper.
The news press did not develop in Wales until the nineteenth century, the golden age
of Welsh printing; until then the Welsh were satisfied with imports.

By the mid-seventeenth century the distribution networks (mainly carriers and the
penny post) were already in place to ensure that news publications reached a broad
audience. The built-in obsolescence of newspapers limited the extent of the dissemination of any single issue, whereas some pamphlets turned into runaway successes,
with multiple editions. One extreme case was Dr Henry Sacheverell's notorious
sermon at St Paul's in 1710, in which the Tory minister railed against Dissenters; over
thirteen months his sermon ran to fourteen editions, and it was said to have sold
40,000 copies within a few days. It provoked dozens of responses and counter-
responses, and his trial prompted even more; hundreds of items in all, some brief,
some long, some sermons, some satires. Many pamphlets, however, were printed in
editions of as low as 250, and reached a smaller audience than newspapers; and
through the eighteenth century periodicals partly displaced occasional pamphlets as
vehicles for polemic. The print-run for a pamphlet or newsbook from the 1640s could
be as low as 200, and 1,500 was the upper limit for most editions. Expansion
happened in fits and starts, though the overall pattern was upward between the mid-
seventeenth and late eighteenth century. In the early years of the eighteenth century
the London dailies could reach into the thousands, though sales of fewer than a thousand remained common. Provincial newspapers of the 1710s were printed in runs as
small as 200–300; within two decades figures had risen to as high as 1,000–2,000.
The increase was not universal: Defoe's influential *Review* (1704–12) was printed in
editions of 400–500. However, Addison reported that 3,000 copies of his *Spectator*
were distributed, and that by 'a modest Computation' each reached about twenty
readers, hence 'I may reckon about Three-score thousand Disciples in *London* and *Westminster*'. The *Craftsman* (1726–47), the opposition paper which attracted many readers
to its attacks on Walpole's ministry, sometimes reached sales of 10,000; a similar figure
was estimated by Dr Johnson for the *Gentleman's Magazine*, the most successful of the
monthlies that thrived during the 1730s. Total figures offer some guide to the overall
circulation of newspapers, though they must be treated with care, as they are gathered from different sources and are potentially unreliable. With these caveats it can
be noted that in 1704 approximate sales of all newspapers were in the region of two-
and-a-quarter million; in 1712 between three-and-a-half and four million; in 1750
in the order of seven-and-a-half million, reaching to fourteen million by 1780, and
by 1851 total sales had reached eighty-five million.

It is not fanciful to infer from these figures that the influence of the newspaper was
disseminating further down the social hierarchy. As Addison suggested, each copy of
a paper might reach numerous readers, ensuring a far greater audience than modest
print-runs promised. Customers of coffee-houses, at the cost of a penny for their sober
drink, could peruse the day's and week's papers for hours, if they had the time. Charles
Leslie wrote in the preface to the first collected volume of *The Rehearsal* (1708):

the greatest Part of the *People* do not Read *Books*, Most of them cannot *Read* at all. But they will Gather together about one that can *Read*, and Listen to an *Observator* or *Review* (as I have seen them in the streets) where all the *Principles* of *Rebellion* are Instill'd into them.

The continuity in stereotypical and formulaic complaint about the pernicious effects of the popular press makes it difficult to asses the extent of real change. There is some consensus that the social status of the audience was diverse. In 1650 Marchamont Nedham planned a newsbook because he wished to sway the 'Vulgar Judgements' of the 'Multitude'. In 1678 Henry Care wrote in the first issue of his newsbook, *The Weekly Pacquet of Advice from Rome*:

> This good Design may possibly seem contemptible by being Attempted in a Pamphlet-course; but 'tis considered, that though there be good Books enow abroad, yet every Mans Purse will not allow him to buy, nor his Time permit him to read, nor perhaps his Understanding reach to comprehend large and elaborate Treaties. This Method is therefore chosen, as most likely to fall into Vulgar hands, and agreeable to their circumstance, who have most need of such Assistances.

He spoke to 'the middle or meaner Rank'. In 1725 Nathaniel Mist, in *Mist's Weekly Journal* (1725–8; previously *The Weekly Journal*, 1716–25; continued as *Fog's Weekly Journal*, 1728–37), identified 'the middling and poorer sort of People' as the general readers of newspapers. The *British Observator* (1733–5) claimed to speak to 'The middle part of mankind'. Contemporaries also agreed that the weekly periodicals containing essays and literary discussions were consumed by a more elite audience.

This breadth of audience led to concerns over influence, both literary and political. Though the news periodical led to such worthy projects as *The Spectator*, which purveyed Addison's superb essays on literature, it was widely perceived as an antagonist to literary endeavour. The tradition stems from the civil war, when an increasingly pessimistic royalist party identified vulgar printed matter as the natural ally of the parliamentary cause, and themselves as the true preservers of aesthetics, foredoomed by the times. A 1645 pamphlet-poem, *The Great Assises Holden in Parnassus*, written by an avid reader of newsbooks, lamented that the press, 'This instrument of Art, is now possest / By some, who have in Art no interest.' Poetry was integral to the pamphlets and newsbooks of the 1640s, and the inexpensive pamphlet became a conventional medium for publishing a poem, particularly one concerned, like Dryden's *Absalom and Achitophel* (1681), with contemporary politics. Pope's *Dunciad* saw in bad poets and journalists the same prostitution of the muse in the unprincipled and ill-educated pursuit of a living:

Hence Journals, Medleys, Merc'ries, Magazines:
Sepulchral Lyes, our holy walls to grace,
And New-year Odes, and all the Grub-street race.

(ll. 42–4)

Poets' descriptions, however hostile, can evoke a sense of the dynamism of the eighteenth-century news media, and the excitement they elicited. George Crabbe's poem *The Newspaper* (1785) captures both their physical presence and their Babelish impact:

> I sing of NEWS, and all those vapid sheets
> The rattling hawker vends through gasping streets;
> Whate'er their name, whate'er the time they fly,
> Damp from the press, to charm the reader's eye:
> For soon as Morning dawns with roseate hue,
> The HERALD of the morn arises too;
> POST after POST succeeds, and, all day long,
> GAZETTES and LEDGERS swarm, a noisy throng.
> When evening comes, she comes with all her train
> Of LEDGERS, CHRONICLES, and POSTS again.

Though newspapers roused his poem, Crabbe claims they 'banish every Muse'. He also testified to their impact upon the provinces, where newspapers bred 'the Whig farmer and the Tory swain'; and he suggested that those 'who abhor a book' and ignore the Bible nonetheless 'think it hard to be denied their News'. In fact many poems, most paradoxically *The Dunciad* itself, were inspired by matters read in newspapers. A quote from *The Dunciad* prefaced *The Grub Street Journal* (1730–7), a lively literary magazine which was, through many layers of irony, a continuation of Pope's war with the Dunces by another means. Some poets published in newspapers: William Wordsworth in the *Morning Post* (1772–1937) and Robert Burns in the *Caledonian Mercury*. The interaction between traditional muses and the new printed media, the concrete detail they offered and the sense of change they provoked, could be fertile.

The social and political influence of pamphlets is contested. Studies of public opinion during the Popish Plot, and during the allegiance controversy of 1688–9, suggest that the political pamphlet was already capable of exerting a significant influence over a broad spectrum of the public. *The Tatler* defined its potential audience in 1709 as 'Politick Persons, who are so publick-spirited as to neglect their own Affairs to look into Transactions of State', and evidence for circulation indicates that newspapers and pamphlets had the potential to play an important role in governing and manipulating opinion. Yet studies of public opinion focus on particular moments of crisis, and may not reflect the permanent condition of the power of the press; more large-scale research on individual and collective responses to propaganda and news is necessary before the authority of the fourth estate is fully appreciated.

Printing nevertheless seemed fundamental to radical groups who could not hope to participate in government through channels of patronage or personal influence. The careful coordination of public demonstrations and printed petitions and pamphlets had been central to the success of the Leveller movement in the late 1640s and early 1650s. Two of the longer-lasting opposition journals of the early eighteenth century, *Mist's Weekly Journal* and the *London Evening Post*, were perceived to play a role in keeping the excesses of the Whig ministry in check; and it was during the periods of their most vociferous censuring that they seem to have sold most copiously. A similar popularity was enjoyed by 'Cato's Letters', a column by John Trenchard and Thomas Gordon in the *London Journal* between 1720 and 1722. These were then reprinted in book form (as were many periodical essays). The cry of 'Wilkes and Liberty' would not have been heard were it not for the careful use of the printing press, and the exploitation of both the periodical and pamphlet by the Aylesbury MP and his followers. John Wilkes founded the weekly *North Briton* in 1762 as a counterblast to *The Briton* (1762–3), pro-Bute propaganda by Tobias Smollett. *The North Briton* remonstrated against George III, his family and his ministry, and in 1763 issue 45 led to the arrest of Wilkes (and many others) for libel. Wilkes became a popular hero, and 'No. 45' emerged as a reformist slogan; this was an expressive change from a decade earlier, when the slogan 'the '45' had quite different connotations, and the Jacobite press received most hostile attention from the government.

Wilkes' cause raised the pressure for fuller reports on parliamentary proceedings. Strict controls were restored to such reporting after 1660. Several magazines offered accounts during parliamentary recesses in the early eighteenth century, but in 1738 the loophole which permitted this was closed. Thereafter magazines resorted to the use of fictional devices: *The Gentleman's Magazine* published the debates of 'The Senate of Lilliput'. Between 1768 and 1774, a period of expansion of newspapers, the press began to infringe upon parliamentary privilege; the Commons offered a limited resistance, and then accepted this new franchise of the press. James Boswell, in his *Life of Johnson* (1791), celebrated this 'unrestrained freedom, so that the people in all parts of the kingdom have a fair, open, and exact report of the actual proceedings of their representatives and legislators, which in our constitution is highly to be valued; though', he added with a note of caution, 'unquestionably, there has of late been too much reason to complain of the petulance with which obscure scribblers have presumed to treat men of the most respectable character and situation'.

The combination of this belief in the right of public access to information concerning government and the close association between certain radical groups and the press, resulted in a rhetoric that freely associated the liberty of the press with other liberties. An editorial in the *London Evening Post* in 1754 (reprinted in the *Salisbury Journal*) opined:

> Those who declaim against the *Liberties* taken by *News Papers*, in representing Grievances, proposing Remedies, and censuring Persons, know not what they say, or what they mean: it is *this Liberty*, that not only protects the *rest*, but without *this Liberty*, the constitutional *Levity* of our *Government* would be *prejudicial* to the *Subject*; the *News Papers* expose *Crimes*, detect *Impositions*, bring *Contrivances* to *Light* that would be too *high*, too *low*, or too *hard* for the LAWS, and *Impunity* would render *intolerable*.

The newspaper perceived itself and was perceived as 'the History of the present Times' (*Mist's Weekly Journal*, 28 July 1722), not only in the metropolis, but, as Johnson commented in the *Idler* (no. 30, 1758), 'almost every large town has its weekly historian'. Nonetheless, many, especially in the radical press, deployed historical examples for evidence of the dangers of despotism, especially in the form of an encroachment on civil liberty and the liberty of the press. The letters of 'Junius' in *The Public Advertiser* in 1769 warned the King to listen to 'the complaints of your people', and gestured to the precedent of the Stuarts: 'The Prince who imitates their conduct . . . should remember that as [the crown] was acquired by one revolution, it may be lost by another.' The first issue of *The Whisperer* in 1770 compared popular opposition to the 'arbitrary proceedings' of Charles I with those of 'G—— the t——', and offered itself as a public voice to expose these infringements. While there was no serious attempt to write a history of the newspaper in Britain until George Chalmers' *The Life of Thomas Ruddiman* (1794), essayists looked back to the Stuart revolutions as milestones on the road to the liberty of the press.

Such associations were enhanced by the English counter-revolutionary campaign that followed the French Revolution. During the 1790s the press gained a radical, dynamic edge evocative of the 1640s, one which impressed itself on the imagination of William Blake. One of John Thelwall's formidable lectures, serialized in his weekly paper *The Tribune* (1795–6), explored the 'Differences between the English Revolution of 1649, and that of France, in 1792', and, surreptitiously, the parallels between England in the seventeenth century and in the 1790s:

> Charles I shut up the coffee-houses, lest sedition, as it is called, should be talked . . . The elastic spring of British energy was not destroyed. The more it was compressed, the greater its reaction.

Parliament took action against the printers, publishers and authors of radical sentiments: initial moves in 1792 were followed by a series of arrests (including Thelwall's), and by more extensive legislation against the press in 1797–9.

A 1794 trial suggests the continuities in the role of pamphlets and news periodicals between the 1640s and the 1790s. A speech purportedly made by 'Citizen Thelwall', relating the fable of the execution of a tyrannical rooster, 'King Chanticleer', appeared in one of the most spectacular of the weekly papers of the 1790s, *Politics for the People: Or, A Salmagundy for Swine* (1793–5), edited and published by Daniel Isaac Eaton. Eaton's title responded to Edmund Burke's expostulations against the 'swinish multitude', and he offered a lively blend of radical politics, satire and rhetorical virtuosity. Eaton was charged with libel for this two-pence 'pamphlet', as the prosecution called it, reflecting the close association that still obtained between occasional pamphlets and periodicals. The counsel for the prosecution complained:

> it is calculated to find it's way among the lowest of the people, and to excite them to discontents and commotions, such and such only can be it's purpose; the very nature of the publication, the price, the title of it, all manifest this. (*The Trial of Daniel Isaac Eaton*, 1794)

The counsel's words attest to widespread perceptions of the power of cheap print, its readership, and its association with radical politics. The defence's response endorsed these perceptions, but with an entirely different perspective on the benefits of polemical intervention in public, which, aside from its secularism, is the heir of Milton's defence of publication in *Areopagitica*:

> Political pamphlets, I think, should be cheap. I am very sure that public order and tranquility will never be maintained so well as when every man reads and understands political pamphlets, because there is no obedience to law so exemplary, there is no attachment to a good constitution so strong, as that which results from a knowledge of the reason and obligation of the law, and the true principles as well as beneficial effects of the constitution.

During the seventeenth and eighteenth centuries the pamphlet developed as an important form for the communication of news, politics and theology; as such it had a transformative impact, if sometimes subliminal, on literary writing. It was defined both by its physical format and appearance and by its engagement with topical matters of public concern, but also by a series of engaging styles, some demotic, some self-conscious. During the same period the newspaper was invented and developed into something like its modern form. Initially as an adjunct to the newspaper, critical journals and weekly reviews appeared, and the critic was eventually accepted as a legitimate mediator between author and reader. Journalism also emerged as a real mode of writing, polemical, plain, sometimes breathless, occasionally disposed to strategic allegory and allusion. In time, nineteenth-century historians began to appreciate the historical significance of the popular press, and linked it to the growth of democracy, attributing to apparently ephemeral publications the dignity demanded in *Areopagitica*. Men and gods did not conspire the fall of Grub Street, but in 1830 it was renamed Milton Street.

REFERENCES AND FURTHER READING

Black, Jeremy (1987). *The English Press in the Eighteenth Century*. London and Sydney: Croom Helm.

Craig, Mary Elizabeth (1931). *The Scottish Periodical Press, 1750–1789*. Edinburgh: Oliver and Boyd.

Cranfield, Geoffrey A. (1962). *The Development of the Provincial Newspaper, 1700–1760*. Oxford: Clarendon.

——(1978). *The Press & Society: From Caxton to Northcliffe*. London: Longmans.

Downie, J. A. (1979). *Robert Harley and the Press: Propaganda and Public Opinion in the Age of Swift and Defoe*. Cambridge: Cambridge University Press.

Downie, J. A. and Thomas N. Corns, eds (1993). *Telling People What to Think: Early Eighteenth-century Periodicals from 'The Review' to 'The Rambler'*. London: Frank Cass; and *Prose Studies* 16.

Ferdinand, C. Y. (1997). *Benjamin Collins and the Provincial Newspaper Trade in the Eighteenth Century*. Oxford: Clarendon.

Frank, Joseph (1961). *The Beginnings of the English Newspaper, 1620–1660*. Cambridge, Mass.: Harvard University Press.

Habermas, Jürgen (1989). *The Structural Transformation of the Public Sphere: An Inquiry into a Category of Bourgeois Society.* Trans. Thomas Burger. Cambridge, Mass.: MIT Press. Original work published (1962).

Hanson, Laurence (1936). *The Government and the Press, 1695–1763.* Oxford: Clarendon.

Harris, Michael (1987). *London Newspapers in the Age of Walpole : A Study of the Origins of the Modern English Press.* Rutherford, N.J. and London: Fairleigh Dickinson University Press.

Llyfrddiaeth cylchgronau Cymreig 1735–1850: A Bibliography of Welsh Periodicals 1735–1850. (1993). Aberystwyth: Llyfrgell Genedlaethol Cymru.

McDowell, Paula (1998). *The Women of Grub Street: Press, Politics, and Gender in the London Literary Marketplace 1678–1730.* Oxford: Clarendon.

Munter, Robert (1967). *The History of the Irish Newspaper, 1685–1760.* Cambridge: Cambridge University Press.

Nelson, Carolyn and Matthew Seccombe (1986). *Periodical Publications 1641–1700: A Survey with Illustrations.* Oxford: Occasional Papers of the Bibliographical Society, 2.

Nelson, Carolyn and Matthew Seccombe (1987). *British Newspapers and Periodicals: A Short Title Catalogue.* New York: Modern Language Association of America.

Raymond, Joad (1996). *The Invention of the Newspaper: English Newsbooks, 1641–1660.* Oxford: Clarendon.

Raymond, Joad, ed. (1999). *News, Newspapers and Society in Early Modern Britain.* London: Frank Cass; and *Prose Studies* 21.

Rea, Robert R. (1963). *The English Press in Politics 1760–1774.* Lincoln: University of Nebraska Press.

Rogers, Pat (1972). *Grub Street: Studies in a Subculture.* London: Methuen.

Siebert, F. S. (1952). *Freedom of the Press in England 1476–1776: The Rise and Decline of Government Controls.* Urbana: University of Illinois Press.

Smith, Nigel (1994). *Literature and Revolution in England, 1640–1660.* New Haven and London: Yale University Press.

Sutherland, James (1986). *The Restoration Newspaper and its Development.* Cambridge: Cambridge University Press.

Tercentenary Handlist of English & Welsh Newspapers, Magazines & Reviews (1920). London: Published for *The Times* by Hodder and Stoughton.

Wiles, R. M. (1965). *Freshest Advices: Early Provincial Newspapers in England.* Columbus, Oh.: Ohio State University Press.

49

Political Writing

David Wootton

In 1776 a recent immigrant from England to Philadelphia published *Common Sense*, a small pamphlet which immediately became a runaway success, and inaugurated the age of democratic revolutions in which we still live. For Tom Paine it was common sense that monarchy was not an efficient form of government, that government should represent the people, and that, if a government refused to respect the wishes of the people, it should be overthrown by revolution. He believed, in short, in popular self-government through representation. He took it for granted that a self-governing people would allow each individual freedom of religious conscience and of expression, yet if we go back to 1640 very different principles would have seemed common sense. Everyone (or very nearly everyone) would then have agreed that human beings are wicked, and therefore ought not to choose those who rule over them; that rulers should answer only to God, not to their subordinates; and that, since monarchy most closely resembles God's own rule, it is therefore the best form of government. And everyone (with the exception of a few, mostly exiles in Holland or America) would have agreed that membership of the established church should be compulsory, and that church and state both had the right to restrict freedom of speech. Could one have carried Paine's little pamphlet back in time to 1640, the individual words and sentences (with few exceptions) would have made sense to an educated reader, but the argument would have appeared mere nonsense. What we have to chart, therefore, is the process whereby one kind of common sense – that expressed in theories of divine right monarchy – was replaced, at least for some people, by another – that articulated by Paine. It is true that most Englishmen (unlike Americans) would not have found Paine's views persuasive, but the mixed constitution, the limited monarchy which they took for granted would have been scarcely more comprehensible to an Englishman from 1640 than the arguments of the American revolutionaries, and the American and French Revolutions delayed, but did not halt, the seemingly inexorable process whereby Painite arguments came to be accepted (though not until the twentieth century) even in conservative England.

The disappearance of divine right monarchy is not the only major transformation that took place in this period, indeed it was only made possible by three other, inter-related cultural shifts – the rise of egocentric, market-oriented, and sentimental ways of thinking. Our period also saw a major alteration in the governing metaphors which could be used to conceptualize politics. Images drawn from the human body and from cosmology, both as understood by ancient Greek and Roman scientists, were slowly replaced by a new language of mechanism, of motivation (above all of self-interest), and (drawn from economic thinking) of unintended consequences. The new physics, the birth of psychology, and the emergence of political economy meant that politics was now discussed within an entirely new intellectual framework.

It is conventional to say that modern political theory begins with the composition of Machiavelli's *Prince* (*c.*1511) and More's *Utopia* (1516). The first invented the notion that politics is primarily a study of how power is used in practice, not of how people would like it to be used. The second argued that any satisfactory account of how power ought to be used would require us to reject all our existing political institutions. Thus was born a fundamental dichotomy between realism and utopianism, a dichotomy which brought about the slow demise of traditional formats for discussing politics – such as books on the education of the prince – which had assumed a fundamental harmony between the realistic and the moral.

Much political thought in our period is post-Machiavellian: often it is concerned with what is called 'reason of state', the rational calculations of rulers seeking to max-imize their power at home and abroad; a tradition that leads just outside our period to Clausewitz. Even theorists who never mention Machiavelli, such as Hobbes (q.v.) seem to take for granted a Machiavellian view of human nature as involved in an unceasing quest to maximize power and security. And much of it, by contrast, is utopian – from Winstanley (*Law of Freedom*, 1652) to Proudhon, with Godwin (*Politi-cal Justice*, 1793) in between, theorists followed More in attacking contemporary society for pitting individuals against each other rather than seeking to maximize the welfare and happiness of society as a whole. We can imagine Machiavelli reading Clausewitz, or More reading Godwin, and, eventually, making sense of their succes-sors; but neither of them would have known where to begin if presented with a copy of Paine, since Paine is barely interested in what both the Machiavellian and utopian traditions took to be a fundamental task: that of creating rulers and citizens with the right moral qualities. Political theory as we know it today may be indebted to the Renaissance, but it is in large part the creation of the English Civil War, the Scottish Enlightenment, and the French Revolution. Let us consider these three influences in turn.

When the English Civil War broke out in 1642, theorists on both sides had at their disposal an extensive armoury of arguments. Most of the issues had previously been faced during the French wars of religion, and arguments for royal authority, a mixed constitution, historical precedent and even tyrannicide could be reconstructed on the basis of French examples. Further back, exactly the same issues had been at the heart of the disputes between the popes and church councils during the middle ages. The arguments of medieval canon lawyers were still alive in 1642, although translated from Latin into English and from religious into secular terms.

By 1660 much had changed. First, the modern theory of revolution was born. Before 1642 there were a number of arguments available to support resistance against tyranny. But the universal assumption was that once a tyrant was deposed the original constitution must be restored – there was an immensely strong presumption in favour of historical continuity and against radical change. As the royalists appeared on the brink of victory in the winter of 1642–3, and parliament appeared prepared to settle, and to abandon key opponents of the monarchy who would inevitably be executed, a group of diehards argued that if parliament allied with the king to become an instrument of tyranny then the people would be back in a state of nature: entitled to resist all established authority and to establish a new constitution (should they survive – they well knew the most likely outcome was hanging). This argument, that power can revert to the people, who are not bound by the decisions of their ancestors, is the modern, Painite argument for self-government and revolution, and was powerfully restated a few years later by the Levellers. On the basis of this claim to popular sovereignty it is fairly easy to claim, as the Levellers did, that virtually every adult male should have the vote, for it is hard to see otherwise how government can be made responsive to the will of the people. Moreover, the Levellers not only insisted that the right of revolution was inalienable; the same was true, they said, of the right to freedom of conscience. The state was thus to be detached from divine authority, and turned into a secular institution.

Second, the king, who had often claimed to be God's representative on earth, was tried and executed in 1649. When monarchy was restored in 1660 the theory of divine right monarchy was also brought back to life; so much so that Locke wrote his *First Treatise* (c.1682) in opposition to Sir Robert Filmer's *Patriarcha*, a work which was written (though not published) before the Civil War and which insisted that God had made clear his preference for hereditary absolute monarchy when he made Adam lord of all he surveyed. But the Revolution of 1688 was a further blow against divine right monarchy, which thereafter was upheld only by Jacobites and non-Jurors. After the final defeat of Jacobitism in 1746, divine right theories were an anachronism throughout the English-speaking world. Divine right theory was tied up with a traditional way of thinking about the world in which the microcosm (the human body) was analogous to the macrocosm (the Ptolemaic universe, with the earth at its centre), and both were similar to the body politic. Thus the king was comparable to the head on the body, with the right to take all decisions, and to the sun in the heavens, before whom all stars disappeared from the sky. Like the head, his function was to rule over the lower parts; like the sun he was an emblem of God himself. The demise of divine right political theory implied a new view of human nature and of the cosmos: John Aubrey tells us that it was only after the execution of the king that most people were willing to believe the Copernican theory that the earth goes round the sun.

Third, after the victory of the parliamentary side in the Civil War, James Harrington (*Oceana*, 1656) was the first to seek to adapt republican principles to fit the nation-state. Prior to the Civil War republicans had always thought in terms of city-states, where citizens were capable of participating in politics on their own behalf. In monarchies, on the other hand, representative institutions had no continuing existence – in England, parliament never met between 1629 and 1640, while in France the Estates General failed to meet for almost two hundred years – so that the representatives of the people were incapable of exercising control over the administration of government. Harrington was the first to conceive of a representative republic where the executive was subordinate to the legislature. With Harrington, elections become the key moment in the political process.

Fourth, Harrington produced a general theory of political order. According to him, the distribution of wealth in society – in particular of landed wealth, for it is land that feeds soldiers and cavalry horses – determines the distribution of power. The English Revolution was, in Harrington's view, the result of a slow transfer of landed wealth from aristocracy to gentry which had taken place over several hundred years. Harrington, drawing on Machiavelli, opens the way to the sociological interpretation of politics which we later find in Montesquieu and the Scottish Enlightenment.

The demise of divine right theory, the modern theory of popular sovereignty, a representative republic, and an economic account of political power: these were major and adaptable innovations to which other figures made significant contributions. Thus Hobbes played his part in attacking divine right theory, while seeking to ground a new absolutism in a modified theory of popular sovereignty – with the result that neither monarchists nor republicans could approve his views. Instead Harrington's successors (known to recent scholarship as the neo-Harringtonians) adapted Harrington's theories to allow for the Restoration of both the king and the House of Lords, arguing that a monarchy where Lords and Commons each had a decisive role was the best and most stable form of government.

Underlying these intellectual developments we can see the beginnings of broader, more amorphous cultural changes. Hobbes believed that all human beings are machines, and that the state should be an artificial mechanism; this argument was taken up by Harrington who believed that a well-constructed state would be able to endure indefinitely. Previous ways of thinking about government had relied on organic metaphors; but this new emphasis on mechanical metaphors does not simply reflect a new way of thinking about politics. Rather, it is a new way of thinking *tout court*: we can trace its development in the introduction of new words: mechanics (1648), mechanism (1662), mechanize (1678). Mechanized systems have to be self-correcting, and they are therefore a precondition for the idea that the market is a self-correcting mechanism, a precondition for economic thought as we now understand it, which first makes its appearance in Adam Smith's *Wealth of Nations* (1776 – the same year as Paine's *Common Sense*).

Even more important is the appearance of words such as selfish (1640), self-interest (1649) and egotism (1714). Before the Civil War people assumed they had a place in a larger order, and that their actions should conform to that order. In the end it was not they but their superiors who should judge of right and wrong – and everyone has a superior, for God rules over all. Hobbes (who coined 'self-defence') and Harrington assumed that each person must and should pursue their own interests – their theories assumed that each person has an egocentric view of the universe. Similarly, the advocates of popular sovereignty, along with the advocates of freedom of religious conscience, believed that each individual must in the end judge where right and wrong lies in deciding whether to resist tyranny or religious oppression. They assumed a high degree of personal autonomy. It used to be said that political theories could be divided into those which placed authority in God (in which authority descended from on high) and those which placed it in the people or a popular assembly (in which authority ascended from below). From this point of view the Civil War marked the triumph of ascending over descending theories. But equally it marked the triumph of self-centred as opposed to other-centred theories, for in the Civil War theorists deference and subordination are replaced by personal autonomy and self-interest. It is assumed that citizens are masterless men.

The transition to thinking of societies as systems of competing self-interests meant that any modification in ways of thinking about either political economy (the phrase dates to 1767) or human psychology (the word dates to 1653) would have an immediate impact on political and social theory. An important figure in this respect is Bernard Mandeville. Mandeville's *Fable of the Bees* (1714) portrayed a world in which private vice is the foundation of public strength and wealth. Imagine, Mandeville said, a society of true Christians. Parsimonious and meek, they would quickly be conquered by richer and more warlike communities. On the other hand qualities which had traditionally been regarded as vices were, Mandeville argued, socially beneficial. The dandy, the gambler, the drunkard provide employment, and ensure that money, instead of lying idle, is put to use. Thanks to them the economy grows. Where previous thinkers had assumed that a virtuous and godly community could best satisfy the legitimate needs of its citizens, Mandeville believed that it is in our interests to live in a society which is selfish and godless. At the heart of Mandeville's theory was the notion (which can be traced back before Mandeville to Bayle and before him to Nicole) of unintended consequences: the general good is an outcome which can be achieved when no one is actually aiming at it, and cannot be achieved when it is their true objective.

Of course, conflicting interests might seem bound to lead to conflict. But Mandeville argued that it is a fundamental characteristic of human nature that we are vain and desire to be well thought of by others. Thanks to this, parents are able to socialize children. By the same means, politicians have encouraged people to interiorize values which are socially useful: they have, as it were, domesticated human beings. These values may traditionally be thought of as 'virtues', but in fact they are grounded in base and self-centred motives such as vanity and shame. Such arguments not only ran counter to the views of contemporaries who were trying to promote Christian values; they also directly attacked the traditional republican emphasis, grounded in a reading of Cicero, on the need for virtuous citizens. Where republicans had always regarded Spartan austerity as admirable, Mandeville praised luxury.

Mandeville's insistence that prosperity was the key to any political community's survival was taken up by Hume (*Essays*, 1741–70), who noted that politicians were now required to be interested in the economy because in modern society national wealth and military power go hand in hand. Political theory was thus inextricably linked to the emerging discipline of political economy. Smith's *Wealth of Nations* not only relied on mechanical imagery in order to present the market as a self-regulating mechanism, and thus to reject attempts by government to regulate prices or control investment. It also relied on a picture of the economy as consisting in a circulation of goods and money. This picture, drawn from the French physiocrats, seems to have originated in a new type of organic metaphor: Harvey's discovery of the circulation of the blood (1628), which had been followed by the discovery of the circulation of sap in plants, made it easier to conceive of systems of circular transfer, exchange and transmutation.

Adam Smith was, with David Hume, a leading member of the Scottish Enlightenment. Like a significant number of other Scots philosophers, Smith came to believe that one could identify certain key stages in human economic development. Hunting and gathering had been followed by the herding of sheep and cattle; next had come settled agriculture; and that had made possible the growth of cities and of trade. Each stage implied a different conception of property, a different system of justice, and a different political order. Harrington's simple economic model of political change had thus now been developed into a sophisticated three-stages theory of history (which allowed one not only to look back in time, but outwards in space, so that native Americans could be regarded as closer to their historical origins than Tartar tribes). The three-stages theory of history is merely one example of a new discipline, now referred to as 'conjectural history', which sought to explain how savagery had developed over time into civilization, polytheism into monotheism, and hunting into commercial prosperity, and whose leading exponents were Rousseau, Hume and Smith. The Scottish Enlightenment marks the coming of age of the new intellectual framework of Newtonian physics, Harveyan anatomy, Lockean associationist psychology, Mandevillian unintended consequences and conjectural history.

It may seem surprising that I have advanced from the English Revolution to the Scottish Enlightenment without mentioning John Locke except in passing. But it is important to remember that while Locke's *Essay Concerning Human Understanding* (1689) soon had a national and international reputation, his *Two Treatises* (1689) were published anonymously and provoked little discussion. Paine claimed that he had not read Locke when he sat down to write *Common Sense*. In many respects the arguments of the Second Treatise – the state of nature; the social contract; the separation of legislative, executive and judiciary; the right of rebellion – are simply more sophisticated versions of arguments developed during the Civil War. But Locke had one major innovation to offer. The assumption of all theorists before Locke was that property was analytically dependent on government. If one declared government tyrannical, with the consequence that the social contract was dissolved and the state of nature was returned, then it seemed to follow of necessity that people's property rights must disappear with the government that had established them. Any theory of revolution must therefore appear to be a theory of anarchy. Against this whole tradition Locke argued that men in a state of nature had property rights because one acquired a right to something by mixing one's labour with it, and once one had acquired it one then had the right to trade it. Thus the fish in the sea belong to anyone and everyone; but if I pull a fish out of the sea it becomes mine, and you are wrong to take it from me.

Hume's political theory was in many respects a straightforward attack upon Locke. Locke claimed that legitimate government was founded on consent, on a social contract. Hume claimed we had never been asked to consent, had never entered into a contract. The very idea of a contract implied a promise, but promises, Hume argued, are highly artificial conventions – society must therefore precede the promise, not vice versa. Locke claimed that property had a foundation in nature. But why, Hume wanted to know, were the apples that grow on the tree I have planted mine not yours? Are the birds that feed on your grain yours, or can I hunt them? Why can I own land, but not sea? Property too, Hume argued, was an artificial convention; indeed different societies had different regimes of property, different rules for determining who could own what. So too artificial conventions determined whether a government was legitimate. In England a woman might inherit the throne; in France she might not. It was local convention that made a Queen of England a legitimate ruler, a Queen of France no ruler at all.

Hume's arguments are delicately balanced. On the one hand he wants to argue that we need conventions and that it is dangerous to disrupt them. It is much better to have a system of property and justice than disorder, so that one should preserve the order one has, whatever its minor defects. Thus a French subject should uphold the powers of the king, and an Englishman should stand by the rights of parliament. On the other hand Hume argued that conventions regarding promises, property, justice, and government had come into existence because they served useful purposes. If a convention became destructive rather than useful, or if it became clear that one could reform it without serious risk of disruption, then use and function were the only ultimate test of whether it was appropriate or not. Two quite separate traditions thus grow out of Hume's approach.

On the one hand one can argue that use and function can be rationally analysed, in which case one should reform outmoded conventions in order to increase the happiness and welfare of the community. This argument leads straight to the technocratic utilitarianism of Bentham, who published his *Fragment on Government* in the crucial year of 1776. Bentham argued that the purpose of morality and politics was to minimize pain and maximize happiness (inventing the words minimize and maximize to clarify his argument), and that the duty of government was to ensure that individuals who sought to maximize their own happiness were led to act in ways which did not detract from the happiness of others (the duty–interest juncture principle). Government should thus act, not on the basis of traditional or customary wisdom, nor on the basis of public opinion, but on the basis of rational calculation.

Alternatively one can argue that conventions are delicate and arbitrary, and need to be preserved for fear that the alternative is chaos or military dictatorship: this is the argument of Burke's *Reflections on the Revolution in France* (1790). In Burke's view the whole attempt to rationalize politics is misconceived – good order depends on tradition, sentiment, loyalty, deference, and past practice. At the core of Burke's argument are two ideas. The first is that one must nurture all those elements in society which run counter to individualism. The second is a new view of history, crystallized in the word 'prescription'. An innovation may be unjustified to begin with, but the passage of time changes its character and gives it legitimacy. Thus one can acquire a customary right to walk on a footpath or vote in an election, but neither right is founded in reason or nature. A prescriptive right is a right whose character has been changed by the passage of time itself. As opposed to the traditional insistence of the common law tradition that legal principles went back to time immemorial, the new emphasis on prescription meant that one could trace the evolution of rights, in the process acknowledging that they were historical, not natural. Both the proto-liberalism of Bentham and the proto-conservatism of Burke may thus be traced back to Hume, while Hume himself is indebted to Mandeville (for his stress on self-interest and the public benefits of private vices), and to Harrington (for his notion that a political scientist might be able to identify causal connections, to analyse the system of government as if it were a machine).

Any account of the conceptual framework within which politics was discussed in the mid-eighteenth century must include a further term which balanced words such as self-interest and selfish: 'sympathy'. The word is first used to mean 'feeling another's feelings' in 1662, and from then on we find a growing stress on the idea that human beings are not motivated simply by selfish concerns, but that they have a genuine concern for the welfare of others. It is important to stress that a preoccupation with sympathy or benevolence could not develop except in the context of a picture of human beings as egocentric and autonomous. We see this new preoccupation reflected in new turns of speech, such as Burke's determination to 'identify . . . with the people' (1780). This concern with sympathy received its most influential expression in Shaftesbury's *Characteristicks* (1711). Despite Mandeville's bitter hostility to Shaftesbury, much of eighteenth-century moral philosophy consisted in an attempt to find a middle way between Mandeville's emphasis on the selfish and Shaftesbury's emphasis on the benevolent motives of humankind. The preoccupation with motive is in fact characteristic of the eighteenth century, for Locke's *Essay* (1689) was generally understood to have powerfully reinforced a relativistic account of morality which denied that morality had been promulgated by God or was supported by a universal consent of mankind. In the absence of any fixed law, motive became the guide to behaviour and the key to judgement.

How far does this take us towards understanding *Common Sense?* Paine can put his trust in popular sovereignty because he believes there is a natural harmony of interests. He need not worry about an education for virtue because he assumes that the public good is in large part the result of unintended consequences. He is preoccupied with prosperity and the new science, designing an iron bridge for example. He attacks monarchy because the king's interests are different from those of his subjects and because courts are wasteful: his tests are functional and utilitarian. He has no respect for tradition, but believes each generation has the right to remake the world – and thereby he opposes himself not to divine right or immemorial custom, but to convention, tradition, and prescription. A good few of these themes can thus be traced back before *Common Sense* and we can begin to get some idea of why Paine's views seemed sensible.

Focusing on *Common Sense* enables us to measure something of the degree of change across our period. But there are other issues which are brought to the fore if we turn to Paine's *Rights of Man* (1791–2), a work written under the impact of the French Revolution. One of the important features of that work is that it provides a sketch of a new welfare state and focuses on the question of what revenue from taxation should fund. *Common Sense*, written in an American context, assumes a virtually non-existent state apparatus; *Rights of Man*, written in a European context, assumes a powerful state machine. Paine himself had worked for the customs, and was therefore familiar with the new government bureaucracy, and it is vital to grasp that by the mid-eighteenth century the British state, which had been so fragile and feeble a hundred years before, was immensely powerful: capable of raising a vast revenue (Britain was now heavily, not lightly taxed), of funding an enormous public debt, of operating an efficient and pervasive revenue-collecting bureaucracy, of conquering first one empire and then another, of engaging in warfare on a global scale, and of manipulating nationalist sentiment to ensure support for government objectives. Yet one might say that for the most part these changes were invisible to political theory: not until the nineteenth century do themes such as the legitimacy and purpose of taxation and the proper scope and purposes of state action begin to be addressed; and not until the twentieth is there any serious attempt to theorize bureaucracy or nationalism.

These gaps are partly to be explained in terms of the emergence of the idea that certain themes and certain texts lay at the heart of political theory. Read Rousseau or Hume and you will catch echoes of Machiavelli, Grotius, Hobbes, Locke and Mandeville: of an emerging classical tradition (in which Mandeville was to be supplanted by Smith) concerned with power, legitimacy, representation, rebellion, and self-interest/benevolence. The late seventeenth and early eighteenth centuries had seen a lively debate in England on the subject of standing armies – the key institutions of the new state. But no classic text addressed itself to this subject, and eighteenth-century commentators were quite happy to live in a world of impressment for the navy without expressing any serious concern about the rights of those kidnapped for service. There was a good deal of discussion regarding the nature of the English (after 1707, British) constitution, but the edge was taken off such arguments by the virtual collapse of the Tory party for a full half century after 1715 and by the transformation of the Whig party into a party of the establishment. Oppositional True Whigs and Tories might campaign against high taxation, government debt, corruption, placemen, and foreign wars, but such campaigns did not offer a new theory of representation (extension of the franchise was long assumed to be a recipe for a more, not less, corrupt electorate) or a new picture of the nature and purposes of government, implying instead a return to some lost, Elizabethan ideal. Political parties had been central to the political process since the Exclusion Crisis (1681), but their existence was at odds with a conceptual framework which assumed that politics was concerned with general not sectoral interests, and Burke's defence of party (*Thoughts on the Cause of the Present Discontents*, 1770) appears a hundred years after the first emergence of party, even if it usefully heralds a new party-political era.

Paine sought to extend the range of political analysis to include unemployment, pensions and insurance, but the crisis of the French Revolution made it harder, not easier, to think about the relationship between citizen and state, or between public opinion and political parties, or between legislative assembly and nation. The anti-revolutionary stance of the British state, the triumph of Burke, and the failure of the French Revolution to deliver, as initially expected, an improved version of the British constitution, served as an effective obstacle to serious analysis until the generation of Tocqueville and John Stuart Mill.

A final issue remains to be addressed. There may have been an emerging consensus about the 'classical' texts of political thought, but we do not know whether Paine had ever read any of them. We know he had read an obscure attack on monarchy by John Hall (1650), which he had found reprinted by the radical freethinker John Toland, who had mistakenly included it in a collection of Harrington's works (1700). And we know he had read the English translation of Jacinto Dragonetti's *Delle virtù e de' premi* (*c*.1768). Dragonetti's work, which advocated social equality, pensions and support of the unemployed, was inspired by Beccaria's *Of Crimes and Punishments* (1764), an appeal for rational punishments based on a principle of deterrence, and an argument (against judicial torture) that people should be treated as innocent until proven guilty. Beccaria himself was inspired by the *De l'esprit* of Helvétius (1758), an attack on despotism from a radical republican viewpoint. Helvétius, Dragonetti and Beccaria were all three rapidly translated into English. Helvétius admired Locke's *Essay* and Hume's *Treatise* and was attacked by his opponents for having been influenced by Mandeville. *De l'esprit* was in part a radical reworking of Montesquieu's *Esprit des lois* (1748), itself a work influenced by Harrington. What we are dealing with here is a complicated exchange of texts across national boundaries, between languages, and over time.

In the eighteenth century – and increasingly as the century wore on – readers and writers lived in what was called the republic of letters: an international community in which Rousseau, for example, read Mandeville, and Hume reviewed Helvétius, while Smith reviewed Rousseau. And the educated travelled: Montesquieu, Voltaire, Rousseau and Helvétius visited England; Locke, Hume and Smith went to France. Mandeville was educated in Holland, where it seems he was taught by the great sceptical philosopher Pierre Bayle.

Censorship was one of the great forces at work within this republic. Helvétius could be legally published in England; in France his book was banned and burnt by the hangman. The numerous editions after the first were smuggled in from Switzerland, Holland and other places where printers did a roaring trade in books banned by the authorities. Even banned books are shaped by censorship, for there are degrees of illegality. Thus a book that advocated tyrannicide would be hunted down without mercy, while a blind eye would be turned to the circulation of copies of one (like *De l'esprit*) that attacked oriental despotism. And censorship alters the way in which people think. It encourages displacement (not French despotism, but oriental) and abstraction (not the faults of this king, but of rulers in general). One might thus say it is an open question whether freedom of speech or imperfect censorship is most conducive to intellectual progress. Hume, who had lived in France, chose as the epigraph of his *Treatise* a quotation from Tacitus: 'Oh happy day in which one can say what one thinks!'; but, when Wilkes began to campaign for constitutional change, Hume quickly reached the view that there was too much, not too little liberty in England. At some point he tried to persuade Diderot that censorship was a good thing, to which Diderot replied: 'You think that our intolerance is more favourable to the progress of thought than your unbounded liberty? Helvétius, D'Holbach, Morellet, and Suard do not share this view.' But in his posthumous *De l'homme* (1773) Helvétius agreed with Hume, not Diderot: it was partly censorship, he claimed, which accounted for the greater sophistication of political thought in France than in England.

There was no censor to muzzle the presses on which Paine wrote *Common Sense*, but the text of Dragonetti that he read had been translated from a book published secretly in order to be smuggled into Italy and France, and only a handful of copies of *Common Sense* were smuggled into England. Paine knew no language other than English, yet he could follow debates in France and Italy. It is a fundamental paradox of our period that it sees the decline of Latin as a universal language (Milton had been employed to justify the execution of the king to the intelligentsia of Europe in Latin, not English), but its replacement by a new internationalism symbolized by the Republic of Letters. This community was destroyed by the French Revolutionary wars, and has never been rebuilt.

References and Further Reading

There is no good general survey of political theory in our period. Immensely influential, but covering a longer period, is J. G. A. Pocock, *The Machiavellian Moment* (Princeton: Princeton University Press, 1975). For a more recent discussion of the republican tradition see Quentin Skinner, *Liberty Before Liberalism* (Cambridge: Cambridge University Press, 1997). On the new values of the commercial society see A. O.

Hirschman, *The Passions and the Interests* (Princeton: Princeton University Press, 1977). Full of insights is Don Herzog, *Happy Slaves* (Chicago: Chicago University Press, 1989). A collection of essays that surveys our period is Nicholas Phillipson and Quentin Skinner, eds, *Political Discourse in Early Modern Britain* (Cambridge: Cambridge University Press, 1993).

50

Philosophical Writing

Peter Walmsley

Pray, Sir, in all the reading which you have ever read, did you ever read such a book as *Locke*'s Essay upon the Human Understanding? —— Don't answer me rashly, – because many, I know, quote the book, who have not read it, – and many have read it who understand it not: – If either of these is your case, as I write to instruct, I will tell you in three words what the book is. – It is a history. – A history! of who? what? where? when? Don't hurry yourself. —— It is a history-book, Sir, (which may possibly recommend it to the world) of what passes in a man's own mind; and if you will say so much of the book, and no more, believe me, you will cut no contemptible figure in a metaphysic circle.

(Sterne, 1978, 70)

Here, in *Tristram Shandy* (1759–67), Laurence Sterne is playing two competing senses of *history* against one another. Our modern sense of the word – as the narrative of the past life of a person or nation – had gained ascendancy in Sterne's generation. So when Tristram teases us to say how Locke's *Essay Concerning Human Understanding* (1689) is a history book, we are at a loss: surely it is not history, but metaphysics. Only when Tristram condescends to tell us that it is 'a history of what passes in a man's own mind' do we see he means *history* in that other sense – a descriptive account of observed phenomena – and that Tristram is just relaying a commonplace. By the 1760s every educated Briton knew that Locke, now a canonized Whig worthy, had set metaphysics on a new, experiential footing. Locke's *Essay* was the most widely read philosophical book from its publication until well into the nineteenth century, in both the imposing original and the more manageable abridgement for students. And if there inevitably remained a sizeable, if embarrassed, segment of the population who had not read it, the philosophers who followed Locke all felt compelled to write in careful dialogue with his great natural history of human thought.

Locke's *Essay* opens with a strong display of allegiance to the new natural philosophy. The book's dedicatee, Thomas Herbert, eighth Earl of Pembroke, was not just Locke's old friend and protector, but President of the Royal Society in the year the *Essay* was published. But it is with the Epistle to the Reader, with its tribute to the leading lights of the Royal Society, that Locke, himself a member of the Royal Society, clearly pitches his tent with the moderns:

> The Commonwealth of Learning, is not at this time without Master-Builders, whose mighty Designs, in advancing the Sciences, will leave lasting Monuments to the Admiration of Posterity; But every one must not hope to be a *Boyle*, or a *Sydenham*; and in an age that produces such Masters, as the Great – *Huygenius*, and the incomparable Mr. *Newton*, with some other of that Strain; 'tis Ambition enough to be employed as an Under-Labourer in clearing Ground a little, and removing some of the Rubbish, that lies in the way to Knowledge; which certainly had been very much more advanced in the World, if the Endeavours of ingenious and industrious Men had not been much cumbred with the learned but frivolous use of uncouth, affected, or unintelligible Terms, introduced into the Sciences, and there made an Art of, to that Degree, that Philosophy, which is nothing but the true Knowledge of Things, was thought unfit, or uncapable to be brought into well-bred Company, and polite Conversation.

While Locke in this passage makes a very conventional rhetorical gesture of humility, he also clearly claims a place for himself and his book in the Royal Society's ambitious schemes for the advancement of material knowledge. In France the breadth and coherence (not to mention the institutionalization) of the growing Cartesian canon inspired many zealous apostles, but in Britain few philosophers were strict disciples of Descartes, Gassendi or Paracelsus, though each had enormous influence. Indeed, a repudiation of systems of any kind was central to the rhetoric of British philosophy at this time, a reflection of the religious and political latitude espoused by many of its practitioners. Locke presented himself as a theoretical loner, taking considerable pride in his professed ignorance of Descartes. Bacon certainly had influence as a philosophical father who was both indigenous and noble, but it was as much the vigilant inclusiveness of all his work, that he does not lay down a system but rather opens innumerable avenues for investigation, that made him so attractive to the founders of the Royal Society and, ultimately, to Locke.

The elevation of natural history was Bacon's peculiar legacy to British philosophy. Bacon had envisioned all the divergent disciplines of natural philosophy being harnessed to a single ambitious public project, a great anatomy of the world to which the *Novum Organum* (1620) was meant to serve as a preface. And if Bacon's catalogue of the myriad 'instances' by which our knowledge of the world might be ordered seems, at points, hopelessly eclectic, it is not without a clear intellectual purpose and a new sense of the necessary integration of scientific practices. In the *Parasceve* (1620), for example, Bacon accounts unanalytical history that contents itself with the mere description of individual natural kinds of as little help as ancient authors or superstitious tales. A truly progressive natural history demands a strategic and fully integrated programme of *'Experimenta lucifera'*: 'by the help and ministry of man a new face of bodies, another universe or theatre of things, comes into view' (*Works*, IV, 255, 94 and 253). As Locke himself puts it in 'The Conduct of the Understanding' (1706), which was originally intended as a final chapter for the *Essay*'s fourth edition, Bacon 'did not rest in the lazy approbation of what was because it was; but enlarged his minde to what might be'. In this rare invocation of learned authority, Locke depicts Bacon not as a mere anatomist of nature, but as the author of a potent heuristic method which has already vanquished the formal logic of scholasticism.

Locke applies the methodology of observation and experiment so vigorously promoted by Bacon and, in turn, by the fellowship of the Royal Society in investigating human understanding. When, in Book I, Locke casts doubts on the Cartesian assumption that active thought is the essence of mind, pointing out that in dreamless sleep the mind seems to be at rest, Locke privileges common sense over traditional metaphysical distinctions and opens our mental life to a novel empirical scrutiny. In fact throughout the *Essay* Locke blurs the established boundaries between material and spiritual substances. Suggesting that our knowledge of each is equally limited, he can claim, in his concluding chapter 'Of the Division of the Sciences', that the study of mind and that of matter fall within the same intellectual discipline. He calls this branch of knowledge *'natural Philosophy'*, admitting he does so 'in a little more enlarged sense of the Word', and defines it as 'The Knowledge of Things, as they are in their own proper Beings, their Constitutions, Properties, and Operations, whereby I mean not only Matter, and Body, but Spirits also, which have their proper Natures, Constitutions, and Operations as well as Bodies' (IV, xii, 2). In this light, Locke's empirical approach to the understanding appears as the appropriate expression of his larger vision of the categories of human knowledge. By jettisoning essentialist assumptions about the nature of spirit and subjecting human thought to the cautious scrutiny of the scientific gaze, Locke hopes not only to bring the mind within the compass of the Royal Society's universal natural history of all substances, but to lay the ground for discoveries in the operations of the mind equal to those so recently attained in optics, botany and anatomy.

In the introductory chapter of the *Essay*, Locke lays out his intellectual agenda in terms that candidly, if quietly, signal how very novel the ensuing study will be:

> It shall suffice to my present Purpose, to consider the discerning Faculties of a Man, as they are employ'd about the Objects, which they have to do with: and I shall imagine on this Occasion, if, in this Historical, plain Method, I can give any Account of the Ways, whereby our Understandings come to attain those Notions of Things we have, and can set down any Measures of the Certainty of our Knowledge, or the Grounds of those Perswasions, which are to be found amongst Men, so various, different, and wholly contradictory. (I, i, 2)

Locke's 'Historical, plain Method' will prove just that – an attention to fact and detail, an interest in narrating the processes of thought undistracted by questions of the physiology of the brain or by the problems raised by scholastic maxims about mental forms and essences. Locke's method is, as John Yolton has argued, 'descriptive, not justificatory' (*Compass*, 14) – the method not of a metaphysician, but of a natural historian of the understanding. In fact Bacon himself had hinted at the possibility of just such a project, imagining that his inductive method will invade the provinces of syllogistic logic – ethics, politics, even metaphysics: 'I form a history and tables of discovery for anger, fear, shame, and the like; for matters political; and again for the mental operations of memory, composition and division, judgement, and the rest; not less than for heat and cold, or light, or vegetation, or the like' (*Works*, IV, 112).

Locke's historical method is not immediately apparent; the first book of the *Essay*, as it presents and then attacks theories of innate knowledge, tends to follow the conventions of philosophical disputation and deductive logic. Here we find Locke battering innatist positions with volleys of refutations one moment and playfully elaborating innatist principles *ad absurdum* the next. At the very end of Book I, however, he promises to lay the haphazard tactics of 'Controversial Discourses' aside; having cleared the ground, he can now 'raise an Edifice uniform, and consistent with it self, as far as my own Experience and Observation will assist me'. Locke warns his reader 'not to expect undeniable cogent demonstrations' in what follows: 'All that I shall say for the Principles I proceed on, is, that I can only *appeal* to Mens own unprejudiced *Experience*, and Observation, whether they be true, or no' (I, iv, 25). Locke seems to have predicted, accurately enough, that many would find this experiential approach to metaphysics bewildering. Thomas Burnet, for one, expressed considerable anxiety over Locke's refusal to argue from explicit principles (*Remarks*, 44). Locke's rejection of logical demonstration for mere observation is a necessary consequence of his view of the character and extent of our possible knowledge of mind. He readily accepts that demonstration is capable of great advances in those sciences in which absolute principles are work, such as mathematics and, possibly, ethics. When, however, we seek to improve our knowledge of *'substantial Beings'*, whose essences elude us, *'Experience here must teach me*, what reason cannot' (IV, xii, 9–10).

Locke works, like the natural historian, to isolate, describe, and name each species of idea, and he makes it clear that what little certainty he can lay claim to depends entirely on the care with which he observes the habits and objects of his own mind. Underlying this process, it would seem, is a faith that there are natural kinds to our ideas: that simple versus complex ideas or ideas of substance versus those of relation can be clearly and consistently distinguished by any careful observer. Throughout the *Essay* he exhibits the natural historian's preoccupation with marking the boundaries between natural species, a preoccupation that informs his larger account of our mental abilities. Our powers of *discerning* ideas one from another are for Locke fundamental to human understanding, second only to perception and memory: 'Unless the Mind had a distinct Perception of different Objects, and their Qualities, it would be capable of very little Knowledge' (II, xi, 1). Here the precise and highly particularized knowledge sought by the natural historian is identified as a precondition to all thought. Ideas are naturally discrete for Locke and, lifted from the fluid environment of thought, can themselves be objects for reflective scrutiny. He promotes 'distinctness' as a virtue of thought, and seeks to establish 'determined' ideas. At moments Locke's model of mind seems a version of the scientist's cabinet of curiosities, a closet where determined ideas can be ranged in order and stored, readily accessible for personal inspection or public display.

Locke sees that his task is, however, more than simply descriptive. It is not enough simply to recount his observations; he must present the species of ideas he has identified in an order that is at once rational and, as far as is possible, natural. This desire to paint the larger prospect of the understanding is reflected in the geographic metaphors Locke chooses in the *Essay*'s opening chapter. Here he proposes to undertake a 'Survey of our own Understandings' in order to discover the 'Extent of our Knowledge' and find the 'Horizon . . . which sets the Bounds between the enlightned and dark Parts of Things' (I, i, 7). The mind – and, by association, the *Essay* itself – is frequently figured as a 'little World' (II, ii, 2), a landscape populated with ideas, a 'little Canton' surrounded by 'a huge Abyss of Ignorance' (IV, iii, 24). The contours of this landscape are clearly drawn in the structure of Book II which mirrors what Locke sees as the natural 'progress of the Mind' (II, xxix, 1) from passive sensation to the most abstract speculation. Book II begins by describing simple ideas of sense and reflection (ii–viii) and proceeds, after a brief consideration of our powers of perception, retention, discerning, comparing, and abstracting (ix–xi), to account for our complex ideas under the following categories: modes, simple followed by mixed (xiii–xxii); substances, single and collective (xxiv–xxv); and relations, both natural and those of human design (xxv–xxviii). Throughout Book II as a whole, and within each category he establishes, Locke organizes ideas along a spectrum that extends from simple to complex, particular to general, concrete to abstract, and natural to artificial.

Locke's taxonomic obsessions are perhaps nowhere more evident than in the layout of the *Essay* itself, which provides many different avenues of access to the whole. Draft A of the *Essay* (1671) was itself written in a commonplace book, and Draft B, composed soon after, already has summary headings in the margins and an extensive table of contents. By the time the *Essay* reaches print, Locke provides not only two tables of contents with descriptive headings for chapters and sections, but a comprehensive index and even a system of italicized keywords that delivers, in condensed form, the prevailing theme of each passage. These tools facilitate skimming, cross-reference and review, permitting different patterns and depths of reading, different levels of generality and speed to suit the interests and abilities of the reader. The *Essay* is physically designed not as a linear treatise carefully building a single strain of argument but as a natural history, a comprehensive reference work consisting of many discrete discourses to which we are invited to return again and again.

Locke clearly saw that his particular contribution to the great instauration was in large part linguistic. Recall that in the Epistle to the Reader he proposes to rid philosophy of 'uncouth terms' so that it might, in the end, be fit to enter 'polite conversation.' That the advancement of learning depends upon the elimination of 'unintelligible Terms' was a common theme in seventeenth-century natural philosophy, part of a broad, well-established critique of the obfuscating abstractions of scholasticism and the impassioned cant of religious enthusiasts. But Locke proposes that by exploding such jargon in the course of his argument he will be 'clearing Ground' for the likes of Huygens, Boyle and Newton to advance 'the true Knowledge of Things'. More than this, the *Essay*'s vocabulary of ideas will provide a way of talking about thought and sense experience wholly complementary with Restoration science's programme of collection, experiment, and observation.

This discursive mode, appropriate to Locke's self-consciously novel metaphysics, was the same as that promoted by such apologists for the Royal Society as Thomas Sprat and Joseph Glanville. And like these, Locke attacks scholastic disputations, the Socratic debates that were central to teaching and examination in the Restoration universities, as unnatural and unproductive of knowledge. In the *Essay* Locke expresses his strong aversion to the violence and competitiveness of disputes, which turn students into captious 'wranglers' rather than careful thinkers. Plato had compared elenctic debates to wrestling matches, a metaphor frequently revived in Restoration accounts of the disputation. It often happened that the answerer, with no chance to qualify, entrenched himself in his publicly declared position, whatever its merits, and fought to protect his intellectual reputation. Locke objects that this combative forum stunts intellectual growth: 'Men even when they are bafled and silenced in this Scholastique way, are seldom or never convinced, and so brought over to the conquering side' (IV, xvii, 4). In any case, 'Victory' in the universities is 'adjudged not to him who had Truth on his side, but the last word in the Dispute' (III, x, 7). Locke seeks above all to deny the dispute its imagery of masculine contest by claiming that the subtle feints and labyrinthine defences of the beleaguered disputants are 'more like the Dens of Robbers, or Holes of Foxes, than the Fortresses of fair Warriours' (III, x, 9). Locke's main objection, however, is to the traditional logic which governs these exercises, a consequence of his conviction that true knowledge is far more limited than is commonly conceded. Locke's sweeping prospect of the understanding consigns much of the business of the human mind to the realm of probability. Locke fears that, in applying the rules of deduction indiscriminately to all themes that present themselves, the disputant more often than not ends up treating matters of probability as if they were capable of certainty. From Locke's informalist perspective, the way of maxim and syllogism presents a gross caricature of our natural processes of reasoning. In its close scrutiny of abstract terms, the dispute becomes nothing more than verbal play; the disputants, with victory in their sights, do not hesitate to 'perplex, involve, and subtilize the signification of Sounds' (III, x, 7).

In striking contrast, the voice of the *Essay* is candid but cautious. Locke repudiated the learned authority commonly assumed by philosophical writers; we are 'not to expect any thing here, but what being spun out of my own course Thoughts, is fitted to Men of my own size'. The familiar, first-person voice of the *Essay* speaks comfortably from a domestic interior; among Locke's favourite examples are 'the Ring I have on my finger' and 'the Paper I write on' (II, xxxi, 6 and 12). Consider how he argues for the existence of an external world: 'Thus I see, whilst I write this, I can change the Appearance of the Paper; and by designing the Letters, tell before-hand what new *Idea* it shall exhibit the very next moment, barely by drawing my Pen over it' (IV, xi, 7). These deictic moments of authorial self-display, as they dramatize the act of literary creation, draw us into Locke's closet. The sound of common conversation is imitated in

Locke's loose, accumulative syntax, an easy plain style enlivened by occasional descents into colloquial diction. He most often deploys low words in the service of common sense against the excesses of scholasticism, as when he shows how the learned make 'a pudder' about essences, mixing only 'a small pittance of Reason . . . with those huffing Opinions they are swell'd with' (III, v, 16). And throughout the *Essay*, Locke draws our attention to the fact that he is writing in 'very plain *English*' (IV, viii, 3), frequently stopping to search out more accessible equivalents for traditional metaphysical terms. *Substantia* thus becomes 'Under-propping' (II, xiii, 20), and *species* and *genera* are translated as 'Sorts and Kinds' (III, i, 6). Locke's strategy is not simply one of denying his opponents the authority of the Latinate; he appeals to the vernacular to determine whether or not these words conjure up clear and distinct ideas in our minds. As he pursues this programme of rendering scholastic jargon 'into intelligible *English*' (II, xxiii, 21), Locke comes to rely more and more on the testimony of the common speaker. Locke establishes our roles as conversants, not just by addressing his opening Epistle to us, but by making large gestures of deference to our judgements. He can claim 'I consider my self as liable to Mistakes, as I can think thee.' Such flattering diffidence comes, however, with heavy demands on our energies as readers. Writing in Book III about the abuse of words, Locke rounds on those who refuse to define their terms when writing about ethics, saying 'it must be great want of ingenuity, (to say no worse of it) to refuse to do it' (III, xi, 17). *Ingenuity* as Locke uses it here – meaning something close to the old moral sense of *candour*, an intellectual openness and generosity that verges on charity itself – is perhaps the chief virtue of his own rhetoric. And Locke makes it clear that much depends on our ingenuity as readers, and that the pleasing diversion of excursive reflection is available only to the active reader who will make use of his or her own thoughts: ''Tis to them, if they are thy own, that I referr my self . . . this Book must stand or fall with thee, not by any Opinion I have of it, but thy own.' True to his word, Locke repeatedly appeals to our experience to validate his case: his style is distinguished by phrases which seem to initiate not dispute but dialogue, such as 'Let any one examine his own Thoughts, and throughly search into his Understanding, and then let him tell me' (II, i, 5) or 'I ask every one whether he has not often done so' (II, xxi, 69). The second person is employed sparingly but to considerable effect in the *Essay*. In the midst of his case against an innate and universal notion of God, Locke turns to us and reflects 'Had you or I been born at the Bay of *Soldania*, possibly our Thoughts, and Notions, had not exceeded those brutish ones of the *Hotentots* that inhabit there' (I, iv, 12). At such moments he seems intent on goading the complacent reader into self-consciousness, making him or her consider the full personal consequences of the argument.

Writing in Book IV of the degrees of assent we grant in matters of probability, Locke makes a plea for charity and forbearance:

> We should do well to commiserate our mutual Ignorance, and endeavour to remove it in all the gentle and fair ways of Information; and not instantly treat others ill, as obstinate and perverse, because they will not renounce their own, and receive our Opinions,

or at least those we would force upon them, when 'tis more than probable, that we are no less obstinate in not embracing some of theirs. (IV, xvi, 4)

Locke observes that we are inevitably hurried into our opinions, denied leisure for reflection by the 'conduct of our Lives, and the management of our great Concerns' (IV, xvi, 3). Just the same, any belief, once owned, is cherished as true, and we are all the more obstinate in defending it for fear that a sudden change of opinion would incur charges of folly or ignorance. Time and care, then, are needed to bring any mind to see its error, and the mind that refuses to relinquish its beliefs must be respected: 'It would, methinks, become all Men to maintain *Peace*, and the common Offices of Humanity, *and Friendship, in the diversity of Opinions*' (IV, xvi, 4). Locke displays these irenic virtues when, confronted with the density and elusiveness of the material world, he turns to dialogue. His exchanges with his reader are indeed 'gentle and fair ways of Information' in which the violence of learned dispute dissipates before admissions of 'mutual Ignorance'. Dramatizing our resistance to his argument, Locke marks out within his text the time we need to come to a cautious and measured assent. The *Essay*'s philosophical conversations plot the difficult negotiations by which we make our way through this twilight of probability.

The rise of Locke's *Essay* to its place of ultimate authority in the British imagination was slow, and if it met with many detractors on its first publication, it was not until twenty years later that the anxieties over the consequences of Locke's method were given their fullest and most forceful articulation. In *The Principles of Human Knowledge* (1710) and again in the *Three Dialogues between Hylas and Philonous* (1713), George Berkeley, later Fellow of Trinity College Dublin and Bishop of Cloyne, repudiated Locke's epistemology as promoting a radically sceptical materialism and even irreligion. Promoting himself as a champion of 'common sense' he admits part of the Lockean agenda: all 'ideas' originate in either sense or reflection (*Works*, II, 41). Where Berkeley's principal objection lies is with Locke's refusal to distinguish clearly between material and spiritual substances, indeed to subject spirit to a method developed for dealing with matter. Berkeley's response is to attack the idea of material substance altogether. Laying down the principle '*esse* is *percipi*', he challenges the notion that we can have any notion of matter separate from our sensible ideas – we have no access to any of the invisible and intangible minute parts of matter upon which Locke and many other scientists of his day believed our ideas of colours, tastes and smells depended. According to Berkeley's 'immaterial' system, we only have evidence of the existence of ideas and of the minds that have them. Since ideas of sense are not of our own doing and seem to burst upon us with order and vivacity, they must be the creations of a greater and more powerful mind, the mind of God. Berkeley's argument is the antithesis of Locke's sprawling taxonomy of ideas; focused and concise, it is a revaluation of traditional formalist logic. In fact, the *Three Dialogues*, with its carefully managed Socratic exchange, reads as a defence of the university disputation. Berkeley strives, above all, to reclaim a place for theology in epistemology by lacing his texts with lines of Scripture:

nothing can be more evident to any one that is capable of the least reflexion, than the
existence of God, or a spirit who is intimately present to our minds, producing in them
all that variety of ideas or sensations, which continually affect us, on whom we have an
absolute and entire dependence, in short, *in whom we live, and move, and have our being.*
(*Works*, II, 109)

Immaterialism, for all its ingenuity, is chiefly aimed at bringing Locke into line
with St Paul and at denying that observation alone is an adequate source of human
understanding.

Where Berkeley had seen the twin spectres of materialism and irreligion in Locke's
Essay, David Hume found a powerful and heuristic new logic. In *A Treatise of Human
Nature* (1739–40), Hume embraces Locke's scientific method and rhetoric. Early in
the *Treatise* Hume clarifies his allegiance to Locke's anti-innatist stance: our *ideas* are
derived from what he calls *impressions* – lively mental experiences of sense and reflection. Borrowing an exotic example from Locke, he reminds us that 'we cannot form
to ourselves a just idea of the taste of a pine-apple, without having actually tasted it'
(I, i). Moreover, Hume follows Locke in repudiating the formalist, geometrical
methods of scholastic metaphysics; the purpose of logic is not, he tells us in his introduction, to provide an artificial deductive discipline to our thought, but 'to explain
the principles and operations of our reasoning faculty, and the nature of our ideas'. In
this vein, he goes on to create a genealogy for the *Treatise* that affiliates it with modern
rather than ancient authorities, and in particular with a British tradition of scientific
thought:

> As the science of man is the only solid foundation for the other sciences, so the only
> solid foundation we can give to this science itself must be laid on experience and obser-
> vation. 'Tis no astonishing reflection to consider, that the application of experimental
> philosophy to moral subjects should come after that to natural at the distance of above
> a whole century; since we find in fact, that there was about the same interval betwixt
> the origins of these sciences; and that reckoning from Thales to Socrates, the space of
> time is nearly equal to that betwixt my Lord Bacon and some late philosophers in
> *England*, who have begun to put the science of man on a new footing, and have engaged
> the attention, and excited the curiosity of the public.

Here Hume places himself within a second golden age of metaphysics, a great flourishing of thought only possible in 'a land of toleration and of liberty'. This instauration begins with Bacon (whose inspiration Hume traces through the work of Locke
and the third Earl of Shaftesbury) and clearly culminates in Hume's own Baconian
commitment to 'experience and observation'. Moreover, he insistently advertises that
he will employ experimentation to disclose the nature of our ideas. Experiment, the
carefully witnessed and recorded production of natural phenomena in controlled envi-
ronments, was associated with the most prestigious discoveries in British natural
philosophy – Harvey's of the circulation of blood, Boyle's of the elasticity of air, and
Newton's of the heterogeneity of light. True to his word, Hume tackles the problems

that confront him as natural occurrences and repeatedly stages mind experiments to elucidate the nature of ideas. Consider, for example, how he tests his hypothesis that our ideas are much more vivid when stimulated by a sensible object than when not:

> I place my chief confidence in experience to prove so material a principle. We may, there-fore, observe, as the first experiment to our present purpose, that upon the appearance of the picture of an absent friend, our idea of him is evidently inliven'd by the *resem-blance*, and that every passion, which that idea occasions, whether of joy or sorrow, acquires new force and vigour. In producing this effect there concur both a relation and a present impression. Where the picture bears him no resemblance, or at least was not intended for him, it never so much as conveys our thought to him: And where it is absent, as well as the person; tho' the mind may pass from the thought of the one to that of the other; it feels its idea to be rather weaken'd than inliven'd by that transi-tion. (I, iii, 8)

Here are all the conventions of experimental discourse: the invitation to visualize a scenario and the careful modification of circumstances to produce new phenomena. As in Newton's *Opticks* (1704), the strategic use of the first person here encourages us to become virtual witnesses of the scene, to place before ourselves – albeit in our mind's eye – the portrait of an absent friend and then remove it, and so to confirm Hume's argument about 'present impressions'. With an implicit appeal to the ethic of labour, Hume everywhere insists on the rigours of the experimental discipline, where human thought is tested by meticulously designed and repeated trials: 'we must carefully separate whatever is superfluous' and enlarge 'the sphere of . . . experiments as much as possible' (I, iii, 15). And as Hume moves from ideas to passions and virtues, he brings experiment to bear on human behaviour as well as thought. Having, for example, just finished staging his mind experiment about the portrait of the absent friend, he turns with unnerving ease to the 'ceremonies of the *Roman Catholic* reli-gion', which 'may be consider'd as experiments of the same nature'. For Hume the 'mummeries' of the devout – the various postures and gestures of their rituals – are necessary for 'inlivening their devotion, and quickening their fervour, which other-wise would decay away, if directed entirely to distant and immaterial objects' (I, iii, 8). Experiment is not just the natural method of intellectual enquiry for Hume, but also the only possible proceeding for a pragmatic moral philosophy. Hume founds his ethics, not on any universal natural virtues, but on psychological and behavioural evidence, garnered through a 'cautious observation of human life' (introduction). Like Addison and Steele's Mr Spectator or Johnson's Rambler, he is a canny, even scathing observer to the follies of humanity.

Hume's willingness to stand as an unflinching witness to the profound illogic of human behaviour, indeed to insist that morality is only valid in so far as it could account for the full spectrum of human life, seems in large part inspired by Locke's account of the association of ideas, a chapter Locke added to the fourth edition of the *Essay* (1700). Here Locke describes the absurdity that occurs when ideas are connected in the mind 'wholly owing to Chance or Custom', as when the patient, once cured, cannot bear the sight of the surgeon who performed the painful operation, or when the child, after too many nurse's tales, comes to connect sprites and goblins with darkness (II, xxxiii, 5–18). What was an anomaly of the understanding for Locke, a troublesome afterthought, becomes for Hume normative mental process. All thought is, naturally, a product of chance and custom for Hume; objects inevitably become cemented together in our thought patterns because, in the vagaries of our experience, they have tended to appear together. Where Locke had depicted our faculties industriously extending our knowledge, building a full understanding from the careful comparison of ideas, Hume is more hesitant to grant us mental agency. Habit, and not reason, determines the regular workings of the mind. We do not reason that heat will follow from fire, we do not even appeal to our memories of previous conjunctions of heat and fire, we are just used to thinking of heat and fire together. In this vein, Hume's working analogy for thought is drawn from Newton's account of the universe. The connection or association of ideas is 'a gentle force', 'a kind of ATTRACTION, which in the mental world will be found to have as extraordinary effects as in the natural' (I, i, 4). In Hume's *Treatise*, thought is not a chain of reasonings, or even a sequence of pictures thrown up on a screen, but a gravitational field – a web of connected ideas, all of shifting intensity and each pulling a host of others along with it.

More than either Locke or Berkeley, Hume saw himself as a professional writer, and he did eventually attain the recognition he sought from his massive *History of Great Britain* (1754–61). The *Treatise*, a work of Hume's twenties, was less warmly received, and he went on to recast its argument in several forms in the course of his life. But even in its original form it is evident that Hume saw himself as the man of letters he was to become, eagerly 'waiting on the approbation of the public' (introduction). Like Locke and Berkeley before him, he makes a conventional attack on the use of rhetoric in philosophy, as the resort only of scholastic disputations where 'the victory is not gained by the men at arms, who manage the pike and the sword; but by the trumpeters, drummers, and musicians of the army' (introduction). Hume goes on, of course, to play the stout yeoman in the battlefield of philosophy; plain dealing, hard working and unflinching when things get a little gory. But behind the straightforward voice of the *Treatise*, there is a concern to orchestrate the reader's response. Eschewing Berkeley's concision and directness for amplitude, Hume pursues problems in extensive digressions, works out points with ample illustration, and carefully anticipates and answers objections. Above all, Hume is careful not to confront the reader directly with the radically sceptical conclusions of his epistemology. Where Berkeley honestly if ill-advisedly laid out his *esse* is *percipi* for scrutiny in the first few pages of the *Principles*, Hume opens with reassuring gestures to a modern metaphysical tradition that is scientific, progressive, even useful. Book I of the *Treatise* begins as an inviting declivity in a familiar landscape, and if the way becomes steeper and the light fails, we have nonetheless the company of Hume, who seems as startled as do we by the turn of events. In effect Hume re-enacts before us his own original process of sceptical enquiry. Thus he registers, as if for the first time, his bafflement over our ideas of cause and effect, which he finds to be nothing but a 'constant conjunction' of ideas in the mind, with no 'ultimate connection' available to reason: ''tis by EXPERIENCE only, that we can infer the existence of one object from that of another' (I, iii, 6). Our belief that one object will, when it strikes another, cause that second object to move is an act of what Hume calls 'imagination' – the power of mind that 'enlivens' or intensifies ideas (I, iii, 13). Casting, as we have seen, our ideas of relation as operative mental 'customs', Hume now suggests that 'all probable reasoning is nothing but a species of sensation'. Where Locke had depicted thought as natural and as anchored by the resemblance of ideas to the real external substances that cause them, Hume describes our mental worlds as highly artificial. Indeed, Hume hints that our largely imaginative reckonings of the world might best be described in the language of art criticism – 'taste and sentiment' determine not just our moral choices, but our very way of seeing the world around us (I, iii, 8). For Hume all our ideas are inextricably entangled with emotions and appetites, a view he enforces by daring us to form an idea of £1,000 without an attendant *frisson* of greed.

Hume subtly introduces and then presses home the theme of the tenuousness and arbitrariness of our mental assumptions by illustrating his argument with gaming metaphors. He challenges our ideas of cause and effect by showing that we do not know what happens when one billiard ball strikes another, and he laboriously unravels the thoughts of a gambler throwing a die to display the character of probabilistic projection. These analogies are then brought to bear on the vaunted experimental method of the *Treatise* itself to concede that 'every past experiment may be consider'd as a kind of chance; it being uncertain to us, whether the object will exist conformable to one experiment or another' (I, iii, 12). The reader ploughing through Book I feels a growing sense of vertigo as the sureties of the world disappear one by one: 'reason is nothing but a wonderful and unintelligible instinct in our souls' (I, iii, 16); external objects are a necessary self-delusion (I, iv, 2); our very selves nothing but 'a bundle or collection of different perceptions . . . in perpetual flux and movement' (I, iv, 6). Our sense of instability is heightened by an alarming atheistical subtext that surfaces here and there throughout the *Treatise*. Hume himself repressed the infamous digression on miracles until the *Philosophical Essays* (1748), but he keeps the footnote proving that 'God is' – the first and most crucial conclusion in the version of natural religion widely promoted by Anglican apologists – is in fact the worst form of tautology (I, iii, 7). Ironically posing as one tender of religious themes and an enemy only to the excesses of Catholicism, he manages to attack many central tenets of Christianity, pointing out for example that we have no impression of God and no notion of the immortality of our own souls (I, iii, 9 and 14).

Throughout this gradual descent into radical doubt Hume stops from time to time to recognize the apparent absurdity of his conclusions and to provide a vent for the growing anxieties of the reader: 'I doubt not but my sentiments will be treated by many as extravagant and ridiculous. What! The efficacy of causes lies in the determination of mind!' (I, iii, 14). A gulf grows between the philosopher and the common thinker as Book I of the *Treatise* unfolds, with Hume even devoting several chapters to a sectarian history of philosophical delusion. The ancients with their substantial forms and occult qualities are mere dreamers, and the moderns with their distinction of primary and secondary qualities little better (I, iv, 3–4). The only option seems to be to play the parasitic sceptic, one who lives off the follies of dogmatic philosophers in a strange suicidal symbiosis (I, iv, 1–2). Just as Hume has registered the fully emotional character of our ideas, so he dramatizes at length, in the conclusion to Book I, the melancholy and restlessness that attend the philosophical life:

> I am first affrighted and confounded with that forelorn solitude, in which I am plac'd in my philosophy, and fancy myself some strange uncouth monster, who not being able to mingle and unite in society, has been expell'd all human commerce, and left utterly abandon'd and disconsolate. (I, iv, 7)

Almost manic depressive, Hume's sceptic endlessly circles between the solitary glory of gazing into the abyss and the necessity of living a life in which such visions are wholly irrelevant, a life more easily, indeed more reasonably lived by labourers and even animals than by philosophers.

Locke had consistently avoided morality in his *Essay*, saying it was a separate science and, like geometry, formally demonstrable, and though friends pressed him to write an ethics he never did. In fact, Locke's attack on innatism was initially read as an attack on morality and religion, since innatists typically cast our distinctive ethical and religious knowledge as a special gift from God, a seed of divinity we bring with us from a higher world and the mark of our mastery over creation. Even Newton, admittedly when his paranoia was at its most violent, would claim that in attacking innatism Locke 'struck at the root of morality' (*Correspondence*, IV, 727 and 731). Certainly, Locke's way of ideas ostensibly works against assumptions of universal concepts of virtue and vice. Hume is much more comprehensive in his probabilism than Locke, and he is ultimately capable of imagining a stable working morality that makes no reference to immutable laws, natural or revealed, but is founded upon the experimental observation of human behaviour. Having reached a terrible epistemological aporia at the end of Book I of the *Treatise*, he can proceed in Book II to offer a descriptive account of the human passions, and finally in Book III to elaborate an ethical system that is emotional rather than rational: 'the distinguishing impressions, by which moral good or evil is known, are nothing but *particular* pains or pleasures' (III, i, 2). Experience shows that we have unmistakable feelings of displeasure on witnessing a vicious act. Armed with such 'moral sentiments' and enjoying a natural sympathy with our fellow creatures, we are clearly able to act in a way capable of sustaining civil society. Hume's *Treatise* is, then, both the *reductio ad absurdum* and the salvation of the project of rewriting metaphysics as natural philosophy begun by Locke. Hume's godless, affective morality answers the objections of Locke's detractors in a way they could never have imagined. Hume clearly relished the irony: 'thus the most abstract speculations concerning human nature, however cold and unentertaining, become subservient to *practical morality*; and may render this latter science more correct in its precepts, and more persuasive in its exhortations' (III, iii, 7).

REFERENCES AND FURTHER READING

Bacon, Francis (1857–8). *The Philosophical Works of Francis Bacon*. Ed. J. Spedding et al. 5 vols. London: Longmans.

Berkeley, George (1948–57). *The Works of George Berkeley, Bishop of Cloyne*. Ed. A. A. Luce and T. E. Jessop. London: Nelson.

Burnet, Thomas (1989). *Remarks on Locke by Thomas Burnet*. Ed. George Watson. Doncaster: Brynmill Press.

Flew, Anthony (1986). *David Hume: Philosopher of Moral Science*. Oxford: Blackwell.

Glanville, Joseph (1665). *Scepsis Scientifica*. London: H. Eversden.

Hume, David (1975). *Enquiries concerning Human Understanding*. Ed. P. H. Nidditch. Oxford: Oxford University Press.

——(1978). *Treatise of Human Nature*. Ed. P. H. Nidditch. 2nd edn. Oxford: Clarendon Press.

Locke, John (1976–89). *Correspondence of John Locke*. Ed. E. S. de Beer. 8 vols. Oxford: Clarendon Press.

——(1975). *An Essay concerning Human Understanding*. Ed. P. H. Nidditch. Oxford: Clarendon Press.

Newton, Isaac (1704). *Opticks*. London: S. Smith.

Norton, David Fate, ed. (1993). *The Cambridge Companion to Hume*. Cambridge: Cambridge University Press.

Richetti, John (1983). *Philosophical Writing: Locke, Berkeley, Hume*. Cambridge: Harvard University Press.

Shaftesbury, Anthony Ashley Cooper, third Earl of (1714). *Characteristicks of Men, Manners, Morals, Times*. 2nd edn.

Sprat, Thomas (1959). *The History of the Royal Society*. Ed. J. I. Cope and H. W. Jones. London: Routledge.

Sterne, Laurence (1978). *The Life and Opinions of Tristram Shandy*. Ed. M. and J. New. 3 vols. Gainesville: University Presses of Florida.

Stewart, M. A. and John P. Wright (1994). *Hume and Hume's Connections*. University Park: Pennsylvania State University Press.

Tipton, I. C. (1974). *Berkeley: The Philosophy of Immaterialism*. London: Methuen.

Walmsley, Peter (1990). *The Rhetoric of Berkeley's Philosophy*. Cambridge: Cambridge University Press.

Yolton, John (1956). *John Locke and the Way of Ideas*. Oxford: Oxford University Press.

——(1970). *Locke and the Compass of Human Understanding*. Cambridge: Cambridge University Press.

51

Historical Writing

Karen O'Brien

David Hume's declaration, in 1770, that 'this [is] the historical age, and this the historical nation', may have been effusive, but it was no great exaggeration. The period witnessed a remarkable flowering of historical writing, in which individual achievements as enduring as Clarendon's *History of the Rebellion* and Gibbon's *Decline and Fall* were accompanied by a more general transformation in the country's historical culture and awareness. This was a transformation which differed from other subsequent movements and changes in historical practice, in the sense that it took place largely before history became a professional discipline. Throughout the late seventeenth and eighteenth centuries, history remained primarily the domain of amateur writers, albeit of amateurs who became increasingly competent and specialized in the business of historical scholarship. Scholarly standards improved and there was an expansion in the number of areas which came under the purview of history, yet it continued to be understood as a liberal art within the general field of literature.

The generic identity of history as a species of literary writing, which proved so resilient throughout the eighteenth century and beyond, derived from classical prescriptions and models. The rhetorical model of history defined by the traditional *ars historica* was not generally perceived to be at odds with its status as a branch of knowledge, even after the scientific revolution of the early seventeenth century. Francis Bacon himself assigned history a secure position within his scheme of knowledge, which he subdivided into the faculties of memory, imagination and reason, corresponding, respectively, to the genres of historical writing, poetry and philosophy. It was, he observed, a matter of debate as to which faculty and genre offered the best access to truth – a debate which remained unresolved during the next two centuries, although commentators increasingly came to regard the struggle between memory, imagination and reason, as something internal to history itself. It was not until the nineteenth century, that commentators suggested that there might be a tension between the narrative form of history and its empirical or philosophical content. In the 1820s, the historian Thomas Babington Macaulay wrote of history as a battleground 'under the jurisdiction' of 'two hostile powers', reason and imagination: 'it is sometimes fiction', he wrote, 'it is sometimes theory'. In recent times, critical theorists (most influentially, Hayden White) have made a good deal more of the tension between the truth claims of history and its narrative textuality. Historians of the late seventeenth and eighteenth centuries had no such doubts about the capacity of history as a mode of knowledge, but they were preoccupied with the philosophical problems posed by the narrative ordering of factual material. History, as historians of this period would have acknowledged, is obliged to make connections between causes and effects in the past without which it would be devoid of truth content — merely meaningless data. Yet this inevitably entails a measure of creative intervention on the part of the author, and the paradox for the historian is that truthful, meaningful history is inseparable from conjecture and the art of rhetorical persuasion.

Seventeenth- and eighteenth-century practitioners of history, like their Renaissance forebears, looked to classical models as their chief source of inspiration. They adopted the classical idea of history as linear, political narrative written either by a retired statesman or soldier with first-hand experience of the events described (such as Thucydides, Caesar, Sallust, and after them Clarendon, Gilbert Burnet and Bolingbroke), or by an amateur man of letters chronicling his times or the history of an empire or kingdom (such as Livy or Tacitus, and after them Gibbon, Hume and Catharine Macaulay). With the weight of classical authority behind them, these 'particular' and 'general' histories enjoyed a position at the top of the hierarchy of eighteenth-century prose genres, some way above the novel and their nearest rivals, biographies and memoirs. The public perception of history as a venerably classical genre enabled historians to benefit from its prestige and authority even while they adapted and renewed the genre, often extending its analytical and thematic scope far beyond the range of their predecessors. The classical idea of history as the record of exemplary deeds was steadily transformed into one which was less concerned with political lessons, and more with the economic, social and cultural dimensions of historical change. Over and above supplying examples of human conduct to be imitated or avoided, historians aimed to give their readers a broader understanding of their inherited English, Scottish, British and European identities. Historians also broadened their conception of political history to include many aspects of what was then considered private life (see Mark Phillips, 'Adam Smith and the History of Private Life'). In the hands of Scottish historians, in particular, political history became civil history by incorporating such subjects as the development of legal systems, modes of economic subsistence, and changes in the organization of the family and the position of women; thus, 'society', rather than the political realm, became the primary object of historical enquiry.

Historians also experimented in other ways, even as they continued outwardly to observe classical protocols. For example, Clarendon, in his self-consciously Thucydidean *History of the Rebellion*, breaks with tradition in his thoroughly unclassical incorporation of copious documentary material, as does Gilbert Burnet in his *History of the Reformation* (1679–1715). Both works paved the way for the massive scholarly endnotes to Robertson's *History of the Reign of the Emperor Charles V* and for the erudite footnotes to Gibbon's *Decline and Fall*. The progressively scholarly orientation of history seems to have promoted, rather than inhibited, experimentation at the formal level. Throughout this period the generic, as well as the scholarly, possibilities of history were enlarged as writers imported stylistic techniques, registers and vocabularies from other kinds of writing. Contemporary commentators tended to point out similarities between history and poetry – a traditionally close relationship – but it was from the newer form of the novel that historians borrowed most of their innovations. The language of sentiment, developed in mid-eighteenth-century fiction, proved especially attractive to historians seeking to involve their readers emotionally in the plight of historical figures, and, frequently, to generate a sense of common adherence to a particular version of the national past.

Some historians, for example Oliver Goldsmith in his *History of England* for children of 1764, made use of the epistolary form, more commonly associated with fiction, while others, such as Robert Henry in his multi-layered *History of Great Britain on a New Plan* (1773–93) followed novelists of the later eighteenth century in their attempts to dismantle linear narrative. Historians were sufficiently secure in the superiority of their genre not to feel compromised by their borrowings from novelists. Novelists, meanwhile, played upon their secondary status to historians, drawing attention to the derivative relationship between their works and history. From titles of novels (*The History of Tom Jones, A Foundling* or *Clarissa: Or the History of a Young Lady*) to strategies of factual authentication (such as supporting documents, pseudo-editorial prefaces, precise dates and places), novelists positioned their works in an ambivalently deferential or parodic relationship to historical writing. By the end of this period, historical novelists such as Walter Scott started to mount a serious challenge to the pre-eminence of traditional history, but not before historians themselves had experimented with novelized presentations of characters and events.

The generic evolution and enlarged thematic scope of narrative history simultaneously reflected and instigated a broadening of its audience. Historians increasingly wrote with a sense of a wider, less elite readership than the one addressed by earlier writers. By the mid-eighteenth century there was a large enough historical reading culture in Britain to sustain sizeable print runs of expensive, multi-volume works. As well as narrative history, this culture favoured works of antiquarian scholarship. The early eighteenth-century culture wars between the ancients (who favoured polished, classical narrative history) and the moderns (who defended scholarly study of documents, artefacts and ruins) polarized British intellectual life for a number of years, but it did not quench the market thirst for either kind of history (see Levine, *The Battle of the Books*). On the one hand, there was strong public demand for a classically polished history of England by a British writer (before Hume's *History of England*, the best available was by a Frenchman, Rapin-Thoyras, and publishers tried continually to fill this gap by commissioning, compiling and rehashing sub-standard works). On the other hand, the market supported a large number of antiquarian publications, such as county histories, chorographical works (most notably William Gibson's monumental re-edition of Camden's *Britannia*, 1695), and surveys of vernacular or religious architecture (such as Richard Gough's *Sepulchral Monuments*, 1786). Alongside this market for works of rural antiquarianism, urban histories increased rapidly in number and popularity, reflecting the growth of a metropolitan reading public with a sense of civic pride in its past (see Rosemary Sweet, *The Writing of Urban Histories*).

As well as encompassing a range of social and regional interests, the historical reading public was also genuinely mixed in terms of gender. Historians such as Hume and Gibbon were fully aware of the female constituent of their readership, and endeavoured to reflect female concerns and interests in their works. History was the kind of writing most often recommended to women by the authors of conduct books and educational works; it could offer them insights into the male world of public affairs, and, in the case of the many histories of Rome written or reprinted in this period, it could compensate for their lack of a classical education (see, for example, Hester Chapone's essay on 'The Manner of Reading History' in her *Letters on the Improvement of the Mind*, 1773). Women historians or historical scholars were comparatively rare in this period: Catharine Macaulay, Mary Wollstonecraft and the Anglo-Saxon scholar Elizabeth Elstob were conspicuous exceptions. However, as D. R. Woolf has shown, women made a significant contribution to what might be called the 'social circulation' of historical knowledge ('A Female Past?'); some edited historical miscellanies or excerpted passages from history in educational anthologies (Mary Wollstonecraft included extracts from Robertson and Hume in her *Female Reader* of 1789), whilst others translated historical works (for example Susannah Dobson's 1784 translation of Sainte-Palaye's influential *Memoirs of Ancient Chivalry*) or popularized episodes or characters from history in poems, novels or plays (for example, Hannah More's highly successful play *Percy*, 1777). Women also played an important role in the general extension of the generic range of narrative history. By the end of the period, women featured prominently as authors of historical biographies (for example, Elizabeth Hamilton's *Memoirs of Agrippina*, 1803) a field in which, along with art history, they were to excel during the next century.

Among the major historical works of this period, the work which conformed most closely to the classical ideal of political narrative written by a man of affairs was Edward Hyde, Earl of Clarendon's *History of the Rebellion and the Civil Wars of England*. This was a first-hand 'particular history' of political events from the years leading up to the Civil War to the Restoration which, with its minute analysis of the complex human dynamics and hidden workings of conflict, clearly recalled Thucydides' *History of the Peloponnesian War*. An adviser to Charles I, Clarendon started writing his history in 1646, at the king's request, after royalist military defeats forced him into exile in the Scilly isles, Jersey and Paris. After the Restoration, Clarendon returned to office as Lord Chancellor, effectively ruling England until a series of political defeats forced him into a second exile in France in 1667. It was during this time that he composed a long autobiography, partly to vindicate his own conduct; he then resumed his history of the Civil War, incorporating portions of the autobiography into the revised whole,

and delivered the finished manuscript to his son in 1671. The political stance of the
work – firmly, though never uncritically, loyal to the dynasty and prerogative of the
Stuart monarchs yet committed to the idea of a balanced English constitution of
church and state – rendered it more, not less, controversial as the century wore on;
and it was not until 1702–4, during the reign of Clarendon's grand-daughter, the
Stuart Queen Anne, that the work was finally touched up by his sons and published.
The remaining portions of the autobiography, including the account of his chancel-
lorship, were published in 1758.

The general framework of the *History of the Rebellion* is didactic and providential.
It is Clarendon's conviction that the Civil War was the result of national deviation
from righteousness followed by divine deliverance which powers the rhetorical movement of the two magnificently sustained opening periods (much abbreviated below):

> That posterity may not be deceived . . . he who shall diligently observe . . . will find all
> this bulk of misery to have proceeded, and to have been brought upon us, from the same
> natural causes and means which have usually attended kingdoms swoln with long plenty,
> pride, and excess, towards some signal mortification, and castigation of Heaven. (I, 1–2)

The opening reveals the moral essence of Clarendon's history, centring upon the apostasy of a foolish and wicked nation, and also points towards the narrative substance
of the work, the 'natural causes and means' which lie in his minute, fascinating
accounts of the loyalties, betrayals and power struggles between individual men.
Politics, for Clarendon, is a larger, more complex dimension of friendship; moral relations between men, the willingness and courage of one man to set aside flattery and
self-interest and speak truthfully to the other, are the true stuff of politics. It is the
failure of those closest to Charles I to counsel him honestly and warn him, as Clarendon himself tried to do, against interfering too much with England's traditional
constitution, which precipitates disaster.

Clarendon's prose is forensic, with its dense weave of precisely modulated adjectives and carefully marshalled syntax, but it also rises to elegiac or tragic heights
at key moments in the narrative. One such moment occurs towards the beginning of
the history when he recalls the early years of Charles I's reign as a kind of pastoral
scene before the fall: 'the kingdoms we now lament were alone looked upon as the
garden of the world [with] arts and sciences fruitfully planted there; and the whole
nation beginning to be so civilized that it was a jewel of great lustre in the most royal
diadem' (I, 94). A second moment of stylistic flight occurs during the famous scene
of the trial and execution of Charles I. Here, the tragic dignity of the king ('the saint-
like behaviour of that blessed martyr') is emotively contrasted with the coarseness and
insulting behaviour of his accusers: 'the several unheard of insolences which this excellent prince was forced to submit to [. . .], his majestic behaviour under so much insolence, and resolute insisting upon his own dignity [. . .] are all so well known [. . .]
that the farther mentioning it in this place would but afflict and grieve the reader'
(IV, 488).

The History of the Rebellion reinforced Charles's image, in the eighteenth century, as a martyr to dangerous radicalism, despite Clarendon's measured assessment of his failings as a king. Catharine Macaulay caused public outrage when, in her *History of England*, she dared to suggest that the execution was justified on political grounds. Yet, despite its role in perpetuating consensus about Charles I, Clarendon's history was otherwise received by its early readers as a controversial, party-political work. The publication of the *History of the Rebellion* was timed by Clarendon's sons and their associates to promote the fortunes of the Tory party. For much of the eighteenth century, public perception of the history as a work tied to the Tory party-political agenda limited its artistic appeal (though not its phenomenal sales) to Whig readers.

Anti-Whig writers, most notably the Tory and sometime Jacobite politician Henry St John, Viscount Bolingbroke, were happy to embrace Clarendon's literary legacy. Bolingbroke's *Letters on the Study and Use of History*, written in the late 1730s and printed in 1752, were addressed to Clarendon's descendant Lord Cornbury, and, like his predecessor's history, imparted the accumulated insights of a man of state into the meaning of history. Bolingbroke's work was innovative in its attempt to bridge the gap between the classical, Clarendonian idea of history as recorded experience and the idea, developed in France a few decades earlier, of historical writing as the application of *philosophical* principles to the data of the past. Bolingbroke's aphorism, adapted from the Greek, that 'history is philosophy teaching by examples' marks the beginning of a new era of historical thought in Britain. British historians of the second half of the eighteenth century, whilst still, for the most part, committed to linear, narrative history, opened up a number of new areas of philosophical investigation, including the general insights into human nature which the past provides, the verifiability or otherwise of historical facts and truths, and the nature and laws of causality. Theoretical questions such as these were investigated exhaustively by French critics in the early part of the eighteenth century, and motivated the historical work of Voltaire, Montesquieu and other writers of the French Enlightenment. French histories were translated and widely read in Britain, whetting a public appetite for British 'philosophical' history. This was only partly satisfied by Bolingbroke's brief sketches, and it was Scottish writers who first supplied the public with a British version of philosophical history, distinctive in depth and scope, and free of the polemical animus which sometimes marred French works.

A much fuller answer to the British demand for a national philosophical history came in the form of David Hume's *History of England*, the first volume of which appeared in 1754. At last British readers had a history by a British writer (Hume's Scottishness was less significant to English reviewers than his non-Frenchness) good enough to replace Rapin, which was, moreover, dazzling in its narrative orchestration of its source material, and in its agile, wry, detached (but never dry) style. Hume wrote his history backwards, beginning with two volumes on the seventeenth century (1754, 1756), moving back to the Tudor period (two volumes in 1759), and ending with two medieval volumes (1762). Hume approached his subject as a moral philosopher already deeply interested in the peculiarities of human nature, the unpredictable yet decisive role of beliefs in motivating human action, and the mismatches, in all areas of human endeavour, between causes and effects. He also adopted the standpoint of a social philosopher searching (like Gibbon after him) for the secular origins of religious belief, the political effects of economic change, and the cultural basis of political stability. Hume claimed, with some justification, to have produced an 'impartial' history detached from the Whig and Tory party prejudices of his day, and, from the outset, he began dismantling cherished party myths about the political meaning of the English past. Yet critical discussion of the work then, as, to some extent, now has been dominated by the question of its party allegiances. Some contemporary critics were happy to report that Hume had, indeed, given Britain an impartial, 'general' history, but many more complained that the work was either too Whiggish or, more often, too Tory.

In a letter of 1756, Hume explained: 'With regard to the politics and the character of princes and great men, I think I am very moderate. My view of things are more conformable to Whig principles; my representations of persons to Tory prejudices.' This simplifies Hume's political vision of the past, but it does encapsulate Hume's sense of post-medieval British history as a general momentum of 'things' (economic growth, the spread of literacy, Protestant ideas of individual conscience, the decline of the personal power of the aristocracy) towards greater political liberty; this process is on a collision course with the ideas which royal 'persons', in particular, legitimately hold about their inherited power and rights. The seventeenth-century volumes tell the story, in the spirit of sceptical, historically nuanced Whiggism, of religious and political liberties improvised and then precariously established in 1688–9; but stylistic interludes of tragedy, sentimental drama and mock epic capture the cost and contradictoriness of this 'progress' for many of the persons involved.

The *History of England* contains a broad repertoire of styles, from the ironic to the overtly sentimental, thus eliciting from its readers a complex range of responses to the events of their past. Hume was keenly aware of the female portion of this readership, and bore them in mind when making use of novelistic effects in the history. His account of the execution of Charles I, a person whom he presents through the lens of 'Tory prejudices', outdoes even Clarendon in its emotional intensity, and is rendered in the feminized language of sentimental fiction: 'if Mrs Mure be not sorry for poor King Charles', Hume wrote to his friend William Mure, 'I shall burn all my papers and return to Philosophy'. Like Robertson after him, Hume used the language of sentiment to register and absorb the disruptive political significance of painful historical memories. The subject of religious fanaticism, however, seemed to him to demand a different stylistic approach, and here he combined a satiric voice with the analytical detachment which characterized his other works such as *The Natural History of Religion* (1757). Like Swift, Hume saw 'enthusiasm' (the kind of radical Protestantism which engendered the Civil War) as the product of sincere delusion rather than hypocrisy, and all the more dangerous and demented for that reason. The *History* does advance a number of social explanations for enthusiasm, but, for Hume as for

Swift, its origins lie deeper in the human psyche, and it is part of the black comedy of human nature.

The Tudor and medieval volumes of Hume's *History* are, by comparison, less colourful, though, in many respects, more philosophically ambitious as works of social and economic history. The Tudor volumes place less emphasis upon royal personalities and dilemmas, and more upon the story of the establishment of the centralized, monarchical English state out of the ruins of the medieval feudal order. Hume's perspective in this part of the *History* is consistently European, with each development in England measured against contemporary events on the continent. Elizabeth I – a monarch reinvented in the 1730s by Bolingbroke and others as the good and liberal 'Queen Bess' – is presented as an absolute (but not despotic) European sovereign who drew power away from the church, nobility and commons in order to create a firm and stable political system. In the medieval volumes, Hume traces this process of national state formation back to its origins in a pioneering interpretation of the rise and fall of feudalism. In addition, Hume gives a surprisingly generous account of the medieval Catholic Church as a force for social justice and change, although he is otherwise conservative, by the standards of his day, in his mainly negative attitude towards chivalry and other aspects of medieval culture.

After initial controversy, Hume's *History* met with growing public acceptance, and, in its final, revised form of 1778, achieved enduring canonical status. The Stuart volumes faced a serious rival in the form of Catharine Macaulay's *History of England* (1763–83), a work which, along with its sequel *The History of England from the Revolution to the Present Time* (1778), set out to offer a radical alternative to Hume's reading of the seventeenth century. Macaulay (no relation of her namesake, Thomas Babington) was a leading radical Whig salonnière and pamphleteer who achieved enormous fame in her own lifetime both in Britain and North America. In tone and substance, Macaulay's history is diametrically opposed to Hume's. Where Hume is cosmopolitan, sceptical in religious matters and politically impartial, Macaulay is a passionately engaged writer, committed to Protestantism, classical-republican politics and the forgotten but retrievable cause of English liberty. In both her histories, Macaulay replaces Hume's detached authorial voice with a brisk, self-confident persona, dedicated to liberty in England, and dismissive of all those who have stood in its way. When it comes to liberty, she complains with characteristic impatience, 'the people of Great Britain always are, half stupid, half drunk, and half asleep' (1778 *History*, 372).

Macaulay saw few signs of progress in English history, despite many exemplary cases of individual selflessness and heroism. Certainly, she considered the events of 1688 as neither glorious nor a revolution, and the corruption and greed of modern politics filled her with despair, despite the economic improvements which, she acknowledged, had been brought by commerce. For Macaulay, the golden age of English history was the Commonwealth of 1649–53, but this was quickly ruined by the 'base, vain-glorious' Cromwell, and thereafter liberty made little progress. Thus, rather than searching for signs of progress, the real purpose of Macaulay's history is to re-educate her readers politically as a preparation for the campaign for the extension of civil and voting rights to a wider section of the English middle class.

Macaulay never advocated female suffrage, and it was only in her later work, the *Letters on Education* (1790), that she made the case for the civil and intellectual equality of women. Yet, in rejecting the notion of the 'progress of society', which less radical historians such as Hume and Robertson always claimed to have been favourable to the equality of women, she established a link between feminism and republicanism which Mary Wollstonecraft and other subsequent writers would develop further. In a general way, the foray of a woman writer, with her name and picture at the front of each volume, into the male genre of narrative history constituted in itself an assertion of equality: 'The invidious censures which may ensue from striking into a path of literature rarely trodden by my sex', she remarked in the preface to the first volume of 1763, 'will not permit a selfish consideration to keep me mute in the cause of liberty' (I, x). Macaulay's prose is not presented as, in any sense, the product of a feminine sensibility; instead, she approaches liberty, natural rights and civic virtue as abstract ideals which transcend the gender and historical limitations placed upon those who articulate them.

Despite their radicalism, Macaulay's histories were not innovative at the formal or philosophical levels. Macaulay had political, and possibly feminist, reasons for rejecting the newer, philosophical history in favour of political narrative, but this was a decision which would cost her readers in the longer term. Meanwhile, Hume's medieval volumes revealed to a wider public the possibilities of the new sociology and political economy currently being developed in Scottish universities. His Scottish intellectual circle included Adam Smith, the literary critic Hugh Blair, the philosophers Adam Ferguson and Lord Kames, and the historian William Robertson. Scotland was incorporated into Great Britain by the Union of 1707, yet the country continued to be regarded with some suspicion or condescension south of the border, particularly after the 1745 Rebellion. Scottish Whig writers of Hume's generation were anxious to redeem Scotland's reputation, and to enhance its standing within Britain and the British empire. Few did more to accomplish this objective than Robertson, a leading Church of Scotland minister and, later, Principal of the University of Edinburgh whose status as a historian equalled that of Hume and Gibbon until well into the nineteenth century.

Robertson's first historical work, *The History of Scotland* (1759) simultaneously exemplified and promoted this idea of Scotland as a place of learning, polite culture, and religious and political moderation. Dealing mainly with events in the sixteenth century, it took a Whiggish, but politically tactful and stylistically decorous, approach to some of the most controversial moments in the country's past: the violence of the Reformation, the murder of the husband of Mary, Queen of Scots, and Scotland's loss of separate nationhood after the Union of the Scottish and English crowns. At the end, the history looks forward to the Union of 1707 as a framework for progress and prosperity in the province, but it also conveys some emotional allegiance to the enduring virtues of Scottish culture, such as its martial spirit of independence and self-reliance, its ethos of public service, and its capacity for communal loyalty. Most notably, the work handles with great diplomacy the story of Mary, Queen of Scots, a potent symbol for eighteenth-century Jacobites, by depicting her as a sentimental heroine rather than as a fully responsible political agent. In this, Robertson laid the ground for the subsequent reinvention of Jacobitism, by Walter Scott and others, as an aesthetic attitude only.

Robertson was more typical of his age than Hume or Gibbon in regarding historical events as, at the deepest level, embodiments of God's providential purpose. Like generations of Scottish Presbyterian historians before him, he characterized individuals and peoples as unwitting 'instruments' of providence, and saw his own role as that of an elucidator of God's guiding hand through history. This fundamentally Protestant sense of history precluded the kind of ironic distance between narrator and narrative content characteristic of Hume and Gibbon's work, but did not prevent him from sharing their cosmopolitan and ecumenical spirit of historical enquiry. This spirit is more clearly exemplified in Robertson's next book, *The History of the Reign of the Emperor Charles V* (1769), which is really a 'general' history, rather than a biography, and which documents the difficult birth of a new, multi-denominational political order in sixteenth-century Europe. The history is prefaced by an extended essay entitled 'A View of the Progress of Society in Europe' from Roman to late medieval times. An exploration of the form and nature of 'society' in Europe (not of 'European society'), the 'View' built upon Hume and Smith's work to present a highly influential analysis of the transition from feudalism to the modern world of commercial, civil polities. The 'View' also contained an important discussion of the positive contribution of medieval chivalry and the Crusades to the civilizing process in Europe, thus paving the way for a more general 'gothic revival' in British historical culture.

Robertson's last, and greatest, major history, *The History of America* (1777) expands still further his work on the Renaissance period by telling the story of the Spanish and Portuguese discoveries and conquests in Central and South America. Once again, his approach to history proved highly innovative for its day, incorporating the latest Scottish social and anthropological theory into detailed surveys of Inca, Aztec and other native American civilizations. Robertson also gives a compelling narrative of the conquistadors' sense of excitement (his history was famously the inspiration for the closing lines of Keats's sonnet 'On First Looking into Chapman's *Homer*'), as well as the intoxication of sudden wealth, and the dangerous delirium of unlimited power. Despite his commitment to Protestant historiography, Robertson also took a balanced view of the role of the Catholic Church and the Spanish state in the cruelties of conquest, ascribing most of the worst excesses to the greed and inhumanity of the privateers and officials on the ground.

Around the same time as the *History of America*, Scottish philosophical history acquired a notable English disciple, albeit one with a profound sense of the limitations of theoretical categories and sociological generalizations. Edward Gibbon, in his *History of the Decline and Fall of the Roman Empire*, 1776–88, far exceeded all other historians of this period both in historical erudition and narrative breadth and mastery.

Yet there are significant continuities between Gibbon's history and the works of the Scottish Enlightenment; these reside in the work's central preoccupation with the nature of civil society, the balance between liberty and political stability, encounters and wars between peoples at different levels of social development, and the historical consequences of religious fanaticism. In the context of eighteenth-century historical writing, Gibbon's work can certainly be considered as one of the 'general', philosophical histories of its age, providing, like the works of Hume and Robertson, a linear, causal narrative of a great chronological sweep of political events.

Committed, at least at the outset, to the modes of explanatory, causal narrative he had developed from his reading of Hume, Montesquieu and Robertson (though not the providential aspects of his writing), Gibbon searches for the hidden political, social, economic and military springs of the slow decline of Rome. At the political level, he shows how the Roman citizens' sense of public responsibility was slowly depleted by years of remote, autocratic government. At one point, Gibbon suggests that the Emperor Septimius Severus (AD 193–211) could be plausibly considered 'the principal author of the decline of the Roman empire' because he ended a long tradition of political supervision of the army by Rome's ruling class (I, 148). Gibbon believed that balanced constitutions, with power dispersed among different institutions and groups of people, were necessary for the political health and stability of a state. Rome, however, was long subjected to the absolute governments of individual emperors; although the empire continued to survive for many centuries on the ideological capital of the republic and so command respect from its people, it became little more than an eastern despotism, even before it relocated itself to the east.

A more obvious cause of decline was the repeated raids of the northern barbarians who weakened and disrupted the western empire before taking it over completely. In this case, however, Gibbon opts for a less conventional approach (and one which is more in line with late twentieth-century scholarship on the subject) which is to emphasize the paradoxical role of the Ostrogoths, Franks, Saxons and other northern tribes in absorbing many aspects of Roman life into their culture, and so effecting the continuation of the empire by indirect means. Most notoriously, Gibbon associates the decline of Rome with the rise of Christianity, initially by delaying all mention of the subject until chapters 15 and 16 at the end of the first volume in which this new religion is suddenly and ironically revealed as the destroyer of the civic life of the empire. In chapter 15, Gibbon ironically postulates five principal reasons for the success of the early Christians (by which he means their erosion of Rome's tolerant, sociable religious and civic culture): their inflexible temper and zeal, the novelty and power of their doctrine of the immortality of the soul, their virtues, their active involvement in church government, and the miracles which occurred. Gibbon then demonstrates, in chapter 16, that the numbers of Christian converts, and especially of Christian martyrs, was greatly exaggerated by pious commentators ('the whole might consequently amount to about fifteen hundred, a number which, if it is equally divided between the ten years of the persecution, will allow an annual consumption of one hundred and fifty martyrs', I, 579). Christianity was statistically insignificant,

Gibbon concludes, until everybody discovered that it was in their interest to convert to the faith after Constantine hypocritically did so in AD 337.

Yet, below the surface of the coruscating ironies of these two chapters, and in the volumes which follow, Gibbon's sense of the causal relationship between Christianity and the decline of Rome turns out to be far more complex. Before it becomes the official state religion, Christianity is presented as the only dynamic element in an otherwise complacent and stagnant culture; in an empire sinking into the 'languid indifference of private life', the Christians create their own public world (I, 83). By emphasizing the discontinuity between Christianity and the pagan culture of the empire, Gibbon also implicitly acknowledges that the significance of this new religion lay in its radical restructuring of social and sexual values, and its capacity to generate new modes of consciousness and individual autonomy at a point when, among pagans, 'the minds of men were gradually reduced to the same level, the fire of genius was extinguished' (I, 83). Chapter 15 incorporates a statement, unusually direct for Gibbon, of what he considers to be the best qualities in the most 'virtuous and liberal' people; these are the 'love of pleasure', leading to civilized sociability, and the 'love of action', leading to the good of the public realm (I, 478). Whereas the pagans appear to cultivate the first at the expense of the second, the Christians exhibit both of these qualities in an intense, but perverse form: a 'love of pleasure' through their secret sociability and paradoxically erotic asceticism (Gibbon, who was remarkably frank on sexual matters, describes how the Christian 'virgins of the warm climate of Africa [. . .] permitted priests and deacons to share their bed, and gloried amidst the flames in their unsullied purity', I, 481); and a 'love of action' in their eager promotion of their church, discussed in a section entitled 'The Christians active in the government of the church' (I, 482).

All this goes beyond the compliment which satire pays to the ebullience of its target; Gibbon, even at the moment when his causal narrative appears most determinate, points his readers towards the paradoxical, long-term historical consequences of the Christian revolution. What follows in subsequent volumes is the story of how western Christianity in the long run adapted and protracted the Roman imperial culture which it had originally helped to undermine. Eastern Christianity, by contrast, proves to be more of a force for cultural inertia, and does not adopt such a flexible, syncretic approach to its pagan imperial heritage. Yet here, too, Gibbon's causal narrative gives way to productive complexity, and he reaches the explanatory limits of philosophical history. It is the eastern empire's sheer persistence, through hundreds of years of continuity and unperceived change, which impresses, and not the incremental process of decline. There could be no doubt that the Roman empires in the west and east did fall (to the barbarian king Odoacer and to the Ottoman Turks, respectively), but Gibbon allows the question of decline to slip beyond the readers' imaginative, as well as philosophical, grasp.

Enlarged and enriched by Gibbon's achievement, the Scottish tradition of philosophical history persisted to the end of the century and well beyond. In the 1790s historians found this form of history particularly serviceable when seeking to narrate and explain the French Revolution in something other than purely political terms. Mary Wollstonecraft's *Historical and Moral View of the Origin and Progress of the French Revolution* (1794), for example, followed Macaulay in its avoidance of an identifiably female historical voice, and applied the analytical categories of works such as Robertson's 'View of the Progress of Society in Europe', to the background and first year of the Revolution; through the lens of her own, politically radical version of philosophical history, the Revolution emerges as an event noble in its ideals, but doomed to violence and failure because it attempted to propel an uneducated, uncivilized populace into a higher stage of social evolution.

REFERENCES

Bolingbroke, Henry St John, Viscount (1752). *Letters on the Study and Use of History.* In *Lord Bolingbroke: Historical Writings* (1972). Ed. Isaac Kramnick. Chicago: Chicago University Press.

Clarendon, Edward Hyde, Earl of (1704–6). *The History of the Rebellion and Civil Wars in England.* (1888, reissued 1992). Ed. W. Dunn Macray. 6 vols. Oxford: Oxford University Press.

Gibbon, Edward (1776–88). *The History of the Decline and Fall of the Roman Empire.* Ed. David Womersley (1994). 3 vols. Harmondsworth: Allen Lane.

Hume, David (1754–62). *The History of England.*

Ed. William B. Todd (1983). 7 vols. Indianapolis: Liberty Press.

Macaulay, Catharine (1763–83). *The History of England.* 7 vols. London: J. Nourse, R. Dodsley and A. Hamilton.

Robertson, William (1759). *The History of Scotland.* 2 vols. London: A. Millar.

——(1769). *The History of the Reign of the Emperor Charles V.* 3 vols. London: W. Strahan.

——(1777). *The History of America.* 2 vols. London: W. Strahan.

Wollstonecraft, Mary (1794). *An Historical and Moral View of the Origin and Progress of the French Revolution.* London: Joseph Johnson.

FURTHER READING

Braudy, Leo (1970). *Narrative Form in History and Fiction: Hume, Fielding and Gibbon.* Princeton: Princeton University Press.

Brown, Stewart J., ed. (1997). *William Robertson and the Expansion of Empire.* Cambridge: Cambridge University Press.

Hicks, Philip (1996). *Neoclassical History and English Culture: From Clarendon to Hume.* Basingstoke: Macmillan.

Hill, Bridget (1992). *The Republican Virago: The Life and Times of Catharine Macaulay, Historian.* Oxford: Clarendon Press.

Levine, Joseph (1987). *The Battle of the Books: History and Literature in the Augustan Age.* Ithaca N.Y.: Cornell University Press.

O'Brien, Karen (1997). *Narratives of Enlightenment:*

Cosmopolitan History from Voltaire to Gibbon. Cambridge: Cambridge University Press.

Phillips, Mark (1989). 'Macaulay, Scott and the literary challenge to historiography'. *Journal of the History of Ideas* 50, 117–33.

——(1997). 'Adam Smith and the history of private life: social and sentimental narratives in eighteenth-century historiography'. In *The Historical Imagination in Early Modern Britain.* Ed. Donald R. Kelley and David Harris Sacks. Cambridge: Cambridge University Press, 318–42.

Phillipson, Nicholas (1989). *Hume.* London: Weidenfeld and Nicolson.

Rawson, Claude (1997). 'Gibbon, Swift and irony'. In *Edward Gibbon: Bicentenary Essays. Studies on*

Voltaire and the Eighteenth-Century. Ed. David Womersley. 355, 179–201.

Rendall, Jane (1997). '"The Grand causes which combine to carry mankind forward": Wollstonecraft, history and revolution'. *Women's Writing* 4, 155–72.

Smitten, Jeffrey (1985). 'Impartiality in Robertson's *History of America*'. *Eighteenth-century Studies* 19, 56–77.

Sweet, Rosemary (1997). *The Writing of Urban Histories in Eighteenth-century England*. Oxford: Clarendon Press.

White, Hayden (1987) *The Content of the Form: Narrative Discourse and Historical Representation*. Baltimore: Johns Hopkins University Press.

Womersley, David (1988). *The Transformation of The Decline and Fall of the Roman Empire*. Cambridge: Cambridge University Press.

Woolf, D. R. (1997). 'A feminine past? Gender, genre and historical knowledge in England, 1500–1800'. *The American Historical Review* 102, 645–79.

Wootton, David (1993). 'Hume, "the historian". In *The Cambridge Companion to Hume*. Ed. David Fate Norton. Cambridge: Cambridge University Press, 296–307.

Wormald, B. H. G. (1951). *Clarendon: Politics, History and Religion, 1640–1660*. Repr. 1976. Cambridge: Cambridge University Press.

52

Religious Writing

Brian Young

Eighteenth-century Britain witnessed a continuing demand for religious books, not all of which were contemporary productions. The Bible naturally continued to be produced in prodigious quantities, with translations into the minority languages of Welsh, Irish and Scots Gaelic making an occasional, usually sponsored appearance. Within England, Wales and Ireland, and amongst the Episcopalians in Scotland, the Book of Common Prayer had quickly established itself after its revision in 1662 as a central component of the Anglican liturgy, and it maintained its authority into the twentieth century, despite the attempts of some less orthodox eighteenth-century clergy, such as Samuel Clarke and Theophilus Lindsey, to reform it in line with their own advanced doctrinal beliefs. A sense of continuity was particularly important for members of the Church of England during years of considerable religious antagonism, and this is apparent in the reverence which some felt for writings which marked out a specifically Anglican heritage. Consider the introductory remarks made by an Evangelical clergyman, Cornelius Bayley of Manchester, to an 1811 edition of the piously inscribed *Sermons or Homilies, appointed to be read in churches in the time of Queen Elizabeth, of famous memory*:

> The excellency of this work appears not so conspicuous for the ornaments of its diction, as for the piety and importance of its doctrines, which were sealed with the blood of the martyrs of the 16th century; and, together with the Liturgy and Articles of our justly admired Church, form a bulwark against the united efforts of papists and dissenters.

Such a very Protestant language of martyrdom could, nonetheless, serve also, despite Bayley's fear of nonconformists, occasionally to *unite* Anglicans and Dissenters, hence the central fact that Foxe's *Acts and Monuments of the Protestant Martyrs* continued to enjoy huge popularity nationally, an icon of that very Protestant sense of identity which historians have seen as integral to the fabrication of 'Britishness' between 1707 and 1837.

In an age in which religious identity was central to political and social identities, religious writing encompassed a notably wide spectrum, often crossing several genres, and remaining an essential component of literature in the widest sense. From Milton to Blake, both themselves enthusiasts for often heretical theological debate, religion was frequently a major preoccupation of creative writers as much as of professional theologians, and it is this common ground between laity and clergy which provides such a marked feature of the religious literature of the period. Indeed, much of the most effective and affecting religious literature was very often produced by lay people, as instanced most remarkably by the prayers and allied writings of Samuel Johnson, and this was to be a distinctive feature of Anglican apologetic that would continue immediately beyond the period charted in this survey in the important theological writings of Samuel Taylor Coleridge.

The literary importance of a devout laity was also felt among Dissenters, and the most popular book of the seventeenth and eighteenth centuries, Bunyan's *Pilgrim's Progress*, affirmed the cultural centrality of the laity in a period which also witnessed a dramatic decline in nonconformity's numerical strength. The ecumenical popularity of the hymns written by Isaac Watts, an early eighteenth-century nonconformist divine, was another important aspect of the inescapable cultural presence of nonconformity in an otherwise predominantly Anglican society. Watts's unmistakable rhythms were later to be accurately and affectionately parodied in Lewis Carroll's *Alice* poems, a vivid testimony to the long-term Anglican acculturation of what originated as a specifically Dissenting musical and liturgical tradition. Watts and Philip Doddridge, whose educational and theological writings were widely read, had many contemporary Anglican admirers, but the times were against even the notably gentlemanly form of Dissent which they represented. *Pilgrim's Progress*, an altogether less gentlemanly work, thus continued to be enjoyed as an inspiring statement of a generalized, non-denominational form of Protestantism over the eighteenth century, rather than as a uniquely powerful nonconformist testament. Bunyan, in common with other nonconformists, had also been a severe critic of what he considered heretical speculation, and in this respect his prose writings ran counter to much of the thinking of the most influential poet of the age, Milton.

Milton's *Paradise Lost* (1667) was, arguably, the most intellectually significant religious book of this period, determining as it did so much of the poetic activity of the following century and a half, a period in literary history economically defined by the critic Harold Bloom as 'the Milton-haunted eighteenth century'. Both *Paradise Lost* and *Paradise Regained* set the style for the long poem as an influential site of theological and philosophical reflection, as can be seen in such religiously motivated contributions to the genre as Pope's *Essay on Man* (1733–4) and Edward Young's *Night Thoughts* (1742–5). Milton the poet was also inescapably Milton the philosopher and the theologian, and so, while his prose writings were often either disregarded, or else excoriated as political and religious extremism (as in Johnson's notoriously disapproving *Life* of Milton), his theological notions could still often be traced in his poems. The explicitly heterodox nature of Milton's theology still awaited its discovery in the form of the long-lost manuscript of *De Doctrina Christiana*, the publication of which in 1825 was the occasion of one of Lord Macaulay's best known essays, but much of its content could have been surmised through the tendency of his religious poems, as Macaulay himself noted. *Paradise Lost* and *Paradise Regained* were startlingly potent testimonies to Milton's profound and sometimes unsettling theological reflection, and they remained as potentially subversive of the theological landscape in the age of Blake as they had when they emerged in the no less theologically contentious atmosphere of Charles II's reign.

Even without the provocations of *De Doctrina Christiana*, Milton's prose writings had acted as a repository of ultra-Protestant argument that would long continue to be drawn upon by like-minded apologists for the right to private judgement, and which would equally strongly continue to be opposed by those defenders of an established episocopalian church which so much of Milton's work had been designed to subvert. Indeed, one could chart a history of Protestant identities through the uses to which Milton's writings, and even his name, were put between the Restoration and the French Revolution. At one extreme stands Johnson, with his determinedly orthodox, extraordinarily partisan repudiation of Milton the resolutely heterodox Protestant; at the other, the reply made in 1779 to Johnson's *Life* by the ultra-Protestant Anglican divine Francis Blackburne, demonstrates a marked desire to continue the work of 'further Reformation' to which Milton himself was so notably and dauntlessly devoted. Blackburne's reply to Johnson's critique had originally appeared in his two-volume biography of Thomas Hollis, a bibliophile and political agitator who had been determined to keep Milton's Commonwealthman politics alive in England and the American colonies, not least through the public gift of books by Milton and like-minded writers. Milton the poet was thus central to later poetic explorations of Protestant Christianity, whilst Milton the ultra-Protestant propagandist was a troubling source of apologetic instability throughout the eighteenth century. This ambivalence regarding both Milton the man *and* the reception of his writings indicates the central tension in English religious writing in the long eighteenth century, between the desire for stability and an acceptance of the inherited religious apologetic of earlier centuries, on the one hand, and an often equally strong desire to explore the parameters of Protestant freedom, wherever they might be found to lead, on the other.

This exploration of religious freedom was championed by such men as John Toland, whose *Amyntor, or a Defence of Milton's Life* (1699) used the poet as an icon of this ultra-Protestant enterprise. The parameters of Protestant freedom were to grow very wide indeed, and ultra-Protestant engagement frequently began to shade into religious scepticism and the rejection of a belief in revealed religions such as Christianity itself. In Toland's most notorious work, *Christianity Not Mysterious* (1696), the bounds of Protestant freedom merged with those of an apology for natural religion which repudiated the miraculous foundations of revealed Christianity in favour of belief in an increasingly distant, largely unknowable deity. Appeals to the admittedly already somewhat dubious authority of such Protestant paragons as Milton thus served a more intricate purpose amongst freethinkers such as Toland, since they seemed to validate even the most extreme interpretation of religious freedom, an interpretation which paradoxically undid the very religion which they claimed to be purging of unnecessary additions to its essentially simple, and utterly reasonable core. Toland would take his speculations concerning God to such new levels of self-consciously esoteric reflection as were conducive to his introduction of the notion of pantheism into England, accompanied by a suggested liturgy for its adherents in *Pantheisticon* (1720). Toland and his small circle of admirers effectively sought to undermine Protestantism from within, and Milton, the most Protestant of poets, was the authority figure to whom they frequently made appeal in so doing. This championing of religious freedom would prove a major source of theological dispute throughout the eighteenth century, and something of the attendant ironies can still be heard in such notoriously subtle adumbrations of its language and strategies as chapters 15 and 16 of Edward Gibbon's *History of the Decline and Fall of the Roman Empire* (1776–88).

Freethinking, or deism, of the sort pioneered by Toland was a marked feature of the theological landscape of the first half of the eighteenth century. It put Christianity on the defensive, leading to some apologetic writings of no small quality, and a great many of very little immediate, still less long-term importance. The most durable of such replies was indeed an acknowledged apologetic masterpiece, Joseph Butler's *The Analogy of Religion, Natural and Revealed* (1736), which subtly and effectively used those very appeals to the natural and moral worlds so often made by freethinkers in order to undermine their claims, and to further those of revealed religion. Butler's *Analogy* won him a geat deal of respect, but it was only gradually that it acquired its reputation for philosophical supremacy, eventually achieving the dubious eminence of textbook status, as it became a necessary part of undergraduate reading at Oxford until the middle of the nineteenth century. Similarly, the works of George Berkeley frequently engaged with the onslaughts of freethinking, but his writings were found too subtle and indeed philosophically eccentric to gain him anything but the grudging admiration of his contemporaries, and his was a reputation which built up over time even more gradually than did that of Butler. One of the most gifted of the apologists for Christianity who proved so desirable in the first half of the eighteenth century, and a writer whose prose gained him many admirers not all of whom by any means shared his religious convictions, was William Law.

It is one of the nicest ironies of eighteenth-century literary history that William Law had been engaged to act as tutor to Edward Gibbon's father, and many approving as well as critical comments regarding him can be found in Gibbon's *Autobiographies*. Amongst the many significant exercises in religious apologetic which Law penned were replies to two of the more extrovert freethinkers of the early eighteenth century, Matthew Tindal and Bernard de Mandeville. Tindal's *Christianity as Old as the Creation* (1730) tendentiously claimed that the only religion which rightly and properly existed was natural religion, which was discovered through the overwhelming evidence in the natural world of a superintending, supremely creative intelligence, and also in the moral world through the perceived efficacy of right behaviour. Law dismissed Tindal's claims as being both impiously minimal and badly reasoned.

Mandeville's notorious *Fable of the Bees* (1714), with its frank and challenging claim that private vices acted as inducements to public virtue, was likewise denigrated by Law as betraying the morals of a presumptuous and blasphemous, if not downright devilish, thinker. Such negative accounts naturally followed from Law's altogether more positively conceived and decidedly popular encomia to a well-regulated, properly devotional Christian life, *A Practical Treatise upon Christian Perfection* (1726) and *A Serious Call to a Devout and Holy Life* (1729). Samuel Johnson had a famously high regard for Law's devotional writings, with their calls to moral vigilance and selflessness, and he equally famously condemned himself for always failing to meet those standards. A prodigiously prolific writer who did attempt to meet those standards, and whose followers were noticeably methodical in their lives, was John Wesley, but Wesley was an early critic of a later turn in Law's writings which had the effect of losing him not only readers, but also the widespread respect which his earlier writings had won for him.

Law, the fierce critic of worldliness in Walpole's notably worldly and frequently anti-clerical England, increasingly turned for inspiration of the most direct kind to the mystical writings of the seventeenth-century German author Jacob Boehme, most of which had been translated into English by various divines, both Anglican and decidedly radical and nonconformist, in the period of the Civil War and its immediate aftermath. In so doing, Law continued his assault not only on freethinkers, but also on rationalist Christians, whose appeals to reason and the intricacies of a universe newly charted by Isaac Newton (himself a dedicated reader of Scripture, and lifelong commentator on a wide range of sacred writings), Law found both immensely distasteful and apologetically dangerous. The reasonable belief promoted by such late seventeenth-century Anglican divines as John Tillotson and other well-placed 'latitudinarian' clergy, which neatly chimed with the Newtonianism which developed alongside it, was, in Law's view, the antithesis of true faith, a faith increasingly predicated on a mystical apprehension of a universe saturated by God and His creative principles of love and spirit. The universe was understood by Law in Behmenist fashion as having been constituted by a titanic struggle between God's loving spirit and fallen matter, which was merely the compromised and compromising product of Satan's fall from grace. Law's was a universe of symbols, a never-ceasing contest between different principles of light and darkness which could be traced across the cosmos by proper application to Boehme's God-inspired writings.

Such a profoundly mystical understanding of a largely life-denying existence and the roots of true religion held considerable attractions for those many men and women who were all too apprehensive of the 'reasonableness' which they saw as compromising Anglican divinity; to them, reasonable belief was worryingly close to the rationalism of the freethinkers, and it was not at all the way of the Cross: the redemption of fallen humanity was not to be achieved by an appreciation of the higher mathematics or by living a life according to merely 'formal', dangerously this-worldly moralism. Mysticism was not without its political correlates, and Law the nonjuror, whose religious principles made it impossible for him to take the Oath of Allegiance to

George I when the House of Stuart remained the legitimate dynasty in his eyes, was but one of several Tory-inclined mystics at work in the eighteenth century. Not that such theologico-political associations are always so readily discernible, and it is interesting that complicating permutations in such associations can also be traced. The radical artisanal world in which William Blake worked was productively open to a legacy of mystical imagery and counter-rationalism in which Law played at least as great a part as any putative underground inheritance (or rediscovery) of the more obviously radical elements of Civil War and interregnum theology. Blake's own very personal brand of Behmenism can be seen to have made its way into his mind through at least two channels: Law's writings *and* those of the radical sectaries of the mid-seventeenth century. Law would certainly have appreciated the impulses animating Blake's anti-iconic portrayal of a naked Newton, pointlessly measuring out the universe which dwarfs him, and echoes in sentiment between the two writers can be found in their respective works. Thus Law berating the modern soul for 'living in, and loving the things of time', when it ought to be 'loving and living in the truths, which are the riches of eternity' (injunctions to be found in his Behmenist treatise, *The Way to Divine Knowledge*), is suggestively close to one of Blake's more celebrated *Proverbs of Hell*: 'Eternity is in love with the productions of time.' The nonjuring mystic and the radical prophet situated themselves against what they saw as the comfortable Whig-Anglican hybrid cult of reasonableness, which they likewise condemned as a compromising parody of true faith in their mystically apprehended universes of signs and portents.

Mysticism was, then, a significant element in the religious thought of eighteenth-century England, albeit a much neglected one in a secondary literature which has long given itself over to analysis of the influence of Newton and John Locke on a religion which placed greater emphasis on probability than unimpeachable certainty, and on adhering to a rewardingly moral conception of the good life rather than on giving oneself up to the all-consuming claims of world-denying self-sacrifice. Even Wesley saw himself as working somewhere between these two worlds, and, critical though he was of the Anglican formalism which troubled Law, he was equally wary of the *contra mundum* extremism of a man he had once treated as a source of enormous moral and religious authority. Wesley was also the creator and editor of a large number of texts which were designed to influence the religious lives of a large mass of people, many of whom he felt to have been largely untouched by the altogether too worldly moralism of Anglican reasonableness. Several of these works comprised selections from mystical writers such as Thomas à Kempis, who had had their no less important place in Law's library. It was not, however, only mystics who made their presence felt in the positively industrial quantities of material which Wesley poured out of the appropriately named Foundry in London. Redactions of Locke's philosophy and Newton's mathematical works, medical treatises, studies of electricity and astronomy, pedagogical tracts, lives of inspired and inspiring men and women, editions of sermons and theological writings, hymnals and aids to devotion (including Law's *Practical Treatise* and *Serious Call*), all were produced in large numbers by Wesley's encyclopaedic intelligence, an intelligence very much of the age which produced such more obviously secular but decidedly similar enterprises as Ephraim Chambers' *Cyclopedia*, and Johnson's *Dictionary*, and even, much to Wesley's distaste, that pet project of the *philosophes* whom he otherwise so consistently deplored, the *Encyclopédie*. Wesley was a one-man publishing phenomenon, and one in whom the Protestant gospel of the word had found its ultimate champion.

Indeed, the gospel so promoted was but a part of a larger phenomenon in eighteenth-century England, one which had enormous literary consequences. Students of the Evangelical Revival, which had its roots in Germany, in America's Great Awakening, and in Scotland's Cambuslang, as well as in the Methodism of Wesley and Whitefield, have seen in William Law and other High Church exponents of a methodically devout life what one scholar called heralds of the Evangelical Revival. Its roots were certainly fed by such intense High Church spirituality as much as by Calvinist Puritanism, and it proved equally promiscuous in its choice of literary influences and models. An early champion of the Revival, James Hervey, even turned to the notion of philosophical rhapsody which he found in the writings of the freethinking Earl of Shaftesbury when composing his popular invocations of Christian glory overwhelming mere worldliness, *Meditations and Contemplations* (1746–7) and *Theron and Aspasio* (1755). Worldliness would out, however, and something of the varied flavour of eighteenth-century English life can be tasted in a satirical print which took Hervey's *Meditations Among the Tombs* as its mockingly pious title. Here is depicted an all too obviously priapic gentleman, shamelessly ravishing a woman of doubtful morals in a churchyard otherwise populated only by the notably unregarded dead. In a cultural world dominated by Henry Fielding and William Hogarth, albeit a dominance contested by the religious sensibility of Samuel Richardson, the 1740s saw the Evangelical Revival mocked mercilessly in print, both by pronouncedly secular opponents *and* by clerics who saw in such 'enthusiasm' the fanatical antithesis of their own reasonable belief and temperate practice and a distant funeral party.

Evangelicalism would grow in importance as the century progressed, gaining adherents who discovered in it a living faith which they contrasted with the supposedly dry and arid pastures of self-consciously 'reasonable' Anglicanism. The liberalism of the ultra-Protestant party, which the Evangelicals vehemently opposed, reached its limits in the debate over subscription to the Thirty Nine Articles of the Church of England which was enforced on clergy when taking up their livings, and on undergraduates at the English universities (on matriculation at more consciously orthodox Oxford, and graduation, at more consciously liberal Cambridge). A petition was made to parliament in 1772 by a small but well-placed group of Anglican liberals for relief from such subscriptions to articles which were found by many to be internally inconsistent, and which were seen as forming a hindrance to the Protestant right to private judgement. Their chief apologist in print was Francis Blackburne, a Cambridge-educated liberal, who was soon to be Milton's champion against Johnson, an Oxford-educated adherent of Anglican orthodoxy. The petition failed, but it had immediate consequences which would dictate a good deal of religious discussion in the ensuing decades. On the one side, it obliged Anglicans seriously to examine the content of the articles, leading some, such as Augustus Montague Toplady – the celebrated writer of several fine hymns, that major arsenal of Evangelical Revival – to encourage a revival of the Calvinism which they found to be the guiding philosophy of the articles; on the other, it led to a small but intellectually significant secession from the Trinitarian Church of England to a new denomination, that of Unitarianism. Unitarianism would attract significant numbers of self-consciously intellectual adherents, such as its founders, the former Cambridge dons Theophilus Lindsey and John Disney, and Thomas Cadell, Gibbon's publisher, as well as such important representatives of what is now called 'Rational Dissent' as Joseph Priestley, whom Gibbon would later somewhat richly denounce in print as an enemy to orthodox Christianity. Alongside this examination of the dogmatic roots of Anglicanism came the political crisis of the 1770s, when the war with America led many thoughtful men and women to examine the nature of the society in which they lived, and thence to consider the prospects of the lives they might want to lead in future, both in this and the next world. This second-wave of Revival brought in such major writers as the poet William Cowper, the hymn-writer and former slave-ship captain John Newton, and, perhaps most importantly, Hannah More, until then best known as a playwright. More turned from the worldly attention of the stage to the provision of works of practical application for the poorer classes which supplemented the strictures on the morals of the upper classes made in *A Practical View of the Prevailing Religious System of Professed Christians in the Higher and Middle Classes in this Country, Contrasted with Real Christianity* (1797) by her friend, William Wilberforce. Her tracts of the 1790s denounced the radical politics championed by the likes of Blake, calling the poor to reform their own lives rather than seeking to undermine the constitution at the behest of Thomas Paine, whose attempt at introducing freethinking to the artisanal classes, *The Age of Reason* (1794–5), was almost as widely deplored as his earlier invocations to *Common Sense* (1776) and *The Rights of Man* (1791).

Evangelicalism thus profited from the political uncertainties of the 1770s, and it even, to some extent, dictated important elements in the intricate dynamic of domestic politics in the troubled 1790s and early 1800s. This influence was out of all proportion to numbers, and most Anglicans remained committed to an altogether less strenuous version of their faith, just as Dissenters, always a very small minority in English society, were very far from being united in support of 'Rational Dissent'. Indeed, the 'enthusiasm' of Evangelicals and Methodists was but one half of the opposition to reasonableness which the 'superstition' of Catholicism completed in the eyes of 'reasonable' Anglicans. When the unbelieving David Hume wrote a subversive essay 'On Superstition and Enthusiasm' in the 1740s he was knowingly pushing 'reasonable' belief to its limits; his opponents knew this, but his command of irony, in this instance at least, was beyond their powers of retaliation. Not that Hume was held by his contemporaries in anything like the regard he has long since assumed in the history of philosophy. To Johnson he was notoriously but a 'beggarly Scotchman', a follower of the long-exploded freethinking of Pope's former patron, Lord Bolingbroke. Towards the end of Pope's life, Bolingbroke was replaced in his affections by one of the most ambitious clergymen of the eighteenth century, William Warburton, who eventually became the Bishop of Gloucester.

Warburton's career fascinatingly and importantly intersects with most of the trends already examined in this survey. He came to prominence by defending Pope's *Essay on Man* against those who found in it dangerous traces of the freethinking promoted by Bolingbroke, his erstwhile 'guide, philosopher and friend'. Warburton also promoted the established interests of the Church of England and the toleration of Dissent from a firmly political, even worldly perspective, in *The Alliance Between Church and State* (1736), and he denounced the excesses of freethinking in *A View of Lord Bolingbroke's Philosophy* (1756). He also coupled the 'fanaticism' of Whitefield and Wesley with a repudiation of the 'insults of infidelity' in a long exposition of *The Doctrine of Grace* (1763). Although privately he wondered at the wisdom of attacking Hume in print, concerned that such a move might serve only to keep his otherwise worthless name before the reading public, he colluded with his disciple Richard Hurd in producing *Remarks on Mr Hume's Essay on the Natural History of Religion* (1757). He also frequently did battle with his fellow clergy, so zealous was he to win the high ground of theological apologetic, ground he clearly lost to one such opponent, Robert Lowth, in an engagement over the true nature and import of the Book of Job, the subject of considerable controversy in eighteenth-century biblical exegesis. Lowth's Oxford lectures on the poetry of the Old Testament have been seen by literary historians as considerable components in the growth of the sublime as an aesthetic category in the eighteenth century, and his appreciation of Hebrew writing within its historical context would have a revolutionary effect on biblical criticism. Lowth's *De sacra Poesi Hebraeorum* (1753), delivered in Oxford as lectures between 1741 and 1750, would also prove a profound and seminal source of the British experience of Romanticism, especially after appearing in an English translation as *Lectures on the Sacred Poetry of the Hebrews* in 1787. Blake's firmly radical musings on Jerusalem and the Old Testament are not without their debts to Lowth's learned lectures.

Warburton's greatest work also earned him the most opprobrium from his contemporaries, both inside and outside the Church. The full title of this work firmly demonstrates its ambitions, and also bears telling witness to the apologetic dangers it consequently incurred: *The Divine Legation of Moses Demonstrated, On the Principles of a Religious Deist, From the Omission of the Doctrine of a Future State of Reward and Punishment in the Jewish Dispensation* (1738–41). The principles of the work are adumbrated in this deliberately provocative title. Moses had been considered by unbelievers to be a fraudulent founder of a so-called 'revealed religion'; to cite the title of a notorious clandestine tract which found favour among freethinkers, he was one of the titular figures in *The Treatise of the Three Impostors*, the others being Jesus and Muhammad, the founders of two equally groundless faiths, Christianity and Islam. It was Warburton's declared aim to undermine this dangerous critique by establishing the unique claims for religious veracity which were to be made through a proper understanding of the Judaism which Moses actually founded. This he achieved to his own satisfaction, but not to that of many other readers of what is a dense, difficult, often frustrating, and decidedly argumentative text. Accepting that all founders of ancient religions had deployed the consolations of a future life as a cover for their exploitation of other people in this life, a central element in what freethinkers called 'priestcraft', Warburton aimed to show that Moses did not proclaim any doctrine of a future life, and, hence, that his was the true faith, and not a fraudulent means of securing power over his deluded followers. Only gradually was knowledge of a future life vouchsafed to the Jews, and only in the passion of Christ was the doctrine fully revealed. This was, to say the least, a controversial claim, and one which several clerical readers thought conceded far too much to freethinkers, several of whom enjoyed themselves hugely in using Warburton's contention to their own ends. This pivotal paradox in a work which made much use of paradoxes required a great deal of scholarly enquiry to look even remotely plausible, and Warburton duly sought to analyse an enormous area of classical and biblical scholarship. Inevitably, he made a large number of mistakes, and his interpretations were open to criticism from an equally large number of scholars. Not that his work was entirely without merit; he developed a theory of hieroglyphic writing, for example, which won for him the admiration of Condillac (and, consequently, a somewhat unlikely but very important presence in the argument of Jacques Derrida's major work on language, *Of Grammatology*). Replies to this dogmatic divine acquired something of the nature of a cottage industry, and it is interesting to reflect on the fact that Gibbon's first venture into print in English took the form of *Critical Observations on the Sixth Book of the Aeneid* (1770), an examination of one of the many subsidiary arguments in the *Divine Legation*.

Any examination of religious books in the eighteenth century reveals a surprisingly acerbic tone amongst the adherents of a confessedly irenic religion, and Warburton's blustering, dictatorial tones take this tendency to excess. Even sermons could instance this blisteringly argumentative disposition on the part of clergy contending not only with freethinking and the imagined rivalries of 'Popery', but also among themselves for the palm of 'orthodoxy' or the merits of consistent Protestantism. This was a culture of 'replies', 'examinations', 'observations', of pamphlets and books which took to task whatever was considered to be unorthodox or otherwise unsound, and it is primarily in this context that one can best understand the large number of offended replies to the studied ironies of Gibbon's *Decline and Fall* which made their first appearance alongside the first volume in 1776, and which continued to be produced into the 1780s and even beyond. One of the earliest replies was made by Richard Watson, a clergyman of decidedly liberal principles who rose successively to be Regius Professor of Divinity at Cambridge and Bishop of Llandaff. Watson's apologetic career mirrors the religious atmosphere of the closing decades of the century as effectively as Warburton's did that of its middle decades. After taking on Gibbon in *An Apology for Christianity* (1776), composed as one gentleman responding to another, a somewhat older Watson (who was personally unsympathetic towards, but politically astute enough not to ignore, Evangelicalism), replied to Paine's widely detested *Age of Reason*, very much *de haut en bas*, in *An Apology for the Bible* (1796). So identified had Watson become with this calming service for the worries of nervous clergy, that he seriously contemplated a request made by a troubled Bath clergyman for a reply to a work by a Cambridge liberal of the younger generation, Thomas Robert Malthus. With the first edition of Malthus's *An Essay on the Principle of Population* (1798), replete with closing chapters very directly and controversially concerned with theological matters (chapters which were dropped from subsequent editions), one reaches a new era in the religious history of England, one in which secular interests are beginning to compete more openly with those of a culture hitherto preoccupied with the status of Christianity as an arena both of true knowledge and of ethical motivation.

Not that transitions can be so easily made, and recent interpretations of the history of England in the early nineteenth century emphasize the strongly religious roots of social, cultural and political understanding in that period, but this was a Christianity which was even more aware of competing interpretations of the world and humankind's place in it than had been its eighteenth-century predecessor. William Paley, Watson's younger Cambridge colleague, may well have produced the seminal apologies in the 1800s for a natural religion leading to an acceptance of revealed religion in his *Natural Theology* and *A View of the Evidences of Christianity*, along with a defence of the Acts and Pauline epistles as genuinely the work of St Paul in *Horae Paulinae*, but he did so in a period of political crisis in which Evangelicalism and what has been called the 'politics of atonement' precariously prevailed against the unsettling elements of unbelief, but their air of confidence belies the troubled atmosphere in which they were composed. By 1825, however, Macaulay, a favourite when a child of Hannah More, and the product of a Cambridge in which Paley's works were a staple of instruction, nonetheless felt able to laud the religious freedoms which Milton represented in the pages of the religiously rather sceptical *Edinburgh Review*. Macaulay had little patience for the radical milieu in which Blake worked, but his defence of Milton was that of a man free from any doctrinal commitment, but happy to identify himself, culturally at least, as a Protestant. In Macaulay's dogmatically minimal Protestantism can be traced elements of many of the trends sketched in this survey, and the reception of the otherwise doctrinally combustive *De Doctrina Christiana* in 1825 contains many lessons for students of English religious writing.

REFERENCES AND FURTHER READING

Bennett, G. V. and J. D. Walsh, eds (1966). *Essays in Modern English Church History in Memory of Norman Sykes.* London: A. and C. Black.

Champion, J. A. I. (1992). *The Pillars of Priestcraft Shaken: The Church of England and its Enemies, 1660–1730.* Cambridge: Cambridge University Press.

Claydon, Tony and Ian McBride, eds (1998). *Protestantism and National Identity: Britain and Ireland* *c.1650–c.1850.* Cambridge: Cambridge University Press.

Colley, Linda (1992). *Britons: Forging the Nation.* New Haven, Conn.: Yale University Press.

Derrida, Jacques (1976). *Of Grammatology.* Trans. Gayatri Chakravorty Spivak. Baltimore, Md.: Johns Hopkins University Press.

Drury, John (1989). *Critics of the Bible 1724–1873.* Cambridge: Cambridge University Press.

Engell, James, ed. (1984). *Johnson and his Age.* Cambridge, Mass.: Harvard University Press.

Evans, A. E. (1932). *Warburton and the Warburtonians: A Study in Some Eighteenth-century Controversies.* London: Oxford University Press.

Garnett, Jane and Clin Matthew, eds (1993). *Revival and Religion Since 1700: Essays for John Walsh.* London: Hambledon Press.

Gascoigne, John (1989). *Cambridge in the Age of the Enlightenment: Science, Religion and Politics From the Restoration to the French Revolution.* Cambridge: Cambridge University Press.

Gibbons, B. J. (1996). *Gender in Mystical and Occult Thought: Behmenism and its Development in England.* Cambridge: Cambridge University Press.

Griffin, Dustin (1986). *Regaining Paradise: Milton in the Eighteenth Century.* Cambridge: Cambridge University Press.

Haakonssen, Knud, ed. (1996). *Enlightenment and Religion: Rational Dissent in Eighteenth-century Britain.* Cambridge: Cambridge University Press.

Hilton, Boyd (1988). *The Age of Atonement: The Influence of Evangelicalism on Social and Political Thought, 1785–1865.* Oxford: Clarendon.

Jacob, Margaret C. (1981). *The Radical Enlightenment: Pantheists, Freemasons and Republicans.* London: Weidenfeld and Nicolson.

Keeble, N. H. (1987). *The Literary Culture of Nonconformity in Later Seventeenth-Century England.* Leicester: Leicester University Press.

Lamb, Jonathan (1996). *The Rhetoric of Suffering: Reading the Book of Job in the Eighteenth Century.* Oxford: Clarendon.

Lund, Roger D., ed. (1995). *The Margins of Orthodoxy: Heterodox Writing and Cultural Response 1660–1750.* Cambridge: Cambridge University Press.

Mee, Jon (1992). *Dangerous Enthusiasm: William Blake and the Culture of Radicalism in the 1790s.* Oxford: Clarendon.

Prickett, Stephen (1986). *Words and the Word: Language, Poetics and Biblical Interpretation.* Cambridge: Cambridge University Press.

Rivers, Isabel (1991). *Reason, Grace and Sentiment: A Study of the Language of Religion and Ethics in England, 1660–1780, Vol. 1: From Whichcote to Wesley.* Cambridge: Cambridge University Press.

Thompson, E. P. (1993). *Witness Against the Beast: William Blake and the Moral Law.* Cambridge: Cambridge University Press.

Walsh, J. D., Stephen Taylor and Colin Haydon, eds (1993). *The Church of England c.1689–c.1833: From Toleration to Tractarianism.* Cambridge: Cambridge University Press.

Womersley, D. J. (1988). *The Transformation of 'The Decline and Fall of the Roman Empire'.* Cambridge: Cambridge University Press.

Young, B. W. (1998). *Religion and Enlightenment in Eighteenth-century England: Theological Debate from Locke to Burke.* Oxford: Clarendon.

53

The Novel

Simon Varey

In *Joseph Andrews*, Henry Fielding boasted that he was introducing 'a new species of writing' to the reading public, although his method of doing so appealed to the precedents of Cervantes, who had been dead for a hundred and fifty years, and Homer, who had been dead considerably longer. By the time Fielding was writing his prose fictions in the 1740s, Aphra Behn, Daniel Defoe and Eliza Haywood had already marked out the territory of what is now, but was not then, called the novel. These three writers had proved popular without relying on an exaggerated claim and without drawing much attention to the genre. One might argue that they – and Fielding, and Samuel Richardson as well as dozens of others – made up the genre as they went along. There were no rules, although occasionally someone cited some, usually from an anachronistic source such as Aristotle or Madame Dacier. If this looks like a case of justification after the fact, it is so because the forces that gave the novel its impetus were as much economic as aesthetic.

Fielding's claim to novelty does not stand much scrutiny anyway because he used it in the service of narrative self-consciousness. In *Joseph Andrews* and *Tom Jones*, Fielding created extravagant stories built upon the accidents of birth and a sequence of coincidences, culminating in revelations that depend on established conventions of romance. What happens in *Tom Jones* is not impossible, just wildly improbable. A pregnancy is concealed, allowing the true origin of young master Jones to be revealed by a sequence of incidents orchestrated by the grand master of the narrative. Jones turns out to be the country squire's nephew, so he inherits and marries money, and lives comfortably ever after in an ending that is too tidy for belief. If there is a god who rewards a wayward but good-hearted young man with material wealth and the girl of his dreams, then this novel is the gospel. In reality, events do not cooperate with such tidy human desires. Literary history's efforts to pinpoint the beginnings of the form of the novel run up against this same reality. Unlike *Tom Jones*, the genre itself has no single, ultimately identifiable moment of birth, but a succession of moments, from conception to emergence, with no one orchestrating developments.

The novel emerged from a complex of literary origins more or less established in the seventeenth century, but the modern sense of the term did not gain currency until about 1800. Until then, the novel was all kinds of things, evolving pragmatically from narrative types that are unfamiliar and largely unread today.

Confusingly, the noun 'novel' usually meant a short tale of love, yet it was distinguished from 'romance'. One of the best-known attempts to distinguish the formal meanings of these two terms occurs in the preface to William Congreve's *Incognita*:

> Romances are generally composed of the Constant Loves and invincible Courages of Hero's, Heroines, Kings and Queens, Mortals of the first Rank, and so forth; where lofty Language, miraculous Contingencies and impossible Performances, elevate and surprize the Reader into a giddy Delight . . . he is forced to be very well convinced that 'tis all a lye. Novels are of a more familiar nature; Come near us, and represent to us Intrigues in practice, delight us with Accidents and odd Events, but not such as are wholly unusual or unpresidented . . . Romances give more of Wonder, Novels more Delight.

Congreve's definition of romance belongs to the world of Spenser's *Faerie Queene* and Sidney's *Arcadia*. In 1692, when these words were published, hardly anyone was writing romances conceived like this. But Congreve hit home by saying that novels dealt with matters of everyday life. During the English novel's first century, roughly 1680 to 1780, hundreds of writers introduced innovations of style, subject and technique, and just as quickly abandoned some of them. If any one principle can apply to so many novels (perhaps 4,000 titles in all), it would be that most of them presented recognizable types of human being, human predicament, and human behaviour. The dominant subject, not surprisingly, is love, especially love's place in discourses of desire and power.

By 1780 formal distinctions about genre had become normal. In that year Thomas Holcroft gave the world his aesthetic opinion that a novel should demonstrate unity of design, meaning that incidents irrelevant to the story should be excluded. This is hardly sophisticated critical theory, but it serves as a useful reminder of what the novel had become by the end of its first century. With the exception of Laurence Sterne's *Tristram Shandy*, in which the irrelevant becomes the relevant and the margins take over the centre, prose fiction had by then gradually pruned its 'irrelevant' outgrowths. The outgrowths never were wholly irrelevant except in a formal way, but Defoe, Fielding and many others had perfected the art of introducing an apparently irrelevant story, often a moral tale that mirrored their thematic concerns. *Tristram Shandy* buries this convention of the interpolated tale in mockery, when Corporal Trim finds a piece of paper folded inside a book and reads it aloud, the irrelevant side first. It is like finding a letter with a shopping list scribbled on the back, and reading the list. The point is that Trim cannot know the difference until he has read both sides. Sterne opts to include it all. There is still a randomness about Sterne's narrative world, just as Defoe's sprawling narratives sometimes seem arbitrary when they describe an incident only in order to let it peter out.

As the publishers of novels sought ways to find a niche for these new books, alongside the more predictable forms of sermons, poetry and essays, many novels promised more than they delivered. Eighteenth-century books had no dust jackets, so title pages did the job of attracting readers, and many a title page suggested that the prurient reader would be in for a treat. *Moll Flanders* delivers what its title page promises in the sense that the narrative does concern whoredom, adultery and incest, as well as a range of crimes in the theft category. Yet this is no book for those seeking graphic descriptions: it is much more concerned with morality, usurping social conventions, and showing that a woman stuck in a series of difficult circumstances can survive and prosper. This disparity is not false advertising: the relationship between title page and narrative suggests that the novel's packaging and marketing were as uncertain and unsettled as the genre itself. In the changing world of developing capitalism, literature was coming to depend far more on retail sales than on the safe haven of patronage. Commercial success thus prompted sequels such as Defoe's to *Robinson Crusoe* and imitations such as the anonymous *History of Charlotte Summers*, a supposedly female *Tom Jones*.

Early writers of novels found commercial success with the scandal chronicle and the secret history. Even with the expansion of the press, relatively little information became public and there was no such thing as investigative reporting or really much extensive news gathering. Newspapers published official announcements, arrests and court decisions, shipping movements, results of distant battles weeks after the event, and editorials on current parliamentary politics. Although censorship of the press was officially allowed to lapse in 1695, successive governments practised it in a variety of ways. At the level of national government and public information, Britain lived with a curious culture of censorship and secrecy. In the early eighteenth century, writers of scandal chronicles, secret histories, and true histories exploited the effects of this culture, not by leaking government secrets but by exposing covert actions – usually to do with sexual relationships, adultery and personal gain, rather than covert deals by European diplomats in Vienna over national alliances. Writers also sought – more interestingly – the psychology behind the secrecy. Three closely related fictional forms blended fact and fantasy, historical material and pure speculation, all with the clear intent to reveal the usually dirty secrets of people (named or not) in high places. This revelatory fiction seems to have its roots in the journalist's desire to expose, together with the satirist's desire to cut someone down to size. Personal memoirs, too, played their part in the evolution of the novel, with their carefully constructed selves and their sense of revelation.

Some of the most popular novels of the century purported to reveal secrets, including now largely neglected fictions narrated by inanimate objects or inarticulate creatures. In this subgenre, typified by Charles Johnstone's *Chrysal; or, the Adventures of a Guinea*, the narrator might be a coin, a flea, even an atom. These 'narrators' see everything – the intimate and seedy as well as the public aspects of people's lives. Non-human narrators could go into places – in the case of a flea, into the most intimate human place of all – where people could not. Whatever else these novels may have been, they were voyeuristic. Uncovering scandal, reading other people's letters – these too are voyeuristic activities that feature everywhere in hundreds of novels. Voyeurism by itself quickly becomes unsavoury prurience, but in the hands of so many of the early writers, voyeurism leads directly to the psychological motivation required, for example, by Lovelace to rape and, in effect, kill the 'charmer' he desires to possess, Clarissa.

As a popular phenomenon, the voyeuristic tendency is still obvious today in western culture's worship of celebrity, even if celebrity status is now manufactured by the entertainment industry to which the news media belong. In eighteenth-century Britain, people interested in news and politics were interested in celebrities, too: criminals, devious politicians and the privileged whose behaviour was scandalous. There was never a shortage of biographies of thieves and murderers, whose notoriety would be relatively widespread because of print coverage of their crimes, trials, and (frequently) executions. Criminal biography became a subgenre, but the activities of criminals also became woven into the fabric of novels that did not belong to the subgenre at all, such as Defoe's *Colonel Jack*. There was also no lack of gossip, which became grist to the mill of the scandal chronicler who barely concealed true identities in sketching amorous and adulterous affairs. These too became subjects for novels that were not dependent on revealing the identities of recognizable people in public life.

A part of the reason that the novel as a genre was such a grab bag in its early years was that no one could make a living by writing only novels. Professional writers were in any case a recent phenomenon, but all of the authors of early novels that are read today were men or women who published other kinds of writing. Aphra Behn was a playwright who also wrote poetry. Delarivier Manley was a partisan journalist who wrote scandal chronicles and secret histories with a satirical flavour. Having written virtually every kind of prose that an Englishman of his time could conceive (except sermons), Defoe turned to fiction at age fifty-nine and wrote *Robinson Crusoe*. Fielding had established himself as England's leading playwright before he wrote a word of prose fiction, and he relied on the law, not his pen, to pay his ever-recurring debts. Haywood, also a playwright and journalist, was perhaps the nearest of them all to a professional novelist, but she too brought to her novels the insights and experience garnered from other kinds of writing. Until novels were established in the marketplace, authors wrote in the genres that did pay as well as this new one that might. The resulting genre of the novel is a hybrid in which almost anything goes.

In the 1680s probably the most popular writer of novels, as well as plays, was Behn, who drew on political events, personalities and scandals for much of her raw material. The three volumes of *Love Letters Between a Nobleman and His Sister* (1684–7) were based quite closely on a scandal that was the subject of London gossip in 1682. Behn turned real people into Sylvia and Philander, set the whole narrative in France, and presented the affair as a tense struggle between passion and honour.

As with most of Behn's writing, *Love Letters* is especially interesting for her psychological intuitiveness, although, with its generous servings of lips imprinting kisses on cheeks and arms clasping yielding necks, the novel is clearly a bodice ripper designed to bring money to the impoverished author. The language is drawn, like the characters' names, from Arcadia, so that Sylvia looks 'ten thousand times more charming' and Octavio 'one thousand times kneeled and begged pardon', and characters experience 'transports' of passion. Like the English language itself, the idiom for prose fiction of this sort would change radically over the following hundred years. Behn's narrative artfully blends sexually explicit language with political satire on events so topical that Behn seems as if she is writing about them as they are happening. This is one reason that her narrative is an unusually interesting treatment of the complex interaction between politics and fiction – at least for those aware of the actual scandal.

For later readers unfamiliar with the scandal, Behn's more enduring contribution was her ability to catch the rhythms of a relationship between lovers, the thrill of infatuation, the throbbing excitement of hope, the bleak despair and rage that accompany fear of a broken promise or a broken trust. These qualities are surely the reason that *Love Letters* continued to be immensely popular long after the scandal that prompted it was forgotten. Secret histories did not always titillate; this one did.

Behn's much slighter novel *Oroonoko* probably grew from the perceived need for propaganda in the royalist cause at a time of crisis. Set in Surinam, this narrative moves from Old World to New, from romance in Congreve's sense to the uncomfortable realities of slavery. Behn begins by making twin narrative claims that would become familiar in a great deal of fiction over the next few decades:

> I was myself an Eye-witness to a great part of what you will find here set down: and what I could not be Witness of, I receiv'd from the mouth of the chief Actor in this History, the Hero himself, who gave us the whole transactions of his youth.

The claims – to having a story from one of its participants and being an eye-witness to the events narrated – typify the early novel's efforts to reach a public unaccustomed to narrative fiction. Behn was influenced by her own experience in Surinam, by what she considered the political need to draw a booster portrait of a victimized ruler (she supported James II, who was soon forced to abdicate), and by the literature of travel. On all counts she was doing far more than merely reworking three kinds of influence or experience into fiction.

Oroonoko explores the mentality that made a supposedly primitive man admirable. To pin the old label 'noble savage' on Behn's creation is too limiting, especially as it conceals debate – notably among earlier Spanish writers on the Americas – about whether indigenous peoples of a land previously unknown to Europeans were capable of civilization. Behn's 'noble savage' depends on a literature that began in the early sixteenth century, firmly placed in the context of ecclesiastical, moral and philosophical debates. Yet she did something that Spanish monks in the New World did only perfunctorily: she explored qualities of mind rather than interpreting outward behaviour as a sign of inner being. She did not object to the oppression of people of low social standing, yet *Oroonoko* is an indictment of the cruelties of enslavement by colonizing powers. The grotesque ending of *Oroonoko* shows Behn's contempt for the excesses of the ferocious colonizers whose attitude to all things foreign is to fear it or kill it. The ending also puts paid to any thought that this novel is realistic: while the hero is being mutilated and dismembered, he continues to smoke his pipe and serenely utters not a word of protest. The realism lies only in the ferocity of his tormentors.

Defoe gave his fictions the appearance of autobiography and a more convincing sense of the authority of the eye-witness. Not that people who write the stories of their own lives are especially fond of the truth. *A Journal of the Plague Year* carries many typical marks of supposed veracity. H. F., the narrator, strives for authority thus:

> If I may be allowed to give my opinion, by what I saw with my eyes and heard from other people that were eye-witnesses, I do verily believe that there died at least 100,000 of the plague only, besides other distempers and besides those which died in the fields and highways and secret places out of the compass of the communication, as it was called, and who were not put down in the bills though they really belonged to the body of the inhabitants. It was known to us all that aboundance of poor despairing creatures who had the distemper upon them, and were grown stupid or melancholy by their misery, as many were, wandered away into the fields and woods, and into secret uncouth places almost anywhere, to creep into a bush or hedge and die.

In addition to the basic eye-witness claim, H. F. is in the know: he has knowledge of 'secret' places. The narrative encourages a sense of verisimilitude as well, with the piteous howls of people who have caught the plague, or Defoe's famous image of a single open window in a deserted London street – the sort of detail an actual observer would note.

Even though several of Defoe's fictions are set in the seventeenth century, his protagonists resist changes and demands that Defoe's own society would have imposed on them in the 1720s. His protagonists are survivors who resist being incorporated. Moll Flanders, Roxana and Colonel Jack are essentially outsiders who retain their individualism (especially economic), their sturdy independence. The only time they blend in with the society around them is when they need the cover of anonymity. The first half of *Moll Flanders*, an account of Moll's parade of lovers and husbands, focuses so relentlessly on Moll herself that most of the men in her life have very little presence, even when she (or Defoe) remembers to give them names. The issue of Moll's identity comes to dominate the second half, her life of crime, because exposure of her identity will result in her arrest. Defoe does not treat identity only at this simple level: he explores the complex triangular relationship of subjectivity, individualism and society. But society seems almost an abstraction, as Defoe's London – Defoe's world, really – does not offer much in the way of community. A crowd tends to be a dangerous thing because so many individual wills might converge, as they do when Moll callously abandons one 'poor boy' to 'the rage of the street'.

It was common once to talk of Defoe as the instigator of the novel, which he clearly was not, and as the purveyor of picaresque fictions to a rising middle class. There are many things wrong with this image, most notably the wrenched and misunderstood conceptions of class that are still put forward. There was a rising middle class, but when Defoe was writing it was not the coherent, recognizable stratum of British society that it became by about the 1760s. As E. P. Thompson put it: 'a purposive, cohesive, growing middle class of professional men and of the manufacturing middle-class . . . did not begin to discover itself . . . until the last three decades of the century'. In *The Fool of Quality* (1764) Henry Brooke was able to glorify that most bourgeois of characters, the merchant, in a way that would have been impossible in Defoe's time. For Brooke, it is the merchant

> who furnishes every comfort, convenience, and elegance of life; who carries off every redundance, who fills up every want; who ties country to country, and clime to clime, and brings the remotest regions to neighborhood and converse; who makes man to be literally the lord of creation, and gives him an interest in whatever is done upon earth; who furnishes to each the product of all lands, and the labours of all nations; and thus knits into one family, and weaves into one web, the affinity and brotherhood of all mankind.

In contrast, Defoe's typical heroes are Jack, a lad who sleeps in ashpits, and Moll, an orphan who is taken in by a family and aspires (as a little girl) to grow up to be a gentlewoman. Crusoe is the only one even from middle England.

Class looms large in Richardson's narratives of power and desire, *Pamela* and *Clarissa*. Literary history has done a disservice to Behn by giving Richardson dispro-portionate credit for the 'invention' of the novel in letters, although Richardson perhaps took the form a step further than anyone before him. In *Pamela* he blended letters with a narrative that amounts to a fictional diary, but the epic *Clarissa* pur-ports to be a collection of correspondence. Where Behn's running narrative in *Love Letters* connected the letters and added narrative commentary, in *Clarissa* Richardson let his characters do the talking while he restricted a separate narrative voice to a few solemnly editorial notes.

Clarissa is probably the greatest work of fiction the eighteenth century produced: tragic, epic, psychologically complex, the longest and most detailed novel of its time. The pace is incredibly slow, as everything that happens to the two main characters is written down in a letter and mailed to a friend (who replies in detail). The premise of *Clarissa* is that the young, beautiful, strong-willed woman of the title is being pushed into a marriage that she does not want. The greedy, boorish members of her *nouveau riche* family try to force their collective will on her because they see a mar-riage of estates on the horizon. The one man they detest is Clarissa's seductive nemesis, Lovelace, who eventually abducts her, tries to seduce her, drugs and rapes her. The rape begins a long sequence culminating in her death. The moment of rape, the creative centre of the novel, is left scarcely described as a moment. Lovelace knows what he has done and uses evasive language in telling his friend Belford in the shortest letter in the novel. Richardson presents rape not as a single event but as a long, terrifying, agonizing mental process of reliving, absorbing the full horror of the violent invasion of a woman's body and psyche. Thus the rape takes about one hundred pages of piece-by-piece reconstruction as the truth of the incident is assembled from multiple points of view and gradually revealed by the power of narrative. That revelation is the centre of the novel, as it is a sign that the genre has reached a high level of sophistication. In the process, Clarissa learns what has happened to her, realizes the unpalatable truth about Lovelace, who has destroyed her, and discovers much about herself. *Clarissa* is not a novel about a rape, however; it is a minutely detailed examination of an articulate young woman's sensibility, and in Lovelace, Richardson presents as convincing a portrait of evil as any writer has ever achieved. The impact of *Clarissa*'s pathos on early readers would be hard to exaggerate: it provoked tears from readers in sympathy with its explicit sentiment.

It is customary in literary history to pair off Richardson and Fielding as complementary opposites. It has become a posthumous critical rivalry with a life of its own. Fielding parodied *Pamela* hilariously in his lascivious, crude imitation, *Shamela*, and then wrote what amounted to an alternative form, *Joseph Andrews*, an episodic novel of the road, in which the travelling characters meet a series of people and get into usually unexpected situations. Each set of incidents is in some way a moral vignette. Building on this model in 1749, Fielding published his alternative to *Clarissa*. Where *Clarissa* is tragic, *Tom Jones* is comic, but still full of moral commentary. Where Richardson all but obliterated the author as narrator, Fielding thrust in the most intrusive, talkative, bossy narrator yet encountered in fiction. Both novels are ultimately about power, but in technically opposite ways, as befits the tragic and comic modes. The repressive social machinery exemplified by Clarissa's family contributes to her destruction, while Fielding's comic resolution depends on the conservation of the same system.

Contemporary with Richardson and Fielding and far more prolific was Haywood. Her substantial novel, *The Adventures of Eovaai, Princess of Ijaveo*, is a masterpiece of political writing in tune with the satiric outpourings of the opposition to Robert Walpole's administration. Here Haywood demonstrated her control of the power of innuendo, just as she did again five years later in writing her devastating satire, *Anti-Pamela; or, Feign'd Innocence Detected*, one of the many popular books and pamphlets that ridiculed *Pamela*.

Haywood's importance as a writer is contingent on the theme that informs virtually all of her fifty or so novels: the power of a woman's desires. Her female characters express themselves through their desires – usually sexual – and by doing so assert their individual identities as women in a masculine world. Like their creator, Haywood's female characters strive for, and obtain, independence. Even if her novels of the 1720s are more titillating, those of the 1740s and 1750s more thoughtful, this theme still rings loud and clear. Haywood's life, despite the barrage of criticism she had to endure, showed what a woman could do. In her novels she turned one of the most fundamentally important human attributes into material for a sequence of best-sellers that paid her enough to live independently as she desired. In this context, it is easy to argue that Haywood's female characters, like their creator, are subversive, the exact opposite of Fielding's. It should be said, though, that for every fictional female character (not just Haywood's) who expresses this form of subversiveness there are two who marry, one who dies, and one whose sexuality expires with her entry into a convent.

Those enduring human assets, love and sexuality – combined with courtship and marriage, family, even gender itself – become narrative ends in themselves as well as means of cultural control or subversion. This is as true of *Tom Jones* or *Clarissa* as of their contemporary John Cleland's *Fanny Hill* (properly entitled *Memoirs of a Woman of Pleasure*). *Fanny Hill* is a pornographic potboiler that provides numerous fascinating insights into the culture's inability to find a vocabulary for discussing sexuality. Cleland's novel is far more subversive and in many respects more revealing, because it highlights something that *Moll Flanders* and *Pamela* take for granted: that sexual relations in fiction typically adopted even the modern vocabulary of financial transactions. Cleland replaced it with a vocabulary more allied to engineering (a man's penis is his 'machine'), which suggests that, in other novels, sex is a commercial transaction like a retail sale. Paradoxically, it often is in *Fanny Hill*, too, because Fanny is a prostitute.

Sex is obviously not the sole theme of the eighteenth-century novel, but it is among the most important. Richardson's treatment of sentiment in *Clarissa* requires a powerful sexual current to run through the narrative, even though his own statements about sentiment suggest that it is a matter only of shedding tears in sympathy with someone else's distress. Sterne's extraordinary, and funny, treatment of sentiment in both the substantial *Tristram Shandy* and the slim *Sentimental Journey* demonstrate that sex and sentiment are near allies. Sterne's brief career as an author coincided with a fashion for novels that depict a 'man of feeling', a composite figure with visible ancestors among earlier eighteenth-century fictions. The true man of feeling is benevolent, charitable, and good-natured, capable of sympathy and pity. The chief character in *A Sentimental Journey*, Yorick, is capable of being charitable – to a bird as well as a coach – and yet he does not really want to be charitable to a poor monk until his Christian conscience jogs him. Yorick weeps at the right moments, yet he is not always content to do so. All this would not be exceptional were it not that Sterne connects Yorick's libido with his sentiments and his benevolence, and so puts an ambiguous cast on the concept of virtue that Richardson gave such prominence.

In both of his novels, Sterne usurps all the conventions. *Tristram Shandy* is the supreme example, with its preface appearing in volume 3, ten pages supposedly missing, a black page, a white page, a marbled page, squiggly lines on the page indicating narrative lines. These usurp the conventions of the physical book, but Sterne does not stop there. Although there are numerous nods in the direction of Scriblerian satire, Sterne's narrative is unlike any novel that had gone before, as he invites his readers to take the potential of language to its limits, to look for innuendo and *double entendre*, to see that an innocent gesture may be an explosive in disguise, as on the last page of *A Sentimental Journey*.

One character who appears, unflatteringly, in Sterne's fiction is Tobias Smollett, another prolific writer in a wide range of genres. Reading Smollett is a little like reading the history of the novel in English. Defoe's picaresque, Fielding's comic characters, Richardson's letters, benevolence and sentiment, social themes, crime – these all come together in Smollett's epistolary novel, *The Expedition of Humphry Clinker*. Like Joseph Andrews, Humphry Clinker is a servant and minor character who undermines the presumed significance of the title. This novel is filled with jokes, incongruous visual images, caricatures, coincidences and contradictions in the service of humour. The humour is double-edged, for it points to the huge social changes that had taken place in Britain since the days of Behn and Manley, such as the erosion of the power of land and the corresponding shift of power towards money. Where Fielding, for example, for all his slapstick humour, would present an image of control as a way of holding on to the old, established order, Smollett is more likely to show it breaking down, in recognition of the power of the new. Smollett's benevolent man, Matt Bramble (in *Humphry Clinker*), is a grumpy old invalid who sighs for the better days of a bygone era. Smollett's middle class consists of a crowd of people who rush in a comic stampede to get to the dessert table in the Assembly Rooms at Bath – but by the 1770s, these are the people who have replaced the socially privileged as the patrons of Bath.

Humphry Clinker points to a growing trend in novels of the 1770s. In the letters that Smollett's characters write, the contrast between exciting city life, which appeals to the young, and quiet, wholesome country life, which attracts their elders, allows for the narrative integration of environment and individual character. The subgenre that triumphantly blended these (and sentiment, too) was the gothic. Gothic novels specialize in melancholy; dark forests and caves, cemeteries at midnight, and thunderstorms suggest corresponding mental states. Touches of the supernatural, suspense, and mystery appear together in fiction for the first time since the old romances. Mary Shelley's Frankenstein creates a monster that speaks (very eloquently), Horace Walpole introduces a painted portrait whose subject jumps out of the picture frame, and so on. A rich vein of prose fiction lay ahead of *The Castle of Otranto*, Walpole's short, slight novel of gothic horrors, which hardly compares with William Beckford's *Vathek* or with the most compelling and seductive example of the gothic, Ann Radcliffe's *Mysteries of Udolpho*. All the typical elements are in Radcliffe's masterpiece, from the chill of her portrait of tyranny to the sentiment of thwarted romantic love, from the suffocating, enclosed spaces in which the heroine is trapped to the sublime vistas of Alpine landscapes. The theme of entrapment and imprisonment underlines a discourse of power in which the real tension is between civilization and passionate impulses.

Criticism today, with its emphasis on race, class and gender, pays scant attention to the values that eighteenth-century readers placed on their novels. Early twenty-first century criticism reads novels, and everything else, as political documents that reflected, entrenched, or reinforced the power of a socially dominant white male elite. Certainly, the servant Pamela marries her repugnant employer, a member of the landed gentry; Roxana, the protagonist of Defoe's *Fortunate Mistress*, is a feisty woman who makes her own way in the world of banking and finance, where few women normally ventured; Henry and Sarah Fielding's female characters (the fortunate ones, anyway) marry into opulent estates; even Haywood's women tend to look for a good marriage as a way out of financial difficulties. Radcliffe's Emily is in the power of the villainous Montoni, unable to do much about her predicament except chafe at it. These examples all share a root in common everyday life, in which women and the poor had little chance of subverting the status quo. No revolution took place in the British Isles. The novels lean toward a kind of political realism, but few readers in the eighteenth century interpreted them this way. All the evidence suggests that readers looked for finely drawn characters, good moral fables, the moving pathos of tragedy (such as Clarissa's long-drawn-out death) and good humour.

Modern criticism of the eighteenth-century novel has perhaps never been sufficiently historical. Although A. D. McKillop's studious *The Early Masters of English Fiction* was published in 1956, modern criticism of the novel began the following year with Ian Watt's *Rise of the Novel*. Watt posited formal realism as the main characteristic of the eighteenth-century novel, and a rising class of literate consumers as the fuel for the engine that was the novel. Controversial at the time and ever since, Watt's book has remained the starting point for discussion of the novel for more than forty years. Despite its reductive and self-contradictory thesis, this book was responsible for establishing the canonical authors, or at least reflecting what was then current American academic practice. Either way, the eighteenth-century novel was seen and taught for far too long as the exclusive preserve of Defoe, Richardson, Fielding and Sterne. Even Smollett had to fight for his place. No women needed apply. The novel thus began in 1719 with *Robinson Crusoe* and ran on through to about the 1760s, when it entered a lean spell typified by *The Castle of Otranto*, and the genre was then rallied and revived by the divine Jane Austen's comedies at the beginning of the nineteenth century. F. R. Leavis and his cronies could then conveniently dismiss the eighteenth century altogether and begin the history of the English novel with Austen.

The picture has been redrawn radically. The most important change in criticism is the overdue recognition of women as authors as well as consumers of prose fiction. Approaches borrowed with mixed results from cultural anthropology and social history have led to the dropping altogether of the 'rise' of the novel, which is now seen as a much more inclusive genre, subversive in some hands, conservative in others, though rarely acknowledged as the experimental laboratory it was. What we now call the novel evolved as its already literate reading public's taste evolved, but it evolved because the conditions of a capitalist economy enabled it to do so. A large enough readership was in place, disposable income was shifting toward a broader mass of readers, and the metropolitan printing and distribution system was sufficient to market these books successfully. The search for origins is best conducted as a search for all the genres that the reading public was willing to buy, because this accounts for the experimental forms that gradually settled down to produce, by about 1800, a genre whose definition could be agreed.

The number of titles published in the eighteenth century was high, but many titles need not mean a large readership for each one. Novels that went into second, third or fourth editions were clearly in continuous demand, but cautious print runs might still amount to only 5,000 copies altogether. It may not be that much, especially when we remember that the best-selling subjects were not fictional at all, but moral and theological. Reading novels requires time, and most reading takes place in solitude. Busy men and women do seem to have been widely read, which suggests that reading on the run was common, too. Through the solitude of reading, especially reading a novel, one could learn, as one still can, about self and community.

References and Further Reading

Armstrong, Nancy (1987). *Desire and Domestic Fiction: A Political History of the Novel*. New York: Oxford University Press.

Ballaster, Ros (1992). *Seductive Forms: Women's Amatory Fiction from 1684 to 1740*. Oxford: Clarendon.

Castle, Terry (1986). *Masquerade and Civilization: The Carnivalesque in English Culture and Fiction*. Stanford: Stanford University Press.

Davis, Lennard J. (1997). *Factual Fictions: The Origins of the English Novel*. Philadelphia: University of Pennsylvania Press.

Doody, Margaret (1996). *The True Story of the Novel*. New Brunswick, N.J.: Rutgers University Press.

Gallagher, Catherine (1994). *Nobody's Story: The Vanishing Acts of Women Writers in the Marketplace, 1670–1820*. Berkeley: University of California Press.

Hunter, J. Paul (1990). *Before Novels: The Cultural Contexts of Eighteenth-Century English Fiction*. New York: Norton.

Making Genre: Studies in the Novel or Something Like It, 1684–1762 (1998). *Studies in the Novel* 30, 2.

McDowell, Paula (1998). *The Women of Grub Street: Press, Politics, and Gender in the London Literary Marketplace, 1678–1730*. Oxford: Oxford University Press.

McKeon, Michael (1987). *The Origins of the English Novel, 1600–1740*. Baltimore: Johns Hopkins University Press.

Richetti, John (1969). *Popular Fiction Before Richardson: Narrative Patterns, 1700–1739*. Oxford: Clarendon.

Spencer, Jane (1986). *The Rise of the Woman Novelist: From Aphra Behn to Jane Austen*. Oxford: Basil Blackwell.

Todd, Janet (1989). *The Sign of Angellica: Women, Writing and Fiction, 1660–1800*. New York: Columbia University Press.

54

Poetry

David Fairer

The poetry of the period from 1660 to the 1780s has tended to suffer from the Wig View of literature: how can genuine poetry be written by people in false hair-pieces? Many students in the past encountered this unspoken question through a survey course in which Dryden and Pope, and possibly Swift, were used to establish a category of the 'Augustan' which could act as a foil for the 'Romantic movement'. More ambitious surveys added Gray, Goldsmith or Johnson in order to introduce a concept called 'eighteenth-century poetic diction' – very useful for beginning a seminar on Wordsworth's *Lyrical Ballads*, or Blake's *Songs*. Artifice gave way to nature, conservatism to radicalism, false curls to a powerful simplicity. The scheme was an alluring one that offered a set of tidy critical judgements and a reasonably coherent 'long eighteenth century' for students to digest.

This narrative is thankfully now breaking down, and the poetry of the period is coming to be seen as richly varied, fraught with contradictions and controversies, and open to experiment of many kinds. Various factors are playing a part: the rediscovered work of women poets and labouring-class writers has introduced a range of new and strong voices that demand to be heard; the availability through anthologies and databases of a much greater variety of poetry for classroom use has widened the scope for discussion; and in scholarship and criticism there has been a growing stress on continuities not only between eighteenth-century poetry and the pre-1660 tradition, but with the work of the 'Romantic' poets themselves. The fact that it is now far less easy to provide a brief survey of the subject is a welcome sign of eighteenth-century poetry's increasing popularity as a subject in its own right.

One way of beginning to appreciate the cross-currents and tensions is to look back from the vantage-point of 1781–2, and ask how some writers at the end of our period viewed the poetic developments of the previous 120 years. In his *Lives of the English Poets* (completed 1781) Samuel Johnson saw the great national achievement as being the work of Dryden and Pope in bringing elegance, harmony and correctness to English verse during the period 1660 to 1744. For Johnson, Pope's heroic couplets were supreme ('to attempt any further improvement of versification', he wrote, 'will be dangerous') and he thought that the mid-century poets who looked back to Spenser, Milton and the Greek lyric (Gray, Collins, the Wartons, Mason and Akenside) had lapsed into fanciful self-indulgence; in deserting the heroic couplet for their 'ode and elegy and sonnet' they merely produced verse that was harsh and irregular. The year 1781, however, also saw publication of the third volume of Thomas Warton's *History of English Poetry*, where the shape of literary history was presented very differently: Warton celebrated the reign of Queen Elizabeth as 'the most poetical age' before invention and imagination had been stifled by the wit and correctness of Charles II's court, and in his edition of Milton's early poems (1785) he went on to rejoice that during his own century a 'school of Milton' had arisen to counter the 'school of Pope'. In 1782, his brother Joseph Warton completed his two-volume *Essay on Pope*, in which the poet was consigned to the second class of didactic and moral verse, beneath the 'pure poetry' of 'our only sublime and pathetic poets, Spenser, Shakespeare and Milton'. No wonder, then, that Vicesimus Knox in his essay 'On the Prevailing Taste in Poetry' (also 1782) saw the recent poetic landscape in terms of two opposed critical camps:

> I think it is not difficult to perceive, that the admirers of English poetry are divided into two parties. The objects of their love are, perhaps, of equal beauty, though they greatly differ in their air, their dress, the turn of their features, and their complexion. On one side, are the lovers and imitators of Spenser and Milton; and on the other, those of Dryden, Boileau, and Pope. (*Essays Moral and Literary*, II. 186)

By including the French poet and critic Boileau, Knox sets an older native tradition alongside a more recent French neoclassicism; but he does not see one ousting the other. For him they exist side by side as evidence of the glorious diversity of English poetry. Once we remember that eighteenth-century poetry encompassed both of these lines simultaneously, we shall be less eager to see a gradual move during the period from classic to romantic (or from neo-classic to pre-Romantic). These neatly labelled building-blocks with their simple half-truths ought to be put away and replaced by a subtler sense of poetry's character. Throughout the eighteenth century, poets were aware of conflicting traditions and of lively critical debate.

Milton and Dryden, the two great poets of the Restoration period (1660–1700), do seem to offer different trajectories through the eighteenth century. Between them they suggest a temptingly easy division of poetry into two distinct kinds: heroic couplet verse of social comment and satire, and blank verse (unrhymed) of solitary vision and imagination. We can set Dryden's *Absalom and Achitophel*, focused on specific political events of November 1681, alongside *Paradise Lost* (1667), the blind poet's universal epic encompassing all history and all space. But as soon as we do this, complications arise. The most obvious influence on Dryden's couplet satire is *Paradise Lost*; its central scene is one of temptation and Fall that repeatedly echoes Milton's; and Dryden's King David (Charles II) intervenes to end civil discord as decisively as

God ends Milton's War in Heaven. Conversely, it is possible, thanks to Christopher Hill and other Milton critics, to view *Paradise Lost* as a poem embedded in its own precise political moment – the immediate aftermath of the monarchy's Restoration in 1660 – and offering an analysis of issues of state power, legitimacy, rebellion, justice – the very things that concern Dryden in his poem. Any division of English poetry between Milton and Dryden into separate 'schools' is therefore fraught with complication at the outset. In such an extensive and diverse field covering some 130 years of writing there are many individual voices, many varied innovations in form and subject, as well as surprising returns to past literary modes.

Yet a distinction between Milton's architectural paragraphs of blank verse and Dryden's pointed and polished couplets is a crucial one for the way poetry was to develop, and the particular characteristics of these two verse forms would be exploited in many of the finest poems of the next century. A comparison of two related passages from *Paradise Lost* and *Absalom and Achitophel* can suggest what different possibilities these basic forms opened up.

A crucial moment in Book 9 of Milton's epic occurs when the serpent has led Eve to the Tree of Knowledge, and his speech of temptation has aroused in her a desire for the forbidden fruit:

> He ended, and his words replete with guile
> Into her heart too easy entrance won:
> Fixed on the fruit she gazed, which to behold
> Might tempt alone, and in her ears the sound
> Yet rung of his persuasive words, impregned
> With reason, to her seeming, and with truth;
>   (*Paradise Lost*, IX. 733–8)

The sinuous quality of blank verse is here ideal for insinuating Eve's weakness and susceptibility into our minds. The lines set up a sympathetic guileful motion, like Milton's 'sly snake' itself. With no rhymes to halt the line-endings we are not stopped in our tracks by eye or ear (*behold*, *sound*) but drawn across into the next line as Eve watches the fruit and recalls the serpent's words. When the flow is interrupted (*to her seeming*), it is for a purpose, to part *reason* and *truth* – though the crucial phrase is slipped in as a quiet mid-line parenthesis. We sense through these fluid lines how easy Eve's transgression is going to be. The drama is sustained through the paragraph as we await her response: the verse works from within, so to speak.

At the equivalent moment in Dryden's satiric poem, after the speech in which the smooth-talking Achitophel has tempted Absalom to rebel against his father, the heroic couplets immediately distance us from the dramatic moment so as to make us draw wider conclusions:

> What cannot praise effect in mighty minds,
> When flattery sooths, and when ambition blinds!
> Desire of power, on Earth a vitious weed,

Yet, sprung from high, is of celestial seed:
In God, 'tis glory: and when men aspire,
'Tis but a spark too much of heavenly fire.
                (*Absalom and Achitophel*, 303–8)

Dryden is fascinated by dualities: the human set against the divine; forces working from without (flattery) and from within (ambition); what comforts us (sooths) and what injures us (blinds); the power and glory of God, and the low vices of men. Holding these in place are the couplets, which tie each statement up in an ironic point and block off any developments or evasions that might take place if the lines could flow further. There is no escape from the conclusive rhymes: even the mightiest human *mind* is *blind*; a divine *seed* can grow into a mortal *weed*; *aspire* and *fire* combine to hint at dangerous excess, even destruction. One of the powers of couplet writing exploited by its best practitioners (Dryden, Pope, Swift, Johnson, Goldsmith, Crabbe) is to hold and control the wayward, and make us face facts. As in this passage, couplets tend to bring things, often literally, to an immediate point, and they are therefore ideal for juxtaposing contrasting elements of a thought or experience, and encouraging choice or judgement. The flow of experience is regularly checked, and measured; an idea does not set its own terms as can often happen in blank verse (where the lines may move in sympathy with more wandering thought and less clearly defined feeling), but is placed under pressure within an established paradigm. For the skilled poets of the Restoration and eighteenth century, the heroic couplet is far from being a limitation, but becomes a powerful resource.

The key to the character of this verse form, which established itself so widely after 1660, lies in its original title of the 'English heroic' (as distinct from the 'French heroic', or rhymed alexandrine, on which it was partly modelled). It was felt to have a compactness and strength that made it suitable for dignified modes like epic and tragedy, and for the concise wit of a verse essay or epistle, and it tended to be seen as the native equivalent of the Latin hexameter of Vergil's *Aeneid* or the satires and epistles of Horace. When Dryden translated the works of Vergil (1697) he spoke in his preface about the compact quality of Vergil's lines and the classical strength of the epic structure ('there is nothing to be left void in a firm building'). To him these were linked. Although he admitted that blank verse offered advantages over rhyme in being less restricting, it was the more succinct and disciplined heroic couplet that he chose.

The French neo-classicists used rhyme, but the poets of Greece and Rome had not, and indeed not everyone agreed that rhyme was appropriate for a longer poem. Milton's rejection of it for his epic of *Paradise Lost* was deliberate, and for the second edition in 1674 he added a note on its verse form (or 'measure'):

The measure is English heroic verse without rhyme, as that of Homer in Greek, and of Virgil in Latin; rhyme being no necessary adjunct or true ornament of poem or good verse, in longer works especially, but the invention of a barbarous age, to set off wretched matter and lame metre.

There is more than a hint of national pride when Milton concludes that blank verse 'is to be esteemed an example set, the first in English, of ancient liberty recovered to heroic poem from the troublesome and modern bondage of rhyming'. The republican Milton, who narrowly avoided execution when the monarchy was restored (and had seen his hopes for liberty end in new bondage), makes a veiled political comment on the Francophile court of Charles II and all the elegant rhymers who were anxious to model themselves on the neo-classical poets of politeness and elegance patronized by Louis XIV and the Académie Française. Milton's identification of heroic couplets with an enslavement to French taste, and of blank verse with ancient British liberties, was repeatedly echoed by those eighteenth-century poets who wanted to re-establish the native literary tradition.

Dryden's friend and admirer, the Earl of Roscommon, in his *Essay on Translated Verse* (1684), summarized the respectful attitude of many English poets of the Restoration towards the French achievement:

> When *France* had breath'd, after intestine Broils,
> And Peace, and Conquest crown'd her foreign Toils,
> There (cultivated by a Royal Hand)
> Learning grew fast, and spread, and blest the Land;
> The choicest Books, that *Rome*, or *Greece* have known,
> Her excellent *Translators* made her own:
> And *Europe* still considerably gains,
> Both by their good *Example* and their *Pains*.
> From hence our generous Emulation came,
> We undertook, and we perform'd the same.

Appropriately enough, Roscommon's verse essay is modelled on that of Boileau's *L'Art Poétique* (1674), itself a version of Horace's critical epistle, *Ars Poetica*. (In 1711 the young Alexander Pope would draw on all three poems for his *Essay on Criticism*.) We note that Roscommon associates the classical inheritance with a new peace and internationalism after years of civil war ('intestine Broils'). There does seem to have been at this period, when Britain was recovering from its own internal conflict, the first stirrings of a European-wide classicism, especially among writers within the range of court patronage.

But however much the French were admired, they were also there to be outdone. Their renowned wit and elegance could be more than matched in English poetry, and Roscommon goes on to make this very point:

> *Vain* are our *Neighbours Hopes*, and *Vain* their *Cares*,
> The *Fault* is more their *Languages*, than theirs.
> 'Tis Courtly, florid, and abounds in words;
> Of softer sound than our perhaps affords.
> But who did ever in *French Authors* see
> The Comprehensive, *English Energy*?

With brilliant compression, Roscommon makes each line shorter than the one before, until he ends with the kind of succinct, vivid phrase that Dryden was to praise in Vergil – one that does not count syllables on its fingers (as the first line does), but bounces with triumphant emphasis, At their best, Dryden's heroic couplets have a similar energy, combining compactness and rhythmic verve: the pentameter does not plod, but forms itself into natural phrasing. In the following lines from his verse epistle 'To Sir Godfrey Kneller' (1694) Dryden is praising the most successful painter of the Restoration period:

> Shadows are but privations of the Light,
> Yet when we walk, they shoot before the Sight;
> With us approach, retire, arise and fall;
> Nothing themselves, and yet expressing all.
> Such are thy Pieces, imitating Life
> So near, they almost conquer'd in the strife;
> And from their animated Canvass came,
> Demanding Souls; and loosen'd from the Frame.

This complex passage can tell us a lot about the poetry of the Restoration period. It is playfully serious; its art copies life (the classical *mimesis*) but with a touch of mimicry too, and a delight in the way nothingness can suggest substance; the wit of the passage, like the wit of the playful shadows, celebrates animation while being conscious of surface. The sudden image of the dead demanding to be brought back to life literalizes the word *animated* ('having a soul'), but at this moment of greatest animation, Dryden reminds us of the canvas and the frame – that it is art after all, and art at its wittiest. He relishes the power of his own words and delights in the idea that something so insubstantial can 'shoot before the Sight' in this way.

In the Restoration period, wit of such a kind became particularly prized, so long as it did not believe in its own illusions. As Dryden said in *Absalom and Achitophel*, 'Great Wits are sure to Madness near ally'd; / And thin Partitions do their Bounds divide.' To be a wit was at this time to be much more than a humorist: it was closer to our modern idea of genius. The term 'wit' assumed a combination of intelligence, creative sparkle, sophistication, originality and imagination – but also self-conscious artifice (the canvas and frame).

At this time, when the literary world (authors and readers) was still a narrow one of only a few thousand people centred on the capital, the taste of the court circle and aristocratic society was supreme. Wit was therefore at a premium, and the ability to turn a few skilful lines enhanced a person's social reputation. Most poetry circulated in manuscript among friends and lovers, perhaps transcribed for a patron or into a private commonplace book, and some copies made their way into printed miscellanies, or appeared as complimentary dedications. This was an age of the prologue and epilogue, the occasional poem, the epigram, or impromptu. The neat turn of an idea or 'conceit' was much prized, and when the subject was love, the idea of 'serious play' came into its own:

What cruel pains Corinna takes
   To force that harmless frown;
When not one charm her face forsakes,
   Love cannot lose his own.

So sweet a face, so soft a heart,
   Such eyes, so very kind,
Betray, alas! the silly art
   Virtue had ill designed.

This poet-seducer is the Earl of Rochester, perhaps the most notorious wit and rake at Charles II's court. The wit of his poem is to construe Corinna's resistance to him simply as bad art, forced and unnatural; the ideal art during this period was an unlaboured ease, but Corinna's is an artifice that is all too obviously the product of 'cruel pains' (her hardworking virtue is as painful to herself, Rochester suggests, as it is cruel to him). Her face and heart reveal the truth by simply being themselves – an ideal of natural ease, whereas her virtue is laboured and false. Stepping aside from the song, we see its outrageous egotism: having sex with him will be natural and honest: to refuse will betray her own desires. Rochester's poetic artifice is concealed by the lyric's easy natural flow: its power to seduce depends on its apparent spontaneity. The game of wit is well practised.

In the early decades of the eighteenth century Restoration wit of this kind was regarded with some ambivalence by writers like Pope, Swift and Gay. They were uneasy about 'the Mob of Gentlemen who wrote with Ease' (Pope's phrase), and Swift opened his *On Poetry: A Rapsody* (1735) with the complaint: 'All Human Race wou'd fain be *Wits*, / And Millions miss, for one that hits.' The three of them, together with their friend Dr John Arbuthnot, formed the Scriblerus Club to satirize false wit and learning. The Scriblerians felt that poetry was in danger of becoming predictable and ephemeral, and had lost its wider responsibility as a cultural force. Later in the same poem, Swift speaks of

The trivial Turns, the borrow'd Wit,
The *Similes* that nothing fit;
The *Cant* which every Fool repeats,
Town-Jests, and Coffee-house Conceits
        (ll. 151–4)

The possibility of creating a broader national market for literature had been demonstrated by the huge success of Addison and Steele's *Spectator* (1711–14), a periodical which reached out through its critical and moral essays to help create a public sphere which was interested in cultural debate. With such a readership in mind, poets could speak as critics of urban or court vices, and appeal to the polite aspirations of an expanding professional middle class. The poet as cultural commentator was a role the Scriblerians readily embraced. In this context, heroic couplets gained a new impetus through their ability to retain shape and poise in the face of human waywardness and stupidity. This is Pope in *Epistle to a Lady* (1735) commenting on the sad end of the Duchess of Buckinghamshire:

> Strange! by the Means defeated of the Ends,
> By Spirit robb'd of Pow'r, by Warmth of Friends,
> By Wealth of Follow'rs! without one distress
> Sick of herself thro' very selfishness!
>
> (ll. 143–6)

The couplet is ideal for condensing and summarizing (hence its appropriateness for epitaphs, of which Pope was a master). The poet tolls the knell and the ironic pairings pass like mourners before us: her life of excess has become a sad procession of contradictions. The formality of couplets is part of their potential. But to use 'form' does not mean being static or stiff. In Pope's *Epistle to Cobham* (1734) the moment of death is caught in couplets that compress a whole lifetime of fussy vanity into one final gesture:

> 'Odious! in woollen! 'twould a Saint provoke,
> (Were the last words that poor Narcissa spoke)
> No, let a charming Chintz, and Brussels lace
> Wrap my cold limbs, and shade my lifeless face:
> One would not, sure, be frightful when one's dead –
> And – Betty – give this Cheek a little Red.'
>
> (ll. 242–7)

In the midst of the lively chatter expressed in the varied weighting of the stresses, the fourth line is noticeably slower and heavier as we glimpse her stiff corpse. The heroic couplet can be a marvellously flexible vehicle for registering the slightest nuance of pace and rhythm. In a poem like Pope's 'Eloisa to Abelard' (1717) the verse form is simultaneously expressive and constraining – like a violin string – imposing discipline on the speaking voice and therefore increasing its eloquence. At a time when the implications of Newtonian gravity were making their impact, this concept of energy through order was easy to comprehend.

Being the 'heroic' measure of Dryden's Vergil and of Pope's translation of Homer (1715–26) brought a further range of possibilities for the pentameter couplet. Its association with classical epic meant that a strong satiric effect could be achieved by mimicking heroic dignity, and some of the finest poems of the early eighteenth century exploit this 'mock-heroic' potential. Works as various as Pope's *The Rape of the Lock* and *The Dunciad* ('The Mighty Mother, and her Son who brings / The Smithfield Muses to the ear of Kings, / I sing'), or Gay's *The Fan* and *Trivia*, or Swift's 'Description of a City Shower', create a comic indecorum, or mismatch, between the concerns of the present and those of the classical past. As Swift watches a rainstorm create havoc in the streets, he focuses on a well dressed young spark not daring to leave his sedan chair:

> Box'd in a Chair the Beau impatient sits,
> While Spouts run clatt'ring o'er the Roof by Fits,
> And ever and anon with frightful Din
> The Leather sounds, he trembles from within.
> > ('Description of a City Shower', ll. 43–6)

Swift's parallel is with the Greek soldiers hiding in the Trojan horse, who tremble with fear when the priest Laocoön strikes it with his spear. The climax of the Trojan War as told by Vergil is being humorously re-enacted in the London street, and the unheroic young fashion victim shrinks from the raindrops on the leather roof, as if they were the drumbeats of battle.

The aim of the mock-heroic poem is not to mock the heroic, but to create an extra dimension and complicate the *now* and *here* by recalling an epic parallel. There is often some satirical judgement behind it (as in Swift's poem), but the writing is also driven by a creative delight in incongruity and a play of allusion that enlivens a scene or enriches a traditional genre. Pope's *Dunciad* and *The Rape of the Lock* show how varied the results could be, and both poems can even be viewed as miniature epics themselves, transposed into modern terms – epics for an unheroic age. Vergil's Georgics (descriptions of rural labour) and Eclogues (pastorals) were subjected to similar reworkings. Where Vergil had instructed his readers in the country labours of farming and bee-keeping, Gay's urban georgic, *Trivia*, is a guide to walking the London streets; and Lady Mary Wortley Montagu produced six *Town Eclogues* (1716) in which Arcadian shepherds have become the leisured upper classes gathered round the card table or at their morning toilette. In this way, supposed mock-forms were themselves established as genres. They went beyond humorous parody to offer new modes of capturing experience:

> There was a time (oh! that I could forget!)
> When opera-tickets pour'd before my feet;
> And at the ring, where brightest beauties shine,
> The earliest cherries of the spring were mine.
> > (ll. 17–20)

The once beautiful Flavia (from Lady Mary's 'Saturday. The Small-Pox') laments her scarred face in the tones of pastoral elegy. Her scene of triumph is the fashionable 'ring' in Hyde Park instead of the village green, and her treats extend to opera-tickets as well as the traditional rustic fruit; but the lines do not mock Flavia: they offer a more complex note of self-irony as the court beauty laments her own spring and the loss of the fiction in which she had lived.

Through the work of poets like Dryden, Rochester, Pope, Gay, Swift and Lady Mary Wortley Montagu, the formal constraints of French neo-classicism were adapted to the freer stress-patterns of spoken English, and the result is linguistically rich and subtle. In their poems elegant conventions engage with actual human experience: their heroes, nymphs and shepherds lead pressurized lives in hot drawing-rooms or busy

London streets. To call such writing simply 'neo-classical' is not specific enough, and the term 'Augustan' has now become so freighted with philosophical and political baggage ('Augustan values' etc.) that it blurs rather than clarifies. Whatever we term this kind of poetry, it was the dominant mode of the period 1660–1740, and, as Vicesimus Knox saw, it continued through to the end of the eighteenth century – and beyond. The pointed heroic couplet remained popular for verse epistles and satiric writing (with poets as diverse as Mary Leapor and Charles Churchill), and was developed further as an effective moralizing mode in the poetry of Samuel Johnson, whose *Vanity of Human Wishes* (1749) offers powerful generalizations about the inevitability of human fate; Oliver Goldsmith used it in *The Deserted Village* (1770) to set a satirized present against a sentimentalized past; and in George Crabbe's *The Village* (1783) it expresses the relentless pressures of rustic poverty.

But as we saw at the beginning, the literary critics of 1781–2 were conscious of another tradition: alongside those who looked back admiringly to Dryden and Pope were Knox's 'lovers and imitators of Spenser and Milton'. This line of writing emerged confidently in the 1740s to challenge Pope's pre-eminence (a move Johnson strongly resisted); but it had already been in place for several decades. A division in taste within the literary world was recognized even in the 1690s. In his critical writing Dryden carefully distanced himself from Milton's language (in particular from his outdated poetic vocabulary), and it became clear that *Paradise Lost* had shattered the convention that blank verse should be confined to drama. Taking all time and space for his subject, Milton at once made poetry's possibilities seem boundless. We can sense the rousing effect of his epic voice by returning to the Earl of Roscommon's *Essay on Translated Verse* (1684). For the second edition the following year he made an extraordinary move by taking the poem (after 375 lines of heroic couplets) into Miltonic blank verse for a tribute to *Paradise Lost*. Not merely does Roscommon offer an extended imitation of the War in Heaven, but he also attacks rhyme (in rhyme) as an inheritance of the barbarian hordes who overthrew the Roman empire ('For *That*, in *Greece* or *Rome*, was never *known*, / 'Till by *Barbarian* Deluges o'reflown'). For him, Milton represents the genuinely classical style and shows how Britain might become the new Rome or Athens ('Why should not *We* their *ancient Rites restore* / And *be*, what *Rome* or *Athens* were *Before*?'). It is important to understand that the Miltonic tradition, which we can see being inaugurated in Roscommon's *Essay*, was not simply a proto-Romantic movement set in opposition to 'neo-classicism', but was seen by many as an alternative and more genuinely classical style. Many later Miltonists took this view, and the most notable of them (John Philips, Mark Akenside, Thomas Warton, Thomas Gray and William Cowper) were all classical scholars deeply imbued with Greek and Latin poetry, who felt they were returning to a pristine classicism rather than one overlaid with French elegance.

The British Miltonic tradition brought a resurgence in blank verse as a poetic medium, particularly through the work of John Philips (who came to be thought of as Milton's poetic 'son'). In three very different popular poems, *The Splendid Shilling* (1701), *Blenheim* (1705), and *Cyder* (1708) Philips showed the range of possibilities offered by 'Miltonic verse' (as blank verse tended to be called in these early years) from mock-epic comedy, to heroic celebration, to rural georgic. In Philips's hands, blank verse was a flexible resource capable of handling a wide range of tone and subject. Not surprisingly, it became the favoured medium for extended pieces of a descriptive and meditative kind in which the poet's thoughts interacted with the shifting moods of nature. James Thomson in *The Seasons* (1730) exploited its range to convey the breath-taking power of his *varied* GOD', and his poem's unprecedented popularity brought many admirers and imitators. Mark Akenside in *The Pleasures of Imagination* (1744) developed the potential of blank verse for an extended philosophical argument, which in his hands seemed to unfold organically in tune with the natural responses of the human mind. In *The Pleasures of Melancholy* (1747) Thomas Warton used it to indulge the wandering thoughts of his moody egoist exploring the landscape of his mind; and Joseph Warton in *The Enthusiast: Or The Lover of Nature* (1744) showed the ease with which the verse form could move in a single sentence from satire to celebration, from art to nature:

> Can gilt alcoves, can marble-mimick gods,
> Parterres embroider'd, obelisks, and urns
> Of high relief; can the long spreading lake,
> Or vista lessening to the sight; can Stow
> With all her Attick fanes, such raptures raise,
> As the thrush-haunted copse, where lightly leaps
> The fearful fawn the rustling leaves along,
> And the brisk squirrel sports from bough to bough . . . ?
>   (ll. 5–12)

By the 1790s blank verse had come to be associated with the meditations of a first-person 'I', whether a solitary visionary or a genial observer. At one extreme was Edward Young's grandiose *Night Thoughts on Life, Death, & Immortality* (nine books, 1742–5) with its exclamations and rhetorical questions, and at the other was William Cowper's *The Task* (six books, 1785) in which the speaking voice is modulated in the subtlest ways – witty, rueful, indignant, warm-hearted – in what Coleridge called 'divine chit-chat'. In their blank verse of the 1790s Coleridge and Wordsworth, both steeped in the work of Akenside, the Wartons, Young and Cowper, found themselves able to move naturally between prophetic and conversational modes within a single poem.

If the Miltonic tradition had its natural expression through blank verse, it also dis-covered a congenial form in the ancient Pindaric ode, which had been assimilated into English by Abraham Cowley in 1656. Unlike Cowley and Dryden, Milton wrote no Pindaric odes, but the metrical daring of the form and its association with sublime subjects and visionary ambitions, led eighteenth-century poets to infuse it with the spirit of Milton. As early as 1709 (the year Pope wrote his *Essay on Criticism*) Isaac Watts used the Pindaric form to celebrate Milton's imaginative daring and refusal to be bound by French critical rules:

Immortal Bard! Thus thy own *Raphael* sings,
   And knows no Rule but native Fire:
All Heav'n sits silent while to his Sovereign Strings
   He talks unutterable Things;
With Graces Infinite his untaught Fingers rove
     Across the Golden Lyre
           (*The Adventurous Muse*, ll. 56–61)

English poets were becoming increasingly conscious of the sound of verse and its links with the music of the Greek lyre and Hebrew harp: the lofty tones of Pindar, the ancient lyric singer, were joined to those of the Old Testament Psalmist. In the year of Pope's *Windsor-Forest* (1713), which celebrated a nation at peace, Anne Finch published 'Upon the Hurricane', her vision of national chaos and destruction. This long irregular Pindaric on the Great Storm of 1703 is directly inspired by the language of the Psalms. The ode's irregular line lengths and varied rhyme patterns are suitably fluid and unpredictable as they unfold a revelation in which the 'Great Disposer' has suspended nature's laws and threatens to erase human history at a stroke.

The lyric-prophetic mode marked a return to poetry's origins as an inspired art concerned less with social forms than elemental forces, and it was Milton who brought all this into focus. His spirit presided over an increasingly confident national poetry which valued its continuities with the medieval-Elizabethan inheritance of Chaucer and Spenser, but also found links with ancient Greek and biblical traditions. Such a return was confidently announced in Thomson's preface to the second edition of *Winter* (1726): 'let POETRY, once more, be restored to her antient Truth, and Purity; let Her be inspired from Heaven, and, in Return, her Incense ascend thither'. Lofty declarations were suited to the ode form, and in 1746 Joseph Warton announced his *Odes on Various Subjects* as 'an attempt to bring back Poetry into its right channel' on the principle that 'Invention and Imagination are the chief faculties of a Poet'. By mid-century, an assertion of the creative powers of the *poeta* ('maker') went along with a widening interest in literary history and the nature of poetic development. In William Collins's 'Ode on the Poetical Character' (1747) and Thomas Gray's 'The Progress of Poesy: A Pindaric Ode' (1757) the self-conscious poet traced his own inheritance down from the original enchantments of Apollo and Venus, and in both poems one of the mediators is Milton – he who 'rode sublime / Upon the seraph-wings of Extasy' (Gray). Collins is the more tentative about matching his master, and though he pursues the 'guiding Steps' with genuine dedication, he trembles to think that Milton may have been the last poet to speak with true godlike power.

During the 1750s and 1760s a growing interest in the literary past opened up new avenues for poets to explore, and led some to take on the voices of psalmist, bard, or minstrel. Christopher Smart, for whom King David was the supreme poet of nature, not only translated the Psalms (1765), but offered in the dazzling *Song to David* (1763) his own hymn of praise for all living things. Thomas Gray's researches into the history of Welsh poetry left their mark on his popular Pindaric ode, 'The Bard' (1757), in which the last of the ancient bards sings out from the top of a mountain, and before plunging to his death curses the English invader and prophesies like a Celtic Ezekiel ('loose his beard, and hoary hair / Stream'd, like a meteor, to the troubled air'). The notion of the poet as a doomed elemental force found its essence in *The Works of Ossian* (1765), a phenomenon which left its mark on European Romanticism. These supposed translations by James Macpherson (which included two epics, *Fingal* and *Temora*, and various shorter episodes) were in fact imaginative re-creations based on bardic materials he had collected from old Gaelic singers and storytellers. In Macpherson's haunting rhythmical prose the reader hears a primal voice rising and falling like the wind: 'When now shall I hear the bard; or rejoice at the fame of my fathers? The harp is not strung on Morven; nor the voice of music raised on Cona. Dead with the mighty is the bard; and fame is in the desart no more' (*Fingal*, VI).

The excitement of recovering a lost tradition of poetry could be enjoyed by the polite literary world, so long as the language was smooth and the emotions attuned to the sentimental tastes of the time (Ossian's noble princes and maidens spoke with courteous dignity and fine feeling). This was the key to the success of Thomas Percy's ballad collection, *Reliques of Ancient English Poetry* (three vols, 1765), in which the medieval and Tudor material was rendered more elegant by creative editing and the inclusion of some modern pieces. Percy's minstrels (as he argued in a prefatory essay) performed at court and were welcomed into the noblest houses. This was not, alas, the fate of the only modern minstrel, Thomas Chatterton, a youth completely suffused in the imagined world of fifteenth-century Bristol who took on himself the persona of Thomas Rowley, poet and 'secular priest'. Chatterton died in 1770 in a London garret at the age of seventeen, leaving an array of invented 'Rowley' documents and poems which when published aroused admiration for their genius, but fierce dispute over their authenticity. Romantic myth soon seized on the doomed poet, and both Coleridge and Wordsworth found inspiration in 'the marvellous boy'; but it was John Keats who most absorbed Chatterton's genius, considering him 'the purest writer in the English language'. Keats loved to recite 'Mynstrelles Song', especially stanza eight:

> Comme, wythe acorne-coppe and thorne,
> Drayne mie hartys blodde awaie;
> Lyfe and all yttes goode I scorne,
> Daunce bie nete, or feaste by daie.
>   Mie love ys dedde,
>   Gon to hys death-bedde,
>   Al under the wyllowe tree.

The eighteenth-century poet who most absorbed Milton's genius and who understood its implications most deeply was William Blake (1757–1827). In his fifty-plate illuminated poem, *Milton* (composed *c*.1800–4), the poet of *Paradise Lost* enters Blake's consciousness in order to undergo a purging of his errors. Reanimated within Blake, he removes the false rational superstructure from his epic and recovers its profound truth: that God is not a distant law-giver but the imaginative faculty within every individual. In his work of the 1780s and 1790s Blake re-imagined, verbally and visually, the eighteenth-century poetry of the Miltonic tradition. He passionately admired Ossian and Chatterton, and painted 537 watercolours illustrating Young's *Night Thoughts*; but it was Thomas Gray (whose poems he also illustrated) who most helped to shape Blake's early work, in which the humane sentimentalist becomes the national prophet. Both Gray's 'Ode on a Distant Prospect of Eton College' and 'The Bard' trace the dilemma of a visionary artist confronting human fate, and their haunting images are infused into Blake's *Book of Thel* (1789) and *Songs of Innocence and of Experience Showing the Two Contrary States of the Human Soul* (1794). In his concern with seeing progress through contraries, and with finding a place for imaginative energy within artistic order, Blake wrestles creatively with that duality in the poetic tradition which Vicesimus Knox had identified in 1782. He seeks to integrate form and vision. No longer should we see Blake overthrowing a single *ancien régime* of eighteenth-century poetry, but as engaging with the tensions and contradictions that make the poetry of the period 1660–1789 so fascinating.

References and Further Reading

Barrell, John (1983). *English Literature in History 1730–80: An Equal, Wide Survey.* London: Hutchinson.

Budick, Sanford (1974). *Poetry of Civilization: Mythopoeic Displacement in the Verse of Milton, Dryden, Pope, and Johnson.* New Haven and London: Yale University Press.

Chalker, John (1969). *The English Georgic: A Study in the Development of a Form.* London: Routledge and Kegan Paul.

Doody, Margaret Anne (1985). *The Daring Muse: Augustan Poetry Reconsidered.* Cambridge: Cambridge University Press.

Dowling, William C. (1991). *The Epistolary Moment: The Poetics of the Eighteenth-century Verse Epistle.* Princeton: Princeton University Press.

——(1992). 'Ideology and the flight from history in eighteenth-century poetry'. In *The Profession of Eighteenth-century Literature: Reflections on an Institution.* Ed. Leo Damrosch. Madison: University of Wisconsin Press.

Fairer, David and Christine Gerrard, eds (1999). *Eighteenth-century Poetry: An Annotated Anthology.* Oxford and Malden, Mass.: Blackwell.

Feingold, Richard (1978). *Nature and Society: Later Eighteenth-century Uses of the Pastoral and Georgic.* Hassocks: Harvester Press.

Ferguson, Moira (1995). *Eighteenth-century Women Poets: Nation, Class, and Gender.* Albany: State University of New York Press.

Fox, Christopher (1990). *Teaching Eighteenth-century Poetry.* New York: AMS Press.

Griffin, Dustin (1986). *Regaining Paradise: Milton and the Eighteenth Century.* Cambridge: Cambridge University Press.

Johnston, Arthur (1971). 'Poetry and criticism after 1740'. In *History of Literature in the English Language, Vol. 4: Dryden to Johnson.* Ed. Roger Lonsdale. London: Barrie and Jenkins.

Landry, Donna (1990). *The Muses of Resistance: Labouring-class Women's Poetry in Britain, 1739–96.* Cambridge: Cambridge University Press.

Lonsdale, Roger, ed. (1984). *The New Oxford Book of Eighteenth-century Verse.* Oxford: Oxford University Press.

——ed. (1989). *Eighteenth-century Women Poets: An Oxford Anthology.* Oxford: Oxford University Press.

Price, Martin (1964). *To the Palace of Wisdom: Studies in Order and Energy from Dryden to Blake.* Carbondale and Edwardsville: Southern Illinois University Press.

Rothstein, Eric (1981). *Restoration and Eighteenth-*

century Poetry 1660–1780. The Routledge History of English Poetry, Vol. 3. Boston, London and Henley: Routledge and Kegan Paul.

Sitter, John (1982). *Literary Loneliness in Mid-eighteenth-century England.* Ithaca and London: Cornell University Press.

Sitter, John, ed. (2000). *The Cambridge Companion to Eighteenth-century Poetry*. Cambridge: Cambridge University Press.

Spacks, P. M. (1967). *The Poetry of Vision: Five Eighteenth-century Poets*. Cambridge, Mass.: Harvard University Press.

Wasserman, Earl R. (1959). *The Subtler Language: Critical Readings of Neoclassic and Romantic Poems.* Baltimore: Johns Hopkins University Press.

Weinbrot, Howard D. (1993). *Britannia's Issue: The Rise of British Literature from Dryden to Ossian.* Cambridge: Cambridge University Press.

55

Shakespeare and New Drama
Paulina Kewes

'O *Marius, Marius*! wherefore art thou *Marius?*' – thus the Restoration Juliet (renamed Lavinia) to her Romeo in Thomas Otway's *The History and Fall of Caius Marius* (1680), a play which appropriates the love plot from Shakespeare's *Romeo and Juliet*. Transplanted from modern Verona to late republican Rome, and set against a background of political strife rather than mere family feud, Shakespeare's tragedy of star-crossed love becomes strange and unfamiliar. The Restoration and the eighteenth century produced numerous other redactions of Shakespeare which to the modern sensibility may appear startling, perhaps even bizarre: the love- and sex-obsessed *Tempest* (1667) in which even Ariel has a girlfriend; the happily ending *King Lear* (1681) in which the old king regains his throne only to abdicate in favour of Cordelia and her beloved Edgar; the poetically just *Troilus* (1679) in which Cressida commits suicide to prove her innocence; or the operatic *Midsummer Night's Dream*, re-christened *The Fairy-Queen* (1692), and embellished with a masque of four seasons, singing and dancing by Chinese men and women, and a dance of six monkeys. These adaptations, some of which were performed well into the nineteenth century, set forth the familiar in an unfamiliar guise. Occasionally the changes were minor, involving no more than a few deletions and stylistic revisions as in the case of *Hamlet* which was staged by the Duke's Company with production cuts (very likely made by Sir William Davenant); at other times the alterations were far more radical. Only two of the Shakespearean plays known to be in the active repertory were performed unaltered, *Othello* and *1 Henry IV*, though given the thematic emphases both of them acquired when staged – for instance the Moor tended to wear British officer's red uniform – we can legitimately consider them as production adaptations.

Taking Shakespearean plays, especially as adapted, as a key indicator of generic evolution, let us see what kinds of plays were written for, and produced on, the English stage in the century following the Restoration of the Stuart monarchy in 1660. Did the adaptations conform to the dominant generic trends of the day or were they themselves trend-setters? What do they tell us about the theatrical culture of the later seventeenth and eighteenth centuries, in particular about the standing of Shakespeare? By examining the ways in which Shakespeare's plays were produced, rewritten and judged, we can better understand and appreciate the theatrical conditions, generic modes and politics of drama. By looking closely at new plays appearing in the intervals between clusters of Shakespearean adaptations, we can identify and define the distinctive generic forms of contemporary serious and comic drama, that is, the genres which emerged and proved lastingly successful in our period.

The Stage

The two most radically innovative theatrical developments after 1660 were the introduction of movable scenery and the appearance of female performers on the public stage. Following his auspicious return from continental exile, Charles II authorized two of his courtier-friends, Thomas Killigrew and Sir William Davenant, to set up theatre companies, the King's and the Duke's respectively. In the early 1640s Davenant's plans for a scenic playhouse had been foiled by the outbreak of the Civil War. In the later 1650s he was allowed by the Cromwellian Protectorate to stage operatic theatricals such as *The Siege of Rhodes* (1656) and *The Cruelty of the Spaniards in Peru* (1658). Now, in 1660, he launched his new theatrical venture by investing heavily in scenes and machines. And, since the pool of pre-1642 scripts granted to the Duke's Company in Lord Chamberlain's orders of 1660 and 1668 was severely limited, he mounted spectacular revivals of his own plays and equally spectacular productions of new and revamped shows. The commercial attractiveness of Davenant's novelties forced Killigrew's troupe, which held rights to most Elizabethan, Jacobean and Caroline scripts, to strive hard to match them. Vigorous competition between the two acting companies lasted until the formation of the United Company in 1682 (and re-emerged with the break-up of that company in 1694). Thus from the early 1660s onward the audiences at London's public playhouses were treated to the kind of lavish visual spectacle that before the Civil Wars had been the privilege of those select few who had gained admittance to masques staged at court.

In Renaissance playhouses, both open-air ones such as the Shakespearean Globe and indoor ones such as Blackfriars, spectators facing a bare stage had had to imagine, with the help only of off-stage sound effects, the storm with which *The Tempest* opens. Their Restoration successors who attended the play's recent off-shoots, Sir William Davenant and John Dryden's *The Tempest, or the Enchanted Island* (1667), and the musical recension of that adaptation (1674), not only were regaled with an elaborate pictorial representation of the storm on the painted scenery but were also entertained with the sight of spirits and devils traversing the stage in flying machines. The special effects called for by the production of the operatic *Tempest* are usefully glossed by the edition of 1674. It describes the background canvas as portraying *a thick Cloudy Sky, a very Rocky Coast, and a Tempestuous Sea in perpetual Agitation. This Tempest (suppos'd to be rais'd by Magick) has many dreadful Objects in it, as several Spirits in horrid shapes flying down amongst the Sailers, then rising and crossing in the Air. And when the Ship is sinking, the whole House is darken'd, and a shower of Fire falls upon 'em. This is accompanied with Lightning, and several Claps of Thunder, to the end of the Storm.*

We can gauge the attraction of such multimedia shows from a comment by a contemporary Londoner, Samuel Pepys, upon a performance of Davenant's version of *Macbeth* (1664). 'A most excellent play in all respects', he enthused, 'but especially in divertissement, though it be a deep tragedy'. That 'divertissement' was augmented in a revival mounted by the Duke's Company in 1673 at their fancy new Dorset Garden theatre which was recorded by the company prompter, John Downes. Downes attributed the success of '*The Tragedy of Macbeth*, alter'd by Sir *William Davenant*' to its 'being drest in all it's Finery, as new Cloath's, new Scenes, Machines, as flyings for the Witches; with all the Singing and Dancing in it'.

The architectural innovations which made possible the dazzling special effects in public theatres emulated the technological sophistication of the pre-Civil War court stage presided over by Inigo Jones. The permission, which was endorsed in the royal patents of 1662 and 1663 respectively, for women's parts to be played by female actors, legitimated the practices characteristic of the production of court masques under James I and Charles I in which the two successive queens and their female attendants had routinely taken part. The ostensible motive cited by the authorities for allowing women on to the stage was their ambition to extirpate the immorality fostered by transvestite acting. In the event, the immorality was boosted rather than reduced by the theatres' extensive exploitation of female bodies for sexual titillation; while transvestite acting – both ways round – became a staple of many a comic production.

Though the identity of the first actress to appear on the public stage is uncertain, we know that she took the part of Desdemona in a revival of *Othello* late in 1660. However, as Restoration dramatists were acutely aware, Shakespeare's plays did not afford nearly enough substantial female roles. In order to remedy what they saw as a serious deficiency, they set about rewriting Shakespeare by inserting new female characters and expanding existing ones. As with the addition of music and spectacle, Davenant led the way. In his version of *The Tempest*, written in collaboration with Dryden, Miranda gains a sister, Dorinda; Caliban a sister (and lover), Sycorax; and Ariel a female companion, Milcha. In Davenant's operatic *Macbeth* the corruption of Lady Macbeth is offset by the exemplary virtue of Lady Macduff whose part has been considerably enlarged. The new possibilities created by the arrival of the actress were thus exploited by the adapters who, within a short time, developed several distinct character types – the gay and witty heroine, the ingenue, the sinister villainess, the pathetic victim – and the corresponding plots and scenes centring on courtship, seduction, cuckolding and sexual violence. Scenes of rape and attempted rape were added to several redactions of Shakespeare. In Nahum Tate's *The History of King Lear* the chaste and pious Cordelia is assaulted by two villains in Edmund's pay and escapes being raped by him only through a serendipitous intervention of her suitor Edgar disguised as Poor Tom. In the final scene of Tate's *The Ingratitude of a Common-Wealth* (1682), a remake of *Coriolanus*, the hero's wife Virgilia stabs herself to avoid violation by Coriolanus' arch-enemy Aufidius.

Precisely because they allow for a comparison between the original and the adaptation, post-Restoration redactions of Shakespeare throw into relief the transformations of the drama prompted by the introduction of movable scenery and stage machinery and by the advent of the actress. The same process of change is reflected in the 'original' drama of the period. In both serious plays and semi-operas we find scenes which call for elaborate staging. The provision for fancy special effects became, alongside the emphasis on music, dance and song, the distinguishing feature of semi-opera, sometimes also called dramatic opera or English opera. In such multimedia spectaculars, which were pioneered by Thomas Betterton and the Duke's Company in the 1670s, and which again came to prominence with Purcell in the early 1690s, the spoken text was interspersed with more or less contextually relevant singing and dancing, and set off by splendid scenery, costumes and flamboyant staging. Unable to match their rivals' sumptuously mounted operatic shows *The Tempest* (1674) and *Psyche* (1675), the King's Company had to content themselves with parodying them in bawdy burlesques by Thomas Duffett: *The Mock-Tempest* (1674) and *Psyche Debauch'd* (1675). For example, *The Mock-Tempest* opens not with a sea-storm but with a storming of a brothel by an angry crowd ('*A great noyse is heard of beating Doors, and breaking Windowes, crying a Whore, a Whore, &c*'); Prospero, surnamed Whiffe, is demoted from duke to keeper of Bridewell, a house of correction for prostitutes; and Miranda and Dorinda are transformed from innocent if ignorant adolescents into sexually experienced, indeed promiscuous young women, for whom the real unknown is 'that thing call'd Husband . . . with a great pair of Hornes upon his head'.

In both serious and comic plays we find a range of major parts for women; in all manner of drama the musical element, whether in the form of incidental songs and dances or more closely integrated musical interludes, is prominent. Thus *The Indian Queen* (1664) a rhymed heroic play written by John Dryden and Sir Robert Howard, shows its passionate and wicked heroine, Queen Zempoalla, solicit assistance from a necromancer in a scene complete with sung incantations and conjurings. (In 1695 that play was turned into a successful semi-opera by a modest amount of cutting and the addition of the music by Henry Purcell.) And in Dryden's later *Tyrannick Love* (1669) Saint Catharine is assailed in her dream by two spirits, Nacar and Damilcar, who, being suspended in the air, insinuate sinful thoughts to her in a sensual song cast in rhyming couplets.

The creation of powerful female characters across the spectrum of dramatic genres, and the prevalence of fancy staging in serious plays and semi-operas and of discovery scenes in comic drama, were trends which affected both new plays and adaptations of old ones throughout our period. To understand changes in dramatic form, however, we need to examine not only those general developments but specific circumstances of chronology and short-term change. Dramatic genres and themes grew and altered in response to the political concerns and crises of the time. Again the example of Shakespearean adaptation will point up the pattern of change.

Politics and Genre

In the early 1660s the dominant generic form was the tragicomedy, which by featuring a near-catastrophe metaphorically recalled the recent horrors of Civil War and regicide only to dispel them in a fortuitously happy ending. The underlying model for early Restoration tragicomedies was supplied by Beaumont and Fletcher's plays such as *A King and No King* and *Philaster* whose contemporary revivals outnumbered those of all other 'old plays'. The tragicomic schema is well illustrated by the first in the line of Shakespearean adaptations, Davenant's *The Law against Lovers* (1662), a hybrid of *Measure for Measure* and *Much Ado about Nothing*. In it the seemingly puritanical Angelo turns out to have been merely testing Isabella whom he had loved long before, and the righteous rebellion headed by his brother Benedick (a vivacious and noble Cavalier and suitor of the spirited Beatrice) claims no casualties. Roughly contemporaneous was James Howard's lost revision of *Romeo and Juliet* which, as Downes tells us, 'preserv[ed] *Romeo* and *Juliet* alive; so that when the Tragedy was Reviv'd again, 'twas Play'd Alternately, Tragical one Day, and Tragicomical another'. Answering the collective desire to exorcise the memory of the recent political trauma, the Dryden–Davenant *Tempest*, too, defuses the potentially disturbing themes of rebellion and usurpation by expunging both Caliban's plot to overthrow Prospero and Sebastian's to kill Alonso; by showing Alonso and Antonio to be duly repentant from the outset; by satirizing the Commonwealth experiment in the low comic scenes involving the drunken sailors; and by staging two triumphant restorations rather than one: Prospero's to the throne of Milan and Hippolito's to the throne of Mantua.

Awash with more or less exalted tragicomedies, the early 1660s provide few varieties of tragic drama *par excellence* other than horror tragedies such as Thomas Porter's *The Villain* (1662), which was closely modelled on the enduringly popular *Othello*. As if by way of compensation, that decade saw the emergence of the most curious – and the most short-lived – dramatic form of the later seventeenth century: the rhymed heroic play. In *The Law against Lovers* the characters occasionally speak in rhyming couplets. In full-blown heroic plays such as those by the Earl of Orrery, John Dryden, Sir Robert Howard, and, later, Elkanah Settle, Nathaniel Lee and Thomas Otway, rhyme is the exclusive mode of expression. It is used to figure forth the emotional and rhetorical excess generated by the conflicts between good and evil, between love and honour, between public duty and private gratification, which are played out by the larger-than-life heroes and heroines in the fantastically remote settings of Mexico, Peru, Morocco and Turkey, and less often medieval England. Though they may appear far-fetched and perhaps even slightly ludicrous to the modern reader, heroic plays enjoyed an intense if brief vogue. Despite the exoticism of their settings, the grandiosity of their protagonists and diction, and the ostensible royalism of their ideological stance, some of these plays provided astute and timely commentaries upon the nation's political past and present. The most renowned of them all, John Dryden's two-part ten-act *The Conquest of Granada* (1670–1), features several usurpations and evokes the spectre of civil war in its dramatization of the conflict between the Moorish tribes of the Abencerrages and the Zegrys. It also explores the dangers inherent in weak kingship and highlights the threat posed to it by the power that resides in the multitude.

The period of the ascendance, flowering and demise of the Restoration rhymed heroics, approximately 1664–77, did not result in the rewriting of any play by Shakespeare as a heroic extravaganza. Nor did the boom in sex comedy in the mid-1670s lead to the appearance of racy revisions of Shakespeare's comedies (though the witty banter of Beatrice and Benedick in *The Law against Lovers*, and the sexually suggestive dialogue of the Restoration *Tempest*, may well have contributed to the development of that generic form). The most famous, or perhaps infamous, sex comedies of the decade were William Wycherley's *The Country-Wife* (1675) and *The Plain-Dealer* (1676), Sir George Etherege's *The Man of Mode* (1676), Thomas Shadwell's *The Virtuoso* (1676), and Aphra Behn's *The Rover* (1677). Although united by their flaunting of libertine philosophy 'derived' from Hobbes and fixation on sex at the level of both plot (which typically featured seductions, couplings, and cuckoldings) and language (which brimmed with *double entendres*, innuendoes, and raunchy exchanges), those plays exemplify a wide range of comic modes and styles: from hard-hitting social satire and milder satiric forms often tinged with farce, to wit comedy, sword-and-buckler play, and romance-*cum*-intrigue. However popular *The Man of Mode* or *The Country-Wife* may have been, in the late 1670s salacious comedies of town life populated by handsome rakes, beautiful and clever virgins, preposterous fops, ageing coquettes, and humorous cuckolds, did not constitute the only or even the dominant variety of comic drama. The comedies of Spanish romance and intrigue stimulated by the stupendously successful (and impeccably chaste) *The Adventures of Five Hours* (1663) by Sir Samuel Tuke continued to hold the boards, as did the imitations of Jonsonian humours comedy by Thomas Shadwell and the native renditions of Molière's farces. The vogue for sex-driven comedy on which the notoriety of Restoration drama rests to this day was short-lived (in 1678 obscene pieces by Dryden, Shadwell, Otway and Behn flopped). And it did not preclude the successful production of radically different kinds of comic plays, some of them earnest and moral.

In the late 1670s the mood of the drama darkens, with comedies becoming more cynical, sinister and bawdy, and with the rhymed heroics relying increasingly on shock and horror and eventually giving way to more genuinely tragic forms of blank verse drama. That change parallels a shift in the political climate. Since the early 1660s the Stuart regime had been steadily losing the capital of public trust and support that had made the Restoration possible. By the late 1670s the monarchy came under the gravest threat it had experienced since the upheaval of the 1640s. A period of intense political crisis was triggered by the largely fabricated allegations, made in the autumn of 1678 by Titus Oates, a Jesuit-*manqué*-turned-informer, of a Popish Plot against the king. During the next three years the opposition, who came to be called Whigs, exploited the anti-Catholic hysteria sparked by Oates's spurious revelations in their bid to exclude Charles II's Catholic brother, James Duke of York, from succession to the throne. The drama, both comic and tragic, responded to the unfolding crisis, some pieces foregrounding an unflinchingly loyalist (Tory) message, others purveying an oppositional (Whig) one. Understandably, given the alertness of the government to the danger of political subversion, several playwrights tried to outwit the censor by smuggling politically sensitive material on to the stage under the name of the 'immortal Shakespeare'. (That tactic, though generally effective, did not shield from suppression Tate's injudicious dramatization of a deposition of an English king in *The History of King Richard The Second*.) The result was as many as ten adaptations of Shakespeare's plays between 1678 and 1682 which conscripted the Bard as a champion sometimes of Whig, sometimes of Tory positions.

The common feature of this group of adaptations is their preoccupation with abuses of power by those in positions of authority, and with the various kinds of threat to rulers, whether military coups, conspiracies or popular insurrections. That preoccupation is reflected already in the choice of originals for revision, chief among them being Shakespeare's Roman plays *Antony and Cleopatra*, *Titus Andronicus*, and *Coriolanus*, and his English and British histories, *Richard II*, *1–3 Henry VI*, *King Lear*, and *Cymbeline*. *Troilus and Cressida*, *Timon of Athens*, and *Romeo and Juliet*, too, were converted into vehicles for political commentary by subtle and not-so-subtle additions of topical material. To illustrate: forceful warnings against the horrors of internecine strife are issued in John Crowne's *The Misery of Civil-War* (1680, a version of *2–3 Henry VI*), his *Henry the Sixth, The First Part* (1681, a version of *1 Henry VI*), and Thomas Otway's *The History and Fall of Caius Marius* (1680, partly based on *Romeo and Juliet*). Crowne, in particular, is adept at manipulating scenic emblems to enhance, by theatrical means, his essentially loyalist message in *The Misery of Civil-War*. In an episode vividly dramatizing the merciless plunder, mass rape, and other atrocities committed by a band of soldiers upon the population of an enemy village, '*The Scene is drawn, and there appears Houses and Towns burning, Men and Women hang'd upon Trees, and Children on the tops of Pikes*'. There is a parallel scene in Otway's *Caius Marius*, in which the now victorious Marius Senior (father to Romeo *alias* Marius Junior) orders the summary execution of scores of Roman citizens who have opposed him; he spares only virgins, 'for my Warriours to rejoice in'. When begged for mercy by a young child, he cries: 'Take hence this Brat too; / mount it on a Spear, / And let it sprawl to make the Grandsire sport'. Equally menacing if occasionally less bloody are the scenes of mob violence in: *The Misery of Civil-War* (which opens with Jack Cade's rebellion presented in such a way as to satirize Oates's perjured testimony); *Richard II* (in which the seditious rout are manoeuvred by the wily Bullingbrook into agreeing to the execution of their own leader); and *The Ingratitude of a Common-Wealth* (in which the plebeians, blackened in comparison with their Shakespearean counterparts, rise against the patricians and are later stirred by the tribunes into opposing Coriolanus's election to a consulship).

To the tyranny of the multitude, some adapters juxtaposed the tyranny of the individual or individuals. In Tate's *The History of King Lear*, the despotism and cruelty of Regan and Gonerill, and the oppressive taxation imposed by them, enable Gloster to rouse the British peasantry to rise in support of the old king. (That popular rising replaces Shakespeare's French invasion.) And in Edward Ravenscroft's *Titus Andronicus, Or The Rape of Lavinia* (1678–9?), the gory revenge exacted by the Andronici upon the Emperor Saturninus and his adulterous wife, Tamora Queen of the Goths, appears fully justified, the regicide Lucius being hailed as '*Romes* Royall Emperour'.

Political themes such as these are as a rule overlaid with, indeed reinforced by, the treatment of love, passion and sexual transgression. As we have seen, the influence of Hobbesian libertinage upon adaptations of Shakespeare's comedies was infrequent (even if that creed was the driving force behind the representation, in the Dryden–Davenant *Tempest*, of Hippolito, the 'natural man' who has never seen a woman, but who, upon seeing one and learning that there are more of them in the world, decides to win them all). By contrast elements of libertine comedy surface in the Popish Plot and Exclusion Crisis reprises of Shakespeare's serious plays. For instance, the Bastard in Tate's *The History of King Lear* dallies amorously with Regan in a quasi-pastoral grotto, receives billets-doux from both Regan and her equally depraved sister Gonerill, and hatches a plan to rape Cordelia whose beauty and innocence arouse his voracious sexual appetite. Similarly, in Thomas Shadwell's *The History of Timon of Athens, the Man-Hater* (1678), Timon is in the process of leaving his devoted mistress Evandra for Melissa, a mercenary coquette. And in Crowne's *The Misery of Civil-War*, Edward Plantagenet (the future Edward IV) carries on an affair with Lady Elianor Butler, initiates negotiations for a French match, and eventually falls for and marries the pretty widow Lady Grey, thereby alienating the self-proclaimed king-maker Warwick who has also pursued her. The representation of royal promiscuity on the stage serves sometimes to palliate, sometimes to stigmatize, the real-life promiscuity of the Stuart males: the king, his brother and heir, and the king's bastard son, the Duke of Monmouth.

Though it is tempting to classify the adaptations according to the dominant political outlook they purvey, and to emphasize the implicit Whiggery of, for example, Shadwell's *Timon*, or the explicit Toryism of, for instance, Tate's *King Lear*, the theatrical impact of those plays could be and frequently was politically complex and ambivalent. (And whatever the topical appeal of any of the new versions, several of them held the stage long after all possible topical application was forgotten.) There are two sets of reasons that account for this ambivalence. First, given that until the spring of 1681 the outcome of the power struggle between the king and the Commons was uncertain, and that the playwrights aimed to please heterogeneous and factious audiences on whose approval their livelihood depended, it should come as no surprise that the writers tended to hedge their bets and equivocate. Second, a number of dramatic tropes and techniques such as, for example, the figuration of the martyrdom of loyal heroes (e.g. Humphrey Duke of Glocester in Crowne's *Henry the Sixth*) or of the deposition of just kings (e.g. Richard II in Tate's play of that name) by wicked rebels, could have an effect contrary to that intended by the dramatist. For if loyalism brings no earthly reward or if legitimate monarchs can be effectively replaced by competent usurpers, what is the point of being loyal or of keeping faith in divine-right kingship? Furthermore, the infusion of anti-Catholic sentiment could subvert, or at least complicate, the political intent of a play. That is the case in Crowne's *Henry the Sixth*, which both demonizes and ridicules popery's grounding in human hypocrisy, greed and superstition; and in Dryden's *The Spanish Fryar* (1680), whose reassuringly loyal high plot featuring a propitious restoration is countered by the comic antics of the corrupt Catholic priest, friar Dominick, in the low plot.

The ambiguity of impact arising out of the interplay of conflicting tropes, generic forms, and modes of characterization, is a notable feature of two of the finest tragedies of the period, Nathaniel Lee's *Lucius Junius Brutus; or, The Father of His Country* (1680) and Thomas Otway's *Venice Preserv'd; or A Plot Discovered* (1682). The former, which depicts the expulsion of the Tarquins and the founding of the Roman republic, was swiftly banned for its allegedly 'very Scandalous Expressions & Reflections upon ye Government'; the latter, which shows the failure of a conspiracy against the Venetian senate, became a celebrated Tory piece. Yet neither the Whiggery of *Lucius Junius Brutus* nor the Toryism of *Venice Preserv'd* is straightforward and uncomplicated. Though, in Lee's play, the republican regime seems preferable to the tyranny of the Tarquin kings, it is by no means flawless, as Brutus's opportunistic manipulation of the masses and his ruthless treatment of former supporters and his own family forcefully remind us. Moreover, even if the audience's political judgement is firmly on the side of the republic, their emotional response, which is likely to involve intense sympathy and pity for Brutus's son Titus and Tarquin's daughter Teraminta (whose passionate love ends in tragic death decreed by Brutus), tend to undermine that judgement. In Otway, any possibility of jubilation at the preservation of the Venetian state is checked, first, by the representation of its senate as no less corrupt than the conspirators and, second, by the demonstration of the pernicious and ultimately tragic influence of politics upon human love and friendship.

In contrast to the often equivocal serious plays, the politics of comic drama are relatively simple. Satiric butts and heroes are predictable and easy to recognize. Among the former are the Whiggishly inclined city husbands and Roundhead rebels whose punishment routinely consists in being cuckolded by Tory blades/dashing Cavaliers, for example in Otway's *Souldiers Fortune* (1680), Edward Ravenscroft's *The London Cuckolds* (1681), Thomas D'Urfey's *Sir Barnaby Whigg* (1681) and Aphra Behn's *The Roundheads* (1681). Less numerous are Whig comedies. The prime example is Shadwell's *The Lancashire Witches, and Tegue O Divelly the Irish Priest* (1681), a biting political satire aimed at (Irish) Catholics and Anglican temporizers alike, which mingles that theme with sexual romp and farce, and which capitalizes on the spectacle of flying witches.

Though the political crisis of the late 1670s and early 1680s produced a rich and varied crop of plays, its overall effect on the drama was damaging. Attendance at play-houses dwindled, many dramatists suffered penury and turned away from writing plays to fiction and translation, and the long-struggling King's Company was reduced to seeking union with the more fortunate Duke's Company. Their merger in 1682 was followed by a lull in dramatic activity, the repertoire of the United Company con-sisting mostly of revivals. The condition of the theatre was not assisted by the death, in 1685, of drama's greatest royal patron, Charles II, and the accession of James II whose inflexible implementation of pro-Catholic policies led to another political upheaval, the Glorious Revolution in 1688. With William and Mary declared joint sovereigns in 1689, a measure of stability was restored, though steadfast Jacobites such as John Dryden found it difficult to reconcile themselves to the new order. Among the few dramatic highlights of the early years of the new regime are Dryden's crypto-Jacobite plays: *Don Sebastian* (1689), a split-plot tragicomedy combining sex, pathos and politics; *Amphitryon* (1690), an exuberant, witty and erotically charged, but also moving farce inspired by Plautus and Molière, which, through its humorous interrogation of Jupiter's kingly powers, offers a teasingly elusive commentary on the Williamite status quo, and which, through an account of Jupiter's philandering, provides a retrospective gloss on Charles II's sexual habits; and *King Arthur* (1691), a dramatic opera deftly blending fake Arthurian lore, material from Shakespeare, Spenser and Tasso, and scenic wonders, and songs and dances memorably set by Henry Purcell.

The theatrical scene becomes more animated in the 1690s. That revival begins with the injection of new talent, with plays by William Congreve, Thomas Southerne, Colley Cibber, John Vanbrugh and George Farquhar. It is further boosted by the re-emergence of competition after the split of the United Company in 1694 and the establishment of two rival companies in 1695. Serious drama of the turn of the century is largely unremarkable in quality, a fact confirmed by a high rate of flops. Comedy, by contrast, experiences a veritable renaissance. Shifting from the focus on courtship characteristic of the early Restoration, comic plays of the 1690s and 1700s increas-ingly centre on marriage, exploring, with varying degrees of sympathy, humour and insight, the diverse manifestations of marital discord and failure. Perhaps most strik-ing in this respect is Congreve's *The Double-Dealer* which presents a young though not very light-hearted couple, Cynthia and Mellefont, whose matrimonial future we are invited to judge by the example of as many as three dysfunctional marriages: the Touchwoods, the Plyants and the Froths. However sympathetic and serious the young lovers may appear, statistically their prospects for marital felicity must seem bleak given the rampant adultery, hypocrisy, evil, and downright stupidity of the older generation.

The drama's moral impropriety was severely castigated by Jeremy Collier, a non-juring Anglican divine, in his *A Short View of the Immorality and Profaneness of the English Stage* (1698). That tract generated several more or less convincing responses from playwrights and critics, notably Congreve and Farquhar, though it did not have as decisive an impact on new drama as Collier and other moralists would have wished. The trend towards exemplarity in comedy, and pathos and poetic justice in serious drama, predates Collier's blast and does not become more pronounced in its wake. Instead, the dawn of the new century is marked by two developments which, though unrelated, were to affect the London theatre scene in more important and lasting ways. The first of those was the appearance of a spate of adaptations of Shakespeare's comedies: Charles Gildon's *Measure for Measure, Or Beauty the Best Advocate* (1700), into which was spliced the Tate-Purcell opera *Dido and Aeneas*; George Granville's *The Jew of Venice* (1701), a more comic and more bawdy version of *The Merchant of Venice*, with Shylock as the chief butt; John Dennis's *The Comical Gallant, Or the Amours of Sir John Falstaff* (1702), a revision of *The Merry Wives of Windsor*; William Burnaby's *Love Betray'd; Or, The Agreable Disapointment* (1703), based on *Twelfth Night*; and, slightly later, Richard Leveridge's *Pyramus and Thisbe* (1716), an extrapolation from *A Midsummer Night's Dream*. Even if only one of these adaptations entered the repertory, their very appearance suggests a new readiness, on the part of both writers and audiences, to extend the generic canon of stageable Shakespeare. The second, and very different, theatrical novelty was the advent of, and almost instantaneous craze for, Italian opera in 1705. Performed by prima donnas and castrati imported from the continent at exorbitant cost, all-sung Italian opera offended nationalist sensibilities. Yet despite the outcry against its foreignness and alleged promotion of aberrant sexuality, features epitomized by the idolized and lionized eunuch singers, the form attracted enthusiastic support among the aristocracy, gentry, and the middle classes. Even so, the gloomy predictions of an imminent demise of native musical drama did not materialize. From Davenant's musical updatings of Shakespeare in the 1660s, through the series of spectacular productions of dramatic operas in the 1670s and again in the 1690s, to Purcell's all-sung English opera, *Dido*, and the contribution of Daniel Purcell and John Eccles at the turn of the century, that tradition had a lot to offer. Plenty of musical shows in English remained in the repertory, and as late as 1706 George Granville's *The British Enchanters: or, No Magick Like Love* (1706) proved a hit and became a stock piece. The vogue for ballad opera sparked by John Gay's *The Beggar's Opera* (1728) declined in the 1730s, but by the 1750s and 1760s English burletta was in the ascendant. It ultimately gave rise to a host of 'English operas' that flooded the stages of Drury Lane and Covent Garden in the 1780s and 1790s. Thus musical shows in English, of whatever generic form and provenance, were a major presence in the repertory of London theatres in every decade from the 1670s to 1800.

Diversity, Development, Decline?

The original plays written for, and produced on, the Restoration and early eighteenth-century stage exemplify a wide range of serious and comic forms. So do the adaptations of Shakespeare's plays mounted in that period. Contrary to what earlier generations of critics have claimed, the Shakespearean corpus, far from having been uniformly debased by the gratuitous addition of bawdry or formulaically rewritten according to an imaginary set of rigid neo-classical rules, was accessible to audiences and readers in a variety of timely and exciting versions which responded to contemporary social, cultural, and political concerns. Chronologically, we can discern several broad generic trends affecting the kinds of drama written in that period, from the tragicomic bent of the 1660s, and the succeeding vogue for heroic drama, to the surge of sex-comedies in the mid-1670s and the proliferation of tragedies during the Popish Plot and Exclusion Crisis which was reflected in a spate of adaptations of Shakespeare's serious plays. Yet even among the Shakespeare-based tragedies and histories of the late 1670s and early 1680s there are radical disparities. If some of the originals were bowdlerized, as was Dryden's *Troilus*, others became signally more bawdy, as did Ravenscroft's *Titus*. If some were made more socially decorous, as was Tate's *King Lear* which excises the Fool and contracts the part of Mad Tom, others became more boisterous and rowdy. Thus Thomas D'Urfey's version of *Cymbeline* called *The Injur'd Princess* (1682) not only turns Cloten into 'A Fool' and Jachimo into 'A roaring drunken Lord, his Companion', but supplements these two native comic butts with a foreign one, Shattillion, who is described in the Dramatis Personae as 'An opinionated *Frenchman*'. If some rewritings became more 'neo-classical', as did the story of Antony and Cleopatra when reconceived by Dryden in *All for Love* (1677), others became more violent, gory and depressing as did *Romeo and Juliet*, *Coriolanus* and *Titus Andronicus* when rewritten by Otway, Tate and Ravenscroft respectively.

The adaptation of Shakespeare's plays after the Restoration illustrates an evolving paradigm of dramatic types. It reflects, too, the changing status of Shakespeare as author. At the outset of our period, in 1660, he was so little regarded that Davenant could get the rights to some of his plays without incurring a protest from his rivals in the King's Company. In early Restoration stage revivals and emergent criticism, Shakespeare trailed behind both Fletcher and Jonson. Those who mined his work for raw materials rarely bothered to acknowledge that they had done so. Shakespeare gained ground slowly, with more plays, both unaltered ones and adaptations, entering the repertory. His assent was reinforced by the crisis of 1678–82 when it became expedient to claim him as source in order to evade accusations of subversive intent. After 1700 Shakespeare became a significant presence on stage and in criticism, a process assisted by the publication, in 1709, of Rowe's collected edition of his *Works*, and by the proliferation, in the 1730s, of cheap editions of his plays. It was further bolstered by a spate of major revivals *c.*1740 which came in the wake of the Licensing Act of 1737.

That legislation limited the number of legitimate theatrical venues to the two patent houses, and required all new scripts to be submitted to the licenser, who was to remove anything immoral, irreligious, or offensive to the government. The Licensing Act had a thoroughly detrimental effect on the production of new plays and on the theatrical culture more generally. It brought to an end the recent expansion in the number of acting companies which set the scene for vigorous competition. (In 1737 London boasted as many as four theatres performing plays and two opera companies. The monopoly of Drury Lane and Covent Garden prevailed until 1843, when more than two venues for regular spoken drama were finally sanctioned by Act of parliament.) It also cut short the lively dramatic experimentation of the 1720s and early 1730s, which saw the emergence of exciting new work by Henry Fielding, John Gay, George Lillo and many others. Fielding produced innovative comedies, burlesques, and political satires disguised as mock-operas, foremost among them *The Tragedy of Tragedies*, *The Grub Street Opera*, and the savage anti-Walpole skit *The Historical Register for the Year 1736*. Gay was the author of a series of imaginative generic hybrids and, in 1728, launched the genre of the ballad opera with *The Beggar's Opera*. Lillo inaugurated bourgeois domestic tragedy with his *The London Merchant; or, The History of George Barnwell* (1731), and followed it through with a distinctly middle-class version of Shakespeare's *Pericles*, called *Marina* (1738). London would not see so varied, so vibrant, and so creative an outburst of theatrical activity until the twentieth century.

The Licensing Act may have stifled original playwriting, yet, paradoxically, it ensured the dominance of Shakespearean drama on the stage, and substantially contributed to the cultural elevation of Shakespeare. And if the mid- to late eighteenth century cannot boast a rich vein of dramatic masterpieces beyond the comic works of Richard Brinsley Sheridan and Oliver Goldsmith in the 1770s and 1780s, there are a series of distinguished performers (Garrick, Macklin, Kemble, Mrs Siddons), editors (Theobald, Warburton, Johnson, Capell, Steevens, Malone), and critics (Montague, Johnson, Duff, Gentleman) of Shakespeare whose efforts confirmed and disseminated his status as the nation's foremost literary genius. By the time of the Stratford Jubilee of 1769 Shakespeare had become the Bard as we know him.

The passage of the Licensing Act caused major changes in the London theatre and in the kinds of new plays that found their way to the stage. Granted a monopoly, the managers of Drury Lane and Covent Garden were largely content to stage perennial favourites varied with occasional revival of seventeenth- and early eighteenth-century classics. This led directly to the rush of revivals of Shakespearean comedies in the 1740s, and the rapid expansion of Shakespeare's place in the repertory. The results for playwrights, however, were severely deleterious: few new plays got staged, and most of those that did get produced were formulaic and unadventurous. Censorship robbed the drama of any possibility of serious social or political commentary. Since making a living as a playwright became virtually impossible for nearly half a century the energy that had earlier gone into playwriting was quickly redirected into the boom in novels that characterizes the 1740s.

REFERENCES AND FURTHER READING

Bevis, R. W. (1988). *English Drama: Restoration and Eighteenth Century, 1660–1789*. London: Longman.

Brown, L. (1981). *English Dramatic Form: An Essay in Generic History, 1660–1760*. New Haven, Conn.: Yale University Press.

Danchin, Pierre, ed. (1981–8). *The Prologues and Epilogues of the Restoration, 1660–1700*. 7 vols. Nancy: Presses Universitaires de Nancy.

Dobson, M. (1992). *The Making of the National Poet: Shakespeare, Adaptation and Authorship, 1660–1769*. Oxford: Clarendon.

Holland, P. (1979). *The Ornament of Action: Text and Performance in Restoration Comedy*. Cambridge: Cambridge University Press.

Howe, E. (1992). *The First English Actresses: Women and Drama 1660–1700*. Cambridge: Cambridge University Press.

Hughes, D. (1996). *English Drama 1660–1700*. Oxford: Clarendon.

Hume, R. D. (1976). *The Development of English Drama in the Late Seventeenth Century*. Oxford: Clarendon.

——(1983). *The Rakish Stage: Studies in English Drama, 1660–1800*. Carbondale and Edwardsville: Southern Illinois University Press.

——(1988). *Henry Fielding and the London Theatre, 1728–1737*. Oxford: Clarendon Press.

Loftis, J. (1963). *The Politics of Drama in Augustan England*. Oxford: Clarendon.

Loftis, J., R. Southern, M. Jones and A. H. Scouten (1976). *The Revels History of Drama in English, Vol. V: 1660–1750*. London: Methuen.

The London Stage, 1660–1800. Part I: 1660–1700. Ed. William Van Lennep, Emmett L. Avery and Arthur H. Scouten (1965). Carbondale: Southern Illinois University Press. *Part II: 1700–1729*. Ed. Emmett L. Avery. 2 vols (1960). Carbondale: Southern Illinois University Press.

Maguire, N. K. (1992). *Regicide and Restoration: English Tragicomedy, 1660–1671*. Cambridge: Cambridge University Press.

Markley, R. (1988). *Two-Edg'd Weapons: Style and Ideology in the Comedies of Etherege, Wycherley, and Congreve*. Oxford: Clarendon.

Marsden, J. I. (1995). *The Re-imagined Text: Shakespeare, Adaptation, & Eighteenth-Century Literary Theory*. Lexington: University Press of Kentucky.

Marsden, J. I., ed. (1991). *The Appropriation of Shakespeare: Post-Renaissance Reconstructions of the Works and the Myth*. New York: Harvester Wheatsheaf.

Owen, S. J. (1996). *Restoration Theatre and Crisis*. Oxford: Clarendon.

Powell, J. (1984). *Restoration Theatre Production*. London: Routledge.

Rothstein, E. (1967). *Restoration Tragedy*. Madison, Wis.: University of Wisconsin Press.

Rothstein, E. and Kavenik, F. M. (1988). *The Designs of Carolean Comedy*. Carbondale and Edwardsville: Southern Illinois University Press.

Staves, S. (1979). *Players' Sceptres: Fictions of Authority in the Restoration*. Lincoln: University of Nebraska Press.

Styan, J. L. (1986). *Restoration Comedy in Performance*. Cambridge: Cambridge University Press.

Weber, H. M. (1986). *The Restoration Rake-Hero: Transformations in Sexual Understanding in Seventeenth-Century England*. Madison: University of Wisconsin Press.

Zwicker, S. N. (1993). *Lines of Authority: Politics and English Literary Culture, 1649–1689*. Ithaca: Cornell University Press.

Index